THE PAPERS OF ULYSSES S. GRANT

THE PAPERS OF

ULYSSES S. GRANT

Volume 19: July 1, 1868 – October 31, 1869

Edited by John Y. Simon

ASSISTANT EDITORS
William M. Ferraro
J. Thomas Murphy

TEXTUAL EDITOR
Sue E. Dotson

——

SOUTHERN ILLINOIS UNIVERSITY PRESS

CARBONDALE AND EDWARDSVILLE

Library of Congress Cataloging in Publication Data (Revised)

Grant, Ulysses Simpson, Pres. U.S., 1822–1885.
    The papers of Ulysses S. Grant.

    Prepared under the auspices of the Ulysses S. Grant Association.
Bibliographical footnotes.
    CONTENTS: v. 1. 1837–1861—v. 2. April–September 1861.
—v. 3. October 1, 1861–January 7, 1862.—v. 4. January 8–March 31,
1862.—v. 5. April 1–August 31, 1862.—v. 6. September 1–December 8, 1862.—v. 7. December 9, 1862–March 31, 1863.—v. 8.
April 1–July 6, 1863.—v. 9. July 7–December 31, 1863.—v. 10.
January 1–May 31, 1864.—v. 11. June 1–August 15, 1864.—v. 12.
August 16–November 15, 1864.—v. 13. November 16, 1864–February 20, 1865.—v. 14. February 21–April 30, 1865.—v. 15. May 1–
December 31, 1865.—v. 16. 1866.—v. 17. January 1–September 30,
1867.—v. 18. October 1, 1867–June 30, 1868.—v. 19. July 1, 1868–
October 31, 1869.
    1. Grant, Ulysses Simpson, Pres. U.S., 1822–1885. 2. United
States—History—Civil War, 1861–1865—Campaigns and battles
—Sources. 3. United States—Politics and government—1869–1877
—Sources. 4. Presidents—United States—Biography. 5. Generals—
United States—Biography. I. Simon, John Y., ed. II. Ulysses S. Grant
Association.
E660.G756   1967   973.8′2′0924   67–10725
ISBN 0–8093–1964–0 (v. 19)

Contents

Introduction

Six weeks before election day in 1868, Ulysses S. Grant, declining yet another invitation to a political gathering, observed "I have had the most quiet, pleasant time this Summer that has fallen to my lot since the opening of the rebellion in /61." He had toured the West for two weeks in late July, returned to Galena in early August, and remained there with his wife, Julia, family, and staff officers until leaving for Washington, D.C., two days after his election as president. Only brief trips in Illinois, to Wisconsin, and to Missouri interrupted his seclusion in Galena.

Western travel, residence in Galena, and a determination to follow "the rule of silence" did not insulate Grant from all political questions. His wartime General Orders No. 11, issued in December, 1862, expelling Jews from his military jurisdiction, distressed Jewish voters, prompted "hundreds of letters" to Grant, and became a public issue. Grant discussed his decision in an unusually lengthy letter, taking care to express regret and to assert "that I have no prejudice against sect or race but want each individual to be judged by his own merit." Characteristically he delayed publication of the letter until after the election to avoid any appearance of seeking votes.

Paralleling his intention to keep quiet on the political front was Grant's desire to administer the army effectively yet unobtrusively. Unrest and sporadic violence still plagued the South and Indians remained a challenge out west. Fortunately for Grant, nothing catastrophic occurred while he was away from Washington, and Secretary of War

John M. Schofield and close friend and chief of staff John A. Rawlins, now seriously ill, handled routine business satisfactorily, the latter forwarding to Galena all matters requiring special attention. Rawlins's death less than one year later was a painful blow to Grant.

Winning the election ended the period of repose. Grant's return to Washington necessitated meeting numerous government, military, and party officials and signaled the start of hectic weeks of travel, speeches, dinners, and interviews. Demands on Grant ranged from cabinet selections to disposal of his home in Washington and covered a spectrum from matters of great public concern to the purely private. Grant also retained army command and needed to monitor changing military situations as well as to prepare for the transfer of command.

Grant's inauguration as president increased concerns and drudgery. His cabinet selections confounded observers, caused personal embarrassment, made him the target of newspaper abuse, and evoked a prickly response inconsistent with his famous reserve. Bowing to the wishes of new Secretary of War Rawlins, Grant revoked an order reforming the relationship between the War Department and the commanding general less than a month after its issuance. This decision angered General William T. Sherman and distanced a friend from Grant. Callers from every walk of life competed for his attention and letters of application and recommendation deluged his office. Grant responded by limiting hours for visitors and directing correspondence related to appointments to pertinent departments, but the crush of work and worry during his first weeks as president left him suffering from exhaustion by late March.

Grant rallied. By early April he was heavily engaged with his presidential duties and striving earnestly to "establish the credit of the country" and to initiate his own policies. The most novel was his Indian policy. Convinced that unscrupulous whites were at least as much to blame as Indians for hostilities and outrages, Grant decided to appoint only Quakers or ordained ministers as Indian agents. He believed that such agents would inspire trust and persuade Indians to give up nomadic lives for residence on reservations. Other aspects of Indian policy included the appointment of former staff officer Ely S. Parker, a Seneca, as commissioner of Indian Affairs, and the formation of an Indian Commission comprising notable philanthropists and humanitarians to advise on Indian matters and to oversee actual practices. Quandaries, rather than miracles, accompanied implementation of this policy, but Grant determined to give reform a fair trial.

Grant's good intentions toward blacks equaled his good intentions toward Indians. He openly favored the Fifteenth Amendment and hoped to speed Reconstruction to a peaceful conclusion, prodding Congress to authorize voting on new state constitutions in Virginia, Mississippi, and Texas. He then used every means at his disposal to facilitate equitable balloting. Grant met prominent blacks to consider issues and to receive recommendations for appointments. Early in his presidency, he signed a bill securing equal rights for blacks and whites in Washington, D.C. Grant further expressed social reform sympathies by prohibiting reduction of wages for government workers under the terms of the eight-hour-day law passed the previous year.

Grant's involvement in foreign policy was less straightforward. He denounced Fenian agitation along the Canadian border. At the urging of Secretary of State Hamilton Fish, he resisted persistent pressure for U.S. intervention on behalf of Cuban insurgents seeking to overturn Spanish rule and issued an order authorizing officials in New York to interdict filibustering expeditions. In July, 1869, he assigned his private secretary Orville E. Babcock as special agent to investigate affairs in Santo Domingo, a quiet beginning to what became a deafening foreign policy debate.

Grant balanced public duties and private interests. He gave minute attention to his farm and property in St. Louis. Future financial independence was never far from his mind. Grant's fondness for vacationing with family and friends at his new home in Long Branch, N.J., created a tug between official obligations and personal inclinations. Strong feelings for family and friends led Grant to give access and latitude not always in his best interest. In some instances, such as reviewing the torrent of patronage requests from his father Jesse in Kentucky, indulgence was simply irritating. In other instances, such as the involvement of Grant's brother-in-law Abel R. Corbin in gold speculation, indulgence was nearly disastrous.

We are indebted to Timothy Connelly for assistance in searching the National Archives; to Harriet F. Simon for proofreading; and to Christina M. Desai and Rebecca A. Phillips, graduate students at Southern Illinois University, for research assistance.

Financial support for the period during which this volume was prepared came from Southern Illinois University, the National Endowment for the Humanities, and the National Historical Publications and Records Commission.

JOHN Y. SIMON

September 30, 1993

Editorial Procedure

1. Editorial Insertions

A. Words or letters in roman type within brackets represent editorial reconstruction of parts of manuscripts torn, mutilated, or illegible.

B. [. . .] or [— — —] within brackets represent lost material which cannot be reconstructed. The number of dots represents the approximate number of lost letters; dashes represent lost words.

C. Words in *italic* type within brackets represent material such as dates which were not part of the original manuscript.

D. Other material crossed out is indicated by ~~cancelled type~~.

E. Material raised in manuscript, as "4th," has been brought in line, as "4th."

2. Symbols Used to Describe Manuscripts

AD	Autograph Document
ADS	Autograph Document Signed
ADf	Autograph Draft
ADfS	Autograph Draft Signed
AES	Autograph Endorsement Signed
AL	Autograph Letter
ALS	Autograph Letter Signed
ANS	Autograph Note Signed

D	Document
DS	Document Signed
Df	Draft
DfS	Draft Signed
ES	Endorsement Signed
LS	Letter Signed

3. Military Terms and Abbreviations

Act.	Acting
Adjt.	Adjutant
AG	Adjutant General
AGO	Adjutant General's Office
Art.	Artillery
Asst.	Assistant
Bvt.	Brevet
Brig.	Brigadier
Capt.	Captain
Cav.	Cavalry
Col.	Colonel
Co.	Company
C.S.A.	Confederate States of America
Dept.	Department
Div.	Division
Gen.	General
Hd. Qrs.	Headquarters
Inf.	Infantry
Lt.	Lieutenant
Maj.	Major
Q. M.	Quartermaster
Regt.	Regiment or regimental
Sgt.	Sergeant
USMA	United States Military Academy, West Point, N.Y.
Vols.	Volunteers

4. Short Titles and Abbreviations

| ABPC | *American Book-Prices Current* (New York, 1895–) |

CG	*Congressional Globe* Numbers following represent the Congress, session, and page.
J. G. Cramer	Jesse Grant Cramer, ed., *Letters of Ulysses S. Grant to his Father and his Youngest Sister, 1857–78* (New York and London, 1912)
DAB	*Dictionary of American Biography* (New York, 1928–36)
Garland	Hamlin Garland, *Ulysses S. Grant: His Life and Character* (New York, 1898)
HED	*House Executive Documents*
HMD	*House Miscellaneous Documents*
HRC	*House Reports of Committees* Numbers following *HED, HMD,* or *HRC* represent the number of the Congress, the session, and the document.
Ill. AG Report	J. N. Reece, ed., *Report of the Adjutant General of the State of Illinois* (Springfield, 1900)
Johnson, Papers	LeRoy P. Graf and Ralph W. Haskins, eds., *The Papers of Andrew Johnson* (Knoxville, 1967–)
Lewis	Lloyd Lewis, *Captain Sam Grant* (Boston, 1950)
Lincoln, Works	Roy P. Basler, Marion Dolores Pratt, and Lloyd A. Dunlap, eds., *The Collected Works of Abraham Lincoln* (New Brunswick, 1953–55)
Memoirs	*Personal Memoirs of U. S. Grant* (New York, 1885–86)
O.R.	*The War of the Rebellion: A Compilation of the Official Records of the Union and Confederate Armies* (Washington, 1880–1901)
O.R. (Navy)	*Official Records of the Union and Confederate Navies in the War of the Rebellion* (Washington, 1894–1927) Roman numerals following *O.R.* or *O.R.* (Navy) represent the series and the volume.
PUSG	John Y. Simon, ed., *The Papers of Ulysses S. Grant* (Carbondale and Edwardsville, 1967–)
Richardson	Albert D. Richardson, *A Personal History of Ulysses S. Grant* (Hartford, Conn., 1868)
SED	*Senate Executive Documents*
SMD	*Senate Miscellaneous Documents*
SRC	*Senate Reports of Committees* Numbers following

SED, *SMD*, or *SRC* represent the number of the Congress, the session, and the document.

USGA Newsletter *Ulysses S. Grant Association Newsletter*

Young John Russell Young, *Around the World with General Grant* (New York, 1879)

5. *Location Symbols*

CLU University of California at Los Angeles, Los Angeles, Calif.

CoHi Colorado State Historical Society, Denver, Colo.

CSmH Henry E. Huntington Library, San Marino, Calif.

CSt Stanford University, Stanford, Calif.

CtY Yale University, New Haven, Conn.

CU-B Bancroft Library, University of California, Berkeley, Calif.

DLC Library of Congress, Washington, D.C. Numbers following DLC-USG represent the series and volume of military records in the USG papers.

DNA National Archives, Washington, D.C. Additional numbers identify record groups.

IaHA Iowa State Department of History and Archives, Des Moines, Iowa.

I-ar Illinois State Archives, Springfield, Ill.

IC Chicago Public Library, Chicago, Ill.

ICarbS Southern Illinois University, Carbondale, Ill.

ICHi Chicago Historical Society, Chicago, Ill.

ICN Newberry Library, Chicago, Ill.

ICU University of Chicago, Chicago, Ill.

IHi Illinois State Historical Library, Springfield, Ill.

In Indiana State Library, Indianapolis, Ind.

InFtwL Lincoln National Life Foundation, Fort Wayne, Ind.

InHi Indiana Historical Society, Indianapolis, Ind.

InNd University of Notre Dame, Notre Dame, Ind.

InU Indiana University, Bloomington, Ind.

KHi Kansas State Historical Society, Topeka, Kan.

MdAN United States Naval Academy Museum, Annapolis, Md.

MeB	Bowdoin College, Brunswick, Me.
MH	Harvard University, Cambridge, Mass.
MHi	Massachusetts Historical Society, Boston, Mass.
MiD	Detroit Public Library, Detroit, Mich.
MiU-C	William L. Clements Library, University of Michigan, Ann Arbor, Mich.
MoSHi	Missouri Historical Society, St. Louis, Mo.
NHi	New-York Historical Society, New York, N.Y.
NIC	Cornell University, Ithaca, N.Y.
NjP	Princeton University, Princeton, N.J.
NjR	Rutgers University, New Brunswick, N.J.
NN	New York Public Library, New York, N.Y.
NNP	Pierpont Morgan Library, New York, N.Y.
NRU	University of Rochester, Rochester, N.Y.
OClWHi	Western Reserve Historical Society, Cleveland, Ohio.
OFH	Rutherford B. Hayes Library, Fremont, Ohio.
OHi	Ohio Historical Society, Columbus, Ohio.
OrHi	Oregon Historical Society, Portland, Ore.
PCarlA	U.S. Army Military History Institute, Carlisle Barracks, Pa.
PHi	Historical Society of Pennsylvania, Philadelphia, Pa.
PPRF	Rosenbach Foundation, Philadelphia, Pa.
RPB	Brown University, Providence, R.I.
TxHR	Rice University, Houston, Tex.
USG 3	Maj. Gen. Ulysses S. Grant 3rd, Clinton, N.Y.
USMA	United States Military Academy Library, West Point, N.Y.
ViHi	Virginia Historical Society, Richmond, Va.
ViU	University of Virginia, Charlottesville, Va.
WHi	State Historical Society of Wisconsin, Madison, Wis.
Wy-Ar	Wyoming State Archives and Historical Department, Cheyenne, Wyo.
WyU	University of Wyoming, Laramie, Wyo.

Chronology

July 1, 1868–October 31, 1869

JULY 4.   Democratic party nominated Horatio Seymour for president and Francis P. Blair, Jr., for vice president.

JULY 7.   USG arrived in St. Louis eight days after leaving Washington, D.C.

JULY 16.   Due to a strike by railroad engineers, USG arrived at Fort Leavenworth a day later than anticipated.

JULY 18.   USG, Lt. Gen. William T. Sherman, and Maj. Gen. Philip H. Sheridan began a two-week tour of the West that included stops at Denver; Benton, Dakota Territory; and Omaha.

JULY 28.   Ratification of the Fourteenth Amendment to the U.S. Constitution.

AUG. 1.   USG recommended removal of civil officers in Miss. unable to take the oath prescribed by Congress and approved a request to appoint blacks to offices in Va.

AUG. 7.   USG spoke briefly to a welcoming crowd at Galena, where he resided for most of the next three months.

AUG. 27.   USG and Julia Dent Grant left Galena to visit Orvil L. Grant in Chicago. On Aug. 29, USG addressed a crowd gathered at his brother's home.

SEPT. 9.   USG spoke briefly at the dedication of a normal school in Platteville, Wis.

SEPT. 26.   USG arrived in Chicago, accompanied by Bvt. Brig. Gen. Adam Badeau, for a two-day visit with Orvil Grant.

OCT. 1.   USG went from Galena to his farm near St. Louis.

OCT. 5.   At Springfield, Ill., USG attended the laying of the cornerstone of the Ill. State House.

OCT. 7.   USG attended the meeting of the U.S. Indian Commission at Chicago and returned the next day to Galena.

OCT. 10.   President Andrew Johnson directed USG to issue General Orders No. 82 to regulate elections in southern states.

OCT. 14.   Election returns reporting Republican victories in Ohio, Pa., and Ind. reached USG at Elihu B. Washburne's home in Galena.

NOV. 3.   USG and Schuyler Colfax won election as president and vice president.

NOV. 4.   USG delivered a short speech in Galena acknowledging his electoral victory.

NOV. 5.   USG left Galena by train for Washington, D.C., arriving on Nov. 7.

NOV. 13.   USG and Julia Grant, en route to USMA to visit their son, stayed overnight in New York City.

NOV. 21.   USG returned to Washington, D.C., following a day in Philadelphia.

NOV. 24.   USG recommended transferring the Indian Bureau from the Dept. of the Interior to the War Dept. and maintaining existing troop levels.

NOV. 30.   USG spoke at the annual dinner of the St. Andrew's Society, Philadelphia.

DEC. 2.   USG arrived in Boston and was declared a guest of the city. During his stay he visited Harvard College and the manufacturing centers of Waltham and Lowell.

DEC. 6.   USG returned to New York City after spending the previous day in Providence visiting Governor Ambrose E. Burnside of R.I.

DEC. 8.   USG attended the wedding of Julia Kean Fish, the daughter of Hamilton Fish. In the evening, USG spoke at a Union League Club dinner.

DEC. 11.   USG returned to Washington, D.C.

DEC. 15.   In Chicago, USG addressed a reunion of former officers of the Army of the Tennessee.

DEC. 18.   On his return trip to Washington, D.C., USG visited his father, Jesse Root Grant, at Covington, Ky.

DEC. 31.   USG spoke at Girard College, Philadelphia, a school founded for the instruction of orphans.

JAN. 4.   USG returned to Washington, D.C., from Philadelphia.

JAN. 12.   Suffering a severe headache, USG canceled all appointments.

JAN. 19.   USG met a committee of the National Convention of Colored Men.

JAN. 21.   USG attended a meeting of the trustees of the Peabody Education Fund in Baltimore and remained there until Jan. 23.

FEB. 3.   USG attempted to settle a dispute with Sayles J. Bowen involving the purchase of USG's Washington, D.C., home by offering to make good personally any loss Bowen sustained.

FEB. 4.   USG and Julia Grant took rooms at the Fifth Avenue Hotel in New York City and departed for Philadelphia on Feb. 8.

FEB. 10.   Congress formally declared USG the winner of the presidency. On Feb. 13, a congressional delegation presented a certificate of election.

FEB. 19.   Businessmen in New York City agreed to purchase USG's house for $65,000 and transfer the property to Sherman. On Feb. 26, USG transferred the deed to Sherman.

FEB. 27.   Congress proposed the Fifteenth Amendment to the U.S. Constitution.

MAR. 4.   USG inaugurated as eighteenth president. Congress convened. Horace Porter, Frederick T. Dent, and Orville E. Babcock became private secretaries to USG.

MAR. 5.   Sherman assumed command of the U.S. Army, replacing USG. Sheridan replaced Sherman as commander, Division of the Mo. USG nominated Washburne as secretary of state, Alexander T. Stewart as secretary of the treasury, Adolph E. Borie as secretary of the navy, Jacob D. Cox as secretary of the interior, Ebenezer R. Hoar as attorney gen., and John A. J. Creswell as postmaster gen.

MAR. 6.   USG asked the Senate to pass a joint resolution exempting Stewart from the 1789 law prohibiting those engaged in trade or commerce from holding office in the Treasury Dept.

MAR. 9.   Stewart withdrew his acceptance of a cabinet post.

MAR. 10.   Washburne resigned as secretary of state. USG tendered the office to Hamilton Fish.

MAR. 11.   Secretary of War John M. Schofield resigned. USG nominated Fish as secretary of state, John A. Rawlins as secretary of war, George S. Boutwell as secretary of the treasury, and Washburne as minister to France.

MAR. 12.   After first declining USG's nomination, Fish agreed to become secretary of state.

MAR. 15.   USG met representatives of the Cherokees, Choctaws, Creeks, and Chickasaws and assured them of his goodwill.

MAR. 18.   USG's family moved into the White House following repairs and the installation of new wallpaper and carpets.

MAR. 19.   USG signed a bill securing equal rights for blacks in Washington, D.C.

MAR. 30.   Recovered from facial neuralgia and exhaustion, USG received visitors for the first time in three days.

APRIL 2.   USG held a private interview with Lt. Governor Oscar J. Dunn of La., the first prominent black public official to visit the White House.

APRIL 7.   USG asked Congress to authorize elections in Va. and Miss. to ratify state constitutions.

APRIL 10.   Congress adjourned after creating the Board of Indian Commissioners and passing the Judiciary Act to increase the number of U.S. Supreme Court justices from seven to nine.

APRIL 12.   The Senate convened a special session in accordance with USG's proclamation of April 8.

APRIL 13.   USG nominated Ely S. Parker as commissioner of Indian Affairs.

APRIL 20.   USG met Rabbi H. Z. Sneersohn, who discussed the plight of Jews in Palestine.

APRIL 21.   USG met John W. Forney and others traveling through the South to promote the investment of northern capital.

APRIL 29.   Traveling by U.S. Navy steamer, USG and an excursion party visited Mount Vernon and George Washington's tomb.

MAY 1.   USG met privately with Robert E. Lee.

MAY 10.   The Union Pacific and Central Pacific Railroads completed the first transcontinental track.

MAY 19.   USG offered George H. Stuart appointment as secretary of the navy.

MAY 19.   USG issued a proclamation clarifying the eight-hour-day law for government employees by prohibiting any reduction in wages to compensate for reduced hours.

MAY 25. USG visited the U.S. Naval Academy and returned the next day.

MAY 29. USG participated in a memorial service for Union soldiers at Arlington Cemetery.

JUNE 4. USG distributed diplomas to U.S. Naval Academy graduates.

JUNE 9. USG, family members, and Rawlins left Washington, D.C., for USMA and the Boston Peace Jubilee.

JUNE 16. USG spoke in Boston and toured the city.

JUNE 21. USG left New York City for Washington, D.C.

JUNE 25. Borie resigned as secretary of the navy. On the same day, George M. Robeson assumed this office.

JUNE 30. USG visited Baltimore and the machine shops of the Baltimore & Ohio Railroad as the guest of John W. Garrett.

JULY 1. USG distributed diplomas and awards at the Georgetown College commencement but avoided meeting Andrew Johnson, whose son was among the graduates.

JULY 13. USG assigned Babcock as special agent to investigate affairs in Santo Domingo and designated Nov. 30 for the ratification vote on the proposed Miss. state constitution. On July 15, USG designated Nov. 30 for a similar vote in Tex.

JULY 15. USG and family left for Long Branch, N.J., arriving on July 19 after stopping at Fort Monroe, Va., and Cape May, N.J.

JULY 22. USG, Julia Grant, and their daughter, Nellie, visited New York City.

JULY 26. USG presided over a gala evening ball and reception at the Stetson House, Long Branch.

AUG. 3. USG announced that he had purchased a seaside summer home in Long Branch. USG left Long Branch by steamer to visit Wall Street, USMA, and Fish at his home in Garrison, N.Y.

AUG. 7. USG attended a parade and banquet in his honor at Newburg, N.Y.

AUG. 10. USG returned to Washington, D.C., for a cabinet meeting, while his family remained in New York City.

Aug. 13.   Traveling in a car provided by the Erie Railroad, USG visited that company's locomotive works at Elmira, N.Y.

Aug. 14.   USG went to Kane, Pa., and spent the next four days trout fishing and visiting coal and iron mines.

Aug. 19.   USG stopped briefly in New York City on his way to Newport, R.I.

Aug. 25.   USG visited manufacturing mills at Manchester, N.H., and attended a reception at Concord.

Aug. 28.   USG arrived in Saratoga, N.Y.

Aug. 31.   In Washington, D.C., for a cabinet meeting, USG departed the next day for Saratoga, arriving on Sept. 2.

Sept. 3.   USG gave a reception at the Union Hotel, Saratoga.

Sept. 6.   Rawlins died in Washington, D.C., before USG could return from Saratoga. On Sept. 7, USG contributed $1,000 to the Rawlins Family fund.

Sept. 9.   USG left Washington, D.C., for New York City after attending Rawlins's funeral and appointing Sherman as temporary secretary of war.

Sept. 14.   USG spoke briefly in Johnstown and Pittsburgh on his way to Washington, Pa., where, on Sept. 18, he took part in laying the cornerstone of the town hall.

Sept. 24.   Gold prices, inflated by speculation, plummeted in a "panic" after USG ordered the sale of U.S. government gold, thwarting the market-cornering scheme of Jay Gould and James Fisk but creating enough financial havoc to earn the designation "Black Friday."

Oct. 3.   USG told the Associated Press that he had done nothing to influence the money markets.

Oct. 5.   Abel R. Corbin, USG's brother-in-law, denied complicity in the gold panic.

Oct. 13.   USG named William W. Belknap as secretary of war.

Oct. 14.   USG spoke briefly at an agricultural fair in Frederick, Md. On Oct. 15, he toured the battlefield at Antietam.

Oct. 19.   U.S. naval vessels seized the filibuster ship *Hornet* at Wilmington, N.C.

Oct. 26.   USG and Julia Grant left Washington, D.C., to attend the wedding of Anna Simpson and James R. Weaver in Philadelphia.

The Papers of Ulysses S. Grant
July 1, 1868–October 31, 1869

To Bvt. Maj. Gen. John A. Rawlins

By Telegraph from St Louis Mo [*July*] 8 *1868*
To MAJ GEN JNO A RAWLINS
CHIEF OF STAFF.

No person ineligible to hold office under the 14th Article of the Constitutional amendment should be allowed to qualify. District Commanders are the judges of the qualification of Civil Officers until all the requirements of the different acts of Congress, to complete reconstruction of the seceded states, are fully complied with

U. S. GRANT,
General.

Telegram received (at 10:00 P.M.), DNA, RG 107, Telegrams Collected (Bound); *ibid.*, RG 108, Telegrams Received; copy, DLC-USG, V, 55. On July 6, 1868, Maj. Gen. George G. Meade, Atlanta, had telegraphed to USG. "Both houses of the Legislature of this state organised on the 4th inst, by electing a Presidents of the Senate & Speaker of the House—Indications would seem to point to a democratic majority in the Lower House, and probable rejection of the 14th article—When the houses were organised, all members who had received the largest number of votes, were allowed to qualify by taking the oath prescribed by the Constitution of the State, and no reference was made to the eligibility of members under the 14th article—It is believed there are several in both houses who are disqualified, but of course it is not to be expected that a democratic majority will make any haste to unseat such—The question is have I any authority in the premises—A Legislative body is undoubtedly the judge of the qualifications of its own members—but has a legislature convened under the reconstruction acts & therefore provisional, under these acts & the act of June 25th, until it has passed the 14th article, the right to pass the 14th article or do any act beyond mere organisation, until it has purged itself of disqualified members, and can I in view of the powers conferred by the reconstruction acts, exercise any control over them in case of their failure so to do—An early reply to this telegram is requested." ALS (telegram sent), Meade Papers, PHi; telegrams received (2—at 8:00 P.M.), DNA, RG 107, Telegrams Collected (Bound); *ibid.*, RG 108, Telegrams Received. On July 7, 2:00 P.M., Bvt. Maj. Gen. John A. Rawlins telegraphed to Meade. "Your dispatch relative to the eligibility of members of the Georgia Legislature, and your authority touching the same, has been received and forwarded to Gen Grant for instructions. It is clear to my mind that, under the reconstruction acts, including the one passed June 25, 1868, that no person prohibited from holding office under the United States, or any state, by section three of the proposed amendment to the Constitution of the United States known as Article 14 unless relieved from such disability, is eligible to a seat in the Legislature; and is, therefore not competent to take part in its deliberations or to pass upon the ratifications of said Amendment. Under ordinary circumstances the Legislature itself would be the proper judge of the qualifications of its members, and bearing upon this latter point I send you herewith copy of dispatch of Hon J. F. Wilson, Geo S Boutwell and others to Governor Warmouth of Louisiana. I also send one from Gen Grant to me for General Buchanan, which most unmistakably defines his views of the character of these governments and authority of the District Commanders. The Reconstruction Acts are required to be construed liberally to the end that all the intents thereof viz: the reestablishment of civil governments, in the states lately in rebellion, may be fully and perfectly carried out, and it would seem that persons ineligible to hold office under their provisions should not be permitted to defeat them. . . . 'June 30 1868. Gov. WARMOUTH New Orleans. We think that persons disqualified by the 14th Article of the Amendment to the Constitution of the United States are not eligible to your Legislature. This is to be determined by the respective Houses; but no oath can be imposed, except the oath prescribed by the State Constitution. signed JAS F WILSON, Chairman Judiciary Committee, GEO. S. BOUTWELL, J. F FARNSWORTH H. E. PAINE, Reconstruction Committee.' 'Relay House Md., June 30, 68. To MAJ GEN RAWLINS. Instruct General Buchanan that the government of Louisiana is provisional and the Lieutenant Governor is bound by the decisions of the District Commander, right or wrong, whilst it remains so. (signed) U. S. GRANT. General' " Telegram sent, *ibid.*, RG 107, Telegrams Collected (Bound); telegram received (at 11:00 P.M.), Meade Papers, PHi. At 7:45 P.M., Rawlins telegraphed to USG. "Herewith please find dispatch from Maj. Gn. Meade, with my reply to same." LS (telegram sent), DNA, RG 107, Telegrams Collected (Bound); telegram sent, *ibid.*; copies, *ibid.*, RG 94, Letters Received, 834M 1869; *ibid.*, RG 108, Telegrams Sent; DLC-USG, V, 56.

On July 8, Meade wrote to USG. "I have the honor to report that on receiept of official information from His Excellency Harrison Reed Provl-Govr of Florida, that the Legislature of that state, had adopted the amendment to the Constitution known as Article 14—and had otherwise complied with the requisitions of the Act of Congress which became a law June 25 /68 I issued the accompanying General Order requiring the Military Commander in that state, to turn over to the civil authorities the government of the state, and to desist from any further interference upon any pretext whatever with civil affairs so soon as he secured official notification that the civil Government was duly inaugurated—I now enclose copies of letters from Col Sprague Comd in Florida & Govr Reed, announcing the accomplishment of these orders and that military rule under the Reconstruction Laws has ceased in the State of Florida." ALS, DNA, RG 94, Letters Received, 922M 1868.

On July 16, Meade telegraphed to Rawlins. "I am officially advised by the Commanding Officer Sub-District of Alabama, that the Legislature which convened on the 13th inst adopted on that day the 14th Article Constnl Amendment, and otherwise complied with the requisitions of the Act of June 25–/68 and

that on the 14th the Governor elect was duly inaugurated & installed in office."
ALS (telegram sent), Meade Papers, PHi; telegram received (at 6:00 P.M.),
DNA, RG 107, Telegrams Collected (Bound); *ibid.*, RG 108, Telegrams Re-
ceived. On July 8, George P. Rex, Selma, "late Surgeon, 33, Ills Reg, Vet, Inf,
Surg in Chief 1 Div 16. A. C. Army of Tennessee," wrote to Rawlins. "I have
learned that there is a probability of the removal of Brev Brig Gen O. L. Sheppard from the command of the Sub. Milt. Dist. of Alabama. In behalf of the
loyal people of this state, we would earnestly remonstrate against his removal,
Gen Sheppard is a true man, and true to the intrests of the loyal people of this
State, and has discharged his duties with fidelity & impartiality; he has endeared himself to every loyal man in the State, by his course of strict honor and
justice, and no greater calamity could befal us, than his removal from the command of the State, at this time. You will do us a great favor, if you will have
him retained in his present command" ALS, *ibid.*, Letters Received. On July
25, Rawlins endorsed an undated petition. "The undersigned Members of the
General Assembly of the State of Alabama, beg leave most respectfully to represent that the retirement of General O. L. Shepperd from the command of the
District of Alabama, either by his removal, or by an order relieveing him of duty
at his own request—would in our judgment operate most disastrously to the
cause of peace, law and order, in this State, at this particular crisis in our political history,   The necessity for an efficient officer, one who commands the
entire confidence of the people, has at no time during the process of reconstruction, been more manifest than at this particular juncture,   Gen Shepperd commands the respect & Confidence of the entire people, and the moral effect of his
mere presence, in the capacity of commander of the State, will of itself secure a
strict observance of the law, and suppress violence and disorder, without a
resort to harsh and extreme measures   Such results might not follow, if a
new commander were introduced, a stranger to the masses and one who had
not yet won their confidence,   We therefore respectfully protest against his
removal, and against an order relieving him of duty here, at a period fraught
with so much danger to the peace of society, and to the cause of the Union, and
successful reconstruction   And in behalf of these great interests we earnestly
invoke your timely interposition, to prevent the terrible calamities that will
probably flow from a change of commanders at this time," DS, *ibid.*, RG 94,
Letters Received, 467B 1868. On July 25, six Ala. representatives wrote to
USG. "The undersigned members of Congress from the State of Alabama do
most earnestly and respectfully request the General of the Army to retain in
command of the District of Alabama, Genl O. L. Shepherd,—the present commandant. All union men of the State regard his retention as indispensable to
peace and good order; and we cordially unite in the petition of the General Assembly of the State to have him retained even against his own request to be
removed." LS, *ibid.*, RG 108, Letters Received.

On July 18, Meade telegraphed to USG. "On the 8th (eighth) instant having been officially notified by the Provl-Gov of Georgia, that both Houses of the
Legislature, had reported to him they were organised, and ready for any com-
municatn from him—I instructed the Govr to communicate to both houses, that
until compliance was had with the laws of Congress, I considered them as
provisional, and subject to my control, and that I could not consider either
house legally organised until, it had examined into & decided on the eligibility

of its members under the 14th Article—On receipt of this communication both house appointed a committee to investigate and report—In the senate a majority of the Comee reported all eligible—one member of the minority reported two ineligible—another member of the minority reported nine ineligible—The Senate after hearing the report of the committee, and excluding the senators reported against from voting endorsed and adopted the report of the majority declaring none ineligible.—This action is today transmitted to me by the Provl Governor, who adopts the extreme report of the minority—gives his judgement that the action of the majority of the committee and of the Senate is illegal, and that the nine members are ineligible—states however that he has official information that certain of these members, have had their disability removed by Congress, and calls on me to over-rule the decision of the Senate and declare vacant the seats of those members reported against by one member of the minority, whose disabilities have not been removed.—I am not disposed to alter the position I have assumed, that it is the prerogative of each House to judge of the facts & the law in the cases of members of their Houses—I consider I have performed my duty, when I called their attention to the law & required action to be taken under it I do not feel myself competent to over-rule the deliberate action of a Legislative body, who report they have conformed to the rule I laid down for their guidance If I was the sole and exclusive judge of the qualifications of members, I should have exercised my prerogative before allowing the houses to organise—I construed the despatch of Mr Wilson to Govr Warmouth prohibiting any oath, but such as the constitution prescribed, as prohibiting any test in advance of the House having control, and as leaving to each House the right to decide—My judgement therefore is to acquiesce in the decision of the Senate and leave to Congress, such action as may hereafter be deemed proper, in case the Senate has failed to comply with the law. To adopt the course proposed by the Provl Govr and over-rule the action of the Senate— will bring me in immediate conflict with the Legislature, and produce results— which in my judgement will be worse than allowing a few doubtful members to retain seats under the vote of their own body.—It is proper I should add that there appears at present no doubt but that the congressional acts will be complied with, even if members whose seats are questioned are left undisturbed— So far as I can ascertain the trouble is a personal one, arising out of the contest for U-S. Senatorship. I should also add that the Senate whose action is reported, has a decided republican majority, and could have purged itself of such members, as are clearly ineligible—What I desire to know, is whether in your judgement, my duty requires me to override the deliberate act of the Senate, and judge for myself on the qualifications of members—I have no doubt of my power in the premises but do not feel, that I am called on to do more than I have done—" ALS (telegram sent), Meade Papers, PHi; telegram received (at 10:00 P.M.), DNA, RG 107, Telegrams Collected (Bound); *ibid.*, RG 108, Telegrams Received. See *HED*, 40-3-1, III, part 1, p. 113; *SED*, 41-2-13, p. 50. On July 21, USG, Denver, telegraphed to Rawlins. "Meades dispatch received, His conclusions are approved—Ask Secretary to recommend Gen'l. Augur for Brigadier General" Telegram received (on July 22), DLC-John M. Schofield; (dated July 22, received 5:00 P.M.) DNA, RG 107, Telegrams Collected (Bound).

On July 21, Meade telegraphed to USG. "Both houses of the Legislature of Georgia having examined into & decided upon the qualifications of their respective members under the 14th Article Constitutional Amendment I yesterday instructed the Provl Governor to communicate to each House, that I considered their organisation legal & withdrew any opposition to their proceeding to the business which called them together. Today both Houses by decided majorities have passed the Constitutional Amenendment known as article 14, and will without dout at once otherwise comply with the requisition of the act of June 25th /68" ALS (telegram sent), Meade Papers, PHi; telegram received (at 4:20 P.M.), DNA, RG 107, Telegrams Collected (Bound); (at 5:00 P.M.) *ibid.*, RG 108, Telegrams Received. On July 22, Meade telegraphed and wrote to USG. "Yesterday the Govr Elect of Georgia notified me officially that both Houses of the General Assembly of Georgia had by solemn act, complied with the requisition of the Act of Congress, which became a law June 25–1868—and to day I have witnessed the inauguration of the Govr Elect   The state of Georgia is therefore under the acts of Congress entitled to representation—The official documents will be carried by todays mails to-day by Brvt-Brigr Genl—R—C. Drum sent to Washington for this purpose—" ALS (telegram sent), Meade Papers, PHi; telegram received (on July 23, 9:30 A.M.), DNA, RG 107, Telegrams Collected (Bound); *ibid.*, RG 108, Telegrams Received. "I have the honor to transmit herewith inclosed official copies of the Joint Resolutions of the General Assembly of the State of Georgia, 'ratifying the amendment to the constitution of the United States proposed by the 39th Congress' and 'to declare the assent of the State to the fundamental conditions imposed by Congress to entitle the State of Georgia to representation in Congress,' which passed both branches of the Legislature of Georgia, yesterday." LS, *ibid.*, RG 107, Letters Received from Bureaus.

On July 30, Meade telegraphed to USG. "The Govr of Georgia, advises me there is reason to believe, the municipal authorities of Augusta are about being resisted, by a combination made for that purpose.—These authorities, were the appointees of my predecessor, and it is probable the resistance anticipated, is on the ground that military authority having ceased, all agents deriving their power from the Military are functus officio.—The Govr calls on me to sustain the civil authorities if necessary—Instructions, and advice is requested, on the position the military power now occupies—In my judgement I have no right to interfere or use the military forces under my command except where so instructed to do, from superior authority—And that the Govr should report to Washington his inability to preserve order and enforce the law, before any orders are sent to [me]—If I am to preserve order in these states, and do the police duty of municipalities, whenever the civil authorities choose to call on me—I shall have my hands full, as the facility of having order preserved thro the U. S. forces, will act to deter proper efforts on the part of the Civil Power—Besides my force will be inadequate to do this duty—Not expecting any such duty, I consented to the withdrawal of the 15th Regt of Infantry.—I am not disposed, and do not desire, to use my command, on the judgement of others or at their dictation—As the reconstruction laws, and the powers given me under them no longer exist—I must ask explicit & distinct instructions as to my powers, and their proper exercise—This despatch can be shown to the Secy of War, if Genl. Grant is not at Hd

Qrs—" ALS (telegram sent), Meade Papers, PHi; telegram received (at 6:30 P.M.), DNA, RG 107, Telegrams Collected (Bound); *ibid.*, RG 108, Telegrams Received. On July 31, 6:30 P.M., Rawlins telegraphed to Meade. "Your telegram to the Genl Commanding requesting instructions and advice on the position the military power occupies in Georgia has been submitted to the Secretary of War and by him laid before the President and Cabinet. Your views as to when and how the military forces under your command may be used ~~are~~ were approved of, and I am instructed by the Secretary of War to say to you that he will prepare and send to you instructions for your guidance. Also that should any insurrection or riot break out before you receive them to advise the Governor to telegraph to the President for the requested authority to use the troops in quelling the same—By referring to Gen Grants letter to you dated June 27th 1868, you will find his opinion upon the tenure of office of military appointees which is against their continuance unless provided for by state authority—" Telegrams sent (2), *ibid.*, RG 107, Telegrams Collected (Bound); telegram received, Meade Papers, PHi. See *HED*, 40-3-1, III, part 1, pp. 121–23.

To Charles R. Morehead, Jr.

———

ST. LOUIS, Mo., July 14, 1868.

Hon. C. R. Morehead, Jr.:
Mayor of Leavenworth, Kansas:

DEAR SIR: Your favor of the 11th inst., enclosing resolution of the Council of Leavenworth City, extending to me a public reception, and asking when I shall be in your city, is received. I expect to leave this city for Leavenworth in the train which starts in the afternoon to-morrow. I will probably be in Leavenworth one day, at the quarters of General Sheridan, when I will be happy to meet all the citizens of Leavenworth who do me the honor to call. But allow me to decline a public reception. I fully appreciate the compliment conveyed in the resolution which you forward, and thank the City Council and citizens for it; but while travelling for recreation, and to inspect personally a country with which I have so much to do and have never seen, I would much prefer avoiding public demonstrations.

Believing that you and the citizens of Leavenworth, to whom I reiterate my thanks, will fully appreciate this feeling, and the

motive which induces me to decline this proffered kindness, I subscribe myself.

> Very respectfully, your obedient servant,
> U. S. GRANT.

Washington Chronicle, July 25, 1868. Born in Mo. in 1836, Charles R. Morehead, Jr., a merchant in Leavenworth since 1860, became mayor in 1868.

To Julia Dent Grant

———

FORT LEAVENWORTH, KANSAS, July 17th *1868*.

DEAR JULIA,

We arrived here last evening, seven hours behind time, and
after all sorts of delays. Owing to a stryike among the engineers
on the road we were detained at Webster station, awaiting the
train, untill between 9 & 10 O'Clock at night. The country to this
place is beautiful, and this is one of the most beautiful military
posts in the United States. We leave it in the morning for the far
West, Gens. Sherman and Sheridan accompanying us. Instead of
returning from the end of the road, as I had intended, we will cross
over to the other road and return by by that. This arrangement will
extend my trip about four days beyond what it would have been
had I returned from the end of the road. This will probably be the
last chance I will ever have to visit the plains, and the rapid settlement is changing the character of them so rapidly, that I thought
I would avail myself of the opportunity to see them. It will be
something for Buck too, in after life, to know that he had traveled
on the plains whilst still occupied by the Buffalo and the Indian,
both rapidly disappearing now. He is delighted with the prospect.
Sherman, Sheridan, Fred Buck & myself each carry with us a
Spencer Carbine and hope to shoot a Buffalo and Elk before we return. There are military stations all the way across only ten miles
apart. The time taken in travel is three days to the other road.

About Tuesday week is the time you may look for me back.—Love and kisses to Nellie Jess & yourself.

ULYS.

ALS, USG 3.

On July 17, 1868, USG, Fort Leavenworth, telegraphed to Bvt. Maj. Gen. John A. Rawlins. "Dispatches from twentieth 20 to twenty third 23 will reach me in Denver   Will leave here tomorrow" Telegram received (at 1:20 P.M.), DNA, RG 107, Telegrams Collected (Bound); *ibid.*, RG 108, Telegrams Received; copies, DLC-USG, V, 55; DLC-John M. Schofield.

To Julia Dent Grant

———

D[en]ver C. T.
July 21st 1868,

DEAR JULIA,

We have just arrived ~~a~~in this city of the Mountains, all well, enjoying the trip by stage, across the plains, very much. I would not have missed it for a great deal, and Buck has enjoyed it hugely. Yesterday we rode One hundred & twenty miles in stage, over the plains, between 6'.30" a. m. and 10 p. m. firing from the stage frequently at Antelope. We killed two, ~~one of~~ one of which was shot either by Buck or Gn. Sheridan, we could not tell which. Buck will have a great deal to tell when he gets home which will be about the 30th of this month. We will be detained here two ~~delay~~ days longer than I would have staid on account of our baggage. From Leavenworth our baggage was all checked through, but when we got to the end of the rail-road we found that Freds & my trunks were not along. By telegraphing back we found that in changing cars at Lawrence, Kansas, the baggage man had left our trunks on the platform. Next day being Sunday no train was coming up, consequently it put the baggage back two days. I do not regret it now however because I shall spend the two days in the gold mines in the mountains which probably I would never see but for this accident.

Buck has enjoyed his trip beyond any he has ever yet taken. He has seen wild horses, Buffalo, wolf & Antelope and had frequent shots at the two latter. I have regreted so much not bringing Jesse with me. He would have enjoyed the trip and this high mountain air would have made him strong and well, given him an apetite for anything. We have felt no oppression from heat for three days.

Love and kisses to you, Nellie & Jesse.

> Yours Affectionately
> ULYS.

The towns we visit are Golden City, Central City, Black Hawk & Georgetown, the latter sixty miles from here. We go to-morrow and return next day.

> U.

ALS, USG 3.

To Isaac N. Morris

July 31st 1868.

DEAR SIR:

I will leave here, with my family, for Galena on Thursday next,[1] by rail. Having my children, servants, and Mrs. Grant's father, we will go direct and make our visit to you from there. Mrs. Grant says now she will accompany me to Quincy. But I doubt it. She is very hard to get started when once settled. I will be there however if nothing unforeseen happens in the mean time.

You are severe on Frank Blair.[2]

> Yours Truly
> U. S. GRANT

To HON. I. N. MORRIS.

ALS, ICarbS. On Aug. 8, 1868, USG, Galena, twice wrote to Isaac N. Morris. "Your letter of the 2d inst. asking me to drop you a line to let you know when I would leave St. Loui[s] was duly received. As I had written to you but the day before your letter was written, informing you of my proposed plann of movement, I supposed it would be answer enough.—I can not say exactly the day

I will be in Quincy but think it will be on Friday next. If I can get off from here Wednesday evening I will remain Thursday with my brother in Chicago and go on to Quincy Thursday night. If I start later than that I will go direct to Quincy without making any stop at Chicago." ALS, *ibid.* "I shall be in Quincy on Wednesday morning one day earlyer than I wrote you in my last." Daniel F. Kelleher Co., Inc., Oct. 8, 1985, no. 62.

On Aug. 15, USG visited Quincy and responded to speeches of welcome made by Morris and Benjamin M. Prentiss. "LADIES AND GENTLEMEN OF QUINCY—It is impossible for me to find words to express my gratification for this kind and enthusiastic reception. I thought that I was visiting your city very quietly to pay a visit to my lifelong friend, Colonel I. N. Morris. What was my surprise to find what seems to be not only the whole city, but the county of Adams, turned out to welcome me to your midst. I cannot properly thank you for this ovation, but permit me to return my heartfelt thanks for this undeserved mark of your partiality and kind feelings." Clippings in DLC-Edward McPherson; Morris Family Papers, IHi. On Aug. 16, USG wrote to Morris concerning the visit. *ABPC*, 1905, p. 556.

On Oct. 3, Morris wrote to USG. "I hope you will not be alarmed at the number or magnetude of the enclosed Documents. Dr Pierce is the brother-in-law of Senator Hendricks. I mentioned him to you when you were here He must, of course, sustain Mr H but after the state election passes he will render you good service. His position is now delicate When you look over the publications relating to him please return these to me as I have to return them to him The long one, however, I am going to have first published if I can get it in some paper in this state. I suppose you may notice I still continue my letters to Blair. The 8th I enclose you. I know very well you do not get time to read them all, but the one I send and the two or three which shall follow it I hope you will read I have not yet consented to go upon the stump for three reasons 1st I doubt if my health would permit it 2d I think I am doing and can do more good with my pen. 3rd The Republican politicans do not act as if they wanted to recognise any Democrat as a helper. They certainly take no pains to put these forward for the reasons they want to claim all the glory of your election after it transpires. The course of the Central State Comt of this State is strange. But let it go We are determined to help you any how all we can. Simply as the Republican candidate you could not be elected. This you must very well understand. I suppose you will allow us to perform as a *side-show* at least if we pay our own bills and give a free exhibition! Our regards to Mrs Grant God bless you! . . . I received a letter from Horace Greely to day and send you a copy thereof" ALS, USG 3. On Oct. 9, USG telegraphed to Morris. "Your letter received will be glad to See you on Monday" Telegram received (at 1:20 P.M.), ICarbS.

1. On Wednesday, Aug. 5, USG spoke in St. Louis. "GENTLEMEN AND FELLOW-CITIZENS: I can scarcely find words to thank you for this very hearty and warm reception. It is peculiarly gratifying to me to meet so many friends in St. Louis, a place which has arisen since I have been a man grown, and where I have interests, AND WHERE I INTEND TO BECOME A RESIDENT AT SOME FUTURE DAY. Thanking you again, I will bid you good night." *New York World*, Aug. 7, 1868. On Aug. 7, USG responded to a speech by J. A. Smith welcoming him to Galena. "GENTLEMEN AND FELLOW-CITIZENS OF

GALENA—After an absence of three years from your midst, it affords me great pleasure to return here again to see you all, and, as I hope, spend an agreeable and quiet fortnight with you. During that time, I will be happy to see you at your homes, and at mine whenever you can make it convenient to call I shall not on this occasion, nor upon any other, make you a speech, which I suppose you are well aware of. I am very glad to see you." *Chicago Journal*, Aug. 8, 1868.

2. During the campaign, Morris wrote a seventeen-page pamphlet, *Grant: And Why He Should Be Elected President*, and published at least eight letters addressed to Francis P. Blair, Jr., Democratic candidate for vice president. *New York Times*, Oct. 16, 1868. In a much-publicized letter of June 30, Blair proposed to overthrow "the Radical plan of reconstruction" by having a Democratic president-elect "declare these acts null and void, compel the army to undo its usurpations at the South, disperse the carpet bag State Governments, allow the white people to reorganize their own Governments and elect Senators and Representatives." *Ibid.*, July 3, 1868. In his letter accepting the nomination, Blair added an attack on the "military leader under whose prestige this usurping Congress has taken refuge since the condemnation of their schemes by the free people of the North in the elections of the last year, and whom they have selected as their candidate to shield themselves from the result of their own wickedness and crime, has announced his acceptance of the nomination and his willingness to maintain their usurpations over the eight millions of white people at the South, fixed to the earth with his bayonets. He exclaims: 'Let us have peace.' " *Ibid.*, July 22, 1868.

To Bvt. Maj. Gen. John A. Rawlins

Cipher   *By Telegraph from* St Louis Mo [*Aug.*] 1 *1868*
To GEN. JNO. A. RAWLINS,
CHIEF OF STAFF.
Have not received letter on subject of remitting sentence of military commission. Exercise your judgement in my name
U. S. GRANT
General

Telegram received (at 2:30 P.M.), DNA, RG 107, Telegrams Collected (Bound); (at 2:50 P.M.) *ibid.*, RG 108, Telegrams Received; copy, DLC-USG, V, 55. On July 30, 1868, 3:00 P.M., Bvt. Maj. Gen. John A. Rawlins telegraphed to USG. "Have you received my letter on subject of remitting sentences of military Commissions." Telegrams sent (2), DNA, RG 107, Telegrams Collected (Bound); copies, *ibid.*, RG 108, Telegrams Sent; DLC-USG, V, 55.

On Aug. 2, USG wrote to Rawlins. "Recommends remission of all sentences by Military Courts in states lately in rebellion—now having adopted reconstruction measures of Congress." DNA, RG 108, Register of Letters Received.

This is probably the same letter from USG to Rawlins, catalogued as dated Aug. 21, concerning "persons now serving out sentences of Military Commissions, convened under the reconstruction Acts of Congress, in those states where these laws have become inoperative. . . . The States of North Carolina, South Carolina, Georgia, Florida, Alabama, Louisiana and Arkansas having been restored to self government, by law, and the Acts of Congress authorizing Military trials in these states being inoperative . . . I wish you would recommend to the Sec. of War, in my name, the remission of all unexpired sentences against citizens of all of the above states, inflicted by Military Courts." *The Collector* (Jan., 1949), 155. On Aug. 5, Rawlins wrote to Secretary of War John M. Schofield. "I am authorized by General Grant to recommend to you the remission of the remainder of the sentences, and the release from imprisonment, of all persons now in confinement under sentence of military commissions organized under the reconstruction acts of Congress, in the States in which the reconstruction laws have ceased to be operative." LS, DLC-Andrew Johnson.

To Bvt. Maj. Gen. John A. Rawlins

Cipher   *By Telegraph from* St Louis Mo [*Aug.*] 5 1868
To MAJ GEN JNO. A. RAWLINS,
CHIEF OF STAFF.
Direct General Meade to leave troops as now stationed in Alabama if they have not been already concentrated. If they have been sent to Huntsville, direct that, at least four 4 companies be stationed at the state capital of Alabama, and the rest held in reserve to answer calls should they be made by the Governor of the State.

U. S. GRANT
General

Telegram received (on Aug. 6, 1868, 8:45 A.M.), DNA, RG 107, Telegrams Collected (Bound); *ibid.*, RG 108, Telegrams Received; DLC-USG, V, 55. On Aug. 4, 3:00 P.M., Bvt. Maj. Gen. John A. Rawlins telegraphed to USG. "Gen. Meade's order of the 30th ulto concentrates the troops in Alabama as follows: Eight companies at Huntsville and two companies at Mobile. These are all the troops to be left in the State, and will leave Montgomery—the State capital and where the legislature is in session without troops. It seems to me one company at least should be stationed at Montgomery, and the others distributed in different parts of the State, where their presence will in a measure preserve peace. Senators Spencer and Warner say Huntsville and vicinity is the most orderly part of the State, and the worst are Jacksonville, Talledega, Tuscaloosa, Selma, Mobile and Montgomery. I suppose the concentration of them at Huntsville is in view of their health, ~~and~~ economy and supposed availability. The Secretary of War is absent. Have you any instructions?" LS (telegram sent), DNA, RG 107, Telegrams Collected (Bound); telegram sent, *ibid.*; *ibid.*, RG 94, Letters Received, 377A 1868; copies, *ibid.*, Annual Reports, 1869; *ibid.*, RG 108, Telegrams Sent; DLC-USG, V, 56. On Aug. 5, 12:20 P.M., Rawlins telegraphed to USG. "If the troops in Alabama are to be concentrated at any point it strikes me most forcibly that Montgomery is that point. Its river and railroad facilities would enable them to reach more readily the most disaffected districts than from any other place. To reach them from Huntsville would require them to march from Decatur or move by railroad via Atlanta; this of course you know from your own familiarity with army operations there. Gen. Meade's proposed disposition of the troops I am informed alarms the law and order men. They regard it as a virtual withdrawal of them from the State." LS (telegram sent), DNA, RG 107, Telegrams Collected (Bound); telegram sent, *ibid.*; *ibid.*, RG 94, Letters Received, 376A 1869; copies, *ibid.*, Annual Reports, 1869; *ibid.*, RG 108, Telegrams Sent; DLC-USG, V, 56. See *HED*, 40-3-1, III, part 1, pp. 116–17.

On Aug. 6, Maj. Gen. George G. Meade, Charleston, S. C., telegraphed to Rawlins. "Please get from Adjutant Genl. and forward to Genl. Grant my telegram of yesterday to Secr of War giving reasons for concentration of troops— It was not with any intention of not answering any proper calls made on me by the constituted civil authorities—tho' I am of the opinion that said calls should be made thro' the authorities at Washington—on the contrary my disposition of troops was made with a view of promptly acting by moves if action was required—I did not station any at Montgomery because the place is unhealthy, and I thought it better to remove the troops from the centre of political agitation—but I have 4 companies at Mobile and 8 at Atlanta that can be sent to Montgomery in less than a day—It is now too late to change without great confusion existing orders, and I trust the Genl. in chief has that confidence in my judgement that when he is apprised of my reasons and himself examines the disposition of the troops that he will refrain from over-ruling me—If however he is still of the opinion that 4 companies should be at Montgomery—they can be sent from the troops now in this command the late 2d District—I would state there never has been over three companies at Montgomery—and that I do not know of a single reason for troops being at Montgomery, than any other town in the state—" ALS (telegram sent), Meade Papers, PHi; telegram received (on Aug. 7, 9:00 A.M.), DNA, RG 107, Telegrams Collected (Bound); *ibid.*, RG 108, Telegrams Received.

On Sept. 14, Meade, Philadelphia, telegraphed to Rawlins. "On the twelfth 12 instant I telegraphed the Secretary of War urging my being permitted to retain the squadron of the Fifth 5 Cavalry hitherto at my Head Quarters—the other four companies in the Dept to go west. There are duties to be performed in the mountainous portion of N. and S Carolina Georgia and Alabama which can only be performed by disciplined cavalry—mounted infantry of no avail. This consideration in addition to my desire to have a reserve at Atlanta for contingencies impel me to ask at least for the present a suspension of the order removing the squadron from Atlanta. Should the exigencies of the public service not admit of the squadron being left I would ask for the retention of Capt Mealys company as they are familiar with Head Quarter duty. Please see the

Secretary and let me know decision today and aid me in having my request granted." Telegrams received (2—at 1:45 P.M.), *ibid.*, RG 107, Telegrams Collected (Bound); copy, Meade Papers, PHi. On Sept. 17, Meade telegraphed to Rawlins. "War Dept advises me that orders for movement of cavalry from the Dept of South, were issued by Genl in Chief—My telegram of 14th inst was predicated on the supposition these orders were from the War Dept—The four companies from N & So Carolina have moved, but the squadron hitherto at my Head quarters at Atlanta, ~~are~~ is awaiting action on my application to retain it— which I beg leave earnestly to renew and to ask action thereon—repeating my request that in case I can not retain the squadron, I may be allowed to retain Capt Maly's company.—" ALS (telegram sent), *ibid.*; telegrams received (2— at 1:00 P.M.), DNA, RG 107, Telegrams Collected (Bound); *ibid.*, RG 108, Telegrams Received. At 2:50 P.M., Rawlins telegraphed to USG transmitting the final sentence of Meade's telegram. Telegrams sent (2), *ibid.*, RG 107, Telegrams Collected (Bound); copies, *ibid.*, RG 108, Telegrams Sent; DLC-USG, V, 56. On the same day, USG, Galena, telegraphed to Rawlins. "Let squadron of Cavalry at Atlanta Remain there" Telegram received (at 6:52 P.M.), DNA, RG 107, Telegrams Collected (Bound); *ibid.*, RG 108, Tele-grams Received; copies, *ibid.*, RG 94, Letters Received, 440A 1868; DLC-USG, V, 55.

To Lt. Gen. William T. Sherman

Gn.

I have sent the following dispatch in reply,

Galena, Aug. 8th /68

Gov. R. Fenton,
Albany N Y.

I would respectfully but urgently add my recommendation to the thousands of others that the place occupied by Gn. Halpine be filled by a competant person who will bestow the profits of the of-fice upon his berieved family. Gn. Halpin's devotion to his adopted country entitle his family, it seems to me, to this acknowledgement of the value of his services.

U. S. Grant

ALS, DLC-William T. Sherman. Written on the reverse of a telegram received on Aug. 7, 1868, 7:40 P.M., dated Aug. 6, from Horace Greeley, Charles A. Dana, and Robert B. Roosevelt, New York City, to USG, Lt. Gen. William T. Sherman, and Maj. Gen. Philip H. Sheridan. "Governor Fenton has the power to fill the vacancy caused by General Halpines death with some person who will appropriate the profits to his Family   may we ask that from friendship for the deceased you will Telegraph to Governor Fenton a recommendation of such Kindness to the family of one who deserved well of his Country—" Telegram received, *ibid.* Charles G. Halpine, born in 1829 in Ireland, emigrated to the U.S. in 1850, where he became known as a journalist, poet, and humorist. A Civil War staff officer for Maj. Gen. David Hunter, he later wrote an enthusiastic poem about USG, hoping that he would be the Democratic nominee for president in 1868. See William Hanchett, *Irish: Charles G. Halpine in Civil War America* (Syracuse, 1970).

To Jesse Root Grant

[*Aug. 14, 1868*]

DEAR FATHER, When I leave here I will go directly to West Point without passing through Cincinnati. The Judge Levitt[1] you speak of I presume is the Israelite who called on me at the time; if so I received his communication but not for three weeks after it was written. It was sent to St. Louis. . . . I was not in St. Louis . . . until my return from the Rocky Mountains. If this is the letter you refer to all I can say is the Judge has written out our conversation substantially correct. He wanted me to indorse it and make corrections if any were to be made. I could not do this. It would be a departure from a rule I have established and would lead to interminable correspondences. There was in the letter an allusion to a letter received by me before the publication of my June [*Jew*] orders, correctly given, as I recollect it . . . I sent it to Mr. Rawlins in Washington for verification, and with instructions to have the Judge's letter returned to him with or without remark from him. . . . The family are all well. I have enjoyed my summers vacation very much, and look forward with dread to my return to Washington. . . .

ULYSSES

Christie's, Dec. 8, 1989, no. 29. See letter to David Eckstein, Aug. 24, 1868.
   On April 22, 1868, Bvt. Brig. Gen. Adam Badeau wrote to Simon Wolf. "General Grant directs me to acknowledge the receipt of your letter of April 14th, in which you allude to an order issued by him in 1862, 'banishing the

Jews from the Department of the Tennessee', and in which you 'most respectfully ask as an American citizen and Israelite whether this order was intended
then or since to reflect in any way or manner on the Jews as a class, or whether
it was not an order directed simply against certain evil designing persons whose
religion however ~~certain~~ was in no way material to the issue' While General
Grant is extremely anxious to avoid thrusting himself into anything approaching a controversy on such a matter, he yet cannot fail to observe the cordial tone
and spirit of your note; and out of respect to that he instructs me to say that the
order was, as you suppose, 'directed simply against evil designing persons,
whose religion was in no way material to the issue' He fully appreciates the
services to which you allude rendered at various times to literature religion and
science, by Israelites and recognizes the fact that many of them were thoroughly
loyal to the country in the recent struggle for its existence. In the case in question, however, those who were guilty of carrying contraband articles and information across the lines were without exception, Israelites, and no others had
done this with success. This fact brought out the order, which would have been
made just as stringent against any other class of individuals who should have
interfered in the same way with his rules. When the order was made the guilty
parties happened to be Israelites exclusively, and it was made to reach the guilty
parties without intending to wound the feelings of any. It would have been made
just as stringent against any other class of individuals, religious, political or
commercial This communication is intended in no way to be made public, and
you will confer a favor on Gen Grant by withholding any notice of it from the
public press" ADfS, USGA. Another letter from Badeau to Wolf is described
as written later than April 22 and dated March. "I have brought your request
to the attention of General Grant, and while he would like very much indeed to
comply therewith, yet he fears that any statement made by him would be mis-
construed by the general public. He therefore prefers not to make any explanation other than that you have already received. He desires me to express his
hearty and sincere appreciation of the interest you have taken, knowing that your
motives are actuated by friendship and a desire to do justice not only to himself,
but to the people whom you so worthily represent." Simon Wolf, *The Presidents
I Have Known from 1860–1918* (Washington, [1918]), p. 66. On Dec. 11,
Badeau wrote to Wolf. "I can see no reason why the letter I wrote you last
summer relative to General Grant's Order No. 11, should not be published, as
you request." *Ibid.*, p. 67.

   Wolf published a letter dated Aug. 6. ". . . No one, even the General, denies
that the order was proscriptive, but in one sense not uncalled for. The General
never meant then, since, or now to proscribe the Jews because they were such,
but simply to banish from his camp the Lazzaroni who infested it. Unfortunately
the order was ill-worded, but that is no reason why *American citizens* should
be betrayed from their allegiance to principles, and turn to a party that advocates the reverse of what is right and true. . . . I know General Grant and his
motives, have corresponded with him on this very subject, and assert unhesitatingly *that he never intended to insult any honorable Jew; that he never thought
of their religion;* that the order was simply directed 'against certain evil-design-
ing persons, who respected neither law nor order, and who were endangering
the morale of the army.' . . . The order never harmed me—never harmed anyone, not even in thought, except those whom *we as Jews despise and hold in*

contempt. It would be perfect folly to suppose for a moment that the Jews have found in Grant another Titus, for he is fully aware of the noble deeds performed by thousands of Jewish privates, and hundreds of Jewish officers during the late war; and I know that some of his warmest friends, even in Washington, are Jews. The bugbear of what he may do when he becomes President is childish. He will do his duty as the law and the will of the people, through their chosen representatives, prescribe; *no more—no less. . . ." Boston Transcript*, Aug. 6, 1868. For Wolf's reliability, see *PUSG*, 7, 52.

On March 6, 1869, Wolf wrote to USG. "I have the honor to apply for a position in the foreign service of the Government. I am a German by birth, an Israelite in faith, and I trust a thorough American by adoption. Should I be appointed I will ever aim to uphold the dignity and integrity of the Government, and reflect credit upon the Country that has so kindly protected me." ALS, DNA, RG 59, Letters of Application and Recommendation. On March 12, Isidor Bush, St. Louis, wrote to U.S. Senator Carl Schurz of Mo. "Permit me to introduce to you herewith Mr Simon Wolf, or if he is already known to you—as he most probably is,—permit me to say that Mr Wolf has been one of the warmest and ablest supporters of President Grant during the last campain; This may not seem to be anything deserving special notice or any thanks. But if you remember the fierce opposition created among his (& my) correligionists against Grant—it took required more than ordinary firmness, fidelity to principles and party—character, nay boldness, in an Israelite—and more especially in a young Jew—who as attorney had principally Jews as his clients—to avow and to work zealously for the election of Genl Grant. Mr Wolf has done this most ably and successfully & has done perhaps more than any other to break down and to change this at first very violent opposition. Moreover he is a very amiable talented and learned young man, loved and esteemed by all who know him, and he is widely and favorably known especially among Israelites. Now if Presidt Grant wants to prove his impartiality towards toward Israelites and to disprove any unfriendliness attributed to him on account of Order No 11—there is probably no better opportunity than by appointing Mr Simon Wolf to the position for which I am informed, he is an applicant. And I hope therefore that you will gladly extend to him your influence in this matter." ALS, *ibid.* On March 29, Wolf wrote to George E. Baker. "By accident a letter from I. Bush of St Louis to Senator C. Schurz has been filed among my papers, please see that *bearer* receives the same." LS, *ibid.* Wolf noted that the letter had been retrieved. See David H. and Esther L. Panitz, "Simon Wolf as United States Consul to Egypt," *Publication of the American Jewish Historical Society*, XLVII, 2 (Dec., 1957), 76–100. USG appointed Wolf recorder of deeds, D. C.; President James A. Garfield appointed Wolf consul in 1881.

On May 3, 1869, Benjamin G. Goldberg, New York City, wrote to USG. "Relying on your former knowledge of my services to your cause in which I spent some four months, writing in the press and canvassing for your previous to your election—not forgetting that I risked my life for you in Missourie I venture to solicit your sympathy and kind assistance in my present distressed circumstances. I lost all my fortune in Cheyenne, and you may remember, I made application for a consulship and had an interview with you twice in Washington. Your personal knowledge of me induces me to solicit your aid now; afflicted as I am with sickness, being consumptive, and having a large family to support. As you have been favored by a beneficent Providence in attaining the highest point of good fortune, perhaps your assistance to me may be but the commencement of good fortune also. Trusting to be favored with a prompt and gracious reply to this my application . . ." ALS, DNA, RG 59, Letters of Application and Recommendation. Related papers, *ibid.*, include a newspaper clipping of Goldberg's letter. ". . . The candidate of this party for President, is General U. S. Grant, the man who led the national armies to victory and who has since shown his attchment to the great principles of right and justice. But this man, once in his life, in the midst of an exciting military campaign—when much was done to vex and harass him—and whilst he was manfully fighting for his country, made one mistake, and now that mistake, that single fault, is seized upon by the enemies of peace and friends of rebellion, to prejudice the Israelites against him and the great party he now leads. But we should, and as a general thing, I believe Israelites do, look beyond this single act, and weigh the good deeds of this man and his party against this single fault: Shall one fault outweigh all that is good in both man and party? . . . General Grant sees and acknowledges now that his order against the 'Jews' (as he called them) was too broad. We see it—we saw it then, and we did not like it. Yet his career has been so grand and his party of principles so conspicuous on every occasion, that I cannot consent to throw him aside for the single fault referred to. Who, amongst us, is perfect? He that is without a fault let him speak."

Newspaper debate concerning General Orders No. 11 persisted throughout the presidential election of 1868. See Bertram Wallace Korn, *American Jewry and the Civil War* (Philadelphia, 1951), pp. 132–38; Joakim Isaacs, "Candidate Grant and the Jews," *American Jewish Archives*, XVII, 1 (April, 1965), 3–16. On June 16, 1868, Joseph Medill, Chicago, wrote to U.S. Representative Elihu B. Washburne. ". . . What can be done in regard to that Jew order of Gen Grant issued in 1862 expelling 'all Jews as a class' from his department. We have in this city at least 600 Republican Jews, headed by Gen. Salomon who served under Gen. Grant when the latter was only a Colonel commanding a brigade. The Gen. has written to Grant on the subject but has received no answer. It would only be necessary for General Grant to write a letter to Salomon or some other influential Jew saying that he has no prejudice against Jews, that he is in favor of full toleration of all religious opinions; that his subsequent experience in the army convinced him that other classes of men were just as likely to violate any regulations in relation to trading with the enemy, as Jews. Something to this effect would mollify the Jews and save us a good many thousand votes. The Jews of Cincinnati and St. Louis are numerous enough to defeat our ticket in both cities, and they are strong enough to hurt us in Chicago also, as they include many of our most active Republicans. That they are deeply aggrieved by the General's order is undoubted. The cops [*Copperheads*] are making a handle of the matter in all parts of the country and we shall lose large numbers of Jew votes everywhere, besides converting them into very active bitter opponents. Let the General write a private letter to Salomon or Greenebaum, or some other leading and influential man among them, smoothing the matter over. We shall have no votes to spare. . . ." Typescript, DLC-Elihu B. Washburne.

On Jan. 29, William S. Hillyer, New York City, had drafted a letter to the editor, *New York World.* "Your correspondent whose letter you published in yesterdays world is sadly at fault in his statement as to the origin of Gen Grants Jew order. There is not one word of truth in his letter. I ~~shall not vote for~~ am not in favor of General Grant for the Prsidency; ~~I think the highest interest of the country will be served by his defeat, and I shall~~ but and will do what I honorably can to secure the success of the democratic ticket. But I cannot permit his private character to be assailed when I personally know the charges made are without foundation. You have published the record against the Elder Grant. Whatever the public may think of the transactions of the father General Grant did not countenance them. On the contrary the history of the celebrated 'Jew order' which I am about to narrate is a complete vindication of General Grant from complicity with his father. At the time of the issuing of this order General Grants headquarters in the field were at Oxford Mississippi. His ~~d~~Department headquarters were at Holly Springs. I was then a member of his staff and acting Provost Marshal General of the Department. At the date of the order I was I was ~~at Ch~~ a member of his Staff and acting Provost Marshal General of the Department. On the day this order was issued I was in Holly Springs. I had previou[s]ly under direction of the General issued an order prohibiting *all civilians* not connected with the army to pass south of the Tallahasse river—On this day ~~spoken of~~ Col Lagow of Grants Staff ~~came to my office~~ notified me that old man Grant was in town and had some arrangement with a cotton trader and would come to me for a pass for both of them to go to Oxford. A few moments after Mr Grant came in and after a preliminary conversation he stated to me that he wished a pass for himself and friend to go to 'Ulysses headquarters.' I replied 'certainly Mr Grant. ~~as your friend I presume is a fr I will give you the a pass and your~~ Is your friend a friend of the Generals who wishes to make a ~~personal~~ friendly visit?' 'He is a friend of mine', ~~he replied,~~ 'I presume that is sufficient.' he replied To which ~~I remarked 'Mr Sir' said I~~ I said 'Is he a ~~trader or a~~ cotton buyer, does he wish to go for any purpose of trade? If so I can not give him the pass. I ~~w~~could not give you a pass if you desired it for such a purpose'. 'Very well' said he 'I suppose I can get through without your assistance'—Thereupon he left me. I immediately called Col Lagow and told him the old gentleman was going to telegraph to the General for a pass and requested Lagow to go and telegraph that I had refused 'the friend' a pass. Mr Grant went to the ~~office~~ telegraph office and ~~sent this~~ dispatched to the General as follows 'I am here with a friend and desire permission to come to your headquarters Can we come?'. Lagow thereupon telegraphed 'Your father's friend is a Jew. Hillyer has refused him a pass'. In a few moments ~~the Gen~~ General Grant sent back ~~the following~~ this reply 'You can come your friend cann[o]t' and ~~immediately~~ immediately thereupon wrote the noted order No 11, expelling all Jews from the Departments. This is the exact history of the Jew order. The facts which I state can be further verified by the telegraph records and by Gen Jno A. Rawlins the only member of the old staff now with Gen Grant. This explanation ~~would probably I should have made long ago~~ would probably have been made long ago but for the connexion with the transaction of the Elder Grant. As he has voluntarily placed his case on the ~~public~~ records and it has been given full publicity by the press, it is due as a matter of simple justice to Gen Grant that he should have the benefit of this explanation . . ." ADf, Hillyer Papers, ViU. The remaining page of the document contains a revision of the earliest section that conveys no additional information. See *PUSG*, 7, 52.

1. Jesse Root Grant probably mentioned U.S. Judge Humphrey H. Leavitt, Southern District, Ohio, a resident of Cincinnati since 1855. USG, however, meant someone else. See letter to David Eckstein, Aug. 24, 1868.

To Bvt. Maj. Gen. John A. Rawlins

Quincy Ill.
Aug. 16th 1868,

DEAR RAWLINS,

I have just seen a letter shewing that Capt. Wilcox, (I do not know what regiment he belongs to) has been ordered from Ft. McIntosh, Tex. to Washington, by the Sec. of War. The order was obtained, I presume, by his father-in-law, Col. Craig of Mo.[1] with the view of ultimately getting him detailed on some duty in the West. Capt. W. has performed a great deal of duty as Asst. Qr. Mr. and as we have not officers enough in the Dept. to do the duty I wish you would enquire of the Qr. Mr. Gen. for his record whilst in his dept. and if he cannot employ him in Shermans Division, either in Sheridan's or Augur's Dept. If so I would like him to be detailed by the Sec. of War according. I would like very much to have this detail made if not detrimental to the service.

As you will see by the papers, no doubt, I have been making a short visit to Mr. Morris.[2] I flattered myself that I was getting here quietly; Bbut the telegraph seemed to notify every body on the route after we (Jones is with me) got about halfway and every body was out on the platforms to meet us. I felt sorry that I had concented to come. The enthusiasm of the people seemed to be very great, but I feel a little out of place putting myself in a position where I may be misunderstood.

Yours Truly
U. S. GRANT

ALS, NRU.

1. James Craig, former Democratic U.S. Representative from Mo. (1857–61) and brig. gen. of vols., was the father-in-law of Capt. John A. Wilcox, 4th Cav.
2. See letter to Isaac N. Morris, July 31, 1868.

To Bvt. Maj. Gen. John A. Rawlins

————

Galena Il.
August 18th '68.

DEAR RAWLINS,

On Monday next I expected to start East to wind up in Washington about the 10th of September. I find it so agreeable here, however, that I have concluded to remain until about the close of September and then go direct to Washington.—I see by the papers that Mrs. Rawlins has been alarmingly ill? I hope all case of alarm has now passed. Mrs. Grant, and the children, desire to be remembered to her and yourself.

Whilst I remain here I shall avoid all engagements to go any place at any stated time. The turn out of people is immense when they hear of my coming. I was invited to visit Dubuque and I agreed to go over this evening but positively refused to agree to any reception. I find however that the papers have noticed the fact that I was to be there, and no doubt it will prove an uncomfortable evening for me. I would disappoint the parties who invited me if none but them were concerned but there will be so many persons from the country that I feel that I must keep my engagement.

Yours Truly.
U. S. GRANT.

Copy, Bender Collection, Wy-Ar. On Aug. 18, 1868, USG spoke in Dubuque, Iowa. "MY FRIENDS: I am very glad to see you and thank you for your kindness. Dubuque being near my old residence, I have a number of friends here whom I desire to see. I have come among you for no political purpose, and do not design to make you any speech; nor do I desire that any speeches should be made on my account. I thank you all, and wish you good evening." *New York Times*, Aug. 23, 1868.

To Bvt. Brig. Gen. Adam Badeau

~~Washington, D. G.~~, Galena Ill, Aug. 18th/68

DEAR BADEAU,

As I have concluded to remain here until about the close of Sept. I think you had better open the letters that have accumulated in Washington. Such as are on official business refer to Rawlins. All others do with as your judgement dictates, only do not send any to me except such as you think absolutely require my attention and will not keep 'till my return.

If you are not otherwise more agreeably engaged I think you will find it pleasant here for a while and then to return with me. I have also written to Comstock to come out if he feels like it.[1]

The family are all well.

Yours Truly
U. S. GRANT

ALS, MiU-C.

1. On Aug. 30, 1868, Bvt. Brig. Gen. Cyrus B. Comstock telegraphed to USG. "Letter just received. I start tonight for Galena." ALS (telegram sent), DNA, RG 107, Telegrams Collected (Bound); telegram sent, *ibid.*; copies, *ibid.*, RG 108, Telegrams Sent; DLC-USG, V, 56.

To Richard Yates

~~Washington, D. G.~~, Galena, Ill, Aug. 21st/68

MY DEAR GOVERNOR,

Your invitation to me to visit you at Jacksonville on my return from Quincy to this place, only reached me since my return from Dubuque. I could not have gone that way however if I had received your letter in time. I had committed my self to visit Dubuque on Tuesday last. To keep that engagement left no time to tarry by the way.

I have concluded to remain in the West longer than I contemplated when in Quincy, and will avail myself of the opportunity to visit about a little if I can do so quietly.

Yours Truly
U. S. GRANT

HON. R. YATES,
ɟU. S. SENATOR,

ALS, IHi.

To David Eckstein

————

Galena Ill.
Aug. 24th 1868

DEAR SIR;

Your favor of the 20th inst. is received. Your determination relative to the publication, or rather nonpublication, of the substance of our conversation, suits me very well. Although I dislike to see what I say in conversation printed, yet, in this case, I could not have objected if you had deemed it advisable.

I answer, as you request, to inform you that your letter ~~was~~ is received. Your first letter was not received by me for some three weeks after it was written. It was registered, and directed to St. Louis. All my letters were forwarded to the country where I was staying, but this one, being registered, could not be forwarded from the post office to which it was addressed. Hence the delay in its return

With great respect,
Your obt. svt.
U. S. GRANT

TO DAVID ECKSTEIN,
CINCINNATI, O.

ALS, American Jewish Archives, Cincinnati, Ohio.

On July 9, 1868, David Eckstein had written to USG. "You will I trust remember me as the Jew who sought an interview ʏwith you, recently in Covington, concerning the order issued by you during the war to which many of our persuasion are taking exception. That interview was so entirely satisfactory to me, that I am quite sure a promulgation of your explanation would do good. I understood you to say that you had no objections to the publication of your sentiments then expressed and I desire the privilege of doing it; but I have deemed it better to first submit my recollection of the conversation for your consideration, and correction if I have not faithfully narrated it. May I ask you to make such correction as may be necessary to conform to the facts." LS, CSmH. USG endorsed this letter to Bvt. Maj. Gen. John A. Rawlins. "I leave it to your judgement whether to return this with authority to publish it or not. The paper ought to be returned however. The statement is more nearly correct than such things usually are." AE (initialed), *ibid.*

On Oct. 12, Eckstein wrote to Adolph Moses. "Please excuse the liberty of thus informally addressing you as a perfect stranger. I am induced to do so, desiring to express my pleasure and satisfaction derived from your letter to the NEW YORK HERALD relative to General Grant and the Israelites. I, too, am an Israelite and have been a republican since the breaking out of the late war. About Order No. 11, I have been as much incensed and condemned it as much as any Israelite or citizen in the country. In my last, prior to the meeting of the Chicago Convention, I wrote to Governor Geary, of Pennsylvania, a friend of mine for years, setting forth to him in the strongest terms the objections I had, and Israelites generally, against General Grant, and why they desired, both republicans and democrats, that he should not be nominated. He was afterwards nominated; but in the meantime I had gained information through Israelites bearing upon the matter, which if it did not amount to a satisfactory solution considerably mitigated my embarrassment on the subject. About that time I observed the democratic press throughout the country taking the matter up and representing to the people that the Jews, as a class, would oppose the election of General Grant for President. I felt then already confident that a reaction in favor of the General would eventually take place, especially on the part of all Jews who have formerly been and still remain republicans. In consequence thereof I published an article in the Cincinnati *Commercial* on the 3d of July last for the purpose of dispelling the then generally prevailing opinion that the Jews as a class were really opposed to General Grant. I experienced at the time considerable abuse and contumely here and elsewhere, but soon had the satisfaction to find that my sentiments expressed in that article were being taken up, endorsed and corroborated all over the Northern States by most able and influential coreligionists. The opposition press seems entirely silenced now on the subject everywhere, and even Dr. Wise, editor of the *Israelite*, has long since become reconciled. I must further state to you that afterward I went to see General Grant while on a visit at his father's, in Covington, and was received by him in a most cordial manner, without even the formality of an introduction. I stated to him the object of my visit, being to receive from him some information in regard to Order No. 11, to which his humble servant and the Jews generally take serious exception. I approached him very reluctantly. He thereupon in the kindest manner assured me of his perfect willingness to furnish me all the information relative to Order No. 11. He conversed with me near two hours and chiefly about this order matter. The explanations which I received from him, I venture to assert, are sufficient to remove and obliterate every vestige of objection against him on the part of every fair-minded and reasonable Israelite, and would impel them to a still more hearty support of the party which put the General in nomination, unless he were an Israelite who never acted and does not now sympathize with the republican party and its principles. General Grant gave me permission to publish the substance of our conversation if I desired so to do, but I refrained for the following reasons: — First, because I know the democratic press would make it appear a bid for Jewish votes on the part of General Grant, though laudable his motive; and, second, when the time arrived when I intended to publish it there had already such a great change taken place in the sentiment of the Israelites on the subject that I regarded it then, as now, needless. Knowing full well how ably you wield the pen and how great your influence among our coreligionists, I concluded to volunteer the information herein contained for you to make use of, and also permit you to use my name if you deem it essential." *New York Herald,* Oct. 23, 1868. An unsigned manuscript in the Eckstein Papers may provide the account hinted at elsewhere. "On the 17th of De. 62, I was at Oxford, Mississippi, and saw Gen. Grant receive and open a large number of letters and dispatches that evening received. On opening one of them he remarked: 'Here is instructions from Headquarters which I have been expecting,' and read as follows: We are reliably informed that the Jews are in the various cities buying up the gold, to take to the South to invest in Cotton. That will place in the hands of the Rebels additional means to carry on the war. That should be prevented. You will therefore take measures to prevent it in your Department. Upon this instruction the Jew Order No 11 was issued. All Jews then within Gen. Grant's lines, who could give a satisfactory account of the honesty of their intentions were relieved from the effect of that order. Last week I wrote to a gentleman in Washington, that was present at the time assisting the Gen. in looking over his dispatches, to know if my recollection of that circumstance was correct. In reply the gentleman says I am substantially correct. But that the General does not wish any publication made by any special friend. 'This statement you can use as you choose, but not give my name as authority.' " Bertram Wallace Korn, *American Jewry and the Civil War* (Philadelphia, 1951), pp. 140–41.

Thirty citizens of Cincinnati (including Henry Mack) signed a petition dated Feb. 6, 1869, addressed to USG requesting Eckstein's appointment to office. DS, DNA, RG 59, Letters of Application and Recommendation. Numerous other papers, some addressed to USG, are *ibid.* A petition of Jan. 4, 1870, signed by many citizens of Cincinnati, asked that Eckstein be appointed assessor, 1st District of Ohio. DS, American Jewish Archives. On Feb. 18, USG nominated Eckstein as consul, Victoria, Vancouver Island. In Nov., 1872, Eckstein, Victoria, wrote to USG. "Thanks be to Providence! It has once more bestowed its smiles approvingly upon those illustrious founders of our beloved Republic, who so nobly struggled for Liberty, Union and Equality; and upon all patriotic union-defenders, scions of freedom and equal justice to all—Your Excellency's triumphant re-election for President of the United States betokens, in my humble estimation, that above expressed as much as anything else—I can not refrain sincerely to congratulate you, without violence to my feelings; and express the heartfelt wish that God may keep and protect you. May He grant you long life in the circle of your family; ever viewing with satisfaction and delight our county united and proud, our nation progressive, prosperous and happy." ALS, USG 3.

To William Elrod

_____

Galena, Ill,
Aug. 24th 1868

Dear Elrod.

It is now the time I expected, when I came here, to have started back East. It is so pleasant here however that I have concluded to remain one month longer. I wish you would [— — —]e and let me [— — —]u are getting on. Tell me whether you had good rains after I left? How the crops are likely to turn out? wWhether you have bought cows yet? What progress has been made on the barn, &c. Do you think all the mares are in foal? If you have not yet got money from Benoist I can send you $500 00 from here. If your crop of potatoes turn out well it will bring you in considerable money. Potatoes must be high this year for there will be none in this section to send to market.—In setting out grapes next year I think I would try about one acre of the Catawby. . . .
P. S. The first time you go to the city call at Grant's Livery Stable, on 7th St back of the Courthouse, and pay my bill. How have you fixed the carpets & furniture at my house? Mrs. Grant thinks camphor should be ~~mixed~~ sprinkled in the carpets;

U. S. G.

AL (signature clipped), Illinois Historical Survey, University of Illinois, Urbana, Ill.

To Charles S. Hamilton

———

Chicago, Ill. Aug. 28th *1868*

Dear Hamilton,

Your favor of the 25th inst. was rec'd yesterday. You could not have received my letter of about one week before, notifying you that I had determined to extend my visit to the West some weeks more, and would visit you before going back? I wrote you such a letter and left Galena yesterday with the expectation of spending to-day with my brother here,[1] and going to Fond du' Lac to-morrow. Mrs. Grant and one of the children are with me and expected to be your guest over Sunday. We were unfortunate enough however to have our baggage (a single trunk) go East this morning, through mistake, and leaving us "nothing to wear." This will defer our visit and possibly prevent Mrs. Grant from going all together. I will visit you though before going East; possibly next week. I want to go quietly, unannounced, directly to your house, and from there I will see such of the good people of Fond du Lac, as choose to call.

Please present my regards to your family.

Yours Truly

U. S. Grant

ALS, Hamilton Papers, Illinois Historical Survey, University of Illinois, Urbana, Ill. Written on ornate stationery of "Grant & McLean, Manufacturers & Dealers in Leather, and Saddlery Hardware."

On Oct. 11, 1868, USG, Galena, wrote to Charles S. Hamilton. "It may be that I will yet be disappointed in my proposed visit to Fon-du-Lac though I cannot say so positively now. I have been compelled to visit Chicago and St. Louis as much on business as pleasure, and now I am having company at my house which may detain me until I have to start for Washington. If I get to Fon-du-Lac at all, it will be during next week early. . . ." Kenneth W. Rendell Catalogue [1970], no. 113. Dated Oct. 16 in Parke-Bernet Sale, Feb. 17, 1970, no. 129.

On Feb. 20, 1869, Bvt. Maj. Gen. John Pope, Detroit, wrote to USG. "It seems superfluous for me to ask your remembrance of C. S. Hamilton of Wisconsin as you have known him as long and as well as I do, & I therefore only write this note because he wishes me to do so—He desires to be Marshal of Wisconsin, & I suppose that it is only necessary to let you know it—He will himself communicate with you about it—I know nothing about such matters &

only write because I cannot refuse such a small favor to a friend both of yours
& mine" ALS, DNA, RG 60, Records Relating to Appointments. On March 1,
Hamilton wrote to USG. "I respectfully ask for the appointment of United
States Marshall for the District of Wisconsin. You know me, and can judge
whether I can properly fill the position. I have no political record, other than a
faithful support in my humble way, of the Republican party & principles. I came
here with a majority of the Wisconsin delegation distinctly pledged to my support.—A portion one of this delegation find it for their political interest, to forego
these pledges, but I speak without egotism in saying that no candidate has yet
been named, whose appointment, will be so satisfactory to the loyal people of
our State. I have done some service to the Country. I ask the office in view of
those services, and to save my family from the fangs of ~~P~~poverty. The office is
now vacant." ALS, *ibid.* On March 30, USG nominated Hamilton as marshal,
District of Wis.

1. On Aug. 29, 1868, USG spoke to a crowd assembled at the home of
Orvil L. Grant. "Gentlemen: I thank you for this spontaneous compliment.
As this audience knows I do not make speeches, and I could hardly find language in the presence of so large a gathering of my fellow-citizens even to express my thanks, you must simply, upon this occasion, allow me to return from
the bottom of my heart my sincere thanks for this kind call." *Chicago Journal,*
Aug. 31, 1868. Following a speech by J. Y. Scammon, USG said: "Gentlemen—I thanked you once for your kindness. All I can do now is to thank you
again for this unexpected greeting and for the magnificent turn-out. I feel that
I should like to speak to each of you, and to shake hands with each of you, but
that is impossible. So I can but say I thank you—I thank you." *Ibid.*

To William Elrod

Galena Ill,
Sept. 4th /68

Dear Elrod,

Your letter is received. I am rather glad you have bought no
cows. I think now it will be better to buy none except you can do it
from the proceeds of the farm. You can build your barn and the
fence I told you about, and cultivate to the best advantage to give
money and gradually get it stockd and improved just as we want it.
What I sa~~y~~id about grapes however I want carried out. Buy enough
in the ~~s~~Spring to complete the lot you have commenced planting
on, and then from your own cuttings extend as far as looks proffit-
able.

Get barely money enough from Benoist to pay up square, and what your sales lack of running you untill next harvest I will supply.

All are very well. I do not know now when I will go back to Washington. You had better make paper payable to Benoist fall due the last of Oct. If you have already borrowed however make no change, but notify me of what you have done and I will arrang to meet it.

Yours Truly
U. S. GRANT

ALS, Illinois Historical Survey, University of Illinois, Urbana, Ill.

On Sept. 4, 1868, Horace Capron, commissioner, Dept. of Agriculture, wrote to USG. "This Department has lately received from Europe, a quantity of Autumn seed wheat for distribution to Members of Congress, Agl Societies and a few practical farmers who have the facilities for giving it a fair trial and the disposition to make a full report of the result to the Department. It affords me pleasure to say that, I have forwarded by the mail of to day, (marked as per memo, enclosed) three bushels, consisting of one bushel each, of 'Talavera' 'Rough Chaff' and 'Polish'; the two former of English, and the latter of Russian growth. Mr Ford will be advised by this mail, to forward the wheat to Mr, Elrod as soon as it arrives in St Louis. These wheats bear a high reputation, in the sections of Country from which they came, as as hardy, early maturing and very prolific, and I trust they will prove a valuable acquisition to your cereal products." LS, *ibid.* USG endorsed this letter. "I did not intend to have any wheat sewn on my place; but this coming as it does you may prepare a piece of ground and try it." AES, *ibid.*

To Bvt. Maj. Gen. John A. Rawlins

———

By Telegraph from Galena Ill [*Sept.*] 5 *1868*

To GEN J A RAWLINS

Send to Omaha all the Cavalry in Thomas, Meade and Stonemans command. Let them turn in their horses and order Quarter Master to supply their places at Omaha

U. S. GRANT
General

Telegram received, DNA, RG 94, Letters Received, 428A 1868; (2—at 5:55 P.M.) *ibid.*, RG 107, Telegrams Collected (Bound). On Sept. 5, 1868, Lt. Gen.

William T. Sherman, St. Louis, telegraphed to USG. "Just arrived all the
frontier Governors are dreadfully Exercised by the recent outbreak of the
Cheyennes and arrapahoes their acts seem desperate & the result of a perfect
cooperation. augur Should have another regiment of Cavalry and I ask for it
Earnestly Even if we have to Exchange for it a regiment of Infantry. John E
Smith just in from the ~~the~~ Powder River Forts—Should you Conclude to grant
this request let their horses be sold where the regiment now is the men sent by
Rail to Omaha and an order for the purchase there ~~i~~of new horses—I think this
a more Economical and rapid Course than to Ship horses from the east I have
no doubt now we must settle this business with the Cheyennes for Ever and the
approaching winter will be a good time" Telegram received (at 3:15 P.M.),
ibid., RG 108, Telegrams Received; copies, *ibid.*, RG 107, Letters Received
from Bureaus; DLC-USG, V, 55. On the same day, Speaker of the House
Schuyler Colfax, Denver, telegraphed to Secretary of War John M. Schofield
and Bvt. Maj. Gen. John A. Rawlins. "For past ten days hostile Indians have
been striking simultaneously at isolated settlements of Colorado Territory for
a circuit of over two hundred miles, men, women and children have been killed
daily and hundreds of thousands of dollars of property been stolen, these
atrocites have been mainly near the three lines of travel from this focal point
towards the Union Pacific R R. The last division of Pacific R R & the road via
Colorado City towards Santa Fe, especially the two latter, This Territory has
no means with which to put volunteers in the field. it is almost bare of arms
and literally defenceless, I beg leave respectively to suggest to your consideration that a strong cavalry force be sent with the utmost speed to Denver under
an efficient authorized commander with orders to use it for prompt protection
of settlers and punishment of these enemies, the news of these outrages reaches
this place quickest as the common centre and from hence the scenes of the outrages can be most quickly reached, I venture to suggest also that a supply of
arms and ammunition should in addition be sent to the Territorial Authorities"
Telegram received (at 7:15 P.M.), DNA, RG 107, Telegrams Collected
(Bound).

On Sept. 6, Sherman telegraphed to USG. "Dispatch of Fifth (5th) recd
if you Could Send a Couple hundred recruits to Omaha for the second (2nd)
Cavalry and the same number to Fort Leavenworth for the seventh (7) it would
be a good thing." Telegram received (on Sept. 7, 8:40 A.M.), *ibid.*, RG 108,
Telegrams Received; copy, DLC-USG, V, 55. On Sept. 7, Bvt. Brig. Gen. Cyrus
B. Comstock, Galena, telegraphed to Rawlins. "General Grant wishes the Ad-
jutant General to send two hundred 200 recruits to Omaha for the Second 2
Cavalry and, if possible, as many more to Fort Leavenworth for the Seventh 7
Cavalry." Telegrams received (2—at 12:20 P.M.), DNA, RG 107, Telegrams
Collected (Bound); *ibid.*, RG 108, Telegrams Received; copies, *ibid.*, Telegrams
Sent; DLC-USG, V, 55, 56.

On Sept. 9, Sherman wrote to USG. "I am glad to notice that you have
taken up a long and quiet sojourn at Galena, and hope you enjoy the 'Otium.'
The Indians as you have observed have without one particle of reason broken
out again, and have committed a good many murders along the Kansas border,
and also in Colorado. I still believe this is confined to the young bloods, not exceeding 300 who by their rapid motion, have seemed to be many thousands—
The Governor of Kansas is dreadfully Exercised, and says he cant sit still and

see his people murdered. I have assured him he need not sit still but may in person, or by his people keep in motion and protect themselves against these Raids, which Cannot be prevented by any reasonable number of troops. He offers two Regimts of Cavalry, but I decline any, unless Sheridan asks, for them and he also declines. The Governor of Colorado also represents matters as awful, and he prevailed on Colfax to make to me a lengthy despatch, to the Effect that I ought to send immediately to Denver, and keep there one full Rgmt of Cavalry on the theory that from Denver as a Centre they can better protect the Settlements than from any other point.—In my whole Division I have four Regiments of Cavalry. Augur has one and Sheridan three (3)—One of these is in New Mexico Scattered, and from there come constant calls for more Cavalry. Sheridan has two Regimts 7th & 10th with him operating against the Cheyennes. He is now at Fort Dodge, and has one body of Cavalry moving towards Colorado, and another to the South of the Arkansas towards the Cimaron where he thinks the Cheyennes have their families and herds. I hope he may get hold of them and obliterate them. I am acting on this theory to attract all Indians within the two big Reservations, and afterwards to get the President to make his Proclamation that in the interving space Indians have no right to be, ordering all troops to proceed against them as hostile, and permitting Citizens to do the Same. By our treaties we allowed the Indians to hunt game in this Region, provided they Kept the Peace—but they have not Kept the Peace, and from the nature of things they Cant keep the Peace—As soon as Sheridan heard you had promised me some more Cavalry he asked for it—I told him that Augur needed it more than he did, and could operate South from the Union Pacific Road, without regard to boundary lines and therby Cooperate with him as against the hostiles, but I would give him if he wanted it the Infantry Regimt that Augur has in Excess of his Absolute wants, the One we proposed to keep in reserve at Omaha. I expect his answer to-day Minnie was badly hurt in her fall at fort Sanders. She is still weak and sore, but is able to walk about the house—My best regards to Mrs Grant, Buck, Jesse, Nellie & all the family." ALS, DNA, RG 108, Letters Received.

On Sept. 23, Sherman wrote to USG. "I wrote you some days ago, since which time seven companies of cavalry have arrive, and been despatched up the Road to Fort Harker, whence they will scout all the tributaries of the Republican and reach Fort Kearney or Sedgwick—These are the only companies that can come at this time, as I infer from a telegram of Genl Kelton. Sheridan is now at Fort Hayes & reports now that Sully found the Indian Camps on the Canadian to the South of Fort Dodge, but they Eluded him, and he came in for reinforcemts. This is the same old story, but I have given them all notice that the troops will keep out all winter, till they can report two dead indians for evry one we lose, or until the Cheyennes and Arapahos are completely subdued & impoverished—The Rascals say they prefer War to Peace, because it is more profitable. It is cheaper they say to Steal than to work, and they profess to find war more profitable than Even Govt annuities. There is no alternative but a steady persistent war on our part, till they are wiped out. In the mean time, we protect the cars, coaches &c, so that the regular trade & travel goes on without interruption, and the Governors have subsided. Dont you want to see St Louis during the Fair, and Races. The Races begin next week, & last six days—viz Sept 28. to Oct 3—The Fair also lasts a week, beginning with Oct 5. I have to be in Chicago Oct 7. to attend a meeting, the last I hope of the Indian Peace Commission, but hope to get back to See the last of the Fair. I think you ought to attend the Fair. It would not Compromise your political position, and be perfectly consistent with yr idea to Encourage and Stimulate agriculture, and the peaceful Arts. I think there is not a shadow of doubt of yr Election, and begin to sympathise with the new budget of trouble that is in wait for you." ALS, USG 3.

On Sept. 24, Sherman telegraphed to USG. "Colonel Forsyth with sixty (60) scouts mounted were attacked four (4) days ago ninety (90) miles north of Wallace by seven hundred 700 Indians One 1 Lieutenant Beecher killed. The Doctor mortally wounded and Forsyth badly. Forsyth sent in two (2) men on foot & immedeately Col Bankhead and one hundred 100 men started to their relief. Genl Sheridan reports today that another messenger is in and That Forsyth could bring his party in only for his wounded. He reports He killed thirty five 35 Indians & lost besides his officers all his Horses two (2) men killed & eighteen 18 wounded. I feel easy that he will not suffer further loss as the movement of Bradleys Column from North-Platte & another force of Cavalry to his west will relieve him & Bankhead is guided by the very men who Came in. All is being done the case admits of and I hope the parties out will not only relieve Forsyth but kill a good many Indians, Sheridan is at Fort Hays & the fifth 5 Cavalry seven 7 companies have all gone up the road to him" Telegram received (on Sept. 25, 8:50 A.M.), DNA, RG 108, Telegrams Received; copy, DLC-USG, V, 55. See letter to Lt. Gen. William T. Sherman, Sept. 25, 1868.

To Charles H. Ray

Galena Ill,
Sept. 6th /68

Dr. C. H. Ray,
Dear Sir:

I expected Gn. Corse[1] and yourself at my house to spend the day and dine with me. Finding you did not come I called at the hotel for you. Your being out I leave this not to request both of you to come up to my house as soon as you return to the hotel. Expecting you I will not go to church to-day.

Yours &c
U. S. Grant

ALS, USGA. Charles H. Ray, born in 1821 in Norwich, N. Y., studied medicine, moved to Iowa and then to Ill., where he edited the Democratic *Galena Jeffersonian* (1851–54). Republican affiliation led to his becoming editor of the *Chicago Tribune*. Ray sold his interest in the paper (1863), returned briefly as editor (1865), and became editor of the *Chicago Evening Post* (1867). See *PUSG*, 13, 413; letter to Schuyler Colfax, Aug. 21, 1870; letter to William A. Richardson, Aug. 22, 1870.

1. Former Brig. Gen. John M. Corse, collector of Internal Revenue, Chicago.

To George K. Budd

Galena Ill.
Sept. 11th 1868

GEO. K. BUDD, ESQ,
DEAR SIR:

Your favor of the 3d of Sept. is received. Your previous letter, asking for some position for Capt. Wade[1] to keep him from his company, was also duly received. I sent that letter to Washington with an indorsment favorable to the granting of your request, but what I asked for I do not now remember. I presume it has been acted upon befor this and the Capt. been notified.

Yours Truly
U. S. GRANT

ALS, MoSHi. George K. Budd, born in 1802 in Philadelphia, worked on merchant ships, moved to St. Louis (1836), opened a store, turned to banking, and founded the Boatmen's Savings Institution. Active in local politics, publisher of the *St. Louis Intelligencer* (1850–53), he sold bonds during the Civil War as an agent of Jay Cooke & Co. and served as city comptroller (1850, 1864–68).

1. Capt. Robert B. Wade, 17th Inf., USMA 1865, married Budd's daughter Belle.

To William Coffin

~~Washington, D. C.~~, Galena Ill. Sept. 11th *1868*

WM COFFIN, ESQ,
MY DEAR SIR:

Your favor enclosing check for Quarter's rent due Sept. 1st is received. You need not have hurried about sending it before Mr.

Baugh had paid. I wish also to express my thanks for the trouble you have taken in arranging for the lease of my house, and to express my entire satisfaction with what you have done. Of course if anything should occur to make the amt. agreed to be paid by Mr. Baugh exorbitant, such as a finantial convulsion, I would not expect to demand from him anything unreasonable.

I am just in receipt of a letter from Mr. Davis notifying me that he has expressed to me a book from Mr. Coddington. The book has not yet reached me, but will, no doubt, within a day or two. Please thank Mr. Davis, and Mr. Coddington too, for me.

I have had a most delightful and quiet time, and so have my family, since leaving Washington. I dislike to think about starting back but must go in a few weeks more. Mrs. Grant joins me in presenting regards to Mrs. Coffin, Miss Coffin & yourself.

I will be in Phila soon after my return to Washington.

Yours Truly
U. S. Grant

ALS, Richard E. Longacre, Wayne, Pa.
On March 13, 1869, William Coffin, Philadelphia, wrote to USG. "My Brother E W. Coffin of New Jersey is anxious to obtain one of two appointments, under your Administration either the Collector of Customs at Brownsville Texas or United States Marshall of New Jersey he Served through the Rebbelan as an officer of the Comisary department with credit to himself and friends, and is intirely competent to fill either position if consistant with your views and dont interfere with your promises to others you will place me under many obligations by appointing him I enclose but one certificate as to his charictor but can get any number of them if wanted he is honest gentlemanly and diceded—he is a Republican altho not a Politian—if there Should be any chance for him you will much oblige by letting me know I have had numbers of applications for letters to you but have refused in all cases except my Brother"
ALS, DNA, RG 56, Collector of Customs Applications.

To Isaac N. Morris

Galena, Ill,
Sept. 14th /68

DEAR SIR:

I am in receipt of your favor enclosing one from Mr. A. Moses, of the 3d inst.[1] My first inclination was to answer Mr. M. because you asked it of me; then I thought it would be better to adhere to the rule of silence to all questions. Were I to commence once answering all political questions asked me there would not be time enough between now and the 3d of Nov. to get through. Mr. Moses, I think, will fully understand this.—In regard to Order No 11 hundreds of letters have been written to me about it, by persons of the faith affected by it. I do not, nor did not, answer any of them, but permitted a statement of the facts concerning the origin of the order to be made out and given to some one of the writers for publication.[2] I do not pretend to sustain the order. At the time of its publication I was insensed by a reprimand received from Washington for permitting acts which the Jews, within my lines, were engaged in. There were many others within my lines equally bad with the worst of them, but the difference was that the Jews could pass, withe impunity, from one Army to the other. Gold, in violation of orders, was being smuggled through the lines by them. At least so it was reported. The order was made and sent out, ~~by~~ without any reflection, and without thinking of the Jews as a sect or race to themselves, but simply as the persons who had succesfully (I say successfully insted of persistently because I know there were a plenty within my lines who envied them their success) violated an order, which violation innured greatly to the help of the rebels.

Give Mr. Moses assurances that I have no prejudice against sect or race but want each individual to be judged by his own merit. Order No. 11 does not sustain this statement, I admit, but then I do not sustain that order. ~~nor never did~~ It never would have been issued if it had not been telegraphed the moment penned, without one moments reflection.

My kindest regards to Mrs. Morris and the rest of your family. I have had a delightful time here, and feel inclined to continue it as long as possible.

Yours Truly

U. S. GRANT

ALS, ICarbS.

1. Adolph Moses, born in Speyer (Germany) in 1837, moved to New Orleans in 1852, was admitted to the bar in 1861, served as capt., 21st La., C.S. Army, then settled at Quincy, Ill. *Publications of the American Jewish Historical Society*, 16 (1907), 200–3. On Sept. 3, 1868, Moses, Quincy, wrote to USG. "I address you at the earnest solicitation of your friend, Hon. I. N. Morris, in relation to the matter now generally known as Order No. 11. It will hardly surprise you that we, as a people, already over-sensitive through former oppression and contumely, should lament the issuance of that order, whatever the immediate causes might have dictated. I am assured by high authority, some of which I might call Jewish, that no idea of special dislike to the Jews prompted you; on the contrary, that you regret the sweeping effect of the order. However generous this avowal may be on your part, yet you are well aware that a word spoken or a sentence written ceases to be the property of the speaker or writer, and passes into the domain of history, particularly when spoken or written by a man of super-eminent position and worth. I regret that our people who love to enjoy the quiet retreat of private life should be so prominently paraded in this campaign; but the instinct of self-defence presses utterance, however unwelcome the task. Our demands are simply to be judged like other people, and not to have the vices and shortcomings of our bad men illuminated at the expense of the many virtues and excellent qualities of our good men. Whatever the issue of this campaign may be, Mr. M. assures me that you bear no ill-will to the Jewish people, and, if they feel the severe compulsion to cast their suffrage against you in this campaign, they do so, in many instances, under protest, for with them their long-assailed reputation demands the greatest sacrifices, even at the risk of being misunderstood by the jud[g]ment of the hour. Excuse the liberty of addressing you. I have the encouragement of one of your friends." *Chicago Times*, Nov. 30, 1868.

2. On May 6, Bvt. Maj. Gen. John A. Rawlins wrote to Lewis Dembitz, Louisville. "Your letter relating to the order of General Grant, dated Oxford, Miss., December 17, 1862, expelling Jews as a class from his department, is before me. You are doubtless aware that General Grant has never, either by himself or through the aid of friends, attempted to defend any military order which the emergencies of the service seemed at the time to require. However, as my name is attached to it as Assistant Adjutant General, it may not be improper to state that at and previous to its date our military affairs were in a most critical condition, and important movements were transpiring. General Sherman was collecting forces at Memphis and Helena. General Grant was moving steadily against Pemberton, at Granada, keeping up appearances of immediate attack, to divert his attention from Sherman, and in co-operation

with Grant Dodge was moving south from Corinth. The success of Grant's plans depended in keeping the enemy in ignorance of his real purpose—namely, the surprise and capture of Vicksburg by Sherman—and it was therefore of the utmost importance that every avenue of information to the enemy should be closed. The most stringent orders had previously been published forbidding persons going or coming through our lines, limiting traders to certain boundaries and prohibiting the passage of corn South or the payment of it for Southern products. Persistent violations of these orders by persons principally of the Jewish race were the subjects of constant reports by many of General Grant's subordinates, some of whom had even issued orders expelling them from the lines, but which General Grant had promptly revoked. Reports of the same character were also received from other than military sources. At length, on the evening of December 17, 1862 (the date of the order), the mail brought from Washington a large number of complaints, officially referred to him by the General in-Chief of the army, against this class of persons for violations of the above mentioned orders. The general felt, on reading them, that some immediate action was demanded of him. He realized to its full extent the critical condition of military affairs, and judged, whether wisely or unwisely, that to meet the exigency action must be immediate, thorough and in a form not to be evaded. The order you refer to was the result. It was written and telegraphed to his subordinates without revision, leaving all persons not justly amenable to its terms to be relieved on their individual application. The idea that it was issued on account of the religion of the Jews cannot be seriously entertained by any one who knows the General's steadfast adherence to the principles of American liberty and religious toleration." *New York Herald*, June 23, 1868.

Printed with a letter from "A True Republican" to the editor. "General Rawlins' letter in explanation of General Grant's order No. 11 is dated Washington, May 6, 1868, and why it should be given to the public only six weeks after it was written is not proper for me to inquire; but considering that said order has been creating quite a controversy among newspapers, it might have appeared sooner. Without questioning the stability of the ground upon which General Rawlins rests his defence, without arguing the probable result of such defence, I take the liberty of asking the General a few questions, which if properly answered will do a good deal towards satisfying the minds of the American people in general and of the Jews in especial in regard to this order. *First*—Did General Grant feel satisfied at the time when the order was issued that all the Jews crossing his lines or trading near or within their boundaries intended to violate his orders or to give the enemy information in regard to his movements or plans? *Second*—Did General Grant know that Jews only were apt to commit such offences? *Third*—Was General Grant satisfied in his mind that among those of other religious denominations crossing his lines there were none who would or might violate any of his orders or reveal any of his plans to the enemy? Was he positive that no Methodists, Catholics, Baptists, Quakers, Mormons or anybody else belonging to one of the thirty and odd different religious sects (Jews excepted) which live peacefully in this free country would act contrary to his orders? If General Rawlins should be able to answer these questions satisfactorily, then the Jews may, perhaps, be willing to admit that General Grant's order No. 11 was justifiable." *Ibid*.

To Bvt. Maj. Gen. John A. Rawlins

———

Galena Ill.
Sept. 17th 1868.

GEN. J. A. RAWLINS,
CHIEF OF STAFF, U, S, A,
GENERAL:

The enclosed order are returned approved. There is one change in the assignment of Officers of the Corps of Inspectors Gen.l which I would suggest, though do not insist upon. It is the change of places given to Gens. Sacket and Totten. Gen. Sacket has served, if I am not mistaken, Twenty-three years, nearly continuously in the West, without a single detail in the East, except it may have been with the Army during the War.

Very Respectfully
your obt. svt.
U. S. GRANT
General

ALS, DNA, RG 159, Letters Received.

To John D. Platt

———

Galena Ill,
Sept. 19th 1868

JUDGE PRATT
DEAR SIR:

I owe you an apology for not replying to your polite invitation for me and Mrs. Grant & myself to visit you during the Fair, just held, in Warren. I could not go but would have replied promptly only that I got your invitation, and read it, down town, and after reading it put your note in my pocket and forgot it. The excuse is a poor one and shews my general neglegence. I hope you will excuse it.

Please present Mrs. Grant's & my regards to Mrs. Pratt.

Yours Truly

U. S. GRANT

ALS, Jackson C. Wenner, Naples, Fla. John D. Platt of Warren, Ill., county judge, Jo Daviess County, delegate to the 1860 Democratic Convention, Charleston, S. C., had signed the call for the first war meeting in Galena. On Sept. 29, 1871, USG, Galena, telegraphed to Platt. "It will afford me pleasure to stop a few minut[es] at Warren tomorrow" Telegram received, *ibid*.

To Isaac N. Morris

Galena, Ill,
Sept. 20th 1868,

DEAR SIR:

Your last favor is rec'd. I would prefer that no letter written by me between the time of the Chicago Convention and the election in November should be published. Any written before that time I have no objection to the publication of, nor will I object to the publication of any others, having any significance, after the election.

I will not be able to go to Quincy again this trip. With the exception of a visit to my brother in Chicago Mrs. Grant has not left Galena since we came here. If Mrs. Morris & yourself could pay us a visit here Mrs. Grant would be pleased. Why can you not come?

Mrs. Grant joins me in in kindest regards to Mrs. Morris and yourself.

Yours Truly

U. S. GRANT,

HON. I. N. MORRIS
QUINCY, ILL,

ALS, IHi.

To Elihu B. Washburne

Galena Ill,
Sept. 23d 1868,

DEAR WASHBURNE,

I am glad to see Congress found it expedient to adjourn without further legislation. I feared the effect of legislation at this time, and then too if Congress had remained in session it would prevent A. J. from taking his proposed trip to East Tenn. I have as much affection for him as Frank Blair[1] had for the "Fennigans" and would go just as far as Frank was willing to go to see him off, and would hold out every inducement to have him remain.

My time passes very pleasantly and quietly here and I have determined to remain until some time after the October elections. I will aim to be in Washington a few, but a few, days before the Nov. election There is nothing particularly stiring going on here. A person would not know there was a stiring canvass going on if it were not for the accounts we read in the papers of great gatherings all over the country.

Please remember me to Mr. A. T. Stewart Mr. Grinnell and Mr. Dodge[2] who all have ~~seemed~~ taken a great interest in my wellfare, even before they knew me personally. The same might be said of hosts of other New Yorkers, but the names of all cannot be innumerated in a single letter.

Yours Truly
U. S. GRANT

ALS, IHi.

1. See letter to Isaac N. Morris, July 31, 1868.
2. See *PUSG*, 18, 131. Moses H. Grinnell, born in 1803 at New Bedford, Mass., prospered enormously as commission merchant and shipping firm owner in New York City, served as Whig U.S. Representative (1839–41), became a financial mainstay to the Republican Party, and received an appointment as collector of the port of New York from USG. See letter to Moses H. Grinnell, March 19, 1869. William E. Dodge, born in 1805 in Hartford, son of a reformer and businessman, began work in a dry goods store at age thirteen, joined the firm of Phelps, Dodge & Co., acquired a fortune dispensed to further

the Republican Party and the cause of temperance, and served as U.S. Representative (1866–67).

To John M. Schofield

Galena, Ill
Sept 25th 1868

DEAR GENERAL

I find it so retired and pleasant here, and anticipate so much pulling and hauling after returning to Washington, that I have concluded not to go back until about the close of October. If any thing however should require my presence there earlier, and you will telegraph me here, I will go on at once.—My summer vacation has been a very pleasant one. The trip I took to the Rocky Mountains was both instructive and agreeable—It gave me the key to the topography of the country, so that now when Indian hostilities are reported, or the establishment of a new post, at a particular place is recommended, I can have more distinct ideas about what should be done than can be got merely from maps. I advise you, if you take a trip next summer, to [go] to the mountains. The climate is delightful and the scenery grand. A sick person must get well there, and a well one must go away to die; if he escapes the three epidemics of the country, pistols, bowie-knife and whiskey.

I presume military affairs get on as well without me, as they would with me in Washington; I hear from there often, and all matters requiring my special action are referred to me by Rawlins

I feel very grateful that the War Dept has fallen where it has, where I not only can communicate with the department freely, but feel that it is administered ~~freely~~, entirely in the interest of the nation. Is is a rare thing that Govt Depts. are so administered. They are generally administered in the interest of a political party and not to subserve the public interest

Mrs Grant joins me in regards to Mrs Schofield, the children and yourself

Yours Truly
U S GRANT

GEN JNO M SCOFIELD
SEC OF WAR

Copy, DLC-Adam Badeau. On Sept. 28, 1868, Secretary of War John M. Schofield wrote to USG. "Your letter of the 25th reached me this morning. I am
glad your recreation this Summer has been so pleasant and think you are quite
right to protract your vacation as long as possible. Not only is it important for
you to be free from contact with Washington people at this time, but this rest
after seven years of hard work will the better fit you for what is to come. It is
by no means the least, to me, gratifying result of my occupation of the War office that it has made you feel at liberty to go where you please for this Summer.
My experience since you left Washington has been as nearly as possible the
reverse of yours. But I need hardly tell you that, for you clearly foresaw it. Indeed I have only realized what I had full reason to expect. However I have got
along so far quite as well as could have been expected, and in some respects
better. I am now like a third class Cadet, counting the days till furlough. I feel
pretty confident that all will go on smoothly now, but if any thing happens to
make your presence here necessary I will telegraph you at once. Mrs Schofield
joins me in kindest regards to Mrs Grant, yourself and the children." ALS,
USG 3.
        On March 11, 1869, Schofield wrote to USG. "The recent Act of Congress
reducing the Army is now in rapid process of execution, and the desired changes
in the relations of the General of the Army, the War Department and the staff
of the Army have been perfected. Hence I take pleasure in placing my resignation at your disposal at this early day, so that you may be entirely free to complete the organization of your Cabinet at your convenience. Please accept my
sincere thanks for your kind and generous recognition of my efforts to serve the
country, and my warmest wishes for the complete success of your Administration." ALS, DLC-John M. Schofield. On April 2, Schofield, Fort Leavenworth,
wrote to Orville E. Babcock. "Accompanying my letter of resignation as Secretary of War was a private letter to the President, written before I knew who
was to be my successor, and rendered rather inappropriate to the circumstances
by the appointment of General Rawlings. Moreover subsequent events seem to
have proved the statements of the letter not altogether correct. For these reasons
I would like to have the letter returned to me if the President has no objection.
Will you also be so kind as to inquire what is the condition of my brothers application for a consular appointment." Copy, *ibid*. On March 13, USG had endorsed papers recommending J. V. Schofield for a consular appointment. "I
would like the Sec. of State to give Rev. Mr. Schofield a Consulship which will
be a support for himself and family." AES, DNA, RG 59, Letters of Application and Recommendation. On April 15, USG nominated Schofield as consul,
Hakodadi (Hakodate); he did not fill the post. See William Cathcart, ed., *The
Baptist Encyclopædia* . . . (Philadelphia, 1883), pp. 1034–35.

To Lt. Gen. William T. Sherman

———

Galena Ill.
Sept. 25th 1868.

DEAR SHERMAN.

On account of improvements I have had made on my farm since my visit to it, and money expended in further stocking it, I want to visit it before going back East. I shall be there about next Friday. I would like to meet you there if your engagements do not take you out of the city. If I change my plans so as to take me there any other day I will telegraph you. I hope you will be able to squelch the indians this time effectually. Is it not advisable to push after their villeges and families? The possession of them would bring them to terms.

Yours Truly
U. S. GRANT

ALS, DLC-William T. Sherman. On Sept. 27, 1868, Lt. Gen. William T. Sherman, St. Louis, telegraphed to USG. "Will expect you next Friday to stay at my house if agreeable to you Indian peace Commission meets at Chicago October seventh 7 I am very anxious that Genl Terry should be there. But he is on Dyers Court of Inquiry to meet in Washington October fourth Cant you so order as to delay Dyers Court one 1 week as Terrys presence may enable me to secure such action by the peace Commission will save us much Conflict & Confusion in the future Genl Sheridans first movement against the Indians was committed to General Sully & aimed at their Camps on the upper Canadian Sully got among them but I infer he failed in nerve or activity & Sheridan asks for the services of Gen'l Custar I approved & asked of the adjutant Genl The remission of the balance of his sentence But have no answer Cannot you Expedate that also as Sheridan wants Custar now I want to give him everything he asks for He. reports he has killed about seventy (70) Indians & proposes to keep all his men active till Winter will put them at our mercy I have nothing new from Forsyths Camp But feel easy that he has been relieved & that good execution will result from the movements about the head of the Republican" Telegram received (on Sept. 29, 8:40 A.M.), DNA, RG 108, Telegrams Received; copy, DLC-USG, V, 55.

On Sept. 28, USG, Chicago, telegraphed to Secretary of War John M. Schofield. "Please remit unexpired portion of General Custars sentence and order him to report to General Sheridan. Cannot the Dyer Court be postponed one 1 week to give General Terry opportunity to meet with the Indian Commission which convenes here on the seventh 7 of October. It is important that Terry should meet the other Commissioners." Telegram received (at 9:00 A.M.),

DNA, RG 94, Letters Received, 631W 1868; (2) *ibid.*, RG 107, Telegrams Collected (Bound). At 9:40 A.M., Schofield telegraphed to USG. "I have remitted Genl Custers sentence and ordered him to report for duty. I will also postpon[e] the meeting of the Court of Inquiry one week a[s] you suggest" ALS (telegram sent), *ibid.*, Telegrams Collected (Unbound); telegram sent, *ibid.*, Telegrams Collected (Bound); telegram received (at 11:50 A.M.), *ibid.*, RG 108, Telegrams Received.

On Sept. 28, Sherman telegraphed and wrote to USG. "Dispatch received and am very glad you will spend week at my house This is Race week and next the Fair—Forsyth is all right & Sheridan says he must have killed & crippled seventy five 75 of the Indians. He will follow this up and I hope this winter will teach those Indians a lesson that will last our day" Telegram received (at 11:15 A.M.), *ibid.*; copy, DLC-USG, V, 55. "I have your letter of Spt 25, and your despatch of today, and am particularly glad you will stay at my house during your visit. A good many persons have written to me, and spoken to me, as though your opponents had whispered that Mr Ewing and Tom Ewing Jr had moved me from my Constant friendship to you, and your election. I have abstained from all politics because really and in fact I have had a deep seated aversion to them from old experience in California, and the curious combinations now make me more & more averse to putting faith in mere political men. To all who apply to me, I say you will be elected, and ought to be elected, and that I would rather trust to your being just & fair, yea even moderate to the South, than Seymour and Blair. I remember too well Blairs indignation at Gen G. W. Morgan, at Chickasaw, and at McClernand at Vicksburg to have ~~his~~ faith in his judgmt of men. To talk of such men and *principle*, is like trusting convicts with property. I'm afraid the Republicans as a party have set some examples that may embarrass Govt in the future, but in this they but followed the example of the Democrats when in power, and dominant.—All men when clothed with power will use it, and sometimes abuse it. Your staying with me during your visit here will answer that question, and I will so arrange that you can see whom you choose, and do as you like. Besides my family carriage I will have a buggy and pair of horses at your service at the house. Let me know at what hour you come, or go to the Planters, and send me word, and I will come for you there. If Mrs Grant will also come we have plenty of room, and every convenience." ALS, USG 3.

To Silas A. Hudson

Galena Ill.
Sept. 25th 1868.

DEAR COUSIN,

Your favor of the 22d is just received. I shall not go East until after the October elections. On Wednesday next however I shall leave here to visit my farm in St. Louis Co. and, returning, will spend Sunday in Springfield, Ill. I will get back here about Tuesday of the following week.

If you come up here you must not return the same day. We are very comfortably fixed and will be glad to have you pay us a visit.

I was very glad to hear what you had to say about Senator Grimes.[1]

Yours Truly
U. S. GRANT

To S. A. HUDSON,

ALS, Gary Erickson, Wauwatosa, Wis.

1. Although U.S. Senator James W. Grimes of Iowa had delivered a key vote against the conviction of President Andrew Johnson, he announced support for USG's election.

To William W. Smith

Galena Ill.
Sept. 25th 1868.

DEAR SMITH.

I am just in receipt of Mr. M Kennan's[1] letter inviting me to visit Washington about the 1st of October. We have made up our minds to remain here about one month yet, and as I have declined all invitations to be present at political gatherings I must decline this one too. It has been my intention to visit you this Fall, and I still hope to do so. It will be after the state election however.

I have had the most quiet, pleasant time this Summer that has fallen to my lot since the opening of the rebellion in /61. I want to make the most of it not knowing when the same opportunity will present itself again.

All send love to Emma & the boy and you too.

Please present my kindest regards to Mr. Kennan.

Yours Truly
U. S. GRANT

ALS, Washington County Historical Society, Washington, Pa.

1. Born in 1816 in Washington, Pa., William McKennan graduated from Washington College in 1833 and began to practice law in 1837. McKennan, father-in-law of William W. Smith, dined with USG at Washington, Pa., on Sept. 16, 1869. *New York Herald*, Sept. 17, 1869. On Oct. 20, Robert B. Carnahan, U.S. attorney, Pittsburgh, wrote to USG recommending McKennan as judge, 3rd Judicial Circuit. ALS, DNA, RG 46, Papers Pertaining to Nominations. Additional recommendations are *ibid.* On Jan. 1, 1870, McKennan, Washington, Pa., wrote to USG. "I have received from the Attorney General my Commission as Circuit Judge, for the third Judicial Circuit of the United States— In announcing my acceptance of the Office, it is due to you that I should acknowledge my profound and grateful sense of the kindness which prompted its bestowment—That I did not, by the remotest solicitation, seek it, that it is a spontaneous and generous manifestation of *your* confidence, invests it with a higher value, in my estimation, than that which springs from the personal distinction conferred by it—And the ever fresh recollection of this will furnish me an incentive, and inspire me with zeal, to strive that no discredit shall be reflected upon you—" ALS, *ibid.*, RG 60, Letters from the President.

To Julia Dent Grant

Chicago Ill.
Sept. 26th 1868

DEAR JULIA:

No train leaves here Sunday evening so it will be Monday evening before I get home.

Orvil and the family are very well. If I had not come over Orvil would have gone this evening. It is pleasant for me however to have a change occasionally so I do not regret coming over.

Good buye

U. S. G.

AL (initialed), USG 3.

To Bvt. Maj. Gen. Christopher C. Augur

Galena Ill,
Sept. 29th 1868,

DEAR AUGUR:

Enclosed I return you Hodges letter, as you request. I had no doubt about where Hodges stood before. In the matter of the telegram which was sent to Washington I merely supposed Hodges & Eddys names had been transposed. I know that Governor Woods, the Republican Governor of Oregon, had striven hard to get Eddy removed, and Hodges put in his place, to prevent the former from using the patronage of his place for political purposes. This he asserted Eddy was doing unscrupulously. I take all such statements with a good deal of allowence, and do not allow myself to be influenced by such statements without proof of their accuracy. I shall not go back to Washington until just before the November election.

Yours Truly
U. S. GRANT

ALS, IHi. See *PUSG*, 18, 268–69.

To Jesse K. Dubois

Galena Ill.
Sept. 29th 1868

HON. J. K. DUBOIS,
DEAR SIR:

Either to-morrow evening, or the evening of the day following, I will start, with two officers of my Staff, to visit my farm in St. Louis Co. where I left some improvements making; and, on the return, will pay you a visit. It will be either Saturday or Sunday night when we will get there. (to Springfield)   I would like to get there quietly, unannounced, to see you and a few of your particular friends who might drop in. I have declined so many invitations to visit different sections that I would much prefer this course to having any thing like a demonstration. It would be much easier to explain that I had gone to visit a few acquaintance, made when we were to-gether organizing the first troops to put down the rebellion, and save the nation, than if a big parade were made. I went to Quincy with the understanding that I was to do so quietly. Mr. Morris I have known all my life and had been promising to visit him for three years back. It got out that I was to be there and the result was thousands of people were out. I am not a very good hand at entertaining such crouds either which is another very good reason why I should want to avoid them.

Yours Truly
U. S. Grant

ALS, Willard Bunn, Jr., Springfield, Ill.

To Bvt. Maj. Gen. John A. Rawlins

[*Sept., 1868*]

Dear Rawlins,

Badeau and Comstock are both here. Badeau says that you intend leaving as soon as Mrs. Rawlins' health will permit of her removal. I do hope that will not be long and that you will go where you can be quiet, and the climate suited to recuperate your health. Give any order to yourself you think best. If a southern trip would suit you make an inspection tour in that direction. Go through in the direction best suited to your inclination, and if travelling orders do not feel that it is necessary to get through at any fixed time or that your route is determined by your orders.—I am getting fat, weigh now over 160 pounds. Do not know that I will start back before the middle of Oct. The family are all well.

Yours Truly
U. S. Grant.

Copy, Bender Collection, Wy-Ar.

To Bvt. Brig. Gen. Frederick T. Dent

Galena, Ill,
~~Sept~~Oct. 1st 1868,

DEAR DENT,

Rawlins has arrived apparently, very well. He thinks of remaining about here, St. Paul, and the NorthWest generally, for some time. I go this evening to St. Louis again and will be gone about one week.—To anxious enquirers about when I will be back to Washington tell them that you do not know. In reality I do not know; probably just before the Nov. election however. I have not been followed here yet by the Army of office seekers. Tell Parker & Leet not to send any more letters here to me, or ~~m~~the family. We can wait until we get to Washington. The great majority of them prove to be begging letters.

The family are all well and send a great deal of love to Hellen & the children.

Yours Truly
U. S. GRANT

ALS, John D. Burt, Redwood City, Calif.

To Bvt. Lt. Col. George K. Leet

By Telegraph from Galena Ill [*Oct.*] 8 *1868*

To COL G. K LEET
ARMY HEAD QRS

Submit General Meade's order to Secretary of War, I approve as the order now reads, or with such modification as the Secretary may think proper

U. S GRANT

Telegrams received (2—at 11:05 A.M.), DNA, RG 107, Telegrams Collected (Bound); *ibid.*, RG 108, Telegrams Received; copies, *ibid.*, RG 94, Letters Received, 481A 1868; DLC-USG, V, 55. On Oct. 6, 1868, Maj. Gen. George

G. Meade, Atlanta, telegraphed to USG. "I forward an outline of order to be at once issued on which I desire the comments of yourself Secr—of War & The President—I am of opinion the moral effect of this order and the distributn of troops, will tend greatly to allay existing excitement, and to remove some existing delusions—In connection with this measure, it would have a very beneficial effect—if a movement could be made say of one or two companies, to each of the following places—Raleigh Columbia—Atlanta & Montgomery—indica to act as reserves until after the election—the mere arrival & passage through the country will have a great effect, as indicating the determination of the authorities at Washington to sustain me.—" ALS (telegram sent), Meade Papers, PHi; telegram received (at 9:00 P.M.), DNA, RG 107, Telegrams Collected (Bound); *ibid.*, RG 108, Telegrams Received. For text of the major portion of the order, see *SED*, 41-2-13, p. 61. On Oct. 7, 1:10 P.M., Bvt. Lt. Col. George K. Leet transmitted Meade's telegram to USG at Galena. Telegrams sent (2), DNA, RG 107, Telegrams Collected (Bound); copies, *ibid.*, RG 108, Telegrams Sent; DLC-USG, V, 56.

On Oct. 3, Meade had written to USG. "You have been apprised, that on receiving intelligence of the disorders occuring in this state, on the 19th ulto at Camilla in Mitchell County—that I at once had troops in readiness, to meet any call of the civil authorities, such as are referred to in the letter of instructions from the Genl. in Chief of date Aug. 25th 1868—and that at the same time I despatched Capt. Mills a most reliable, and intelligent officer on whose cool sound judgement and freedom from any prejudice or party bias I could depend—to investigate thoroughly and report the facts in the case—The affair passing off with the riot or rather collision of the 19th inst—and no call having been made on me—the Legislature, (as I think properly) declining the request of the Governor to authorise him to make the call—no troops were sent—The report of Capt Mills was yesterday received and after its persual I deemed the only thing for me to do, was to transmit it to the Governor of the State, the officer with whom I am required to communicate and to assure him, that in any measures that might be taken by the civil authorities in the investigation of the affair and punishment of derelict civil officers or citizens—that in case he met with resistance or he or they found themselves unable to execute the laws I was prepared on being so informed to aid and co-operate with him to the fullest extent of the force under my command. My letter to the Governor, the Report and accompanying documents of Capt Mills are herewith forwarded by the hands of Capt McKibben U. S. Army, and I should be pleased to receive any comments thereon which yourself—the Hon Sec. of War or the President may please to make—I deem it proper to add that in a few days I shall distribute the troops in the Dept. with a view of 'aiding the civil authorities to keep the peace' during the approaching Presidential election" LS, DNA, RG 108, Letters Received. The enclosures are *ibid.*

On Oct. 9, Meade wrote to USG. "I have the honor to submit herewith, copies of a correspondence between Brvt. Maj Genl N. A Miles Comd. Dist of No. Carolina & myself in relation to the exercise of the military power, and to invite your special attention to the same.—It will be seen from this correspondance that Genl Miles not only differs in toto, with me as to the authority given by the Laws, and instructions of the War Dept. but that after the clear and positive enunciation of my views, he continues to make labored arguments in opposition to the same. It is hardly necessary for me to say that no one has a higher respect personally for Genl Miles than myself and that no one appreciates more fully, the distinguished reputation acquired by him for deeds of gallantry enacted during the War—but I find myself in a peculiarly embarrassing position—one probably of greater delicacy than usually falls to a military commander—and one in which it is of the most essential importance, not only that obedience should be given on the part of Subordinates but that there should be harmony of judgement as well—Maj. Genl. Miles & myself are in direct issue on an important point—which is the basis of all my duties,—and as it is impracticable for me to assume the responsibilities which my duties impose on me, unless I receive the warm support & hearty co-operation of my subordinates— and as it must be in the highest degree unsatisfactory for Genl Miles to have to conform to instructions so totally at variance with his judgement & sense of duty; I have to ask a decision on the issue raised, and that the officer whose judgement is not approved whether it be myself or Genl Miles be relieved from further command in this Department." ALS, _ibid._, RG 94, Letters Received, A375 1868.

To John M. Schofield

—————

Galena Ill. Oct. 19th _1868._

MAJ. GEN. J. M. SCHOFIELD,
SEC. OF WAR,
GENERAL:

In as much as I will not return to Washington before you will want to make out your Annual report I have directed Col. Leet to turn over to you all reports of Division, District & Dept. Commanders. I will make no report myself further than to write "Letter of Advice" accompanying these reports, which can be done after I get back. Have not yet fixed upon time for starting.

Respectfully &c.
U. S. GRANT
General,

ALS, DNA, RG 107, Letters Received from Bureaus.

To Francis Lieber

Galena Ill.
Oct. 19th 1868.

DEAR SIR:

Your esteemed favor of the 4th inst. together with the pamphlet on "Nationalism" which you have honored me with the dedication of,[1] is received.

Your friendship for me, shewn so frequently and so flatteringly, is a source of great gratification to me, personally almost a stranger to you, and all the more so because I see in your friendship a patriotism and love of country which actuates it much more than any regard for mere person. Again allow me to thank you for many kindnesses.

> With great respect
> your obt. svt.
> U. S. GRANT
> General

FRANCIS LIEBER, L L D,
NEW YORK CITY

ALS, CSmH. Francis Lieber, born in 1800 in Berlin, emigrated to the U.S. in 1827. He edited the *Encyclopædia Americana* (Philadelphia, 1829–33) and wrote books and essays on government and law while teaching history and political economy at South Carolina College (1835–56) and at Columbia College, N. Y. Lieber advised the U.S. government on legal matters during the Civil War, during which one of his sons joined the C.S. Army and two sons joined the U.S. Army. See *PUSG*, 4, 266; *ibid.*, 9, 63; *ibid.*, 18, 335–37, 591–92; Frank Freidel, *Francis Lieber: Nineteenth-Century Liberal* (Baton Rouge, 1947). On Oct. 4, 1868, Lieber, New York City, wrote to USG and to Bvt. Brig. Gen. Adam Badeau. "I have not hesitated to dedicate to you the accompanying publication, since a large po~~pulation~~rtion of it is occupied with that Nationality for the preservation of which you have lead our hosts to victory: Accept, I pray, the dedication as kindly, as I have made it heartily and conceived it in the spirit of truth. May my wishes expressed in it be largely verified in November next, and may nothing happen which would make the Nation anxious, and feversh in its wish that it could ~~could~~ advance the dial of history from November to March!" "The enclosed is much enlarged, and Sec. III, which I would ask you to read, is entirely new—and, I believe, original Be pleased to present one copy to General Grant with my respects and best wishes; and *with* the enclosed letter to him, if you think he will acknowledge it, If you think he

will not do it, then simply tear ~~it~~ the letter. You as a literiteur will at once perceive that the dedication to Gl Grant has been chiselled a good deal. I think
it is now lapidary, earnest and I know it to be truthful   Let me hear when this
arrives so that I may kno whether you received it. Many of The commonest
Roman Catholic Pro-Fernando Irish men are turning Republican here and
speak of the 'Poor Negro'! You, as a New-Yorker will fully appreciate this fact.
To say the truth Genl Grant owes very warm thanks to the Seymourites and
Blairians. No one could have worked more sincerely for Grant and Colfax than
they have. And Dix! !" ALS, USG 3.

On Oct. 26 and Nov. 9, Lieber wrote to USG. "Allow a veteran—a Water-
loo man—to say to *his*, far younger, general, that your letter gave him great
pleasure. A new victory is approaching; there can hardly be any doubt now;
but we, in New York, have serious doubts concerning our State—at least I
have. Yet it is ~~of~~ for us here of the *greatest* importance that the next State
Legislature and governor be Republican. If you are elected President we here
will do our utmost to make Congress pass a statute giving back the power of
naturalization to the U. States Courts, or U. S Commissioners, as it was originally, and we hope we shall not have a veto on such a bill. The present unlawful
naturalization is *gigantic*. May we have fair weather on the next great election
day! Foul weather, I have observed, always keeps voters of the *good* side at
home." "Although this my most sincere congratulation will arrive long ~~before~~
after that of many others, I take care as you will see, that I make *the first application* of the many millions to which you will be exposed. My friend, the Hon.
Samuel B. Ruggles, has requested me to send you a copy of a short speech of his
on the proposed uniformity of coins—a subject which doubtless will come before
you officially, after the fourth of March, and to invite you to read the latter
portion   You may have observed that the new government of Spain proclaimed
itself with the followg few measures: Expulsion of Jesuits, freedom of education, abolition of slavery and adaptation of the old Spanish dollar to the French
monitary system. If we, with our Continental Commonwealth, could join this
movement, I should consider it as marking an epoch in the history of civilisation.
Let me repeat my most hearty congratulations, although a New-Yorker cannot
rejoice on the result of the election, otherwise than a man rejoices in a great
victory, when some of his kinsfolk have falen in the battle. The loss of the
State of New York is the effect of the most degrading and most openly shame-
less fraud, in which the crimes of forgery and treason against the very funda-
mentals of our polity were mired. It can be plainly proved that you and Mr
Colfax had ~~the~~ a goodly majority of all the lawful voters of the State of New-
York." ALS, *ibid.*

On March 5, 1869, Lieber wrote to USG. "When people send their congratulations from my native city of Berlin to the President of the United States,
I hope I may be permitted to send you mine from this city—now that the '*coming Fourth of March*', has come. I wish the richest blessings on you administration. I enclose the translation of a letter to me, on account of the significant
allusion to your assuming the chief magistracy of the Country. Whatever you
may think of the probability that war will break out in Europe or not, I beg to
say that the letter of a portion of which I send a translation, was written by a
most prominent and far-seeing man. If war does break out, it will be like a
gigantic prairie fire, and the position ~~which~~ of the United State to-ward the rest

of the World will be of the greatest influence. We should then, as we have already done in former times, calmly, connllectedly and *imposingly* contribute to the developmt of the Law of Nations. Accept once more the congratulatio[ns] of a very sincere friend—" ALS, Smithsonian Institution.

On April 8, Samuel B. Ruggles *et al.* wrote to USG. "The undersigned loyal citizens of New York respectfully ask the privelege of expressing to the President the high estimation, in which in common with the great body of the loyal portion of this community, and of the country at large they hold their distinguished fellow-citizen *Francis Lieber*. . . . They cannot but think that his ripe and varied acquirements, his well-established reputation both at home and abroad, his deep philosophical knowledge of the history of nations and their public law, and above all, the pure and lofty tone of political morality and justice, pervading all his writings—not to mention the important, super-added power of giving efficiency to the whole by his ready and happy command of the continental languages most in use in diplomatic intercourse preeminently qualify him to serve our country abroad in a representative capacity or in *international arbitrations*. . . ." Copies (12 signatures), DLC-Hamilton Fish; CSmH. No appointment followed.

On April 22, 1870, Lieber wrote to USG. "One of my sons in the army, Captain Hamilton Lieber, Brvt Lt. Colonel Vol., now Milit. Store Keeper, has applied to the proper authority to be recommended to you to be placed before a retiring board. He lost his arm at the capture of Fort Donelson, in the 9th Regiment Illinois Infantry, served in other portions of the army, during the civil war, and was ultimately appointed Military Store Keeper, by our great friend, Secretary Stanton. His station was Fort Union, New Mexico, where the peculiar climate increased in an alarming degree the swelling of his liver, first contracted, I believe, in the cold water through which your troops had to march in that memorable April, in alarming degree. He has applied, as I have stated, to be retired, and I take the liberty of begging you not to withhold your attention from this case, before the number of retirements admitted by Congress, be exhausted. My son is now at Fort Snelling, Minnesota." ALS, DNA, RG 94, ACP, 4337 1873. On July 21, 1875, Martin R. Thayer, Philadelphia, wrote to USG. "Capt. Hamilton Lieber U S Army has applied to be placed upon the retired list in consequence of wounds and disease sufferred and contracted in the public service. The meritorious character of the application and the great benefits rendered to his country in a civil capacity by Capt Lieber's father—the late Francis Lieber L. L. D—the author of the Military Code promulgated during the war in General Order No 100 (1863) and of many other most valuable works to the Country—induce me to ask respectfully for a favorable consideration of his application—. . ." ALS, *ibid.* On Dec. 13, Capt. Hamilton Lieber was retired.

1. "On the eve of a momentous national election the writer of these few pages makes bold to dedicate them to General U. S. Grant. May the American people confer upon him the chief magistracy of this nation, conscious of its freedom and its grandeur and now assailed again in its best and noblest interests by those enemies against whom but a short time ago he lead the national hosts to victory and patriotic glory. And let the people of this continental republic on the coming fourth of March greet him as Charlemagne was hailed at Rome:

pacific victor." Dedication (original typefaces not reproduced), *Fragments of Political Science on Nationalism and Inter-Nationalism* (New York, 1868).

To Isaac N. Morris

———

Galena Ill.
Oct. 22d/68

HON. I. N. MORRIS,
DEAR SIR:

Soon after you left here I changed my intention of going to Washington before the Nov. election. I write this in reply to your kind note proposing to accompany me, or to send your son along. I do not apprehend danger, but after getting back there I shall have but little peace   I want to put off the evil day, day of all work, as long as possible.

My family are all well, and ask to be remembered to Mrs. Morris and yourself.

Yours Truly
U. S. GRANT

ALS, ICarbS.

To Lt. Gen. William T. Sherman

———

Washington, D. C., Oct. 26th *1868.*

DEAR GENERAL;

Your letter enclosing one from your brother was duly rec'd. As I did not want to change your determination in regards to the publication of the correspondence between us, and am getting to be a little lazy, I have been slow in answering   I had forgotten what my letter to you said but did remember that you spoke of the probable course the Ewings would take, or something about them which you would not probably want published with the letters.

The fact is General I never wanted the letters published half so much on my own account as yours. There are a great many people who do not understan[d] as I do your friendship for me. I do not believe it will make any difference to you in the end, but I do fear that, in case I am elected, there will be men to advocate the abolition of the Gn. bill who will charge in support of their motion lack of evidence that you supported the union cause in the canvass. I would do all I could to prevent any such legislation and believe that without my doing any thing the confidence in you is so genuine with the great majority of Congress for any such legislation to succeed. If any thing more should be necessary to prove the falsity of such an assumption the correspondence between us heretofore could then be produced.

I agree with you that Sheridan should be let alone to prossecute the indian war to its end. If n[o] treaty is made with the indians untill they can hold out no longer we can dictate terms, and they will will then keep them. This is the course that has been pursued in the Northwest, where Crooke has prossecuted war in his own way, and now a White man can travel through all that country with as much security as if there was not an indian in it.

I have concluded not to return to Washington untill after the election. I shall go very soon after that event however. My family are all well and join me in respects to Mrs. Sherman and the children.

Yours Truly
U. S. GRANT

LT. GN. W. T. SHERMAN,
U. S. ARMY,

ALS (facsimile), DLC-John Sherman. On Oct. 22, 1868, Lt. Gen. William T. Sherman, St. Louis, wrote to USG. "I wrote to John, abot your expression of preference that both our letters should be published in full, instead of that mere extract given in my letter to Bowman. I enclose you his answer. Of course he will do, what you think should be done: but I agree with him perfectly, that you cannot better your position, and I advise against the publication of the letters. I have seen no allusion to your advice that officers in service should keep out of politics, construing it as reflecting on Sickles or any other of your friends though it has been interpreted as against Granger. Sickles being an old politician, & having lost a leg, which will likely make it impossible for him to aspire for higher military Rank is an exception to the general Rule. Therefore unless you report your preference I will let the matter rest. I have not a copy of my letter to you from NewMexico, but I have your reply—the copies of both John says are in Washington. Your election now is as certain, as any event can possibly be. The recent movements among Democratic Candidates, leaders, and committees all manifest weakness confusion, and despair. Within the past week I have had many democrats, Southern men by association or birth, say that you are as good as elected, and they are glad of it, because they regard it as ending the political quarrel, incident to the close of the War. I get occasional items from the Indians, not important enough to make public, but satisfying me that Sheridan is doing all the case admits of. His troops are all out, Sailing on the Ocean, occasionally getting a glimpse, and occasionally a small fight. To day he reports a fight between two Co's of the 10th Cavalry, (Black,) & some Indians on Beaver Creek in which 8 Indians were killed, and only two of our men wounded. He is pushing them from Creek to Creek, where alone they can camp, and is preventing the Indians from collecting their winter supply of buffalo meat & robes.—and as soon as snow comes he will go for their camps. He fears that an effort will be made to stop him as soon as the Indians are tired, which usually occurs about this season of the year, but I pledge him my influence, and that of Schofield and yourself, that we will not check him till the Indians are in his judgmnt subdued, and beg for quarter. I will have my annual Report for you at Washgton by the 4 of Nov—which I judge to be about the time you will be ready for it in Washgton. All well here." ALS, USG 3. Sherman enclosed a letter of Oct. 16 to himself from U.S. Senator John Sherman of Ohio, Mansfield. "Your note of the 14th is rec'd—Gen Grant sent me a copy of your letter to him & his reply—but I did not feel at liberty to publish them though the correspondence is highly creditable to both of you and could have done no harm—Still I would not have advised the publication even if I had felt at liberty to do so—Your letter contained one or two expressions about the Ewings and his letter stated rather broadly his reason for accepting so that it is as well that neither was published. The position of Grant as an independent Candidate—whose nomination was generally demanded by the People—is so admirable that he ought to add not one word to his letter of acceptance—The copies sent me are in my files at Washington—I have access to them without going there—but acting upon the discretion given me—I will not make them public unless you request it—In that event you had better send me a copy of Grants letter which I returned to you & which I could readily introduce it. in a speech & thus give it to the public without the formality of a published correspondence—All well here I am gathering apples and potatoes and getting ready for winter in Washington" ALS, *ibid.*

On Oct. 28, W. T. Sherman wrote to USG. "I have yours of 28, and am glad you do not care about the publication of those letters. I'll take all the Chances of Congress abolishing the office of General, and if the members do it because they think I am not a good enough Union man, it is their business not mine. Congress cant add to or take away from Military Reputation and as to pay I will manage to live—The family and others dependant on me are far more interested in the pay question than I am. Sheridan was to have had his annual Report here by the 20th but was very busy. He has telegraphed me that it is coming by Mail. I already have Terry's and Augurs, so that Comstock may safely count on my Report being in Washington by or before the Election is over. If you would prefer having these reports come to you at Galena, telegraph me on receipt of this and I will mail them to you there instead of Washington. I hope you will keep in mind your promise to be at the meeting of the Armies at Chicago in December. Your promise is written and printed in the last report of the Army of the Tennessee, and very many have asked me if you would surely be there. I have always said, that I felt sure you intended to come, unless some over riding necessity at the moment made it impossible. The young men go to much expense on such occasions and we ought to gratify their wishes. I hope you will not call for me to Washington, till you are prepared to Step from your office into the White House. Sheridan is Counting on giving the Indians their quietus in the Winter, and will prefer to be up in Kansas, and I can be of much service to him here. Besides you appreciate the fact that I dont want to be in Washington—until I have work to do—In any Event I will leave the family here till next May, because the schools where the children are do not let out till May or June. Mrs Sherman & Minnie are over in Ohio on a visit to Mr Ewing. Seymour & Blair have weakened their already hopeless chances, by speaking against him. I am rejoiced that you have taken the canvas so quietly, & that you still enjoy the quiet of Galena." ALS, *ibid.*

On Oct. 26, USG wrote to John Sherman. "Your invitation to Mrs. Grant & myself to break our journey East, and spend a day or two with you was duly received, and should have been sooner acknowledged. I thank you for the invitation and would gladly accept it, but my party will be large, and having a special car it will inconvenience so many people to stop over. Mrs. Grant too, and her father, are anxious, when they start, to get through to Washing[ton] before they unpack." ALS (facsimile), DLC-John Sherman.

To William Elrod

————

Galena Ill.
Oct. 29th 1868,

Dear Elrod:

I think there had better be some insurence on my farm property, and I want it taken in a reliable company. I leave you to be the judge of that. You make no mention whether you received a check from me for $500 00? I sent you that amt. after leaving St. Louis the last time. I want you to draw on me for the least amount you can possibly get along with. I have just had to pay $1,500 00 for Mr. Dent which I knew nothing of, and now I hear of another note of his which, with the interest, will come to about $1,200 00. This puts me in debt a good deal, and every dollar I send to the farm adds to the amount.

If you do not write by the day of election your letter will not probably reach me here.

Family all well,

AL (signature clipped), Illinois Historical Survey, University of Illinois, Urbana, Ill. On Nov. 26, 1868, USG wrote to William Elrod. "In sending money to Ford to pay him what he has paid out for me I have sent him several hundred dollars over, with instructions to pay the balance over to you." AL (signature clipped), *ibid.*

To Bvt. Brig. Gen. Frederick T. Dent

[*Nov. 3, 1868*]

I will make no formal reply, but I wish you would say to the gentlemen in charge of the movement that I would much prefer returning quietly to my home without demonstration. I appreciate their motives, and will take the will for the deed. I do not know, either, what day I will be home. I leave Galena on Thursday[1] evening, and may or may not stop on the way.[2]

New York Times, Nov. 7, 1868. Members of the Boys in Blue, Republican veterans, had requested the date of USG's return to Washington, D. C., in order to hold a public demonstration in his honor. *Ibid.* On Nov. 10, 1868, USG responded to a delegation of Washington Republicans led by Mayor Sayles J. Bowen. "GENTLEMEN: I am very glad to meet you all and receive your congratulations, but hope you will spare me any public demonstration. I much prefer having none, and none will be had with my consent. I reside here in this city privately, and will be glad to receive my friends at any time without display, either at my residence or here at my office. This will be much more agreeable to me, and I hope will be agreeable to you. I am not unmindful of the feeling which induces you to tender me this honor, but I will take it all for granted and appreciate your motives all the same." *Ibid.*, Nov. 11, 1868. Variant text in *New York Tribune*, Nov. 11, 1868.

On Nov. 4, Bvt. Maj. Gen. Nelson A. Miles, Raleigh, N. C., telegraphed to USG. "North Carolina goes strongly Republican. Quietude unparalleled. Officers send congratulations." Copy, DNA, RG 393, District of N. C., Letters Sent. On Nov. 5, Governor William W. Holden of N. C. telegraphed to USG. "I am glad to inform you that N C has voted for Grant & Colfax by a handsome ma-

jority, We have elected six of the seven members of Congress, We were
fortunate in having Genl Nelson A Miles as our Military Commander acting in
concert & in support of the civil authorities, He aided materially in securing a
free election There was no disorder but the election was quiet & peaceable as
far as heard from." Telegrams received (2—at 1:25 P.M.), *ibid.*, RG 107, Telegrams Collected (Bound); *ibid.*, RG 108, Telegrams Received.

On the same day, Maj. Gen. Philip H. Sheridan, Fort Hays, Kan., wrote to
USG. "Please accept my Congratulations. on the result of the Election. All
that is now necesary is to collect the revenues of the govermnt & have them
paid in honestly." ALS, USG 3. On Nov. 6, Bvt. Maj. Gen. Montgomery C.
Meigs wrote to USG. "I must add my hearty congratulations to the voices of
millions rejoicing in confidence of victory under your leadership. The contest is
to my mind as much a struggle with rebellion as that in which you led us at
Mission Ridge. I rejoice that the people have again affirmed their determination
to suppress rebellion and to maintain liberty. And I believe that the malcontents
now despairing of success through aid from the ranks of the victorious loyal,
will soon address themselves to peace and labor & will strive to regain the justly
forfeited privilege of taking part in the government by the only legitimate &
honest mode submission to the will of the majority of the people of the whole
United States" ALS, *ibid.* On the same day, Gerrit Smith, Peterboro, N. Y.,
wrote to USG. "I send you herewith a copy of a public Letter addressed to
yourself, I am not unconsious how great is the liberty which I, a stranger to
you, have taken in writing that Letter, You will, however, forgive it, if you
will let your & my friend, Hon. E. B. Washburne, tell you that my long life
has been earnestly devoted to the assertion of the equal rights of all men." Copy,
Syracuse University, Syracuse, N. Y. Smith enclosed a lengthy printed letter
to USG, dated Nov. 4, urging him to remove "the barriers of race and setting
up in their stead the law of impartial justice and the reign of fraternal love."
Copy, *ibid.* Printed (in part) in *New York World*, Nov. 10, 1868.

On Nov. 7, Alfred Pleasonton, New York City, wrote to USG. "Accept my
warmest congratulations upon the triumphant result of your election as President of the United States. The immense majorities cast in your favor are the
highest tribute the people could offer of the confidence & Support they will give
your Administration. In this state alone the result does not show the facts—for
you received an honest legal majority of at least five thousand votes in this state;
but the corruption, venom, & low partisanship in this city made voters much
faster than the human race has ever been manufactured before under the most
favored circumstances—To correct this, the natural period of *nine months*, should
be made the shortest period of probation for the naturalized citizen—This would
place him on an equal footing with the *native born*, at least so far as coming
into the country is concerned. But I am satisfied you will straighten out all these
little matters & make the Empire State second to none in supporting your Government. With my best wishes for your success—. . ." ALS, USG 3. On the
same day, Pleasonton wrote to USG. "Major Clifford Thomson, at present one
of the Editors of the NewYork Times, is an applicant for the position of Consul
at the port of Hong Kong, China. . . ." ALS, DNA, RG 59, Letters of Application and Recommendation.

On Nov. 10, Speaker of the House Schuyler Colfax wrote to USG. "On your
kind hint, when you handed me the valued autograph for Miss Wade, I read

it before sealing it, & cannot leave the City, without thanking you sincerely for the warm & friendly manner in which you allude to me in it. I had only expected a line 'with congratulations of &c,' but you have made me a grateful debtor to you for the earnest & cordial manner in which you speak of me to one who will prize the note so highly. Despite the annoyances that I foresee are to almost overwhelm you, growing out of the insatiate desire for office in this country, I have no doubt you will have a happy & successful Administration. Besides the incidental interest I have in it, as your Lieutenant in the struggle through which we have passed, I shall feel a great solicitude for your success, because of the warmth of my attachment to you, which I am so glad to see, over your own hand, is so fully *reciprocated*. Always command me whenever you desire any thing within my power; & I need not add that, while I shall not obtrude opinions or advice, except to add suggestions to the common stock you will receive, from which you will make up your judgment & action, I shall be only too glad, whenever you desire to advise with me confidentially as to men or measures, to do so frankly between ourselves alone; for whatever you tell me is for my own ear, shall be as safe as locked up in your mind. I shall return with my wife, mother, sister, stepfather Thursday night of next week, 19th inst & we shall remain here till the succeeding Monday, when we go to N. Y. shopping & visiting relatives by the way & there. Please hand the enclosed to Mrs Grant . . ." ALS, USG 3.

On Nov. 19, eight Methodist bishops signed a letter of congratulation to USG. Copy, *ibid*. Printed in *Washington Chronicle*, Dec. 12, 1868. Other telegrams and letters to USG concerning the election are in USG 3; DNA, RG 107, Telegrams Collected (Bound).

1. Nov. 5.
2. On Nov. 4, Mayor Charles F. Wilstach of Cincinnati telegraphed to USG. "The city of Cincinnati sends greetings for your splendid victory, and asks you to accept its hospitalities on your way to Washington." *Washington Chronicle*, Nov. 7, 1868. On the same day, USG, Galena, telegraphed to Wilstach. "Many thanks to citizens of Cincinnati for their tender of hospitalities, but I shall not be able to accept. I shall not pass that way on my return East." *Ibid*.

To Julia Dent Grant

Galena—Nov. 3d *1868*

DEAR JULIA;

Jones telegraphs to know if Mrs. Harry Wilson[1] can go East with us. Jones goes himself. I would like to say yes to this. It will be a great accomodation to Wilson. Answer yes or no, by bearer.

Election returns are coming in very fast and most favorably from all quarters, Pittsburg & Phila. about six thousand better than three weeks ago. Corresponding Republican gains from all quarters.

Ulys.

ALS, USG 3. Written on stationery of the Union Republican National Committee, New York. Perhaps about this time, USG wrote a note to Julia Dent Grant on stationery of L. S. Felt. "Mrs. Blood has made a pilgrimgage to Galena to secure for her husband the position of private secretary to me when I am President." ALS, Meissner Collection, Washington University, St. Louis, Mo. Victoria Woodhull then considered herself to be the wife of James H. Blood of St. Louis, former col., 6th Mo. See Emanie Sachs, "*The Terrible Siren*" *Victoria Woodhull* . . . (New York, 1928), pp. 42–46. On Jan. 2, 1880, Blood, Auburn, Maine, wrote to Secretary of State William M. Evarts. "I want to obtain copies of the papers filed with my application for Consul, in your office in 1869. They refer to my war record as Colonel of the 6th Infantry, Mo Vols. and consist of letters of Genl's Sherman, Blair Smith; and sundry endorsements on orders and recommendations. If you will have the same made so that I can g[e]t them the 8th inst, when I shall be in Washington, I will call and pay the customary fees for such service" ALS, DNA, RG 59, Letters of Application and Recommendation. On Jan. 8, Blood signed a receipt for the return of these letters. DS, *ibid.*

1. Mrs. James Harrison Wilson.

Speech

[*Nov. 4, 1868*]

Friends and Fellow Citizens of Galena:

I thank you for this additional mark of your kindness. Sufficient has now been heard of the result of the late election to show upon whom it has fallen to administer the affairs of the nation for the next four years. I suppose it is no egotism in me to say that the choice has fallen upon me. The responsibilities of the position I feel, but accept them without fear, if I can have the same support which has been given to me thus far. I thank you and all others who have fought together in this contest—a contest in which you are all interested personally as much, and perhaps more than I am. I now take occasion to bid you good bye, as I leave here tomorrow for Washington, and shall probably see but few of you again for some years to come; although it would give me great pleasure to make an annual pilgrimage to a place where I have enjoyed myself so much as I have here during the past few months.

Galena Gazette, Nov. 5, 1868. On Nov. 5, 1868, USG spoke in Belvidere, Ill. "Gentlemen, I see many of you in uniforms. You laid them off three years ago. You can now lay them off again and we will have peace. Good night." *Chicago Journal*, Nov. 6, 1868.

To J. Russell Jones

~~Washington, D. C.~~, Galena Ill. Nov. 4th *1868*

DEAR JONES:

I think it will be best to remain in the sleeping cars until 6. I do not know of any one I want to invite to accompany us from Chicago. John E. Smith will probably go from here.[1]—Also glad to learn that you *went for Seamour*.[2] A man that can hold office under Johnson, and go that way can't expect anything from the next administration.

Yours
U. S. GRANT

ALS, IHi.

1. On Nov. 11, 1868, Bvt. Lt. Col. George K. Leet wrote to the AG. "The Adjutant General will issue the following orders: The verbal instructions ~~of~~ given by the General of the Army the 5th inst. to Bvt. Maj. Gen John E. Smith, Col. 27th Infantry, to proceed from Galena, Illinois, to Washington City and report at the Headquarters Army of the US. are hereby confirmed. Bvt. Maj. Gen. John E. Smith, Col. 27th Infantry, having completed the duty for which he was directed to report at the Headquarters Army of the US., will return to Galena, Illinois, and avail himself of the remainder of his present leave of absence." DS, DNA, RG 94, Letters Received, 974S 1868.

2. Horatio Seymour, born in 1810 in Pompey Hill, N. Y., son of an associate of Martin Van Buren, rose through the state Democratic ranks, becoming governor (1853–55, 1863–65). As wartime governor, he supported the Union but was criticized for his role in the New York City draft riots (1863). Nominated as Democratic presidential candidate in 1868, Seymour made a campaign tour through Cleveland, Chicago, and other northern cities, emphasizing USG's sympathy with radical Republicans.

To Maj. Gen. George G. Meade

Washington, D. C., Nov. 8th *1868*

DEAR GENERAL:

Enclosed I send you resolutions prepared by M. Carpenter,[1] *our* Atty. in the case of Georgia vs. Meade & others which he desires passed by the Ga. Legislature. That body may not be of just the right complexion just now to aid us but I submit the matter to you to see what can be done.

Yours Truly

U. S. GRANT

General,

ALS, Meade Papers, PHi. On Nov. 4, 1868, Matthew H. Carpenter, Milwaukee, wrote to USG. "As election is now over and all right, I enclose you a draft of resolutions which I wish you would transmit to Genl Mead or some one else & have passed by the Legislature of Georgia, so we can end that suit in Supm Court, on the first day of the next term   Congratulating you & the country on the result of the election, . . ." ALS, *ibid.* On Nov. 23, Maj. Gen. George G. Meade, Atlanta, telegraphed to USG. "Letter in reference to resolutions desired passed by Georgia Legislature received and sent to Governor who promises to endeavor to have action taken—Legislature does not meet till January.—Will it be necessary for myself, Ruger, or Wheaton to appear, as summoned on the Sixth proximo when the case comes up—Please reply on latter point as soon as practicable—" ALS (telegram sent), *ibid.*; telegram received (at 4:00 P.M.), DNA, RG 107, Telegrams Collected (Bound); *ibid.*, RG 108, Telegrams Received.

On Nov. 8, Meade had written to USG. "I hardly think it necessary to go thro the form of congratulating you on your grand success—I think you must know that whilst I studiously abstain from all political matters that from the moment you accepted a nomination, I most earnestly desired your success, and am correspondingly gratified at the result as you were pleased to say of me *once* you are the right man in the right place—God grant you success in it which I dont doubt your having if you will only follow the dictates of your own sound judgment and not be led away by others—I have already been applied to for recommendations to you for all kinds of offices, from members of the Cabinet down—to all of which I have declined—because I never want you to see my signature except when it will carry weight from my personal knowledge of the facts in the case, and your knowledge of me.—There is one thing however I wish you to do for me, and that is notify Townsend that he is not to take away from me Capts Sanders & McKibben, whom you *allowed* me to bring here & whom I wish to retain so long as I am kept South—With congratulations to Mrs G . . . It was all quiet here during the elections   The October elections settling that—At present the state officers in Florida are fighting among themselves—but I do not anticipate any serious trouble—beyond individual outrages upon men, who make themselves specially obnoxious to their political enemies.— I hope congress will let these people alone, and let them work out their own case—If not nothing short of *martial law* & a purely military government will do—and if this is established they ought to *foot the bills.*—" ALS, USG 3.

On Nov. 23, Meade wrote to USG. "*Personal* . . . This letter will be handed to you by the Honl. H. V. M Miller Senator elect from Georgia—Mr Miller desires to form your acquaintance and from personal knowledge of Mr Miller and his political status I am very anxious you should know him.—I think it will be conceded by all parties that Mr Miller was one of the most active supporters of the Congressional plan of Reconstruction, but in the convention which framed the Constitution he differed with the extreme men of the Republican party, on the rights that should specifically be given to the Negro—Mr. M desiring to confine these to such civil & political rights as would give the Negro protection in his person & property the franchise but not the right to make expound or execute laws—Subsequently he was together with Mr J. R. Hill elected to the Senate of the U. S—but it is understood their taking their seats has become questionable, in consequence of the Legislature subsequent to their election— and thru a considerable proportion of Republican votes—declaring the negro under the Georgia Constitution ineligible to office & ejecting the colored members of the Legislature—I have reason to believe the admission of Messr Hill & Miller would be acceptable to the main body of the Republicans of the State— and I certainly believe, it is for the interest of the State, and the whole country, that all issues in the future should be avoided, and these gentlemen allowed to take their seats—If after conversing with Mr Miller & posting yourself in the facts of the case you could come to this conclusion & aid Mr Miller I should be greatly gratified—the object of this note is to gain him an interview with you & to commend him as a gentleman most worthy of your consideration" ALS, *ibid.*

1. Carpenter, born in 1824 in Vt., attended USMA without graduating, studied law, practiced in Boston, then moved to Beloit, Wis., in 1848. He moved to Milwaukee in 1858, switched political support from Democratic to Republican at the onset of the Civil War, and gained national standing as a lawyer, especially for his arguments in *Ex parte Garland* and *Ex parte McCardle.* Secretary of War Edwin M. Stanton had employed Carpenter as counsel to defend the officers named in *Georgia v. Grant*, a case questioning the jurisdiction of military officials and southern state governments under the Reconstruction Acts. See E. Bruce Thompson, *Matthew Hale Carpenter: Webster of the West* (Madison, Wis., 1954); Charles Fairman, *Reconstruction and Reunion, 1864–88* (New York and London, 1971), I, 433–37.

To William W. Smith

———

Washington, D, C,
Nov. 8th 186[8],

DEAR SMITH:

We arrived here Saturday evening last,[1] all well. When we went West it was our intention to pay you a visit before returning to Washington; but our stay was protracted so long that we felt obliged to come directly to Washington. I do not think now that any of us will get to your place this Winter, but next Summer I shall hope to, All send love to Emma and the boy, the principle member of the household.

Yours Truly
U. S GRANT

ALS, Washington County Historical Society, Washington, Pa.

1. Nov. 7, 1868.

To Matías Romero

———

Washington, D. C., Nov. 11th *1868*,

DEAR SR.

I returned to this City last Saturday evening after an absence from it of more than four months. On my return I find three of your esteemed letters, one of which was written before you left Mexico to visit this Country. I now write not that I have any thing particular to say, but to continue an acquaintance, and friendship, which I prize because of your patriotism towards your own *republic* during its trials, and sympathy ~~for~~ with ours when also tested. I sincerely hope for you every prosperity and advancement as a nation, and that the utmost good feeling may always exist between this country and all the republics of the American continent.

Before you receive this you will have heard the result of the late election. Already the bitterness and animosity, always engendered by a Presidential campaign, are subsiding. I hope now for national quiet and more looking after material interests.

I shall not be able to visit Mexico as I hoped to do. My presence in the United States will be required from now until Spring.

Please remember me kindly to your family and to the family of the President.

Yours Truly
U. S. GRANT

S. D. M. ROMERO MEXICO

ALS (facsimile), DLC-Matías Romero. On Oct. 9, 15, and Nov. 9, 1868, Matías Romero, Mexico City, wrote to USG. "It gives me pleasure to inform you that political affairs in this country continue to improve. The people is really tired of war and earnestly decided to support the government. Enclosed I send you an English copy of my report on the condition of the finances of Mexico during the last fiscal year which shows a satisfactory result. The action of our Congress on the VeraCruz rail road is not a final one, nor will it cause, in my opinion any serious difficulty We have heard here of the appointment of Gen Rosecranz as U S Minister to Mexico. I hardly believe that in the present condition of things he would come We feel great interest here in the coming election in the United States although we are almost certain of its result. I hope you have returned safely from your western trip after a pleasant tour With my best regards for yourself and family, . . ." "My brother sent me by last mail from the United States copy o[f] a letter addressed to him by Gen Badeau and dated Galena Illinois Sep 13th 1868 relating to Gen Rosencranz. I am very much obliged to Gen Badeau and to yourself if you requested him to write that letter, for the important information it conveys Gen R.'s appointment as Minister to Mexico was received here with distrust for the well known religious views of [the] General I knew full well [t]hat he was not a friend of yours, and was not surprise at [hi]s appointment by the President as I was to his confirmation by the Senate. His course in the United States after his appointment has seemed to us very strange We have heard from reliable sources in the United States [—] indications of what he intends to do here, which if true, would be in open contradiction with you views about Mexico After all these facts have transpired my impression has been that if he is a man of sense, he will not come to Mexico He would remain here only two or three months and in that time and in the present condition of things I am sure he could not accomplish any thing at all On our part, if he comes with the views we have reason to believe he entertains about Mexico, it is better that he should not come I am quite anxious to be [in] Washington during your inauguration as President of the United States and if possible I shall do so if it is only to remain there for a few days With my best compliments for yourself, Mr Grant, Mr. Dent, and your children . . ." "We heard this morning by telegraph from VeraCruz that you was elected President of the United States on the 3d instant This news we received almost with as much pleasure as we did the late capture of Puebla or of this city. We could desire nothing better than this This election does not surprise me at all From the moment I knew that you had accepted the nomination of the Chicago National convention I had not the slightest doubt of your election   When I saw the candidates of the democratic ticket and their plataform, that certainty was still greater. I consider you election, General, as a blessing not only for the United States, but for mankind at large and for Mexico specially. I have no doubt you will succeed in afecting the union between both sections of the contry and in promoting the development and well fare of the United States   I have hastely written an editorial article for the Official paper about this matter, which I will enclose you in this letter   As for Mexico you have often heard me express my views on this subject. I do not think any thing better could have taken place in the United States than to have as President such Just and able man as you are. I feel satisfied that at least for four or eight years we will have nothing but a real friendship and a sincere good will from our great neighbour. It would afford me very great pleasure if I can go to congratulate you and be present at your inauguration   I do not know if my duties here will allow me to do so, but I will try my best to be in Washington by the next 4th of March. I hope you will cary out your idea of coming to Mexico during this month. The President will be very glad to see you here   I will go to meet you to VeraCruz and Mr Lerdo will in all probability accompany me   With my best regards for yourself Mrs. Grant, your children and Mr. Dent, . . ." ALS, USG 3.

To Capt. Daniel Ammen

———

WASHINGTON, D. C., Nov. 23d, 1868.

DEAR AMMEN,—

Your welcome and very interesting letters, up to September, have been received. Since that date the Presidential election has taken place, and the result before this reached you. The Democracy made the most desperate and unscrupulous effort of their lives to change the result, but without effect. Now there seems to be a general acquiescence, North and South, in the result. Appearances now are about what they were in '65. I would write you a long letter on public and home affairs, but that I hope you will be on your way home soon after the receipt of this, if you are not before. I am not on speaking-terms with your venerable Chief, therefore cannot ask him to relieve you from your present duties. I did, however, some ten days since, write to Admiral Porter, asking him to effect your release. Immediately on writing that letter I went North, and have but just returned; so I do not know what success he met with.

I know, however, the admiral came to Washington a day or two after the receipt of my letter. If you are not relieved by orders from the Navy Department, I hope your immediate commander will take the liberty to relieve you himself in time to reach here by the 4th of March, 1869, and trust to orders then justifying his action. I am anxious that you should be here at that time.

Mrs. Grant received a letter from Mrs. Ammen yesterday, from which we learn your family are now well. We hope to have a visit from her soon, when Mrs. Grant and myself will do what we can to make her time pass agreeably.

My family are all well. The children were much pleased with the presents received from you.

Yours truly,

U. S. GRANT.

Daniel Ammen, *The Old Navy and the New* (Philadelphia, 1891), pp. 536–37. On Nov. 23, 1868, USG wrote a check for $300 to Mrs. Zoe Ammen, wife of Capt. Daniel Ammen. DS (facsimile), Sotheby's, May 1, 1985, no. 15.

On Aug. 5, Ammen, Yokohama, wrote to Julia Dent Grant. "Now that I have fulfilled my commission as far as the China ware is concerned and my wishes and what I promised myself, that of presenting you with a pair of bronze candlesticks of the stork pattern, I feel that my mission so far as it has been personal, has been fulfilled.—The candle sticks I feel sure are far more elaborate and beautiful than the pair of which you spoke.—They stand about fifteen inches high and have a spread of some ten inches.—It Each one is formed of a lilly branch containing five leaves and two lilly pods or rather flowers just opening, in the upper one of which the candle is placed.—The stork some eight inches high stands under this stem. The bird as well as the branch is inlaid with fine silver wire, which I believe is only done in Japan and the effect is very pretty. I have not been able to find a bronze *Yuuk* and therefore will not be able to send one to the General as I had wished.—I sent in a large box some two months before this will reach you several articles which I hope have reached you safely and not being able to get in the box on account of its being full, a glove box for Nellie it occurred to me to send it by the official mail bag to the General which left one month before this.—I sent also a 'number 2' box and wrote to the General to be good enough to send it to my wife by Adams Express. On our reaching the Coast of China about November I suppose, your ware will be completed and it is not at all unlikely that I will ship it by a sailing vessel so as to have it reach home by the time or soon after you have to remove to the White House.—In that case I may send the storks also, or they may go through the Pacific mail. I am quite content with both the ware and the bronzes and doubt not that they will realize your expectations.—as you are aware you have a list of 315 pieces, upon a basis of 30 soup plates and 60 large size dinner and other plates and if you wish the supply increased either before or after seeing them, there will be no difficulty about the matter. I have to thank you for your kind attentions to my poor little wife who I doubt not enjoys much the change from York which is very quiet. The rains which for two months were excessive have now ceased or are at least only occasional.—The weather too although warm is not excessively so, as on the Coast of China, and my family of 460 persons on board are as healthy as I could hope for.—The summer is passing away and then we will probably go to the Coast of China unless these people get actually to hard fighting, which it is said they will do to obtain possession of the rice crop now growing.—The Southern daimios or feudal dukes, are united against those of the North and the question will be which party can secure the rice in this region. To-morrow evening we will have theatricals on board.—I think I sent the General one of our bills and have to regret that I cannot have the pleasure of seeing you on board at one of them.—They are by no means bad, but parts of them of course are absurd enough. The rides over the hills near at hand are very beautiful and I take a gallop with some of the younger officers very frequently. We do not talk politics and I don't expect to be at home in time to vote for the General, nevertheless I expect him to be elected all the same.—Then we will have to defer our European trip four years at least, unless he is disposed to make a summer cruize which we might do, but we would I fear be too much in a hurry to enjoy it.—If it were not for worthless fellows now retired and some of them who took care to remain so during the war, being brought back on the active list I would be entitled to command a squadron about March '73. Aug 22nd.—Your china ware is to be completed by the 1st of September but very often they are a little behind time and we will probably not reach Canton before about the 1st of December when I probably will take a proper bill of lading and send per sailing vessel to New York, of course forwarding the bill of lading to the General. Please give my love to the children.—I hope the few little things that I have sent by box to you and to them have duly arrived." ALS, USG 3. On Aug. 10, Ammen wrote to USG. "The summer is wearing away and generally we have delightful weather with occasional rainy days of which to-day is one. Through the kindness of Gen'l Stahel the consul I have a very nice Japanese pony and I take frequent rides over a very picturesque and beautiful country which I regret you cannot see.—It is too rough to drive fast. Gen'l Stahel is a Hungarian by birth and withal a very agreeable and creditable representative abroad and I say this because there are so many who are not. Owing to the civil dissensions we see nothing of Japanese of rank and little of the merchants.—Phelps who co-operated with you on the Mississippi is here the agent of the Pacific Mail steam ship company and is very kind and polite.—Pecuniarily he did well no doubt in resigning, but it is a pity that the service has to lose such men. The exports of Japan most necessary to foreigners are raw silk and silk worm eggs, the latter of almost vital importance to Italy and southern France where silk worms no longer produce healthy eggs; those from China and other parts of the world have not succeeded as a whole at all comparable to those of Japan.—A paste board containing a superfice of about two hundred square inches covered with the eggs is worth some four or five dollars here.—Two years ago it was worth from fifty cents to one dollar.— Last year the exportation amounted to about $6.000.000 and probably this year will be of greater money value, although the quantity will be less owing to the disturbed condition of affairs. Tea of excellent quality is made in Japan but the art of drying it by fire as is done in China is not practised in this country; it is brought in and subjected to the operation at the port of shipment, so as compared with China this country furnishes little, all of which goes to the U. S. In a month the seeds will be ripe and I will send you some, though I fear the plant will not live in the open air north of Richmond and perhaps not even there. It seems to me the way to introduce the culture would be to disseminate widely the seeds carefully put up with the recommendation to cultivate the plant for family use and with directions when to pluck the leaf and how to dry it.—In the localities where it would succeed it would soon have a local market and sooner or later we would supply at least our home market. Japan has a number of plants, as the paper tree, varnish trees, nuts and beans that yield abundant and excellent oils and some water plants that I doubt not would find suitable habitats at home.—Many would no doubt fail but others that succeeded would make the trials as a whole successful.—Out of a bean they make an excellent condiment or sauce.—I shall try to learn how it is made and to get the bean. The coarser paper of which I have sent you specimens as wrappers is very superior to ours in strength of fibre.—Of a yet coarser heavier and stronger kind they make overcoats and umbrellas that for ordinary uses are more effective than ours at a tenth part of the cost.—Of course the fibre or material is oiled. The small glove box that I sent you is a fair specimen of the ordinary laquer work of the country.—Very expensive is also made but it requires one who is accustomed to it to tell the one from the other.—They make a very beautiful thin china ware but no complete sets of that or any other ware have been obtainable by us. The Japanese fear the encroachments of Russia very much; recently the Russians seized upon the island of Saughalia, lying as you will see off the Amoor river, and extending south a long distance to the island of Yesso populated by the Japanese and also by a hairy race.—All that region abounds in excellent harbors and the sea in excellent fish.—As the Amoor is closed by ice during the winter the Emperor no doubt is looking to having harbors that will not freeze and also to an abundant supply of coal lying near the sea and said to be of a better quality than any known in this whole region from Bornea to our west coast inclusive.—Phelps is going up in two days in one of their steamers for the purpose of testing it and of which I will inform you. The Russians, the English and the French regard each other with great jealousy as regards Asia and Japan, but I think before long France will think more economically than at present.—I see by the papers that Major Bonaparte has come over on a visit I presume and suppose that he has seen you ere this and no doubt knows the popular feeling in France as well as any one in his position.—Both England and France seem to be undergoing a violent political ferment and both seem uncertain as to the future. The Shanghae papers insist that the Chinese Empire is defunct and that it must be taken possession of by European powers; they denounce Mr Burlingame too, roundly no doubt because they think the Embassy may lead to a better understanding and prevent their plunder.—The Hiogo News too insists upon regarding as an offence to us and other christian powers that should lead to immediate war, that the Japanese officials are punishing persons supposed to be Christians; however much we may sympathize with those who are persecuted, it seems to me that unless we are prepared to kill thirty nine out of the supposed forty millions of inhabitants of these islands we would better let them rule their own people in their own way. If the foreigners in Japan and China taken as a whole should be regarded as the exponent of christianity and certainly they have a right to suppose that this is the fact, I can well understand the aversion which they may justly have against their people becoming such christians. We would I feel sure really act more as christians in insisting upon all the Missionaries leaving Japan and that all the merchants and others should follow, than in proposing a protectorate over all those who would then profess christianity.—They would I doubt not be all the rascals in the land and every hundreth perhaps an honest man. By the time this reaches you the Presidential election will be near at hand.—I have no doubt of the result no matter who may be nominated by the democrats.—The papers say that the Chief Justice has written a letter to a friend stating that he will support the nominee of the democratic party no matter who he may be, and one may infer no matter upon what 'platform' he may be nominated.—If this is so it shows a blind faith worthy of a martyr—as their candidate, but even this bid will be of no avail. It seems to me that there will be little or no animosity shown at the polls, and that in fact the discordant views of the democrats will make it impossible for them to fairly unite on one candidate.—They will probably have one Electoral ticket for the slave or rather old slave states and another for the North, and thus 'divide' to conquer and divide. It seems to me that the only States that you will probably not carry by a large majority will be Maryland, Kentucky and Texas all of them being in the hands of the meanest and most contempible of rebels few of whom fought.—I doubt not that in the other States you will get the votes of tens of thousands of rebel officers and soldiers who fought squarely through the war. I know it will be your aim to get around you the ablest men and those of most integrity that the country will afford and as we have not been blessed with a good Secretary of the Navy for a long time I do not hesitate to say that the only person known to me who would make a good one is Jas. S. Biddle of Philadelphia, a gentleman whose name I have frequently mentioned to you.—Had he been assistant Sec'y during the War the Navy would not now be the meritricious representation of a force instead of a real power, due to what Mr Boynton calls in his 'Naval History' the '*genius*' of Mr Fox. Biddle was a lieutenant in the Navy and resigned about '55.— Since then he has been President of the Shamokin Valley rail road and lived quietly at home.—On the breaking out of the War he offered his services to the Government, only remarking that if it continued for years, so as to shut off his other means of living, he would hope to be again permanently attached to the Navy.—His services were not accepted which was a source of mortification to him and his three sisters who labored assiduously the whole war to promote the health and comfort of the soldiers. He has never been a candidate for any office and is in all respects a model man, unless it is in being a democrat which I think should be forgiven him, he being a nephew and his wife the daughter of Nicholas Biddle of U. S. Bank memory.—He is a man of great culture and of business as well as Naval ability and of sterling integrity, and I write so much at length that you may think it worth while to ask Admiral Porter and such other Naval men in whose opinion you have confidence, whether I overvalue Biddle.—Without being wealthy his income is ample for his family which I state that you may know that I am not influenced in my sympathy by knowing a worthy person struggling for existence.—In fact I am speaking for the interests of the Navy, and necessarily for the country and not for the man. The

Isthmus I suppose will be explored this winter as I see by the papers that the Colombian Government has assented.—I beg to call your attention again to the narrowness between the head, or rather navigable waters of the river Chepo and the Gulf of San Blas on the Northern shore.—It seems to me, that this river should be closely examined with reference to making a slack water navigation as high up as may be deemed advisable, by means of dams and locks and then tunneling the remainder of the distance. First of all by having slack water navigation, or a canal above the Ocean level, even if it were possible otherwise, at suitable times the water could be drawn off as low as necessary and the canal dredged or cleared of the obstructions.—Heavy falls of rain will from time to time sweep rocks trees and earth into it which will have to be removed. The part tunneled would be secure against this accumulation of debris and would not require culverts, which perhaps as a whole would render tunneling as cheap and far more permanent or less liable to injury at least than any other part of the work.—Nor should this particular examination preclude a similar one to the head waters of the Savanna, based upon a tunnel to the North shore, or a canal from thence to the head waters of the Chuquenaque through an alluvium, and from thence by means of slackwater & a tunnel, to the North Coast. August 22nd.—We are getting ready for the mail which leaves one day in advance of the arrival of the steamer from California.—We have nothing new here and only a telegram that on the 4th of July Mr Johnson had issued a General Amnesty Proclamation which I suppose he regards as entitling every one concerned to vote, otherwise it seems to me he is like the sick man who was making his will and left somebody twenty thousand dollars; as the lawyer who drew up the document knew that he had not the wherewithal he stated this fact, and was replied to '*Never mind if I havn't the money, its so much the worse for him, I have the will at least that he should have it.*'—So the man was left the legacy that he could obtain by labor or otherwise. I enclose a note for Mrs Grant relating to the china ware and bronze stork candle sticks which I think pretty. I shall bring my wife home some simple small nice bronzes but as I don't know exactly where we will locate, will as far as possible avoid *impedimenta.*—I have a great disposition towards Berkeley springs and as on the completion of the Point of Rocks road we would be within four hours of Washington, we would hope that during the summer you Mrs Grant and the children would pay us frequent visits. Please remember me very kindly to your staff. . . . The mail via Europe has just arrived and we learn of the nomination of Seymour & Blair— so you will lose the 'influence' of the Blair family—& of Chase too." ALS, *ibid.*

On Oct. 16, Ammen, Nagasaki, wrote to USG. "We find ourselves here after a very pleasant run from Yokohama and on our passage stopped several days at Hiogo. If you have a large map convenient you will see a remarkable interior water extending from Osaca to the Straits of Simonosaki, a distance of about 250 miles and styled the Inland Sea. The navigation is in some respects dangerous, there being sunken rocks discovered from time to time by vessels striking on them and in addition the tides are very strong and curves sharp.— This is much the longest vessel that has ever passed through & I congratulate ourselves upon it as we arrived without damage unless to a small junk which the current set us down upon but which we did not injure much, only to the value of a few dollars though I feared we would capsize the vessel and drown the crew. On our passage we anchored at favorable times for target practice and our people did very well, demolishing three targets of ten feet square at a distance of twelve hundred yards with 9 inch and other shells. One evening I landed at a village; it happened to be a *fete* day and all the youth beauty and fashion as well as all those whose legs would yet bear them along were out to look at the sports.—There were a number of men engaged in wrestling entirely naked except the cloth around their loins and who showed extraordinary strength and agility.—They were remarkably well made men and very courteous to an opponent when he was thrown.—He was at once courteously raised from the ground, carefully brushed to rid him of the dust and sand and at once proffered a glass of *saki*, a species of rum.—although the amount taken each time was quite small yet a continued repetition had evidently exhilirated the party. As a place had been provided for us to witness the sport, by and by we had the usual visit of the man with the hat, and gave the liberal sum of ten cents.— This extraordinary munificence excited cupidity and another and another man with a hat came along who were rewarded in the same munificent manner.—I don't think my pocket book would have been long in my possession had I been in one of our own towns in such a crowd.—I was glad to leave however as their attentions became too marked owing to the promptings of the saki which they had drank so copiously. The islands lying North along the inland sea are mostly so poor as to show little vegetation whilst the Southern were passably fertile; but it was quite apparent that the inhabitants drew their sustenance from the sea rather than from the land.—The waters abound in very fine fish. I had not the pleasure of a visit to Osaca although we were so near, being anchored at *Kobe* actually forming a part of Hiogo which is purely a Japanese town.—How far Kobe and Osaka, both now open to commerce will become important I will not pretend to predict.—The present style of vessel of the Japanese is so insecure and is so badly managed that it is said one fourth of those going outside a distance of a little more than a hundred miles are said to be wrecked; if this is only partially true, say one in ten or even twenty lost it should give a great advantage to the port on the inland sea at least so far as the productions of the lands adjacent those waters are concerned. By the last mail I sent a box to you which I hope has arrived safely.—As I sent a duplicate list of contents I send none now.—I have yet a nest of waiters and some other articles which I trust Mrs Grant will find to her taste.—I bought a small box of porcelain for Nellie but on remembering that a year or so at her age makes a great difference in taste I have reserved them for Miss Ammen who I doubt not in a year or so will delight in setting a baby tea house. I send you by this mail the seeds of a persimmon which would be an acquisition if it will grow in our country; also some pistache nuts. and a couple of red peppers of a superior kind—The persimmon seed should be soaked in water for 24 hours as soon as received in which some soot and wood ashes had been thrown.—I shall bring several small persimmon trees with me when I come home. In regard to my coming my dear General do not ask anything of the Navy Department after your election that is not entirely agreeable.—When you assume office you can use your pleasure as regards having me ordered if you wish me home but I cannot flatter myself that I would be of any particular use.—Several of my Navy friends have suggested that I should be Chief of Bureau of Navigation.—If it were simply a question of usefulness between Jenkins the present occupant and myself I would think I could take his place to advantage,—but the question is a broader one. I probably will not write you again until we arrive in Hong Kong and in the mean time, beg you will inform me of any thing additional that I can do here or on the Coast of China.—I think I will ship your chinaware in a merchant vessel as soon as I reach Hong Kong as less likely to be broken than via Panama. I have bought a considerable quantity of laquer ware which I think pretty and useful and if Mrs Grant has the same opinion on seeing it a part is at her disposition.—Any note will reach me as directly by sending it to Yokohama as elsewhere and there is less likelihood of there being delay. I have a small bow for Jesse and have sent a very long and powerful one on board the Shenandoah for you.—Of course unless the boys use it it will only serve you as an ornament as I don't expect you to be disposed *to draw the long bow.* Please remember me very kindly to all . . ." ALS, *ibid.*

On Nov. 30, Ammen, "off Woosung, China," wrote to USG. "Last mail I did not write you not wishing to believe that I could not spare an opportunity. On referring to your map you will see that we are now at one of the mouths of the Yang-tse-Kiang, the great river of China.—It is also the mouth of the Woo-sung a small river upon which Shanghai is, about a dozen miles up the river.— Owing to the flatness of the country all are alluvium, and the disposition of the Chinese to make canals, there are several connections or branches above, so that in fact the Woosung river itself is another mouth of the great river, but the connecting channel ways above this point have only an inconsiderable depth. On my visit to Shanghai in '46 it had perhaps not more than thirty European inhabitants,—now it has as many thousand and is the wealthiest city as far as foreigners are concerned, on the whole Coast not even excepting Hong Kong. Owing to natural causes it seems like San Francisco a city of magic growth.— It is the depot and port of the Yang-tse-Kiang and at the same time a centre for the trade of Ning-po and for the Coast generally.—If you have examined the enlarged charts of China you will see that the whole Coast is really a succession of excellent harbors and the periodical winds enable the Junks to make round voyages yearly.—They carry enormous ~~house~~ cargoes and whilst in port serve as commodious houses to the perambulating merchants who live on board.— Often one of these vessels has a dozen owners who live on board all having their allotted space to live and to carry cargo. The 'monsoons' that afford periodical means of transit are much more irregular and local in force, season and direction than one might suppose on reading a school Geography, but I shall reserve their discussion until I am near you and indeed will not do so then unless the subject has special or particular interest to you. The '*typhoons*' or great winds as the word implies occur from July to November and are of the same character as what we know as West India hurricanes.—They are acknowledged now as *cyclones* or whirlwinds invariably rotating against or in the opposite direction to the hands of a watch in the Northern hemisphere and the reverse in the Southern. The actual rate of the violent part of the wind is supposed to be from one hundred to one hundred and fifty miles per hour and the progressive motion of the axis very variable, sometimes particularly in these seas being almost stationary and at others moving off at a mean rate of about fifteen miles per hour. This part, indeed all of the immediate Coast of China north of the Chusan islands is low.—The grounds here are embanked and thoroughly cultivated.— In whatever direction the vision is directed numerous clumps of foliage arrest the eye. In every clump are houses or villages; the foliage however is principally bamboo instead of veritable timber as one might suppose it to be.—The stalks are usually some thirty or forty feet in height and the uses so infinite to which it is applied I have already in part informed you of.—There is no doubt that it would grow at least as far North as Wilmington and it would soon become apparently indispensable wherever grown. Every where looking over the flat land, little hillocks of from five to twenty feet are seen; these are the sepulchral mounds of inumerable dead no doubt raised to keep the body out of water which it would be in if buried below the surface level.—The same care is not shown here for the memory of the dead that is seen on the solid ground as around Canton and even there there is not the adornment beauty and attention which the Japanese show their dead.—At Nagasaki a whole hill side of perhaps fifty acres in extent is covered with tomb-stones beneath the shade of magnificent trees.—I looked in vain for a tomb however old that had not its recent offering of green boughs or flowers placed in its little cup of bamboo or porcelain. Strange as it may seem where the agricultural population living over the whole country is hundreds to the square mile and not a clump of bamboo or wood without its houses the country abounds in pheasants and rabbits.—This arises from the passive nature of the Chinese and that to obtain the necesaries of life they are pressed to labor.—They do not seem to have the number of holidays known to our Japanese friends nor do they seem capable of enjoying them.—As artisans, shop keepers and agriculturists and in what might be called material civilization they seem to be superior to the Japanese but they have not their artistic taste and they have not the sympathy of the European race as that people have.—I never experience difficulty in having something to say to a Japanese but with these people I do not care to hold intercourse.—Along the Coast a surprising number of Chinese speak what is called *pidgeon* (business) English, but when *business* is called *pidgeon* you may well believe we can hardly recognize what is supposed to be our own language.—A gentleman recently arrived on being informed by his servant that his friend who had sent his card wished to see him, instead of saying 'can' which means I wish to see him said to his servant tell him to walk in, when the visitor was surprized to hear 'You maky walky' which being translated means *clear out*.—I will send you a specimen of '*Norvel*,' rendered into just such English as is used to express the subject matter to a Chinese as far as '*pidgeon*' language will serve. The weather is growing cold,—ice has made in the shallow pools and thick enough to resist an unclouded sun.—The Tiensin river is about closing and travel with Pekin for the season is about over.—I have waited impatiently to hear something of our Presidential election, not that I have doubted the result but as yet no news has arrived although it may at any moment and it must arrive *via* India in a week probably will via California at the same time.—From the result of the local elections although the Electoral vote will be very large I confess that the popular vote or the majorities will be less than I supposed they would be.—The ignorant and particularly the Irish have a great dislike and prejudice towards the negro, nor do I suppose a large proportion of the Irish voted for you.—With men of little education there is a dislike to 'manhood suffrage' as it is called and the negro in their mind represents a considerable body of 'manhood suffrage'.—The mere fact that a man, black or white cumbers the earth is not a reason to them why he should vote and through some democratic juggling to many of them the negro seems to be the point at issue.—The democrats too with great address made Butler your Sec'y of War and many persons very friendly to you and not at all so to him have been silly enough to think that possible. I trust if you have not done so that you will read attentively what Gov. Orr said in his valedictory relating particularly to negro suffrage. It seems to me that the present may be a favorable opportunity to correct a great cause of corruption particularly in our cities.—I allude to the fact that men without interest in the country, without any knowledge of it and without a farthing of property or the ability to read vote, and for men too pledged to run our cities hopelessly in debt.—Were it not for this loose and venal element as voters probably a more honest class of men of either party would be nominated.—The indebtedness of our cities is something alarming and surprizing and will ere long end in bankruptcy unless checked.—I am aware that politicians will endeavor to shirk and will probably vote for 'manhood suffrage' or its continuance but it seems to me very much against the interests of the whole country and particularly of the South where there are so many ignorant whites and negroes.—Again, the negro voting and the negro holding office (without of course considering the question except as an affair of policy) is quite different.— In the former case he will probably be secured against invidious legislation, in the latter it looks to a social equality and eventually to inter-marriages *for which the South are far more prepared than the North whatever may be said by them and others*. Hybridity of well defined races seems to impose upon the offspring the vices and the diseases of both races.—When the offspring intermarry and continue to do so the descendents soon run out as they are now doing rapidly in South America and Mexico. For a preservation of vital forces and notably for reproduction the hybrid has to fall back on pure blood of one or the other race.— I wrote several articles that were published in the Ohio State Journal touching upon this subject as illustrated through observations on Brazil and Peru in '56.—I mention this simply to show that my ideas on this subject and the evils necessarily growing out of hybridity are not recent. 2nd Dec'r.—To prevent the chances of breakage and delays as far as your china ware is concerned, I have directed that it be shipped from Whampoa by a vessel now lying there about the 15th or 20th which should bring it to New York early in April.—It will be consigned to the house of Olyphant & Co No 114 Pearl street N. Y. who will await special instructions from you after passing it through the Custom House.— Owing to the shameful manner in which express companies handle packages I thought it better to defer sending it on until one of our tugs should go from the Washington Navy Yard to New York which occurs frequently.—However if you should prefer it sent without delay very well but I would be sorry to have it broken. I have taken the liberty to have mine addressed to you also but it will be in red and a letter A in the corner of the box will prevent any mistake.— Please have it stowed away for the present as I am sure my wife does not want it at York.—I do not know how many boxes there will be but think it likely you will have six or eight and I half as many.—I hope the monogram has been properly done & have directed that one of my peeces and one of yours be left out of the boxes which I will take home when I go be it sooner or later.—Owing to the severity of the season we will only hear of the election by the French mail which will arrive on the 5th.—I shall write you more fully on this subject after I reach Hong Kong, or rather as relates to the China ware. 12th Dec'r.—Three days ago we had news via the California steamers, the steamer also from British

India and a telegram to Kiatka all announcing your election but as yet the returns are not full.—I confess my surprise at New York going against you due no doubt to rascality in the city and the Irish vote.—They feel instinctively and their leaders practically that with you as President *fenianism* will not flourish.— Indeed it seems that owing to reforms likely to occur in Irish affairs that very soon there will be no substantial grievance in which case they will have one sooner or later in our Country. It is gratifying to see how rapidly the Pacific railroad is approaching completion.—Once in running condition and it seems to me that the Indian and the Mormon questions have an easy and a natural solution.—With a railroad through the country we will soon have a heavy population along its line wherever the land will serve. Comparing the Chinese with the Japanese the f[or]mer are far less agreeable and seemingly will never make soldiers.—With such a teeming population as China possesses and the arts especially as applied to War purposes had they the character of the Japanese they would be most formidable.—But they have neither the curiosity nor the cleverness nor the courage of the Japanese.—I was quite surprized at the remarks of Mr Medhurst English Consul at Shanghai to our Admiral that Russia should seize on to & hold China and that no other Power could do it with advantage to themselves and to the Chinese.—The fact is the Chinese seem to be subject to so many and such grievous rebellions as to destroy first one section and then another of the Country, hence were it not for the bamboo and willows they would be almost wholly without material for construction.—The bamboo has so many uses with these people that it would be difficult to conceive how or what they would do without it. I do not doubt my dear General that your persecutions have been begun by the politicians who love their country so much that they always want to serve her.—Bear your vexations with equanimity—it is a grand position to be ~~able~~ chosen to serve a great people in their hour of perplexity and peril.—I beg you will remember me most kindly to Mr Dent, to Mrs Grant and give my love to the children." ALS, *ibid.*

To John M. Schofield

Washington, D. C., Nov. 24th *1868*

GENERAL J. M. SCHOFIELD,
SECRETARY OF WAR.
SIR:

I have the honor to submit the reports of Division, District and Department Commanders for the past year. These reports give a full account of the operations and services of the army for the year and I refer to them for details.

I would earnestly renew my recommendation of last year that

the control of the Indians be transferred to the War Department. I call special attention to the recommendation of General Sherman on this subject. It is unnecessary that the arguments in favor of the transfer should be restated; the necessity for the transfer becomes stronger and more evident every day.

While the Indian war continues I do not deem any general legislation for the reduction of the army advisable. The troops on the plains are all needed; troops are still needed in the Southern States, and further reduction can be made in the way already used and now in operation where it is safe, namely by allowing companies to diminish by discharges without being strengthened by recruits, and by stopping appointments of second lieutenants.

If it should be deemed advisable, the veteran reserve regiments might be discontinued by absorption and retirement of officers and discharge of men, without detriment to the service.

> Very respectfully
> Your obedient servant
> U. S. GRANT
> General.

LS, DNA, RG 107, Letters Received from Bureaus. For the enclosures, see *HED*, 40-3-1, III, part 1.

On Oct. 30, 1868, Bvt. Maj. Gen. Edward D. Townsend forwarded to USG's hd. qrs. a telegram of Oct. 28 from Maj. Gen. Philip H. Sheridan, Fort Hays, Kan., to Bvt. Maj. Gen. William A. Nichols. "The following dispatch from General Sheridan just received: 'In the Field, Fort Hays, Kansas, Head Quarters Dept. of the Missouri, October twenty-eight 28, eighteen hundred and sixty-eight 1868 BVT MAJ. GEN. W. A NICHOLS. General Carr, with seven 7 companies of the Fifth 5 Cavalry and Forsyth scouts under Lieut. Pepoon, struck the indians on Shutness Creek, south of Beaver, on the twenty fifth 25 instant, killed ten 10 indians and five 5 ponies, and captured three 3 ponies. Next day he followed the indians, who disputed his advance to protect their lodges and stock, the indians burning the prairie to the windward, but not stopping the advance of the troops. They forced the indians to abandon robes and camp and lodge equipage, capturing and killing seventy-two 72 ponies. General Carr is still pursuing them. Colonel Bankhead is also in the same section and I think before this has joined General Carr. (Signed) P. H. SHERIDAN, Maj. Gen. U. S. A.' " Copy, DNA, RG 108, Letters Received.

On Nov. 18, Lt. Gen. William T. Sherman, St. Louis, wrote to USG. "I have no doubt you want to be advised of Sheridans movements. I send herewith his last letter. Thus far he has directed his attention to get the Indians out from the country between the Railroads, and we believe all are gone—Some went

north, crossing the Railroad on the 1st of Novr at Alkali station, which is between North Platte and Sedgwick, on the Old Ash Hollow trail.—All the rest
in scattered bands have gone south of the Arkansas. Sheridan supposes them
to be on small streams that run into the Canadian and Red Rivers, about south
of Fort Dodge.—One Column, mostly 3rd Cavalry is moving east down the
Canadian from Fort Bascom in NewMexico—Another commanded by Sully &
Custar, mostly of the 7th Cav. is moving due south from Dodge,—and the
Kansas Regiment under the former Governor Crawford is moving from the
Little Arkansas South west towards the Antelope Hills, which you will find on
our Map, about where the Canadian is crossed by the Western boundary of the
Southern Reservation, Hazens. We expect Cold weather will force the Indians
to gather, and they will naturally retreat to the Wichita Mountains in the South
Western Corner of Hazens Reservation. Sheridan has an escort and will go first
to a camp & depot he has made on a branch of the Canadian south of Fort
Dodge where the Moving Columns can come in to get bread corn &c. In his
letter you see he expects to be out some time, and he feels confident that he will
punish these Indians severely. It looks easy enough on the Map, but the country
is very large, and we must not expect too much. Hazen is at Fort Cobb, where
have assembled 6 or 7000 Indians whom he will provide for till this business is
settled. Sheridan fears that the hostile Indians, now alarmed at the general
movemt, may take refuge under Hazen, but I give Sheridan full swing, and
authorise him to follow to Fort Cobb, and if he finds any of the Indians who
were concerned in this Outbreak to punish them summarily. During his absence
his Adjt Genl McKeever is at Fort Hays, and he communicates with me on all
points when he has not clear instructions. Should any thing happen on Sheridans
line during his absence, I will go up at once. Since the election every thing has
settled down as quiet as a New England village. All people are figuring on a
four years peace. My folks are all well—" ALS, *ibid*. Sherman enclosed a
letter of Nov. 12 from Sheridan to Sherman. "Your notes of the 5th & 7th have
come to hand. I have for some time seen the necessity of going in person South
of the Arkansas & had made all my arrangemts to start on the morning of the
15th The movement of the Indians, in the direction of Fort Cobb, had been
reported to me, & I will after my arrival at Beaver Creek try & reach that—
point. The breaking up of those on the north of the R. Road gives me more
liberty, and the arrangemts for the winter campaign are now nearly compleate.
It has been attended with much labor, & hard work. I do not know when I will
get back, & will not be able to communicate with you as often as I desire, but
will write by every opportunity I will not break up the arrangemts at Fort
Cobb, but will aid &. assist it, but, the guilty should be punished & the doubtful
held as prisoners at Levenworth, in case we should be successful. We can make
this the last of our Indian troubles if by a just punishmt of the guilty. it is due
to humanity and to life & property of citizens to accomplish this end. I hope
to do things so fairly that you will be satisfied I do not intend to leave this
country by my own accord, or to relax my exertions until the Indiains who
maimed Forsyth, &. murdered others, are punished. I am glad you wrote to
Gen'l Grant He should not resign until the day of his inauguration. It would
give to corrupt politicns the power to place bad men in high places. No president
since Washington will go to the White House stronger than he & no one elected
has caused so little chagrin to to his political opponents as he has—all that is

now necessary for him to do, is to collect the revenues of the Governmt & have them paid in honestly when collected. Prosperity, & diminished taxation will grow out of this,—& prosperity will ally dissentions & the peace so much desired will come. Tell miss Minnie that we will only be too happy to see her at Levenworth on the 22d should we get back there at that time, & that we will all be so happy at getting back from this uninviting desert, that we will give her a very merry time. Then Miss Lizzie must come also, for, I feel quite an interest in my first acquaintance with the young lades of your family. We are all in good health with splendid appetites & living on Antelope & Buffalo. We m[iss] Forsyth always so cheerful. I saw him on last Sunday & hope to get him to Levenworth soon. It will take a year to set him fairly on his pins again but his leg will be all right. Goven. Crawford I presume thinks he is going to glory but he will find his path strewn with some hard old 'Northers' which will make his lean lanky bones rattle before he gets back. I will order Gen'l McKeever up here & will direct him to consult you by telegraph should there be any question requiring my action." ALS, *ibid.*

On Nov. 23, Sherman wrote to USG. "I suppose before you become too much immersed in business incident to your new office, you want to know the exact condition of affairs all over the country. I now enclose you a private letter from Augur, which contains much that official letters do not possess. Please read & return it. I also make up some interesting matter from General Hazen, which should be read by the Secretary of War. I have not heard from Sheridan since he started from Fort Hays, on Sunday the 15th inst." ALS, USG 3.

To Maj. Gen. George G. Meade

————

Washington, D. C., Nov. 24th *1868* [*10:35* A.M.]

Gn. G. G. Meade,

Atlanta Ga

I can not know whether your presence will be required here or not until the council arrives. I will then inform your by telegraph.

U. S. Grant

General.

ALS (telegram sent), DNA, RG 107, Telegrams Collected (Bound); telegram sent, *ibid.*; telegram received, Meade Papers, PHi.

On Nov. 4, 1868, Maj. Gen. George G. Meade telegraphed to USG. "So far as heard from the election in the several states of this Department passed off quietly with the exception of Augusta *Georgia*, where there was a disturbance requiring the intervention of the military to suppress, and an emeute at Savanna which was controlled & suppressed by the Police without military intervention.—" ALS (telegram sent), *ibid.*; telegram received (at 1:30 P.M.), DNA, RG 107, Telegrams Collected (Bound); *ibid.*, RG 108, Telegrams Received. On Nov.

19, Meade wrote to Bvt. Maj. Gen. John A. Rawlins. "I have the honor to transmit, herewith endorsed, the official reports of Major Henry E. Maynadier, 12th Infantry and Captain Samuel E. St. Onge, 16th Infantry, of the occurrences at Savannah and Augusta, Georgia, on the day of the Presidential election, referred to in my telegram of the 4th instant. I suggest a referrence of Captain St. Onge's report to the Honorable the Secretary of War for his consideration in connection with the application of the Mayor of Augusta, forwarded endorsed by me on the 14th instant" LS, *ibid.*, Letters Received. The enclosures are *ibid.*

On Nov. 24, 11:00 A.M., USG telegraphed to Meade. "Order two companies of troops from such points as can best spare them to Augusta Ga. to assist in maintaining peace." ALS (telegram sent), *ibid.*, RG 107, Telegrams Collected (Bound); telegram sent, *ibid.*; telegram received, Meade Papers, PHi. On Dec. 3, Meade telegraphed to USG. "The election (municipal) in Augusta Geo, passed off quietly yesterday—The troops now there two companies—were sent by your order to preserve the peace—It was my intention to have sent troops just prior to the election to have remained there until the election was over—then to be withdrawn—but as they were sent under your order & perhaps on information not known to me—I do not feel authorised to with draw them without your sanction.—I am not aware myself now the election is over of there being any occasion to keep troops in Augusta, except in answer to the universal clamor for them every where—based on many considerations mostly foreign to the object for which troops are here.—" ALS (telegram sent), *ibid.*; telegram received (at 6:30 P.M.), DNA, RG 107, Telegrams Collected (Bound); *ibid.*, RG 108, Telegrams Received. On Dec. 11, 10:15 A.M., USG telegraphed to Meade. "Let the two companies now at Augusta, Ga., remain there for the present" Telegrams sent (2), *ibid.*, RG 107, Telegrams Collected (Bound); telegram received, Meade Papers, PHi.

To Catherine M. Dix

Washington, D. C., Nov. 24th *1868*

MY DEAR MRS. DIX;

Your very welcome congratulatory letter of the 4th of Nov. after traveling over the country, has just reached me. The very hearty support which your esteemed husband gave me, and his purely patriotic course from the breaking out of the rebellion to the present day, makes it specially gratifying.—I fully intended when in New York last to call on you and express in person my appreciation of the General's services to the country in the past, and the good offices he has rendered to me personally recently.

When writing to him please present my kindest regards and assurences of esteem.

With great respect
your obt. svt.
U. S. GRANT

ALS, Columbia University, New York, N. Y. On Nov. 4, 1868, Catherine Morgan Dix, New York City, wrote to USG. "Let me be among the first, as my husband would have been, if he were here at home instead of in Paris, to offer my homage of felicitations to yourself and Mrs Grant—whose heart must respond so deeply, at this hour of your and the Nation's triumphs to all the good wishes and prayers, that surround and follow you—My husband's 'savage' letters, leave no room for doubt as to his hearty satisfaction—Imagine his delight, as the glorious tidings of your election are flashed across the Ocean, and proclaimed abroad—for you know he has been for you for the Presidency, steadily and persistently, all the way through, and always wanted the Democrats, to try and secure you as their candidate—Having—if by all right now—the rebels are routed and beaten again by you—In the state—as well as in the field—At the first glance, one might mourn the humiliating position of New York in this present result, yet the knowledge that it was accomplished only by *illegal* voting renews the hope, that some way may be found, as the years pass on, to prevent this shame, and frauds from elections, which ought to proclaim the honest and intelligent will and choice of our people, from being converted instead, by corrupt and abominable management, only into hopeless frauds and failures—" ALS, USG 3.

John A. Dix, born in 1798, long active in Democratic politics in N. Y., had served as secretary of the treasury in the cabinet of James Buchanan (1861) and maj. gen. of vols. (1861–65) before appointment as minister to France (1866–69). From Paris he wrote to support USG for president. "I have thought for a year that Grant should be President. The prestige of his name will enable him to do more than any other man to heal the national dissensions which seem to me, at this distance, to be as far from any satisfactory solution as ever. Then he is honest both from instinct and habit; and he has good sense, perseverance and a modest estimate of his own capabilities. I have no doubt that he would call able men to his councils and listen to their advice, and I believe that he would be a firm, conservative and successful Chief Magistrate." *New York Herald*, Sept. 30, 1868. See *ibid.*, Sept. 23, 1868.

In June, 1869, newspapers carried the story that "Gen. Dix is reported as saying that President Grant has fallen at last into the hands of politicians, and though he may mean well, he cannot resist the influences around him. His appointments have been disappointments, and unless he retrieves himself soon, his ruin is accomplished." *Illinois State Journal*, June 30, 1869. On June 30, Dix, New York City, wrote to USG. "*Private.* . . . If you read the newspapers (I congratulate you if you do not) you may have seen that I have been 'interviewed'—a fashion, which has come up in my absence, & of which I was entirely ignorant until last evening.—Some part of the conversation, which I supposed to be private, was correctly reported; but that which relates to you was almost entirely without foundation. I did not say your appointments were disappointments, or that you would be ruined unless you cast off the politicians. But I did say I had entire confidence in your integrity & the purity of your purposes.— I should feel annoyed if I thought you had attached any importance to a conversation thus given to the public, & which could hardly be otherwise than distorted. There never has been a moment when I have felt a stronger interest in the success of your administration than I do now.—I leave for West Hampton Long Island tomorrow." ALS, NHi.

On Aug. 18, Catherine Dix, New London, Conn., wrote to USG. "Since writing the accompanying letter—I understand from a friend just arrived from *Nice*, that the Consulate there—is vacant—or to be vacated—How much the General and I would be gratified, to have it for Mr. Vesey—" ALS, DNA, RG 59, Letters of Application and Recommendation. On Aug. 21, USG endorsed this letter. "Refered to the Sec. of State." AES, *ibid.* The enclosed letter of Aug. 6 to USG recommending William H. Vesey is *ibid.* On Dec. 6, USG nominated Vesey as consul, Nice.

To Henry Wilson

Washington, D, C,
Nov. 24th 1868.

Hon. II. Wilson; Dear Sir:

Your favor is rec'd and has been read by me alone, not another being knowing anything of its contents. I am much oblig[ed] to you for the kind expressio[ns c]ontained in your letter towards me personally, and for the support and friendship promised, under any circumstances. Your past course towards me has been a sufficient guarantee of that if my future cour[se] will only justify it. In regard to the matter you write specially about I will talk to you upon when I meet you. I will say this however; there is no person who would be more agreeable to me personally than yourself but in regard to the place of Sec. of War I would say to you what I do not care to commit to paper.

Please present my regards to Mrs. Wilson, and believe me sincerely your friend.

U. S. Grant

ALS (facsimile), DLC-Henry Wilson.

To Maj. Gen. George G. Meade

Washington, D. C., Nov. 27th *1868.* [*noon*]

GN. G. G. MEADE,
ATLANTA GA.

J. J. Knox, Agt. Freedmen's Bureau, Athens Ga. reports danger of of mob violence against him. Please see that he is protected from such violence and that he has a fare trial.

U. S. GRANT
General.

ALS (telegram sent), DNA, RG 107, Telegrams Collected (Bound); telegram sent, *ibid.*; telegram received, Meade Papers, PHi. On Nov. 27, 1868, Bvt. Brig. Gen. Richard C. Drum, Atlanta, telegraphed to Bvt. Maj. Gen. John A. Rawlins. "Telegram of Gen. in chief relative to agent Knox just received, a company was sent to athens Ga on the 22nd and has since been ordered to return all danger of violence having passed Major Knox after examination before a Justice of the Peace was discharged from arrest, Maj Genl Meade is in Alabama," Telegrams received (2—on Nov. 28, 9:00 A.M.), DNA, RG 107, Telegrams Collected (Bound); *ibid.*, RG 108, Telegrams Received; copies, Meade Papers, PHi; DLC-USG, V, 55.

To Alberto Blest Gana

WASHINGTON, D. C.,
Nov. 27th, 1868.

SR. D. A. BLEST-GANA,
Minister, etc.

DEAR SIR,—Your esteemed congratulatory letter is rec'd. Please accept my thanks for the kind expressions it contains both towards me personally and to the government of the United States.

The tendency of the world at this time seems to be towards free government. May it go on until all are as free as we are, and as prosperous. I hope the day is not far distant when Republican Governments, especially those on this continent, will be in such

sympathy with each other as to be a mutual support, and be
an —— to all others.

Please present my kind regards to Madame Blest, and accept
the assurance of my esteem.

Yours Truly,

U. S. GRANT.

Adam Badeau, *Grant in Peace* (Hartford, Conn., 1887), pp. 571–72 (word
omitted in source). Presumably in Nov., 1868, Alberto Blest Gana, London,
former minister of Chile to the U.S., then minister to Great Britain, wrote to
USG. "It is with great pleasure that I address you, congratulating you on the
result of the Presidential election in the United States. I think that your countrymen have given a new proof of their wisdom and fitness for republican institutions, by bestowing on you the first place in their important Commonwealth;
and I feel confident that under your administration both union and freedom
will be strengthened in that great and happy country. I wish you every success
and glory in the high position you have been placed in by your fellowcitizens.
With my best respects to Mrs Grant and kind remembrence's to your daughter
and sons, . . ." ALS (undated), USG 3.

To John Jay

———

Washington, D. C., Nov. 28 *1868*.

JOHN JAY, ESQ,
PRES. UNION LEAGUE;
DEAR SIR:

Your letters to Gen. Badeau and myself fixing Monday the 7th
for a morning reception to Mrs Grant & myself, and the evening
for a dinner with the League, are received. I regret troubling the
League to fix any other evening than the one already selected by
them, but a previous engagement compels me to do so.—It is not
certain that Mrs. Grant will be with me, so I will beg to decline
the morning reception, and ask that the dinner be on either Tuesday, the 1st of Dec. Saturday, the 5th, or Tuesday the 8th of the
same month.

On the 8th I promised the family of Gov. Fish, with whom I
have the pleasure of a friendly acquaintance, to attend the wedding

of Miss. Fish. I presume it takes place in the morning, but as I have not yet received a card, do not know positively. Should the wedding and dinner occur the same evening, hardly a probable supposition, I will go to the former late.

Hoping that this arrangement will not inconvenience the Union Leage,

I remain
Very Truly, your obt. svt,
U. S. GRANT

ALS, ICarbS. See letter to Julia Dent Grant, Dec. 7, 1868.

On Nov. 28, 1868, USG telegraphed to Alex Taylor, New York City. "My Engagements preclude my being in New York next Monday evening." ALS (telegram sent), DNA, RG 107, Telegrams Collected (Bound).

To Julia Dent Grant

New York, N. Y.
Dec. 6th 1868,

DEAR JULIA;

We are just back here having been detained over three hours last night by the snow. My visit among the New Englanders has been very pleasant but shorter than I would have liked.[1]—Gen. Comstock and myself will spend the afternoon today with Mr. & Mrs. Tweed,[2] and dine with them. I am stoppin at the St. Nicholas this time.

Kisses for you and the children.

ULYS.

ALS, USG 3.

1. On Nov. 28, 1868, Nathaniel B. Shurtleff, mayor of Boston, telegraphed to USG. "The city council of Boston having with much pleasure heard of your intention to visit this city has directed me to extend to you its hospitalities, When the city authorities are informed of your approach they will wait upon you, to ascertain your wishes in this respect" Telegrams received (2—at 2:30 P.M.), DNA, RG 107, Telegrams Collected (Bound). On Nov. 29, 10:30 A.M., USG telegraphed to Shurtleff. "Thank for your invitation to Boston. Do not know by what train I will arrive. Please make no arrangements for public demon-

stration. I have written to you to-day." ALS (telegram sent), *ibid.*; telegram sent, *ibid.*; copy, MHi. On the same day, USG wrote to Shurtleff. "Your despatch, inviting me to hospitalities of Boston, was duly received. I cannot say by what train I will reach Boston. I fully appreciate your kindness, however, and that of the citizens of your city in extending the hospitalities they have, but would ask to be excused from any and all public demonstrations. I have received an invitation to the St. James to stay during my visit, where I will be happy to receive such citizens as may call." *New York Herald,* Dec. 2, 1868.

On Nov. 28, William Gray, Boston, telegraphed to USG. "Will you dine with me next friday at six [o']clock? Receive friends in evening." Telegram received (at 10:30 A.M.), DNA, RG 107, Telegrams Collected (Bound).

On Nov. 30, USG spoke at the annual dinner of the St. Andrew's Society, Philadelphia. "I am more pleased than I expected to see the manner in which I have been received by you all. I expected to have a great deal of pleasure, but my anticipations have been more than realized." *New York Herald*, Dec. 2, 1868.

On Dec. 1, Secretary of War John M. Schofield wrote to USG, Boston. "I enclose a letter from Hon Elisha Dyer of Providence. R. I. dated Nov 29th, which explains itself. Also that you may know who he is, I enclose another letter from him of Nov 9th including a letter of interduction from Prof. Bartlett. I hope you may find it convenient to acccpt the hospitalities thus offered." Copy, DLC-John M. Schofield. On Dec. 2, Shurtleff wrote to USG. "Your safe arrival here will much gratify the citizens of Boston. This will be handed to you by Charles H. Allen, Esq., President of the Common Council, Alderman Jarvis D. Braman and Councilman Francis A. Osborn. I have requested them to communicate with you and ascertain when it will be convenient for you to receive a representative of the city government for the purpose of expressing in an unobtrusive manner the respect which is retained for you by the citizens of Boston." *New York Herald*, Dec. 3, 1868. On Dec. 2, Governor Alexander H. Bullock of Mass. wrote to USG. "Permit me to introduce to you Colonels Peirson and Russell, members of my Staff, and through them to tender to you a cordial welcome to Massachusetts. I beg that during your stay here you will receive from them and in my behalf any service which may promote your comfort or convenience" LS (press), Massachusetts State Library, Boston, Mass.

2. See *PUSG*, 15, 433; letter to George S. Boutwell, Jan. 14, 1870.

To Julia Dent Grant

New York City
Dec. 7th 1868.

DEAR JULIA:

To-night I dine with the St. Nicholas Society;[1] tomorrow attend the wedding of Julia Fish,[2] in the day, and in the evening dine with the Union League.[3] Wednesday evening I attend the reception at M. O. Roberts,[4] and Thursday go home. My visit has been a pleasant but fatiguing one.

Kisses for you and the children.

ULYS.

ALS, USG 3. On Dec. 8, 1868, Bvt. Maj. Gen. Daniel E. Sickles, "St. Nicholas," wrote to USG. "Pleasonton and I called to pay our respects and to suggest— (say for to-morrow) a visit to Mr Bennett of the Herald at his residence Cor. 5th Av. & 38th St—Mr B. is nearly Eighty years old & unable to call and I know would be very much gratified to have you Lunch with him, accompanied by any friends you desire, and on any day and hour most Convenient to yourself—This mark of Consideration for the veteran journalist of the Country who has manifested so much interest in your Career would have the happiest effect. If our suggestion accords with your arrangements please let Gen'l Comstock notify me by a line sent to the Brevoort House—to-day if Convenient—and we will see to it" ALS (dated only Tuesday), DLC-Cyrus B. Comstock.

1. For an account of the banquet of the St. Nicholas Society, which commemorated New York City's Dutch origins, see *New York Times*, Dec. 8, 1868.

2. On Tuesday, Dec. 8, Julia Kean Fish, daughter of Hamilton Fish, married Bvt. Lt. Col. Samuel N. Benjamin, a mathematics professor at USMA. Benjamin, USMA 1861, had served in the 2nd art. and had been wounded at Spotsylvania.

3. On Dec. 8, USG spoke at the Union League Club. "GENTLEMEN OF THE UNION LEAGUE:—It is with extreme regret that I find myself unable to respond in appropriate language to the warmth of feeling with which this toast has been received. You all know how unaccustomed I am to public speaking— . . . —how undesirable a talent I think it is to possess, how little good it generally does— . . . —and how desirous I am to see more of our public men follow the good example which I believe, in this particular, if in no other, I have set them. . . . I must, however, express my acknowledgments to the Union League of this city, as well as to the Union Leagues of other cities, for the great benefits they conferred upon the government during the rebellion through which we have passed of late years. I wish to acknowledge their liberality toward myself and toward the soldiers serving against the rebellion, and to thank them for it." *New York Herald*, Dec. 9, 1868.

4. Marshall O. Roberts, born in 1814, held steamship mail contracts during the Calif. gold rush and leased steamships to the U.S. government during the Civil War. He contributed substantial amounts to the Republican Party.

To Charles D. Drake

Washington, D. C., Dec. 12th *1868*.

Hon. C. D. Drake,
Dear Sir:

This will introduce to you Capt. T. H. Stevens, of the Navy, who I have known personally for many years. Capt. Stevens is interested in having corrected an injustice which has been done him; and, as I understand, a resolution passed the lower house, unanimously, at its last session, effecting this. It is now pending in the Senate. I do not hesitate to speak for Capt. S. your favorable offices, in Committee, in regard to this. Capt. Stevens is known both as a gallant and efficient officer, facts, I think, which Adm. Farragot & Porter, with hosts of other Naval officers, will attest.

Very respectfully
your obt. svt.
U. S. Grant

ALS (incomplete facsimile), Superior Galleries, Dr. Thomas Chalkley Sale, Jan. 28–31, 1990, no. 5350. On March 11, 1868, the House Committee on Naval Affairs reported that Capt. Thomas H. Stevens should advance "not exceeding twenty-one numbers on the list of captains on the active list of the navy" to remedy "grave injustice" concerning his rank. *HRC*, 40-2-22. On Jan. 29, 1869, U.S. Senator Charles D. Drake of Mo., Committee on Naval Affairs, reported unfavorably on the proposed joint resolution as establishing unsound precedents. *SRC*, 40-3-196.

On March 20, USG wrote to the Senate. "I nominate, for meritorious service during the War, and in accordance with the provisions of the Act of 25 July 1866, Captains Thomas H. Stevens, Thomas H. Patterson and Edward T. Nichols, to take their former positions on the Navy Register." DS, DNA, RG 46, 41st Congress, 1st Session, Nominations. See *New York Herald*, March 30, 1869. For USG's relationship with Stevens, see *PUSG*, 1, 420–21; *ibid.*, 10, 516–17.

To Julia Dent Grant

Chicago, Ills Dec. 14th *1868*

Dear Julia,

We arrived here this afternoon. Had a very pleasant trip though a little detained. There will be about 2000 officers of the Western Armies present at the gathering. We return, leaving here Thursday[1] evening, in the same cars we came in. Will probably go back by way of Cincinnati, stopping over however but a few hours. This will take us into Washington Saturday evening. If we do not go via Cincinnati we will arrive same day in the morning. Orvil thinks Mary[2] will loose one of her eyes if not both. She is worse than when we left here.

Kisses for you and the children.

Ulys.

ALS, USG 3.

On Dec. 6, 1868, USG, New York City, wrote to J. Russell Jones. "I shall be in Chicago during the soldiers convention, two days, and will put up with Orvil. I will stop one night of the two at your house however to cut off callers." ALS, George R. Jones, Chicago, Ill. On Dec. 11, USG telegraphed to Vice Admiral David D. Porter, Annapolis. "Can you not, with such officers of the Navy as served on the Miss. river, go with the party from here to the Chicago convention of soldiers? We leave here, by special car, generously furnished by the different roads from here to Chicago, Saturday evening, to-morrow, at 4:30 p. m." ALS (telegram sent), DNA, RG 107, Telegrams Collected (Bound). On the same day, Porter telegraphed to USG. "Thank you kindly, I would like to accompany you but am not able, Wish you a pleasant time" Telegram received (at 4:00 P.M.), *ibid.* Also on Dec. 11, USG telegraphed to Thomas A. Scott, Pennsylvania Railroad, Philadelphia. "The offers of the managers of the different roads from Baltimore to Chicago to furnish a palace car to the soldiers convention in Chicago & return is thankfully accepted. We will leave Baltimore Saturday evening." ALS (telegram sent), *ibid.*

1. Dec. 17.
2. Presumably Orvil Grant's wife, Mary Medary Grant.

To Julia Dent Grant

Chicago Ill,
Dec. 15th 1868,

Dear Julia,

We all start home to-morrow. As you will see by the papers we have had a good time. I have been shaken to pieces however and will be glad to get started home. Will be home Saturday evening. This will give me an opportunity of spending a few hours at home, the last opportunity I may ever have of seeing father and mother at their home.

Kisses to you and the children.

Ulys.

ALS, USG 3.

On Dec. 15, 1868, USG spoke at a meeting of former officers. "Gentlemen of the Army of the Tennessee:—My first associations in the beginning of the rebellion, through which we have so happily passed, was with you, and with the other officers of the army who fought so gallantly with you. I am heartily glad to be with you. I thank you heartily for this reception, and the country thanks you for your deeds. I am now suffering from one of those neuralgic headaches with which I am periodically afflicted, and which prevents me, even were I so inclined, from saying anything farther on this occasion." *Report of the Proceedings of the Society of the Army of the Tennessee, at the Third Annual Meeting, . . .* (Cincinnati, 1877), pp. 161–62.

To John M. Schofield

Washn D. C. Dec 22 *1868*

Gen. J. M. Schofield
Sec. of War
Sir

I have the honor to recommend that the Signal Establishment in this city be broken up, that the Chief Signal officer be ordered to report to Gen. Barry[1] at Fort Monroe to give instruction in signalling at the Artillery School, that the officers & men of the signal establishment be ordered to their proper duties & that the Signal Officer be directed to make a report of all public property now in his charge, with a view to its proper disposal or distribution.

Very Respectfully Yours

U. S. Grant

General,

LS, DNA, RG 94, Letters Received, 640A 1868. On Dec. 24, 1868, Bvt. Brig. Gen. Albert J. Myer, chief signal officer, Washington, D. C., wrote to USG. "The Office of the Chief Signal Officer is established by Law, providing that that office 'shall have charge, under the direction of the Secretary of War, of all signal duty, and of all books, papers and apparatus connected therewith'. It is further established by legislation fixing the clerks to be in the Office, to enable the chief signal officer to discharge its duties. Under this Law, the Post of the chief signal officer has been, for a number of years, in the City of Washington, and the office has been recognized as a Bureau Office, discharging all the duties of purchase and distribution of apparatus with the usual accountability to the Treasury, the duties of auditing accounts, etc. etc. . . . . If this plan is not thought wise, the detachment can be distributed with the officers going to Departments. The Chief Signal Officer can best discharge these duties, and the many others which come to a position like his, with the administration of his office as now provided by Law, unchanged. Whenever, in the opinion of those wiser than himself, the duties of this Office are not actually advancing the interests of the United States, he trusts he will be among the first to recognize the fact. He expresses here his acknowledgement of the confidence and support he has had from the Secretary of War and the General of the Army, with the satisfaction of knowing he has tried to deserve it." LS, *ibid.*, RG 108, Letters Received. Myer prepared a form assigning signal officers to provide instruction that "will enable each Post and, if possible, each Company, to have within itself the practice and the means for transmitting any Simple message, on the ground that Such knowledge will be always of benefit, and may at Some times prevent disaster to troops otherwise cut off from communication." D, *ibid.*, RG 94, Letters Received, 12S 1869. USG endorsed this form. "Letter after this form recommended to be sent to Dist. & Dept. Commanders to whom Signal officers are directed to report." AE (initialed—probably on Jan. 5, 1869), *ibid.* Additional documents concerning signal officers approved by USG on Jan. 5 are *ibid.* See *HED*, 41-2-1, part 2, pp. 185–201.

1. Bvt. Maj. Gen. William F. Barry. See *PUSG*, 18, 501.

To Andrew P. Peabody

Washington, D. C., Dec. 23d *1868*

Dear Dr.

Your favor of the 14th inst. reached here during my absence to the Soldiers re-union in Chicago. I am under many obligations for your kindness, and will see that my son is benefited by it. The set of examination papers of last July, mentioned in your letter as having been sent, did not reach me. It makes no matter however as I have determined to let my son visit Harvard, during the Christmas Holidays, when he can get them if needed.—I know of no recent graduate of Harvard here hence send my son to Boston at this time to ask if you, or þProf. Agassiz,[1] will be so kind as to procure him such an examination as will shew whether he is receiving the proper training, and make suggestions for his guidance from now to examination day. If any other school should be suggested I do not know that I would object. If you think better that he should continue where he is for this year, Academic year, and then go to some other institution to prepare for one year more, I would not object. The boy is very studious, very ambitious and desirous of obtaining a thorough education, and without a favorable start might injure his health. I think however with a knowledge now of what will be expected of him in July he will have no difficulty in preparing.

My son will bear this to you in person as his introduction.

With great respect,
your obt. svt.
U. S. Grant

Dr. A. P. Peabody
Pres. Harvard University

ALS, ICHi. Andrew P. Peabody, born in 1811, Unitarian minister and editor of the *North American Review*, was appointed (1860) Plummer Professor of Christian Morals at Harvard College, where he served as act. president (1868–69).

On Dec. 28, 1868, USG telegraphed to John P. Tweed, New York City.

"Please direct Ulysses to call at the Metropolitan Hotel for letters." ALS (telegram sent), DNA, RG 107, Telegrams Collected (Bound).

1. On March 20, 1871, Secretary of the Treasury George S. Boutwell wrote to USG. "I have the honor to inform you that Professor Louis Agassiz desires to ship a small quantity of Alcohol to Captain Charles Bryant, a Treasury Agent on duty in Alaska, to be used by that gentleman in the preservation of specimens of animals that he is collecting for the museum of Harvard College. Under Executive Order of February 4, 1870. such transaction cannot be authorized. But in view of the commendable object to be attained, I respectfully suggest such modification of said Executive Order as will permit me to grant Professor Agassiz request—and herewith enclose a form of order for this purpose for your signature, if it meets with your approval." Copy, *ibid.*, RG 56, Letters Sent to the President. On March 21, USG signed that order. Copy, *ibid.*, RG 130, Executive Orders and Proclamations.

On Nov. 11, 1872, Louis Agassiz, Cambridge, wrote to USG. "About a year ago I took the liberty to inform you of the valuable services Mr Nicolas Pike, U. S. Consul in Mauritius, was rendering to science by sending collections of the various natural productions of that region to different scientific institutions at home. I might have added that these collections are in themselves evidence that Mr Pike is fully conversant with the wants of science and the best means of providing for them. On the ground of what he had done not only for the Museum in Cambridge, but also for different societies in other parts of the country I ventured to urge the importance of keeping him as long as possible in the post he now occupies. Since my return to these eastern States øafter nearly a year's absence I learn that Mr Pike has had difficulties with mercantile parties in Mauritius, the wrong doings of whom he has checked and exposed, and in consequence of which efforts are now making to have him removed from his place. Will you allow me to state that I have known Mr Pike long enough and have had with him such dealings that I can confidently affirm that he is not only an upright & highminded gentleman; but also thoroughly devoted to the performance of his duties, in a manner which is equaly creditable to himself and to the Government he represents. I know that the charges proferred against him are in the State department with his refutation and I am sure that if there is an opportunity to have the whole matter sifted it will distinctly appear that Mr Pike has been maliciously slandered by parties who want to put him out of the way that they may have the field to themselves to make extortions from american vessels touching at Mauritius." ALS, *ibid.*, RG 59, Letters of Application and Recommendation. On March 10, 1866, President Andrew Johnson had nominated Nicolas Pike as consul, Port Louis, Mauritius. After receiving a flurry of charges against Pike and letters defending him, USG suspended Pike on June 9, 1873. Copy, *ibid.*, Letters of Suspension.

To John M. Schofield

———

Respectfully returned to the Secretary of War.

It seems to me that the question of jurisdiction under the Civil Rights Bill is not whether the persons claiming its protection are negroes or white men, but whether they "can or can not enforce in the Courts or Judicial Tribunals of the State or locality where they may be any of the rights secured to them by the first section of this act," and this is a question to be decided by the judicial officer of the United States, who takes cognizance of any alleged violation of the Act. The responsibility of the Marshal, as also that of the military officer called to his aid, does not extend to this question, but only to the question whether the writ which he is required to execute, or aid in executing, is a lawful writ. It is not the duty of the military commander to inquire into the nature of the offence for which an arrest is ordered by competent judicial authority, but only whether military aid is necessary and proper to the making of such arrest.

U. S. Grant
General.

Hdqrs. A. U S.
Dec. 24. '68.

ES, DNA, RG 94, Letters Received, S1126 1868. Written on a letter of Dec. 19, 1868, from Maj. Gen. George G. Meade, Philadelphia, to the AG. "I have the honor to submit for the information, and action of the Secy of War the subjoined papers being an application on the part of a U. S. Deputy Marshall & a U S. Comn in Georgia for military aid—with my first reply thereto, and their subsequent explanations and a demand for military aid. The gist of the whole matter, is an attempt through the Civil Rights bill, to give some protection to the negro, which it would appear the state criminal law does not furnish—Mr Morrill the U S. Commissioner is an agent of the Freedman's Bureau, has been if I am correctly informed made U. S. Commissioner to take advantage of the power conferred by the Civil Rights bill for the protection of the negro, and this is the first case that has been presented for my action.—There can be no doubt that Section 5 of the Civil Rights bill authorises the employment of the land and naval forces by the Marshal for the execution of this law—but the question on which I desire to be advised is 1st Does the simple murder of a negro constitute an offence under the Civil Rights bill any more than the murder of a white man? 2nd Is the case, as presented in the accompanying papers, one which under your instructions of Aug. 25. /68 justifies my answering the call of the Marshall? 3rd Am I to require such statement of facts, as to shew the specific case is one where there is prima facie evidence the Civil Rights bill has been violated, or am I to act on the simple requisition of the Commissioner & Marshall—I beg to be instructed at the earliest moment practicable, and do not hesitate to say that I shall be glad to ascertain the Civil Rights Bill does afford a means of correcting a very serious evil all over the South viz—the failure of the local civil authorities to execute the Criminal law—whenever the crimes are in any way connected with the political excitements & questions of the day—" ALS, *ibid*. The enclosures are *ibid*.

To Maj. Gen. Philip H. Sheridan

Washington, D. C., Dec. 24th *1868.*

Dear General;

The time is close at hand when a new deal may be expected of Commanders for Dept. Divs. &c. and I now write to know something of your pleasure in regard to your assignment. My expectation has been to give you and Thomas the two Divisions now Commanded by Sherman & Halleck. I do feel a desire however to send you to New Orleans long enough to put matters in good working order there before sending you to a Division. This I will not do, I dont think, against your will. Please let me know how you feel in this matter.

The chances do not seem to me favorable for a transfer of the Indian Bureau to the War Dept. The measure however seems to receive favor from the public, and, in the end, will be accomplished to the great benefit of the public. Indian wars have grown out of mismanagement of the bureau, and a desire to make treaties so as to have the disbursment of money, in my opinion. If the men who have to do the fighting could have the management in time of peace the would be most likely of any people to preserve peace, for their own comfort if for no other reason.

I congratulate you on your successes so far as I understand

them. I hope the indians will soon be brought to a realizing sense of the importance of peace to them.

Yours Truly

U. S. Grant

Gn. P. H. Sheridan.

ALS, DLC-Philip H. Sheridan. On Jan. 19, 1869, Maj. Gen. Philip H. Sheridan, "Camp Medecin Lodge Creek, Wichta Mountains" wrote to USG. "I am today in receipt of your very kind letter of Decr. 24th in reference to new Commands. I would like to Command the Military Division of the Missouri now Commanded by General Sherman. I do not wish to go to the Pacific coast for many reasons. Some of which are personal I have hoped ~~that~~ for a little leasure time when I might be able if I could ~~collect~~ get money enough on hand to spend a year in Europe, & going to the Pacific coast would interfere with this & other personal interests—It ~~would make me by~~ besides I have spent 6½ years ~~there~~ on that coast It would disappoint me very greatly to go there. In reference to New Orleans—I beg of you not to send me there unless it would be of benefit to you, in your administration, to which I would like ~~to have as~~ to contribute my mite in making as pleasant to you as possible. I would like to have more rest than I would have there. I have been on ~~the~~ a tour now for a long time & crave a little rest—This winter has been pretty hard on me, but it was a necessity. I did all I could & from the bottom of my heart to keep the Indian quiet but it could not be done & I hope to end the troubles permanently [as] far as the resident tribes of Indians in ~~my comd~~ this Dept are concerned. There can be no success in dealing with Indians until the mangemt is assumed by the War Dept. Thieves & robbers of the public monies, extend from the lowest agent up to the Halls of Congress connected with the present Indian managemt. It has been a common thing here to issued corn meal costing 4$ per hundred pound to Indians then purchase it back for a cup or two of sugar as the Indn dislike meal, and then take it up—as a fresh purchase & reissue a 4$ per hundred— . . ." ADf, *ibid.*

To John M. Schofield

———

Washington, D. C., Dec. 30th *1868*

Gen. J. M. Schofield:

Sec. of War:

General:

Inclosed herewith I have the honor to send you copies of the letters called for by the President in his letter of the 26th inst. I also send two letters from Gen. Halleck to me, of the 8th & 17th of

January, 1864, respectively, and one from me to him, of the 15th
of January 1864, as shewing the reason for the correspondence.

I have the honor to be,

very respectfully

your obt. svt.

U. S. GRANT

General,

ALS, DLC-Andrew Johnson. On Dec. 26, 1868, President Andrew Johnson
wrote to Secretary of War John M. Schofield. "Will the Honorable the Secretary
of War please furnish me, from the records of the War Department, with copies
of the letters from General Grant to General Halleck, dated respectively Nashville, January 19, 1864, and City Point, July 1, 1864?" LS, DNA, RG 108,
Letters Received. For the letters requested, see *PUSG*, 10, 39–40; *ibid.*, 11,
155–56. For the others sent, see *ibid.*, 10, 14–18, 23–24.

On Sept. 7, Johnson had written to Schofield. "You will please transmit to
me copies of the following papers now on file in your Department, viz—Letters
of General Grant to General Halleck in January and February 1864, protesting
against the ordering of troops to General Banks on Red River. Letters from
General Grant to General Halleck of the same period in 1864, advancing his
ideas of the Campaign of the Potomac Army. Letter (from June 28th to July
5th) from General Grant to the Secretary of War and the President in regard
to the removal of Genl Butler and appointing Genl. Baldy Smith." Copy, DLC-
Andrew Johnson. On Sept. 14, Schofield wrote to Johnson. "In compliance with
your order dated September 7th, I have the honor to transmit herewith the following papers, viz:—Copy of a letter from General Grant to General Halleck,
dated Nashville, Tennessee January 19th 1864, giving his views relative to
a plan of operations in Virginia and North Carolina. Copy of a letter from General Grant to General Halleck, dated City Point, July 1st, 1864, relative to the
removal of General Butler and assignment of General W. F. Smith to command
the Army of the James. Copies of returns of the Army of the Potomac and 9th
Army Corps, for the months of April and May, 1864, and copies of several telegrams from General Grant to General Halleck, dated respectively February 8th,
15th and 16th, and March 12th and 17th 1864, and from General Halleck to
General Grant dated respectively February 8th, 16th and 17th and March 13th,
and 17th, 1864; also one dated March 12th 1864 from General Grant to the
Secretary of War, relative to the movement of General Banks up Red River in
1864. There does not appear upon the records of the War Department or of the
HeadQuarters of the Army, any letter or telegram from General Grant, protesting against sending troops to General Banks, and the telegrams, of which copies
are enclosed, would seem to show that no such letter could have been written.
The letters from General Grant to General Halleck, dated Nashville, January
19th and City Point, July 1st 1864, are of that confidential character that are
not usually filed with the public records of the War Department, and are never
published without the consent of the writer. They have been kindly furnished to
me by General J. A. Rawlins, Chief of Staff, to enable me to comply with your
order." LS, *ibid.*

Speech

————

[*Dec. 31, 1868*]

MR. PRESIDENT ALLEN:[1] I am very much pleased to have the oppo[r]tunity of visiting the work over which you preside. I feel that it is d[o]ing a good that I can scarcely appreciate. When I was a boy I read wit[h] pleasure of Stephen Girard[2] and of the munificent bequest made in h[is] will, and am delighted to see that his wishes have been fulfilled. Boys, [I] hope you may always have as able a President as you now have.

New York Tribune, Jan. 2, 1869. On Dec. 31, 1868, USG had visited Girard College, Philadelphia, accompanied by Augustus Heaton, a member of the board of directors. William H. Allen, president of the college, introduced USG. ". . . And now, General permit me to welcome you most cordially to this home and school of orphans, many of them made orphans in the late war for the life of the Republic. These spacious buildings are their home, and these faithful teachers and officers are the guides of their youth. They are all loyal boys; patriotic to their hearts' core. Hundreds of those who formerly occupied these halls went forth to fight in the armies under your command, and not a few of them laid down their lives for their country. And if the nation should be again exposed to a similar period, which may God avert, when these boys shall become men, I pledge to you and to the country, hundreds more from these benches who will as bravely do, and as nobly die." *New York Times*, Jan. 2, 1869.

On Jan. 1, 1869, USG spoke at a reception at Independence Hall. "To meet you at any time is a pleasure, but on an occasion and in a place like this gives rise to reflections which it is impossible for me to do justice to in words. I will add that I thank you and the citizens of Philadelphia for the many kindnesses I have received at their hands." *New York Herald*, Jan. 3, 1869. On Jan. 2, USG wrote to George H. Stuart. "Thank you. I visited Bishop Simpson today and learnd that he was to preach to-morrow and have arranged to go." ANS, DLC-George H. Stuart. On Jan. 4, USG telegraphed to Bvt. Brig. Gen. Cyrus B. Comstock. "Please send carriage to meet train leaving here at twelve (12) today" Telegram received, DNA, RG 107, Telegrams Collected (Bound).

1. Allen, born in Maine in 1808, graduated from Bowdoin College in 1833, had been president of Girard College (1850–62), and served as president of Pennsylvania Agricultural College before returning to Girard in 1867.

2. Stephen Girard, born in France in 1750, a successful merchant, shipowner, and banker, bequeathed in 1831 much of his fortune for public works and charities. With this endowment, the city of Philadelphia established in 1848 Girard College, a school for orphans.

To Lt. Gen. William T. Sherman

Confidential *Washington, D. C.*, Jan.y 5th *1868*[9]
DEAR GENERAL:

I have been approached by a citizen of New York City to sell to them, to be presented to you, my house and grounds, but expressing a desire to know if you would receive ~~it~~ them if so presented. I told ~~them mos~~ the gentleman most assuredly you would but I would find out in a quiet way. The proposition was to pay me $65.000 for the house and grounds which I insisted was more than the property was worth, or than I would take, but that I would sell it with the carpets, chairs, wardrobes and much of the other furniture, for that price, reserving many little things which were presents to me and I would not like to sell. I hope the arrangement will be agreeable to you as I know it is deserved. You will find that all your pay and income are required to support your family here without paying rent. You know the house is a commodies and good one, and in a locality that is growing. There is so much vacant ground that prospectively it is valuable.

I hope what I said will meet your approval, and further, that the design of the gentleman who spoke to me will be carried out.

Please present Mrs. Grants & my regards to your family.

Yours Truly
U. S. GRANT

LT. GN. W. T. SHERMAN,
ST. LOUIS MO,

ALS, OHi. On Jan. 15, 1869, Lt. Gen. William T. Sherman, St. Louis, wrote to U.S. Senator John Sherman of Ohio. ". . . Grant wrote me last week that some NewYork Gentlemen had approached him, and offered him $65,000 for his house & lot, to be presented to me; and to know how it would suit me. He answered them that the price was much more than he asked but he could throw in the furniture that would make the thing more complete. As to how it would suit me, he said he presumed it would still he would consult me. I of course promptly replied that it would suit me to a T, and more especially would it suit Ellen & the family who want a big house. That of Grant fulfils all conditions, though had I 65,000 cash I would not invest it there, but as a Gift it would be splendid. The house is very large, and all furnished—It has water, gas, stables—

& vacant lot. . . ." ALS, DLC-William T. Sherman. See letter to Lt. Gen. William T. Sherman, Feb. 12, 1869.

To Julia Dent Grant

———

Washington, D. C., ~~D~~Jan.y 7th 186~~8~~9

DEAR JULIA;

Do'nt you cry about Buck. In a day or two you will hear all about how he is situated. If it is not pleasantly he can be brought back. You can go to see him, or I will, betwene this and Spring.

ULYS,

ALS, USG 3.

To Bvt. Brig. Gen. Adam Badeau

———

Jan. 12th /69

DEAR GEN.L

Say to the people who I appointed to-day to meet that I have a severe headach and will not leave the house. I cannot see anyone here on business either during the day.

Yours Truly
U. S. GRANT

GN. BADEAU

ALS, Munson-Williams-Proctor Institute, Utica, N. Y.

To James A. Bayard

———

Washington D. C. Jany. 13, 1869

HON. JAS. A. BAYARD U. S. S.

SENATOR:

I have the honor to return the copy of a letter of Gen. Chas. F. Smith to Clerk of the Committee on Military Affairs of the U. S.

Senate. I recognize the correctness of the principle on which General Smith's claim is based, but there is no law for the payment of such a claim, and I therefore recommend the passage of a special law to cover his case.

In addition to the justness of the principle involved the subsequent services of Gen. Smith to his country seem to me a reason for special legislation. He died during the war, after manifesting great skill, energy and gallantry, and left two helpless orphans who should be regarded as in some sort, wards of the Nation

Very respy your obt servt

U S. GRANT

General

Copies, DLC-USG, V, 47, 60; DNA, RG 108, Letters Sent. See *SRC*, 41-2-34; *CG*, 41–2, 1730–31. James A. Bayard, born in 1799 in Wilmington, Del., graduated from Union College (1818), eschewed a mercantile career to study and practice law, lost elections running as a Democrat for U.S. representative and senator before an agreement between Democrats and Whigs in Del. to support the Wilmot Proviso resulted in his election to the U.S. Senate in 1851. He resigned his seat in 1864 dissatisfied with Radical Republican policies, returning by appointment in 1867 following the death of his successor.

To Edwards Pierrepont

Washington, D. C., Jan.y 15th *1869*

DEAR JUDGE,

Your favor was duly received. I will be pleased to meet you here and to have the talk you propose. I suppose you have other business which fixes the time for your coming to Washington, but in case you have not I want to say that I meet with the other trustees of the "Peabody Educational Fund," in Baltimore, on Thursday next,[1] and will be absent from here the balance of the week. After that I have no engagement for any specified time within this month.

Yours Truly

U. S. GRANT

JUDGE E. PIERREPONT

ALS, DLC-USG. Edwards Pierrepont, born in Conn. in 1817, originally named Munson Edwards Pierpont, graduated from Yale, was admitted to the bar in 1840, and practiced in Columbus, Ohio, before moving to New York City in 1846. A prominent Democrat who supported Abraham Lincoln's reelection, he changed party allegiance in 1868. See *PUSG*, 18, 190, 506. On Jan. 10, 1869, Pierrepont, New York City, wrote to USG. "Within a few days I intend to come to Washington and if opportunity offers, I mean to talk with you upon public affairs—Men of your stamp do not need other mens' *opinions*, but only facts and true information upon which to base their own opinions—Such I hope to give, and your good judgment will advise you as to the fidelity and usefulness of the communications. Having done what I could to elect one who truly represented the better sentiment of the Nation, I mean to do what I can to vindicate my own sagacity and to prove that the same moral and intellectual traits which made a great commander in time of *Civil War*, will make a great statesman in time of peace, and that the honest instincts of the people are much wiser than than the wisdom of politicians—I somehow, believe that you will not misconstrue this letter and that you will not take exception to its frankness.—Good fortune has placed me at the age of fifty, in perfect health and with ample means so that I can devote my time to the public service, asking no other reward than that good name, which comes of duties well done—The vigilant industry, energy and prudent courage which has served me so well in private pursuits, I should like to employ in whatever of public place these qualities may be most useful. I shall talk with you freely upon public men and public measures, and when the *full time comes*, if you need me in any place you will tell me so, and whether you do or not, I shall always remain your faithful friend" ALS, USG 3.

On Oct. 24, 1868, Pierrepont had written to Julia Dent Grant. "Say to the General that notwithstanding the efforts of Grant Democrats *fraudulent* votes may cause us to lose this State—President Johnson has written a letter to Seymour urging him to take the stump, and now every one of the *Cabinet* are silent—The Enemy rally and concentrate all the force and the fraud upon this State—they wish to save Newyork I hope we shall share in the glory of carrying it fo[r] Gen. Grant—" ALS, *ibid.* On Oct. 25 and Nov. 3, Pierrepont wrote to USG. "I do not feel sure of this State—Thousands of the Irish have come to us—but the means of fraud in this City & Brooklyn *are great.* I *know* the vote of the State is with us & *every* day many democrats write me that they go with us, & *many* come to tell me—I pray God & work, . . ." "This day's vote will make you President of the United States.—May God, as heretofore, give you the wisdom and the strength for the heavy duty. Called by the spontaneous wish of every loyal heart, you can call to your aid whomsoever you desire, and all the people will say, *Amen.*—In Newyork, the vote will surely be for you— Fraud in this city may cheat us out of our rights; But as it looks at this writing, you will carry the State in spite of all the fraud—" ALS, *ibid.*

1. Jan. 21, 1869. For USG's activities at this meeting, see *Proceedings of the Trustees of the Peabody Education Fund* . . . (Boston, 1875), I, 116–17, 138–41. See also *PUSG*, 17, 49.

Speech

[*Jan. 19, 1869*]

I thank the convention of which you are the representatives for the confidence they have expressed, and I hope sincerely that the colored people of the nation may receive every protection which the laws give them. They shall have my efforts to secure such protection. They should prove by their acts, their advancement, prosperity, and obedience to the laws worthy of all privileges the Government has bestowed upon them by their future conduct, and prove themselves deserving of all they now claim.

Washington Chronicle, Jan. 20, 1869. USG responded to a speech by John M. Langston, chair of a committee representing the National Convention of the Colored Men of America. "General Grant: In the name of four millions of American citizens—in the name of seven hundred thousand electors of African descent—electors who braved threats who defied intimidation, whose numbers have been reduced by assassination and murder in their efforts, in the exercise of a franchise guaranteed by American law to every one clothed in the full livery of American citizenship, to secure, in the late Presidential canvass, the election of nominees of the national Republican party to the high places to which they were named—we, accredited delegates to the national convention of Colored Men, sessions of which in this city have just closed, come to present to you congratulations upon your election to the Presidency of the United States. Permit us, General, to express, in this connection, our confidence in your ability and determination to so execute the laws already enacted and to be enacted by our national Congress as to conserve and protect the life, the liberty, the rights, no less of the humblest subject of the Government than those of the most exalted and influential. Called as you are to fill the chair of State, your duties will be arduous and trying, especially since, in this reconstruction period of the Government, removing the rubbish, the accretions of the now dead slave-holding oligarchy. You will administer the Government according to the principles of morals and law announced by the fathers. In advance, we bring to you, General, as a pledge of our devotion to our common country and Government, the liveliest sympathy of the colored people of the nation; and in their name we express the hope that all things connected with the administration of the Government, upon which you are so soon to enter as our Chief Magistrate, may be, under Providence, so ordered for the maintenance of law, and the conservation of freedom, that your name, written high on the scroll of honor and fame, may go down to posterity, glorious and immortal, associated with the names of your illustrious predecessors in the great chair of State—Washington and Lincoln. Again, General, we express our congratulations." *Ibid.* On Jan. 18, 1869, Langston had written to USG requesting this meeting. Df, DLC-John Mercer Langston. See Philip S. Foner and George E. Walker, eds., *Proceedings of the Black*

National State Conventions, 1865–1900 (Philadelphia, 1986), I, 378, 386–87, 390–92.

On May 13, George T. Downing *et al.* addressed USG. "MR. PRESIDENT: Having been appointed by the national convention of colored men recently assembled in this city to represent them in all political matters, we have gladly taken advantage of a statement published by trustworthy newspapers of the Republican party respecting your Excellency's intentions in a very important matter to seek this interview. The statement to which we refer is to the effect that your Excellency intends to appoint in the Northern States to important positions such colored men as can discharge the duties with profit and honor to the public service. Knowing this reported intention to be eminently in keeping with the record of your Administration, we have thought that a few suggestions made by this committee, familiar with the North, might lend some support to the policy indicated. We are assured that the appointment of competent and trustworthy colored men to prominent positions in the Northern States would give a death blow to objections against our holding such positions in the South, by convincing the South that it is not true that the North wishes to force a policy upon them which it is not willing to accept itself. If negroes are elevated to important places by the general Government in Rhode Island, the problem of negro office-holding becomes easy of solution in Georgia. . . . We refer to the Northern aspect of the question, not because we are less interested in the South, but because we are of the opinion that the North, in view of its educational advantages and the elevating experiences that belong to free society, should furnish a criterion as to the ability of negroes to fill responsible positions. We desire that the political experience of Northern colored men and the political power enjoyed by Southern colored men may blend so completely as to cause the entire people to forget color or section in the recognition of patriotism. Our rights as men were recognized by Mr. Lincoln, and we are filled with all gratitude in view of this fact; but we come, too, with a feeling of fellowship added to that of a mere sense of gratitude, because you have appointed numbers of our race to important positions, and thus given a rebuke to vulgar prejudices against a class. In this you have gone far beyond our late lamented President; for, while under the necessities of war, he made the nation *ours* by calling us to its defence, you, under the calm influences of peace, have given us to the nation by lifting our race into the enjoyment of its immunities." *Washington Chronicle*, May 14, 1869.

In [*April, 1869*], Isaac Myers and two others had written to USG. "This committee appointed by the City Ex. Rep. Com. of Baltimore Md. in obedience to instructions respectfully submit for your Excelency's high consideration the following: First, With a view of incorporating the *colored element* of the country, as a fixture, in the Republican party for all time, against all local and national issues, that may arise in future, we would suggest such representation under your administration as will give encouragement to our people and show some recognition of the important and esential part taken by them in the November campaign & election. Secondly that the *south* in consideration of its 300.000 votes cast in November and to encourage the 600,000 that will be cast in future, by our people South of the Potomac, is justly entitled to at least a moity of the representation you will give *our* people under your administration.

and Thirdly we reccommend that the Missions to Hayti & Liberia be given to *competent* colored men also, the Missions to *Cosa Rica, Hondurus,* and *Salvador* in *Central America* and the *U. S. of Columbia, Uruguay, Paraguay,* and the *Argentine Confederation* in *South America.* We make the latter reccommendation because of the position of equality occupied by *our* people in these States and the necessity of an advance step of this kind to still the agitation ~~of~~ upon the question of equal rights in our own country and throughout the civilized World; and for the purpose of practically proving the competence of ~~the leading~~ men of our race   If our propositions are favorably considered by your Excelency, we would suggest the following gentlemen, any of whom will be found fully competent to fill any of the positions named above, with credit and profit to the country   Fred. Douglass N. York. Wm Howard Day N. York. Wm Rich N. York. J. Sella Martin N. York. Geo. T. Downing N. York. H. Highland Garnet Penn. Isaac C Weir Penn. Wm Nesbitt Penn. E. D. Bassett Penn. Jno. H. Butler Md. Isaac Myers Md. A. Ward Handy Md. Robert Morris Mass Fred. G. Barbadoes Mass Jno. M. Langston Ohio A. H. Galaway N. Carolina H. M. Turner Georgia Wm U. Saunders Florida" DS (tabular material expanded), DNA, RG 59, Letters of Application and Recommendation. Petitions from Troy, N. Y., and Boston, endorsing Frederick Douglass as minister to Brazil are *ibid.*

In Jan., 1870, Orville E. Babcock wrote to Downing. "The President directs me to acknowledge the receipt of your letter of the 4th inst, and to say that he saw mention made in the newspaper of such an order as you refer to, also to say that it is his rule never to reply to such articles—Recognizing the kind spirit in which your letter is written he wishes it answered, in a private letter, that you may be enabled to correct any erroneous impression. During the morning of Jany 1st one of the Policemen on duty, come to him and asked if the usual custom of dividing the time between the Colored and white people should be observed, and he said to carry out the usual custom, but that a few moments after the gate was opened he was informed that there were a number of colored people wishing to come in, and he at once gave direction to admit all who wished to come. He gave no other orders or instructions in the matter." Copy, DLC-USG, II, 1. Downing's letter is listed in William Evarts Benjamin, Catalogue No. 42, March, 1892, p. 9.

To Lt. Gen. William T. Sherman

Washington, D. C., Jan.y 19th *1869*

DEAR GENERAL;

I enclose you a photograph of the picture which Healy has completed in Rome and which he says draws largely. If it looks like the photograph, you and Porter naked, I presume the ladies wear vaels when they look upon it.

Yours Truly
U. S. GRANT

GEN. W. T. SHERMAN.

ALS, DLC-William T. Sherman. See *PUSG*, 18, 204, 262.

To J. Russell Jones

————

Washington, D. C., ᴀJan. 19th *1869.*

DEAR JONES:

I want all the land you can let me have out of your late purchase, and as soon as possible want the horse rail-road stock converted to pay for it. At present I have no money but expect to have soon, from the sale of my house, when I will pay up all and stop interest. Whatever I have, including the rail-road stock, I want put into Chicago property, and with the exception of what you have bought, central property that will give an income.

I took no notice of that portion of your former letter touching office because I thought that matter settled. The Post Office at Vincennes was your choice and I promised it to you. It is to late to change now after all the other places, including the Marshalship, are mortgaged. Mrs. Jones will like the change to a place where there are no restaurants kept by pretty waiting maids.

Yours Truly
U. S.

AL (initialed), George R. Jones, Chicago, Ill. See letter to Elihu B. Washburne, Jan. 28, 1870; letter to J. Russell Jones, Sept. 5, 1872.

To Thomas L. Tullock

WASHINGTON, D. C, January 20, 1869.
Thomas L. Tullock Esq., Secretary, &c.

DEAR SIR: Understanding that the committee, of which you are secretary meet this evening for the purpose of arranging for the inauguration ball, I venture to drop you a line to say that if any choice is left to me I would be pleased to see it dispensed with. I do not wish to disarrange any plans made by friends in the matter of ceremonies attending the inauguration, but in this matter it will be agreeable to me if your committee should agree that the ball is unnecessary.

With great respect, your obedient servant,
[U.] S. GRANT, General.

National Intelligencer, Jan. 23, 1869.

To John M. Schofield

Washington, D. C., January 25th *1869*

GEN. J M. SCHOFIELD
SECRETARY OF WAR.
SIR:

In reply to the communication of the President of the 23d inst.[1] calling for a complete copy of the report submitted by Bvt. Brig. Gen. Horace Porter under date of the 26th ultimo[2] upon the condition of affairs in Arkansas, together with a copy of the instructions under which he visited that State, I have the honor to state that a complete copy of the report so far as it relates to the condition of affairs in Arkansas, or any other public matter, has already been furnished; and that the instructions under which Gen. Porter visited Arkansas were verbal.

> Very respectfully
> Your obedt. servant
> U. S. GRANT
> General.

LS, DLC-Andrew Johnson.
    On Nov. 17, 1868, Bvt. Maj. Gen. Lovell H. Rousseau, New Orleans, wrote to Secretary of War John M. Schofield. "I have the honor to forward to you the accompanying communications from the Governor of Arkansas, received by mail, and from Brev. Maj. Gen. C. H. Smith, commanding District of Arkansas: . . . You will see that the Governor of Arkansas has taken steps himself to keep the peace of the state by means of the militia. Unless the necessity becomes urgent within the purview of your instructions of Sept. 14, 1868, I shall take no action in the premises until I hear from you; but should that necessity arise, I shall promptly take such action as I am able, to carry out those instructions." LS, DNA, RG 94, Letters Received, 415L 1868. The enclosures are *ibid*. On Nov. 28, USG endorsed this letter. "Respectfully returned to the Secretary of War. The instructions heretofore given with a view to maintaining peace and good order in the Department of Louisiana seem to me amply sufficient for the guidance of the Department Commander, and the action of Governor Clayton in Arkansas should make no difference in the disposition and distribution of troops in that State, except in the counties covered by the Governor's proclamation of martial law, which proclamation, in my opinion, the Governor must maintain by his own militia; or if unable to do so, the Department Commander, upon proper presentment of the fact to him, can render him aid under his present instructions." ES, *ibid*.

    1. See President Andrew Johnson to Schofield, Jan. 23, 1869. Copies (2), DLC-Andrew Johnson.
    2. On Dec. 26, 1868, Bvt. Brig. Gen. Horace Porter, Little Rock, wrote to USG. "General Babcock and I arrived here two days ago. So many contradictory reports have been circulated in regard to Gov Claytons Militia, that it may be well for you to know the facts in the case. The present state goverment was certainly in some danger previous to the presidential election. Senator Barker had been shot, and wounded badly. Upham of the lower house wounded, Hines, an M. C., and a Freedmens Bureau Agent killed, and other agents and a U. S. Marshal driven from their posts by threats. The Gov., Senator Rice, and others had to sleep in the state house under guard for fear of assassination. The Gov. wisely refrained from taking any violent measures until after the election, fearing the opposition might make capital out of it. As soon as it was over however, he organized a militia force of about 800 men, one fourth colored, under Gen. Catterson in the south-west and Upham in the north-east, with orders to live off the country, taking what was absolutely necessary, and giving vouchers. His intention is to pay all loyal holders of vouchers, and no others   Two assassins have already been executed by sentence of a Mil. commission; seventeen others are in prison, and a great number have been run out of

the state. But the best result I can see is the disposition of nearly all business men to voluntarily enroll themselves as a posse, pledged to assist the sheriffs to arrest lawless characters if the Gov. will relieve them from Martial law. He has accepted many such pledges, and Martial law now exists in parts of but seven counties. The entire conservative wing of the republican party was opposed to the declaration of Martial law, including Gen. Smith, U. S. A. commanding the troops in the state. They admitted the reign of terror established by the rebels, but wanted the U. S. troops to make the arrests. Gov. Clayton's arguments in favor of his policy are as follows: The U. S. troops do not know the people and the country. The lawless behave while U. S. T. are in the vicinity, and break out worse than ever when they leave. The rebels are generally anxious to have them, as it creates an expenditure of money in their midst, from which they reap a benefit. Militia punishes all the disloyal, and extorts pledges from them to support the laws. As these people have threatened to break up the state goverment as soon as U. S. troops are removed, this teaches them that the state is able to protect itself. The Militia has been under tolerably good control, and the plundering reported in the press, is the taking of supplies under orders. One negro militia man committed a rape on a white woman, but was immediately arrested by Gen. Catterson (who seems to be a very good man) tried, convicted and promptly executed. The Governor's policy has no doubt seriously interfered with business men where martial law has been proclaimed and injured business men of all parties—hence the opposition from loyalists. It has interfered with travel, taken off hands for the militia, at a season when they are badly needed, and created many panics. It however has accomplished much more good than the most sanguine expected, and Genl. Smith acknowledged that he thought the Governors judgement was better than his own, and that the result would fully justify the action of the former. The Governor is now disposed to relieve each county from martial law as soon as it can safely be done. The Governor is certainly a man of intelligence and nerve and has labored under difficulties that would have detered a less able officer. Four thousand arms were seized by the Ku Kluxes and thrown off the boat below Memphis. He could seldom secure good men for officers and in the eastern counties he had to depend entirely upon negroes for soldiers." Copy, *ibid.* On Jan. 6, 1869, USG endorsed this letter. "Respectfully forwarded for information of the Sec. of War." AES, *ibid.*

On the same day, 2:30 P.M., USG telegraphed to Maj. Gen. George H. Thomas. "Please inform me if Gn. Granger has sent troops into Ark. as reported in the papers, and if so by what authority." ALS (telegram sent), DNA, RG 107, Telegrams Collected (Bound); telegram sent, *ibid.*; copy, DLC-USG, V, 56. On the same day, Bvt. Maj. Gen. William D. Whipple, Louisville, telegraphed to USG. "I understand that Granger sent Captain D. C. Poole 25th Infantry and no other troops into Ark, he had no authority from Head Quarters Dept Cumberland, Gen Thomas left this day for Washington" Telegram received, DNA, RG 107, Telegrams Collected (Bound).

On Jan. 8, Porter, New Orleans, wrote to USG. "Babcock and I went to Galveston, to look after some matters there, and returned last night. We had hoped to meet Gen. Reynolds there, on his way East, but the roads are in a dreadful condition, and he will be a week getting down from Austin. Gen. Rousseau died at 11 o'clock last night. He had been imprudent in the amount he ate during the holidays, and was attacked with constipation of the bowels. etc. Now is the time to send some good man to command this department. Buchanan will *not do* to leave here a month. Reynolds would be immensely better. His heart is in the right place, but his best friends in Texas think he is possessor of very little administrative ability. I think the 1st Infantry ought to leave here with Buchanan. Gov. Warmouth is opposed to trying the militia experiment here, and thinks his main support is to be derived from U. S. troops until the present state government is firmly established. He is not so much of a 'state-rights' man as Clayton. I feel more encouraged than ever before in regard to the success of 'Reconstruction.' The present state governments, with proper moral and physical support from the Government, will be able to maintain themselves, and build up a permanent loyalty without a doubt. True, there are many bad men among the leaders, but such men have often taken the advance in redeeming new countries. Kansas, now one of the best, and most loyal states in the Union, was purged by means of freedom-shriekers, hymn-book-warriors, and jay-hawkers. They were the pioneers who paved the way for better men. Some one must remove the thorns from a path before people will tread it. These states will, in a measure, have to be 'Kansasized'. We shall start on Sunday next for Mobile, Silma, Montgomery and Atlanta. The rebel papers, here, are assuring the people that you and Congress have commenced open war, and out of this quarrel they expect to get their rights. The are a hopeful race. In the new deal here, another quarter master should be sent to replace Tompkins, both for political and economical reasons. Buchanan might be withdrawn from here at once, by ordering him to Washington to give testimony in regard to the riots and intimidatons here previous to the late election." Typescript, DLC-Horace Porter. On the same day, Bvt. Brig. Gen. Orville E. Babcock, New Orleans, telegraphed to USG. "General Rousseau died last night at eleven (11) o'clock from an attack of inflamation of the bowels" Telegrams received (2— at 10:30 A.M.), DNA, RG 107, Telegrams Collected (Bound).

To Maj. Gen. George G. Meade

Washington, D. C., Jan.y 25th *1869*

DEAR GENERAL:

Your favor of the 19th inst. enclosing some slips of paper, is received. Mr. Tift,[1] member of Congress from Ga. has called on me a number of times to advise as to the best course for the Ga. Legislature to pursue. I told him frankly that I thought Congress, by their previous acts, had acknowledged reconstruction in Ga. as complete and that no course was left open to them but to admit their Senators unless they were disqualified under Article 14. But

I thought the Ga. Legislature had acted in a way to cast suspicion upon them by retaining the colored members until they elected Senators, ratified the 14 Article, and had complied in every way with the reconstruction Acts so far as to place them beyond Congressional interference, then refusing to displace men who were disqualified by the very Article ratified by them, but displaced the very men without whom they could not have complied with the requirements of the law. I told him that I thought now the best thing they could do would be to pass a resolution shewing their willingness to submit the question of elegibility of negros to hold office to the Courts & adjourn until Congressional action was had, if any should be taken. I told him particularly however that these were simply my views given becaus they were asked. That under no circumstances did I want to be regarded as advising either Congress or the legislature of Ga.—It is impossible for me to answer a civil question without being misunderstood either as to what I say or as to the motive for saying it. What I say here is about my views upon Ga. matters. But Congress may entertain different views and so may the members of the Ga. legislature. I am not prepared to say that one or t'other of them may not be nearer right than me. I have had but little time for looking into the matter.

Yours Truly
U. S. GRANT

GN. G. G. MEADE,
U. S. ARMY,

ALS, Meade Papers, PHi.

On Jan. 4, 1869, Maj. Gen. George G. Meade, Philadelphia, telegraphed to USG. "I transmit the latest dispatches received from Genl. Sibley commanding in Georgia, in relation to the reported difficulties on the Ogeechee. Genl. Sibley has been instructed not to permit the organization of any armed bodies whatever whether white or black in contravention of law, to preserve the peace at all hazards, to cooperate with the civil authorities in case he finds the same are acting in good faith and that their action is necessary for the preservation of the peace, and not as at Camilla, the law made a pretext for committing outrages on the negroes. At the same time he is instructe[d] to disarm and disperse all assemblages of the negroes and require them to submit to the legal action of the civil authorities" Copy, DNA, RG 393, 2nd Military District, Letters Sent. On Jan. 22, Meade, Atlanta, telegraphed to USG. "I wrote you several days since, on an averred opinion of yours which had been telegraphed here by M. Tift of Georgia Since then I have been approached by reliable & good men asking my opinion of the effect on Congress of the Legislature referring the disputed question of the negro holding office to the Judiciary & abiding the decision—My reply was that as a matter of mere private judgment I thought the effect would be good & might stay any action of congress till the judicial opinion was given—but that my means of forming a judgement were limited but I would endeavor to ascertain from Washington the opinions of others—Will you see Boutwell, Wilson, Bingham & others of the House & such members of the Senate as it is important to see and advise me of result— This is confidential & un-official—" ALS (telegram sent), Meade Papers, PHi; telegram received (at 9:00 P.M.), DNA, RG 107, Telegrams Collected (Bound); *ibid.*, RG 108, Telegrams Received.

On Jan. 28, Meade telegraphed to USG. "Your letter in relation to Tifts telegram is received—Would you object to its publication—I see many reasons for its publication from the good it will do—at the same time I can see the objection that will be made to your views by those who differ from you—Please answer—I have & shall shew it to only two or three reliable men, and to them in the strictest confidence & only for their information & guidance of their action—" ALS (telegram sent), Meade Papers, PHi; telegram received (at 10:00 P.M.), DNA, RG 107, Telegrams Collected (Bound). On the same day, Meade wrote to USG. "*Private* . . . Your letter of the 25th inst is received— It is precisely what I expected and has gratified me very much to find First that your views on the Georgia question are precisely mine—2d that your interviews with Mr Tift are exactly what I told the people here, I presumed they were—simply the opinions of an individual without any intention of advising controlling or influencing either the Legislature or Congress I felt great delicacy in writing you at all, and it was not till I saw what a perversion ~~you~~ was being made of your action that I thought as a friend I ought to apprise you of the condition of affairs—I shall now read your letter *confidentially* to two or three men—who are good & reliable—not for them to make public your sentiments— but simply to guide *their action*, in persuading the Legislature to take a step that may have a softening influence with Congress—Measures have been taken to bring before the courts the question of the eligibility of the Negro and a judicial decision will soon be obtained independant of any legislative action— What the friends of peace & harmony, are now striving for is to get from the Legislature an expression of their willingness & determination to yield their exclusive prerogative, and abide by the decision when made Have you seen the article (editorial) in the N. Y. Tribune of Saturday Jan. 23—headed 'The condition of the South'? If you have not, hunt it up & read it—for it is just what *I* would have written you officially—" ALS, USG 3. On Jan. 29, 11:45 A.M., USG telegraphed to Meade. "I think it better not to publish my letter but let it be seen by such persons as you think proper." ALS (telegram sent), DNA, RG 107, Telegrams Collected (Bound); telegram sent, *ibid.*; telegram received, Meade Papers, PHi.

1. Nelson Tift, born in 1810 in Groton, Conn., moved to Ga., founded the town of Albany (1836), engaged in business and politics, held the rank of capt. in the C.S. Navy Supply Dept., and was elected to the U.S. House of Representatives as a Democrat. On April 15, 1869, Tift, Albany, Ga., telegraphed to

USG. "Please withhold the commission for Arnold as Postmaster at Albany Georgia until you receive my letter" Telegram received (at 1:50 P.M.), DNA, RG 107, Telegrams Collected (Bound). On April 13, USG had nominated Charles W. Arnold as postmaster, Albany. On May [18], Arnold, Albany, wrote to USG. "Having been appointed by your Excellency Post Master at this place it becomes my duty to ask of you protection from the Ku Klux Klan: which infest this State. I discharge the duties of the Office at the risk of my life. since my appointment an attempt has been made to Ku Klux me at Americus Ga. a small village about 35 miles above this place whither I had gone in the discharge of my official duties as Rev' Assr. The men engaged in that attempt are known to me, their names are given to my family. they are likewise known to Col. W. C. Morrill Revenue Collector 2nd Dist Ga. and U S. Dept Marshal Cox, residing at Americus, to whom I am indebted for the information which prevented me from being murdered. this occurrence was on 24th April, at night. Should I be murdered hereafter, I ask of *your Excellency* the arrest and punishment of those men, who are known to have made an attempt on one occasion to murder me every Republican in this section of Country is in danger of loosing his life. . . . This is confidential, as if it were known that I had written such a letter, I would me murdered Instantaneously." ALS, *ibid.*, RG 94, Letters Received, 357A 1869. Related papers are *ibid.*

To Elihu B. Washburne

Washington, Jan. 26, 1869

CHRMN. COM. ON APPROPRIATIONS
HOUSE OF REPRESENTATIVES
SIR:

Understanding that your committee have struck out of the appropriation for River and Harbor improvements the sum of One Hundred Thousand (100 000) dollars, I take the liberty to express to you the opinion that it would be of great public advantage to have that amount restored, and the total sum of Two Hundred Thousand (200 000) dollars transferred from that appropriation for Military Surveys, &c., A work of vast importance to the mining interest of the country has progressed from the Pacific Coast Eastward to the East end of Salt Lake, taking in a belt of country one hundred or more miles in width along the line of the Pacific railroad. The appropriation here asked for is necessary to complete this work to the plains east of the Rocky Mountains. When done, and published for the information of the public, the miner and the agriculturist will have complete information of the resources of the country described agriculturally and mineralogically. In military operations, should any be necessary, the information will be of vast importance.—

I would add to this recommendation the further recommendation that authority be given to the Sec. of War, to publish the results of these surveys when completed, and to pay expenses of the same from any unexpended appropriations under his control.

I have the honor to be
with great respect
Your obt servt
U. S. Grant
General

Copies, DLC-USG, V, 47, 60; DNA, RG 108, Letters Sent. See *CG*, 40–3, 952, 1588.

To Sayles J. Bowen

———

Washington, D. C., Jan. 30, 1869.

Dear Sir: I am just shown your letter to Messrs. Kilbourn & Latta, of yesterday, in which you wish to know what furniture I would like to dispose of with my house. I distinctly understood from our interview that I was at liberty to regard the sale of my house as canceled if I chose, and that you had an equal privilege to cancel it. Since that I have concluded not to sell, unless it is to parties who talk now of purchasing to make a present to my successor as commander of the army. Whether this measure will be consummated or not, I do not know; but if it is not, I would much prefer to hold the property I now have to making a new investment. I hope I was not mistaken in what I understood you to say

in the interview we had on the subject of canceling the sale of my
house, and that you will be put to no inconvenience by it.

Yours truly,

U. S. GRANT.

S. J. BOWEN, esq.

New York Tribune, Aug. 27, 1872. On Feb. 1, 1869, Sayles J. Bowen wrote to
USG. "In reply to your note of Saturday last, I regret to be compelled to state
that my understanding of the conversation that took place between us at your
residence, in regard to the sale of your property on I-st., does not agree with
yours. I certainly understood you to say that you wished the matter to remain
open for a short period, as you had been given to understand that Congress
might legislate so as to reinstate you in your present position as General after
the expiration of your Presidential term. On no other account did you ask or
desire to retain the property; and it was on the basis of this assumption alone
that everything I said was uttered. Finding that Congress would not legislate
as you supposed, and not hearing from you on the subject, I believed that you
expected to carry out the contract and yield possession of the property at the
time indicated. Had I not supposed that such was the fact, and had I not believed that you and I understood each other, and that you, as well as I, considered the contract in force, I certainly would not have written to Messrs.
Kilbourn & Latta on the subject of the furniture as I did. I have made every
arrangement to leave our present residence early in March, and it will be a
great inconvenience and loss, as well as a sorry disappointment to us if we fail
to get possession of the premises purchased from you at the time indicated in
the contract. Regretting the necessity that impels me to write this communication, . . ." *Ibid.* Julia Dent Grant later asserted that she had blocked the sale
of the house. John Y. Simon, ed., *The Personal Memoirs of Julia Dent Grant*
(New York, 1975), p. 173. See letter to Sayles J. Bowen, Feb. 3, 1869.

Bowen, born in Scipio, N. Y., in 1813, a treasury dept. clerk in 1845, held
several local offices before his election as mayor of Washington, D. C., in 1868.
On March 12, 1869, Bowen, David K. Cartter, George P. Fisher, and William
A. Cook wrote to USG. "The term of office of the Board of Commissioners of
Metropolitan Police of the District of Columbia being about to expire we have
the honor to recommend the appointment of the following named persons in
their stead:—*For Washington City.* William J. Murtagh (reappointed) Charles
King *Vice* Peter F. Bacon William H. Chase *Vice* Samuel Norment *For the
city of Georgetown.* Charles H. Cragin *Vice* Charles English *For the county
of Washington.* De Vere Burr *Vice* Charles H. Nichols These are gentlemen
of the highest moral character and integrity—all loyal patriotic men, friends of
the administration, whose appointments will be satisfactory to the loyal people
of the District and whose official acts will prove a credit to themselves and the
appointing power. . . . All the *prominent* republicans here have been consulted
in regard to these persons and would join in recommending them if a petition
was presented them." DS (tabular material expanded), USG 3. On March 9
and 24, Henry D. Cooke and Charles E. Capehart, Washington, D. C., wrote to
USG recommending retention of Peter F. Bacon as police commissioner. ALS,

DNA, RG 48, Appointment Div., Letters Received. On April 7, USG nominated Derrick F. Hamlink, William J. Murtagh, Charles H. Cragin, William H. Chase, and De Vere Burr as police commissioners.

On March 30, Bowen wrote to USG. "John H. Johnson Esq, who takes this to you is a lawyer of this city whom I have known long and well. He is one of our steadfast republicans, was one of your earliest friends and supporters and has performed most excellent service as a friend of equal rights in this city. His kindness to the sick and wounded soldiers during the war was proverbial. He is qualified for most any position and if you think proper to bestow an appointment upon him it will be appreciated by . . ." ALS, *ibid.*, RG 60, Records Relating to Appointments. On March 21, 1870, Bowen again wrote to USG recommending John H. Johnson. ALS, *ibid.* Additional letters of recommendation are *ibid.* On March 29, USG nominated Johnson as justice of the peace, Washington, D. C. On June 18, Cook, chairman, Republican General Committee, Washington, wrote to USG. "Allow me to trouble you in relation to the appointment of Police Judge. I understand that Charles Walter, John H. Johnston and David R. Smith are applicants. The first and last named are simply justices of the Peace;—Mr. Walter an old Democrat and I think I express the opinion of many of our best citizens that his appointment would be very unfortunate. Nor would the others named be proper. The names of Gen: R. D. Musey, J. Sayles Brown and R. S. Bond have been mentioned. They are in all respects superior to the others; are respectible and of good abilities. Whatever may be done, permit me to express the hope that in the exercise of your superior information and wisdom, an appointment will be made of a good lawyer and one whose judicial acts will not be oppresive to the mass of persons who will appear before the Court—poor and ignorant colored people. Such an appointment I know you will desire to make. Pardon this intrusion on your time." ALS, *ibid.* Papers relating to Charles Walter, S. R. Bond, and David R. Smith are *ibid.* On June 29, USG nominated William B. Snell as judge, police court, Washington. Letters recommending Snell's reappointment in 1876 are *ibid.*

In March, 1869, Bowen signed a petition requesting the appointment of Joseph C. Lewis as a member of the levy court of D. C. DS, *ibid.* On Dec. 1, 1870, Bowen wrote to USG. "In my interview with you and the Attorney General I mentioned the name of Judge Nathan Sargent in connection with a position on the Levy Court in place of Mr. Plant whose term of service is about to expire. Since that time I have learned that Benjamin N. Meeds Esq. is an applicant for the vacancy and in case Judge Sargent should not be appointed I recommend Mr. Meeds as in every way worthy of the place and in all respects peculiarly fitted for the discharge of its duties. I know of no one whose selection would give greater satisfaction to the people of the District." ALS, *ibid.* On Dec. 9, USG nominated Nathan Sargent to replace George H. Plant on the levy court of D. C. On Dec. 12, Sargent, commissioner of customs, wrote to USG. "I have been informed this morning—whether correctly or not, I do not know; that an effort has been, or is to be made, to have my nomination as a Member of the Levy Court withdrawn and the name of George H Plant substituted. The *avowed* objection to me, I suppose must be, that I am not as young as I was once; but it is not the real one. If I go into that Court again it may interfere with the plans of certain persons, and perhaps prevent the re-election of some, if not all, of the present Officers of that Court, *not one of whom is a sup-*

porter of your «Administration, and most of whom are avowedly hostile to it.
Mr Plant was a Republican, I believe, until the right of suffrage was given to
the negro but since then has been hostile to it, and if I am not misinformed and
I am pretty sure I am not, he took Judge Moore of this City up to a Democratic
Meeting in Montgomery County, this fall, to make a Speech in favor of the
Democratic Candidate for Congress who was Elected. I have not been an applicant for the position, but have said that if by my appointment a change could
be effected in the Officers of the Court, I would not decline the appointment.
Having been nominated, it would now be somewhat mortifying to me to have
my name withdrawn As to my confirmation, I have not the least doubt of
that. If, I become a Member of the Court, I shall do my duty there, *fully* and
faithfully, of that you need have no apprehension." LS, *ibid.* On Dec. 22, the
Senate confirmed Sargent's appointment.

On Feb. 21, 1871, Bowen wrote to USG. "I have the honor most respectfully, to make application for the office of Governor of the Territory of Columbia. This position is now open to you, and as you have, on more than one
occasion, expressed a desire to bestow an appointment on me, and as this will
suit me better than any other, may I not hope that you will find it consistent
to give it to me? From indications unmistakeable it is the wish of nearly every
true and tried republican in the District (I mean those who have been and still
are the friends and supporters of republican principles and of your administration) that I should have the appointment, which fact will be made manifest to you if an opportunity be afforded for an expression of public opinion
on the subject. It would be very gratifying to me to receive the appointment
inasmuch as it would be a recognition of the republican party here as well as
an earnest of your friendship and good will toward me. I write from a sick bed,
otherwise I would have called in person." ALS, *ibid.*, RG 59, Letters of Application and Recommendation. Related papers are *ibid.* No appointment followed;
see letter to Hannibal Hamlin, Feb. 21, 1871. A report that Bowen had been
appointed minister to Ecuador proved incorrect. *New York Times*, Feb. 11, 1872.

To Jesse Root Grant

Washington, D. C., Feb.y 1st *1869,*

DEAR FATHER:

Your letter of the 28th of Jan.y is at hand. Mrs. Grant says
she does not see how she can invite Mrs. Freeman to our house at
the time of the inauguration. Our house will be entirely filled
[— — —] our relations

In the matter of appointments I make no pledges now, but
when the time comes, say about the 1st of March, write me, all in

one letter, the names you suggest, within your own acquaintance, and I will give them due concideration.

The family are all very well.

AL (signature clipped), Boyd Stutler Collection, West Va. Division of Culture and History, Charleston, West Va. On April 9, 1870, Jesse R. Grant wrote to an unknown person. "I am well-up in my 77th year, and the delapidating hand of time has unfited me for letter writing I have no letter written by the Gen that I can send you—but send a piece of one, cut by cuting out his name to supply some other person—" ALS, *ibid.* On Feb. 4 and 17, 1869, Jesse Grant, Covington, Ky., wrote to Bvt. Brig. Gen. Frederick T. Dent. "I recd a letter from Ulysses, yesterday, in which he says his house will be full—Mrs Freeman & Mrs Broadwell from Georgetown I understand wish to go, & as they will not have husbands with them to take care of them, I write to you to see if you can engage a room for them at some Hotel, or at some respectable privet house— I dont know at what time they will be at Washington, but probably about the 2nd or 3rd of March Dr Freeman *may* be with them Please write soon & let me know what can be done for these Ladies—It is not yet decided whether Mrs Grant or Jennie will go with me, but boath [c]ant go—I want the Mother to go—" ALS, ICarbS. "When I recd your letter, I showed it to Mrs Freeman She said she would like to take her meals where you & your family board—And wants a room for herself, as she expects the Dr there about the 3rd—If you find rooms geting scarce, you better take a good room for her, even if she has to pay from the time of taking it—She will be likely to go with us, & be there friday the 26th—Mrs Broadwell will probably go on the same train but she has company that will provide for her—General Loudon & Mr Nixon will be with us— Jennie will go with me but I have not been able to coax or hire Mrs Grant to be one of the party She has got the idea, that she would have to set up in the place where the Pres stands to be inaugurated—She says, Do you think I want to set up there for 50,000 people to gaze & point at? I would rather go when there are no strangers there Mrs Freeman was at our house yesterday, & left this letter to be sent to you" ALS, The White House, Washington, D. C. Jesse Grant enclosed a letter of Feb. 16 from "Mrs. Freeman" to Dent. "I did not know Mr. Grant intended to favor me by mention of my name to you. For the trouble you have had, and for your kindness, I return my thanks." ALS, *ibid.*

To Ellen E. Sherman

———

Washington, D. C., Feb.y 2d *1869.*

MY DEAR MRS. SHERMAN;

I am in receipt of a letter from the gentleman in New York City who first spoke to me of buying my house to present to Gen. Sherman. He says the arrangement will unquestionably be consumated. I know nothing further however than what I get from his letter. But I sincerely hope, and believe, there will be no failure. I know from experience that if you have to pay for a house out of savings from the pay of the General it will be a job you will not get through with before he is ready to retire by reason of old age.—The Gn. wrote to me some time before starting south to know what the probabilities were of his getting my house, and more particularly to know, if he did get it, what furniture he would have to bring with him. I write to you in answer to that letter because the Gen is absent and I do not know when he will return.—If the purchase is made the house will have in it substantially every thing for housekeeping except bedding, silver ware and perhaps table ware. The pictures, library, mantle ornaments and some little articles will not be left. There is a billiard table & piano too which I shall reserve but probably will leave in the house so long as I remain in Washington. I feel certain you will like the house and its surroundings. It is large and the grounds are capacious.

Please present my kindest regards to Miss Minnie and the children, and believe me,

Sincerely yours
U. S. GRANT

ALS, Sherman Family Papers, InNd. On Feb. 19, 1869, Alexander T. Stewart, Hamilton Fish, Col. Daniel Butterfield *et al.* wrote to USG. "The undersigned acting as a committee in the matter of a testimonial to Lieut Genl. W T. Sherman would respectfully advise you that the amount stated for the purchase of your house (with such furniture as you leave) $65.000—has been subscribed by responsible parties and will be paid by them when ever called upon by us— If our understanding is correct—that this price is satisfactory to you—also that the matter is well understood by yourself & Genl. Sherman we have to request that the necessary deeds & papers for the transfer of the property to Genl. Sherman may be prepared—Upon an intimation from you a few days in advance of the proper time to be fixed by yourself & Genl. Sherman for the transfer of the property some one of our number perhaps several of us will attend at Washington with the funds for payment &c—" ALS, OHi.

On Jan. 30, Butterfield, New York City, had telegraphed to USG. "Can I see you tomorrow if I come [o]ver tonight?" Telegrams received (3—at 12:35 P.M.), DNA, RG 107, Telegrams Collected (Bound). On the same day, USG wrote "Yes" at the foot of this telegram. AES, *ibid.*

To Hamilton Fish

Washington, *D. C.*, Feb:y 3d *1869*.

DEAR GOVERNOR:

Mrs. Grant & myself leave in the 8. a m train to-morrow for New York City. It would be exceedingly pleasant for us to accept your invitation to stay at your house during our visit but I feel a little hesitation about it because I have been pressed several times to stop at private houses there, and once accepted Mr. A. T. Stewarts invitation but afterwards excused myself on the ground that I would have so many callers that I would not like to take them to a private house. I think under the circumstances that it will be better that we should go to the 5th Av. Hotel.

Yours Truly
U. S. GRANT

GOV. H. FISH
NEW YORK CITY

ALS, DLC-Hamilton Fish.

On Feb. 1, 1869, Simeon B. Chittenden, New York City, telegraphed to USG. "If you can give me monday evening the eighth (8th) I will put you on the twelve (12) midnight train for Philada By special boat, excuse my persistence" Telegram received (at 1:20 P.M.), DNA, RG 107, Telegrams Collected (Bound).

To Sayles J. Bowen

WASHINGTON, D. C., Feb. 3, 1869.

The Hon. S. J. BOWEN—*Dear Sir:* Your note of yesterday was received, and I called this morning to see you in regard to the contents of it. As I leave the city tomorrow morning, to be absent about one week, and may not see you before my return, I write this reply. I certainly understood you that I could exercise my pleasure about complying with the contract to sell my house. I certainly should have told you earlier that I would much prefer not selling it, and intended to do so, but my days and evenings have been so taken up that I neglected it. I will say now, that when I reflect on how much furniture I had in the house, how little it will be worth to me hereafter, and how little it will bring, compared to its cost, if sold, and my disinclination to dicker about the price of such portion as any one buying the house might want to take, I concluded that I would much prefer keeping the house and renting it, with the furniture, to selling. Since that, gentlemen in New-York, to whom I am indebted for the house in the first instance, have proposed buying, with the furniture, to present to Gen. Sherman. In a note received, they say on terms satisfactory to me. In reply I acknowledged my indebtedness to them for the house, and stated that I felt as if Gen. Sherman should have it, and the price would not be considered by me. It will save me great annoyance to walk out without care for what is left in the premises. I regret exceedingly that you should suffer disappointment, and feel that you should not suffer loss. If any is sustained by you, I want to make it good. The furniture in my house, purchased, however, when everything was at the highest, cost about $35,000, exclusive of books and pictures. It will be very inconvenient for me to store this, or part of it, as I would have to do under an ordinary sale. Hoping that this will be satisfactory to you, I remain truly yours,

U. S. GRANT.

P. S.—In view of what I state herein, I will ask it for my accommodation and the accommodation of other parties to be benefited, you will release me from the contract referred to in this letter. I repeat that you should be freed from any loss, and that I will regard [it] not only a duty but a pleasure to bear such loss myself.

U. S. GRANT.

New York Tribune, Aug. 27, 1872.

To Walter Q. Gresham

Washington, D. C., Feb.y 11th *1869*

DEAR GENERAL:

Your letter of the 6th inst. to Gen. Rawlins saying that you will accept the office of Collector of Internal Rev. at New Orleans is rec'd. I am truly glad you have come to that determination. I know the parties in New Orleans who expect that office, and all others in the gift of the president, in that City and there is not one of them in whom I have unbounded Confidence. This led me to cast around for some one to send there. My mind first settled on you. You can truly say that the office sought you and not you the office.

You may rest assured that on the 5th of March, or within a day or two of that time, your name will be sent to the Senate.

Yours Truly
U. S. GRANT

ALS, DLC-Walter Q. Gresham. On Jan. 27 and Feb. 22, 1869, Bvt. Maj. Gen. John A. Rawlins wrote to Walter Q. Gresham. "*Private & Confidential* . . . General Grant wants to get an unquestionably honest and efficient man to accept office in the Custom, or Internal [R]evenue branch of the public service in NewOrleans La. and he beleives you to be that kind of a man. There are three Offices there which it is of the utmost importance should be properly filled, viz. 'Collector of Customs' salary $6.000 with perquisites which I am told for the last two years has not exceeded $2.000 per annum. Collector of Internal Revenue, worth about $13.500, per annum and Assessor of Internal Revenue which cannot exceed $4.000 per annum The General desires me to write to you confidentially, that if you will accept either of the Offices named he will send your name to the Senate for it immediately after his Inauguration to the Presidency. He wants you in NewOrleans that he may have the benefit of your judgment formed after a personal inspection of the condition of affairs there, in the appointment of other officers to the branches of service herein named, and while he might not appoint those whom you might recommend, yet your recommendation would have a very controlling influence with him. Please answer this at an early day that he may know your pleasure in the premises. If you decide to accept the appointment the General would like to see you here in person immediately upon your confirmation. Your answer as well as this to be regarded & treated as strictly confidential" "Your letter of the 17th inst. to General Grant in answer to one from him to you of the 11th inst has been received, and in answer thereto he wishes me to say to you that your letter is entirely satisfactory and that he admires a man more who can say no when an office is tendered him unasked for, than one who cannot accept no for an office asked for." ALS, *ibid.* See Matilda Gresham, *Life of Walter Quintin Gresham 1832–1895* (1919; reprinted, Freeport, N. Y., 1970), I, 346.

On March 11, USG nominated Sidney A. Stockdale (see *PUSG*, 13, 536) as collector of Internal Revenue, 1st District, La., in place of James B. Steedman; James F. Casey as collector of customs, New Orleans; and, on March 31, Blanc F. Joubert as assessor of Internal Revenue, 1st District, La. On Jan. 15, Steedman and Perry Fuller, New Orleans, had written to William G. Moore, secretary to President Andrew Johnson. "The personal and political friends of the President in New Orleans, desire to accomplish what they regard as of the highest importance to themselves, and, incidentally to the President himself. To succeed we feel that it is necessary to have your co-operation Maj. Fuller proposes to resign the office of Collector, if the President will nominate Col. James F. Casey—a brotherinlaw of Genl. Grant. Casey is a conservative, a gentleman, well qualified, satisfactory to the people here and friendly to the the friends of the President. Feeling as we do, a deep interest in the future of our friend, the President, we are anxious to place some of his friends in New Orleans in a situation to help him in the fight in Tennessee and this move, which would put Casey permanently in the position, during Grant's Administration, would aid, *materially*, the object we wish to accomplish. Now, what we want you to do, is to talk, confidentially, with the President, and if he will make the nomination suggested, telegraph either of us, 'Send the paper.' We will understand, and Maj. Fuller will forward his resignation" LS, DLC-Andrew Johnson. See *PUSG*, 15, 344.

To Alexander T. Stewart

Feb. 11, 1869

Your favor of yesterday . . . is rec'd. I am glad of your determination to accept. I feel the utmost confidence in your ability to manage the affairs of the Treasury Dept. It will be my endeavor to strengthen the hands of those I call about me in positions of high trust and not embarass them with assistants or subordinates in whom they have no confidence. I feel the sacrifice you must be making in accepting a place of so much responsibility and thank you for it.

Yours truly,
U. S. GRANT.

Robert F. Batchelder, Catalog 17 [1977], no. 1.

To Lt. Gen. William T. Sherman

———

Washington, D, C,
Feb.y 12th /69

DEAR GEN.

I am advised that I may regard the purchase of my house, to be presented to you, as being substantially effected. In a few days I will have the deed prepared to be delivered to you. In your absence I wrote to Mrs. Sherman about what would be necessary to keep house. I now write to say that you can have possession as soon after the 4th of March as I can get out, Say from the 10th to 12th. I wrote to you yesterday to come on here as soon as you can conveniently. This letter seems unnecessary therefore and I would not write it only that I want to relieve Mrs. Sherman of any suspense about the matter as soon as possible.

The house will have in it Carpets, bedsteads, Mattresses, chairs, Wardrobes, tables, side boards &c. But very little will be wanted to complete the furniture and that little probably will be articles which Mrs. Sherman would hardly like to leave in her present house, and therefore has. The house though in a block has a side lot sixty-seven feet front, extending through to the next street, so that no one can build on the other side of you or back of you.

Yours Truly
U. S. GRANT

GN. W. T. SHERMAN.

ALS, OClWHi. On Feb. 16, 1869, Ellen E. Sherman, St. Louis, telegraphed to USG. "General Sherman is south and is expected home on the 21st instant" Telegram received (at 11:20 A.M.), DNA, RG 107, Telegrams Collected (Bound). On Sunday, Feb. 21, Lt. Gen. William T. Sherman telegraphed to USG. "Arrived last night—have read your letters of eleventh (11) and twelfth (12), and if you wish I can easily be in Washington on Friday or Saturday.—Did not intend to start till Sunday next, but will act on your dispatch in answer to this.—" Copy, *ibid.*, RG 393, Military Div. of the Mo., Letters Sent. On the same day, USG telegraphed to Sherman. "Come as soon as convenient" Telegram received (at 2:20 P.M.), DLC-William T. Sherman. On Feb. 22, Sherman telegraphed to USG. "I will start for Washington Wednesday afternoon." Copy, DNA, RG 393, Military Div. of the Mo., Letters Sent.

On Feb. 21, Sherman, St. Louis, had written to U.S. Senator John Sherman of Ohio. "I got back from NO last night, and find all well at home. This is Sunday, and I have an immense accumulatn of letters, and have just written fully to Grant, Scott & others about that house. It seems to have been concluded, and as soon as I reach Washington I will make suitable acknowledgmts. Dan Butterfield claims to have been largely instrumental in it, but I should much prefer that he should not be the chief party. He did the same for Grant some four years ago, and Grant has left him at NewYork all this time on Recruiting duty, when he should have been with his Regimt on the Plains. I will not let such influence move me—I prefer that Scott, Aspinwall, Stewart, Williams &c should be the donors. . . ." ALS, DLC-William T. Sherman.

To William Elrod

Feb.y 12th /69

DEAR ELROD;

Inclosed I send you check for $500 00/100. You may purchase an additional team to work with. Get mares in preference to horses so that when they grow old, or when they can be partially spared from work, they can be set to breeding. You may rent Wrenshal Dents[1] property if you can get it partly put in clover.—Do you find that your sheep eat out the undergrowth? In the Spring & Summer you will have quite a number of lambs and old sheep to sell to keep you going.

Yours &c.

U. S. GRANT

P. S. Put a stamp on the inclosed check before it is cashed.

ALS, Dorothy Elrod, Marissa, Ill. See *PUSG*, 18, 263.

1. George Wrenshall Dent, USG's brother-in-law.

Speech

[*Feb. 13, 1869*]

I can promise the committee that it will be my endeavor to call around me as assistants such men only as I think will carry out the

principles which you have said the country desires to be successful—economy, retrenchment, faithful collection of the revenue,
and payment of the public debt. If I should fail in my first choice,
I shall not at any time hesitate to make a second, or even a third
trial, with the concurrence of the Senate, who have the confirming
power. I should just as soon remove one of my own appointees as
the appointee of my predecessor. It would make no difference.

There is one matter that I might properly speak of here, and
that is the selection of a Cabinet. I have always felt that it would
be rather indelicate to announce or even to consult with the gentlemen whom I thought of inviting to positions in my Cabinet before the official declaration of the result of the election was made,
although I presumed that there was no doubt about what that
declaration would be. But after consideration I have come to the
conclusion that there is not a man in the country who could be invited to a place in the Cabinet without the friends of some other
gentleman making an effort to secure the position: not that there
would be any objection to the party named, but that there would
be others whom they had set their hearts upon having in the place.
I can say that much from the great number of requests which come
to me, in writing and otherwise, for this particular person, or that
one, from different sets and delegations. If announced in advance,
efforts would be made to change my determination; and, therefore,
I have come to the conclusion not to announce whom I am going
to invite to seats in the Cabinet until I send in their names to the
Senate for confirmation. If I say anything to them about it, it will
certainly not be more than two or three days previous to sending in
their names. I think it well to make a public declaration of this to
the committee, so that my intentions may be known.

National Intelligencer, Feb. 15, 1869; variant text in *New York Herald,* Feb.
14, 1869. USG spoke to congressmen presenting a certificate of election to the
presidency. On Thursday, Feb. 11, 1869, U.S. Senator Oliver P. Morton of
Ind. wrote to USG. "I have been appointed by the Senate one of the Joint Committee to wait upon you and inform you of your election as President of the
United States To enable me to discharge conveniently to yourself, as well as
to my own Satisfaction, my share of this most pleasing duty, I desire to know
at what time it will be agreeable to you to receive the Committee: and would
most respectfully suggest, that, unless some other day would better suit your

Convenience, it be Saturday next in the forenoon at such place as you may be pleased to designate," LS, USG 3. On Feb. 13, USG delivered a brief formal response. "Gentlemen: Please notify the two houses of Congress of my acceptance of the important trust which you have just notified me of my election to; and say to them that it will be my endeavor that they, and those who elected them, shall ~~not~~ have no reason to regret their action." AD, James F. Wilson Papers, Fairfield Public Library, Fairfield, Iowa. Variant text in *CG*, 40–3, 1202, 1227.

On Feb. 9, U.S. Representatives James F. Wilson of Iowa and John V. L. Pruyn of N. Y. wrote to USG. "On the occasion of counting the votes for President & Vice President to take place to-morrow, we beg as tellers on the part of the House to say, that ten seats (and more if desired) in the gallery of the Hall on the right of the speakers chair will be reserved for the General of the Army & his family. As there will probably be a large attendance of Spectators, it has been suggested that it is desirable, that reserved seats be occupied by half-past twelve o'clock." LS, University of Iowa, Iowa City, Iowa.

To Maj. Gen. Philip H. Sheridan

Washington, D, C,
Feb.y 15th 1869.

MY DEAR GENERAL:

As soon after Sherman returns from New Orleans as you can make it convenient I wish you would come on to Washington. I will of course give you the Mil. Div. now commanded by Sherman. When you come on however we will talk about matters of assignment. I want to make a number of changes in assignments of army Officers, as well as of civil Officers, and want to consult with you about some of both classes, particularly in the south.

Expecting to see you so soon I will write no more now.

yours Truly
U. S. GRANT

GN. P. H. SHERIDAN.

ALS, DLC-Philip H. Sheridan.

On Feb. 23, 1869, 3:00 P.M., USG telegraphed to Lt. Gen. William T. Sherman. "I wish you would direct Gn. Sheridan to come to Washington as soon as convenient." ALS (telegram sent), DNA, RG 107, Telegrams Collected (Bound); telegram sent, *ibid.*; copy, DLC-USG, V, 56. On Feb. 24, Sherman, St. Louis, telegraphed to USG. "Dispatch of yesterday received and will have immediate attention, I have not heard from or of Gen Sheridan for near a month, I think he is now coming north across the country from the new camp near the wachita mountains, I start at 2.30 this afternoon" Telegrams received (2), DNA, RG 107, Telegrams Collected (Bound); copy, *ibid.*, RG 393, Military Div. of the Mo., Telegrams Sent.

To Alexander R. Rangabé

Washington, D C., Feby 15 *1869*

MY DEAR SIR

Your esteemed and flattering congratulatory letters of the 20th of January, accompanied by an equally complimentary note from your son, is received. I sincerely hope that my country may continue to deserve the high stand among the nations of the earth which you ascribe to it, and be regarded as the friend of those struggling for freedom, and self government, the world over.

For myself I can only strive to deserve the confidence which so great a nation has bestowed on me

Thanking you for the kind expressions contained in your letter, and hoping for your nation and for you individually, the greatest prosperity, I subscribe myself,

Very truly & respectfully
Your obt Servt
U S GRANT

HIS EXCELLENCY M. A. R. RANGABE
E. E & M. PLENIPOTENTIARY OF HIS MAJESTY THE KING
OF THE GREEKS

Copy, Munson-Williams-Proctor Institute, Utica, N. Y. On Jan. 20, 1869, Alexander R. Rangabé, Paris, wrote to USG. "Now that the complications in which Greece has been involved of late leave me some minutes of leisure, I profit by it to express to you by letter, as I have already done verbally through my son, my joy for your glorious and long foreseen election at the head of one of the greatest and the most powerful nations of the world. At the eve of your installation, I am urged by my feelings towards a country where I met with so great and so noble sympathies for mine, to congratulate you, General, for the new glory with which you are called upon to crown your former deeds, and still more to congratulate America for having chosen the man who, after having triumphally restored its unity, and put an end to the horrors of civil war, will lead its destinies in a way worthy of its fame and its increasing power. I can not doubt that under your dignified administration the American flag will not shrink from showing its glorious stars wherever there is a right to defend, an oppressed to be protected. Your election will, I am sure, open a new era to American politics, equal to the political preponderance your country must hitherto assume in the world. All nations eager for right and liberty rejoice heartily at it, and I am sure to express truly the feelings of my own countrymen in saying that it has been greeted in Greece with the utmost enthousiasm. Having had the honour and the advantage of your personal acquaintance, my own feelings are in perfect accordance with theirs; . . ." ALS, USG 3. On Feb. 7, Cleon R. Rangabé, Washington, D. C., wrote to USG. "I have the honor of transmitting herewith a letter from my father, who, having had the advantage of your personal acquaintance, is in a state of justly appreciating, & embodying in his expressions the sentiments cherished by the whole Greek nation for the great soldier to whom the beloved American Republic owes, & will owe so much of her glory. Not having had the good fortune of seeing you, when some time ago I called to beg of you to accept my congratulations together with those of my father, I seize this opportunity of doing so, . . ." ALS, *ibid.* See Adam Badeau, *Grant in Peace* (Hartford, 1887), p. 576.

To William H. Aspinwall

Washington, D. C., Feby 25 *1869*

W. H. ASPINWALL & GENTLEMEN OF COMMITTEE

GENTLEMEN

Your favor of the 19th inst is received. I had anticipated a portion of your request by having the deed to my residence in this city made out ready to be delivered to Gen. Sherman on his arrival. He will be here tomorrow. I can answer for Gen Sherman that your generosity to him will be ever gratefully remembered. I none the less appreciate it, as it is bestowed upon one of the most deserving, brave and generous soldiers of the republic.

The price named or any other proposed by the committee, is satisfactory to me. It is well understood by Gen Sherman: Any time the committee choose to call on me for the purpose named in their letter of the 19th inst. will be agreeable

With great respect
Your obt Servt
U S GRANT
General

Copies, OHi; DLC-William T. Sherman. William H. Aspinwall, born in 1807 in New York City into a prominent merchant family, derived large profits from the Pacific Mail Steamship Co. and the Pacific Railroad & Panama Steamship Co. A Union League Club founder, he served as an emissary to the British government to prevent construction of C.S.A. ironclads. On Feb. 26, 1869, Aspinwall, New York City, wrote to Lt. Gen. William T. Sherman. "I enclose a letter to Gen Grant which please read seal, & send to him if you approve of the purchase of the house & furniture for $65.000. From present appearances I think there will be subscribed beyond this, about $25000 for investment & I can only say the offering, both here & in Boston, has been most spontaneous. I also send, annexed a copy of Genl Grants letter, as I think its tenor will be gratifying to you. . . ." ALS, *ibid*.

To George H. Stuart

Washington, D, C,
Feb.y 26th /69

Geo. H. Stuart, Esq,
My Dear Friend;

You will no doubt see by the report which will be given of a conversation which I had yesterday with Mr. McClure,[1] of your city, that you are the person, in his judgement, who I have selected for a place in my Cabinet. I write to you now to say there was nothing in what I said to justify him coming to such a conclution except the warmth with which I defended you against the charge of obscurity, or lack of acquaintance in the state. The object in my writing now is to state that I have often thought of you, in that connection, and that there is no one who would be more agreeable to me than yourself. I had however come to the conclution that it would be unjust to you to ask you to leave your business to take a place of so much harrassment in your present health.

For this reason, and this alone, I set myself to thinking further of the gentlemen of Pa to find one who I thought would be satisfactory to me and to the country. I have committed myself to no one nor will I before the 3d or 4th of March. If therefore a place in my Cabinet would be agreeable to you and you will say so to me,

I will take the matter into concideration but without pledge. I will repeat however that whether you are in my Cabinet or not there will be none there who I will deem more suited, or esteem higher or prefer to have associated with me.

Yours Truly

U. S. GRANT

ALS, DLC-George H. Stuart. On Feb. 27, 1869, George H. Stuart, Philadelphia, wrote to USG. "Your letter of yesterday has quite overwhelmed me, I do not feel worthy of being thought of in connexion with such an honorable position as a seat in your Cabinet, I have always esteemed it a great privilige to enjoy your confidence, and friendship, and hope that I ever may continue to do so, This is my highest ambition, I am not now, and never have been an aspirant for any public office, nor do I feel myself capable of filling the position to which the papers for the past few days have assigned me, I hope therefore that you will proceed to fill your Cabinet, without the least embarresment arising from the use of my name by the public press, in the selection of loyal honest and capable men, who will serve their country rather than their own or the ends of the party, The public reports of the several interviews in regard to Cabinet appointments which have recently taken place, have raised you, if possible, still higher in the estimation of all good, and true men, and my constant prayer to God is that you may be thus guided to the end of your Administration, I expect to be in Washington Monday or Tuesday evening, and will take an early opportunity of calling at your residence, and if any suggestions of mine will aid you in selecting a member of your Cabinet from this State, I will be most happy to make them, I need hardly add that at all times it will afford me the greatest pleasure to do any thing in my power that will contribute to make your Administration as good, and wise, and successful as that of Washington, . . . *P. S* I have been so pressed for time during the day that I have only been able at a late hour to mail this but hope it will reach you on Monday morning." Copy, *ibid.* Stuart noted on the copy: *"Copy of Letter addressed to General U. S. Grant President Elect of the United States declining a place if tendered in his Cabinet—* IT WAS AFTERWARDS PLACED AT MY DISPOSAL IN PERSON BUT DECLINED."

On Feb. 26, James M. Scovel, New York City, had telegraphed to USG. "The minds and heart of the people are with you in such appointments as [tha]t of Geo H. Stuart" Telegram received (at 10:25 A.M.), DNA, RG 107, Telegrams Collected (Bound).

1. On Feb. 25, Alexander K. McClure spoke with USG to urge a cabinet appointment for former Governor Andrew G. Curtin of Pa. After USG intimated that Curtin would not enter the cabinet, McClure urged the appointment of "a representative Republican politician" from Pa. "The names of Geo. H. Stuart, Borie, Smith, and others have been spoken of, and I must say that not one of them would satisfy the Republican party of Pennsylvania." In reply, USG stated: "I cannot understand why any loyal man should object to the appointment of Mr. Stuart, . . . but I do not say that he is the man." *New York Tribune,* Feb. 26, 1869. See *New York Herald,* Feb. 26–28, 1869; *Washington Chronicle,* March 4, 1869.

Draft Inaugural Address

CITIZENS OF THE UNITED STATES:

Your suffrage having elivated me to the office of Presidnt I have, in conformity to the Constitution of our Country, taken the oath of office prescribed therein. I have taken this oath without a single mental reservation, with the determination to do, to the best of my ability, all it requires of me. [(T)he responsibilities of the position I feel, but accept them without fear] The office having come to me unsought I commence its duties untrammelled. I will bring to it a consciencious desire, and determination, to fill it to the best of my ability to the satisfactorilyion toof the greatest number of the people. On all leading questions agitating the public mind I will always express my views to Congress, and urge them according to my judgement, and where I think it advisable, interpose a veto to secure will exercise the constitutional privilege of interposing a veto to carry them, or to defeat measures which I oppose. But all laws will be faithfully eexcuted whether they meet my approval or not. I shall, always on all subjects, have a policy to recommend but none to enforce against the will of the people. Laws are to govern all alike, whether those opposed to as well as those who favor them. I know no method to secure the repeal of an [bad or] obnoxious, or bad law, so effective as its faithful execution.

Having just immerged from a great rebellion many questions will come before the country for settlement, in the next few years, which preceding administrations have never had to deal with. In meeting them it is desirable that they should be approached calmly, without prejudice, hate or sectional pride; remembering that the greatest good to the greatest number of people is the object to be attained. This requires security of person, and property, of the citizen [and to the for th] religious & political opinions of the citizen of the United States in any part of any state to which he may choose to go, so long as he breaks no Constitutional law our common country, without regard to local prejudice or sectional. All laws to secure this end will receive my best efforts for their enforcement,

A great debt has been contracted in securing to us, and our posterity, forever, a Union. ~~This debt~~ The payment of this, principle & interest, as well as the return to a specie basis, as soon as it can be accomplished without detriment to the debtor class, or to the country at large, must be provided for. The young men of the country, those who from their age must be its rulers twenty years hence, have a peculiar interest in maintaining ~~its financial integrity this~~ [the national honor]. A moments reflection as to our commanding influence among the other nations of the earth, in ~~our greatness~~ their day, if ~~we are~~ true to ~~ourselves~~ themselves should inspire a national ~~pride, and~~ pride. ~~and love of country, above all present advantages.~~ All ~~sections and all~~ geographical, political and religious divisions can join in this common sentiment. ~~and lay equal claim to their share of its blessings. To hasten this era good feeling, and mutual forbearance should be cultivated now between all sections.~~ Let it be understood that no repudiationst of one farthing of ~~this~~ our public debt can be trusted in public place, and it will go far towards strengthening a credit which ought to be ~~better than that of any nation on earth,~~ the best in the world, and will ultimately ~~to its replacement~~ enable us to replace it with ~~other~~ bonds bearing ~~a~~ less interest. Add to this a faithful collection of revenues, a strict accountability to the Treasury for every dollar collected, and the greatest practicable retrenchment in expenditures, in every department of Government. ~~then~~ [When we] compare the ~~compar~~ paying capacity of the Country now, with ten states still in poverty from the effects of war, but soon to immerge, I trust, into greater prosperity than ever before, with its paying capacity twenty-five years ago, and calculate what it may be expected to be twenty-five years hence, ~~and~~ who can doubt the feasibility of paying every dollar with ~~as much~~ more ease than we now pay for useless luxuries. Why: it looks as if providence had bestowed upon us a strong box, the precious mettals locked up in the

sterrile mountains of the ~~this country,~~ ~~but whi~~ far west, and which
we are now forging the key to unlock, to meet the very contingency
now upon us. ~~Let us be faithful to all our obligations.~~ Ultimately
it may be necessary to increase facilities to reach these riches; and
it may be necessary also that the general government should give
aid to secure ~~that end.~~ [access]. But that should be when a dollar of
obligation ~~sho~~ to pay secures precisely ~~at least,~~ the same sort of
dollar to use now and not before. Whilst the question of specie
payments is in abayence the ~~careful~~ prudent business man is careful about contracting debts ~~with a long time to secure and~~ payable
in the distant future. ~~t~~The nation should follow the same rule. How
the public debt is to be paid, or specie payments are to be resumed,
is not so important as that a plan should

It will be my endeavor to execute all laws, in good faith, to
collect all revenues assessed, have them properly accounted for,
and disbursed economically. I will, to the best of my ability appoint to office ~~only~~ those only who will carry out this design. ~~Many~~
~~unsuitable persons may, on the best of recommendations, get into~~
~~offices they are they are unworthy to fill. But no personal consider-~~
~~ations, either for the individual, or his endorsers~~

In regard to foreign policy; I would deal with nations as equitable laws compell individuals, of this nation, to deal with each
other. ~~The law abiding Citizen of the United States, native or~~
~~foreign born, should be protected by his flag wherever it floats~~ and
I would protect the law abiding citizen, whether of native or foreign birth, wherever the flag of our country floats. I would respect
every reasonable right of every nation and demand equal respect
for our rights. ~~These~~ This rule, in my judgement, ~~have~~ has not
been ~~disregarded~~ observed towards us by ~~some~~ all nations of late.
In such ~~cases~~ it is for us to say what reparation shall be made

Unequal suffrage in the different states is a question which will
likely agitate the public mind so long as it ~~continues.~~ remains unsettled. I would suggest on this subject to the concideration of
Congress and the people that it be taken out of politics by making

suffrage ~~equal~~ uniform, all over the United States so far as it applies to, legislative & executive offices.

Asking patient forbearance one to another throughout the land, and a determined effort on the part of every Citizen to do his ~~or her~~ part towards cementing a happy Union, and asking the prayrs of the christian in behalf of this consumation, I leave you.

ADf, NNP. Bracketed insertions in the hand of Adam Badeau, who noted on the docket: "Original autograph draft of Gen Grants *first* inaugural with my corrections as afterwards accepted by him".

Inaugural Address

[*March 4, 1869*]

CITIZENS OF THE UNITED STATES:

Your suffrage having elivated me to the office of President of the United States I have, in conformity ~~to~~ with the Constitution of our country, taken the oath of office prescribed therein. I have taken this oath without mental reservation, with the determination to do, to the best of my ability, all that it requires of me. The responsibilities of the position I feel, but accept them without fear. The office ~~haves~~ come to me unsought, I commence its duties untramelled. I ~~will~~ bring to it a conscienetious desire, and determination, to fill it, to the best of my ability, to the satisfaction of the ~~greatest number~~ of people. On all leading questions agitating the public mind I will always express my views to Congress, and urge them according to my judgement, and when I think it advisable, will exercise the constitutional privilege of interposing a veto to defeat measures which I oppose. But all laws will be faithfully executed whether they meet my approval or not. I shall, on all subjects, have a policy to recommend, but none to enforce against the will of the people. Laws are to govern all alike, those opposed to as well as those who favor them. I know no method to secure the repeal of bad or obnoxious laws so effective as their ~~faithful~~ stringent execution.

The country ~~H~~having just ~~immerged~~ emerged from a great rebellion many questions will come before ~~the country~~ it for settlement, in the next four years, which preceding Administrations have never had to deal with. In meeting ~~them~~ these it is desirable that they should be approached calmly, without prejudice, hate or sectional ~~pride animosity~~ pride; remembering that the greatest good to the greatest number is the object to be attained. This requires security of person, property, and ~~to the~~ for religious and political opinions ~~of the citizens of the United~~ States in every part of our common country, without regard to local prejudice. All laws to secure ~~this end~~ these ends will receive my best efforts for their enforcement.

A great debt has been contracted in securing to us, and our posterity, the Union. The payment of this *principle* and *interest*, as well as the return to a specie basis, as soon as it can be accomplished without material detriment to the debtor class, or to the country at large, must be provided for. To protect the national honor every dollar of Government indebtedness should be paid in gold unless otherwise expressly stipulated in the contract. Let it be understood that no ~~repudiationest~~ repudiator of one farthing of our public debt will be trusted in public place ~~and~~ and it will go far towards strengthening a credit which ought to be the best in the world, and will ultimately enable us to replace ~~it~~ the debt with bonds bearing less interest than we now pay. ~~And t~~To this should be added a faithful collection of [the] revenue, a strict accountability to the Treasury for every dollar collected, and the greatest practicable retrenchment in expenditure, in every department of government.

When we compare the paying capacity of the country now, with ten states still in poverty from the effects of war, but soon to ~~immerge~~ emerge, I trust, into greater prosperity than ever before, with its paying capacity twenty five years ago, and calculate what it probably will be ~~as long~~ twenty-five years hence, who can doubt the feasibility of paying every dollar then with more ease than we now pay for useless luxuries. Why; it looks as if providence had bestowed upon us a strong box,—the precious metals locked up in the sterile mountains of the far West, and—which we are now forging the key to unlock, to meet the very contingency that is now upon us.

Ultimately it may be necessary to increase the facilities to reach these riches; and it may be necessary also that the general government should give its aid to secure this access. But that should only be when a dollar of obligation to pay secures precisely the same sort of dollar to use now and not before. Whilst the question of specie payments is in abeyance the prudent business man is careful about contracting debts payable in the distant future. The nation should follow the same rule. A prostrate commerce is to be rebuilt and all industries encouraged

The young men of the country, those who from their age must be its rulers twenty-five years hence, have a peculiar interest in maintaining the national honor. A moments reflection as to what will be our commanding influence among the nations of the earth, in their day, if they are only true to themselves, should inspire a them with national pride. All divisions, geographical, political and religious can join in this common sentiment.

How the public debt is to be paid, or specie payments resumed, is not so important as that a plan should be adopted, and acquiesced in. A united determination to do is worth more than divided counsils upon the method of doing. Legislation on this subject may not be necessary now, nor even advisable, but the it will be when the civil law is more fully restored in all parts of the country, and trade resumes its wanted channel.

It will be my endeavor to execute all laws in good faith, to collect all revenues assessed, and to have them properly accounted for, and economically disbursed. I will, to the best of my ability, appoint to office those only who will carry out this design.

In regard to foreign policy I would, deal with nations as equitable law requires individuals to deal with each other, and I would protect the law abiding citizen, whether native or of foreign birth, where ever his rights are jeopardised or the flag of our country floats. I would respect the rights of all nations demanding equal respect for our own; but if others depart from this rule, in their dealings with us, we may be compelled to follow their precedet.

The proper treatment of the original occupants of the land, the Indian, is one deserving of careful study. I will favor any course towards them which tends to their civilization, christianization and ultimate citizenship.

The question of suffrage is one which is likely to agitate the public so long as a portion of the citizens of the nation are excluded from its privileges in any state. It seems to me very desirable that the question should be settled now, and I entertain the hope and express the desire that the it may be by the ratifyication of the fifteenth article of amendment to the Constitution.

In conclusion I ask patient forbearance one towards another throughout the land, and a determined effort on the part of every citizen to do his share towards cementing a happy union, and I ask the prayers of the nation to Almighty God in behalf of this consummation.

AD (bracketed material not in USG's hand), DLC-USG, III. Accompanied by two similar notes, one of which states: "Original Inaugural Address, in his own Writing of General U. S. Grant given by him to his eldest Son, Colonel Frederick D. Grant (Later General) U. S. Army at the White House Washington, D. C. 1875"

On March 4, 1869, after delivering his Inaugural Address, USG returned to his home and sent Adam Badeau to the White House to receive messages. On that day, Badeau wrote to USG. "Mr. George H. Stuart is one of a committee, the others being the Chief-Justice and Senator Frelinghuysen, who desire to present you in the name of some religious society with a Bible. They will wait on you whenever you say—except that the Chief-Justice must be at the Supreme Court, and Mr. Stuart leaves here to-morrow night. If you will send word to me what time will suit you, I will let Mr. Stuart know. Mr. Stuart proposes to-morrow morning before ten o'clock, or if the court does not meet till eleven, before that time." Adam Badeau, *Grant in Peace* (Hartford, 1887), p. 160. USG penciled his reply on the letter. "To-morrow before 10 A. M. at my house, or between 10 A. M. and 3 P. M. at the Executive Mansion." *Ibid.* On March 5, Chief Justice Salmon P. Chase presented to Julia Dent Grant the Bible used at the inauguration ceremony and also wrote her a letter concerning the matter. *Washington Chronicle*, March 16, 1870; Robert B. Warden, *An Account of the Private Life and Public Services of Salmon P. Chase* (Cincinnati, 1874), p. 718.

On March 8, 1869, Gen. William T. Sherman issued Gen. Orders No. 12, naming six men to his personal staff, including Frederick T. Dent and Horace Porter, who, by agreement with USG, became private secretaries to the president. ADf, DNA, RG 94, Letters Received, 131A 1869; *Memoirs of Gen. W. T. Sherman* (4th ed., New York, 1891), II, 441. On March 31, Special Orders No. 75 stated that "By direction of the Secretary of War, Brevet Brigadier General *O. E. Babcock*, Major Corps of Engineers will report for duty to the President. This order to date from the 4th instant." Copies, Babcock Papers, ICN; DLC-USG, II, 1, 4. Horace Porter, "Executive Mansion," wrote a note dated March 4. "Bvt. Brigadier General O. E. Babcock reported in accordance with the provisions of the within Order and is assigned to duty as Secretary to the President" NS, Babcock Papers, ICN. On March 15, Porter wrote to Robert M. Douglas. "You are hereby appointed Assistant Private Secretary to the President to date from the 15th March 1869" Copies, DLC-USG, II, 1, 4. Son of the late U.S. Senator Stephen A. Douglas, Robert had been private secretary to Governor William W. Holden of N. C. *New York Herald*, March 22, 1869. On Sept. 16, 1868, Douglas had spoken at Raleigh in support of the Republican Party and USG. *Ibid.*, Sept. 25, 1868.

To Senate

Washington, March [4], 1869.

TO THE SENATE OF THE UNITED STATES.

I nominate the officer herein named for appointment in the Army of the United States.

To be General of the Army of the United States.

Lieutenant General *William T. Sherman*, United States Army, March 4, 1869.

U. S. GRANT

DS, DNA, RG 46, Anson G. McCook Collection. On March 4, 1869, USG also nominated for promotion Philip H. Sheridan to lt. gen., John M. Schofield to maj. gen., and Christopher C. Augur to brig. gen. All dated only "March," *ibid.*, indicating that USG probably prepared them before assuming office. These promotions depended upon USG vacating his military appointment, an act accomplished without the formality of resignation.

On March 5, Secretary of War John M. Schofield issued orders. "By direction of the President, General William T. Sherman will assume command of the Army of the United States. The chiefs of staff corps, departments, and bureaus will report to and act under the immediate orders of the general commanding the army. Any official business which by law or regulation requires the action of the President or Secretary of War will be submitted by the General of the Army to the Secretary of War, and in general all orders from the President or Secretary of War to any portion of the army, line or staff, will be transmitted through the General of the Army." *Memoirs of Gen. W. T. Sherman* (4th ed., New York, 1891), II, 441. On March 6, Bvt. Maj. Gen. Edward D. Townsend wrote to Gen. William T. Sherman. "The President directed me (before the Inauguration) to have the enclosed orde[r] ready to issue the 5th inst. He yesterday changed its form somewhat and now directs that it be shown you before it goes out—I await your instructions—I congratulate you heartily on your confirmation as General, and hope you will very soon be out again," ALS, DLC-William T. Sherman.

On March 26, Secretary of War John A. Rawlins wrote. "By direction of the President the order of the Secretary of War, dated War Department 'March 5. 1869' & published in G. O. No 11, 'Hd Qrs of the Army, Adj Gen's Office, dated March 8, 1869, except so much as directs Genl W. T. Sherman to 'assume command of the Army of the U. S.' is hereby rescinded All official business wh. by law or regulations requires the action of the President or Secy of War will be submitted by the Chiefs of Staff Corps, Departments & Bureaux to the Secy of War All orders & instructions relating to Military operations issued by the President or Secy of War will be issued thro' the Genl of the Army." Copy (issued as General Orders No. 28, March 27), DNA, RG 107, Letters Received, W379 1869. On March 26, Sherman wrote to USG. "Please do not revoke your order of March 5 without further reflection. It would put me in a most unpleasant dilema because the Army and country would infer your want of confidence. The order was yours and had been long contemplated. There has not been a particle of confusion or difficulty in its execution. The matter of discharges asked for by Genl Butler and Senator Williams do not fall under that order at all but under the law requiring all orders of the President and Secretary of War to go through the General of the Army. Neither of these papers contained a reason for the discharge asked for, and I could not order the discharge, and if such requests should be granted for political reasons, or from official courtesy, all the Secretary of War has to do is to endorse his order, which I at once execute as *his* order. General Rawlins is not in his office yet, but I will see him the moment he comes & explain. If you want to define more clearly what class of business the Secretary should have exclusive control of, it is easily done, not by the repeal of Genl Orders No 11 but by making an Executive order saying what class of business should go direct to the Secretary of War from heads of Bureaus. I a[m] perfectly willing Genl Rawlins shoul[d] pick out his own business only leaving me a clear field of comman[d.]" Copies (2), DLC-William T. Sherman.

On March 29, Monday, Sherman wrote to Maj. Gen. John M. Schofield. "*Private* . . . You will notice that Grant has gone back on that order of yours about making all the heads of Bureaux subordinate to the General of the Army. There was no conflict, no case, and no cause for the change here. I was at the Presidents on Thursday night, and just as I was taking my leave, he said, 'I guess we have got to revoke that order of Schofields'—I enquired which one and he explained. I told him that he himself had dictated the order—that he had been of that mind for a long time, and that he had so told me at Chicago,—&c &c. The next morning Friday I wrote him a note begging him to delay a while till he could think further, but after Cabinet meeting I went up to Rawlins Room to talk about some discharges he had ordered, on the application of Butler and Senator Williams, without one reason or Cause assigned, where he shew me the draft of the order which I read carefully, and asked the modification of one or two words, but he said it had been passed on in Cabinet & must stand.

We then had a general discussion of the effect, which I insisted would ultimately defeat me in the Universal army wish that evry branch of the Army should have one head, and one Common duty & interest: but he insisted the change was forced on them by political considerations, that Butler, Logan &c contended your order took from the Secretary duties and powers devolved on him by Law, and that it changed the Civil nature of the Departmt of War. I said I would cheerfully conform to any decision they arrived at, but that I thought a wrong had been done me by not thinking of that beforehand. I will not change my General orders no 12 of March 8, but hold evry officer and soldier of the Army subject to my Command, and sustain the Dept Commanders in the exercise of their corresponding powers. In the end however political influence may and probably will resume the control and command of the army, and put the Staff Departmts over us, or make them independent of us. Generals Grant & Rawlins both say they will favor the adoption by Congress of the Articles of War, and Regulations compiled by Sheridan, Augur and myself, which they contend will put all parties on their proper legal footing. With the Political influence predominant—I hardly look upon that as possible, especially as after but a few days the President himself has backed down from his own orders, based on long experience. I would like you to show this to Sheridan and keep it for the future, as my version of this matter, but to be used only for your own deliberation and use." ALS, CSmH. See letter to Gen. William T. Sherman, July 31, 1870.

To Senate

TO THE SENATE OF THE UNITED STATES

I nominate the persons herein named for the following appointments, to fill vacancies

Elihu B. Washburne, of Ill. to be Secretary of State.

Alex. T. Stewart,[1] of N. Y. to be Secretary of the Treasury.

Adolph E. Borie,[2] of Pa to be Secretary of the Navy.

John A. J. Creswell,[3] of Md. to be Post Master General.

E. BR. Hoar,[4] of Mass. to be Attorney General.

Jacob D. Cox,[5] of Ohio to be Secretary of the Interior.

U. S. GRANT

WASHINGTON D. C.

MARCH 5TH 1869.

ADS, DNA, RG 46, Anson G. McCook Collection. Only the names, states, and signature are in USG's hand. On March 6, 1869, Horace Porter notified members of the cabinet to meet at noon; all were asst. secretaries except Secretary of

War John M. Schofield, held over from the preceding administration. Copies, DLC-USG, II, 1, 4.

1. On March 5, James P. Morris, Washington, D. C., telegraphed to USG. "In your nomination of A. T. Stewart for Sec'y of Treas'y no better selection could be made—the nation should rejoice" Telegram received (at 4:20 P.M.), DNA, RG 107, Telegrams Collected (Bound). See Message to Senate, March 9, 1869.

2. Born in 1809, Adolph E. Borie graduated from the University of Pennsylvania (1825) and was a leading Philadelphia merchant, active in the Union League, who lacked discernible qualifications for management of the Navy Dept. On March 5, Borie wrote to USG declining the cabinet post for family reasons. William Evarts Benjamin, Catalogue No. 42, March, 1892, p. 4. On March 6, USG telegraphed to Borie, Philadelphia. "I take pleasure in announcing to you your confirmation as Secretary of the Navy. I hope to receive notice of your acceptance of the same." Copy, DLC-USG, II, 5. On the same day, George H. Stuart, Philadelphia, twice telegraphed to USG. "Have seen our friend and have some hope," "He adheres to his letter but with real grief at his inability only through want of health, If you desire it and telegraph, both will visit you on Monday" Telegrams received (at noon and 1:25 P.M.), DNA, RG 107, Telegrams Collected (Bound). On the same day, USG telegraphed to Stuart. "Please come to Washington with Mr Borie." Telegram received, DLC-George H. Stuart. On March 6, Stuart again telegraphed to USG. "Will leave with our friend at noon Monday, He wrote last evening" Telegram received (at 3:00 P.M.), DNA, RG 107, Telegrams Collected (Bound). On March 8, Stuart, Wilmington, Del., telegraphed to USG. "On noon train. If thought advisable make no changes until you see us this Evening" Telegram received (at 2:20 P.M.), *ibid.* On March 9, Vice Admiral David D. Porter, Annapolis, telegraphed to USG. "I will be in Washn at one (1) oclock" Telegram received (at 12:20 P.M.), *ibid.*

3. John A. J. Creswell, born in 1828 in Md., graduated from Dickinson College (1848), practiced law in Md., supported the Union in 1861 and was elected U.S. Representative (1863–65) and U.S. Senator (1865–67). See *PUSG*, 18, 560.

4. Ebenezer R. Hoar, born in 1816 in Concord, Mass., graduated from Harvard College (1835) and Harvard Law School (1839), was an active Whig later appointed associate justice, Mass. Supreme Court (1859). On March 6, 1869, USG telegraphed to Hoar, Concord. "I have the pleasure to announce your confirmation as Att'y General of the U. States. May I hope for your acceptance." Copy, DLC-USG, II, 5.

5. Practicing law in Cincinnati when nominated, Jacob D. Cox had resigned as maj. gen. on Jan. 1, 1866, and served as Union party governor of Ohio (1866–68). See *PUSG*, 10, 213; *ibid.*, 18, 107, 118, 125. On March 6, 1869, USG telegraphed to Cox, Cincinnati. "I take pleasure in announcing to you that you have been confirmed as Secretary of the Interior and hope to receive notice of your acceptance of the office." Copy, DLC-USG, II, 5. A variant text dated March 5 is in typescript, Cox Papers, Oberlin College, Oberlin, Ohio. On March 6, Cox telegraphed to USG. "I accept with real diffidence the post

you have assigned me to and will try to report for duty on Tuesday morning next" Telegram received (at 1:40 P.M.), DNA, RG 107, Telegrams Collected (Bound).

To Senate

Washington D. C.
March 6th 1869

TO THE SENATE OF THE UNITED STATES.

Since the nomination and confirmation of Alex. T. Stewart to the office of Sect'y. of the Treasury I find that by the 8th Sec. of the Act of Congress, Approved Sept. 2. 1789 it is provided as follows, to wit:

"And be it further enacted, That no person appointed to any office instituted by this act shall directly or indirectly be concerned or interested in carrying on the business of trade or commerce, or be owner in whole or in part of any sea vessel, or purchase by himself, or another in trust for him, any public lands or other public property, or be concerned in the purchase or disposal of any public securities of any State, or of the United States, or take or apply to his own use any emolument or gain for negotiating or transacting any business in the said department other that what shall be allowed by law; and if any person shall offend against any of the prohibitions of this act, he shall be deemed guilty of a high misdemeanor and forfeit to the United States the penalty of three thousand dollars, and shall upon conviction be removed from office and forever thereafter incapable of holding any office under the United States: Provided, That if any other person than a public prosecutor shall give information of any such offence, upon which a prosecution and conviction shall be had, one half the aforesaid penalty of three thousand dollars when recovered, shall be for the use of the person giving such information."

In view of these provisions and the fact that Mr. Stewart has been unanimously confirmed by the Senate, I would ask that he be exempted by joint resolution of the two houses of Congress from the operations of the same.

U. S. GRANT

Copy, DNA, RG 130, Messages to Congress. *SED*, 41-1-1. On March 9, 1869, Alexander T. Stewart wrote to USG. "Appreciating the high honor conferred by your nomination, and the unanimous confirmation by the Senate of myself to the office of Secretary of the Treasury, I regret that circumstances beyond our control compel me to decline. Could the difficulties presented by the provisions of the act of 1789, which, in organizing the Department of the Treasury, prohibit the Secretary from being 'directly or indirectly concerned or interested in carrying on the business of trade or commerce,' be overcome by any reasonable sacrifice personal to myself, I would willingly make it. I would promptly transfer to the hands of gentlemen in whom the public have felt confidence, every interest in the gains and profits that could possibly accrue to myself in the business of my house during my official term, to be applied to such public charities as their judgment should dictate—and have proposed and sought by the execution of appropriate instruments to accomplish that end; but serious differences of opinion have been expressed as to whether that course would satisfy the requirements of the law. Although I will not hesitate to make this appropriation, provided it would enable me to accept the office, and thus unite my efforts with your own and those of other members of your Cabinet in restoring economy, honesty, and strict frugality in the administration of the Government, and lift as rapidly as practicable for the people the great burdens of taxation, debt, and extravagance resting upon them; yet, the business relations of my firm, in its connections with others largely interested in their continuance, are such that they cannot be severed summarily; nor can my interest in it be wholly and absolutely disposed of without producing fresh embarrassment and loss to those with whom I have been so long connected. I cannot consent to enter upon the administration of laws by any act or course that may be construed into a disregard or violation of law; and while, therefore, I regret that the plan proposed is deemed inadequate to relieve me from legal and, as it seems to me, technical disabilities, I yield to the better judgment of others, rather than seem to be willing to accept the position in disrespect of law. In finally renewing the declination which was tendered at the outset of these objections, I repeat to you, Mr. President, my thanks for the honor done me in offering this high position, and assure you that you will have my earnest efforts to sustain your administration in carrying out the wise and salutary measures indicated by you on entering upon your office." *National Intelligencer*, March 10, 1869. Also on March 9, USG wrote to the Senate. "~~On~~I have the honor to request to be permitted to withdraw from the senate of the United States my message of the 6th inst, requesting the passage of a joint resolution of the two houses of Congress to relieve the sec. of the Treas. from the disabilities imposed by Sec. 8th of the Act. of Congress approved sept. 2d 1~~8~~789." AD, Mr. and Mrs. Philip D. Sang, River Forest, Ill.; DS, DNA, RG 46, Annual Messages. *SED*, 41-1-3.

On March 8, E. L. Carson, Cincinnati, telegraphed to USG. "The people have thought the appointment of Mr Stewart as Secretary meant business They are greatly disappointed that he is ineligible. They hope however that some business man of similar views and ability will be appointed, You was right in asking of Congress an enabling act the law is obsolete and not applicable to the present times. If the holding of government or stat securities is to disqualify as under this law from holding office in the Treasury Department who in the name of Heaven is to fill them? Jeff Davis, Breckenridge & Genl Forrest are undoubtedly qualified" Telegram received (on March 9, 9:30 A.M.), DNA, RG 107, Telegrams Collected (Bound). On March 11, George L. Collins, Providence, R. I., telegraphed to USG. "I suggest Stewart trustee his business profits to go towards paying national debt—" Telegram received (at 2:10 P.M.), ibid.

On March 8, James O'Connor, Pittsburgh, telegraphed to USG. "Permit me to most respectfully suggest General F. E. Spinners name for Secretary of Treasury. His honesty ability and experience are of national reputation and his appointment would be approved of by all." Telegram received (at 7:50 P.M.), ibid. On March 10, John Thompson, New York City, telegraphed to USG. "If not too late I beg to suggest H. H van Dyck for the Treasury. He is preeminently able Experienced Loyal and Honest" Telegram received (at 11:40 A.M.), ibid. On March 11, Aaron Ericsson, Rochester, N. Y., telegraphed to USG. "I think John E. Williams of New York would be a competent man for Secretary of the Treasury" Telegram received (at 6:45 P.M.), ibid. On the same day, USG had nominated George S. Boutwell as secretary of the Treasury. Also on March 11, George H. Stuart, Philadelphia, telegraphed to USG. "Appointments give great satisfaction Gold closes thirty one half (31 ½). Yesterday thirty two (32). The country will stand by you." Telegram received (at 6:15 P.M.), ibid.

To Hamilton Fish

Washington, D. C. March 10th *1869.*

MY DEAR GOVERNOR:

It has been my intention for some months back to offer you the position of Minister &c. to England when the time came. Now however, owing to my inability to secure the great services of Mr. A. T. Stewart in the Treasury Dept. I will have to make another selection of Cabinet officer from New York. I have thought it might not be unpleasant for you to accept the portfolio of the State Dept. ~~and~~ If not will you do me the favor to answer by telegraph to-morrow to the effect that you will be in Washington soon.

With great respect
your obt. svt.
U. S. GRANT

HON. H. FISH

ALS, ICarbS. On March 11, 1869, Hamilton Fish, New York City, telegraphed and wrote to USG. "I cannot. I Will write by mail this afternoon and explain why" Telegram received (at 12:45 P.M.), DNA, RG 107, Telegrams Collected (Bound). "Your letter reached me at a late hour this mornig—I immediately sent an answer by telegraph, & hope that it reached you in time for any action you may desire to take to day—. I feel most profoundly grateful for the tender of the high position you have been pleased to offer—Nothing would give me greater pleasure than to be associated with your Administration, and to give the best of my humble abilities to aid in advancing the high objects which are the aim of your thoughts & your hopes & to which the Country looks hopefully and confidently for the inauguration of a new era in the government— An era of honesty—economy, & fidelity But there are pressing private & family considerations which oppose a removal to, or a residence in Washington—My wife's health forbids it in the present emergency; nor can I see the prospect that it will allow it within the time named by Mr Washburn—Therefore I was obliged to decline the honor you so very kindly placed before me—Be assured my Dear General, that no time will efface my grateful appreciation of this very unexpected, not to say very undeserved, mark of your confidence and friendship." ALS, MiU-C.

On March 10, Secretary of State Elihu B. Washburne wrote to Fish. "You will receive from the President a letter desiring that you should come into this Department and it is my earnest wish that you will accept his invitation to become a member of his cabinet. I know you have exceptional qualifications for the position, and I believe your appointment will be most favorably received by the country. I accepted the position with the understanding that I should be relieved at as early a day as practicable, as the state of my health renders it impossible for me to discharge the duties of the position for any length of time. If you accept, as I sincerely trust you will, I shall to-morrow hand in my resignation to the President to take effect when you shall be qualified and ready to enter upon the duties of the office. I should like to leave the office on Saturday the 20th inst. if that time would be agreeable to you, as it will be to the President. The President expects to hear of your determination in this regard by telegraph to-morrow. I am anxious that your nomination shall go in at the same time as that of the Secretary of the Treasury." ALS (facsimile), USGA.

To Elihu B. Washburne

Washington, D. C. March 11th *1869,*

HON. E. B. WASHBURNE,
SEC. OF STATE,
DEAR SIR:

Your resignation of the Office of Sec. of State, with reasons for the same, is rec'd. In accepting it I do so with regret that your health will not permit you to continue in the office, or in some Cabinet position. Our personal relations have been such from the breaking out of the rebellion to the present day, and your support of me individually, and of the Army and its cause such that no other idea presented itself stronger to my mind, on the first news of my election to the Presidency, than that I should continue to have your advice and assistance. In parting with you therefore I do it with assurances of continued confidence in your ability, zeal and friendship and with the hope that you may soon be relieved from the physical disabilities under which you have labored for the last few years.

> Very respectfully
> your obt. svt.
> U. S. GRANT

ALS, IHi. On March 10, 1869, Secretary of State Elihu B. Washburne wrote to USG. "When you did me the honor to confer upon me the appointment of Secretary of State, I felt constrained to state to you that my health would prevent me from holding the position for any considerable length of time. I am already admonished that a proper discharge of the duties of the office would involve more labor and responsibility than I am willing to undertake, in justice to the public interest and myself. If convenient and agreeable to you I would be glad to have you name my successor at as early a moment as you may deem practicable, and you will please consider this as my resignation, to take effect as soon as my successor is qualified and ready to enter upon the discharge of the duties of the office. I need not add here, Mr. President, how gratefully I appreciate the distinguished honor you conferred upon me by inviting me to become one of your constitutional advisers. Had circumstances permitted it I should have been pleased to have been associated with you officially, and to have aided you, as far as in my power, in carrying out your views in the administration of the Government upon the principles of honesty, retrenchment, economy, public faith and equal and exact justice to all." ALS, OFH.

To Hamilton Fish

Washington D C. March 11 1869

DEAR GOVERNOR

Not receiving your dispatch until about 1.50 p m I sent your— appointment of Sec. of State to the Senate. Immediately on its receipt however I sent to the Senate to withdraw but was too late. Let me beg of you now to avoid another break, to accept for the present and should you not like the position you can withdraw after the adjournment of Congress. I send this by the hands of Gen Babcock who will more fully explain.

yrs truly

U. S. GRANT

HON H FISH

Copies, DLC-Hamilton Fish; DLC-USG, II, 1, 4. On March 11, 1869, Secretary of State Elihu B. Washburne telegraphed to Hamilton Fish. "Your name went in before President received your despatch. He has written you. Do not decline 'til his letter reaches you." Copy, *ibid.*, II, 5. On March 12, Fish wrote to USG. "Genl Babcock has handed me your letter of yesterday—I did not think that my decision of yesterday could be changed—My Wife's health will not allow her to accompany me; & probably will not permit her to come on during the Spring— and her experience & my own assure us that she neither should or could remain there in Washington during the Summer or Autumn I have the most unaffected mistrust of my competence for the high position to which you call me—for I have a slight knowledge of the extent & the importance of its varied & compli- cated duties—& I instinctively shrink from them—I sincerely hoped that my telegram of yesterday (left at the office *before* noon) would have reached you in time for some other result than the presentation of my name to the Senate— & that you should secure the services of some one capable of more efficient aid & counsel; & whose connection with the government would be of longer dura- tion than I can expect to I appreciate the embarassments which circumstances have thrown around the completion of your Cabinet and the earnestness of your desire to avoid another break, & the importance of having the government fully organized, have led me to say to Genl Babcock that I will go to Washington at the earliest time I can—probably on Monday Eveng I cannot contemplate the probability of my Wife's taking up a residence there—or of the removal of my family—& must therefore reserve the permission held out in your letter that I can withdraw after the adjournment of Congress—As to the contemplated temporary duration of my continuance in office, I shall be silent until I know to what extent, if any, you may think proper to make it known" ALS, USG 3. On March 13, Orville E. Babcock wrote to Fish. "I called this morning at the Ebbitt House and secured a parlor & bed room for you, as you wished; (to be ready Tuesday morning.) The President was much pleased on the receipt of your letter as he will assure you on your arrival. Please give my kindest re- gards to Mrs Fish and the other members of your family." ALS, DLC-Hamilton Fish.

Speech

[*March 16, 1869*]

Mr. GARCIA: I welcome you as the diplomatic representative of the Argentine Republic in this country. It shall be my endeavor, during your mission, to reciprocate the kind sentiments which you express on behalf of your Government, and its desire to strengthen those relations of friendship and commerce which now unite both nations. I notice that your letter of credence is signed by your predecessor, now the Chief Magistrate[1] of the Argentine Republic. The personal and official character which he maintained while here warrants the assumption that in selecting you as the Minister of that Republic, he was actuated by his usual discretion, and had no reason to apprehend that your career would not justify his choice. A similar confidence is entertained by me.

New York Times, March 18, 1869. On March 16, 1869, Manuel R. Garcia, Argentine minister, had presented his credentials to USG. "Mr. PRESIDENT: I have the distinguished honor of placing in your hands the credentials which accredit me as the Envoy Extraordinary and Minister Plenipotentiary of the Argentine Republic in the United States. I beg to assure you, in the name of my Government, of the esteem and admiration which it, as well as my whole country, feel toward the great American Republic, and of the lively desire which animates it to have drawn closer and closer the relations of friendship and commerce which unite both nations on the basis of republican institutions, of which we have taken yours as a model. I flatter myself with the hope that during my stay in the United States I shall be so fortunate as to merit your good-will and confidence, in order to enable me to duly fill the honorable charge which the Argentine Government has intrusted to me, and that I may fill up the measure of any personal deficiency by the samed valued consideration which was so freely accorded in this country to my distinguished predecessor." *Ibid.*

1. Domingo F. Sarmiento, born in 1811, a journalist and educator, served as minister to the U.S. (1865–68) prior to his election as president of Argentina. See letter to Domingo F. Sarmiento, April 15, 1874. On Nov. 29, 1868, Bvt. Brig. Gen. Adam Badeau had written to Sarmiento. "I have lately read in the newspapers that the Argentine Republic proposes offering the command of its armies to one of the successful generals of the United States in the recent war. It would of course be impertinent in me to make any suggestion in a matter of so much importance; but if there should be any foundation for the report alluded to, I am sure you will be glad to know the opinions of General Grant. I have several times heard him say that he hoped in case such a plan should be carried out, that the Argentine Republic would secure the services of a soldier of real talent and not any of the adventurers who would be most likely to be

pressed upon its attention. If there should be any probability like that I mention, the advice of some very prominent American soldier would doubtless assist materially in furthering the objects of the Argentine Republic. Trusting that this note may not be deemed officious, and making my warmest congratulations, my dear Sir and President, upon your accession to the chief magistracy of your country, I am, with the best wishes for the success of your administration and the prosperity of your people, . . ." Adam Badeau, *Grant in Peace* (Hartford, Conn., 1887), pp. 572–73. On Feb. 12, 1869, Sarmiento, Buenos Aires, wrote to Badeau. "I have received with pleasure your letter dated 29th November last, in reference to the rumor spared by the european press, that my government intends to profit the talents and practice of an american general to put an end to the Paraguayan war. Perhapps it may have had origen in my own personal opinion, presumed, in this case, for the predelecction I have espresed in others respects for the american institutions. Whatever may be my own wishes, now, after the taking of Angostura and the flight of Lopez to the mountains almost inaccessible of the interior, neither talent nor militar expirience is wanted to pursue a wild beast, who has sacrified the resigned and abyect *Guarani* people, educated for the pasive obedience by the famous Jesuitics missions. After having thrown to death 150.000 soldiers, and shot his brothers, the bishop, generals and secretaries of State, and carried the women and wounded from his hospitals, and hundred of children ten years age, leaving á desert behind him, and entering to the mountains to wait an end from time and eventuality What would á general do with an enemie that has murdered all his prissoners, and desolate his own country? The *Wasp* left yesterday for Paraguay, and á flag of truce escorted by argentine forces will reach Lopez' Camp, procuring general Mac Maham, to hand him letters from the U. S. and to get sure if he is alive and free, what is doubted by many as town months have elapsed without knowing nothing from him. Our army is not an obstacle for this Comunications. I Can't prevent myself to express you the surprise caused amongst us by the singular position General Mac. Maham has assumed, being the only foreign Minister that has joined Lopez; unknoing perhaps, (what is possible) the horrible crimes commited by the monstrous whose good relations he entertains. I am glad of having this occation to congratulate, by your conduit to Genl Grant, whom I had the honour to acknowledge, for his exaltation to the Government, considering this fact as a guarantee for the prosperity of U. S., and of friend and good relations with my own Country." ALS, DLC-Adam Badeau.

Speech

[March 19, 1869]

MR. ROBERTS: I am happy to receive you as the Envoy Extraordinary and Minister Plenipotentiary of Spain in the United States. The recent events in that country, to which you advert, have excited, and will continue to maintain a lively interest here, hoping, as we do, that they may ultimately lead to an increase in the welfare and happiness of the people of Spain. The disposition which you express to exert yourself during your mission, to the end that those friendly relations which have always existed between the two countries may be strengthened, shall be cordially reciprocated by me.

National Intelligencer, March 20, 1869. USG spoke after Mauricio Lopez Roberts. "Mr. PRESIDENT: I have the honor to present to you the letter of credence by which his Excellency the President of the Provisional Government, charged with the executive power, accredits me as Envoy Extraordinary and Minister Plenipotentiary of Spain to the Republic of the United States of America. Spain, carrying out a revolution which has destroyed her ancient institutions, which were opposed to the development of a policy desired by the nation, awaits from the national sovereignty, represented by several Constituent Cortes, the form of Government which is to rule over her future destinies, and cherishes the confidence that the new order of things which is springing up will obtain the sympathies of the United States and of all liberal people, as she obtained them on the news of her glorious revolution. On my part, upon the lot falling to me to discharge the honorable mission to this Republic which my Government has confided to me, I shall endeavor, by all the means in my reach, to maintain and strengthen the friendly relations which have always existed between Spain and the United States." *Ibid.* Variant texts in *New York Herald* and *New York Tribune*, March 20, 1869.

On April 2, David D. Porter, act. secretary of the navy, wrote to USG. "I have the honor to submit herewith a copy of a despatch, dated the 26th ultimo, received from Rear Admiral H. K. Hoff, commanding the North Atlantic Squadron, with which he sends an extract from a communication addressed to him by the U. S. Consul General at Havana, in regard to an expedition which the Spanish Government learns is fitting out at New Orleans to land in Cuba." LS, DNA, RG 60, Letters from the President. The enclosures are *ibid.* On April 21, Porter wrote to USG. "I have the honor to submit herewith for your information a copy of a despatch, dated the 13th instant, received from Rear Admiral H. K. Hoff, commanding the North Atlantic Squadron, relative to his inquiries concerning reported expeditions fitting out at New Orleans to land in Cuba." Copy, *ibid.*, RG 45, Letters Sent to the President. On May 8, Porter transmitted to USG additional dispatches from Hoff. Copy, *ibid.* For dispatches from Hoff dated April 30 and May 1, see *ibid.*, RG 59, Miscellaneous Letters. On March 20, Secretary of State Hamilton Fish had recorded in his diary. "Mr Roberts, Spanish Minister, called. . . . He then produced three memoranda—I. a statement that on satisfactory evidence, it was represented to him that filibustering expeditions were fitting out in N O Mobile & other southern Ports, against Cuba, & in the interest of the insurgents— . . . I assured him that this Govt would take immediate steps to enforce the Neutrality laws—& accordingly communicated the substance of his report, to the Atty Genl the Secr of the Navy, & the Secr of the Treasury, requesting them to take measures to prevent any violation of the Neutrality laws— . . ." DLC-Hamilton Fish. See *New York Herald*, April 8–10, 19, 1869; *HED*, 41-2-1, part 1, p. 35.

On March 18, "An Englishman," Havana, had written to USG. "It has been said here, that the sugar merchants of New York are subscribing 2 millions of dollars to fit out vessels to intercept succor to the Cubans from the U States. The sugar merchants of New York, like those of this place are principally Germans & Scotch and of mean principles; led by their interests and leanings to everything European, are our great enemies. Also there are some rash copperhead Americans, men who would sell their birthright for a mess of potage amongst them. If but to ruin such mean scoundrel, I would like to see every sugar estate burnt down. But like or not like, if the Cubans continue the fight until they are free, there will not be many estates left, when the end comes Spaniards will destroy Cuban estates & Cubans will destroy Spanish estates until all is consumed. I am in business and this state of things is prejudicial to me, but, fromor principle sake and for the sake of the Cubans, I would rather all were destroyed than the wicked Spaniards should remain masters of the place There is only one hope to keep the place from destruction and that is to get some aid from out side, to give a rush to the revolution. The Spaniards are wind bags. So said Wellington In the philibuster expedition of 1867 the 400 americans at las Poyas in this island shot down the picked soldiers of the Spanish army like rabbits. Speaking of that, the 50 men shot in cold blood at that time deserve to be avenged, but you Americans have lost the enthusiasm of your English forefathers Oh that the States were still Colonies that we might send all the Spaniards to Spain! There is a righteousness in doing such things. I am now 53 but still I am not indifferent to the world, and I pray to God to aid the poor Cubans, against the bad Spaniard. They will be avenged if not here in Spain, for the Spaniard is not born yet to be free. He is too unjust, too brutal & ignorant and whether with the name of republican or royalist he is a tyrant and only fit for a tyrannical Goverment. Such are the men the Cubans are so desirous to be free from and may God in his mercy Curse and destroy all their enemies, particularly foreigners from whom they should expect sympathy, but instead receive opposition." AL (probably in the hand of Thomas W. Wilson), USG 3.

On March 27, Wilson, Havana, wrote to USG. "I enclose in this an official document and a translation of it. Bloody enough, Heaven Knows! In addressing you, I am urged solely by a Christian impulse. A native of England, in soliciting for Cuba the friendship of the U States, I cannot be accused of lust of territory, nor in advocating the cause of the Cubans, can I be accused of unchristian principles The Cubans naturally desire their freedom from Spain, and I see no reason why they should not be free. Cuba is a colony, all colonies, sooner or later, become separated from the parent state. The provinces of the Peninsula of Spain, are held as the States of the U States, as it were, by the ties of matrimony, in which there can be no divorce. The relation of Cuba to Spain, is that of a son of age, wishing to be free from a cruel and dissolute father. Spain as the mother of Cuba, you may picture as a horrid ugly hag, with greedy glaring eyes, hanging on the breast of Cuba, with her voracious mouth drawing not only milk, but blood from her unhappy daughter, who with looks of aversion cast her head away My English blood revolts at the idea of Cuba, at your door, American Cuba, being in thraldom to Spain. I would give up Canada and all that England holds in America to see Cuba free from Spain and incorporated in the U States My interests are damaged by the contest, but if the Cubans gain their independence, I shall not regret that, not even should the island be ruined, as it may be, in the contest I fear that the Spaniards will commit terrible excesses in their rage of despair, and that no one will be safe. They are not like other peoples and as Blackwood's magazine says in it last Novr number, they can barely be considered as belonging to the great European family! If Spain were very powerful, she would be the most aggressive and unjust of all nations. As it is, in her extreme ignorance, she considers herself the first of civilization. That all she does is good and just, and that everything contrary to her views is bad Besides being the most unjust, Spain is the most bloody and cruel of all nations, and believe me Sir all Spaniard are alike in sentiment; the only difference is, that some use the Jesuit's cloak more than others. In Mr Roberts, the new minster from Spain, you will find a smooth tongue and smooth manner, but at bottom is the real Spaniard. Be their Govt Republican or what it may, be it will be bad and tyrannic until—the race is changed. During the struggle between the North & South, Spain and the Spaniards here were bitter enemies to the United States, and furnished all the arms and other assistance she could to the enemies of the American Union, and Cuba retained in her hands, would remain a menace to the United States and a harbor of refuge to its enemies at any time—" ALS, *ibid*. A newspaper clipping in Spanish and Wilson's translation of Domingo Dulce's March 24 order authorizing Spanish forces to seize ships carrying aid to Cuban insurrectionists and to shoot persons captured on such vessels are *ibid*. See *New York Times*, May 21, 1880.

To Moses H. Grinnell

Washington, D. C., March 19, 1869.

DEAR SIR: This will introduce you to Colonel G. K. Leet,[1] who served under me from early in the war to the present day—from the fall of Vicksburg forward, as a staff officer. He is a business man of unquestioned integrity. His experience before the war fits him for business of almost any kind. He now proposes to resign from the Army to engage in private life, and I cheerfully commend him as possessing all the qualities necessary to inspire confidence.

Yours, truly,

U. S. GRANT.

M. H. GRINNELL

SRC, 42-2-227, I, 700. On March 8, 1869, Moses H. Grinnell, New York City, telegraphed to USG. "I received and at once yesterday answered Mr Washburne's letter by telegraph. It is scarcely necessary for me to tell you how grati-

fied I should be to received the appointment of Collector"   Telegram received
(at 1:00 P.M.), DNA, RG 107, Telegrams Collected (Bound). On the same
day, Marshall O. Roberts, New York City, telegraphed to USG. "Allow me to
Express to you my Earnest hope and desire that you will confer on mr Grinnell
the Collectorship of this Port. No man is more [wor]thy Capable and Efficient
in all respects & no other appointment for that Position will give Equal satisfaction to your friends here—" Telegram received (at 2:30 P.M.), *ibid.* On March
24, USG nominated Grinnell as collector of customs, New York City. See letter
to Roscoe Conkling, April 12, 1870.

1. George K. Leet, born in Pa. in 1836, a railroad clerk in Chicago when
the Civil War began, enlisted as a private in the Chicago Mercantile Battery. In
July, 1863, he joined USG's staff as capt. Promoted to maj. in 1866, Leet continued to serve on USG's staff. See *PUSG*, 10, 159–61, 220–21; *ibid.*, 16, 126;
ibid., 17, 565–66; *SRC*, 41-3-380, pp. 91–99; *SRC*, 42-2-227, I, 699–761; *ibid.*,
II, 110–12. On May 4, 1870, Horace Porter wrote to Leet. "I do not like to be
the bearer of bad news to you, but I think I ought to tell you what the President
said when he returned from New York. He remarked that he had heard so much
talk about corruption in custom-houses, jobs, the influences brought to bear in
getting positions, &c., that he would never appoint any one who had been
around him to a position in a custom-house, no matter what his qualifications.
In speaking about you he said (I don't know who told him of the offer) that
you ought to accept Don Cameron's proposition, for, though he believes you as
pure as any one, yet he would never consent to have you go to a custom-house.
He said the attacks would be constant, and injure both you and him. He feels
just as I have always felt about such matters. You can now judge of the situation and act accordingly. Yours, in great haste, . . . He told me I could say
this to you." *Ibid.*, I, X.

To Gen. William T. Sherman

Washington, D. C.
March 31st 1869

GENL. W. T. SHERMAN
COM'D'G. U. S. ARMY.
GENERAL.

General Stoneman being relieved from the command of the
First District I would suggest the reïnstatement of Governor
Wells[1] to the Governorship of the state of Virginia.

Very Respectfully
Your obdt. svt.
U. S. GRANT.

Copy, CtY. On March 27, 1869, Maj. Samuel F. Chalfin, Richmond, telegraphed to USG. "I have just received the following order H. H. WELLES GOVERNOR 'Head' Quarters First Military District Richmond Virginia March 27th 1869 Special Orders 280 Sixty two 62 Extract—All the powers conferred upon the Chief Executive Offices of the state of Virginia by its constitution and laws, and heretofore exercised by the Provisional Governor thereof under the Reconstruction Laws of Congress are hereby devolved upon the Commanding Officer of the First Military District and will until further orders by him be assumed and performed. By Command of Brevet Major General Stoneman" Telegram received (at 8:20 P.M.), DNA, RG 107, Letters Received from Bureaus; (press) *ibid.*, Telegrams Collected (Bound).

On March 29, U.S. Representative Benjamin F. Butler of Mass. wrote to Secretary of War John A. Rawlins. "This note will be handed to you by Mr. Wardwell, Mr. Humphreys and Bvt Col. Merrill. Col. Merrill was Depot Commissary at my headquarters through the campaign at Richmond. Mr Wardwell is a gentleman whom you met at my headquarters, having been driven from Richmond for taking care of Union prisoners and aiding the loyal cause. These gentlemen are a committee of Union men who come up here to protest against the action of Gen. Stoneman. As I had the honor to say to you a day or two since when I conversed with you, there is no relief for the Republicans of Virginia except the immediate removal of Stoneman. If he has got a lieutenant even, next in rank, it will be better than to have him there. If you can spare these gentlemen a few minutes to give them a hearing, I think you will be convinced, as I am from many sources that Stoneman ought to be immediately removed without waiting for Canby's arrival, the delay of which may be more or less prolonged." LS, Dartmouth College, Hanover, N. H. Rawlins forwarded this letter to USG. AES, *ibid.*

On March 31, Horace Porter wrote to Rawlins. "The President directs that Major Genl. Geo. Stoneman commanding the First Military District be relieved by a telegraphic order, and the next officer in rank instructed to assume command until the arrival of Gen'l. Canby." LS, DNA, RG 94, Letters Received, 219P 1869. On the same day, Bvt. Maj. Gen. Edward D. Townsend issued Special Orders No. 75. "By direction of the President of the United States Bvt. Major General A. S. Webb, U. S. Army is assigned to command the First Military District, according to his brevet of Major General until relieved the arrival of Brevet Major General Canby to relieve him. He will accordingly repair to Richmond Va. without delay." ADfS, *ibid.* See Richard Lowe, *Republicans and Reconstruction in Virginia, 1856–70* (Charlottesville, 1991), p. 169.

1. Henry H. Wells, born in 1823, raised and educated in Mich., discharged from the army as bvt. brig. gen., practiced law in Richmond until April 16, 1868, when he was appointed provisional governor of Va. See *PUSG*, 14, 82; *ibid.*, 18, 226–27.

To Mary Grant Cramer

WASHINGTON, D. C., March 31, 1869.

MY DEAR SISTER: I received a note from you a few days since which ought to have been answered at once. The fact is, however, that I scarcely get one moment alone. Office-seeking in this country, I regret to say, is getting to be one of the industries of the age. It gives me no peace. With the adjournment of Congress, however, I hope it will be better.

Father and Jennie left here last Thursday after a visit of several weeks. You heard, no doubt, that father got a severe fall on inauguration day. He is not much improved, and I fear never will entirely recover. It is not probable that his injury will shorten his life, but will probably make him lame for life. He had but little peace while here. Office-seekers were after him from breakfast till bedtime. . . .

The family are all well and join me in love.

Yours truly,

U. S. GRANT.

Printed with ellipses in M. J. Cramer, *Ulysses S. Grant: Conversations and Unpublished Letters* (New York and Cincinnati, 1897), pp. 108–9.

On Nov. 12, 1868, Michael J. Cramer, Leipzig, wrote to USG. "In compliance with the request of the merchants, the diplomatic and Consular officers, and the professors of the University of Leipzig, I herewith tender your their hearty congratulations upon your election as President of the United States. They see in it an auspicious omen for the speedy settlement of our national difficulties and the restoration of permanent peace and tranquillity. Though far away from the passions and turmoil of the contending parties, they have all along looked upon your election as an accomplished fact. From the time you became known to the world as a successful general, they have watched your career with increasing interest. They see in you a man, whose modesty and patriotism is only equalled by your talents, decision and firmness of character, devotion to the cause of right and truth, and Knowledge of men. They see in your election a guarantee that our national unity and greatness will be preserved, our finances and commerce improved, and our credit at home and abroad maintained. It is needless to say that both Mary and myself also heartily congratulate you and your family upon your election to the Presidency. Aside from any personal consideration, we look upon your election as inaugurating a new and glorious era in the political history of our country. The wily, intriguing, self-seeking, ambitious politicians will be check-mated by your sagacity and prudence; & political corruption and dishonesty will be banished by your honesty,

stern sense of right, and firmness of character. We see you building up a government which speaks only in wisdom; a guiding and supporting arm for our
nation; a power free from the curse of personal ambition, and inspired through
all its members by mutual love and assured hope. We see you inaugurating a
new system of diplomacy by appointing *competent* men, who shall speak the
truth in sincerity, regulate all our international affairs and relations with Christian courtesy and in the interests of our nation as well of mankind, and who by
their intelligence and nobility of character shall reflect credit upon our land and
honor upon the society, in which they may move. We see under your guidance
a highly organized society, finding its unity in the inspiration of freedom, and
working through each of its earnest, faithful members, for the growth of all.
We see that society take under its protection that infantile black race thrown
upon their hands by Providence, and educating them for the fullest future enjoyment of liberty and civilization. We see public faith firmly built in each individual conscience and rigidly upheld. We see a moral sentiment, intense and
overwhelming, filling every public vehicle of thought, and every private hearth
and heart, with indignation against the man who loves power better than his
country, or who suggests a public immorality or commits a fraud. And we see
the Christian Religion grasping our nation's heart, as it never grasped a community before; deepening daily the foundations of their freedom in their convictions of right, and swelling daily, from all tongues, a national song of praise,
acceptable before the eternal throne. All this, and more, we sincerely believe,
will be the consequences of your elevation to the Presidential chair. The mission
of our nation is a high one, it is that we should be the vanguard and standard-
bearers of advancing civilization; the foremost file of time's explorers, marching
ever into a prouder and more glorious future, and laying the topstone, with
shouting, of the grand temple of liberty in the light of universal freedom's
dawn.—May High Wisdom lead you and us all to the final accomplishment of
this our high and glorious mission! Mary joins me in sending love to you & your
family. We would be pleased to receive a few lines from you. We are in the
enjoyment of good health." ALS, USG 3.

On March 8, 1869, D. W. Clark, Washington, D. C., wrote to USG. "By
special request [o]f parties interested, I hand this petition to you. The signers
are for the most part men of character, position & influence. It is a *strong*
petition; & so far as I know the signatures were freely given." ANS, DNA, RG
59, Letters of Application and Recommendation. Written on a petition. "The
undersigned *Bankers, Merchants & Business Men of Cincinnati Ohio*, would
respectfully petition Your Excellency to appoint *Michael J. Cramer U. S. Minister
resident at Berne Switzerland. . . ."* DS, *ibid.* On Sept. 9, 1870, USG appointed
Cramer as minister to Denmark "until the end of the next session of the Senate
of the United States, and no longer; subject to the conditions prescribed by
law." D, *ibid.*, General Records. On Dec. 6, USG nominated Cramer as minister
to Denmark in place of George H. Yeaman.

On Dec. 29, William B. Lawrence, Newport, R. I., wrote to Secretary of
State Hamilton Fish. "I learn from the Washington letters in the New York
papers that opposition is made on personal grounds to the confirmation of Mr
Cramer's nomination as Minister to Copenhagen. Were the objections of a political or partisan character I should not trouble you with this communication,
being quite aware that my opinion, in such a case, would have little influence

with those whose votes must control the Senate's decision. . . . Having heard, while I was at Berlin, that Mr Cramer was spoken of in connection with the legation at Berne, I was only restrained, by an apprehension that an application from one so little known to him could be deemed intrusive, from addressing the President on the subject: I could not, howr, refrain in a letter to Mr Cramer, from expressing my hope that the President would not be prevented, by considerations arising from their near family connection, from doing for Mr Cramer what his services and talents justified. I cannot conclude, without adding that I had the pleasure of seeing Mr Cramer at his own home, where I found his accomplished wife in her studio, availing herself of the opportunities, which the *chefs d'oeuvre* of German galleries afforded, for cultivating her taste for the fine arts." ALS, *ibid.*, Letters of Application and Recommendation. On Feb. 4, 1871, Fish wrote in his diary. "Saw Chandler, who wants information about Cramers nomination to Denmark—give him what he asks—In the Evening dine at Delanos—Cramer has been confirmed—Chandler & Carpenter are understood to have made very severe speeches—Chandler tells me that after the speeches, the papers from the Dept. which we had sent to Harlan, were read, & the opposition collapsed—he says Sumner 'Cut and ran'—that he said 'he would ~~not~~ consider a vote—of the Senate taking the nomination out of the hands of his Committee a censure of the Committee,' & then took his hat & left the Senate Chamber—A vote was then taken on discharging the Comm. from the consideration of the nomination, & agreed to without a division—the nomination was then confirmed without a dissenting voice" DLC-Hamilton Fish.

On May 10, 1869, Yeaman, Copenhagen, had written to USG. "Private . . . I beg you grant me a moment of your crowded time. I once would have deemed such a letter as this improper, but I discover that others do not hesitate to push their affairs, both in person and by their friends; and the diplomatic servants of other governments are in the habit of freely making known their wishes to their governments—I have in past explained to Mr Fish how my unexpected recall is a terrible inconvenience to me. I now learn it is worse than I then thought, as my own home is disposed of until October of next year (1870). This is neither your fault or mine, but the error of my friends in their perfect assurance that I would remain here as long as I wished—I did not seek for this place, or any other in the diplomatic service—I accepted it when we are all the friends of Mr Johnson and Mr Seward—I was afterwards, in nearly all things, opposed to Mr Johnson's home policy—I have most earnestly and laboriously sought to discharge all my duties, both official and social—with Danes and Americans—I have broken up my professional business by coming here—In trying to make and keep the Legation respectable I have expended several thousand dollars more than I have received from the Government. I have on my hands a large, sickly and helpless family, in no condition for much moving about. I have been constantly and unreservedly in favor of General Grants election to the Presidency, as Mr McPherson and others whom I need not name can most distinctly show— I feel mortified by my recall—I have suggested to Mr Fish that if I could remain here a few months with leave of absence to visit the United States it would assist me some; but further reflection convinces me that for so short a time, I had better remain with my family and all go back together. I have no doubt General Andrews would have been willing to take some other Legation, where the personal and political hardships of the change would not have been so great; and you and he can best judge whether it is now too late to make such a suggestion of any value— . . ." ALS, *ibid*. Papers urging Yeaman's retention as minister are in DNA, RG 59, Letters of Application and Recommendation.

To Congress

TO THE SENATE AND HOUSE OF REPRESENTATIVES:

While I am aware that the time in which Congress proposes now to remain in session is very brief, and that it is its desire, as far as is consistent with the public interest, to avoid entering upon the general business of legislation, there is one subject which concerns so deeply the welfare of the country that I deem it my duty to bring it before you. I have no doubt that you will concur with me in the opinion that it is desirable to restore the States which were engaged in the rebellion to their proper relations to the Government and the country, at as early a period as the people of those States shall be found willing to become peaceful and orderly communities, and to adopt and maintain such constitutions and laws as will effectually secure the civil and political rights of all persons within their borders. The authority of the United States, which has been vindicated and established by its military power, must undoubtedly be asserted for the absolute protection of all its citizens in the full enjoyment of the freedom and security which is the object of a republican government. But, whenever the people of a rebellious State are ready to enter in good faith upon the accomplishment of this object, in entire conformity with the constitutional authority of Congress, it is certainly desirable that all causes of irritation should be removed as promptly as possible, that a more perfect union may be established and the country be restored to peace and prosperity.

The convention of the people of Virginia which met in Richmond on Tuesday, December 3, 1867, framed a constitution for that State, which was adopted by the convention on the 17th of April, 1868, and I desire respectfully to call the attention of Con-

gress to the propriety of providing by law for the holding of an
election in that State at some time during the months of May and
June next, under the direction of the military commander of the
district, at which the question of the adoption of that constitution
shall be submitted to the citizens of the State.[1] And if this should
seem desirable, I would recommend that a separate vote be taken
upon such parts as may be thought expedient.[2] And that at the
same time and under the same authority, there shall be an election
for the officers provided under such constitution; and that the constitution, or such parts thereof as shall have been adopted by the
people, be submitted to Congress on the first Monday of December
next for its consideration, so that if the same is then approved, the
necessary steps will have been taken for the restoration of the State
of Virginia to its proper relations to the Union. I am led to make
this recommendation from the confident hope and belief that the
people of that State are now ready to co-operate with the National
Government in bringing it again into such relations to the Union
as it ought, as soon as possible to establish and maintain, and to
give to all its people those equal rights under the law which were
asserted in the Declaration of Independence in the words of one of
the most illustrious of its sons.

I desire also to ask the consideration of Congress to the question, whether there is not just ground for believing that the constitution framed by a convention of the people of Mississippi for
that State and once rejected,[3] might not be again submitted to the
people of that State in like manner and with the probability of the
same result.[4]

U. S. GRANT

WASHINGTON D. C.,
APRIL 7TH 1869.

DS, DNA, RG 46, Annual Messages. On April 5, 1869, Secretary of State
Hamilton Fish wrote in his diary. "Summoned by the Prsdt. & found Boutwell.
Cox came in afterward—Prsdt said he thought of sending a Message to Congress
frecommending an act or joint resolution authorizing the submission to the people of Virginia of the Constitution adopted by their convention, & to take separate
votes upon certain parts   He read the proposed Message (the same I suppose
which Jud[ge] Hoar told me last Evening he had written at the request of the

President). I questioned whether there was time for Congress to act upon it at this Session—Boutwell concurred in this opinion & then we examined the provisions proposed to be separately submitted—B—thought one of them (relating to division into Counties & Public Education) ought not to be separately submitted—as they wd vote down every thing they could—that they were getting well (materially) at present, &c—Cox concurred—the Prsdt concluded he wd not send the message—" DLC-Hamilton Fish.

On April 7, Daniel C. De Jarnette and Littleton Q. Washington, Washington, D. C., wrote to USG. "Congress having passed a bill, in accordance with your recent Message, to authorize the submission to the voters of Virginia of the Constitution framed by the Convention which met at Richmond on the 3d day of December 1867; we respectfully desire to make some suggestions upon the subject, not claiming any delegated authority to speak for others but sincerely believing that our views are in accordance those of a large majority of the people of the state. We hope it will be agreable to the President before making his order to allow opportunity for some representative citizens of the State to be heard, and our representations are made only because such persons are not here now to speak for the people. . . . We believe that a separate vote on these clauses would largely promote quiet, public order, good feeling among the people, acquiescence in the reconstruction policy, and an instantaneous augmentation of values. We believe each of these three provisions above described would be rejected by majorities ranging from 50 to 100000 votes and that the remainder of the Constitution would be adopted, so that by the 15th June or 1st July next a Va state government may be in full operation. One question alone remains on which we beg to submit a suggestion. It is—'shall these provisions be submitted separately, or shall the counter plan be adopted of a vote on these provisions 'in connection with the other portions of said Constitution.' The first plan is the original idea of the President. It is simple and easy. It is open to the comprehension of plain and unlettered men. Every citizen would know what his vote would come to. If he wanted to have a large number of other citizens disfranchised and ninety nine hundredths of them disqualified for office, he could vote for it. If not, he could vote in the negative. So too, if he wanted an expensive, cumbrous county and local organization, the effect of which would be to make certain counties entirely subject to negro government, he could so vote, or he could vote against it so as to leave it to the legislature to pass suitable laws for such local and county government. Finally, if he was willing to let the legislature act on the subject of a stay law as the people might desire, all he has to do is to vote against this clause in the Constitution. If the other plan be pursued, it will be very hard to put into operation. It will be almost impossible to frame a military order for the election on this plan such as the people can understand, unless the determination be arrived at to allow the people to vote only on one separate clause. Any attempt to submit more than one provision in this way would lead to endless confusion, and whatever may have been the motives of those who offered it in the House of Representatives, we believe it originated with those who saw that by following the plan of the President, the people of Virginia would have an opportunity to shake off at the polls the cruel and despotic features which are embodied in the Underwood Constitution. By following the first plan of a separate vote on each provision, the President may think fit thus to submit, the State may be organized harmoniously at an early day and general confidence restored. The people of Virginia, we think, will be much gratified to learn the large discretion and control vested by this law in the President, not fearing but that he will use his powers with kindness and consideration so as to secure to them as good a State government as is practicable under all the circumstances of the case." LS, USG 3.

About this time, Gilbert C. Walker wrote to USG. "One of the chief objects to be attained in the Election in Virginia is a full free and honest expression of the popular will, not only upon the Constitution as a whole but also upon the *three* obnoxious clauses which may be submitted to a separate vote. The form and manner of submission should be so plain and clear that all may readily comprehend it and that confusion & fraud may be avoided. Some will desire to vote for the Constitution as a whole & others against it. Some (& probably a large majority) will desire to vote for the remainder of the Constitution after the obnoxious clauses are are stricken out & again others may desire to vote against those clauses & against the remainder of the Constitution—while others will vote against the obnoxious clauses and not vote at all upon the ballance of the Constitution And the important question is how to submit the Constitution so as to allow all these different phases of opinion an opportunity of expression. Of all the plans suggested there seems to be but one which will accomplish the object desired viz—Let the Constitution be submitted as follows 1st 'For or *against* the obnoxious clauses' (naming all three of them)   2nd 'For or *against* the *remainder* of the Constitution' This form of submission will allow every voter in the state to fully express his opinions without any liability to become confused or mistaken. . . ." ALS, *ibid.*

On April 20, Washington wrote to USG. "I have the honor to submit for your consideration a letter which has been addressed to me in respect to the mode of submitting the Virginia Constitution by Judge Meredith and Hon R. T. Daniel, as the most appropriate and direct mode of furthering the objects of the signers. These appear to me fair, reasonable, and of great public utility. The request therein contained is strongly recommended by the high personal character of the authors, hardly any persons in Virginia possessing in a greater degree the respect and confidence of the people. Judge Meredith has long filled a judicial position to the entire satisfaction of the community and Mr. Daniel is one of the most conspicuous members of the Richmond bar. The former has earnestly favored the restoration of the State according to the plan of the President's recent message; the latter though heretofore opposed to it, I am led to believe, is prepared now to unite in the same plan. I enclose also a petition from certain citizens of Danville signed irrespective of party, and a letter from Col. Sutherlin on the same subject which have been forwarded to me for presentation." ALS, *ibid.* On April 19, Raleigh T. Daniel and John A. Meredith, Richmond, had written to Washington. "We beg leave to address you on a subject of much importance to the people of this State, and to enlist your active exertions in our behalf—We know you feel the deepest interest in the subject—It relates to the form in which the issues are to be presented, that are to be decided at the approaching election—The Wells' faction are seeking to obtain an advatage by having the issues presented in an involved & confused form, with as many issues as it is possible to make—We wish them presented in their simplest form— in the mode intimated by Genl Grant himself—with a view to avoid confusion and to obtain a clear expression of the popular Will— . . ." LS, *ibid.*

On the same day, William T. Sutherlin, Danville, Va., had written to USG.

"I have the honor to transmit herewith, a memorial of a portion of the Citizens of this place, which you can rely on as reflecting the sentiments of the great body of the people in this part of the State, As a people we feel grateful to you for your late message to Congress, and earnestly appeal to you, to divide the vote on the Constitution, so. that we may have a fair chance to adopt it, with its worst features expurgated, *We really desire re-construction*, we are tired of living outs side the Union, and only ask that we may a have a Constitution that we can live under, Give us the opportunity to secure this, and we will be ever grateful." ALS, *ibid.* On April 17, Powhatan Bouldin *et al.*, Danville, had petitioned USG. "We, the undersigned, voters & citizens of the State of Virginia, desire to return you our thanks for the Message sent to the Senate and House of Representatives on the 7th inst. recommending the passage of a law for an election in this State. It is our earnest wish that civil law may be restored, on the plan provided in the Reconstruction Acts of Congress, and that Virginia may assume her proper relations to the Union. To avoid confusion at the polls, we would respectfully ask, if consonant with the views of the Executive, that the provisions of the Constitution, on which a separate vote may be ordered, shall each be submitted *alone* or *separately*, and not in connection with the other portions of said Constitution. . . ." DS (91 signatures), *ibid.*

On May 10, Daniel wrote to Washington. "It is with deep concern I announce that I have been wholly unable to raise a committee to be in Washington tomorrow. I have spent most of the time since the convention adjourned in trying to get up a body of men to represent us in Washington—all in vain. I have had twenty promises all of which have failed me; not as I believe from any aversion to the duty, but because every body is absorbed in his own affairs,—*fighting* the wolf from the door. In this emergency what to do? I shall have to impose it on You and any other true man, who may be near You to represent the state in what is necessary to be done. Could the subject be deferred (which I suppose is impracticable) we might still hope to get up a committee; faint hope however, from our experience). The best thing I can think of is for You to present the views, of ourselves (Yourself, myself and Judge M) to the President for consideration, which You may safely represent to be the prevailing views in Virginia—insist on a *one days election*—particularly—and impress on him, that the mass is in favor of reconstruction on his plan. Perhaps it will not do, to put the clause about negro eligibility to juries on the separate schedule, as that might make the negroes go against the separate provisions. But I think the interdict against a stay law, ought to be separated, for if it remains in the Constitution it may enlist (I think will) enlist a large white vote against the Constitution How would it do, to refer the form of submitting the Constitution and the clauses to be separately voted on, to Genl Canby to be reported on to the President? I throw it out for consideration. Excuse this scrawl. I am in the midst of a heavy trial before Judge Chase and am writing while the trial is going on. Do not fail to write me, immediately the results of tomorrow. If Mr Dejarnette is in Washington I know it will give him pleasure to act with You. I am of opinion that it will be best to defer the Election. You know the Convention would not Endorse Walker, because it was thought the People were not ripe for it; but it was thought that in time public sentiment would drift that way. *Let it have time to drift.* Every day I think obliterates differences and asperities and strengthens the action of the Convention" ALS, *ibid.*

On April 13, George K. Fox, Jr., Leesburg, Va., had written to USG. "A word in regard to a matter of vital importance. The law authorises you to order an election in Va. on the Constn and also for *all* officers. Now, by the provisions of the Constn this will be impossible; because, if the Const. be adopted, or any portions of it, *then* the districts & townships are to be laid off, and the COUNTY Officers elected under the law. The difficulty grows out of the *total change* in our County Organization; which can only be effected *after* the Constn shall be adopted & *pursuant to its provisions*. It will, therefore, be impossible to elect for any thing except Gov. Lieut Gov. Members of both branches of the Legislature, &c & Members of Congress—in other words, for *State* officers & Congressmen only, & not for *County* Officers. Fearing that these little *details* have been overlooked, I take the liberty of calling your attention to them." ALS, *ibid*. On April 20, John Murphy, Peckatone, Va., wrote to USG. "I am emboldened to address you upon the subject of the 're-construction' of Virginia by the fact that your recent message to Congress, indicates, a desire on your part to see Virginia occupy the place she once held in the Federal councils; by the fact that the whole matter has been confided to you by Congress; & by the additional fact that I have learned through my sister (the wife of Col: John Fessenden of Boston) that you were favorably disposed towards Virginia. To refer to the past, in detail, would be useless. It is enough to say that the Virginia people thought they had a right to sever their connection with the Federal Union & acted upon that opinion & belief— . . . The *people of Virginia* thought that they would be told to send their representatives back to Congress & resume the position they had given up. Had that been done, then, the Union now would have no more honorable supporter of its laws, its honor or its dignity than Virginia. The opposite policy which Congress thought proper to pursue has by no means soothed the asperities of the late war, yet *the true Virginians*—men who met you on every battle field, whose best efforts were directed towards the overthrow of your armies—are anxious to re-establish their State goverment & to resume their relations with the Federal goverment upon such terms as honorable men would choose. The Convention that met in Richmond & framed the Constitution which you propose to submit to her people (or a portion of them) was not framed by Virginians, the sons of Africa were there; the 'sweet brogue' of the sons of 'Erin' was heard in its deliberations, men from the states already in the Union (Northern men) were there, & but a small proportion of these who had the real interests of the state in view were represented. It need not be a surprise therefore if enough is found in the Constitution to render it distasteful to a majority of voters. Should that be the case I respectfully suggest that the *people of Virginia* without regard to race, color, previous or present condition be called upon to send one delegate from each county to Richmond & there let them frame a constitution that will reflect the sentiments of all Virginians, & send it up to Congress for its approval & if approved be sent to the people for ratification. This would give the obnoxious class (secessionists) & all other classes an opportunity to show the world that they are willing to cooperate with the other States in developing the great destiny of this great Republic. As regards suffrage, I believe that a majority of our people believe that it should be restricted. All white men living in a State hav'nt sufficient interest in that State to direct them to a proper exercise of such a privilege. The case is the same with negros. I believe, however that the negro has stronger local attachments than the white man & if let alone they will acquire a permanent interest & be very useful—(as they now are)—members of society. Could they all be transported by some magic hand, in one night from Virginia it would be looked upon as an unfortunate circumstance. There is perfect good feeling (except in isolated places) between the races. Justice is meeted out to them with an even hand by the Courts of the State. I have represented many of them at the Bar & have generally seen their causes prevail—even too—when Confederate officers composed the Court & their opponents were prominent Confederate soldiers. We are greatly misunderstood & misrepresented. And I believe that the Commander who led the armies of the Union so often to victory, whose generous mind dictated the terms of surrender at Appomattox—terms alike honorable to Captor & captives, will not be less prompt & energetic in building up a destroyed State, . . ." ALS, *ibid.*

On April 21, Robert M. T. Hunter, Loyds, Va., wrote to USG. "The great interest which we feel in Virginia upon the questions involved in the so called Underwood constitution which are soon to be submitted to us for a vote will excuse me I hope for offering some suggestions in regard to it. That the adoption of this constitution without amendment would deprive a large majority of the people of Virginia of all hopes of prosperity and happiness for a long time to come is so plain that I forbear to enlarge upon the subject. We have been very happy to learn in this state that your excellency would probably require a separate vote upon the clauses for a test oath for disfranchisement and the county organization. With such an opportunity I believe that a very large majority of the people of Virginia including many members of the Republican party would vote them down. If they do not a very sad future must await our state. There is however another clause in that constitution to which I wish to call your attention. I mean that which forbids the legislature to pass a stay law for the relief of the debtor class in the Community. I am not aware that any state constitution contains such a prohibition to ~~their~~ its legislature and whatever may be ones own opinion on this question it would scarcely seem to be right to deprive the Legislature of this power. If such a law be unconstitutional the courts will so decide and in regard to its expediency there are none so fit to ~~decide~~ judge as the representatives of the people immediately to be affected by it. No legislature would pass such a law unless a decided majority of its constituents required it and such a majority could never be found unless there were some strong necessity for such a measure. It seems to me therefore that the question ought to be left to the courts and the Legislature. I would not urge such a separate vote if I did not know the general indebtedness of the people of this state and if I did not believe that a judicious measure of this sort would not only help the debtor but also the creditor by ensuring more abundant means to satisfy his claims. The value of our lands begin to feel the impulse of the emigration which is setting in upon us and before very long I think that many men who could not pay their debts at present would soon be able to do so. I forbear to press more of the details upon you or to advert to many other very objectionable features of this constitution. The striking out of the first of these ~~features~~ clauses in the constitution to which I have referred would seem to be necessary even to the tolerable existence of a large majority of our people—The amendment in regard to the stay law which I have ventured to recommend would promote very much their chances for prosperity and happiness   It is for the dearest interests of a great and a brave people, my fellow citizens and country men for whom I invite your kind consideration and I hope they will not be disappointed in the trust which they repose in you." ALS, *ibid.*

On May 6, E. P. Phelps, Staunton, Va., wrote to Alexander Sharp, U. S. marshal, Washington, D. C. "You may remember the interview I had with you in your office last week. I am pretty well satisfied that an effort will be made to induce the President to so place the article in the proposed Constitution of Va, as to make its defeat certain. I would have but little fear, as I have confidence in the President, if our opponents were not so given to misrepresentation. I know their Tactics so well, that nothing would surprise me. If they succeed in making an impression upon the mind of the President, I respectfully ask to be heard before he decides to separate the article in question from the main body of the constitution. I send you an editorial from the Richmond Dispatch, in wh we are referred to as 'the Radical Political M. E. Church.' The policies of our church, offends them, yet this paper is in favor of the election of Walker, claiming that he is a Republican. Can any confidence be placed in him or his supporters? We are charged with an attempt to steal *their* property. We want only our own. The Virginia conference in March last said in its Pastoral address, 'we make no claim to the property that under the plan of separation passed to the M. E. Church South.' I wrote this address, and stand by this declaration. Yet they will make the point that we want this property. We only contend for the property that I refer to in the pamphlet that I left with you for Judge Carter, a copy of which I will send you by mail. This property is ours, and we ought to have it. Will you do me the favor to see the President, and in case he should desire any information let me know. I may be personally assailed by the committee of *conservative* rebels that may wait upon the President, and would be perfectly willing to meet them. . . ." ALS, *ibid.* The enclosure is *ibid.* See also DNA, RG 94, Letters Received, 289P 1869.

On May 6, Secretary of War John A. Rawlins wrote to Gen. William T. Sherman. "Please inform Brevet Major General Canby, commanding First Military District, that the President directs that he may designate either the last Tuesday in June or the first Tuesday in July, as the time for holding the election in Virginia for the ratification or rejection of the Constitution, and the election of State Officers and representatives in Congress, authorized by Act of Congress approved April 10th 1869" LS, *ibid.*, 363W 1869. On May 9, Bvt. Maj. Gen. Edward R. S. Canby, Richmond, wrote to Sherman designating July 6 as the election date and assessing the political situation. ". . . I have given a careful consideration to the Constitution, and particularly to the provisions that have been the subject of so much discussion and objection, and that consideration has led to the conclusion that the only provisions which should be submitted to a separate vote are those embraced in the fourth clause of the first section, and in the seventh section of article three, familiarly known as the 'disfranchising' and 'test Oath' clauses. It is urged by many that the submission of the latter to a separate vote is all that is necessary, but the expurgation of the latter from the Constitution will be of little value, unless the former also be removed, for section 2 of the same article would probably be construed as rendering all persons who were not entitled to vote as ineligible to hold office. This construction—and it appears to me to be legitimate, would require the removal of the disability by the Legislature before any disfranchised person could enter upon the duties of any Office to which he was elected or appointed and the Legislature has the same power to dispense with the test Oath that it has to remove franchise disabilities. As all elections must be controlled by the laws of Congress until the new government has been organized, and the State admitted to representation in Congress, the operation will be prospective and some what remote but the effect will be, in my judgment, to gain many friends for the Constitution and for the government that may be organized under it. The County organization Article VII is bitterly objected to by many, Some of its features are, in this State, novel and experimental, and in that relation perhaps objectionable, but these features are so complicated with others that are undoubtedly good and with the subject of education (Article VIII) that it is difficult to see how they can be separated. If the whole article should be submitted to a separate vote and be lost, that loss will carry with it the loss or at least the indefinite postponement of the system of education, and this is so important a feature that it should not, in my opinion, be exposed to greater hazard than the Constitution itself. The result most feared by those who oppose this article is that in Counties where the colored population is in excess,—ignorant, incompetent, or vicious men will be elected to fill the minor county and township offices, and that the effect will be to separate the white and colored population and render them antagonistic. I do not think this fear is well founded. The election for county and township offices will not take place until after the Constitution has been adopted and the Legislature assembled under it has established the details of county organization for which it provides. By that time much of the present political and social bitterness will have passed away by the solution of more important and agitating questions, and selections for office will be made dispassionately and with reference to qualification and fitness. Moreover if the 'disfranchising' and 'test Oath' clauses should be submitted to a separate vote and be rejected, the range of selection will be so enlarged that there will be no difficulty in finding competent and suitable persons to fill these offices, and I do not think there is much reason to apprehend that proper selections will not be made. The number of registrars and Managers of elections that will be required is about three thousand, and as a large majority of these will be new and inexperienced men, it will be important to have as many officers as can be spared for the purpose of superintending the conduct of the registration and election. . . ." LS, *ibid.* Sherman endorsed this letter to Horace Porter. "Please read this to the President and let me know if Gen Canbys opinions meet his concurrence." AES, *ibid.*

On May 14, USG issued a proclamation that designated July 6 as referendum day and authorized separate votes on the constitution's disfranchisement and test oath clauses. Copy, *ibid.*, 1237S 1869. On July 7, Daniel telegraphed to USG. "on behalf of the state Executive Committee of the Walker party I congratulate you upon the triumph of your policy in Virginia. The gratitude of the people for your liberality is greatly enlivened by the overwhelming majority by which the policy prevails" Telegram received (at 11:00 A.M.), *ibid.*, RG 107, Telegrams Collected (Bound).

1. On April 10, Congress passed a resolution authorizing elections in Va. and Miss.

2. On April 3, a Va. delegation, dissatisfied with the proposed constitution, visited USG to ask "the President to recommend to Congress the expulsion from the constitution of the test oath, the State disfranchisement clause and the county election provision, which were the principal objections entertained by the people of the State against the new constitution. The President replied that the subject of the restoration of the State to the Union was one of deep interest to

him; that he thought the best mode of settling these difficulties was for Congress to order an election on the constitution and permit the people to vote upon it by separate sections. By so doing such features as were most objectionable could be defeated. He said he would consult with the members of his Cabinet on the subject, and if they concurred in his views he would at an early day advise Congress accordingly." *New York Herald*, April 4, 1869.

3. On May 18, 1868, the Miss. constitutional convention had adjourned. Officials announced the vote rejecting this constitution on July 10.

4. On March 25, 1869, USG told a Miss. delegation that "he would do all he could to protect loyal men. That General Ames had authority to appoint this class of men to office in Mississippi, and he had no doubt he would do so as rapidly as possible. He favored giving the provisional Governor power to remove and appoint all officers. He thought Mississippi should be reconstructed as soon as this could be done on a loyal basis, and in such a manner as to give peace and quiet to the people." *Washington Weekly Chronicle*, March 27, 1869. Variant account in *National Intelligencer*, March 26, 1869. See Proclamation, July 13, 1869.

Proclamation

By the President of the United States of America,
A Proclamation.

Whereas objects of interest to the United States require that the Senate should be convened at twelve o'clock on the Twelfth day of April. 1869, to receive and act upon such communications as may be made to it on the part of the Executive:

Now, therefore, I, U. S. Grant, President of the United States, have considered it to be my duty to issue this my Proclamation, declaring that an extraordinary occasion requires the Senate of the United States to convene for the transaction of business at the Capitol, in the City of Washington, on the Twelfth day of April 1869, at twelve o'clock noon on that day, of which all who shall at that time be entitled to act as members of that body are hereby required to take notice.

Given under my hand and the Seal of the United States at Washington, the eighth day of April, in the year of our Lord one

thousand eight hundred and sixty nine, and of the Independence
of the United States of America the ninety third

U. S. GRANT

DS, DNA, RG 130, Presidential Proclamations. See *New York Herald*, April 10,
1869.

To Elihu B. Washburne

Washington, D, C,
Apl. 9th 1869.

DEAR WASHBURNE,

I have been pained to learn that a man upon whom I have confered an appointment should have been a lobbyest to Congress, (in
the McGarrahan case) and failing to get the vote he wished from
the Committee having the matter in charge should becom[e] the
traducer of the Committee which, it seems, were within one of
being unanimous in their ~~vote~~ report. It seems that Moore[1] has
been acting in this way, and very much to the prejudice of Wilson
particularly, the chairman of the Committee.[2] It may be that Moore
is misrepresented in this matter, but I understand that the correspondents who are traducing Wilson give Moore as their authority.
Now you know, and I presume Moore did, that there was no man
in the Fortyeth Congress for whom I had a higher regard than for
the Hon. J. F. Wilson, and that he was one of the men who I confidently hoped to have connected with my administration. To have
him slandered, over my shoulders, I feel as I would to have you, who
stood by me through evil as well as through good report, slandered
in the same way. I do not believe you care to have with you as Sec. of
Legation a man guilty of such conduct. Of course this is presuming
his guilt before hearing the other side. I would be but too glad to
have the report authentically contradicted. But as the matter stands
now Wilson feels terribly agrieved and I think very justly so. Moore
has no doubt read what the correspondents ~~Townsend~~[3] Pyatte[4]

and Boynton[5] have said in this matter, and knows how far they are sustain[ed] in them by his statements. His opinion, or their opinion of the merits of the McGarrahan claim, or what they say about the report of the Committee upon it I have nothing to do with. The matter which concerns me is the statemen[t] that I have been influence[d] in my course towards Wilson by reasons of dissatisfaction with his public acts, and that my notice has been called to them through some agency of Moore's.

Yours Truly

U. S. GRANT

ALS, IHi. On April 15, 1869, Elihu B. Washburne, Galena, wrote to USG. "Your favor of the 9th inst has only reached me this morning. Of course it is impossible for me to say what Mr. Moore has, or has not said, in regard to Mr. Wilson. My relations have been intimate with him and I never heard him speak disparagingly of Mr. W. I have not seen the articles of the correspondents you refer to, but I take it that after having made a raid on Wilson and having been called to account for it, they undertook to make a scapegoat of Moore. I have not the least idea he ever made any statements justifying any attack on Wilson. Moore talks a good deal, but generally *in favor* of people rather than against them. I shall see him in N. Y. next week, and will write you further in this regard. I should be very sorry to have your confidence in Mr. Moore impaired.— I have never known him to be guilty of any conduct unbecoming a gentleman. I feel greatly obliged to you for appointing him my second Secretary, for in my present state of health and liable to a recurrence of the attacks to which I have been subject, I felt desirous of having some friend near my person upon whom I could rely. I will now call your attention to another matter, which I would not have alluded to, had I not received your letter, as I feel the greatest reluctance in troubling you with anything personal to myself. I find the accompanying article in the Chicago Tribune of yesterday. Mr. Wilson was in Chicago day before yesterday and you can judge as well as I can whether or not he inspired it. I have considered myself about 'iron clad' in regard to the attacks of the Press, *but* when I saw that article in a republican paper, heretofore friendly to me, I confess it is a little more than I am willing to bear. It is hard to rest under an imputation so false and atrocious, that I abused your unbounded generosity and kindness in assuming the duties of the office of Secretary of State contrary to your expectations, and impliedly, against your wishes. *You* know how utterly false and how cruel such a suggestion is, but yet you are not in a position to vindicate me and so I must bear it with as much philosophy as I am able to command. As to the other matter in the article, in relation to Wilson's being kept out of the Cabinet by my going in there, and his being embarrassed by my actions there, and finally peremptorily declining the office on that account, it is all new to me. I never heard or dreamed of anything of the kind. I trust you know me well enough to believe that no earthly consideration could have induced me to do anything that would embarrass you in the least degree. The personal and friendly relations existing between us brought upon me vast

demand for my 'influence.' In some cases I have been constrained to bring
certain applications for office to your attention, and perhaps you may have been
a little impatient, but if you only knew of the number of cases in which I have
refused to interfere and the enmities I have incurred for such refusal, I think
you would excuse me. I have had no political debts to pay and have had no occasion to call upon the administration to liquidate any political obligations. In
my official position I have endeavored honestly and conscientiously to discharge
every duty imposed upon me and have followed your fortunes with unfaltering
constancy and have sought to serve your interests with fidelity and without hope
of reward. I am sorry I could not have done more. You know how profoundly
thankful I am for the distinguished evidences you have given me of your confidence and friendship and I hope to vindicate both. I start East to-day *en route*
to my post of duty. I would go by Washington to say good-bye to you, but I
fear my presence in the capitol might embarrass you and set all the newspapers
to lying again. So I will send you my adieus from N. Y. before I sail. A great
deal is said in the papers about the breaking of my 'slate' by Gov. Fish. I had no
'slate' to break. All the nominations were made out under your directions and
upon consultation with you. I acted with great delicacy towards my successor
as you know, and I presume he has intended to act with the same delicacy towards me. Circumstances may have dictated changes and I have no disposition
to complain. Every single man in whom I felt any interest has been appointed,
except Mr. Gibbs. As it was deemed proper not to appoint him, I beg leave to
thank you most heartily for the appointment of Genl. Read. No man could have
been more satisfactory to me. . . . My address till I sail on May 1. is Care of
C. & G. Woodman No. 30 Pine St. N. Y. City." ALS, USG 3. Washburne enclosed a clipping from the *Chicago Tribune*, April 14, 1869. "The following
paragraph appeared in a Washington letter in our issue of March 29: 'A Gentleman and a lawyer, high in the esteem of the people and his friends, who was
unanimously adjudged a place in the Cabinet of General Grant, failed to be
invited thereto because he signed the report of the House Judiciary Committee
in favor of this McGarrahan fraud.' Something similar to this appeared in the
Washington correspondence of the Cincinnati *Commercial*, in which, we believe, the name of the Hon. James F. Wilson, of Iowa, was mentioned as the
gentleman referred to. We have seen a letter from President Grant, in which
it is stated that Mr. Wilson was invited to a seat in his Cabinet, and that he (the
President) deeply regretted that Mr. Wilson, for reasons of his own, was constrained to decline it; and, furthermore, that he (the President) knew nothing
about the McGarrahan claim, and that it cut no figure in the case. It is well
known in Washington that Mr. Wilson was tendered by General Grant the
office of Secretary of State in the original construction of his Cabinet, and that
the appointment of Mr. Washburne to that place was intended to be merely
complimentary, the latter having been previously booked for the French mission.
Having been nominated and confirmed as Secretary, Mr. Washburne unexpectedly entered upon the discharge of the duties of the office. Mr. Wilson was
thus placed in a very embarrassing position, which he endured as long as he
deemed consistent with his own dignity and the dignity of the office. He then
declined the position peremptorily, expressing, however, his unabated confidence
in the sincerity and good faith of the President. The choice of a new Secretary
was then made, and Mr. Hamilton Fish was selected. Mr. Fish, however, de-

clined to take charge of anybody's leavings, and his first act was to make a new set of appointments in place of those arranged by his predecessor. . . ."

On May 30, Joseph Medill, Chicago, wrote to USG. "*Confidential* . . . After considerable reflection and some consultation with our mutual friend Jones, I have concluded to let you know that I disavow all responsibility for the editorial criticism of your Cabinet which appeared in the Chicago Tribune about a month ago. I have hesitated to disclaim my general share of the responsibility for the article, and would not do it, but for the warm feeling of friendship for and confidence I have in you, and I can not bear the idea—that you think I was guilty of it. The fact is that I knew nothing of any intention to publish such an article until I read it in the Tribune. Mr White wrote and inserted the article on his sole responsibility. Remember that I am not the Managing Editor of the Tribune, and therefore do not always know what is going into the paper. I had just returned ~~returned~~ home from New York, and on the appearance of the article was greatly vexed and surprised, and had a talk with Mr White about it, in which I pointed out the unfairness of his criticisms and the imprudence of publishing them in our paper. It is not necessary to relate what passed. But since then no articles of similar tenor have appeared in the Tribune. I think he feels that he committed an error. I am really at a loss to understand the influences that led him to write the article for he had previous to your inauguration professed the warmest feelings of friendship for you. It is very true that during the Months of March and April there were loud complaints and great grumbling throughout the country at some of your appointments, but this is always the case at the incoming of a new Administration. Your appointments for this city give general satisfaction except one of them—the last one, and I think the public are becoming pretty well pleased with your administration. The people who voted for you have *not* lost confidence in your capacity, integrity, or wisdom, but will give you a hearty and firm support in well doing. I am impelled to write you this letter of personal explanation because I desire to disabuse your mind of the belief that after my professions of friendship and confidence in you that I had suddenly and for trivial causes 'gone back' on you. Be assured it is not so. My esteem and faith in you have not wavered in the least. During the period I was Managing Editor of the Tribune from 1862 till 1866 the columns of the Tribune attest that I never lost faith in you. Whenever I was in doubt as to some of your movements or tactics I always advised with Washburn or or Jones and they furnished the necesary light or reassurance, and so I never sold a dollar of the stock I took in you after the battle of Donnalson, and I *hold it yet*, and intend to *keep* it. But I never hesitated to puncture such leaders as Fremont, Halleck, Buell, McClellan, or Rosecrans. I placed the interests of the Union high above individuals and sustained or opposed men just in proportion as they served the Republic. I firmly believe now, that your administration will be a perfect success and that the people will reelect you, and I hope to be living to help. I tell all who find fault with your course that 'Gen Grant has the happy faculty of seeing his errors and correcting them and that in the end he always comes out right'. So believing, allow me to renew my former place in your esteem and good opinion." ALS, *ibid.*

1. Frank Moore, born in 1828 in Concord, N. H., and raised in New York City and Washington, D. C., accompanied his father to Calif. in 1849. He published his first book in 1856 and became known for *The Rebellion Record* (New

York, 1861–68) and other historical works. On March 11, 1869, USG had nominated Moore as asst. secretary of legation, Paris. On April 18, Moore, New York City, wrote to USG. "I am surprised to learn, through Mr. Washburne that some one had reported to you that I was the authority, quoted by Mr Piatt, for saying that the reason why Mr. Wilson of Iowa did not have a seat in your Cabinet, was that he signed the report in favor of the 'McGarrahan Claim.' I seize the earliest moment to give the emphatic and unqualified contradiction to this report, in all its length and breadth. I never spoke to Mr. Piatt but once in my life and that was merely an incidental word, in a conversation with another person, in which the 'McGarrahan Claim' was never thought of or spoken of. As to the other correspondent who referred to this matter, I never made any such statement to him, nor have I ever made any such statement to any other person, for such a thing never occurred to me, and I never heard of it. The whole thing, I assure you, Mr. President, is false from beginning to end, as far as I am concerned   Mr. Washburne says further that I was accused to you of being a lobbyist—So it figures up about this way. Somebody accuses me of slandering Mr. Wilson and then turns around and slanders me by calling me a lobbyist. I wish to state to you that I never have been a lobbyist in the sense in which that term is used. A friend of mine, who thought himself in danger of being defrauded out of a large estate, by the passage of the Mc Garrahan claim through Congress, deemed it necessary to have some one there to protect his interest against the lobby that was pressing the claim. I happened to be passing the winter in Washington, and my friend desired me to make explanations of the matter so that his interests might not be jeopardised. In doing so I was careful never to reflect upon the motives of any one, most surely not, upon the motives of Mr. Wilson, as I always regarded him an honest man, and I have never, at any time, spoken in disparagement of his integrity. This is the only matter before Congress in which I ever had any interest. I hope therefore, Mr. President, that what I have here stated will be entirely satisfactory to you. After the confidence you have reposed in me, by giving me an honorable appointment, I should feel deeply mortified to have you believe that I had been guilty of any act which would in the least degree impair your confidence in me as a gentleman and a man holding an official position under your administration." ALS, James F. Wilson Papers, Fairfield Public Library, Fairfield, Iowa. On April 20, Horace Porter endorsed this letter. "I am directed by the President to forward you the within letter" AES, *ibid.*

2. Former U.S. Representative James F. Wilson of Iowa had sponsored a bill in the 40th Congress to grant William McGarrahan's controversial mineral land claim in Calif. See letter to Jacob D. Cox, Aug. 22, 1870.

3. George A. Townsend, born in 1841 in Georgetown, Del., became a war correspondent for the *New York Herald*, and later, the *New York World*, spending the latter part of 1862 in England advocating the Northern cause. Settling in Washington, D. C., in 1867, after reporting the Austro-Prussian War, Townsend contributed columns signed "Gath" to many newspapers, including the *Chicago Tribune* and *Cincinnati Enquirer*.

On Feb. 12, 1869, Edward McPherson, clerk, U.S. House of Representatives, wrote to USG. "George Alfred Townsend, Esq., one of the brilliant young men of America, and an honor to the profession of journalism, will be an applicant for the Consulate at Paris. He is a graduate of the Philadelphia High School,

& a gentleman of unsullied character, whose qualifications and merits eminently justify the application referred to. His services to the cause of the country during the late political campaign were conspicuous and valuable. He would bring to the place special adaptation, and prove a worthy representative of our Nation in the French Capital. I take pleasure in commending him to your favorable consideration." ALS, DNA, RG 59, Letters of Application and Recommendation. On Feb. 13, U.S. Representative James A. Garfield of Ohio wrote to USG. "I respectfully recommend the appointment of Mr George Alfred Townsend to the Consulate at Paris or to some other of equal importance. He possesses qualities, which, in my judgment ought to commend him to the favorable consideration of the Chief Executive. He has literary abilities of high order; is familiar with the language and customs of European countries; and, above all, is a true, independent,—honorable man—I believe he would serve the country faithfully and with credit. I hope it may be in your power to give him such an appointment as I have suggested." LS, *ibid.* On March 9, Donn Piatt, Washington, D. C., wrote to USG. "I have the honor of joining heartily in the recommendation of Mr. Geo. Alfred Townsend as a suitable person to fill the position of Consul at Havre France or a similar position abroad I know Mr. Townsend to be an earnest republican and the country well knows that he is a journalist of emenent ability. His knowledge of languages—business capacity and sober industrious habits fully qualify for a high consular or diplomatic position—" ALS, *ibid.* On March 10, Speaker of the House James G. Blaine wrote to USG. "I unite with great cordiality with those who ask that Mr Geo. Alfred Townsend may be appointed to a Consular position—Mr. Townsend has culture, integrity—independence and sound principles and would I am sure most honorably & creditably represent his country abroad" ALS, *ibid.* Related papers are *ibid.*

On March 9, Townsend, Washington, D. C., had written to USG. "I have the honor to solicit the position of Minister Resident at the Hague, Holland. Accompanying this application I have submitted the good notices of my friends and respectfully request that they be considered." ALS, *ibid.* On the same day, Townsend wrote to "My dear sir," possibly USG. "I gather from some things dropped by my friend, Colonel Donn Piatt, that remarks have been made to you prejudicial to my character. I can afford to lose the consulship I seek but not your respect. I know the sources of these slanders; they are referable either to the convicted blackmailer, Painter; to an ingrateful dog, Ramsdell for whom I obtained a place on the *Tribune* and was obliged to cut for his bad-manners, or to some other evesdropper and scandal-bearer of the newspaper row, whom I have castigated. I will withdraw my application on the testimony of any credible witness who ever saw me intoxicated, or of his personal knowledge found me dishonorable, or who can produce any bill against me which will not be paid at sight. I have been at no pains to conciliate any body having access to your ear and my style of attack is not pacificatory. But whoever is the author or bearer of these perjuries you will live to see exposed and proven infamous. I enclose letters from Ramsdell and from John Young, both of whom I suspect to be of these libelers, testifying to my character. That from Young was providentially received this very day. Mr. Stillson of the New York *World* will himself disprove the slander with which he is connected. I would gladly withdraw my application but that this will oblige some thief or sneak. If I am sent to Europe by the State department I shall have to give bond for my responsibility. Regretting all this, I stand upon the issue raised and shall fight it out." ALS, *ibid.* No appointment followed.

4. USG had spoken recently with Piatt. See Piatt's April 1 "Washington Letter" in *Cincinnati Commercial*, April 5, 1869. Born in 1819 in Cincinnati, Piatt practiced law, contributed articles to newspapers, and participated in Democratic politics before spending 1853–55 in Paris, being commissioned on April 5, 1854, as secretary of legation. He resigned in 1864 from the 13th Ohio Inf. after attaining the rank of lt. col. He later served one term in the Ohio legislature and, in 1868, moved to Washington, D. C., as correspondent for the *Cincinnati Commercial.*

On Dec. 30, 1870, Orville E. Babcock wrote to Secretary of State Hamilton Fish. "*Confidential* . . . I am informed that one *Don Piat,* was once a Secty of the Legation at Paris, and while there he did things not creditable to a gentleman. That he purchased large quantiteis of things, and failed to pay for them and that the *legation* had to pay for them &c &c. I am also informed that he was an aspirant, and perhaps an applicant for office, at the commencement of the present administration. If you have any information in your department on either subject please have it hunted up. You must have some man posted on all such matters—who can put his hand on any such information. Don Piat, is of no especial account, but if we can show him a defeated applicant for office, he will be where the application of your friend *Dana,* placed him, when he applied to Andrew Johnson, for the Collectorship of N. Y. I am in receipt of the messages, many thanks. If you can find any record of Don Piats conduct of interest please let me have it as early as possible." ALS, DLC-Hamilton Fish. On Jan. 9, 1871, Babcock wrote to J. C. Bancroft Davis, asst. secretary of state. "*Confidential* . . . After a thorough examination we cannot find that any of the correspondence in relation to Don Piatt was ever printed by Congress. The President desires copies of all the correspondence from our legation at Paris on his conduct as Sect'y of the Legation. The President also directs me to enquire whether there are in the State Dept. application or recommendations for appointment of Alfred Townsend to any foreign appointment." LS, *ibid.* On Jan. 12, Horace Porter wrote to Davis. "Upon Search, nothing either of record, or in the files is found in this office which has any reference to the conjectural note referred to in your letter of the 10th instant as sent to the President of the United States on the seventh of February 1855." Copy, DLC-USG, II, 1. See following letter; Charles Grant Miller, *Donn Piatt: His Work and His Ways* (Cincinnati, 1893).

5. Henry Van Ness Boynton, born in 1835 in West Stockbridge, Mass., graduated from the Kentucky Military Institute (1858), taught mechanics and astronomy at that school, and, in July, 1861, became maj., 35th Ohio Inf., promoted on July 13, 1863, to lt. col. Wounded at Missionary Ridge, Boynton was honorably discharged on Sept. 8, 1864. As a journalist, Boynton worked as Washington, D. C., correspondent for the *Cincinnati Gazette* and *Commercial Tribune.* See *PUSG,* 8, 323–25; *ibid.,* 11, 207.

To James F. Wilson

———

Washington, D, C,
Apl. 9th 1869.

HON. J. F. WILSON,
DEAR SIR:

It is but an act of simple justice to you that I should state that I have seen, with pain, for the last few days, studied and persistent attacks upon you for a vote which it seems you gave, as a member of the Judiciary Committee in the last Congress, upon the McGarrahan claim. I was not aware that you gave such a vote until I saw these attacks and now have no knowledge or opinion upon the merits of the claim. My opinion of you however is such that I do not doubt but you cast your vote conscienciously and according to the testimony adduced before the Committee. The gossip therefore which says "that a distinguished member lost a seat in the Cabinet, and a place in the confidence of his friends, through his connection with the case" is untrue.[1] If it alludes to you, and it clearly does, it is refuted by the fact that I tendered you a place in my Cabinet, and very much regretted that you felt constrained not to accept, for reasons entirely personal to yourself, and having no connection with any official acts of yours.[2]

With assurances that I still entertain the same high opinion of you that I did when tendering you a Cabinet appointment,[3] I remain,

Very truly,
your obt. svt.
U. S. GRANT

ALS, James F. Wilson Papers, Fairfield Public Library, Fairfield, Iowa. On March 8, 1869, William F. Coolbaugh, Chicago, had telegraphed to USG. "Wilson of Iowa would undoubtedly Command the Confidence of the Business men of the whole north west as secretary of the Treasury or any place in Cabinet" Telegram received (at 1:25 P.M.), DNA, RG 107, Telegrams Collected (Bound).

1. Quoted from Donn Piatt's "Washington Letter" of March 26 in *Cincinnati Commercial*, March 30, 1869. Piatt retracted this statement in his "Washington Letter" of April 6. *Ibid.*, April 9, 1869.

2. On Feb. 23, Charles S. Clarke, George Acheson, and Christian W. Slagle, Fairfield, had written to James F. Wilson. "Take the advice of your real friends. If Gen Grant offers you a place in the Cabinet do not refuse it but accept for the sake of our Country. Do not fear that you will be impoverished. Take the Office and do your duty and all will be well. Your family cannot have a better inheritance than an unstained record of integrity on your part in the public service and with such a record you need never fear that they will have to beg bread or lack friends." LS, James F. Wilson Papers, Fairfield Public Library.

3. On April 11, a Washington, D. C., correspondent wrote: "Before the inauguration, Gen. Grant sent for Mr. Wilson, and tendered him the Attorney-Generalship. This Mr. Wilson refused to accept. On the evening of the day of the inauguration, Gen. Grant again sent for Mr. Wilson to come and see him at his house. Mr. Wilson accordingly went, and the President then asked him to become his Secretary of State. He said that Washburne expected the place, and it was due to him that he should be appointed, but immediately on his confirmation he would resign, and then he would appoint him (Wilson). Mr. Wilson at first declined the offer, pleading that he was unfit for the position, and felt timid of the responsibility, but President Grant urged him, and he finally agreed to accept. The next day he learned that Mr. Washburne had determined on a list of the most prominent foreign appointments, which he insisted should be made before he retired. Unwilling to take office under such circumstances, and not wishing to oppose any recommendations that Mr. Washburne might make, he immediately sent word to the President, withdrawing his previous acceptance of the office, and stating that it would be impossible for him to accept the position, and without seeing the President left for New-York. President Grant dispatched a messenger after him, urging him to reconsider his action, but Wilson stood firm in his declination, and then Mr. Fish was selected for the position." *New York Tribune*, April 12, 1869. See John Russell Young, *Around the World with General Grant* (New York, 1879), II, 276; Allan Nevins, *Hamilton Fish: The Inner History of the Grant Administration* (New York, 1936), pp. 111–12.

To Hamilton Fish

Washington, D, C,
Apl. 15th 1869.

HON H. FISH:
SEC. OF STATE:
DEAR SIR:

Mr. De Lano, whos name was sent in to-day for Singapore, would be much acomodated by having his destination changed to either Yeddo, Nagasaki or Osaca. If the change can be made without prejud[ice] to other applicants I would be pleased also.

Very respectfully

your obt. svt.

U. S. GRANT

ALS, DLC-Hamilton Fish. On April 14, 1869, Milton M. De Lano, Washington, D. C., had written to USG. "I called this A. M. to see you—as per your appointment of yesterday—and was informed by Genl Dent that you had sent a note to Secretary Fish in regard to my case—I called upon Secretary Fish this P. M. to see what could be done for me. He said he had not received your note, but would see you on the subject to morrow I requested that I might be appointed to Shanghai, where Mr Seward has been for the last eight years Or that Mr Sheppard—who was nominated for Yeddo yesterday might be transferred to Shanghai and I sent to Yeddo. I earnestly hope this arrangement may meet with your approval" ALS, DNA, RG 59, Letters of Application and Recommendation. On Feb. 12, U.S. Delegate George M. Chilcott of Colorado Territory had written to USG. "I learn that My Friend M. M. Delano of Denver City Colorado will be an applicant for a Consulship, and I take this early opportunity of Recommending Mr Delano to Your favorable Consideration, Mr. Delano held the Office of Territorial Treasurer for Colorado with honor to himself, as well as the Office of Mayor of the City of Denver, to which position he was twice elected. knowing Mr Delano as a Gentleman in every sense of the term, and knowing him to be well qualified for the Position I take great pleasure in making this recommendation" LS, *ibid.* On Feb. 15, Hiram P. Bennet, Washington, D. C., wrote to USG. "I learn from Mr Delano that he is an applicant for a Consulship It gives me pleasure to add my endorsement to his fitness for such a position. He was one of the early pioneers of Colorado, where I have known him since 1860. Since I have known him he has enjoyed and deserved the Confidence of that Community occupying positions of honor and trust, confered upon him by the people among whom he resided—He was public spirited and reliable at all times during our late struggle for National Life I regard him as capable and competent to fill with credit to himself and honor to his Country any position, such as he aspires to." ALS, *ibid.* On Feb. 21, Governor Alexander C. Hunt of Colorado Territory, Washington, D. C., wrote to USG. "My friend, M. M. DeLano, of Colorado, intends making application for a Consulship. In common with other official and representative men, I cheerfully endorse him, and respectfully ask that he receive the appointment." LS, *ibid.* On March 3, Lt. Gen. William T. Sherman endorsed this letter. "I concur fully with Governor Hunt. I have met Mr DeLano in Colorado many times, and I believe him an honorable & worthy and inteligent Gentleman" AES, *ibid.* On April 2, Sherman wrote to Secretary of State Hamilton Fish. "My Friend Mr M M Delano of Colorado asks of me a letter to you in his behalf, in relation to his application for a Consulship in Japan—I can hardly express my reluctance to depart from a rule to which I have adhered to abstain from all such matters, but he pleads the fact that Colorado is a Territory, almost without representation or influence. Therefor I state that I have known Mr Delano for some years, and I feel assured that if appointed he will fill the office with great credit to the country. He

has all the qualifications usually called for in such an appointmt." ALS, *ibid.*
On April 8, De Lano wrote to USG. "On the 6th ultimo, I handed to you, (by
Gen'l Dent,) my application for the Consulship, at Yeddo, Japan, supported by
the endorsements of the Delegates, from Colorado, Gov Hunt, Hon J B Chafee,
General Sherman, Commissioner Delano, and many others. I understand, that
the case was referred to the State Department—I have called upon the Secratary,
but can get no assurance of my final success—The Secratary, stated, that it was
quite essential that a Consul, should speak the Court language, of the Country,
to which he was sent. I speak the german language fluently, which is the Court,
and Commercial language of Japan—Secy Fish, has also stated, that Consuls,
should be appointed from the Commercial States—I could have obtained the
endorsement, of very many of the leading merchants, of Chicago, and a great
trafic exists, with that City and Japan—I formerly resided in Chicago, and am
well known, in business circles—and am assured, that my appointment would
give as much satisfaction as if I still resided there—I have spent much time, and
considerable means, in quest of this position, and am anxious to know my fate—
believing that my personal friendly relations with yourself, warranted me in
hoping for success—" ALS, *ibid.* Related papers are *ibid.* On April 15, USG
nominated De Lano as consul, Singapore; on the next day, he withdrew that
nomination and substituted consul, Foo Chow.

On March 11, Speaker of the House James G. Blaine had written to USG.
"As a special & personal favor to myself, I respectfully request the appt of
John P. Cowles Jr of Massachusetts as U. S Consul at Foochow China—Mr.
Cowles is a young man of great merit—of remarkable intelligence, and with
such commercial experience in China & Japan as will make him a peculiarly
efficient and valuable officer in the position named—" ALS, *ibid.* Related pa-
pers are *ibid.* On April 16, Blaine, Portsmouth, N. H., telegraphed to USG.
"I beg that you will appoint John P. Cowles Jr. Consul at Foo Chow It is the
only pressing personal request I have made—" Telegram received (at 11:30
A.M.), *ibid.*, RG 107, Telegrams Collected (Bound). On the same day, Blaine,
South Berwick, Maine, telegraphed to Horace Porter or Orville E. Babcock.
"Keims withdrawal opens Foo Chow to my friend John P. Cowles Jr. of Texas.
It is the only personal request I have made of the Administration. I think President will consider me as entitled to this small recognition Please read this
despatch to him and at all events have the place kept open until I can be further
heard." Telegram received (at 11:30 A.M.), *ibid.* On the same day, Blaine,
Portland, Maine, telegraphed to USG. "John P. Cowles Jr. whom I urge so
warmly for the Foo Chow consulate is a man of the highest character thoroughly
familiar with the commerce of the East. He served gallantly in the war and his
only brother lost his life in one of your great battles" Telegram received (at
1:00 P.M.), *ibid.* Also on April 16, Elihu B. Washburne, Chicago, telegraphed
to USG. "Blaine anxious to have his man Consul Foo Choo, Secretary knows"
Telegram received (at 7:00 P.M.), *ibid.*

On July 30, Lewis Dent, Washington, D. C., wrote to USG. "I am cognizant
of the fact that there was committed to my custody, to be presented to you, a
letter of Mr De Lano the recently appointed consul to Fow Chow, China, requesting the appointment of Frank D. Brawner of St. Louis Missouri, as Marshal
to the Consular Court at Fow Chow. This letter had on it also the endorsement
of Messrs Drake and Schurz, U. S. Senators from Missouri, and Nathan Cole

Mayor of St. Louis, strongly recommending the appointment of Mr Brawner, and my impression is that I handed to Col. Douglass to be presented to you for your action. It cannot be found, however, in the Secretarys Office, and I deem it due to Mr Brawner to make this statement and to request your early and favorable action in his case" ALS, *ibid.*, RG 59, Letters of Application and Recommendation. Robert M. Douglas endorsed this letter. "The letter of recommendation herein referred to, was received, and laid before the President; but has been mislaid, and cannot be found." AES, *ibid.* Related papers are *ibid.* No appointment followed.

To Cherokees

Washington DC Apl 23. 1869

COM. OF CHEROKEES.

DEAR SIRS:

It is cause of regret that Congress has not been able to adjust the various matters between the Government of the United States and the Cherokee Nation on the basis of justice and right to both parties, I trust however that this failure may not prove a source of trouble to your nation, but that the peace now prevailing may continue.

As President it will be my endeavor to preserve that peace, and to do all in my power, believing that Congress will cordially cooperate with me, to see that you receive all just dues.

With respect
Your obt sevt
U S GRANT

Copies, DLC-USG, II, 1, 4. On March 15, 1869, USG had told a delegation from the Cherokee, Choctaw, Creek, and Chickasaw nations that "he was glad to be informed that they would aid the policy for peace between the whites and the Indians, and would be glad of any measure which would accomplish that peace and lead to their civilization and ultimately make them citizens of the government. He felt that the march of civilization alone must of itself effect the civilization of the tribes now hostile to the government." *New York Herald,* March 16, 1869.

On Feb. 28, 1870, USG wrote to the Senate. "In answer to the Resolution of the Senate of the 19th instant, requesting to be informed 'if any officer of the Government has, contrary to the 10th article of the treaty of July 19th 1866, with the Cherokee Nation, enforced or sought to enforce the payment of taxes by Cherokees on products manufactured in the Cherokee Nation and sold within the Indian Territory,'—I transmit a Report from the Secretary of the Treasury, to whom the Resolution was referred." DS, DNA, RG 46, Presidential Messages. See *SED*, 41-2-48.

Speech

―――――

[May 7, 1869]

Mr. GARCIA—It gives me pleasure at all times to hear of the prosperity and advancement of the republican States in this hemisphere. Their progress and success encourage the expectation of the future extension of republican principles and their adoption by other communities. As you are taking leave, I shall hope that your successor may commend himself as much to the confidence of this government, and be as careful of the relations which now exist between the government of Peru and of the United States as you have been in the discharge of the duties.

New York Herald, May 9, 1869. USG spoke after José Antonio Garcia y Garcia, Peruvian minister, expressed a desire for closer commercial relations between Peru and the U.S. *Ibid.* On May 5, 1869, Secretary of State Hamilton Fish had written to USG. "Mr Garcia, the Minister from Peru, having asked for the appointment of a time to present to you his letter of recall, I have taken the liberty to say to him that you would receive him for that purpose at half past Eleven o'clock on Friday next, the 7th instant." LS, OFH.

On June 9, Manuel Freyre addressed USG upon presenting his credentials as the new Peruvian minister. "The relations of friendship which the Government of the United States has always maintained with the Republic of Peru, far from being weakened by the vicissitudes of time, have recently been tightened and strengthened in the direction of reciprocal good-will. Numerous are the acts by which the powerful North American nation has proved its sympathies in favor of the Peruvian people. I take pleasure in acknowledging them, and in proclaiming these sentiments for fraternity and of sincere attachment with which they have inspired my country. She, having entered upon the ways of progress and true liberty by acclimatizing upon her soil all those democratic institutions which are compatible with the necessities of her existence, cherishes a constant desire to draw closer those ties which neither distrusts nor a contrariety of principle and interests will ever weaken. . . ." *New York Times*, June 10, 1869. USG replied. "Colonel FREYRE: I welcome you as the Envoy Extraordinary and Minister Plenipotentiary of the Republic of Peru to the United States. You have drawn a correct picture of the friendly relations between our two countries. It will be my pleasure, during your mission, to endeavor to preserve and perpetuate them: and I have entire confidence in your disposition and ability to coöperate with me toward that desirable end." *Ibid.*

Endorsement

When the time comes let this apt. be made for the Class of 1870, with permission to present himself for examination in Sept. /69 should there be two vacancies at that time. The first vacancy, should any exist in Sept. I desire for Bainbridge Reynolds.[1]

U. S. GRANT

MAY 8TH /69

AES, DNA, RG 94, Correspondence, USMA. Written on a letter of May 8, 1869, from U.S. Representative John A. Logan of Ill. to USG. "I would respectfully and earnestly recommend Master John Clem, of Newark Licking Co Ohio who served in the Army, from the age of ten, to fourteen years old, with distinction and gallanttry, for appointment as Cadet to U. S. Military Academy at West Point" LS, *ibid.*

On Jan. 17, 1871, John L. Clem, Washington, D. C., wrote to USG. "I respectfully apply for a reappointment as a cadet 'at large' at the Military Academy at West Point, for June '72   I have to state that I was born at Newark Ohio, Aug. 13. 1851 and am now nineteen years of age. I served three years and seven months in the late War. I enlisted in the 22nd Mich Vol. Infantry, as a drummer when ten years of age, and served as such till the battle of Chickamauga, where I was promoted to a sergeant for killing a rebel colonel, who ordered me to surrender on the field of battle. After this I was placed on the 'Staff of Major General Geo. H. Thomas,' which position I held until the battle to the right of Atlanta Ga. where I was wounded in the right shoulder while handing Gen. Jno. A. Logan a dispatch. Last year the Ohio Assembly sent Your Excellency a petition in my behalf for an appointment as a cadet 'at large' which is still on file at the War Department. I was appointed a cadet June 1869, but failed to pass my preliminary examination in English Grammar. I have since earnestly pursued my studies and feel confident I can pass a creditable examination." ALS, *ibid.* On May 26, Secretary of War William W. Belknap endorsed this letter. "Respectfully transmitted to the Supt. Military Academy, for the action of the Academic Board. The President has named this youth as third alternate, in the event of a favorable recommendation from the Board. Speedy action is desired" ES, *ibid.* Related papers are *ibid.* On Dec. 18, Belknap wrote to Bvt. Maj. Gen. Edward D. Townsend conveying a presidential order to appoint as 2nd lt. "John L. Clem of Illinois—Address Washington D. C. 24th or 25th Infy." ALS, *ibid.*, ACP, 5243 1871. On May 31, 1872, W. W. Carter, Baltimore, wrote to USG sending information about Clem's military service. ALS, *ibid.*, 422 1872. On March 7, 1873, Clem, Washington, D. C., wrote to

USG requesting appointment as capt. and commissary. ALS, *ibid.* In [Dec., 1876], Clem, Fort Whipple, Va., wrote to USG. "In the event that the House of Representatives passes the Senate Bill making a 'Signal Corps' I have the honor to apply for a captaincy in that corps. . . ." ALS, *ibid.* On Feb. 8, 1877, Alexander Martin, president, Indiana Asbury University, Greencastle, wrote to USG requesting Clem's appointment as "Professor of Military Science & Tactics." ALS, *ibid.* On Feb. 20, Townsend endorsed this letter. "Simply reply, Lt. Clem is not available for the detail." AE (initialed), *ibid.* See Greg Pavelka, "Where Were You Johnny Shiloh?," *Civil War Times Illustrated*, XXVII, no. 9 (Jan., 1989), 34–41.

    1. The son of Bvt. Maj. Gen. Joseph J. Reynolds. See *PUSG*, 17, 377, 551.

Order

May 14th 1869.

I have examined the proceedings of the Court of Inquiry in the case of Brigadier and Brevet Major General A. B. Dyer,[1] Chief of Ordnance, and approve the "findings and opinion" of the Court, and they are hereby approved and confirmed.

[U. S. GRANT]

Copy, DNA, RG 130, Presidential Action, Court-Martial Cases. The Court of Inquiry, composed of Maj. Gen. George H. Thomas, Maj. Gen. Winfield S. Hancock, Bvt. Maj. Gen. Alfred H. Terry, and Brig. Gen. and Judge Advocate Gen. Joseph Holt, had found "that no further proceedings are necessary in the matter of the complaints against Brig. and Brevet Major General A. B. Dyer, Chief of Ordnance, in his administration of the Ordnance Department, as contained in the Report of the Joint Select Committee on Ordnance, and the testimony accompanying the same, reported to the Senate of the United States, July 17 1868." Copy, *ibid.* Clifford Arrick, St. Clairsville, Ohio, and others, patentees of the Eureka art. projectile, had brought charges against Bvt. Maj. Gen. Alexander B. Dyer that included favoring contracts for shells in which he held a financial interest and securing his appointment as chief of ordnance through intrigue. *National Intelligencer*, May 19, 1869; *SRC*, 40-2-173; *ibid.*, 40-2-189; *Proceedings of a Court of Inquiry . . . to Examine into the Accusations Against Brig. and Bvt. Major General A. B. Dyer, Chief of Ordnance* (Washington, D. C., 1868–69).

    On June 25, 1869, Secretary of War John A. Rawlins wrote to Arrick. "I have the honor to inform you that your letters of date respectively June 18th and 19th, relative to the Dyer Court of Inquiry, suggesting and urging a re-opening of the case, to enable you to present your views for the annulment of the Executive order therein, has been received, and, after reference to the Judge Advocate General for his remarks thereon, submitted to the President, who, in answer thereto, directs me to inform you that as, after some five months spent in the investigation of the charges against General Dyer, his accusers thought proper to submit the case without comment, and expressly declined to offer any argument either upon the vast amount of testimony or the legal questions arising therefrom, the proposition to re-open it anew, and urge upon the Executive the views of the law and evidence which should have been urged before the Court, is regarded as both unreasonable and inadmissable, and its favorable consideration would be not only unjust to the accused officer, but a reflection upon the distinguished officers composing the Court, whose examination of the case, as attested by the Judge Advocate General—himself a constant attendant upon the inquiry,—was patient, thorough, and impartial; such an investigation, in fact, as was expected at their hands when selected for the important duty imposed upon them, and there is no just reason to believe that this expectation has not been fully realized; and that for these reasons you will please consider that, so far as the Executive is concerned, the case has been finally determined. . . ." LS, DNA, RG 156, Letters Received.

On Feb. 7, 1871, Arrick and Wilson S. Kennon, Washington, D. C., wrote to USG. "Since the personal interview of November 23d and our letter of December 19. 1870, we have endeavored to relieve the subjects under discussion of some collateral proceedings and issues, that arose out of a supposed disinclination on the part of your Excellency to consider them—Prominently among these, was 'the charge of conspiracy against General Dyer', refered to in a certain *equity cause*, now pending in the Supreme court of the District of Columbia, and which, for the corrupt considerations therein named, *was to be accommodated*, and the charge itself, 'to be withdrawn from Congress symultaneously—' The object of this proceeding before Congress, was to secure what we had been advised your Excellency would not grant, and it is withdrawn now because you have granted it—The letter of withdrawal is herewith submitted, and for the sole purpose of forestalling unjust criticism of the act. The case pending in the District Court does not raise the issue before you; *directly*, and through the representatives of our deceased friend, and those of Gen. Butler, we are advised that *it too*, is soon to be *withdrawn* . . . P. S. We will resume our argument with as little delay as our other engagements will admit of." LS, *ibid.* The enclosure is *ibid.* On Feb. 27, Arrick and Kennon wrote to USG. "For the purpose of concluding discussion thereon finally, we respectfully request permission to withdraw from the files of the Department, the motion now pending before you, in the 'Dyer Court of Inquiry case,' together with all other papers and documents filed by us in support thereof, since May 4, 1869." Copy, *ibid.* Related papers are *ibid.*; *ibid.*, RG 107, Letters Received.

1. See *PUSG*, 14, 208.

Proclamation

BY THE PRESIDENT OF THE UNITED STATES OF AMERICA.
A PROCLAMATION.

Whereas the Act of Congress approved June 25th 1868, constituted, on and after that date, Eight hours a day's work for all laborers, workmen and mechanics employed by or on behalf of the Government of the United States, and repealed all Acts and parts of Acts inconsistent therewith; Now therefore, I, Ulysses S. Grant, President of the United States, do hereby direct that, from and after this date, no reduction shall be made in the wages paid by the Government by the day to such laborers workmen and mechanics, on account of such reduction of the hours of labor.

In testimony whereof, I have hereto set my hand and caused the seal of the United States to be affixed

Done at the City of Washington, this nineteenth day of May, in the year of Our Lord, one thousand eight hundred and sixty nine, and of the Independence of the United States the ninety-third.

U. S. GRANT

DS, DNA, RG 130, Presidential Proclamations. In an undated petition docketed April 14, 1869, John W. Browning, secretary, Workingmen's Union, New York City, *et al.* had written to USG. "We the undersigned representing the wishes and desire of the Workingmen of the Country, would respectfully submit that the rejection by the Senate June 24, 1868 of the proposed amendment to the 'Eight hour law'. offered by Mr Sherman to reduce the wages in a corresponding degree, and the unanimous adoption by the House of Representatives april 8, 1869, of an explanatory resolution declaring that the law shall not be construde to authorize a reduction of the wages. which did not pass the Senate for want of time only, clearly shows that the construction of the law by the Honorable Secretary of the Navy and the Honorable Secretary of War is erroneous and unjust, and therefore we humbly petition your Excellency to direct such orders to be issued as shall settle at once the question how many hours shall constitute a full day's work for Laborers, workmen and Mechanics in the employ of the United States, and entitle employés to a full day's wages" DS (9 signatures), *ibid.*, RG 60, Letters from the President. On April 27, Attorney Gen. Ebenezer R. Hoar wrote to USG. "In accordance with your request of the 23d inst. I have the honor to transmit herewith a copy of the opinion of my predecessor, Mr. Evarts, on the construction of the 'Act constituting Eight Hours a Day's Work,' &c—And also a copy of an Opinion rendered by me to the Secretary of the Navy on the 20th inst. on the same subject. The printed petition referred to has no signature at all, but is endorsed by Senator Wilson, and eight Representatives from Massachusetts." Copy, *ibid.*, Letters Sent. A draft of a "Memorandum submitted to President Grant upon the subject of the pay of Mechanics & Laborers of the govt under the law of June 25 1868 by N P Banks, M. C." is in DLC-Nathaniel P. Banks.

On May 27, 1869, William H. Sylvis, president, National Labor Union, Philadelphia, wrote to USG. "When the attorney-general, adversely to the interests of those intended to be benefited by the enactment of the eight-hour law, decided that under it workmen employed in the government shops are entitled to but four-fifths of a day's pay for what that law constituted a full day's work, we almost despaired of securing justice until after the reconvening of Congress; but your proclamation, under date of 21st instant, has pleasurably disappointed us. Though this is prepared as a letter of thanks, we do not feel it a duty to accord express thanks to government officials, who, in remembrance of their obligation, faithfully interpret or administer the law. We regard government officials as public servants, selected because of their honesty, sagacity, wisdom, and affection for the country, and an equitable execution of the law as a duty, to the faithful performance of which they have made a solemn pledge, and not as a favor meriting special thanks. The proper discharge of a pledged duty is certainly incumbent upon the servant of the public equally as upon him who occupies the same relation to the individual, who is meritedly punished for an improper, though not specially thanked for a proper, performance of his pledged or implied promise. The history of our country during the past several years has proven, however, that the faithful fulfilment of official pledges, the rigidly honest construction and administration of law, is not the rule but the exception; so that it has become customary to especially thank officials when, in a moment of aberration, they condescend to equitably legislate, administer, or interpret. In your inaugural address to the country, you pledged yourself to the enforcement of all laws just or unjust, which you very properly told us were enacted for the government as well of those who opposed as those who favored them— and by reason of that pledge we had a right to expect just such an order as was contained in your proclamation of the 21st inst. But you will pardon us, sir, if we say, that, accepting official conduct during the last few years as an index of that to come, we seriously doubted that, in the face of the attorney-general's very learned opinion, you would render to the laborer of the nation—we say of the nation, for a mighty principle is involved—that which the eight-hour law has declared to be their due. But your order came, and coming unexpectedly is doubly welcome, and we experience augmented pleasure in thanking you for it. We plain people believed the provisions of the law to be plain enough. Their being so, perhaps, accounts for the egregious error committed by your learned legal adviser in his interpretation of them. Your practical mind divined its intent; while to his acumen—the accumulated wondrous wisdom of years of varied experience—it was an occult problem, from the solution of which he emerged defeated—which was worse for his legal reputation than for his material condition, seeing that he is still your attorney-general. My position, as official head of the National Labor Union, has brought me into contact with many 'malcontents,' who, deeming that the government deals inequitably by them, attribute it to too much law and a superabundance of lawyers. Whether they are correct or not, they seem determined to combat from that position, and their ranks are numerous. Their success or defeat, the progress of time alone can develop; but a multiplication of instances wherein (as in the one that has just passed into history) the learned decision of a self-puffed lawyer is compelled to give way to the unvarnished rendering of a practical citizen unread in Blackstone and unversed in the technicalities of Coke or Littleton, will make the former extremely probable. If thanks are due for simple justice, the National Labor Union thanks you for your order. Trusting, sir, that your actions throughout your official term may be gauged by the rule of justice that impelled you to treat Mr. Hoar's opinion with the indifference its utter silliness deserved, . . ." James C. Sylvis, *The Life, Speeches, Labors and Essays of William H. Sylvis* (Philadelphia, 1872), pp. 326–28.

On March 30, 1870, USG acknowledged a gift presented by the Mechanics' State Council of Calif. in gratitude for enforcement of legislation establishing an eight-hour workday. "GENTLEMEN: I have no reply to make, only to thank the mechanics of California for this assurance of their approbation of what I have done, being only what the law required me to do." *Washington Chronicle*, March 30, 31, 1870. Variant text in *Washington National Republican*, March 31, 1870.

On Dec. 13, Thomas M. Wallace, Lyndon, Kan., wrote to USG. ". . . I worked as a mechaic at R. I Arsenal Ill from and after my discharge (vet vol 45th Ill Infr) to year 1870 and by the the unjust ruling of the Post Comander under the eight hour law (with other workmen were deprived of a portion (20 per ct) of our pay untill Your Order of May 19th /69 from & after that date placd us squarely under the benificent act   Prior to Your order as above the Govt is indebted to us in various sums for which we have appealed to Congress for redress but hitherto in vain   I would most Respectfuly (both for my self and in behalfe of my fellow workmen) ~~Solicit~~ ask You to Call the attention of Congress to this matter   I do *need* the *money* just as badly as if it was one hundred thousand" ALS, DNA, RG 107, Letters Received from Bureaus.

Order

———

Washington D. C. June 3d 1869.

A commission of citizens having been appointed under the authority of law to co-operate with the administrative departments in the management of Indian Affairs consisting of Wm Welsh[1] of Phila, John V. Farwell[2] of Chicago, Geo. H. Stuart[3] of Phila, Robert Campbell,[4] St. Louis, W. E. Dodge[5] New-York, E. S. Tobey[6] Boston, Felix R. Brunot,[7] Pittsburgh, Nathan Bishop[8] New York, and Henry. S. Lane[9] of Indiana, the following regulations will till further directions. control the action of said commission, and of the Bureau of Indian Affairs in matters coming under their joint supervision.

1. The commission will make its own organization, and employ its own clerical Assistants keeping its "necessary expenses of transportation subsistence and clerk hire, when actually engaged in said service" within the amount appropriated therefor by Congress.

2. The commission shall be furnished with full opportunity to inspect the records of the Indian Office and to obtain full information as to the conduct of all parts of the affairs thereof.

3. They shall have full power to inspect in person or by subcommittee, the various Indian Superintendencies and Agencies in the Indian Country, to be present at payment of Annuities, at consultations or councils with the Indians, and when on the ground to advise Superintendents and Agents in the performance of their duties.

4. They are authorized to be present in person or by subCommittee at purchases of goods for Indian purposes, and inspect said purchases, advising the Commissioner of Indian Affairs[10] in regard thereto.

5. Whenever they shall deem it necessary or advisable that instructions of Superintendents or agents be changed or modified they will communicate such advice through the office of Commissioner of Indian Affairs to the Secretary of Interior, and in like manner their advice as to changes in modes of purchasing goods or conducting the affairs of the Indian Bureau proper. Complaints against Superintendents or Agents or other officers will in the same manner be forwarded to the Indian Bureau or Department of Interior for action.

6. The commission will at their Board-meetings, determine upon the recommendations to be made as to the plans of civilizing or dealing with the Indians, and submit the same for action in the manner above indicated, and all plans involving the expenditure of public money, will be acted upon by the Executive or the Sec'y of Interior, before expenditure is made under the same.

7. The usual modes of accounting with the Treasury cannot be changed and all expenditures therefore must be subject to the approvals now required by law, and the regulations of the Treasury

Department, and all vouchers must conform to the same laws and requirements and pass through the ordinary channels.

8. All the officers of the government connected with the Indian Service, are enjoined to afford every facility and opportunity to said commission and their sub-committees in the performance of their duties and to give the most respectful heed to their advice, within the limits of such officer's positive instructions from their superiors: to allow such Commissioner full access to their records and accounts, and to co-operate with them in the most earnest manner to the extent of their proper powers in the general work of civilizing the Indians, protecting them in their legal rights and stimulating them to become industrious citizens in permanent homes, instead of following a roving and savage life.

9. The Commission will keep such records or minutes of their proceedings as may be necessary to afford evidence of their action, and will provide for the manner in which their communications with and advice to the Government shall be made and authenticated.

U. S. GRANT.

Copy, DNA, RG 130, Executive Orders and Proclamations. On Feb. 15, 1869, Bvt. Brig. Gen. Ely S. Parker wrote to Benjamin Hallowell, secretary, "central executive committee of the seven Yearly Meetings of Friends." "General Grant, the President elect, desirous of inaugurating some policy to protect the Indians in their just rights and enforce integrity in the administration of their affairs, as well as to improve their general condition, and appreciating fully the friendship and interest which your society has ever maintained in their behalf, directs me to request that you will send him a list of names, members of your society, whom your society will indorse, as suitable persons for Indian agents. Also to assure you that any attempt which may or can be made by your society for the improvement, education, and civilization of the Indians under such agencies will receive from him, as President, all the encouragement and protection which the laws of the United States will warrant him in giving." *SMD*, 45-3-53, pp. 396–97. On March 24, USG met for two hours with Secretary of the Interior Jacob D. Cox, George H. Stuart, William Welsh, William Strong, Eli K. Price, Samuel Shepley, John Hilles, and Edward S. Tobey, and in reply to an expressed need for "a humane and Christianizing policy towards the Indians," stated that "it was his desire to make a radical change in the Indian policy of the government." *New York Herald*, March 25, 1869. See *HED*, 41-2-1, part 3, pp. 486-87; *HRC*, 41-3-39, pp. 80–81; *Autobiography of Benjamin Hallowell* (Philadelphia, 1883), pp. 261–69; Robert H. Keller, Jr., *American Protestantism and United States Indian Policy, 1869–82* (Lincoln, Neb., and London, 1983), pp. 72–89.

On July 5, Cox wrote to Welsh, Philadelphia. "The desire to write rather more at length than I had time to do immediately after my return from the West, must be my apology for not sooner replying to yours of the 29th ult in which you 'decline further service as Commissioner' upon Indian affairs. The terms in which your resignation is couched leaves the President no option as to its acceptance, and in recognizing your withdrawal from the Commission he can only express his regret (in which I heartily join) that you should so far differ from the plan of action indicated in the Executive order organizing the Board, as to make you feel that further action upon it is not desirable. For your kind expressions of willingness to coöperate privately in the very important work of Civilization you have our hearty thanks The Commission having been organized under authority contained in an Act of Congress, and the President having exercised his discretion in indicating its duties in accordance with the Law, I did not feel at liberty to enter into any discussion of the history of the passage of the Act whilst you were a member of the Board; but now that you have retired from it, I will venture to make very brief reference to a passage in your letter of 5th June in which you refer to a modification suggested by me in the original draft of the clause of the act giving authority to the President to appoint the Board—I desire only to say that the essential point to remember is that I insisted upon two things as in my view essential to the legislation in question: *First*: that it should be left entirely discretionary with the President as to whether *any* direct supervision & control of the public moneys should be vested in the Commission; and *Second*, That if such supervision & control were granted it must not be independent of this Department which would remain responsible necessarily for the general conduct of Indian Affairs—These two things *were* embodied in the legislation, and you will remember that you again & again said that it was unnecessary even to consider the question whether the appropriations should pass into the Commission's hands, since the whole would now be left discretionary with the President—For myself, I had not yet fully acquainted myself with the working of the Indian Bureau and the machinery of accounting for public moneys, and was so desirous of getting any practical basis for the organization of the Commission, that I insisted upon nothing but the two things referred to above. This is all I desire to say on that subject. Justice to Commissioner Parker requires that I you should be informed you more fully than you seem at present to be, in regard to what took place at his Spring purchases in New York. The facts are these. We were all desirous of having the assistance of the Commission in the purchases to be made in the Spring; but the Commission had not yet been organized & could not get together in time. Under these circumstances Messrs Stuart & Dodge were requested to aid Gen. Parker in his work, & Mr Chittenden of New York was also kind enough to respond to Gen. Parker's invitation extended after he arrived in that city. After consultation with those gentleman as well as with several other very prominent merchants of the City, an inspector was chosen who was an expert in the goods to be bought, and who had never been connected with the Bureau or with Indian purchases. The inspector examined the goods as they were laid out for packing & approved them as being fully up to samples, and no reason is as yet known for doubting either his skill or his fidelity. When the goods were packed Mr Stuart suggested that the prices were *so low* as to raise suspicion of fraudulent intent to pack others than those selected, and proposed that the whole invoice of the goods be taken to a warehouse which Mr Chittenden kindly offered to furnish, & be there unpacked & reëxamined, repacked &

shipped. Gen. Parker agreed that such a reëxamination would be conclusive, but believing that it would occupy a month, and that that delay would make it too late to get the goods to the Upper Missouri by the Spring rise of that river, thus preventing their distribution this year, he determined to vary the method by selecting an entirely new inspector for whose integrity Mr Chittenden vouched, and having some twenty cases (selected at random from the whole mass) opened & reinspected. This was done & the goods found to be correct. As the contractors knew nothing of the purpose to reïnspect, nor of the boxes selected when it was done, this was believed by Gen. Parker to be a sufficient test in view of the absolute necessity for getting the goods quickly shipped, although he would have preferred to follow Mr Stuart's suggestion if there had been time. Upon the facts submitted to this Department and referred to the President, as to the necessity of haste, the probable delay, and the method actually adopted, General Parker's action has been fully approved, though he will in future purchases endeavor so to fix the time of the same, as to be able to carry out fully Mr Stuart's valuable suggestion in regard to ~~the same~~ it. The belief that the best had been done that the circumstances admitted, considering the time of the year & the fact that but for the change of administrations the purchases would naturally have been made in February, made me regret that you should have chosen to embody in a formal communication a complaint in regard to a matter which had been fully discussed by the Commission when in session & on which they had intimated no dissatisfaction. I especially regretted this because in saying in your letter, to which I have referred, that Messrs 'Stuart & Dodge more than suspected frauds' the language is such as might naturally be understood to include ~~the~~ Gen. Parker in the suspicion, instead of indicating that it was based upon the prices of the goods alone, as I have stated above. Mr Stuart has so fully & emphatically expressed his entire faith in Gen. P's integrity & zeal in the transaction, that we who were cognizant of the events as they happened could not misapprehend them; but I am sure from your own expressions in conversation on the same subject that you will be glad to have your attention thus called to what you will see was a very ambiguous ~~expression~~ statement as coming from the Chairman of the Commission, and making part of the public records of the Department. Again repeating my regret that you should feel it your duty, so quickly to terminate an official connection from which I had hoped to get much satisfaction & public advantage, . . ." ALS (press), Cox Papers, Oberlin College, Oberlin, Ohio.

On July [5], Cox wrote to Felix R. Brunot. "A letter has been received from Mr Welsh declining to act further as a commissioner and notifying me that you will perform the duties of chairman until a further formal meeting of the Board I very deeply regret that Mr Welsh should have felt constrained to this course of action, and am pained with the conviction that until the opportunity occurs for a personal conference with the commission, there will be no sufficient mode of explaining as I should desire to do, the motives and purposes of the President in his Executive order organizing your body, and especially in determining that the best interests of the cause we are at work in would not be promoted by making the Commission *directly* responsible for the control & disbursement of money appropriated by Congress for Indian affairs. . . . It would [be] cause of the sincerest grief [both to] the President & to myself if our failure to comply with Mr Welsh's full desire in the matter should cause what we believe may be a great step in the work of Indian civilization to prove abortive.

Our complete faith in the character & motives of all the members of the Commission is such that we desire to assure you in every possible way of its sincerity, and to beg you to believe that no pride of opinion would prevent our yielding at once to Mr Welsh's demand were it not our real conviction that the public interests may be most thoroughly subserved by beginning, at least, upon the plan indicated in the Executive order. Mr Campbell's resignation has had nothing to do with the questions stated by your late Chairman, but is as he assures us based wholly upon conflict of his personal engagements with a thorough performance of this duty. Mr Tobey only renews the expression of his fear that his health will not permit him to continue on the board & tenders a conditional resignation which I hope [to] persuade him to recall at least till your next full meeting. Let me earnestly request, therefore that the plan for an early tour of inspection to the Indian reservations be carried out: that you then meet in this city to compare notes and have full consultation with this department & with the President if you desire it: and that all other considerations be postponed till this can be done—To save to yourself time & trouble I will mail a Copy of this to each me[mber] of the Board   Assuring you of my anxious desire to make the coöperation of the Commission with this department entirely pleasant & satisfactory, and repeating the earnest hope that we shall discover on fuller comparison of views that the dissatisfaction expressed by Mr Welsh was not felt by you generally . . ." ALS (press), *ibid*.

    1. Born in 1807, importer and philanthropist prominently identified with the Episcopal Church.

    2. John V. Farwell, a Chicago wholesale merchant, born in 1825, aided various religious and reform initiatives, especially those related to the work of Dwight L. Moody. On April 15, 1869, Cox had written to Farwell. "The President has directed me to invite you to become one of the Commission provided for by the late Act of Congress to act as auxiliary to this Department in the Supervision of the work of gathering the Indians upon reservations &c. The Commission will serve without pay, except for expenses actually incurred in travelling, and is expected to act both as a Consulting board of advisers, and (through their sub committees) as Inspectors of the Agencies &c in the Indian Country. The design of those who suggested the Commission was that something like a Christian Commission should be established, having the civilization of the Indian in view, and laboring to stimulate public interest in this work, whilst also coöperating with this Department in the specific purpose mentioned—The following gentleman have been requested to become members of the Board with you: William Welsh, Phila Geo. H. Stuart James E. Yeatman, St Louis—Wm E. Dodge, New York, E. S. Tobey, Boston; & Felix R. Brunot of Pittsburg. Perhaps two others will be added & as soon as answers are received a preliminary meeting will be called here. Earnestly hoping you will consent to your own appointment, and that you will in any event withhold any refusal until the preliminary meeting has been held & you have thus been enabled to discuss more fully the objects and the importance of the contemplated movement, . . ." ALS (press), *ibid*.

    3. See *PUSG*, 12, 407.

    4. Robert Campbell of St. Louis, merchant and banker, born in Ireland in 1804, prospered originally as a fur trapper.

    5. See letter to Elihu B. Washburne, Sept. 23, 1868.

6. Tobey, born in 1813, capitalist and president of the Boston Young Men's Christian Association, participated in several social welfare activities.

7. Steel manufacturer, born in 1820, who had sponsored a corps of vol. physicians during the Civil War.

8. Nathan Bishop, born in 1808, had served successfully as superintendent of schools in Providence, R. I., and Boston and assisted numerous charities.

9. Henry S. Lane, lawyer and banker, born in 1811, former Republican U.S. Senator from Ind. (1861–67).

10. On March 1, 1869, Bishops Edward R. Ames, Matthew Simpson, and other Methodist clergy, Washington, D. C., wrote to USG. "Recognizing in Hon. N. G. Taylor of Tennessee, at present Commissioner of Indian affairs, an accomplished christian gentleman, a proven friend of our National Union—who lost most of his earthly substance on account of his patriotism; a statesman of ability, experience and integrity—your unflinching supporter, and our personal friend,—we most respectfully but urgently commend him to y'r most favorable consideration and to entire confidence—Intimately familiar with 'Indian affairs,' we sincerely trust his services in that Department—as its chief—will be continued unless it be made so essentially military, as to exclude a civilian. In any event, however, we beg to say, that the employment of Col. Taylor, in some important relation to your administration will be most gratifying to your friends—" DS (9 signatures), DNA, RG 48, Appointment Div., Letters Received. On the same day, Jay S. Backus and E. E. L. Taylor, American Baptist Home Mission Society, New York City, wrote a similar letter to USG. DS, *ibid.* On March 23, Nathaniel G. Taylor, Washington, D. C., wrote to USG. "I have the honor of tendering to you my resignation of the Office of Commissioner of Indian Affairs to take effect on the 30th Prox. or as soon thereafter as my successor shall have qualified." ALS, *ibid.*

On March 6, U.S. Senator John M. Thayer of Neb. had written to USG. "I desire not to be officious, but I will take the liberty of recommending the appointment of Gen Parker, of your late Staff, to be commissioner of Indian affairs. I can think of no one whose appointment to that position would give greater satisfaction to the country. What appointment so appropriate? Who could exercise so favorable an influence upon the Indians?" ALS, *ibid.*

On April 12, Attorney Gen. Ebenezer R. Hoar wrote to Cox. "In reply to your letter of the 19th inst. touching the question of the eligibility of Gen'l E. S. Parker to the office of chief of a bureau of your Department, I have the honor to state that, on the facts presented, I do not perceive that he is disqualified from holding such office under the Constitution and laws of the United States." Copy, *ibid.*, RG 60, Opinions. On April 13, Cox wrote to USG. "I learn from Mr Taylor Commr of Indian Affairs that his resignation was worded so as to take effect on *30th* April, inst. I had somehow got the idea that it took effect on *1st* April, & so the nomination of Col. Parker is to take the office immediately—At Mr Taylor's request I make the above statement so that if you think best to change the message to the Senate it may be done. Whilst I am desirous of accommodating Mr Taylor's wishes as far as may be, I recognize the importance of that bureau being under the control of the officer who is to be permanently at its head, as soon as possible." ALS, Cooke Collection, MiU-C. On the same day, USG nominated Parker as commissioner of Indian Affairs. See William H. Armstrong, *Warrior in Two Camps: Ely S. Parker Union General and Seneca Chief* (Syracuse, 1978), pp. 134–36.

On March 9, John B. Henderson, William S. Harney, Bvt. Maj. Gen. Alfred H. Terry, and Gen. William T. Sherman, Washington, D. C., had written to USG. "The undersigned members of the late Indian Peace Commission respectfully represent that our associate General John B. Sanborn of Minnesota having just after the close of the rebellion commanded in the Indian country and having been ~~ofa~~ member of several commissions to make treaties with different tribes is a very suitable person for the office of Commissioner of Indian affairs.—In our opinion he possesses very unusual knowledge of and experience in Indian affairs, and we believe that he would administer the Indian bureau with integrity and ability" LS, DNA, RG 48, Appointment Div., Letters Received. On April 6, S. Markham *et al.*, Washington, D. C., petitioned USG. "We the undersigned Delegates, representing in the aggregate fifty thousand settlers on different tracts of Indian lands in Kansas, respectfully, but most earnestly, recommend the appointment of Gen John B Sanborn, to the office of Commissioner of Indian Affairs. We ask his appointment in the name of the people we represent, and in the name of justice to the Indian; and we submit, that it would be hailed as a very great triumph over the corruptionists that have so long controlled and disgraced the Indian Department" DS (5 signatures), *ibid.* U.S. Representatives William Lawrence of Ohio and George W. Julian of Ind. favorably endorsed this petition.

On March 21, John Bell, Richmond, Ind., wrote to USG. "Impelled by a desire to do something for a long neglected and wronged race I thought it best to offer a few suggestions, noticing thou hast evinced a wish that members of our Society should act as Agents and that one should be appointed as Commissioner I beleive. No doubt many will be pressed for these appointments and I think for the Chief office, it ought to be a 'Friend' of *high Standing*, a *Consistent Conscientious* man, *Known* and esteemed at *home* and *abroad*, thou art perhaps aware 'Friends' *as a people* are not what they were in early times, when they were filled with a high sense of their responsibility towards God and man, so that in selecting 'Friends' for these positions it should be with due regard to their standing and real *Moral* and *religious* Character and *Worth*. It seems to me it would be eminently proper to choose a Pennsylvanian for the highest office, a follower of the great and illustrious Penn such a man might be found in the person of *Thomas Wistar* a long tried and experienced man in Indian affairs who has frequently gone on important Missions of mercy to these poor people, . . ." ALS, *ibid.*

To Charles H. Rogers

Washington. D. C. June 9th *1869*

MY DEAR SIR:

Your favor of the 5th inst. is received. I am sorry that it will not be convenient for Mrs. Rogers &and you to meet us at West

Point this week. Mrs. Grant, the two younger children and myself
will be in New York City for a day or two next week however when
we will have the pleasure of seeing you.

Yours Truly
U. S. Grant

C. H. Rogers, Esq.
New York City.

ALS, Mrs. George B. Post.

To Edwards Pierrepont

West Point, N. Y.
June 14th 1869,

Dear Sir:

Your dispatch of the 12th announcing the decision of Judge
Blatchford in the Dupuy case was duly received. I am truly glad
of the result not so much because I wanted the legality of my act
sustained as because I want to see evil doers punished.—I congratulate you on the result and hope you will be successful in bringing
more of the same sort of public plunderers to justice.

I will be in New York City a few hours to-morrow on my way
to Bo[ston.]

Yours [Truly,]
U. [S. Grant]

Judge E. P[ierrepont,]
New Yo[rk City.]

ALS, Forbes Magazine Collection, New York, N. Y. On March 8, 1869, USG
had ordered: "Whereas at a Circuit Court of the United States heretofore held
in the Southern District of New York, Jacob Dupuy and Moses Dupuy were
convicted of a misdemeanor and were thereupon sentenced to imprisonement and
the sentence was by said Court directed to be executed in the Jail at Blackwell's
Island in the said County of New York. And whereas the President of the United
States on the Fourth instant, directed pardons to be issued to the said Jacob and
Moses Dupuy. And whereas said pardons have not been delivered to and accepted by said Jacob and Moses Dupuy or either of them. It is ordered that the

said pardons be and the same hereby are revoked and withdrawn" Copy, DNA, RG 130, Executive Orders and Proclamations. On the same day, in an unrelated case, USG revoked the pardon of Richard C. Enright. Copy, *ibid.* On May 11, "Blatchford, Seward, Griswold & Da Costa," New York City, wrote to former President Andrew Johnson. "You may remember that on the 3rd day of March 1869, you granted a pardon to Jacob, and Moses Depuy. It appears that after the pardons had been received by the Marshal for the Southern District of New York, the same was countermanded by President Grant. As we are about applying for Moses Depuy, for a writ of habeas corpus, to the District Court of the United States for the Southern District of New York, we have taken the liberty of drafting an affidavit, which we should be very much obliged to you, to swear to and forward to us. If you should not desire to swear to the affidavit in the terms in which it has been drafted, please altar the same as you may deem best, and return the same to us. Apologizing for the trouble we give you, . . ." LS, DLC-Andrew Johnson. An unsigned affidavit is *ibid.* On June 12, Judge Samuel Blatchford, U.S. District Court, New York City, sustained the revocation. *New York Times,* June 13, 1869.

To George M. Robeson

Washington. D. C. June 22d *1869*

Dear Sir:

The Hon. Sec. of the Navy, A. E. Borie, to whom I, and my entire Cabinet, have become much attached finds it indispensably necessary for him to sever his official connection with the Administration. At my urgent request he has already remained with it longer than he contemplated when he accepted the position.[1] I must now releive him, and write this to tender to you the position.—I sincerely hope that it may be consistent with your pleasure to accept, and that I may receive your responce, to that effect, at an early day.

> With great respect,
> your obt. svt.
> U. S. Grant

Hon. J Geo. M. Robeson,
Atty. Gn.
State of N. J.

ALS, ICarbS. Born in Warren County, N. J., in 1829, George M. Robeson graduated from Princeton College in 1847 and began to practice law in 1850. During the Civil War, he organized N. J. troops as brig. gen. In 1867, he was appointed attorney gen. of N. J.

1. On May 21 and 22, 1869, George H. Stuart, Philadelphia, wrote to USG. "I am feeling so poorly to day that I cannot explain ~~to you~~ as I desire the reasons which led to the final conclusion which I ~~had expected wd have been different from that which~~ I sent Mr Borie to day by telegraph, I never wrote any thing so reluctantly or with so much deep regret, If better I shall ~~hope to write~~ try and explain myself to-morrow," "I never wrote any thing with so much reluctance as my dispatch of yesterday to Sec.y Borie, I feel sad ever since ~~least I have done wrong~~ thinking perhaps I may have erred. When I parted from you on Wednesday evening I had all but concluded to accept of your kind offer to take his place as Sec.y of the Navy, To be a member of your Cabinet I regard as the higest eartly honor ~~than~~ and one of which I feel quite unworthy, I am with your adminstration heart and soul and hold myself ready to aid you to the extent of my ability, Personal ~~reasons~~ considerations were the ~~alone~~ only cause of my declining this second unexpected and most complimentary offer, The precarious ~~condition nature~~ state of my health ~~with~~ and the fact that in the present unsettled ~~con state~~ condition of business I had no one to leave at the head of my establiment with sufficent experience ~~to manage it~~ to take my place were mainly the ~~cause of leading me to decide as I did~~ reasons that led to my decision, ~~Should~~ Hoping that in other ways I may be able to serve you personally as well as your adminstation and with my daily prayer to God for ~~you~~ yourself and your dear family . . ." ADfS, DLC-George H. Stuart.

To Adolph E. Borie

Washington. D. C. June 25th *1869,*

HON. A. E. BORIE:
SEC. OF THE NAVY:
DEAR SIR:

Your letter of this date, tendering your resignation of the position of Sec. of the Navy,[1] is received. I need not assure you how much I regret the severence of our official connection, nor how confident I am that the high esteem I have always felt for you, increased with further acquaintance, will continue while acquaintance lasts. I accept your resignation with regret therefore, and

hope that the quiet you will find in retirement will restore you to
perfect health.

With great respect,

your obt. svt.

U. S. GRANT

ALS, PHi. On June 25, 1869, Secretary of the Navy Adolph E. Borie had written to USG. "When I assumed, with appreciative pride, the high office of Secretary of the Navy conferred upon me by your flattering, predilection, I stated
that I feared, for reasons of a personal and domestic nature, then explained,
that I would not be able to retain the position, long: I now come to ask your
acceptance of my resignation; the severance of my official and always most at-
tractive relations with you, for whom I entertain so much esteem and attachment, gives me sincere pain, and the abandonment of my public duties, much
regret, but the great confidence I feel in the harmonious and successful progress
of the Administration under your able, honest and glorious lead, is my great
solace and with the warmest wishes and most earnest prayers for the health and
happiness of yourself as well as of all dear to you, . . ." ALS, DNA, RG 59,
Letters of Resignation and Declination. A signed draft is in PHi. On June 26,
the *New York Herald* printed a version of USG's letter to Borie which consisted
of a perfunctory acceptance of the resignation. On July 4, the *Herald* printed
the correct text.

On June 25, Horace Porter wrote to Secretary of State Hamilton Fish.
"The President directs me to request that you bring with you to the Executive
Mansion at 11.45 A. m. to day, a Commission for George M. Robeson to be
Secretary of the Navy." Copies, DLC-USG, II, 1, 4.

1. On July 2, Secretary of the Navy George M. Robeson, Philadelphia,
wrote to USG. "Herewith I enclose to you a copy of your letter to Mr Borie,
accepting his resignation, copied by my own hand & compared by me—Mr Borie
desires me to say, that he does not ask its publication—his exact words were—'as
far as I am concerned, I would prefer that the Presidents letter to me should
not be published (I consider it too sacred to be given to the press) but if it
is thought best in justice to the President's warmth of heart, I will submit'—I
think their publication desirable for many reasons, not only to show what the
letters really were, but to show also what liars some of the reporters are & how
they do not even stick at forgery, in order to do injustice to the President, and
to my friend—I have also enclosed a copy of the letter to Mr Fish to be placed on
file in the state department, pursuant to arrangement—" ALS, OFH.

To Adolph E. Borie

Washington. D. C. July 7th *1869.*

MY DEAR MR. BORIE:

About Wednesday next[1] Mrs. Grant, the children and myself will leave here for Long Branch on the Str. Talapoosa.[2] I would be pleased, and so would all my family, if Mrs. Borie, your Niece and yourself would come down here and make the trip with us. It may be that we will not get off on that day; but if so I will know it some days in advance and will tell you the exact time of starting.

Please present Mrs. Grants and my very best respects to Mrs. Borie, and accept the same to yourself.

yours Truly
U. S. GRANT

ALS, PHi. See letter to Elizabeth M. Borie, July 20, 1869.

1. The presidential party left Washington, D. C., on Thursday, July 15, 1869.

2. On July 13, Alonzo B. Cornell, surveyor of customs, New York City, telegraphed to USG. "It being impossible for the Tallapoosa to land at the Long Branch dock, if it is your pleasure I will have one of our Revenue Tugs in waiting to receive your party inside of Sandy Hook. Please telegraph me from Cape may what hour we shall look for you. when opposite Stetson House please have the vessel fire two (2) signal guns so that the cars may be sent to meet you at Port Monmouth Dock. Please answer" Telegram received (at 12:50 P.M.), DNA, RG 107, Telegrams Collected (Bound). On July 15, George W. Childs, Philadelphia, telegraphed to Horace Porter. "Mr Paul Superintendent Sea Shore Long Branch Railroad has tendered President Grant and party a special train on arrival of steamer" Telegram received (at 10:15 A.M.), *ibid.* On July 16, Albert W. Markley and Peter Gardner, Stockton Hotel, Cape May, N. J., telegraphed to USG. "We see by the papers you are about to visit Long Branch by vessel, Should be pleased to have you make a visit here on your way to the Branch, Will endeavor to make your stay pleasant and agreeable, answer" Telegram received (at 2:00 P.M.), *ibid.* When USG visited Cape May, July 17–18, he reviewed the Gray Reserves, a Philadelphia militia regt. He arrived in Long Branch on July 19. See *Washington Chronicle,* July 16, 17, 19, 20, 1869.

To Mary B. Pitcher

———

Washington, *D. C.* July 12th *1869*,

MY DEAR MRS. PITCHER:

I do not know whether you were replied to or not in answer to your letter in regard to Lewis'[1] re-examination. I attended to your request however and told Mrs. Grant to write to you that he can be re-examined if he wishes it. The matter will be left entirely to him. If he feels, when the time comes, in September, that he is prepared the examination will be given him. I sincerely hope that Lewis may get through if he is re-examined, but if he does not he is still young enough.

My kind regards to the Gn. and your self.

yours Truly

U. S. GRANT

ALS, DLC-USG, 1C. Mary Bradley married Thomas G. Pitcher, later super-intendent, USMA. See Kate Pitcher Whitworth Schultz, "General Thomas Gamble Pitcher," *Indiana History Bulletin* (Dec., 1925), 37–42.

1. William Lewis Pitcher, born in 1852, son of Thomas G. Pitcher, who entered the U.S. Naval Academy in June, 1868, did not graduate. On Dec. 18, 1871, USG nominated him as 2nd lt., 10th Cav.

Proclamation

———

In pursuance of the provisions of the Act of Congress, approved April 10th 1869, I hereby designate Tuesday the 30th day of November, 1869, as the time for submitting the Constitution, adopted on the 15th day of May, 1868, by the Convention which met in Jackson, Mississippi, to the voters of said State registered at the date of such submission, Viz.: November, 30th 1869.

And I submit to a separate vote that part of Section 3 of Article VII of said Constitution which is in the following words:

"That I am not disfranchised in any of the provisions of the Act Known as the reconstruction Acts of the 39th and 40th Congress, and that I admit the political and civil equality of all men: so help me God: Provided that if Congress shall, at any time, remove the disabilities of any person disfranchised in the said reconstruction Acts of the said 39th and 40th Congress, (and the legislature of this State shall concur therein,) then so much of this oath, and so much only, as refers to the said reconstruction Acts, shall not be required of such person, so pardoned, to entitle him to be registered."

And I further submit to a separate vote, Section 5 of the same Article of said Constitution which is in the following words:

"No person shall be eligible to any office of profit or trust, civil or military, in this State, who, as a member of the legislature, voted for the call of the Convention that passed the ordinance of secession, or who, as a delegate to any convention, voted for or signed any ordinance of secession, or who gave voluntary aid, countenance, counsel or encouragement to persons engaged in armed hostility to the United States, or who accepted or attempted to exercise the functions of any office, civil or military, under any authority or pretended government, authority, power, or constitution, within the United States, hostile or inimical thereto, except all persons who aided reconstruction by voting for this convention, or who have continuously advocated the assembling of this convention, and shall continuously and in good faith advocate the acts of the same; but the legislature may remove such disability: Provided, that nothing in this section, except voting for or signing the ordinance of secession, shall be so construed as to exclude from office the private soldier of the late so-called Confederate States army."

And I further submit to a separate vote Section 5 of Article XII of the said Constitution which is in the following words:

"The credit of the State shall not be pledged or loaned in aid of any person, association, or corporation; nor shall the State hereafter become a stockholder in any corporation or association."

And I further submit to a separate vote, part of the oath of office prescribed in Section 26 of Article XII of the said Constitution which is in the following words:

"That I have never, as a member of any convention, voted for or signed any ordinance of secession; that I have never, as a member of any State legislature, voted for the call of any convention that passed any such ordinance."

The above oath shall also be taken by all the city and county officers before entering upon their duties, and by all other State officers not included in the above provision. I direct the vote to be taken upon each of the above cited provisions alone and upon the other portions of the said Constitution in the following manner, Viz: Each voter favoring the ratification of the Constitution (excluding the provisions above quoted) as adopted by the Convention of May 15, 1868 shall express his judgment by voting

For the Constitution

Each voter favoring the rejection of the Constitution (excluding the provisions above quoted) shall express his judgment by voting

Against the Constitution

Each voter will be allowed to cast a separate ballot for or against either or both of the provisions above quoted—

It is understood that Sections 4.-5-6-7-8-9-10-11-12-13-14 and 15 of Article XIII, under the head of "ordinance" are considered as forming no part of the said Constitution.

In testimony whereof, I have hereunto set my hand and caused the seal of the United States to be affixed.

Done at the City of Washington this thirteenth day of July, in the year of our Lord, one thousand eight hundred and sixty-nine, and of the Independence of the United States of America, the ninety-fourth.

U. S. GRANT

DS, DNA, RG 130, Presidential Proclamations. See Message to Congress, April 7, 1869. On April 13, 1869, Robert S. Hudson, Yazoo City, Miss., had written to USG. "Unknown to you as I am, and may ever be, permit me to suggest to you, for the well-being of both colors and races in this state, that no election upon the constitution and for officers of this state be ordered to take place before 1st day of August 1869. My reason is that, if earlier, labor will be so demoralized and neglected that want and failure of crops will certainly ensue, Please save us from this great calamity! The objectionable features of the late constitution of the convention of this state is not only in its proscriptive character but *increase of officers*—About 65, new offices, *salaried*, are created by it,

Lt Governor, Superintendant of Public Works (we have none) Superintendant of Public Schools, with Sub-Superintendants for each county (60 counties) Superintendent of Agriculture—Commissioner of Foreign Emigration &c—is equally offensive in our policy and *poverty*, and can only be supported by taxation of the most oppressive character in our condition—Our people, *both* black & white are *very poor* and need every relief from the burdens of taxation—The proposed constitution must double taxation, for its support and execution—Free the constitution from these objections & it will succeed." ALS, USG 3.

On April 16, Hiram T. Fisher, chairman, Republican State Executive Committee, and editor, *Mississippi Pilot*, Jackson, wrote to USG. "I would respectfully submit as the opinion of the entire Republican party of Miss, that the election on the Constitution should not be held until the 26th of December next, Before that time the planter has every advantage of the colored voter, After that and until the next years crop is begun, the colored people are perfectly free to vote and act as they please without running the risk of being summarily discharged or turned off without pay or settlement, An election at any time before the 25th Dec. would greatly jeopardize the interests of the colored people, and be dangerous to loyal reconstruction, Hoping that these suggestions may recive your careful consideration, . . ." ALS, *ibid.*

On April 15, U.S. Representative George C. McKee of Miss., Jackson, had written to Rawlins enclosing a statement addressed to USG. ". . . There is still another potent reason to all who wish to see the State re-constructed on a loyal Republican basis. The new Commander of this District is filling the offices with straight-out loyal men. Thus far he has met the views of Republicans so well that we are well assured that had he been in command last year re-construction in this State would already have been an accomplished fact, as we are sure it will be if he remains and is given the necessary time. Ever since the Rebellion the loyal men have struggled against the wealth and influence of the aristocracy and the power and patronage of the State and the United States. Every office holder worked against us and prostituted his official power by using it in opposition to re-construction and the Republican party and in persecuting and oppressing members of this party. And now that we are fast obtaining possession of the various offices with their influence we ought to be allowed time to organize and consolidate and solidify our power. Our Sheriffs, who, with their deputies are to protect us from the outrages of the last election ought to be allowed time to at least feel at home in their new duties and become familiarized with the reins of power. . . ." ALS, DNA, RG 107, Letters Received, M170 1869. On April 22, Rawlins endorsed these documents to USG. AES, *ibid.*

On June 7, Alston Mygatt, Vicksburg, wrote to USG. "We learn by 'telegram' that Maj: Wofford (who does not represent the Republican Party of this State—but on the contrary is mongrel, half Democratic and half Conservative) advises the holding of Election in August! The 'new Constitution' fixes the time for holding elections on the first tuesday after the first monday in November— this meets the approval of nineteen twentieths of our citizens:—The Republicans will throw out the fifth section of the Franchise &c We do not wish any change in the judiciary or bill of rights! In the last election we had the Military, the Federal and State government official influence and many of the Registers against us: in the coming contest all this influence will be in our favor beside the great moral weight of the Administration—this is almost certain to insure success to the Reconstruction Party!" ALS, USG 3.

On June 8, Benjamin Leas, Vicksburg, wrote to USG. "Having resided in this place since the winter of 63 & 4, and having not only felt the want of Civil Government, but have been deeply interrested in endevering to procure one, I take the liberty of addressing you on a single point, in relation to the proper time for holding the coming election. I am aware that efforts are being made to induce you to name an early day for said purpose. those efforts are in the interest of the Democratic party. this I know to be the case for the reason that nine tenths of the Republicans are poor, whilst the Democrats can and will raise money to elect their ticket. Give us until the Constitutional day at least, 1st Tuesday after the 1st Monday of November and the Freedmen will have time and means and be in a much more independent condition. I believe this to be the wish of evry reliable Republican, a fact that I think will be made manifest at our coming Republican State Convention to be held on the 1st day of July next. Your attention will greatly oblige your humble Servant." ALS, *ibid.*

On Oct. 5, Attorney Gen. Ebenezer R. Hoar wrote to USG. "I have carefully considered the letter addressed to you by R. C. Powers, of Jackson, Miss., of the date of September 18, 1869, asking that a new apportionment may be made by the military commander in Mississippi, for the election of members of the legislature under their new constitution, or that the article of the constitution which fixes the apportionment of members of the legislature may be submitted separately to the vote of the people of that State. I can have no doubt that the alleged cause of complaint cannot be remedied by any action of yours. The people of Mississippi are to give their vote for or against the adoption of a constitution, and to elect members of the legislature under it. If the apportionment of representatives provided in the constitution submitted, is unequal and unjust, they can reject the constitution for that reason; or, if it shall so appear to Congress, it may constitute a reason for the refusal by Congress to admit the State to representation under such a constitution. But the provision for the apportionment of representatives is an essential part of any constitution. If that provision were submitted separately and rejected, there would be no frame of government adopted for the State, the rest of the constitution not being sufficient to constitute a frame of government. And, on the other hand, if the constitution were adopted and a legislature elected, not according to the apportionment which the constitution provided, but under a different apportionment prescribed by the military commander, it is very clear that such a legislature would not be the legislature provided by the constitution, and would have no power to act under and in pursuance of that instrument. The people of Mississippi must vote upon the constitution as it is; and all essential parts of it, they must accept or reject as one entire instrument. If any essential part seems to them so objectionable that they would be unwilling to adopt it as a whole, they can so decide; but there is no warrant of law for submitting any other constitution than the one framed by the convention, or for electing a legislature on any other basis than that which it has marked out." Copy, DNA, RG 60, Opinions. On Oct. 7, Horace Porter wrote to Ridgley C. Powers, chairman, Republican State Executive Committee, Jackson. "I am directed by the President to acknowledge the receipt of your communication of the 18th ultimo, and to state that the same was referred to the Attorney General for his opinion, which was received this morning, and is herewith enclosed." Copies, DLC-USG, II, 1, 4.

To Buenaventura Báez

Ulysses S. Grant, President of the United States of America, to his excellency Buenaventura Baez, President of the Dominican Republic:

GREAT AND GOOD FRIEND: Deeming it desirable to satisfy my curiosity in respect to your interesting country by obtaining information through a source upon which I rely, I have for this purpose appointed Brevet Brigadier General Orville E. Babcock, of the army of the United States, to proceed to the Dominican Republic in the character of a special agent. Having been one of my aides-de-camp while I commanded the armies of the United States, and having since been intrusted by me with confidential business of importance, I have entire confidence in his integrity and intelligence, and I commend him to your excellency accordingly.

Written at Washington, the 13th day of July, A. D. 1869.

Your good friend,

U. S. GRANT.

SRC, 41-2-234, p. 137. Buenaventura Báez, born about 1810, the son of a wealthy landowner, was educated in France. A founder of the Dominican Republic, he thrice served as president and was thrice overthrown between 1849 and 1866, then returned to power in March, 1868. On July 13, 1869, Secretary of State Hamilton Fish wrote a letter of instruction to Orville E. Babcock. *SRC*, 41-2-234, p. 189; *SED*, 41-3-17, p. 79.

In Sept., 1869, Babcock, Washington, D. C., wrote to William L. Cazneau, Santo Domingo. "I arrived home safely and found the President away. He returned on the 22d. I have conversed with him and find he takes much interest in my report and in the Republic of Sto Domingo. He is unable to send definite information of what he will do by this steamer. Will you see President Baez and ask him to make no definite arrangements with the English loan until he hears from President Grant,—as it will embarrass matters very much if that loan is consumated. The question of 'State' as used in the confidential communication caused some consideration. I assured the President that we had discussed the question and that President Baez assured us that he understood that Sto Domingo *could not be admitted* as a state, but that she would have to be treated as a *territory* until she had conformed to the requirements of the Constitution of the *United States*, for admission as a state. Please see President Baez and converse with him on these subjects of the 'loan' and 'state' and communicate to me by the return of the steamer, should there be any misunderstanding on these points. You can assure him that the President will give him a definite answer at an early day. The President appreciates fully the reasons given by President Baez for secrecy. From the report just received from the Commander of the Tuscarora you can assure President Baez that he need have no fear of the Telegrafo. If she puts to sea she will be seized. With my kind regards to the President and Cabinet and to Mrs Cazneau . . ." Copy, Babcock Papers, ICN. See message to Senate, March 14, 1870; letter to James W. Nye, June 27, 1870.

Order

ULYSSES S. GRANT.

PRESIDENT OF THE UNITED STATES OF AMERICA

TO ALL TO WHOM THESE PRESENTS SHALL COME GREETING[S.]

Whereas, it has come to my kn[ow]ledge that a military expedition has been begun or set on foot within the territory and jurisdiction of the United States against the authority and government, territories and dominions of Spa[in] with whom the United States are at peace, and in violation of public law, and contrary to the provisions and prohibitions of the Eighty eighth chapter of the Laws of the first Session of the Fifteenth Congress, entitled 'An Act in addition to the Act for the punishment of certain crimes against the United States, and to repeal the Acts therein mentioned,' passed April 20th 1818;[1] . . .

Now, therefore, Know Ye, that reposing special trust and confidence in the integrity, prudence and ability of Edwards Pierrepont, District Attorney of the United States for the Southern District of New York, and of Francis C. Barlow, Marshal of the United States for the said Southern District, and of each and either of them, I do hereby, . . . authorize and empower the said Edwards Pierrepont and the said Francis C. Barlow, and each and either of them, to employ such part of the land or naval forces of the United States, or of the Militia thereof, as shall be necessary for that purpose, in order to the execution of the prohibitions and penalties of the said act and for the purpose of preventing the carrying on of any such expedition or enterprise from the territories or jurisdiction of the United States against the territories or dominions of Spain with whom the United States are at peace, The authority and power hereby given, to be held and exercise[d] during the pleasure of the President of the United States.

In testimony whereof, I have caused the Seal of the United States to be hereunto affixed.

Given under my hand at the City of Washington, the fourteenth day of July, in the year 1869, and of the Independence of the United States the Ninety fourth.

U. S. GRANT.

BY THE PRESIDENT:

HAMILTON FISH.

SECRETARY OF STATE.

Copy, DNA, RG 59, General Records. See *New York Times*, July 1–4, 7, 8, 16–17, 1869. On June 30, 1869, Edwards Pierrepont, U.S. attorney, New York City, had telegraphed to Secretary of State Hamilton Fish. "Under your orders as the President directed the prisoners about one hundred and sixty (160) in number have been turned over to the Admiral in command of the Navy Yard. A third tug on its way with other prisoners and will take the same course. I have just returned from an interview with the Admiral at the Navy Yard. Colonel Ryan is believed to be concealed in one of the Tugs. Search is being made. The admiral will write for full orders from the President." Telegram received (at 5:00 P.M.), DNA, RG 59, Miscellaneous Letters. On July 1, Pierrepont wrote to USG. "Knowing that your Secretary of State is absent, I address you directly. There are now in prison of the Cuban expedition. J. H. Norris William Sindorf. J. F. Clancy, Ralph Harmon. & F. W. Conant They are in Ludlow St. Jail, being unable to procure bail. They were indicted for violation of the Neutrality Laws. They are under bonds to appear for trial in the sum of $5000 each and under bonds not to break the peace of Spain in $2500 each As they cannot give bail, I have no power to release them and they will be compelled to remain in prison until next October. I bring their case for your consideration, and any orders that you may see fit to give in the premises will be promptly executed . . ." LS, *ibid.* On the same day, Francis C. Barlow, U.S. marshal, New York City, telegraphed to USG. "The Captured Vessels and men were placed under the charge of Admiral Godon at the Navy Yard; according to your orders he removed the men to the Receiving ship. Today he has received orders to send them back to the Tugs & retain them, there are no provisions on the Tug and the Admiral [ha]s peremptorily ordered not to ration them. They are not in my charge and I have no means for feeding them, Will you issue orders that they be fed by the Admiral otherwise they will starve" Telegram received (at 4:00 P.M.), *ibid.*; (press) *ibid.*, RG 107, Telegrams Collected (Bound). Also on July 1, Barlow telegraphed to USG. "THE ORDER DIRECTING DISPOSITION OF PRISONERS HAS BEEN RECEIVED AND WILL BE OBEYED. I HAVE ARRANGED TO FEED PRISONERS. NAVY

DEPARTMENT NEED NOT DO IT. ALL IS ARRANGED AND RIGHT. THE CONFUSION ABOUT ORDERS WILL BE EXPLAINED BY LET-TER." Telegram received (at 4:20 P.M.), *ibid.*, RG 59, Miscellaneous Letters. On July 2, Horace Porter twice telegraphed to Barlow. "Your despatch of 1st inst. received. Appropriations make no provision for Navy feeding civil prisoners. Can they not be supplied by the same authority that would feed them if confined in the ordinary way." "Navy Department has been directed to feed your prisoners as you requested." Copies, DLC-USG, II, 5. On the same day, Vice Admiral David D. Porter wrote to USG. "I have the honor to acknowledge the receipt of your order of this date, that the Commandant of the Navy Yard at Brooklyn, N. Y. be directed to make provision for supplying the prisoners now in his charge with food. The order has been transmitted to day to the Commandant by tele-gram and by letter." Copy, DNA, RG 45, Letters Sent to the President.

On July 14, Secretary of the Navy George M. Robeson wrote to USG. "I have the honor to acknowledge the receipt of your order of the 13th inst., direct-ing that the Commandant of the Brooklyn Navy Yard, NewYork, be instructed to furnish such assistance as he may have at his command upon the application of the U. S. Marshal on the U S. District Attorney, for the purpose of making arrests and guarding prisoners." Copy, *ibid.* On July 15, Pierrepont telegraphed to Fish. "The Commission of the President and your orders have been received. Will be promptly executed—Present difficulty, as Marshal advised, is in finding the Ship, Every means will be taken." Telegram received (at 12:30 P.M.), *ibid.*, RG 59, Miscellaneous Letters.

1. See *U.S. Statutes at Large*, III, 447–50.

To Adam Badeau

Washington. D. C. July 14th *1869*

DEAR BADEAU:

Your two very welcome letters were duly received. I shall al-ways be glad to hear from you but may not be able to reply very frequently.—The little insight your letters give to public acts and feeling abroad is something which cannot be gathered so clearly from official dispatches. So far I have been pleased with Mr. Mot-leys[1] utterences abroad, and I have no doubt he will prove the very best man that could have been selected for the English mission. It is not half so important that the Alabama claims should be settled as it is that when settled it should be on terms creditable to this nation. I do not see that any harm is to arise from the matter stand-ing in an unsettled state.

I leave here to-morrow for Long Branch, and the North, to be gone all Summer. I will return here however from time to time myself to look after public business. Probably will not remain absent longer than two weeks at any one time.—Public affairs look to me to be progressing very fafvorably. The revenues of the country are being collected as they have not been before, and expenditures are looked after more carefully. This is policy enough for the present. The first thing is seems to me is to establish the credit of the country. My family are all well and join in respects to you. Please remember me kindly to Mr. Motley and his family.

yours Truly
U. S. Grant

ALS, Harkness Collection, NN. On March 31, 1869, Horace Porter wrote to Secretary of War John A. Rawlins. "I am directed by the President to request you to issue an order instructing 1st Lieutenant Adam Badeau Bvt Brig. Gen'l U. S. A. to report to the President for duty at the Executive Mansion." LS, DNA, RG 94, Letters Received, 225P 1869. On April 15, USG nominated Adam Badeau as asst. secretary of legation, London.

1. Born in 1814, John Lothrop Motley graduated from Harvard in 1831, gained fame for his histories of the Dutch Republic and the Netherlands, and served as minister to Austria (1861–67). See George William Curtis, ed., *The Correspondence of John Lothrop Motley* (New York, 1889), II, 210, 301–8. On April 26, 1869, USG wrote to Queen Victoria. "I have made choice of John Lothrop Motley, one of our distinguished citizens, to reside near Your Majesty in the quality of Envoy Extraordinary and Minister Plenipotentiary of the United States of America. He is well informed of the relative interests of the two countries, and of our sincere desire to cultivate and strengthen the friendship and good correspondence between us; and from a knowledge of his fidelity, probity, and good conduct, I have entire confidence that he will render himself acceptable to Your Majesty, by his constant endeavors to preserve and advance the interest and happiness of both nations. I therefore request Your Majesty to receive him favorably, and to give full credence to whatever he shall say on the part of the United States, and most of all when he shall assure Your Majesty of their friendship and good wishes for your prosperity. And I pray God to have Your Majesty in his Safe and holy Keeping." Copy, DNA, RG 84, Great Britain, Instructions.

Proclamation

[July 15, 1869]

BY THE PRESIDENT OF THE UNITED STATES OF AMERICA
A PROCLAMATION

In pursuance of the provisions of the Act of Congress, approved April 10th 1869, I hereby designate Tuesday the 30th day of November 1869, as the time for submitting the Constitution,[1] adopted by the Convention which met in Austin, Texas, on the 15th day of June 1868, to the voters of said State registered[2] at the date of such submission, viz:

I direct the vote to be taken upon the said Constitution in the following manner, viz:

Each voter favoring the ratification of the Constitution as adopted by the Convention of the 15th of June 1868 shall express his judgment by voting—

For the Constitution

Each voter favoring the rejection of the Constitution shall express his judgment by voting—

Against the Constitution . . .

U. S. GRANT

DS, DNA, RG 130, Presidential Proclamations. Printed in *HED*, 41-2-265, p. 12. On April 10, 1869, Andrew J. Hamilton *et al.*, Washington, D. C., had written to USG. "The undersigned, members of the late Constitutional Convention of Texas, and other Citizens of that State, now in this city, and who have actively aided in the work of reconstruction, beg leave to present you with a copy of the Constitution adopted by the Convention, to which we invite your personal attention. It is beleived that it will compare favorably with the most liberal constitutions of the American States. It is framed in exact compliance with the requirements of the reconstruction laws of Congress. The Convention, as was required by law, provided for the submission of the constitution to the registered voters of Texas on the 5th day of July next. The Constitution appears to meet the approval of an overwhelming majority of the qualified electors, and, in our opinion, will be acceptable to those even who are precluded from participating in the election upon its ratification or rejection The only serious objection urged against the constitution by republicans in Texas is the Suffrage clause, which it is insisted disfranchises none but lunatics and felons— in other words that it establishes 'universal suffrage and amnesty'. If this be the true construction, which we do not propose to discuss; our consciences approve and our judgements sanction it as necessary to remove all 'irritating causes' from among our people In the same spirit which animated your Excellency at Appomattox, we have tendered our late opponents the Olive Branch. The tone of the daily press, and the total absence of lawlessness growing out of political causes, forces upon us the conviction that they are sincere in accepting it We perceive, from the bill presented to Congress by the Reconstruction Committee, and which has passed both houses, that Texas is included in the necessary legislation urged in your special message, of the 7th inst, for the States of Virginia and Mississippi, and that the election ordered to be held in July upon the ratification of the constitution has been suspended, subject to your order. As an independent measure it is beleived that no act would have passed affecting Texas, but since the subject has been referred to the wisdom and justice of your Excellency, we are content. Major General Reynolds, now in command of the Fifth Mil. District is an officer possessing the confidence alike of of your Excellency and the loyal people of Texas. He is on the spot—familiar with the condition of affairs, and can at any time interpose and arrest the election, if in his judgement, it could not be safely held. It is therefore in all confidence, we pray Your Exceleny to order, that the election in Texas be proceeded with, as provided by the Constitutional Convention." DS (13 signatures), DNA, RG 107, Letters Received from Bureaus. George W. Paschal endorsed this letter. "This was handed to me ~~by~~ for the President. His assurance to myself and Gov Hamilton rendered the delivery at the time unnecessary. I would now suggest that the election be held 1st Monday in August. This has always been the day of election in Texas. We can carry the constitution." AES, *ibid.*

On May 8, A. Neith, Galveston, wrote to USG. "Enclosed herein find an Extract from a paper in this State from which you can form some slight idea of the prevailing feeling of the people, and it will show how necessary it becomes the authorities to postpone ordering an election until such time as those opinions may be over come Excuse the liberty I take in writing you, but I feel still some interest in a State where I have spent one third of a century in trying to build up a good government, and desire to furnish you information which might not be easily obtained from other Sources I have a slight acquaintance with Gen. Dent and beg to be excused for troubling you—wishing you good health and Success in your administration—" ALS, USG 3. The enclosed clipping praised opposition to the test oath in Va.

On May 15, Bvt. Maj. Gen. Joseph J. Reynolds, Austin, telegraphed to USG. "Referring to Section Three 3 of the Act of Congress of April Tenth 10 eighteen sixty nine 1869, I respectfully recommend that the election on the ratification of the Constitution framed by the late Convention for this State be held commencing on the Third 3 Monday the Nineteenth 19 day July next The revision of registration required by Section [Se]ven 7 of the act of July Nineteenth 19 Eighteen sixty seven 1867 will then begin o[n] the first Monday, the Fifth 5 day [of] July. It is not necessary to submit any portion of the Constitution to a separate vote. The suffrage clause Section one 1 article six 6 page twenty eight 28 is substantially the same as s[ec]tion one 1 article three 3 page s[even and sec]tion twenty one 21 page six 6 There is no disqualification in the State Constitution beyond the Fourteenth 14 Amendment to the Constitution of the U. S." Telegram received (at 7:30 P.M.), DNA, RG 107, Telegrams Collected (Bound); copy, *ibid.*, RG 94, Letters Received, 156T 1869.

On May 24, James A. McKee, Galveston, wrote to USG. "My interest in unconditionally loyal reconstruction in this state and anxious desire that the loyal masses shall have a fair opportunity in the forthcoming election must be my only Excuse for thus intruding upon your time and attention I see from the Public press that influences are at work at Washington pro and con to have the day of Election fixed Earlier or later so as to meet the ends of the parties interested In what I have to say I have no motive other than a sincere desire to serve loyal reconstruction Loyalty must rule or be ruined in the south hence I am in Earnest in this matter and duty demands that I shall speak plainly In order that the unconditionally loyal people may have a fair opportunity to obtain political control of this state it will be necessary to delay the Election to a time as late as Nov And to place this matter on Square grounds I will say that it is necessary as a party measure for the reason that there is discord in the republican party of this state which had its origin in the late reconstruction convention and grew out of side issues not of republican faith These differences are to a large extent now personal as the matters in question have ceased to be issues but the animous engendered still exist on the part of some leaders and has led them into positions antagonistic to loyal reconstruction Gov Hamilton prompted doubtless by a first desire to defeat his political friends who have seen proper to differ with him on these outside issues has seen proper to announce himself a candidate for Govorner independent of any and all nominations and has commenced a Canvass of the State looking mainly for support to the opposition element as he will receive but little from those who have no purpose to serve other than that of loyal reconstruction. The opposition encourage and will support him because they see in his election a stepping stone to political control in this state An early election is his certain success Time will break down the movement Time will cement and harmonise the republican party This desireable end is now in course of consumation Loyal men not consumed with their own madness think the situation is one of life or death to them and are willing and disposed to make large concessions for harmony In considering this matter it will be well to bear in mind that an early election can in no wise hasten reconstruction as it must be consumated by action of Congress after Dec next With a harmonised party and sufficient protection to ensure open and fair discussion the republicans can enter the canvass with reasonable prospects of success Without these conditions reconstruction will be on a basis of positive disloyalty in its results It remains for me to say that in the local issues that caused alienation in the republican party that I took sides with Gov Hamilton but never allowed the differences to become personal It is but just to say that the tone of public sentiment is more pacific than before your election though it is still far from being what it ought to be I am the lately appointed Post Master for this City and Can with pleasure refer to Genl Reynolds Comng this Military District." ALS, *ibid.*, RG 107, Letters Received from Bureaus.

On June 22, Reynolds telegraphed to USG. "Letter in relation to Texas civil affairs mailed today" Telegram received (at 2:20 P.M.), *ibid.*, Telegrams Collected (Bound). On Sept. 4, Reynolds wrote to USG. "After your summer recreation I have determined to add to your fall labors a few words on the political situation in Texas. You will remember that about the 4th of March last there were present in Washington two delegations of Texans, both claiming to be representatives of the republican party of Texas. One of these delegations, headed by General E. J. Davis, was appointed by the Constitutional Convention; the other delegation, headed by General A. J. Hamilton, was self-appointed. Pursuing the policy which I had decided upon in October, 1867, upon my arrival in Austin, of always endeavoring to produce harmony among all classes of republicans, I declined to permit myself to be identified specifically with either faction, but frankly told their leaders (E. J. Davis and A. J. Hamilton) that I would recommend for office men of both factions who I was satisfied would make good officers. . . . The circumstances all considered I am constrained to believe that the coalition which has been charged as existing between the conservative or A. J. Hamilton republicans and the democrats, generally ex-rebels, does actually exist. The platforms of the two wings of the republican party are precisely the same. The radical wing act out their professions of adherence to the Reconstruction laws of Congress and present for office men who are qualified under these laws. The conservative wing frequently nominate men for office who are known to be disqualified under the Reconstruction laws, but who are also known to be acceptable to the democrats. The success of the A. J. Hamilton faction, as it will be produced by democratic votes, will be the defeat of republicanism in Texas, and will put the State in the hands of the very men who, during the period of the rebellion, exerted every nerve to destroy the Union and who have uniformly opposed the Reconstruction laws with a persistency worthy of a better cause. This letter is already too long. Use it as you please." *New York Herald*, Sept. 27, 1869. On Sept. 14, Gen. William T. Sherman telegraphed to USG. "General Reynolds reports from Austin Texas, that it will be impossible to ~~hold~~ poll the complete vote of Texas on a single day, fixed for November 30. He asks that the Election may according to the State Constitution be prolonged for four days" ALS (telegram sent), DNA, RG 107, Telegrams Collected (Bound); copy, *ibid.*, RG 94, Letters Sent. On the same day, USG, Pittsburgh, telegraphed to Sherman. "If the reconstruction acts of congress do not interfere authorize Gen Reynolds to extend the election in Texas to four (4) days commencing November 30th" Telegram received (on Sept. 15), *ibid.*, Letters Received, 566A 1869; (press) *ibid.*, RG 107, Telegrams Collected (Bound). On Jan. 3, 1870, Reynolds telegraphed to Frederick T. Dent. "All the counties in the State have been heard from officially except four, and those have been heard from unofficially, but the result is reliable. Davis' majority in the whole State is 775. An official report will be sent through the Adjutant General for the President as soon as these four counties are made official for it." *Washington Chronicle*, Jan. 5, 1870.

On Jan. 31, 1871, Orville E. Babcock wrote to Secretary of War William W. Belknap. "The President wishes me to request you to telegraph Gen. Jos. Reynolds, Texas, and say that he will be pleased to have him report here as soon as possible and bring with him his records for 1868, 1869, and since that time [c]oncerning political or other outrages in his district." LS, DNA, RG 94, Letters Received, 358 AGO 1871. On April 15, Reynolds wrote to Dent. "*Personal* . . . I enclose a slip from the State Journal Please show it to the President—On turning over the state after the election *the point* was to *maintain* and improve if possible the obedience to law that had, for the first time, been brought about in Texas by military power, used to be sure rather in a passive than an active sense—Gov. Davis & myself were decidedly of the opinion that some *organized* force *must* replace the troops to be withdrawn from the interior of the state—He accordingly urged upon the Legislature the *State Police*

as an experiment It has proved a decided success and accounts for the absence
of Ku-Klux organizations in Texas—So far every thing is encouraging in Texas
for 1872 and *our U. S.* Best regards to all the friends" ALS, Mrs. Gordon
Singles, Alexandria, Va.

1. On Feb. 2, 1869, Hamilton, Austin, telegraphed to USG. "Since your
election all going well, Violence decreasing and hopefulness for the future
prevalent, The general tendency of the public mind all right but the passage
of the proposed act to require all officers to take the test oath would cause a
hurtful reaction of your own memorable words 'In God's name let us have peace'
We will complete a constitution tomorrow or next day, I will witness your
inauguration" Telegram received (at 1:15 P.M.), DNA, RG 107, Telegrams
Collected (Bound); (press) *ibid.*; *ibid.*, RG 108, Telegrams Received; copy,
DLC-USG, V, 55. On Feb. 4 and 11, Bvt. Maj. Gen. Edward R. S. Canby,
Austin, wrote to Bvt. Maj. Gen. John A. Rawlins transmitting reports concern-
ing the Tex. constitutional convention and a letter of Jan. 28 from its president,
Edmund J. Davis, concerning the division of Tex. into separate states. *HED*,
40-3-97. On Feb. 22, USG endorsed this material. "Respectfully forwarded to
the Secretary of War, with request that these papers be transmitted to the
Reconstruction Committee for its information." *Ibid.* On March 16, Hamilton,
Washington, D. C., wrote to USG. "Please find herewith enclosed a copy of the
Constitution ordained by the late Constitutional Convention of the State of Texas,
which is to be submitted to the people of that State for ratification on the 1st
Monday in July next. I think you will find it free from objections which are
to be found in most of the Southern Constitutions while it is just to all classes,
making them all equal before the law." ALS, OFH. The enclosure is *ibid.* On
April 28, Secretary of War Rawlins wrote to USG. "I have the honor to submit
herewith: Constitution of the State of Texas, adopted by the constitutional convention convened under the reconstruction acts of Congress passed March 2,
1867, and the acts supplementary thereto; to be submitted for ratification or
rejection at an election to take place on the first Monday in July, 1869. Also,
Constitution and ordinances of the State of Mississippi, adopted in convention
assembled in pursuance of the reconstruction acts of Congress, and held, by
order of General E. O. C. Ord, in the city of Jackson in 1868. Also corrected
copy of the constitution framed by the Virginia convention" LS, USG 3.

2. On May 5, William M. Scallorn, Winchester, Tex., wrote to USG. "I
write you this that I may have my political disabilities removed My political
Antecedents are as follows. I held the office of Deputy. Post Master in 1856 or
57, at Plum Grove Fayette County Texas I voted for Cecession, not that I
favored it or a dissolution of the Union But as some of the Southern States had
already passed ordinances of Cecession I thought if the South were to be unanimous, Coercion would not be attempted. But in the Course of a few months
reconcilliation could be effected and Cecession would become a nullity. In the
Spring of 1862 I volunteered into the Southern army as a private. I held no
office during the war in the so called Confederate States government nor Army.
In a few months after I inlisted, I was permitted to return home on a sick furlough, where I remained until finally discharged in 1863. Immediately after
the Surrender I took the Amnesty oath in good faith, Appeared before the
board of Registrars to register as a voter, but could not because I had before
the rebellion been county Post Master and afterwards participated in the re-

bellion. I feel solicitous to have the Union restored and to this end would direct my energies I am nearly forty years of age have been a practicing physician but do not now practice Before the rebellion I paid taxes on about $7000.00/10 dollars worth of property. I now pay taxes on about $5000.00/100 dollars worth. I refer you for the truth of what I have above stated to Revd. Henry Renick Winchester Texas Revd Mr Renick was Chaplain of the State Convention which framed the Constitution of the State that is now before the public If in your Clemency you can grant me a special pardon upon the statements made above (which are true) without detrimenting the interest or prosperity of the Country you will confer a favor upon me to do so" ALS, *ibid*. In an undated letter, John E. George, Danville, Tex., wrote to USG. "Permit an humble individual to intrude upon your time one moment—I am under disability by holding civil office before the war and during the war at this place that of Justice of the peace—which I have held continuously 16 years—I immediately applied for pardon and was pardoned May 1 1867—I am by *act* of *Reconstruction according* to *instructions* given to our *board* of *Registrars* not *permitted* to *register* I was by a Resolution of the Convention together—with other names recommended for general relief by Congress (in July, 1868—) See Journal of Convention—1st Session—I am Loyal to the Government of the U. S. I have never been otherwise—my feelings have never been istranged from the U. S. Govt—I endorse the Reconstruction acts—I endorse the adoption the *new Constitution—now being submitted* to the voters of Texas for adoption—I wish to take full action and do all I can to secure its adoption—I am anxious for Texas—to be back in the Union—If you can aid me in removal of disability— you oblige." ALS, *ibid*.

To Elizabeth M. Borie

Long Branch, N. J., July 20th *1869.*

MY DEAR MRS. BORIE,

Your husband is enjoying himself so much here, and we all enjoy his company too, that I drop you a line to ask you to send him immediately back.[1] To make sure of his safe return will you not come with him? On Monday evening next there is to be a grand party given to our party at this house which I know you will enjoy and at which I hope to meet you.

Mrs. Grant joins me in kind regards to you.

yours Truly

U. S. GRANT

ALS, PHi. Elizabeth D. McKean married Adolph E. Borie in 1839. On July 24, 1869, USG telegraphed to Vice Admiral David D. Porter. "Please telegraph

Ammen and wife to come here for party Monday Evening sure" Telegram
received (at 3:30 p.m.), DNA, RG 107, Telegrams Collected (Bound). For
a description of the ball and reception held at the Stetson House on Monday,
July 26, see *New York Tribune*, July 27, 1869.

On July 24, USG telegraphed to Robert M. Douglas. "Horses arrived safely
this noon" Telegram received (at 3:30 p.m.), DNA, RG 107, Telegrams Collected (Bound). On July 25, USG telegraphed to Secretary of State Hamilton
Fish, Garrison, N. Y. "If convenient I would be pleased to see you here to-
morrow or day following" Telegram received (on July 26), DLC-Hamilton
Fish. On July 30, Warren Leland, Saratoga, N. Y., telegraphed to USG. "It is
reported that yourself & family contemplate a visit to Saratoga I hope you will
do so, one of our new cottages is at your disposal" Telegram received (at
12:50 p.m.), DNA, RG 107, Telegrams Collected (Bound).

1. Borie left Long Branch on July 21 and returned on July 24. On Oct. 3,
Borie, Philadelphia, wrote to Adam Badeau, London. "I have received several
very interesting letters from you and am under the impression that I wrote you
upon my resignation, but not quite certain owing to the unsettled condition I
have been in. I have been at home (at our Country-seat) now for two weeks
and only just begin to feel again like a decent orderly citizen; first the President
invited me to accompany him around to and at Long Branch and then the Secy
of the Navy to go with him Admiral Porter Comr Alden Genl Sherman &ca on
their visit (in the Tallapoosa), of inspection of the Yards and Forts and then I
had to take madame mon epouse who met me at Newport, on a visit to the White
Mountains. . . . Poor Rawlins has gone to a happier office! A noble fellow, truly,
he was so pure zealous and earnest! I was very fond of him, tho' we did not
always agree (viz '8 hour law' and 'Cuba' upon both which what he called 'the
voice of the nation' I called 'popular clamor' 'Buncombe' &ca) My successor
Genl Robeson seems to work along nicely to himself and all around him as I felt
sure he would and that he would hold his own *in any Cabinet in the world*. The
Administration is going on nobly and I think gaining ground steadily but I am
a little fearful of result in our coming election for Gov of Penna, Genl Geary
being decidedly a weak candidate, but even if as I fear it will be no test on
other issues: the reduction of the debt (56 millions) is a great card, tho'
t'would have been much more healthy had Congress not forbidden it, to have
been half in legal tenders and not all in bonds A-propos of that what a wonderful shot that was of Genl Grant (I believe it was his) on 24th Sept at the
Gold Room! Never in all his great 'camps' in the War did he strike a surer
blow! I havnt ceased laughing about its effect ever since: that crazy wicked
hole (New York) will long remember it nor cease to feel that there is a power
(when ably & honestly wielded) that can thwart their evil machinations when
at the worst and least expected. . . ." ALS, CSmH.

To Columbus Delano

Washington. D. C. July 30th *1869*

HON. C. DELANO
COM. INT. REV.
DEAR SIR:

After seeing the representatives from Ky. who ask the removal of the Assessor of Int. Rev. for the Louisville District, I think it may be advisable to make the change they ask. If you think with me the change may be made this evening before I go or notice given that it will be made,

Respectfully
your obt. svt.
U. S. GRANT

ALS, DLC-Delano Family. Edgar Needham continued as assessor of Internal Revenue, 5th District, Ky.

To Lewis Dent

LONG BRANCH, Aug. 1, 1869.

DEAR JUDGE: I am so thoroughly satisfied in my own mind that the success of the so-called Conservative Republican party in Mississippi would result in the defeat of what I believe to be for the best interest of the State and country, that I have determined to say so to you in writing. Of course, I know or believe that your intentions are good in accepting the nomination from the Conservative party. I would regret to see you run for an office, and be defeated by my act, but as matters now look, I must throw the weight of my influence in favor of the party opposed to you. I earnestly hope that before the election there will be such concessions on either side in Mississippi as to unite all true supporters of Reconstruction and of the Administration together in support of one ticket. . . .[1] I write this to you solely that you may not be under

any wrong impression as to what I regard, or may hereafter regard, as public duty. Personally, I wish you well, and would do
all in my power proper to be done to secure your success; but in
public matters, personal feelings will not influence me. With kindest regards, yours truly, U. S. GRANT.

New York Tribune, Oct. 29, 1869. On Aug. 14, 1869, Lewis Dent, Washington, D. C., wrote to USG. "I am sorry to lean both from your letter to me and
your conversations with Tarbell, that you are unalterably committed against
us. Is it reasonable to suppose, that a people having the free choice of their
representatives, would elect for their rulers a class of politicians, whose antecedents and conduct hitherto, has been of a nature so aggressive and hostile as to
excite their profoundest antipathy. This is the charge, by the Mississippians,
against the Bitter Enders, as they are called. It is not made because they are
of Northern birth or education, ~~because~~ for many men of Northern birth and
education, are with us in antagonism to the Bitter Enders. It is not made because they fought against the South and Cesession, for many of that party fought
on the side of the South. Neither is it made because they are republicans, for
the leaders of our party, opposed to them, were amongst the first to organize the
Republican Party in the South, were elected delegates by that party to the
Chicago ~~p~~convention, and for their constancy and fidelity to that party have
been rewarded by you with offices of trust and honor. But the charge is made,
because their proscriptive antecedents and aggressive policy towards the people of Mississippi, have properly made them the objects of abhorrance, and
therefore are they unwilling to make them their rulers. Their conduct consists,
not only in continually advocating a proscriptive policy but, otherwise, in preach-
ing to the freedmen, in a time of peace, such denunciatory and revolutionary
doctrines, as excite and direct, against the white men of the South and their
families,—a most dangerous animosity, such animosity indeed, which, with continuation of like fuel, will inevitably lead to a black-man's party and eventually
to a war of races. Neither are these doctrines preached with an honest desire, to
promote the welfare of the negro, or promote Peace, or indeed, to strengthen the
party, but solely to alienate from the planters, the ancient confidenc and affection
of this race, in order, that the new political element, under the name of republican, ~~might~~ay be entirely controled and subordinated to their own purposes for
power and aggrandisement. And this party you take by the hand, and give to
them your countenance and support;—the same party whose infamous attempt to
force a rejected constitution on Mississippi you resisted and rebuked; and spurn
from you the National Republicans, who believing in the sincerity of the Republican Party—flocked in mass, to your invitation, as they did in Virginia and
Tennessee, (and will in Texas and Mississippi), to stand on your platform and
advocate your principles. I am afraid, dear General, you have made a fatal mistake, and that in refusing the National Republicans, a place on the platform,
you will give them into the arms of the Democracy. Be this as it may. If I am
elected I will only be elected as a republican, and come what will of weal or woe,
to your administration, I always will be your firm political and personal friend."
ALS, USG 3. For an account of USG's meeting of Aug. 6 with Jonathan Tarbell,
Mississippi Republican Party, see *New York Times*, Aug. 12, 1869.

On Aug. 8, Frederick T. Dent wrote to J. L. Harrison. "Having just returned last evening from an extended tour on business, throughout the Lake
country of the north I find your Letter—and hasten to thank you for your just
remarks in the Troy Daily Whig—The Budget could readily learn if it would
take the pains to enquire—that no one of the name of Dent holds an office confered by General Grant I am the only one of four brothers who hold a federal
office. I am an officer of the army a possition I have held for twenty six years—
My Brother Judge Lewis Dent is spoken of for Gov of Mississippi so I hear—
the people of Mississippi have as much the privilege of chosing for themselves
a Governor to their liking as the State of New York has—and are as free from
the dictation of Gen Grant in their selection as I presume New York would be
I am not an office seeker and in the humble sphere in which I move have ever
tried to treat all men justly and to transact business with urbanity and politeness—if I failed in the case of the writer of that article in the Budget—he must
have caused it himself by his own conduct or language for I am sure such language and falsifications he has gathered together in that short article—might if
spoken to me induce me to be impolite to the Editor of the Budget to the extent of treating him with 'pompous' contempt" ALS, ICarbS.

1. According to the source, the omitted material dealt with private matters.

Speech

[*Aug. 3, 1869*]

ATTORNEY GENERAL BREWSTER,[1] LADIES AND GENTLEMEN—
I made this visit to Long Branch as a recreation from official duty.
The visit has been made pleasant by you all. I have purchased a
cottage here by the seaside, where I shall make the summer home
of myself and family, or, at least for my family and such portion
of the summer for myself as my public duties will permit.

New York Herald, Aug. 4, 1869. On Aug. 3, 1869, Spencer B. Driggs, Long
Branch, N. J., had written to USG. "Will his Excellency the President allow
the guests of the Stetson House to make special acknowledgment of the pleasure
they have received from the presence of himself and family, socially. Hon. B. H.
Brewster will express our wish in a few words of thanks, not a set speech. Only
a goodby, and no speech, will be expected from you." *Ibid.* On the same day,
USG wrote to Driggs. "It will afford me great pleasure to meet the guests of
the Stetson House before leaving, this afternoon, to say goodby to them, as requested in your note, just received. I am much indebted to these guests, as well
as to the proprietor of the house, for a most delightful visit to Long Branch."
Ibid.

1. Benjamin H. Brewster, born in 1816, graduated from Princeton College in 1834, practiced law in Philadelphia, and was designated as attorney gen. of Pa. in 1866. On Aug. 3, 1869, he spoke on behalf of the guests at the Stetson House to thank USG for visiting Long Branch.

On Oct. 21, Governor John W. Geary of Pa. forced Brewster to resign as Pa. attorney gen. On Oct. 29, Thomas L. Kane, Kane, Pa., wrote to USG discussing his attempt to reconcile the difficulties between Geary and Brewster. Copy, DLC-Simon Cameron. On Sept. 25, Robert J. Walker, Philadelphia, had written to USG. "In recommending the appointment of any one to Office by you, I have a sense of extreme delicacy, and feel that I have no rights in this respect, or claims, except those which appertain to every American Citizen. This is not because of the want of any good feeling for you personally, for in that respect, I could most truly avow the best wishes and kindest feelings for you, but for the reason that my opposition last year to the reconstruction policy of Congress, prevented my support of any of its advocates, however great my respect for some of them might be. That question has however now been finally settled, by a tribunal, from which there is no appeal, and I therefore feel at perfect liberty, regarding that matter as adjudicated, to act upon other living issues of vital importance to the Country. These are chiefly in my judgment, *first*, and of pressing and transcendingant importance, the Annexation to the United States of all British America, *second*, 2d the settlement of the Alabama claims. Having been the Financial Agent of the Government in Europe during a large portion of the period, when these transactions were occuring, and having special authority from the Government in connection with them, I have given the subject great attention, it has already been partially discussed by me, in my letter of April last, and I intend to renew and complete the discussion so soon as my health, (now progressing favorably) will permit. The third is the Cuba question, but this, though vastly important, will settle itself in our favor without a war, which would ruin and devastate Cuba. Spain, however, by a most barbarous and inhuman policy, may force us to come to the relief of suffering humanity at a period in advance of what would otherwise be the best policy Whatever I publish, I will send you at once, in hopes that you may find time to read it before any final decision on your part. And now, having fully explained my present position, I will take Fully conscious of my inability to carry such measures myself, I will at least have done my duty. And now having fully explained my present position, I will take the liberty of making some suggestions, in regard to an important appointment. I ask no questions, but rumor says, today, that, in consequence of there being two Cabinet appointments from Massachussetts, Judge Hoar is likely to become one of the Circuit Judges of the United States, under the new bill. In that event, there will be a vacancy in the Office, of Attorney General of the United States. Should such a contingency arise, I hope, it might not be considered indelicate on my part, to make some suggestions, in favor of my life long friend Benjamin H. Brewster of this City. Mr Brewster stands in the foremost ranks, at the Bar of this City, and is Attorney General of this State. As a Lawyer, I have known him long and well. I possess some familiarity with the duties of the Office of Attorney General of the United States. With many of the points connected with that Office, Mr Brewster's practice has made him very familiar, and, I think, his intrepidity on such questions, and especially the suppression and detection of frauds, would greatly assist the Officers of the Treasury, who seem to be doing their full duty on this subject. Making due allowance for my great friendship and regard for Mr. Brewster, I am influenced in making this recommendations, exclusively by a desire to promote the public welfare." LS, NHi.

On Nov. 27, H. Green, Easton, Pa., wrote to USG. "Observing a concurrence of statement in the public prints, to the effect, that there may shortly be a vacancy in the Office of Attorney General, I am induced to express a desire that it should be filled by a Pennsylvanian—I feel that it would be an appropriate acknowledgment of the eminent position of our Commonwealth as a State of the Union, and also of her fidelity to the Republican party and principles, to give her a position in the Cabinet—And I take an especial pleasure in expressing this feeling because we have a citizen who, it seems to me is peculiarly fitted for this position—I refer to Hon. Benjamin H. Brewster late Atty. General of Pennsylvania—. . . Being myself a lawyer, of Republican faith, and enjoying a pretty wide acquaintance with the Bar and Bench of Philadelphia and of Eastern and Central Pennsylvania I feel authorized to say that such an appointment will be regarded as well deserved and highly popular" ALS, DNA, RG 60, Records Relating to Appointments. On Dec. 4, George Connell, Philadelphia, wrote to USG recommending Brewster for attorney gen. ALS, *ibid.*, RG 59, Letters of Application and Recommendation. On Aug. 23, 1871, Driggs, Long Branch, wrote to USG. "If you will permit one who is not a diplomat, neither a politician—but simply a citizen who feels sensitive pride in all that our Country does in connection with other Nations, to express a desire; you will then pardon me for suggesting the name of Benjn H. Brewster, as Counsel for the '*Alabama Claims*' to attend your appointee to Geneva. Mr Chas O'Conor may be a better constitutional lawyer, and Mr Cutting may be as good an historical lawyer, but, in all this Country I do not know of one who combines the two so fully, as does Mr Brewster, which, together with his intimate knowledge of the manners—customs—rules,—laws and their origin, of other nations; and his high standard of honor and American dignity (You are doubtless aware that he has had large experience in Foreign Countries) And particularly his determined adherence to you and your administration, as well as, a grateful response to delicate exhibitions of kindness to some members of his present family, appear to me, to fit him pre-eminently for that position, as well as a confidential friend in whom you can implicitly rely. Pardon this suggestion, as Mr Brewster knows nothing of my proposing such a thing. My knowledge of his personal feeling towards you, and of his elegant fitness for the position, have alone prompted me to say this much, privately." ALS, *ibid.* See Eugene Coleman Savidge, *Life of Benjamin Harris Brewster* (Philadelphia, 1891), pp. 102–6.

Speech

———

[*Aug. 7, 1869*]

Mr. MAYOR—It affords me great pleasure to visit the city of Newburg[1] and this spot, made memorable in the way it has been.

I should be very glad to respond in fitting terms to the reception which I have received here. You know, however, that I am not accustomed or in the habit of making such responses. I therefore, in a word, thank you for the very hearty welcome and reception which I have received at the hands of your citizens.

New York Herald, Aug. 8, 1869. On Aug. 7, 1869, Newburg, N. Y., had honored USG with a parade and a banquet. *Ibid.* Following a toast by James W. Taylor, USG spoke. "You do not expect any person to make two speeches in one day; therefore you will not expect me to respond." *Ibid.*

On Aug. 4, USG had written to Secretary of State Hamilton Fish. "I leave for Garrisons on Mary Powell at half-past three (3½) to-day" Telegram received, DLC-Hamilton Fish. USG's visit to Fish's home is reported in the *New York Times*, Aug. 6, 1869. On Aug. 6, USG, West Point, N. Y., wrote to Mayor George Clark of Newburg. "Your note of this date, saying that the steamer M. Martin will meet me at the wharf at this place at 10 A. M. tomorrow is received. Governor Fish and myself will leave Garrison's on the ferry at 10:05 A. M., the nearest moment to the hour mentioned in your note at which the boat will be leaving." *New York Sun*, Aug. 7, 1869.

1. On July 6, Clark *et al.* wrote to USG. "At a meeting of the Common Council of the City of Newburg, held on the 17th day of June, 1869, the Mayor of the city reported to the Common Council that he, together with Hon. J. T. HEADLEY and Messrs. ALFRED POST and JAMES W. TAYLOR, had, at the request of citizens of Newburg, waited upon the President of the United States, at West Point, on the Saturday previous, and tendered him an invitation to visit Newburg and Washington's Headquarters, and that the President had stated that it was probable that he could accept the invitation sometime in the present month of July; and, therefore, the Common Council appointed the undersigned a Committee to invite the President to visit the City of Newburg, as the guest of the city on such day as would be most convenient to him. . . ." *New York Times*, July 20, 1869.

To Gen. William T. Sherman

————

Washington, D, C,
Aug. 10th /69

DEAR GENERAL:

Your kind invitation of the 2d inst. sent to me at Long Branch, has followed me up and just this moment reached me. I am much obliged for your invitation and would accept it but that I have

Porter staying with me and have invited the Sec. of State to dine with me to-day and to-morrow and with him to-morrow such members of the Cabinet as are in the city. I also want you and Adml. Porter to join us at dinner at 6 p. m. to-morrow. Please answer that you will come.

[U. S. Grant]

P. S. I accept your invitation for my next return to the City if you should be at home.

U. S. G.

AL (signature clipped), DLC-William T. Sherman.

Speech

[*Aug. 11, 1869*]

Mr. Minister—I am greatly pleased to receive from the republic of Mexico a Minister to this government so acceptable as yourself. Your previous residence in the United States has made you familiar with its institutions and its people and must have satisfied you that its government shares the views of the Mexican statesmen who deem a republic the form of government best suited to develop the resources of that country and to make its people happy. For myself I may say it is not necessary for me to proclaim that my sympathies were always with those struggling to maintain the republic: that I rejoiced when the evident will of the nation prevailed in their success, and that they have now my best wishes in their labors to maintain the integrity of their country and to develop its natural wealth. I am prepared to share in your efforts to continue and increase the cordial, social, industrial and political relations so happily subsisting between these two republics.

New York Herald, Aug. 12, 1869. On Aug. 11, 1869, Ignacio Mariscal, Mexican minister, had presented his credentials to USG. A translation of his remarks is *ibid*. Mariscal had served in the U.S. as chargé d'affaires *ad interim* (Oct., 1867–April, 1868).

To Frederick T. Dent

———

New York City,[1]
Aug. 12th/69

DEAR FRED,

In looking for a lawyer to advise with relative to the Carondelet property[2] avoid Kline, or Cline,[3] whichever is the right way to spell his name. I presume Ford would advise you to go to him because he is his, Fords, lawyer and is a good one too. But I understand that he has been employed, if not now heretofore, by Carondelet. It would be well to get some lawyer who has never been employed in the case. It is likely that Mr. Maguire[4] would be a good person to advise with as to who to employ.

We leave here in the morning for Kane Pa[5] About Thursday[6] next we will start from there to Newport R. I. From thence to the White Mountains, Lake Champlain, Lake George, Saratoga and thence home, which we will reach from the 15th to 20th of Sept.

Yours Truly
U. S. GRANT

ALS, ICarbS.

1. On [Aug.] 11, 1869, John Covode, Philadelphia, telegraphed to USG. "Will you stop in Philadelphia as you go North or when can I see you in New-York   Answer to Continental"   Telegram received (at 10:15 A.M.), DNA, RG 107, Telegrams Collected (Bound). On the same day, Covode telegraphed to Horace Porter. "Am I to understand from your answer that I cannot see him either here or in New York"   Telegram received (at 2:50 P.M.), *ibid.* Also on Aug. 11, Porter telegraphed to Covode. "President will stop in New York 'till to-morrow evening, at 37 West 27th St.—You could meet him there." Copy, DLC-USG, II, 5. This was the home of USG's sister and her husband, Virginia and Abel R. Corbin. See letter to Virginia Grant Corbin, Aug. 21, 1870.

2. In 1840, Frederick Dent filed the first in a series of suits for land in Carondelet, Mo., granted in 1789 to Gabriel Cerre. The Mo. Circuit Court, St. Louis, ruled against Dent's claim to part of the land in 1857. Twelve years later, George W. Dent, who had acquired the claim from his father, filed another suit. Pursuit of the matter required federal legislation to grant "status in court." On Feb. 27, 1869, U.S. Senator George H. Williams of Ore. wrote to Bvt. Brig. Gen. Frederick T. Dent. "Your Bill passed the Senate last night. Accept my Congratulations" ALS, Harry S. Truman Library, Independence, Mo. See *CG*, 40–3, 913–14, 1642; *U.S. Statutes at Large*, XV, 458. Both the U.S. Circuit Court, St. Louis, and the U.S. Supreme Court eventually ruled against

the Dent claim. See *Missouri Democrat*, May 20, 23, 1870; John William Wallace, *Cases Argued and Adjudged in the Supreme Court . . . December Term, 1871* (New York, 1906), XIV, 308–14; letter to Charles W. Ford, April 7, 1870.

3. George W. Cline, St. Louis attorney.

4. Probably John Maguire, St. Louis real estate agent.

5. On June 22, 1869, Thomas L. Kane, Kane, Pa., had telegraphed to USG. "May I expect that you will telegraph me when to order the Presidents special" Telegram received (at 2:00 P.M.), *ibid.* On July 2, USG wrote to Kane concerning a projected trip to Kane, Pa. Ben Bloomfield, List DI [1949], no. 34. On Aug. 13, USG and a party that included his family and the Corbins left New York City for Kane, via Elmira, N. Y. Traveling in a car provided by the Erie Railroad, USG met Jay Gould and James Fisk, Jr., and visited the company's locomotive works and repair shops in Susquehanna, Pa. USG arrived in Kane on Aug. 14 and remained until Aug. 17. Returning to New York City as a guest on U.S. Senator Simon Cameron's personal car, USG toured iron and coal mines in Lebanon and Schuylkill counties and a rolling mill of the Reading Railroad. On Aug. 19, Corbin recorded in his memorandum book: "Returned this afternoon from Pennsylvania with General Grant and family, who went on to Newport without stopping at all." *HRC*, 41-2-31, p. 244. Gould's recollection of USG's trip is *ibid.*, p. 154. See *New York Herald*, Aug. 13, 15–17, 19, 20, 1869.

6. Aug. 19. On Aug. 21, USG spoke at a public reception in Newport, R. I. "MR. MAYOR AND CITIZENS OF NEWPORT—I can only say in reply to your kind remarks that it affords me great pleasure to be in your city at this time. It is a pleasure that I have long desired, but other duties interfering, this is the first opportunity I have had of doing so. I shall be here but a few days, during which I hope to see most of your people and leave with as favorable impressions as I have received on first entering into it." *Ibid.*, Aug. 23, 1869. For variant text, see *New York Sun*, Aug. 24, 1869. On Aug. [21], USG was introduced to Ida Lewis, lighthouse keeper, Newport. "I am happy to meet you, Miss Lewis, as one of the heroic, noble women of the age. I regret my engagements have been such as not to allow me to call on you at your home. Farewell." *Washington Chronicle*, Aug. 28, 1869. On Aug. 24, USG spoke at a reunion of the Grand Army of the Republic, Ocean Cottage, R. I. "It affords me great pleasure to visit the shores of Rhode Island, where I have been so seldom before, and it is also a particular pleasure to me to see so many of my old comrades in arms, as I am sure I meet here to day, as well as the thousands of others who sympathized with them while they were bearing arms." *Ibid.*, Aug. 26, 1869. On Aug. 25, USG spoke in Concord, N. H. "MR. MAYOR AND CITIZENS OF CONCORD—It affords me great pleasure to visit your beautiful city and your granite State. It is the first time I have ever had the opportunity to make such a visit. It would afford me much satisfaction to make a longer stay, but time will not permit. I thank you for your kind welcome." *New York Herald*, Aug. 27, 1869. A variant text appears in *Galena Gazette*, Aug. 30, 1869. On Aug. 29, USG addressed a welcoming committee at Saratoga, N. Y. "GENTLEMEN OF THE COMMITTEE OF RECEPTION—I thank the people of Saratoga for their cordial welcome. I came here for the purpose of enjoying the advantages of your wat[ers]. I intend to remain here for a fortnight, at the end of which time I hope to be able to testify as to

their benefit." *New York Herald*, Aug. 31, 1869. On Sept. 1, Mayor George W. Flower of Watertown, N. Y., wrote to USG. "I have the honor, on behalf of the Common Council of this city, as well as of our whole population, irrespective of party, to ask that you will extend your intended visit to Utica, to this city, also. The fresh remembrance of, and the lively gratitude felt by our people for, the eminent service rendered our common country by you, together with the early associations of yourself with Watertown when your regiment was stationed at Sackets Harbor, prompts this invitation. With the assurance that a cordial and hearty welcome awaits you, we earnestly desire you to signify your acceptance." *New York Daily Reformer*, Sept. 6, 1869. On Sept. 3, USG wrote to Flower. "Your favor of the 1st inst., extending to me an invitation to visit Watertown, is received. Nothing would afford me more pleasure than to visit again a place of which I retain so many pleasant recollections, but my time will not admit of it. I thank you, however, and through you, the citizens of Watertown, for your and their very cordial invitation." *Ibid.*

To Francis C. Barlow

———

New York August 12th *1869*

F. C. Barlow.[1]
U. S. Marshal
Southern Dist of N Y
General

Learning from the District Attorney of the Southern District of N. Y. that Judge J H McCunn N. Y. Superior Court has ordered the discharge of a United States prisoner held by you for the United States. I authorize & direct that, you hold said prisoner against all orders of said Judge McCunn and that the prisoner only be released on the order of a Judge or other authority, having power to direct a United States Marshal.

You are authorized to use all legal means to retain said prisoner and to prevent your own arrest by such authority of State Courts

Yours Respectfully
U. S. Grant

Copy, DNA, RG 94, Letters Received, 592B 1869. A variant text is printed in the *New York Sun*, Aug. 20, 1869. On Aug. 13, 1869, Francis C. Barlow, U.S. marshal, New York City, wrote to Secretary of War John A. Rawlins. "I have the honor to enclose copy of a letter from the President of the United States. I was directed by the President to transmit it to you. Gen. McDowell has furnished sufficient assistance to maintain the authority of the United States. On consultation with the District Attorney, we have agreed that it is proper to ask you so far to modify your order to the Commandant of Fort Schuyler, as to allow me to bring Pratt before the U. S. Commissioner for examination, on Monday next at 12 M. As I now hold him under a warrant of the Court, it does not seem desirable to fall back on the holding of the Military authorities, until we are compelled to, and it i[s] important for the vindication of the authority of the Government that Pratt should be produced before the Commissioner in due course of law, in spite of the illegal action of Judge McCunn. . . . in case the Commissioner should discharge Pratt on Monday, we presume you desire to hold him under the Military power in aid of the Reconstruction Acts We therefore respectfully suggest that orders be given (if you shall so desire) to the Military authorities here, and to the officer who shall command the detachment which shall escort Pratt before the Commissioner on Monday, that in case the Commissioner shall discharge him, and my authority over him under the warrant thereby cease, he the said Military officer, shall detain him under the Military power." LS, DNA, RG 94, Letters Received, 592B 1869. Related papers are *ibid.* On Aug. 16, John H. Pratt, accused of murder in Jefferson, Tex., was released for lack of evidence. *New York Times*, Aug. 8, 10, 12, 17, 1869.

On Feb. 15, Bvt. Maj. Gen. Edward R. S. Canby, Austin, Tex., had telegraphed to Bvt. Maj. Gen. John A. Rawlins. "I propose to appoint a Military Commission for the trial of the parties implicated in the killing of Geo W. Smith at Jefferson the tenth (10th) or fifteenth (15th) of next month and I request that an officer of the Bureau of Military Justice may be ordered to that place to report to me by letter for the purpose of conducting the prosecution of these cases. I find that Major Layton cannot be spared without serious inconvenience and I have no other officer to send. The cases are important in all their aspects and the best legal talent will no doubt be secured for the defence" Telegram received (at 3:00 P.M.), DNA, RG 107, Telegrams Collected (Bound); *ibid.*, RG 108, Telegrams Received; copy, DLC-USG, V, 55. The army arrested suspects in the case, provoking an outcry against the use of military commissions to try civilians. On Oct. 29, Robert W. Loughery, editor, *Jefferson Times*, telegraphed to USG. "My dispatch of Wednesday met no response my appeal was not for clemency but justice for a brief delay that could work no injury, Personal and political malice have triumphed innocent men & defenceless women feel there is no prote[c]tion these men may be outwardly degraded and hearts may be crushed but no earthly power shall save the authors of this great [w]rong from the infamy connected with it" Telegram received (at 2:50 P.M.), DNA, RG 107, Telegrams Collected (Bound). On March 30, 1870, Maj. Nathan A. M. Dudley, superintendent, Tex. State Penitentiary, Huntsville, wrote to USG. "In compliance with the request of a large number of the prominent citizens of Jefferson and several Army Officers, I have the honor to enclose herewith a Petition for the pardon of 'Oscar Gray' one of the Jefferson prisoners now undergoing sentence in this Institution for life. In endorsing this petition, favorable, as I do, I would respectfully say, in explanation of my reasons for so doing, that the evidence against Gray was less strong than against many of those that were tried and acquitted. That he is an ignorant man, inoffensive in himself if left alone, that he was led into the Mob by parties holding highly responsible places in society both in the Church and out of it, He has always up to this difficulty been a quiet hard working steady man, respected by the Community where he lived, since his arrest his wife and only child have both died, his conduct during the trial and since he has been in this Institution has been good. Believing as I do that the object of the trial and conviction of this party and even the few that were convicted has been obtained, and that the Citizens of Jefferson and vicinity have learned a bitter but salutary lesson, I respectfully pray that your Excellency extend the clemency his friends so earnestly solicit for him." LS, *ibid.*, Letters Received, F60 1870. The enclosure and related papers are *ibid.* Papers concerning the case of Ludwick P. Alvord are *ibid.*, Letters Received from Bureaus; *ibid.*, RG 153, Letters Sent. See William L. Richter, *The Army in Texas During Reconstruction, 1865–1870* (College Station, 1987), pp. 177–79; Allen W. Trelease, *White Terror: The Ku Klux Klan Conspiracy and Southern Reconstruction* (New York, 1971), pp. 140–47.

1. On March 24, 1869, Barlow wrote to USG. "I am told that the papers reccommending me as U. S. District Attorney for the Southern District of New York have been laid before you—I also learn that the friends of certain other applicants for the office have represented (whether to yourself or not I do not know) that I am an unsuitable person for the place because of my inexperience at the bar—I can most truly say that I do not expect this appointment, and I have no doubt that you will select some one far more competent than myself for the position—But I do not like to have my professional competency attacked, and I beg that should there be any question of that kind I may be allowed to refer to those who know me, and that the opinions of those who are opposed to me should not be taken—Here I will only say that for three years I have had sole charge of the legal business of the Park Bank, one of the largest banks in the Country—and I take the liberty of enclosing a letter from one of the best known of our Judges—I trust you will excuse this personal letter to yourself— I should not have said a word except on this point of professional fitness, and as I know you like directness, I say it directly to you—" Copy, DLC-Hamilton Fish. The enclosure, a copy of a letter from Judge Charles P. Daly to USG concerning Barlow's legal experience, is *ibid.* On April 10, Attorney Gen. Ebenezer R. Hoar wrote to USG. "I have this moment received a telegram from New York, informing me that Gen. Barlow is inclined to accept, and that I shall have a definite answer this evening—" ALS, OFH. On Oct. 23, Edwards Pierrepont, U.S. attorney, New York City, wrote to USG and to Hoar. "I regret exceedingly that Marshall Barlow has determined to resign—I do not believe that an officer so capable and efficient will be found to take his place. I the more deeply regret the resignation of General Barlow because the administration of that office is so directly connected with my own, that the one cannot be successfully conducted without the coöperation of the other—Between Gen. Barlow & myself there has been at all times and in every respect the most perfect harmony—I feel great solicitude about his successor; I trust that you will not overlook the great importance of having an honest man of energy & sense in this important office. Gen. Barlow and I have talked this matter over soley with refference to fitness and advantage to the Govermt, and we both agree that if the present chief Deputy, Mr Harlow, can be appointed it will secure a most excellent capable &

upright man for that very responsible office—I should not write so urgently upon this subject, were it not for the fact, that no amount of labor or success in my office will avail much against the frauds or blunders of a dishonest or incapable Marshall. The salary is so low that it will be found difficult to retain in that office an honest and efficient man. There are reasons which Gen. Barlow will present why we both think Mr Harlow the best man, likely to want the place— I earnestly hope that no unfit man will will receive that office—It would dampen the zeal which I have felt in trying to bring the office of United States atty. in this District into a more elevated position—" ALS, CtY. On Oct. 25, Moses H. Grinnell, New York City, telegraphed to USG. "If Genl Barlow should resign his position of U. S Marshal of this District I trust his chief Deputy S. R Harlow may be appointed to the vacancy He is just the man for the place" Telegram received (at 1:30 P.M.), DNA, RG 107, Telegrams Collected (Bound). USG appointed Samuel R. Harlow to replace Barlow. On March 10, 1870, Grinnell wrote to USG. "*Personal* . . . A rumor has reached me, that a change is to be made in the office of U. S. Marshall for this district. I trust it is unfounded. I have the most implicit confidence in Mr Harlow's integrity and ability to fill the position, and the expressions of satisfaction at the manner in which he performs its duties that have come to my knowledge, are many and concurrent. he is moreover a thorough going Republican and acts in perfect harmony with the friends of the administration. You will pardon me for troubling you with this, but I feel it my duty on account of the anxiety I feel that so important an office should be properly filled, and that the disgraceful proceedings in that office under the Administration of Mr Johnson, may not be repeated under yours. I may add that I do not know the name of the person suggested in the place of Mr Harlow." LS, DLC-USG, IB. On March 18, USG nominated Harlow as collector of Internal Revenue, 4th District, N. Y., and George H. Sharpe as marshal, Southern District, N. Y.

To Roscoe Conkling

New York City
August 12th /69

My Dear Sir:

Your favor of the 7th inst. kindly inviting Mrs. Grant, the children, and myself to visit you at Utica only come to hand last evening just before starting time, hence apparent neglect in not replying earlyer. It will afford me great pleasure to accept your invitation for a day, longer it is not probable that I will be able to stay. I have cut out about as much visiting as I will be able to get through with in the time that I feel I can remain away from Washington. From here I go to Kane, Pa thence to Newport R. I. the White Mountains and Saratoga. Probably within twenty-four hours of my arrival there I will start for Washington, leaving my family behind, thus making my own stay at the springs short.—I shall hope to meet you there when the other visit can be arranged.

With high regards

your obt. svt.

U. S. GRANT

ALS, DLC-Roscoe Conkling. Roscoe Conkling, born in 1829 in Albany, N. Y., was admitted to the bar (1850) and became active in Whig and Republican politics. Acclaimed for his success as a lawyer and orator, he served as mayor of Utica (1858–59) and U.S. Representative (1859–63, 1865–67) before he entered the U.S. Senate (1867). Conkling had purchased a house in a fashionable section of Utica for his official residence; his wife, a sister of Horatio Seymour, was its principal occupant. See David M. Jordan, *Roscoe Conkling of New York: Voice in the Senate* (Ithaca, N. Y., 1971).

To Hamilton Fish

Kane Pa. Aug. 14th /69

HON. HAMILTON FISH,
SEC. OF STATE:
MY DEAR SIR:

On reflection I think it advisable to complete the neutrality proclamation which I signed before leaving Washington, and to issue it if Gen. Sickles[1] has not received an entirely satisfactory reply to his proposition to mediate between Spain and ~~France~~ the Cubans. In fact I am not clearly satisfied that we would not be justified in intimating to Spain that we look with some alarm upon her proposition to send 20.000 more troops to Cuba to put down, as Americans believe the right of self government on this Continent. Not that Spain has not a perfect right to prosecute as vigorous a war as she pleases, upon her own soil, observing the rules of civilized warfare; but that the rights of our citizens have been so wantonly invaded by Spanish troops, or volunteers, that such a course would arouse the sympathies of our citizens in favor of the Cubans to such a degree as to require all our vigilence to prevent them from giving material aid. The question might well be asked whether Spain would not be weaker with 20.000 more troops in Cuba; and also, by us, whether we would be justified by our own people to let them do so without at least putting the Cubans on the same footing with their adversaries first.—Except the issueing of the proclamation I do not give this as instructions but as something to think of whether it is not sound. If deemed so the policy of acting upon it will be discussed afterwards.

I will be in New York City on Thursday[2] next on my way to New Port. Will be at Mr. Corbins a few hours before sailing.

Yours Truly
U. S. GRANT

ALS, DLC-Hamilton Fish. In an undated document, USG authorized Secretary of State Hamilton Fish to issue the neutrality proclamation. DS, *ibid.* An undated draft of the proclamation states: "Whereas it is to be desired that the present ~~g~~cordial relations existing between the United States and Spain should not be affected by the grave events which are now taking place in Cuba, where a war ~~is being~~ has for some months been carried on between the people of that Island and the authorities of Spain and still exists ~~and also~~ and whereas it is also important that a strict neutrality in the contest shall be maintained by the United States and by the citizens thereof and by all persons residing or being within the territories or jurisdiction thereof   Now therefore, to that end, and in order to avoid the damage which might come to the citizens of the United States, and to their navigation and commerce from the want of clear provisions to which to adjust their conduct, and in order that the laws of the United States may be enforced, I, *Ulysses S. Grant* President of the United States, do hereby warn all citizens of the United States under the pains and penalties in such case made and provided against (~~within the territory and~~ or ~~jurisdiction of the United States~~) accepting and exercising within the territory or jurisdiction of the United States a commission to serve either of the said belligerents. And I do further warn all persons ~~within the territories and jurisdiction of the United States,~~ under the pains and penalt~~y~~ies ~~of the law~~ in such case made and provided, against doing any of the following acts within the territories and jurisdiction of the United States, the same being forbidden by laws thereof—namely—1st Against enlisting or entering himself, and against hiring or retaining another person to enlist or enter himself, or to go beyond the limits or jurisdiction of the United States with intent to be enlisted or entered in the service of either of the said belligerents as a soldier, or as a marine or seaman on board of any vessel of war, letter of marque, or privateer. 2d Against fitting out and arming, or attempting to fit out and arm, or procuring to be fitted out and armed, or knowingly being concerned in the furnishing fitting out or arming of any ship or vessel with intent that such ship or ~~vess~~ vessel shall be employed in the services of either of the said belligerents to cruise or commit hostilities against the subjects, citizens or property of the other belligerent. 3d Against issueing or delivering a commission within the territory or jurisdiction of the United States to any ship or vessel to the intent that she may be employed as aforesaid. 4th Against increasing or augmenting, or procuring to be increased or augmented, or knowingly being concerned in increasing or augmenting the force of any ship of war cruiser or other armed vessel, which at the time of her arrival within the United States was a ship of war cruiser or other armed vessel, in the service of either of the said belligerents by adding to the number of guns of such vessel or by changing those on board of her for guns of a larger calibre or by the addition thereto of any equipment solely applicable to war   5th Against beginning or setting on foot or providing or preparing the means for any military expedition or enterprise to be carried on from the United States against either belligerent. And I do hereby enjoin upon all persons residing within the territories and jurisdiction of the United States, faithfully to observe the laws thereof, and to abstain from every act which can be considered as a breach of strict neutrality in this war, and I do hereby notify all persons violating the law commonly known as the neutrality law, that they will thereby cease to be entitled to the protection of this government. And I do enjoin upon all officers of the Government, civil and military, in their respective spheres, to be faithful vigilant and active in enforcing the laws. In testimony whereof I have hereunto set my hand and caused the seal of the United States to be affixed to these presents." Df, *ibid.* A revised copy of the proclamation is *ibid.*

On Aug. 20, 1869, Horace Porter, Newport, R. I., wrote to Fish. "I should have written you before now to thank you, and your family for your politeness during my visit, and to assure you of the pleasure I enjoyed while with you. The only thing that marred my happiness was the attack of ague, ~~and~~ but I shall hold you, for this, in no wise accountable. Please say to Mrs. Fish that thanks to her dosing I have not had another attack, and hope I have entirely recovered, Mr. Davis has, no doubt, told ~~him~~ you of the Presidents views in regard to Cuba, which coincide exactly with your own. The President says it was not at all necessary for you to have remained in N. York last evening, nor will he expect you to come to Newport, which I told him you were ready to do. The return to W. is fixed for Monday night, 30th With kind remembrances to Mrs. Fish, Mrs. Rogers and the rest of the family; all of whom contributed so materially to my pleasure while with you. . . . Please say to Mrs. Fish that I have found the vest I thought I had left at your house." ALS, *ibid.* On July 10, 1870, Fish recorded in his diary that USG had thanked him for "preventing the issuing last August & September of the Proclamation of Cuban belligerency *which he had signed*, & which he wrote me a note instructing me to sign (which I did) & to issue (which I did *not*)" *Ibid.*

1. On June 28, 1869, USG had written to Francisco Serrano, Regent of Spain. "I have made choice of Daniel E. Sickles, one of our distinguished citizens to reside near the Government of Spain. . . ." Copy, DNA, RG 84, Spain, Instructions. On April 16, Edward W. Whitaker and Fred M. Patrick, Hartford, had telegraphed to USG. "Connecticut soldiers endorse Sickles for Spain against every body" Telegram received (at 11:30 A.M.), *ibid.*, RG 59, Letters of Ap-

plication and Recommendation; (press) *ibid.*, RG 107, Telegrams Collected (Bound).

On April 12, USG had nominated Henry S. Sanford as minister to Spain. On April 13, George P. Smith, New York City, wrote to USG. "The undersigned—from a sense of duty—begs to address you, directly, today, in earnest protest against the reported appointment of Mr Sanford—present Chargè at Brussells, to any post of honor under your Administration. In October, 1861— at the request of General Meigs—to whom, if necessary, I beg to refer, I went abroad, to make certain purchases for his Department. On arrival in London, I found Mr Sanford awaiting me—with a scheme, which he urgently pressed, to transfer my purchases and payments to him—unquestionably, as a speculative operation for his private benefit—in which business he was then very active— some particulars of which are given in Report of House Committee—of 38th or '9th Congress—numbered 67. or 68—I beleive. Failing in his attempts on me— he then despatched his worthy Secretary of Legation to Washington—and but for the prompt and persistent opposition of General Meigs—they would have succeeded in selling to the Government, a large quantity of Army Cloths, utterly unsuited to the service—but at prices would have made a large profit to the operators. When Mr Sanford came over, recently, to get his mission advanced to full grade—I felt it my duty to enclose to a Senator, a letter Mr S. had written me, urging transfer of my business to him, in '61—the reading of which, in the Senate, I had reason to beleive, did not help his promotion." ALS, *ibid.*, RG 59, Letters of Application and Recommendation. USG endorsed this letter. "Refered to the Sec. of State. The writer of this letter is a man of high character, so says the Sec. of the Interior who knows him personally." AE (initialed), *ibid.* Related papers are *ibid.* Expecting nomination as minister to Spain himself, Sickles expressed displeasure regarding Sanford's nomination during an interview with USG on April 14. *New York Herald*, April 15, 1869. On April 22, the Senate tabled Sanford's nomination. See *New York Times*, Feb. 15, 1898; Joseph A. Fry, *Henry S. Sanford: Diplomacy and Business in Nineteenth-Century America* (Reno, 1982), pp. 54–56, 84–85.

2. Aug. 19.

To William Elrod

Newport R. I.
Aug. 23d /69

DEAR ELROD,

Whilst at Long Branch I got an Alderny bull and two heifers to send to the farm. They are of the very purest blood. I expect before going back to Washington to stay to buy some four or six more heifers. It is possible that those already got may have gone to you. When they go I want you to dispose of the bull you now have and keep none but the one I send. *One of the heifers* I send is with calf by another bull. Should she have a male *calf raise it* for the farm, but all male calves by the bull I send out dispose of as best you can. All others raise with the view of ultimately geting a full stock of Alderneys.

Yours Truly

[U. S. GRANT]

AL (signature clipped), Illinois Historical Survey, University of Illinois, Urbana, Ill.

Memorandum

———

Washington. D. C. [Aug. 31,] 186[9]

The United States are willing to mediate between Spain & Cuba, ~~for the independence of the latter~~, on following terms. Immediate armistice   Cuba to recompense Spain for public property &c. All Spaniards to be protected in their persons and property if they wish to remain on the island, or to withdraw with it, at their option. ~~If~~ The United States not to guarantee except with approval of Congress. These conditions to be accepted ~~within a reasonable time or the United~~ by Sept. 25th or the United States to be regarded as having withdrawn all offer to mediate. As time progresses devastation depreciates value of property, and consequently of the sum that can or will be guaranteed.

AN, DLC-Hamilton Fish. On Sept. 1, 1869, Secretary of State Hamilton Fish cabled to Daniel E. Sickles, U.S. minister, Madrid, transmitting these instructions. *HED*, 41-2-160, p. 32; Allan Nevins, *Hamilton Fish: The Inner History of the Grant Administration* (New York, 1936), 243–44.

To Hamilton Fish

Saratoga N Y.
Sept. 3d/69

Hon. H. Fish,
Sec. of State;
Dear Sir:

Please see Dr. McGrew and take such action, after an examination of the papers he presents, as you may deem proper. I know the Dr. personally as a proper and capable man and physician. He was a surgeon in the Western Army serving directly under me, and his family I have known slightly personally, and by reputation well, all my life.

Respectfully Your
U. S. Grant

ALS, DLC-Hamilton Fish. On Aug. 30, 1869, Jesse Root Grant, Covington, Ky., wrote to J. C. Bancroft Davis, asst. secretary of state. "The Bearer Dr. John S. McGrew, was the Medical Attendant on on my son Gen Grant, at New Orleans when he was hurt there by the fall of his Horse. The Dr visits Washington on business with the Dept of which you now have charge . . ." ALS, DNA, RG 59, Despatches from U.S. Consuls in Honolulu. Papers supporting Dr. John S. McGrew's request to be reinstated as surgeon, U.S. hospital, Honolulu, are *ibid.*; *ibid.*, Letters of Application and Recommendation.

On May 24, 1865, McGrew, Lexington, Ky., had written to USG. "I have the honor to request that you give me permission to visit you at Washington City—on business pertaining to my position in the Army. I was, as you will probably remember, one of your Medical attendants when you were suffering from the injury you received by the fall of your horse at New Orleans, last fall a year." ALS, *ibid.*, RG 108, Letters Received. On Feb. 6, 1866, Gordon Granger wrote a letter to U.S. Senator James Guthrie of Ky. describing McGrew as "a conservative in politics & an ardent supporter of the present administration." ALS, *ibid.*, RG 59, Applications and Recommendations, Lincoln and Johnson. On the same day, USG endorsed this letter. "I can endorse what Gn. Granger says of the services and qualifications of Surgeon McGrew except as to his political status. That I know nothing about. I believe he would be a capable and faithful appointee where ever placed." AES, *ibid.*

To Roscoe Conkling

SARATOGA, N. Y., Sept. 5, 1869.

To Hon. Roscoe Conkling:

MY DEAR SIR: It is with extreme regret that the continued
and dangerous illness of Secretary RAWLINS, whose relations with
me have been so intimate from the breaking out of the rebellion to
the present day, compels me to forego the contemplated pleasure
of a visit to your city tomorrow. I know that you, and my other
friends, will appreciate the motive which calls me from a pleasure
trip to the bedside of a comrade, who has rendered such signal service to his country, and whose death will cast a gloom over the
nation. The most recent dispatches scarcely leave a hope that I may
see him alive.

I am, very sincerely, yours,
U. S. GRANT

New York Times, Sept. 6, 1869. On Sept. 3, 1869, USG, Saratoga, N. Y., had
telegraphed to Col. John E. Smith. "Please telegraph me Genl Rawlins present
condition" Telegram received (at 10:30 A.M.), DNA, RG 107, Telegrams
Collected (Bound). On Sept. 6, Horace Porter, Gray's Ferry, Pa., telegraphed
to Robert M. Douglas. "President will reach Washington five twenty (5.20)
this PM. Telegraph Camden Station Balto Rawlins condition" Telegram received (at 12:20 P.M.), *ibid.*

To Mary E. Rawlins

[*Sept. 6, 1869*]

Mrs. Mary E. Rawlins, Danbury, Conn.:

Your beloved husband expired at twelve minutes after four
o'clock this afternoon, to be mourned by a family and friends who
loved him for his personal worth and services to his country, and a
nation which acknowledges its debt of gratitude to him. On consultation with friends, it is determined that he shall be buried in
the Congressional Burying Ground,[1] as the most appropriate place,

unless you have other suggestions to make. The time of the funeral is not arranged, but probably will take place on Thursday[2] next.

U. S. GRANT.

New York Times, Sept. 7, 1869. See *PUSG*, 9, 502–3. On Sept. 7, 1869, William R. Rowley, Galena, telegraphed to USG, then to Horace Porter. "The father of Genl Rawlins desires to know what disposition is to be made of the remains of his son . . . Answer" "The parents of Gen Rawlins desire me to request that his remains be brought to Galena." Telegrams received (at 10:00 A.M. and 4:00 P.M.), DNA, RG 107, Telegrams Collected (Bound). On the same day, Porter telegraphed to Rowley. "Danbury, Conn; Springfield, Ills.; and Washington claim remains of Gen. Rawlins—President and other friends urge burial in Congressional Cemetery here at present. Body is embalmed and can be removed at any time hereafter." Copy, DLC-USG, II, 5.

On Sept. 7, J. C. Duff, New York City, telegraphed to USG. "It is with profound sorrow that we have rec'd the news the death of the Hon John A. Rawlins, the army and country acknowledges his valuable services, we will take care of his family, By order of German veterans, When is the funeral,?" Telegram received (on Sept. 8, 9:40 A.M.), DNA, RG 107, Telegrams Collected (Bound). On Sept. 7, Moses H. Grinnell, New York City, telegraphed to Porter. "Steps have been taken by which thirty (30) or forty thousan[d] 40,000 will be raised for Gen Rawlins family Have written by mail" Telegram received (at 4:15 P.M.), *ibid*. On Sept. 11, Vice President Schuyler Colfax, Oregon City, telegraphed to USG. "Convey to Mrs Rawlins my sincerest sympathy, The nation shares in her great loss, Sorrow in this distant region as universal as at the Capital, Please add one hundred (100) dollars for me to fund, Will remit you from San Francisco" Telegram received (at 1:50 P.M.), *ibid*. Additional telegrams of condolence are *ibid*.

On Sept. 8, Julia Dent Grant, New York City, telegraphed to USG. "I see you are ill, Shall I come home tonight? I feel so anxious, . . . Answer" Telegram received (at noon), *ibid*. On the same day, Abel R. Corbin, New York City, telegraphed to USG. "Mrs Grant & myself on yesterday visited Mrs Gen Rawlins at Danbury We are all well, When can Mrs Grant Expect you," Telegram received (at 1:35 P.M.), *ibid*. On Sept. 18, Adam Badeau, London, cabled to USG. "Please secure General Rawlins historical papers before sold or lost unless prohibited, Will return immediately" Telegram received (at 1:40 P.M.), *ibid*.

1. On Oct. 19, 1870, Porter wrote to O. D. Barrett, Washington, D. C. "The President directs me to acknowledge the receipt of your letter in regard to the remains of Gen: Rawlins, and to convey to you his thanks for your kindness in informing him of the statement of the undertaker in regard to the neglect of the remains, and in obtaining consent to deposit them in another vault. The President on receipt of your letter at once directed Gen: Jno. E. Smith—Gen Rawlins intimate friend who has been engaged in settling his estate—to make a thorough investigation of the circumstances. He reports that the undertakers statement is entirely without foundation, that great care has been taken of the remains and that there is no objection to their remaining in the vault in which they are at present deposited. It is the desire of the many of the General's friends

to have the body buried at Springfield, Ills. and this will probably be done after the cold weather sets in. It is thought proper that these facts should be communicated to you since you have taken such a kind interest in the matter. The contents of your letter caused the President great anxiety, but it is hoped, from what Gen: Smith says, that the undertaker was misinformed." Copy, DLC-USG, II, 1.

On Dec. 11, 1871, Orville E. Babcock wrote to William S. Hillyer. "The President directs me to acknowledge the receipt of your letter about removing the remains of Gen. Rawlins, and also erecting a monument. He requests me to say that he will have the remains transferred and will have a stone placed at the grave. He does not think it best to draw from the estate money for an elaborate or expensive monument, especially as there is a lasting monument, an equestrian statue in bronze, in the process of construction, to be placed on some public reservation in this City. The President thinks the friends of Gen. R. residing here can attend to the matter without putting you to the trouble and expense of coming here to attend to it. At the President's request I shall look to the matter, make the arrangements and submit them to Mrs. R. for her approval." LS, Hillyer Papers, ViU.

2. Sept. 9, 1869.

To Elihu B. Washburne

Washington, D. C. Sept. 7th *1869.*

DEAR WASHBURNE;

ȻOur mutual and much esteemed friend, Gen. Rawlins, expired yesterday after, as you are aware, years of gradual decline. Although he has lived far beyond what his most sanguine frends hoped yet his final taking off has produced a shock which would be felt for but few of our public men. He retained his consciousness up to within a few minuets of his death. Although I was not with him in his dying hours I am told that his greatest concern seemed to be for his destitute family. I was at Saratoga when his rapid decline commenced. The first dispatch I received indicating any immediate danger was on Saturday evening, or night, after the last train had left. I was compelled to remain until sunday evening and arrived consequently about forty minuets after he had breathed his last.

I have been intending for months to write you and have no special excuse for not doing so except that when I do get alone for an hour I always happen to have something to do. Whilst I have been away this Summer I have been very much let alone by people who have an axe to grind but there has scarsely ever been a minuet when there was not callers.—You will see by the official statements that the first six months of the administration have been sucsessful in improving the revenue collections, and somewhat in reducing expenses. The showing is a reduction of over forty-nine Million of the public debt. The actual decrease is greater. McCullough kept no interest account; consequently on the 4th of March no interest due that day, or cupons over due but not presented for payment, appeared as a part of the public debt. We have actually paid about six Million, in gold, of old coupons which the statements give no credit for. In addition to this we have paid probably as much as two Million in currency on contrats fulfilled and purchases made before the 1st of March which is another *dead horse* paid for.—Please give my love to Jones and his family and say to him that I expect to write to him soon, but if I do not it is not because I think the less of him. If I can I will drop you a line also occasionally, but, as I say to Jones, I repeat to you.

I presume Mrs. W. and the children will be with you when this reaches. If so please present Mrs. Grants' and my love. My family are all well and I attribute the fact to having them out of the White House during the Summer. Every one left here have been taken sick and have been obliged to leave by direction of the Dr.

Yours Truly
U. S. GRANT

ALS, IHi.

To George S. Boutwell

NEW YORK CITY, *September* 12, 1869.

DEAR SIR: I leave here to-morrow morning for Western Pennsylvania, and will not reach Washington before the middle or last of next week.[1] Had I known before making my arrangements for starting that you would be in this city early this week, I would have remained to meet you. I am satisfied that on your arrival you will be met by the bulls and bears of Wall street, and probably by merchants too, to induce you to sell gold, or pay the November interest in advance, on the one side, and to hold fast on the other. The fact is, a desperate struggle is now taking place, and each party want the government to help them out. I write this letter to advise you of what I think you may expect, to put you on your guard.

I think, from the lights before me, I would move on, without change, until the present struggle is over.

If you want to write me this week, my address will be Washington, Pennsylvania.

I would like to hear your experience with the factions at all events, if they give you time to write. No doubt you will have a better chance to judge than I, for I have avoided general discussion of the subject.

Yours truly,
U. S. GRANT.

Hon. GEORGE S. BOUTWELL, *Secretary of the Treasury.*

HRC, 41-2-31, p. 359. On Feb. 1, 1870, Secretary of the Treasury George S. Boutwell testified before the U.S. House Committee on Banking and Currency. "About the 4th day of September, I suppose, I think on the evening of the 4th of September, I received a letter from the President, dated at New York, as I recollect it; I am not sure where it was dated. I have not seen the letter since the night I received it. I think it is now at my residence in Groton. In this letter he spoke, I think, somewhat of his purpose of returning to Washington, and when I should be here. In that letter he expressed an opinion that it was undesirable to force down the price of gold. He spoke of the importance to the West of being able to move their crops. His idea was that if gold should fall the West would suffer and the movement of the crops would be retarded. The impression made upon my mind by the letter was that he had rather a strong opinion to that effect, but at the same time, in the letter he said he had no desire to control my purpose in regard to the management of the Treasury; that he was entirely satisfied with it, &c., and he left the matter to my judgment entirely. I saw from the letter that it was his opinion that the sale of gold in any considerable quantity might carry down the price of it, and that if the price were to fall the West would be embarrassed; that they would not be able to move their crops and get a return." *Ibid.*, p. 358. See letter to Robert Bonner, Oct. 13, 1869.

On Sept. 16, 1869, Jay Gould, New York City, wrote to Horace Porter. "We have purchased half a million gold on your account. . . ." *New York Times*, Oct.

18, 1869. On Sept. 19, Porter, Washington, Pa., telegraphed to Gould. "I have not authorized any purchase of gold, and request that none be made on my account. I am unable to enter into any speculation whatever." *Ibid.* See *HRC*, 41-2-31, pp. 445–46.

On Sept. 18 or 19, Julia Dent Grant, Washington, Pa., wrote to Virginia Grant Corbin and later remembered part of the letter. "The General says, if you have any influence with your husband, tell him to have nothing whatever to do with _____. If he does, he will be ruined, for come what may, he (your brother) will do his duty to the country and the trusts in his keeping." John Y. Simon, ed., *The Personal Memoirs of Julia Dent Grant* (New York, 1975), p. 182. Abel R. Corbin remembered the substance of the letter to be: "The President is greatly distressed at the rumors that your husband is speculating, or interested in speculations in Wall street; if it is true, he hopes he will disconnect himself at once." *HRC*, 41-2-31, p. 252. Jay Gould testified concerning the letter. " 'Tell your husband,' or 'tell Mr. Corbin, that my husband is very much annoyed by your speculations. You must close them as quick as you can.' " *Ibid.*, p. 157. Another version stated: "My husband is very much annoyed at your speculations. He tries not to be influenced by them, but fears he is. Another reason why they must be closed is because Cuban matters will soon come up in Cabinet, and the action of our government will influence the price of bonds." *New York World*, Oct. 21, 1869. See *HRC*, 41-2-31, p. 448; *New York Sun*, Oct. 6, 1869.

On Sept. 24, "Lindsay," New York City, twice telegraphed to Orville E. Babcock. "Wall street is wild over the gold question gold six[ty] & one half (60½) Ring associate assert they can carry where they please" "Bears riding bulls hard say they will carry Gold back to 35 before three" Telegrams received (at 12:30 P.M. and 1:50 P.M.), DNA, RG 107, Telegrams Collected (Bound). On the same day, Frank E. Howe, New York City, telegraphed to Porter. "Gold one hundred & sixty (160) immense alarm and indignation among the merchant clique brag and bet are gone . . ." Telegram received (at 1:00 P.M.), *ibid.*

On Sept. 25, Saturday, Mrs. Corbin, New York City, telegraphed to USG. "Myself and husband leave today will be at Your House Sunday morning" Telegram received (at 3:40 P.M.), *ibid.* See *HRC*, 41-2-31, pp. 266, 446–47. On the same day, DeB. Randolph Keim, Harrisburg, Pa., telegraphed to Porter. "Would president allow me to use prudently publicly fact having written letter to Boutwell not to sell gold when in NewYork Sept thirteenth 13th this had effect in demolishing gold Ring and the President deserves credit. Please answer immediately" Telegram received, DNA, RG 107, Telegrams Collected (Bound).

1. On Sept. 4, Horace Porter, Saratoga, N. Y., wrote to William W. Smith. "The President desires me to say that he will arrived with his party at Pittsburgh next Friday night (10th inst) or Saturday morning, and take stages to arrive at Washington, Pa. by Saturday evening." ALS (facsimile), DLC-USG, I, D. On Sept. 7, Smith telegraphed to "Gen H Porter or Gen Dent." "Will President be here Saturday as General Porter wrote me from Saratoga" Telegram received (at 3:25 P.M.), DNA, RG 107, Telegrams Collected (Bound). On Sept. 11, 2:25 P.M., USG, West Point, N. Y., telegraphed to Smith. "Will be in Pittsburgh on Tuesday noon next on way to Washington Pa." Telegram received, Washington County Historical Society, Washington, Pa.

On Monday, Sept. 13, Mayor Jared M. Brush of Pittsburgh and Mayor

Simon Drum of Allegheny, Pa., telegraphed to USG, West Philadelphia. "Can you arrange to remain in Pittsburgh Tuesday night. If so, will you accept the hospitalities of the cities of Pittsburgh and Allegheny." *Pittsburgh Commercial*, Sept. 14, 1869. On the same day, USG, Harrisburg, telegraphed to Brush and Drum. "It will afford me great pleasure to accept your invitation, and remain over night at Pittsburgh." *Ibid.* On Sept. 14, USG spoke in Johnstown, Pa. "This day three years ago I was one of the Executive party which stopped at this place. I trust that no catastrophe like that which occurred that day will happen to-day. I thank you, fellow citizens, for your cordial greeting." *Ibid.*, Sept. 15, 1869. On Sept. 14, 1866, thirteen people died when a makeshift bridge collapsed under the weight of a crowd gathered to welcome the presidential party. See *New York Times*, Sept. 15, 1866. On Sept. 14, 1869, USG spoke in Pittsburgh. "GENTLEMEN: I thank you for the very cordial reception which you have extended me. Since my arrival in this city I have been met on every hand with the most flattering demonstrations of regard. But it is unnecessary for me to say more, for I am very sure that few of you could hear what I say." *Pittsburgh Commercial*, Sept. 15, 1869. On Sept. 15, George B. McMurtry, Pittsburgh, wrote to USG. "The Manufacturers of Pittsburgh cordially tender to yourself and suite, an invitation to the banquet to be held at the Monongahela House, on Thursday evenining, 16th instant." *Ibid.*, Sept. 16, 1869. On Sept. 15, Porter, Pittsburgh, wrote to McMurtry declining the invitation. *Ibid.*

On Sept. 17, John D. Boyle wrote to USG. "The undersigned, the Burgesses and Councilmen of the borough of Washington, representing its citizens, would respectfully solicit you to deposit within the corner stone of the town hall, now in process of erection, on Saturday next (September 18th), a box containing the memorials of the present and the past, so that future generations may learn our history to the present time, when these memorials shall come to light. . . ." Alfred Creigh, *History of Washington County from Its First Settlement to the Present Time* . . . (Washington, Pa., 1870), p. 146. On the same day, USG, Washington, Pa., wrote to Boyle *et al.* "Your letter of this date requesting me, in behalf of the Citizens, to deposit within the Corner Stone of the Town Hall, now in the process of erect[ion] on Saturday, Sept. 18th /69, a box containing memorials of the presnt, is received. It will afford me pleasure to comply with this request; enhanced pleasure because your County, and City, were named in express honor of the Father of our Country, (whos name they bear) ~~and~~ whos name is reverenced by every American Citizen who loves his Country." ALS, Washington County Historical Society, Washington, Pa. See John A. Carpenter, "Washington, Pennsylvania, and the Gold Conspiracy of 1869," *Western Pennsylvania Historical Magazine*, 48, 4 (Oct., 1965), 345–53.

To Hamilton Fish

Dated Washington Pa Sept 17 *1869* [7:09 P.M.]

To HON HAMILTON FISH

I do not think it advisable to authorize direct purchase of Cuba by the United States. It is questionable whether a matter of such importance should be considered without the sanction of Congress

U S GRANT

Telegram received (in cipher), DLC-Hamilton Fish. On Sept. 17, 1869, Secretary of State Hamilton Fish had telegraphed to USG. "General Babcocks . . . I will write by mail this afternoon" Telegram sent (in cipher), DNA, RG 59, Telegrams Sent.

To Ebenezer R. Hoar

Washington, D. C. Sept 25. *1869.*

SIR:

The enclosed papers are hereby referred to you for your opinion.

In view of the fact that Congress created the reconstruction laws and can, if necessary, alter them; and that each house of Congress is, by law, the judge of the qualifications of its own members, I am of opinion that, instead of there being an objection to the election of U. S. Senators[1] by the present legislature of Virginia, it is desirable that they should be elected at the approaching session of that body.

Very respectfully yours

U. S. GRANT

HON. E. R. HOAR
ATTY. GENL.

LS, DNA, RG 60, Letters from the President. On Sept. 23, 1869, Secretary of War William T. Sherman wrote to Bvt. Maj. Gen. Edward R. S. Canby, Richmond. "*Confidential* . . . The President says he has just had a conversation with the Attorney-General, who says he is in receipt of many letters from Virginia, inquiring whether the Legislature soon to meet should elect their Senators, ready to apply for admission on the meeting of Congress; but he cannot with propriety answer such letters—But if you will address me, as Sec'y of War, a letter making the inquiry, he can give a favorable answer, and the Attorney-General can sustain it with an opinion. I should think it would be best that Senators should be chosen, ready to take their seats when the State is admitted, and if you will address me such an inquiry, I will endeavor to answer you in such form as will satisfy the members of the Legislature—" Copy, *ibid.*, RG 107, Letters Received from Bureaus. On Sept. 24, Canby wrote to Sherman. "I was about to submit the enclosed letter for your consideration when yours of yesterday was received I had expressed the same opinion in conversations but had declined to give officially because it would have the appearance of prejudging a question that I thought properly belonged to the Legislature itself. There was however so much anxiety for an official opinion from some quarters that I had prepared the answer to Mr Courtenays note to be sent to him if it should be approved by you. It is of course superfluous now but I send it now as expressing what I have said upon the subject which has been somewhat muddled in the repetitions that I have seen. An opinion from the Attorney General will be eminently satisfactory to the members of the Legislature and will probably save me from some newspaper criticism." ALS, *ibid.* On Sept. 25, Attorney Gen. Ebenezer R. Hoar wrote to USG. ". . . Upon a careful consideration, I am now of opinion that the election of Senators, like voting upon the XIV and XV Amendments to the Constitution of the United States, is a part of the action contemplated by Congress as preliminary to a restoration of the State to its full relation to the Government of the United States, as one of the States of the Union. The Senators thus elected would have no power or authority, until the Senate of the United States should have passed upon the validity of their election and admitted them as members of that body. Under the act of April 10, 1869, the election of members of the House of Representatives was permitted, and has taken place; and when Congress comes to act upon the whole question of the reconstruction of the State, it would seem equally proper that members elected to both branches of the National Legislature should present themselves, and be ready for admission to seats in the respective houses. The election of Senators does not seem to me to transcend the action which comes within the limited and qualified purposes requisite to reconstruction, but rather to be essential to the completeness of that action;—and I think that the military commander should not interfere with or prevent it. . . . The papers sent to me are herewith returned." LS, *ibid.* See *HMD*, 41-2-8, pp. 9–11.

On Nov. 26, U.S. Senator Simon Cameron of Pa., Petersburg, Va., telegraphed to USG. "The party with me from the South will be in Washn tomorrow and if You have time will detail their experience" Telegram received (at 11:00 A.M.), DNA, RG 107, Telegrams Collected (Bound). The next day, USG met with a delegation from Va. to discuss measures for readmitting the state. See *New York Herald*, Nov. 28, 1869.

1. On Oct. 19, Robert M. Douglas, Richmond, telegraphed to USG. "Lewis and Johnston nominated in secret caucus last night, Genl Williams name authoritatively withdrawn without any authority from his friends great dissatisfaction among them" Telegram received (at 11:00 A.M.), DNA, RG 107, Telegrams Collected (Bound). USG had attended the 1866 wedding of Maj.

Robert Williams, a native of Va., and Adèle C. Douglas, widow of Stephen A. Douglas. See *PUSG*, 15, 347; *New York Sun*, Sept. 30, 1869; *Richmond Daily Dispatch*, Oct. 18, 20, 1869.

To Jesse Root Grant

Washington, D. C. Oct. 1st *1869.*

DEAR FATHER;

Your favor of the 13th Sept. was just handed to me yesterday. I presume that the papers informed you long before that your desire had been anticipated. I have borne Mrs. Porter's[1] name in my mind all the time, determined to do something for her. When I found that the apt. of Bayles[2] did not give satisfaction, and that no other would to all parts of the Republican party in Louisville, I determined to make an appointment to please myself.

The family are all well and send much love.

Yours Truly

U S. GRANT

ALS, Mrs. Arthur Loeb, Philadelphia, Pa.

1. On Jan. 11, 1869, USG telegraphed to Mrs. Lucy M. Porter, Annapolis. "Carriage will meet you at the depot this evening." ALS (telegram sent), DNA, RG 107, Telegrams Collected (Bound). On April 26, 10:00 A.M., USG had telegraphed to Jesse Root Grant. "Yours and Mrs Porter's letters recd. No use for her to come will answer by mail." Copy, DLC-USG. On Dec. 6, USG nominated Lucy M. Porter, Newport, Ky., as postmaster, Louisville. The widow of USG's friend Maj. John H. Gore, Mrs. Porter had lost a second husband. See *Louisville Courier-Journal*, Sept. 19, 24, 1869; *PUSG*, 16, 38–39.

On Oct. 7, Jesse Grant, Covington, Ky., telegraphed to USG concerning Porter's son, James M. Gore, U.S. Naval Academy. "For some slight offense midshipman Gore has been turned back Please restore him" Telegram received (at 10:40 A.M.), DNA, RG 107, Telegrams Collected (Bound). Gore graduated in June, 1870, but received no commission. On Nov. 2, 1872, Horace Porter wrote to Commodore Daniel Ammen. "Your letter of the 29th ultimo with enclosure is received, and in reply thereto I have to inform you that Midshipman Gore's orders for examination may be revoked and the President will try and give this young man a place in the Army." LS, *ibid.*, RG 45, Letters Received from the President. On Jan. 6, 1873, USG nominated Gore as 2nd lt., 22nd Inf.

2. On Sept. 1, 1869, USG had endorsed an application of Jesse Bayles,

former col., 4th Ky. Cav. "I designate Jesse Bayles to perform the duties of Postmaster at Louisville, in the county of Jefferson, and State of Kentucky, in place of J. S. Speed, suspended under the act approved April 5, A. D. 1868:" *Louisville Courier-Journal*, Sept. 4, 15, 1869.

Proclamation

BY THE PRESIDENT OF THE UNITED STATES OF AMERICA.
A PROCLAMATION.

The year which is drawing to a close has been free from pestilence—health has prevailed throughout the land—abunda[nt] crops reward the labors of the Husbandman—commerce and manufactures have successfully prosecuted their peaceful paths—the mines and forests have yiel[d]ed liberally—the Nation has increased in wealth and in strength—peace has prevailed; and its blessings have advanced every interest of the People, in every part of the Union. Harmony and fraternal intercourse restored, are obliterating the marks of past conflict and estrangement. Burdens have been lightened—means have been increased—civil and religious liberty are secured to every inhabitant of the land, whose soil is trod by none but freemen.

It becomes a people thus favored to make acknowledgement to the Supreme Author from whom such blessings flow, of their gratitude and their dependence—to render praise and thanksgiving for the same, and devoutly to implore a continuance of God's mercies.

Therefore, I, Ulysses S. Grant, President of the United States, do recommend that Thursday the 18th[1] day of November next, be observed as a day of Thanksgiving and of Praise and of Prayer to Almighty God, the Creator and the Ruler of the Universe. And I do further recommend to all the people of the United States to assemble on that day in their accustomed places of public worship and to unite in the homage and praise due to the Bountiful Father

of all mercies and in fervent prayer for the continuance of the mani-
fold blessings he has vouchsafed to us as a People:

In testimony whereof, I have hereunto set my hand and caused
the Seal of the United States to be affixed, this fifth day of October,
A. D. eighteen hundred and sixty nine, and of the Independence
of the United States of America the Ninety fourth.

U. S. GRANT

DS, DNA, RG 130, Presidential Proclamations. On Oct. 3, 1863, and Oct. 20,
1864, President Abraham Lincoln issued similar proclamations designating a
national day of thanksgiving at the urging of Sarah J. Hale, editor, *Godey's
Lady's Book and Magazine*. The practice continued annually under President
Andrew Johnson and USG. See Lincoln, *Works*, VI, 496–97; *ibid*., VIII, 55–56;
James D. Richardson, ed., *A Compilation of the Messages and Papers of the
Presidents, 1789–1902* (n. p., 1907), VII, 18, 92, 138, 178, 228–29, 277,
325, 397; Sherbrooke Rogers, *Sarah Josepha Hale: A New England Pioneer,
1788–1879* (Grantham, N. H., 1985), pp. 96–102.

On Oct. 8, 1870, Secretary of State Hamilton Fish wrote to Hale. "unofficial— . . . I have to acknowledge your note of 5—inst—& the enclosure containing President Washington's Thanksgiving Proclamation issued in 1789—for
which I desire to offer my thanks—The question of issuing a Proclamation
naming a day of Thanksgiving for the present year has not yet been officially
considered. I will however bring your letter to the notice of the President, at an
early date, with a view to such action as he shall deem proper—I may be permitted to add that I entertain little doubt that the President will have no hesitation in determining to recommend a day of Thanksgiving & that he will adopt
the day which you propose" ALS, CSmH. On Oct. 21, USG designated Nov.
24 as a national day of thanksgiving. DS, DNA, RG 130, Presidential Proclamations.

On Oct. 27, 1871, Fish wrote in his diary. "President signs Thanksgiving
proclamation for 30 Novr but not to be issued until tomorrow—in the mean time
I am to telegraph to Govr Claflin to know whether when there are five Thurs-
days in Novr, Massachusetts observes the the fourth or the fifth—" DLC-Hamilton Fish. On Oct. 28, Governor William Claflin of Mass. telegraphed to Fish.
"The President when here informed me that he had Selected the thirtieth for
Thanksgiving and we have accordingly agreed upon that day." Telegram received, DNA, RG 59, Miscellaneous Letters. USG's proclamation of Oct. 28 is
ibid., RG 130, Presidential Proclamations. On Oct. 11, 1872, USG designated
Nov. 28 as a day of thanksgiving and, on Oct. 14, 1873, designated Nov. 27.
DS, *ibid*. On Oct. 13, 1873, Hale wrote to USG transmitting "the enclosed
paper with the . . . highest esteem for his noble deeds." She enclosed a copy of
President George Washington's proclamation of 1789 and an editorial she had
written in Feb., 1860, promoting a thanksgiving holiday. William Evarts
Benjamin, Catalogue No. 27, Nov., 1889, p. 7; *The Collector*, Dec., 1948,
M2325. See *Godey's Lady's Book and Magazine*, LX (Feb., 1860), 175.

On Oct. 11, 1874, Hale, Philadelphia, wrote to USG. "Trusting that you will pardon my troubling you with another appeal for our National Thanksgiving Day, I must urge the example of President Washington as my excuse—The last Thursday in November of this year falls on the twenty-sixth of the month, exactly eighty-five years from the date of our first National Thanksgiving inaugurated by Washington, in compliance with the request of the First Congress of the United States of America. I feel sure that you will pardon me for suggesting that if President Grant would in his Message to the Forty-fourth Congress recommend the establishment of a National Thanksgiving as the perpetual American festival, the peop[le] of the Republic would gratefully uphold him, and both Houses of Congress would sanction this Holiday—" LS, DNA, RG 59, Miscellaneous Letters. Hale enclosed clippings of her editorials. *Ibid.* See *Godey's Lady's Book*, LXI (Sept., 1860), 271; *ibid.*, LXXXIX, 533 (Nov., 1874), 471. On Oct. 29, Fish wrote to Hale. "The President has referred to this Department your letter to him of the date of 11th instant, relating to a National Thanksgiving Day. In reply I have to state that the issuing by the President of a Proclamation naming a day for Public Thanksgiving appears to have become annually expected on the part of the People and an established custom on the part of the Executive. A Proclamation naming Thursday the twenty-sixth day of November next, as a day of Public Thanksgiving has been signed by the President" LS, CSmH. USG's proclamation of Oct. 27 is in DNA, RG 130, Presidential Proclamations.

On Oct. 26, 1875, Fish met with USG and wrote in his diary. "I remind him of a Thanksgiving Proclamation—He named the last Thursday in November and said he would sign it on any day: we would send it to him." DLC-Hamilton Fish. On Oct. 27, USG designated Nov. 27 as a day of thanksgiving. DS, DNA, RG 130, Presidential Proclamations; copy, *ibid.*, RG 59, Circulars. On Oct. 24, 1876, Hale wrote to USG. "Pardon my calling your attention to our National Thanksgiving—Enclosed are two papers—the first holds the Proclamation of Washington—He first appointed this Holiday for the last Thursday in November 1789—The second paper refers to the coming Proclamation of Gen. Grant, to which the approaching close of his able and faithful services gives special interest—The first American Congress requested President Washington to appoint the day of Thanksgiving—Was not this a National Holiday?—Would it not be fitting to call the attention of the Forty-Fourth Congress, at their last Session 1877 to this Holiday?—To be preserved, it must be made legal—If both Houses of Congress would unite in establishing the last Thursday in November as a Thanksgiving Day, at home and abroad, would it not strengthen the bond of Union, between the American People?—I am thankful that President Grant has had the honors of this great Centennial Year, and I trust that his life will still prove a blessing to his country—" Copy, CSmH. On Oct. 26, USG designated Nov. 30 as a day of thanksgiving. DS, DNA, RG 130, Presidential Proclamations; copy, *ibid.*, RG 59, Circulars.

1. On Sept. 27, 1869, Governor John T. Hoffman of N. Y. wrote to USG. "It has been for several years the custom for the Governor of this State to await the President's designation of a day for National Thanksgiving and Prayer, and then to issue his Proclamation for the State accordingly. The day has usually been the *last Thursday of November*, which this year will be the 25th The 25th of November, is always celebrated in the City of New York as 'Evacuation Day', by a very considerable Military display, and there are serious objections there-

fore to my designating that day for Thanksgiving and Prayer. I should regret exceedingly the necessity of making any designation which was not in harmony with yours, as uniformity in the celebration throughout the Country is desirable. Will you oblige me by considering the matter, and inform me of your determination as soon as convenient. I beg leave to suggest that the *first* Thursday of November, or any except the last would be a convenient day." LS, *ibid.*, Miscellaneous Letters.

To Columbus Delano

Washington. D. C. Oct. 7th *1869*,

DEAR SIR:

On consultation with Senator Drake, and his report of interview with you, I think it will be advisable to suspend the appointment of Col. McDonald, as Supervisor of Int. Rev. for Mo. for the present.

Very respectfully
your obt. svt.
U. S. GRANT

HON. C. DELANO,
COM. INT. REV.

ALS, DLC-Delano Family. John McDonald, in St. Louis from about 1835, was a steamboat agent in the 1850s. As maj., 8th Mo., he served in southeastern Mo. and at Fort Donelson. For letters recommending McDonald for appointment, including an endorsement by Gen. William T. Sherman, see John McDonald, *Secrets of the Great Whiskey Ring* (Chicago, 1880), pp. 20–25. Charles W. Ford, U.S. Senators Charles D. Drake and Carl Schurz of Mo. *et al.* opposed McDonald's appointment. *Ibid.*, pp. 25–26. See *PUSG*, 6, 91; letter to Charles W. Ford, May 16, 1870; *Missouri Democrat*, Oct. 7, 9, 17, 1869.

On Sept. 22 and 23, 1869, Frederick T. Dent had written to Ford. "I had a long talk with the commissioner a day or two since. he said he was glad to hear of the course you took in those distileries and that you should have his support—I told him about the relief of the Sup's father—he said you did perfectly right—that he wanted you to write to him about it frankly and without reserve—he intimated that some doubts existed as to the proper man having been secured as supervisor—The President has arrived and so has your letter about the Ox—which I have just handed him to read—as soon as he reads it I will answer it if he does not do so himself." "Your letter was given to the President he highly approves of your suggestions about the Ox—and is glad you are going to have him exhibited for the benefit of the orphans of the Soldiers he says that he will keep the ox and for the good he has already done, he shall as long as he lives be taken care of on his farm . . . enclosed is a cheque the President sends to Elrod" ALS, DLC-USG. See *Washington Chronicle*, Sept. 25, 1869.

On Dec. 1, William H. Mills, Bangor, wrote to USG. "I beg to state a few facts to your Excellency, and pray that I may be pardoned for so doing. Having made the military profession the study of my life, and having attained to the highest rank in our state militia, I should have been the first man in the War from Maine, had not my hands been so tied that it was utterly impossible. But the moment that General McClellan developed his system of campaigning, as he did from Alexandria *towards* Manssas Junction & back, & thence to York Town and up the Peninsular & back, I denounced him both in the newpapers & to the President, *as a traitor*, and continued to do so, until he was removed from his command. But while *I* was not permitted to take part in the War, my eldest son, Wm H Mills, Jr, went through the war with great credit to himself, both in the Field and in the Recruiting and Pay Departments. And my son-in-law, Mr Carlos Pierce, at the sanitary Fair in New York, actually paid $3000, towards the procurment of the Sword for your Excellency and interested some friends to pay $7000, more, making $10,000.—and then subscribed himself for *ten thousand votes for 'General Grant'*—which carried the sword in your favor. Mr Pierce owned the celebrated *big* Ox and had him at that & other Fairs, and when Mr Lincoln was re-elected, he presented the Ox to Mr Lincoln, who gave him to the Boston Fair, where he was purchased back by Mr Pierce, and at you election, he presented him to your Excellency. This Ox, first & last, brought into the Treasury of the sanitary Commission over $8000. and Mr Pierce, first & last, paid more than $50,000. for the support of the Government & the funds of the sanitary commission. I am not aware that Mr Pierce has ever asked for any favor from the Goverment for himself. But he did ask that my son, his brother-in-law, after serving three years in Aarazona, might be transfer'ed to service in the east;—and he did sign a very strongly written petition by Mr Peters, and signed by the *Maine Delegation* in *Congress*, recommending myself for the appointment of a Consulship, which petition is now on file in the Office of secretary of state and to which, I beg to ask your favorable consideration." ALS, DNA, RG 59, Letters of Application and Recommendation. Related papers are *ibid.* No appointment followed. See Lincoln, *Works*, VIII, 96–97.

To Blanton Duncan

WASHINGTON, October 12. [*1869*]

Blanton Duncan,[1] *Chairman:*

Your dispatch inviting my presence at the Commercial Convention in Louisville, as an honorary member, is received. I regret my inability to be present. The objects of the convention, however, I heartily indorse, and everything calculated to increase the commerce of the country, and especially everything tending to bring the citizens of different sections of our own country together in interest and friendship, as it tends to the allayment of sectional prejudices and bad feeling. I hope your convention may be productive of much good.

U. S. GRANT.

Washington Chronicle, Oct. 15, 1869. Blanton Duncan of Ky. served as chairman of the arrangements committee for the Commercial Convention. See *Louisville Courier-Journal*, Oct. 12–17, 1869.

1. On May 3, 1869, James Speed *et al.* wrote to USG. "The undersigned, citizens of Louisville, Kentucky, have been informed and believe, that *Blanton Duncan*, a resident of said City, is *the only person whose lands, in Kentucky, have been condemned, for the crime of Rebellion on the part of its owner.* In view of that fact and of the fact that he was not a peculiarly prominent Rebel, and of our knowledge of him and his family, and their condition, we ask your Excellency to order, through your Attorney-General, a dismissal of the proceedings against said Duncan's estate, pending in the ~~District~~ Circuit Court of the United States for the District of Kentucky." DS (23 signatures), DNA, RG 60, Letters from the President.

To Robert Bonner

———

WASHINGTON, D. C., Oct. 13, 1869.

ROBERT BONNER, ESQ.—*Dear Sir*: Your favor of the 11th inst. is received. I have never thought of contradicting statements or insinuations made against me by irresponsible parties as those are alluded to in your letter, but as you have written to me in so kind a spirit, I will say that I had no more to do with the late gold excitement in New-York City than yourself, or any other innocent party, except that I ordered the sale of gold to break the ring engaged, as I thought, in a most disreputable transaction. If the speculators had been successful you would never have heard of any one connected with the Administration as being connected with the transaction.

Yours truly,
U. S. GRANT.

P. S.—I have written this in great haste, and without exercising judgment as to the propriety of writing it, but I submit it to your judgment.

U. S. G.

New York Times, Oct. 16, 1869. On Oct. 11, 1869, Robert Bonner, editor, *New York Ledger,* had written to USG. "As I stated to you immediately after your election, that there was no office which I desired either for myself or any friend, I have had no occasion to write to you in regard to such matters. There is a matter now, however, that concerns you personally, and in which I feel that I discern your interest so plainly, that I take the liberty to write to you with reference to it. I do this with less hesitation, because you did me the honor after your election to confide to me pretty fully your views. In the present disturbed state of the public mind concerning the recent gold combination, is it not the quickest and surest way to set at rest the great excitement and uneasiness which prevail, for you to make a brief denial over your own signature of all foreknowledge of that combination, in order to relieve yourself entirely from all responsibility for the acts of others? Of course, those who know you personally do not require such a disclaimer: but the great public, whose minds are liable to be warped by the determined and persistent efforts to injure you, will be, it seems to me, at once satisfied and quieted by such a statement." *Ibid.* On Oct. 16, Bonner telegraphed to USG. "Your letter has already done a vast deal of good. People who were themselves yesterday circulating the report, now swear that they never believed it, just as the Tribune puts it this morning" Telegram received (at 2:10 P.M.), DNA, RG 107, Telegrams Collected (Bound).

On Oct. 8, Caleb C. Norvell, financial editor, *New York Times,* wrote to Postmaster Gen. John A. J. Creswell. "I enclose slips from th[e] *Commercial* which you will find sets the President all right abou[t] the Gould-Corbin *imbroglio.* In regard to our Editorial of August 25, by whomsoever originally prepared, it could not have been seen or [—] by the President. It was placed in type by Mr Bigelow, as originally written, & submitted by Mr B. to my revision. I cut out every thing that appeared to conceal a Gold speculation and interpolated all that I believed to be the true interest & purpose of the Administration. And the article as it appeared, by Gould's own confession, was any thing but the purpose the ring had in view." ALS, USG 3. The enclosure is *ibid.* See *HRC,* 41-2-31, pp. 275–81. On Oct. 12, Lt. Col. James H. Wilson, Keokuk, wrote to Horace Porter. "*Confidential.* . . . I am just back from Davenport, and find your letter of the 7th on my desk. You have doubtless received my last before this time. and hence I shall expect to hear from you again without delay. Apropos to the subject which most interests me now, there are one or two recent developments which taken in connection with your [r]emarks concerning the Fisk Corbin 'Gold combination,' makes me more desirous than ever to have *you go into the Cabinet.* . . . I have never seen Corbin, but from what I know of his wife's attractions—or lack of them—and from what I have read of Corbin, I am just as firmly convinced that he is a scoundrel and married the President's sister for motives of intrigue, as I am that the President himself is essentially pure & good. This is only one of a thou[s]and instances in which the Pre[s]ident has been duped—You & I know the President's purity, but depend upon it, there

will be many who will doubt it, if these things continue to recur. . . ." ALS
(press), DLC-James H. Wilson. On Oct. 13, Wilson wrote to Orville E. Babcock.
"*Confidential.* . . . You have doubtless heard before this time of the recent *Fisk-
Corbin* Gold combination, and the villainous attempt to draw Grant into it. I
needn't tell *you* that it has failed ingloriously—or that the skirts of our friend,
are as clean as virgin linnen. Even Dana, whose course towards Grant has been
marked by exceeding censoriousness and injustice, says Grant is entirely innocent—but what a dog this Corbin must be! An article in the Chicago Tribune
signed 'Gath'—written by Mr Hale unveils his past rascality—and there is now
no doubt in my mind that this fellow married the President's [sis]ter for the purpose of putting himself upon relations of family confidence with the President.
It seems too that Dan Butterfield, is mixed up in this last scheme. This don't
surprise me at all for I have always suspected him of being an unmitigated
scamp, . . . The death of Rawlins is more deeply regretted by the thinking and
knowing men of the country than it otherwise would have been, on account of the
fact that it had come to be recognised by them, that he was the President's best
friend & most useful counsellor when engaged in denouncing rascality, which
the President's unsuspicious nature has not dreamed of being near. You and I
know how necessary, the bold, uncompromising, & honest character of our dead
friend, was to our living one—and how impossible it is for any stranger to
exercise as good an influence over him, as one who has known him from the time
of his obscurity till the day he became the foremost man of the nation. The long
and short of it is that Rawlins, was his Mentor—or if I may say it, his conscience keeper, and although he may not be willing to believe it, he needs some
one for Secretary of War—who can perform the duties that Rawlins did, in this
character. There are a thousand men in the U. S. equal to the mere official
drudgery—but not three nor two who can do and perform those higher and more
important, and at the same time keep Grant in happy ignorance of their existence.
I note with grati[fi]cation and pride what you say in reference to me in that
connection and while I need not assure you that I would feel myself highly
honored by such a call as you indicate, it is my duty to say that there is not the
least possibility of its being given to me. I should not hesitate to accept—and I
hope I should not fail to perform any part of my duty towards the President or
the Country. Of one thing you might rest assured that there would be no stealing,
no family combinations, no Kitchen Cabinet, if I could prevent them. However
there no use in saying what I would or wouldn't do, under a contingency not at
all likely to happen. Porter writes me that the President has not yet made his
selection—& probably will not for a couple of weeks—who it will be he does not
intimate, tho' he says pretty plainly that it will not be Belknap. The same says
it will be John E. Smith or Porter himself if any dependence can be placed in
the signs of the Times—whatever they may be. As between these two you must
pardon me for saying, I regard Porter as being much the abler man—and this
without disparagement to Smith, whom I thoroughly respect. I know Porter better, & well enough to believe him to be a very talented, thoroughly honest, true
& incorruptible man   He is a close observer—in fact one of the closest & keenest
observers—I ever knew, of the idiosyncrasies and foibles of men, and withal
has more tact than *anyone I ever knew* in governing his relations with men. He
has perfect control of all his passions & faculties, & is as sharp as a French policeman in detecting rascality either in *posse* or in *esse*. In the double relations which

the successor of Rawlins shd hold to the President, I think he could & would exert a powerful influence for good. Smith you know too well for me to describe, to you, and much better than I know him. I fear his appointment would not add strength to the Cabinet, in popular estimation—principally because he has nothing but a local or military reputation. The same objection however would apply with as much force to Porter & myself—and as the President ha[s] already ignored this consideration in more than one case, he might do so again if he had any more valuable object to obtain. Whatever he may do, I hope he will not allow Logan or Ben Butler to exercise an undue influence in determining the final choice—for *he'll have to fight these fellows yet*, & had better have an ally than an enemy in the camp, when the fight begins. . . . You have doubtless seen the announcement that Parker is going to deliver an 'Eulogy on the Life & Services of Genl Rawlins' to the Soc: of the A. T. at Louisville—and it is reported that Hilyer is writing his life. This is a duty I would like to perform—but as a matter of course I can't do it without access to his papers. Two years ago he told me that he intended to make me his literary legatee—but I suppose he forgot it. Badeau (so Porter informs me) has suddenly discovered that he must see these papers, & has got leave to visit Washington for that purpose—I suppose we may look for his secd Volume soon.—" ALS (press), *ibid.*

On May 12, Horace Greeley and James B. Taylor, New York City, had telegraphed to USG. "In case a change in the Sub-Treasury here is contemplated, We ask that you defer the nomination to afford time for representation from many friends" Telegram received (at 7:00 P.M.), DNA, RG 107, Telegrams Collected (Bound). On June 8, Simeon B. Chittenden, New York City, wrote to USG. "Having heard Gen'l Butterfield spoken of to day as a candidate for Assistant Treasurer in New York, I cannot help expressing to you my belief that he is eminently fit for the place, and my earnest hope that he will be appointed to it. This is written of my own motion: not at the request of any one." ALS, *ibid.*, RG 56, Asst. Treasurer and Mint Officials, Letters Received. On June 9, Horace Porter endorsed this letter. "Attention of Sec. of Treasury specially called to this letter" AES, *ibid.* On June 12, Cornelius K. Garrison, New York City, wrote a similar letter to USG. *Ibid.* On June 25, Col. Daniel Butterfield, New York City, telegraphed to Porter. "No papers received. My bondsmen are leaving town. Hurry them forward" Telegram received (at 2:35 P.M.), *ibid.*, RG 107, Telegrams Collected (Bound). On July 3, Butterfield received a leave of absence from the army to become asst. treasurer, New York City. See *HRC*, 41-2-31, p. 309.

On Oct. 22, Butterfield, New York City, wrote to USG. "Certain charges have been made by parties here in New York, through the public press, affecting my integrity and honor if maintained and proved true. Some days since I addressed a letter to the honorable the Secretary of the Treasury, asking an investigation of the matter, if the charges had to him any semblance of truth. Otherwise than by this letter I have remained silent under these accusations by the advice of friends and counsel. These charges have at last assumed such definite shape and form that to longer remain silent is to plead guilty, and admit their truth. Being still an officer of the army, on leave of absence, I have the honor to request that a court of inquiry, composed of officers of the army, may be ordered to investigate all these charges, with the usual power to take testimony and affidavits and compel attendance of witnesses, that the whole matter may be thoroughly and carefully investigated. It is due to you, in return for the honor you conferred upon me by this appointment that such an investigation be made, that your condidence in me may be publicly sustained and approved, or, failing in acquitting me of the charges preferred against me, the reverse. I know of no other way that the charges can be investigated in such a manner as to bring forth the truth, which I court and desire, as well as fully and entirely satisfy the public, who have a just and proper right to know the whole truth of the matter." *Washington Chronicle*, Oct. 27, 1869. On Nov. 8, Governor Marshall Jewell of Conn. telegraphed to USG. "Permit me to suggest the name of General Hawley as the successor of General Butterfield." Telegram received (at 10:50 A.M.), DNA, RG 107, Telegrams Collected (Bound). USG nominated Charles J. Folger to replace Butterfield; on June 21, 1870, Folger, New York City, wrote a letter of resignation to USG. ALS, *ibid.*, RG 56, Asst. Treasurers and Mint Officials, Letters Received.

To William W. Belknap

———

Dated, Washington Dc [*Oct.*] 18. *1869*
Received at Keokuk Oct 18 10 15 a D

To HON WM BELKNAP
Your letter accepting the appointment of Secy of War is received I feel the greatest confidence in your ability and disposition to fill your new trust with entire satisfaction to the country   in doing so You will fully satisfy me   General Sherman[1] can continue as secy of war until the time mentioned in your letter the twenty fifth *25* or twenty six *26* instant

U S GRANT

Telegram received, Belknap Papers, NjP. William W. Belknap, born in N. Y. in 1829, educated at Princeton and Georgetown colleges, settled in 1851 in Keokuk, where he practiced law and was elected to the Iowa legislature as a Douglas Democrat (1857–58). He was commissioned maj., 15th Iowa, as of Dec. 7, 1861, fought at Shiloh, commanded the regt. at Vicksburg, and was promoted to brig. gen. as of July 30, 1864, and bvt. maj. gen. as of March 13, 1865. After returning to Keokuk, he was appointed collector of internal revenue. On Oct. 14, 1869, Belknap, Keokuk, had written to USG. "Fully realizing the responsibilities of the office of Secretary of War to which you have appointed me, I have accepted it and will endeavor to execute the duties of the position in a manner satisfactory to the country & to yourself. For this marked manifestation of your confidence I am profoundly grateful." *Autographs,* W. Graham Arader III, [1988], p. 4.

    On Sept. 7, William Vandever *et al.*, Keokuk, had telegraphed to USG. "In considering the claims of a successor to Genl Rawlins the undersigned citizens of Iowa and Missouri respectfully beg leave to invite your attention to the merits of Gen Wm W Belknap whose services and accomplishments we believe could not fail to reflect credit upon the administration" Telegram received (on Sept. 8, 8:40 A.M.), DNA, RG 107, Telegrams Collected (Bound). On Sept. 8, Governor Samuel Merrill of Iowa *et al.* telegraphed to USG. "Permit us to tender name of Gen G M Dodge as Successor of lamented Rawlins" Telegram received (at 4:30 P.M.), *ibid.* On Sept. 9, Judge John F. Dillon *et al.*, Des Moines, telegraphed to USG. "The undersigned judges of supreme court without the knowledge of Genl Grenville M Dodge and reflecting the earnest wishes of the People of Iowa and the northwest desire to join Governor and state officers in dispatchs of yesterday and respectfully urge his appointment to place made vacant by death of the lamented Rawlins" Telegram received (on Sept. 10, 9:00 A.M.), *ibid.* On Sept. 9, U.S. Senator George E. Spencer of Ala., Washington, D. C., wrote to Grenville M. Dodge. "*Confidential* . . . I have just paid the last tribute of respect to our dear friend Rawlins. I have never known a man more universally mourned, ~~than he~~ To night I go to NewYork with the President, We have organized a movement to put you in Rawlins place & I think the position will be tendered to you without a doubt & I *beg* of you not to decline it. You can do Grant more good & the party more good than any man in the Country, Day after tomorrow the '*Times*' in NewYork will have an editorial urging the appointment & all your friends have spoken to Grant about it. I dont know that the place will be tendered you but all your friends repeat it & do not for Gods sake decline it. Poor Rawlins wanted you & I think the *President* will offer it. He did not as usual commit himself but I think it pleased him when it was suggested. Genl Sherman I think is favorable to you. If J. F. Wilson would write the President it would do good. The appointment must be made within ten days. I hope you have recovered your health entirely" ALS, Dodge Papers, IaHA.

On Aug. 19, Secretary of War John A. Rawlins, Danbury, Conn., had written to Dodge. ". . . My health is much improved this summer, though for two weeks past I have been a little under the weather, And right here my dear Dodge if on that account I should have to quit if the President will allow me as they say he did Borie to suggest his successor it is clearly within the range of probabilities there might be more force given to the recent telegram that you were to be the person than some of the papers seem to give credence." ALS, *ibid.* On Oct. 15, Col. John E. Smith, Washington, D. C., wrote to Dodge. "I find among the Papers of our late Friend Jno A Rawlins Deeds for Lots in Cheyenne that are not recorded I presume owing to their being no organization then in the Tery Who 'Can I send them to for record' Rawlins mentions in his will some lots in Golden City, as I find no evidence of such property with his papers, 'Can you give me any information there is nothing new here except a Secratary of War, who has not yet reported' You were the first Choice of the President and would undoubtedly have been appointed but for your Interest & Connexion with the U P R R I regret with many others that there was any obstacle to your appt to a position that you would fill so well and acceptably to the Army and Country." ALS, *ibid.* Correspondence relating to Dodge as a replacement for Rawlins is *ibid.* See Stanley P. Hirshson, *Grenville M. Dodge: Soldier, Politician, Railroad Pioneer* (Bloomington and London, 1967), p. 174.

On Oct. 8, Lt. Col. James H. Wilson, Keokuk, wrote to USG. *"Personal. . . .* I have just seen it stated in one of the New York papers that 'Genl John E. Smith or Genl Horace Porter of the President's military staff will probably become Secretary of War' &c. &c. Feeling an unabated interest in your welfare, as well [a]s in the Success of your administ[r]ation, with the liberty of an old friend, I venture to express the hope, that this statement may prove to be true *so far as it concerns Genl Porter.* I have probably known him longer and more intimately than any one outside of his own family, & hence may be pardoned for saying that I confidently believe him to be capable of administering the War Department with ability fully equal to that of a Stanton or a Rawlins. As this involves not only talents but honesty of the highest order, I can add nothing to the language to make it stronger. You are as fully cognizant of these qualities in Genl Porter as any one, and therefore it only remains for me to say that they cannot be too highly valued, particularly when considered in reference to the duties and responsibilities of the War Office. The 'politicians,' will probably object to his appointment (to an office which they consider as a political perquisites), on the score of *youth,* coupled with the fact that he is a graduate of West Point, but as you have not hitherto regarded these as fatal objection[s] unless coupled with others more worthy of consideration, and as *you will probably have to fight the politicians any how*, I hope you will not allow them to exert an undue influence in the choice of your advisers and most trusted subordinates. As a matter of course I understand that you will make your own selections, in this as in other cases, without any regard to outside pressure. And I am the last one to desire to exert such pressure, or to see it exerted, but it may be some sati[s]-faction for you to know that some of your friends ~~would~~ find ample reason to approve your choice should it chance to to fall upon a man of such honesty, zeal, and ability, as Genl Porter." ALS (press), DLC-James H. Wilson. Wilson had telegraphed to USG backing Belknap for secretary of war and also sought the office himself. Paul Clayton Pehrson, "James Harrison Wilson: The Post-War Years, 1865–1925," Ph.D. Dissertation, University of Wisconsin, 1993, pp. 118–22.

On Oct. 10, Horace Porter wrote to Belknap. "I wrote to Gen. Wilson, a day or two after the death of our valued friend Rawlins, that I was urging your name upon the President as his successor. I spoke about you the night the President and I arrived here from Saratoga, to attend the funeral. The P. was greatly predisposed in your favor, but wisely took no action until he could carefully weigh the matter in his mind, and consider carefully the interests and claims of the various sections of the Country. Yesterday he authorized a note to be written by Gen. Sherman tendering you the office. I cannot express to you how much gratification I feel at the result and write to beg that you will, *under no circumstances, decline.* The country wants a young and vigorous man, who will grow up with the country. I shall give you the history of the whole affair when I see you, which ~~which~~ is no less interesting that flattering to you. Your good friend Gen. Wilson will be highly delighted when he hears of this, He has written me several very kind letters about you. Awaiting anxiously for your telegram *accepting*, and hoping soon to see here fully installed, . . ." ALS, Belknap Papers, NjP. On Oct. 12, Secretary of War William T. Sherman telegraphed to Belknap. "The President tenders to you the appointmt of Secretary of War. Until you arrive here I will execute the office. Take ~~a reasonable~~ your own time, so that you can come on prepared to stay. At present little is doing except to prepare for Congress." ALS (telegram sent), DNA, RG 94, Letters Received, 638A 1869; telegram received (on Oct. 13, 11:25 A.M.), Belknap Papers, NjP. On Oct. 13, Belknap telegraphed to Sherman. "Fully conscious of the responsibilities of the office tendered me by the President, I gratefully accept it. In accordance with your telegram, I will take several days time—Letter mailed today" ALS (telegram sent), *ibid.*; copy, DNA, RG 94, Letters Received, 638A 1869. On Oct. 18, Sherman wrote to USG. "General Wm. W. Belknap having accepted the tender by you of the office of secretary of War, and having signified his intention to leave his home at Keokuk Iowa, for this City on the 25 inst, I hereby submit this my resignation of the office, to take effect on the arrival of Gen Belknap, and upon his taking the oath prescribed by Law. I do this in fulfillmt of the understanding at the time of my appointmt as Sec of War. Thanking you for the Confidence reposed in me, ..." ALS, *ibid.*, RG 59, Letters of Resignation and Declination.

On Oct. 27 and Nov. 3, Porter wrote to Wilson. "It seems a long time since I have written you, but I went to N York last week and returned quite sick with a bilious attack, so that I have not only been off my feed, but considerably off my 'write'. We now have contradictory reports in regard to the exact time of Belknap's arrival, Papers say Friday night. I had intended, when I got your last letter, to run over to Baltimore and meet him, but fear I shall not be able to strike him on the way. I shall heed what you say in regard to all matters connected with him, Without being officious I want to open his eyes to a great many things here, as much for his own sake as for the general welfare. I am satisfied he will make a better officer that the P. could have obtained if he had searched two months longer. I shall never forget the kind partiality you have shown for me in this matter, I am afraid your lenient judgment would place me in many a position, which the world would not look upon approvingly. B. ought not to think I made him, I have rather been what, they would call in English enterprise parlance, a 'promoter.' He cannot help being radical enough when he finds what the devils South are doing to regain their former power, or rather to increase it. Ames writes very encouragingly from Miss. Brother Dent we think will go under, and be handsomely tomahawked right through the centre of the head. I shall cry 'peace to his ashes!' I have had a long talk with Winslow, He talks a heap of sense, He says you and he will come East in Dec. You must bring your wife to our house Bab and I are alone there now, you know, and we shall be 'awful glad' to see you, W. spoke o[n] the directorship of the R. R. &c. We shall talk it up when you come on. I declined to be an officer in the Balt. & Potomac R. R. on general principles, being an officer of the governmt, and fearing some of the hounds here who have nothing else to do, might talk. This small road at such a distance may be a very different thing, and the same objections might not hold good. We shall see when we talk over the details. ~~The~~ I appreciate fully the suggestion, and the offer to 'sail in' with you in the enterprise, which will be a great service to that section of the country. The Historian and his English valet (you must pronounce the *t* I find) are here, and will be for six weeks probably. He has written as much as eight or ten pages on his second volume in all, and will be able to put it in press about the time our grandchildren get married. I return you LaGrange's papers We hear nothing but good from him, and I shall continue to look out for him. Good men are scarce now. I have talked with the Old Man about Bluford and Col. Logan, so that he has a full understanding of the matter,   Babcock and I are back with our ~~families~~ families, and he sends his regards, and unites with me in an invitation to come on and see us. I might have known your dams were all right, as the newspapers stated they were washed away. With kind regards to Mr W. and a kiss for the little one" "Belknap ~~has~~ is taking hold, and is very well received here. I had several hours talk with him the day he came, and gave him all the information he seemed to desire, without being unnecessarily officious and have seen a good deal of him since,   I assured him that you had done more than any other one person in making him what he is, which he seems fully to appreciate. I told him the 'history of his appointment' commenced when you urged him for the Internal Revenue Dept. last spring. I posted him fully on Washington etiquette, and gave it as my opinion that he could take rooms of proper style at a private boarding house ~~of proper~~ without violating for a moment any proprieties of his office, that it is now a recommendation for an officer to be seen living strictly within his means. He has taken two fine rooms in the Seward house. The Historian immediately asked him and me to dine with him. I see B. understands him thoroughly, sees both the good and bad points in his composition. You may be expected to be sent for this winter to render a very important verbal report on the subject of your works to the Hon. the Sec. of War. As you know more about the time ~~time~~ you can be best spared, just send me a line fixing the time, and bring your wife to our house, when you will be treated in the most hostile manner"   ALS, DLC-James H. Wilson.

1. On Sept. 9, USG appointed Sherman as secretary of war ". . . to execute and fulfil the duties of that office according to Law, and TO HAVE and TO HOLD the said office, with all the powers, privileges and emoluments ~~thereunto~~ to the same of right appertaining; . . . until the end of the next session of the Senate of the United States, and no longer; subject to the conditions prescribed by law. . . ." Typescript, DNA, RG 107, Letters Received, S435 1869. Sherman's appointment was not officially designated *ad interim* but was regarded as temporary. "I was appointed to perform the duties of [the] office till a successor could be selected." *Memoirs of Gen. W. T. Sherman* (4th ed., New York, 1891), II, 443.

To Columbus Delano

————

Washington. D. C. Oct. 18th *1869*

Hon. C. Delano;
Com. Int. Rev.
Dear Sir:

After a conversation with Gen. Croxton[1] relative to the Collectorship of the 7th Dist. of Ky. I am disposed to think we have done wrong in removing Col. Kelly. As Gen. Kelly proposes to go into other business early next year, and as there has really been nothing against him, except the persistent efforts of some mempers of his party to effect his removal, I think it advisable to withhold the appointment of Dr. Moore. This is more proper because of charges which Gn. Croxton makes against the Dr. which, if proven, shew him to be an improper person to appoint. This latter however I would not have stated as a reasn for suspending the appointment because I would not wish to be put in the position of having to prove a mans unfitness for office, or appoint him in case of failure. Sufficient reason for the action suggested lays in the fact that we have done a good officer an injustice in removing him, without giving him an opportunity to be heard.

Respectfully &c
U. S. GRANT

ALS, DLC-Delano Family. On May 25, 1869, Samuel W. Price, president, Grant Club, Lexington, Ky., had telegraphed to USG. "I understand that a movement is on foot to remove R M. Kelly Collector of the Seventh 7 District of Kentucky which would be highly detrimental to the interests of the Government, as he is a most excellent officer—a staunch republican, and a gentleman of great personal worth and was one of your most active and zealous supporters and contributed more material aid than any man in the District toward your election Was also a gallant officer in the union army and served with great credit to himself and Government from beginning to close of war and as an evidence of his standing with the republican party in Fayette County Kentucky—his home—was appointed one of the Committee on resolutions and to nominate delegates to the Twenty Seventh 27 May State Convention, which resolutions endorsed your administration fully including the Fifteenth Amendment" Telegram received (at 7:00 P.M.), DNA, RG 107, Telegrams Collected (Bound). Additional telegrams to USG concerning the removal of Robert M. Kelly are *ibid.* On May 26, John T. Croxton, Lexington, telegraphed to Horace Porter. "It is reported the President has ordered the removal of Colonel Kelly the Collector of this District. Is it true" Telegram received (at 2:00 P.M.), *ibid.* The next day, Porter telegraphed to Croxton. "No order has been given in regard to Kelley." Copy, DLC-USG, II, 5.

Kelly, former col., 4th Ky. Mounted Inf., had been appointed in 1866 by President Andrew Johnson. On Oct. 16, 1869, USG designated Noah S. Moore, Paris, Ky., to replace Kelly; on Oct. 18, USG reappointed Kelly. See *Louisville Courier-Journal*, Oct. 19, 1869. After Kelly resigned in 1870, USG appointed him as pension agent, Louisville.

1. Croxton, born in 1837, graduated from Yale College (1857) and began to practice law in Paris, Ky., in 1859. He commanded the 4th Ky. Mounted Inf.,

then a cav. brigade, which he led through Ala., capturing Tuscaloosa. See *PUSG*, 13, 125; *ibid.*, 14, 497–98; *ibid.*, 15, 19–20.

On March 2, 1869, Bvt. Maj. Gen. James H. Wilson, Keokuk, wrote to USG. "Understanding that the friends of General John T. Croxton of Paris Kentucky desire to present his name to you for an appointment under your administration, I take the liberty of bearing my testimony to his eminent abilities and distinguished services as a soldier. He was one of the very few native southerners who had the independence to be an abolitionist before the war, and the courage from boyhood to maintain his right to such opinions at all times and in all places. As a matter of course when the war broke out he enlisted in the Union army and steadily rose through the various grades to the rank of brigadier General, with the brevet of Major General for gallant and meritorious services. The last year of the war, he served under my command in Kentucky, Tennessee, Alabama, and Georgia, in command of a brigade and division, and by his coolness in danger, resolute and courageous bearing at all times, by his discretion, promptitude, zeal and intelligence he won for himself general recognition as being an officer of great merit in every sense of the word. Being highly educated, young, ambitious, and well trained in the legal profession, I regard him as a man of great promise—and one who will prove himself hereafter as heretofore, fully equal to any position which he may be called upon to fill. I know of no man who more eminently typifies that New South, which it should be the desire of every good citizen to see replace the south of other days. Hoping that his hands and those of the Union party may be strengthened for the good work which yet remains to be done in Kentucky, and that you will pardon the liberty I have taken in behalf of a comrade, whom I have learned to trust thoroughly & completely, ..." ALS, DNA, RG 59, Letters of Application and Recommendation. On March 16, Maj. Gen. George H. Thomas, Washington, D. C., favorably endorsed a copy of Wilson's letter. AES, *ibid.* On March 11, Theodore D. Woolsey, president, Yale College, wrote a recommendation. "I have known General Croxton since 1853 when he came to New Haven and entered Yale College. He was a faithful and successful student here, particularly distinguishing himself in mathematics. He was remarkable, and was respected, for his manly independence and honesty in avowing his convictions, even when the avowal made him unpopular among the southern students. The same manliness and honor seem to me from frequent accounts I have had of him, to have shown themselves in his life and character since. I could give several characteristic traits during the war greatly to his credit, but I will mention one just before the war,—that, as I have understood, he voted for Lincoln, the only man at the polls, and under threats of being shot if he should do so. . . ." ADS, *ibid.* On March 15, Allen A. Burton wrote to Secretary of War John A. Rawlins. "(Confidential) . . . The papers in behalf of Gen. Croxton were filed in the Department of State to-day, briefed and will be ready whenever the President may be pleased to have them ordered. The mission to Bogotá, United States of Colombia, Honduras, or some Spanish American Republic, with a preference for the first, would be satisfactory to the friends of Gen. C. This suggestion is made on the suggestion that Lisbon, Copenhagen, and other European legations, filled by Ministers Resident are provided for. An appointment to Europe would, of course be preferable. In case it be not convenient to give the General a mission, then a Governorship of a territory would be acceptable. I beg to be allowed to repeat what I had the honor to state this morning, to-wit: that I am not authorized to state positively that Gen. C. would find it convenient to accept either of the positions above indicated. That the action in his favor has been taken by some of his civilian friends who believe that the first and most important step towards a permanent peace in our unfortunate State, is, a pronounced recognition by the President, of the services of Kentuckians who have proved Soldiers indeed. The adoption of the XVth Amendment will enable Kentucky to send four, probably five, loyal representatives to Congress. These representatives ought to be, and most likely will be, men who fought the enemy during the war and who have not surrendered to him since. Gen. C. is the leader and worthy representative of this class of men in Kentucky, as he is first in Military rank; and we think it desirable beyond measure, that the State finally pass under their control. Until this shall have been accomplished, there can not be law, order and liberty in the State, and that regeneration which every patriot should pray for. To this end, the President can strengthen the arms of the friends of the undertaking, giving the *true* soldier the preference in Kentucky appointments, by which lawless men there will see at once what must inevitably overtake them in case they continue their resistance to authority." ALS, *ibid*. Related papers are *ibid*.

On Nov. 21, 1872, Wilson, New York City, wrote to USG. "I take the liberty of recommending Genl John T. Croxton of Paris, Kentucky as a gentleman in every way qualified for and deserving of the Office of Minister Resident at Bogota, Republic of Colombia. which will soon become vacant by the resignation of Genl Hurlbut, who has just been elected to Congress. . . . Genl Croxton's sacrafices for the Country & its cause, coupled with his feeble health, have crippled his private means to a certain extent, and while he would make no claim on this ground his friends and the Administration may well advance it as an additional reason for making an appointment excellent in itself, particularly as Genl Croxton has been compelled to give up his private business for the purpose of seeking the restoration of his health by a temporary residence in Colorado. Trusting that the appointment may be made, . . ." ALS, *ibid*. A related telegram is *ibid*. On Nov. 22, Benjamin H. Bristow, Philadelphia, wrote to USG. "Genl Wilson and I took the liberty to telegraph you from New York yesterday, asking that the Mission to Bogota be given to Genl John T. Croxton of Ky, and I now beg leave to put on file in this more formal way my unqualified endorsement of Genl Croxton for the position. He is now in Colorado by advice of physicians and cannot live long in the climate of Ky. His physicians have said to me that he can be saved from fatal disease, if he will remain in a more equable & milder climate. His ill health is directly attributable to arduous labors, and exposure while in the Military service of the Country. By education and talent he is well qualified to do honor to the Country abroad. He was among, the first, living in a slave state, to take up arms in the cause of the Country, and has been a life-long friend to the principles of liberty which have now taken such firm and deep root in the United States. I know him to have been a consistent supporter of the Republican party and your Administration. A better man for the place, I do not think can be found, and I earnestly recommend his appointment." ALS, OFH. On Dec. 10, USG nominated Croxton as minister to Bolivia.

To Adolph E. Borie

Washington. D. C. Oct. 20th *1869.*

MY DEAR MR. BORIE.

During the Summer vacation Mrs. Grant & myself promised ourselves the pleasure of a visit to Mrs. Borie and you. Our course however laid in such directions that we did not get to pay the visit. You were then at your country place and, it may be, were better prepared there to receive visitors than at your City home. But as you have so kindly and frequently invited me to pay you a visit I now write to say that Mrs. Grant & myself, and possibly her sister, Mrs. Dent, without any of the children, will go to Philadelphia on Tuesday[1] next to spend about three days. I write, not to ask a renewal of your invitation but, to have you say frankly whether you will be at home at that time, and whether it will be entirely agreeable to you to accept the visit in the City.

We miss you here, though the new secretary is all you said of him, and more too. I am very much pleased with him as I am with all the advisers I have been so fortunate in selecting.

Please present Mrs. Grant's and my kindest regards to Mrs. Borie, and to my friend Mr. Steward, when you meet him.

With high regards
your obt. svt.
U. S. GRANT

ALS, PHi. On Oct. 21, 1869, Adolph E. Borie, Philadelphia, telegraphed to USG. "Will be but too happy   I write by mail"   Telegram received (at 10:45 A.M.), DNA, RG 107, Telegrams Collected (Bound). On Oct. 23, USG wrote to Borie. "Unless I otherwise inform you, by telegraph, I will leave Washington on Tuesday next, in the 12:30 p. m. train. The children being at school now it is not our purpose to take them with us. If Mrs. Dent goes I will probable take her husband also. Mrs. Grants' and my best regards to yourself & family." ALS (facsimile), USGA. On Oct. 28, USG spoke at a benefit sponsored by the Methodist Episcopal Church. "LADIES AND GENTLEMEN AND CHILDREN: I can only thank you for your very kind reception whenever I have visited Philadelphia. I have alwa[y]s been warmly welcomed, but never in a more gratifying manner than on the present occasion. I take an interest in Sunday Schools, and am very much gratified at the success of the present movement." *New York Sun*, Oct. 30, 1869. See *Washington Chronicle*, Oct. 29, 1869. On Oct. 30, USG wrote to Borie, "My Dear Ex." "We arrived here on time last evening my having recovered from the effects of your hospitality before reaching Baltimore. We shall of course expect a visit from you and Mrs. Borie during the Winter and promise you in advance not to put you through any thing like Phila hardships. Mrs. Grant joins me in kind regards to you and yours." ALS, James S. Copley Library, La Jolla, Calif.

1. On Tuesday morning, Oct. 26, USG addressed members of the Brotherhood of Locomotive Engineers. "GENTLEMEN: I am very glad to meet you as the representative class of one of the branches of industry of our country which does more towards its development than any other. Without the aid of the railroad the interior of so vast a country as we have could be made of but very little use. You have my best wishes, gentlemen, for your success and prosperity." *New York World*, Oct. 27, 1869. At 12:30 P.M., USG left for Philadelphia for the wedding of Anna Simpson and James R. Weaver. See *New York Sun*, Oct. 29, 1869. On Oct. 29, USG, Philadelphia, telegraphed to Horace Porter. "Send carriage to Depot at 5 oclo[c]k today"   Telegram received (at 2:25 P.M.), DNA, RG 107, Telegrams Collected (Bound).

Bishop Matthew Simpson had written an undated letter to USG. "PERSONAL. . . . Will you allow me to ask your consideration of a matter personal to myself. My second daughter will in a few months be married to Prof. J. R. Weaver, of West Virginia. He was Capt in the army—was a prisoner in *Libby* for eighteen months—was breveted Lt. Col,—and is now Professor of Mathematics, Military Tactics &c in West Virginia College at Morgantown. He is a young gentleman of about 28,—a college graduate,—of unblemish character, and of more than ordinary energy, but of very little means. I am anxious that he should have opportunities of fitting himself for the best literary positions, and hence would be glad to have him reside a few years in Europe. If he could obtain a Consulship that would yield a fair support for him and my daughter for two or three years the plan could be carried out. I do not wish to see him enter political life—nor do I ask for office for him, if he cannot serve the country well, while he can also improve himself. I prefer making this frank statement to you alone. I do not care for a position for him for several months yet—and if in your arrangements no good place can be given him consistently with the public interests, I shall be satisfied with yr decision. If a good place may be obtained and recommendations of Senators or others are desired, I think any number may be obtained. But I prefer making no formal application to be placed on file, unless there is a fair prospect of success. Asking your indulgence for the only application I have ever made for a member of my family, I place the matter in your hands. I ought also to add that I have signed a few applications at the urgent request of friends that I esteem, and in whose success I wd delight, but do not expect to trouble you with many such, as I have declined further representations. With profound regard, and with my sincere desire for your triumphant success . . . P. S. If such a position [as] Consul Genl at Frankfort-on the Maine cd be procured it wd be very gratifying—If the formal application is made it will come from WEST VIRGINIA which I presume will not have many applicants." ALS, *ibid.*, RG 59, Letters of Application and Recommendation. USG endorsed this letter. "Refered to Sec. of State with hope that petition can be granted." AE (initialed—docketed as March 15), *ibid.* Related papers concerning a consulship for Weaver are *ibid.* On Aug. 31 and Sept. 1, Simpson, Philadelphia, telegraphed to USG. "Matters have changed.   do not want Glasgow   Let it remain Italy.

sorry to trouble you 'Strictly confidential' " "I now desire Prof Weavers transfer to Glasgow. Have been perplexed" Telegrams received (at 1:00 P.M. and 12:20 P.M.), *ibid.*, RG 107, Telegrams Collected (Bound). On Sept. 3, USG, Saratoga, N. Y., telegraphed to Secretary of State Hamilton Fish. "Bishop Simpson, asks leave for Prof. Weaver to remain away from his post until November. If not incompatible with public interest, please telegraph him authority." Telegram received (at 12:50 P.M.), *ibid.*, RG 59, Miscellaneous Letters. On the same day, Fish telegraphed to USG. "Have telegraphed to Bishop Simpson giving him until thirtieth November for Professor Weaver." Telegram sent, *ibid.*, Telegrams Sent. On March 4, 1870, USG nominated Weaver as consul, Antwerp.

To Roscoe Conkling

Washington. D. C. Oct. 30th *1869*

DEAR SENATOR:

Your favor of the 27th is rec'd. I directed Gen. Babcock to say, in reply to your first letter, in substance, that no choice has been indicated for any of the Judgeships created by the last Congress, nor would any choice be indicated until about the time the nominations are sent to the Senate. My intention is to go over all the recommendations, with the Atty. Gen. a short time before the meeting of Congress, say a week, and select what we will think the best names for nomination. As however no notice will be given to parties so selected, before the meeting of Congress, changes can be made up to the last moment. This arrangement will give Members of Congress an opportunity to be heard without putting them to the inconvenience of making a trip to Washington for that special purpose.

Yours Truly
U. S. GRANT

HON. ROSCOE CONKLING,
U. S. SENATOR.

ALS, DLC-Roscoe Conkling.

Calendar

1868, July 1.   C. Caldwell and three other delegates to the Tex. constitutional convention to USG. "A vacancy occurred in the office of Mayor in the city of Jefferson by the death of J S. Elliott. The loyal citizens of said city suggested the name of *A. Grigsby*, a man of tried fidelity to the Government. and an earnest Laborer in the work of reconstruction; the nomination of Mr Grigsbee was approved by Gov. Pease. and Maj Genl Reynolds and forwarded to Hd Qrs of 5th military District   Genl Buchanan however refused to make the appointment and in lieu thereof designated at the instance of the entire rebel population *W. N. Hodge* as Mayor. Mr Hodge is in full sympathy with the unreconstructed element and if permitted to retain the office will use all its power and patronage to the injury and oppression of Loyal men. His appointment was made upon the petition of the disloyal men exclusively, not one single union man concurring. We therefore beg in the interest of our suffering Union friends. that *W. N. Hodge* be removed, and *A. Grigsby* be appointed in his stead."—DS, DNA, RG 107, Letters Received from Bureaus. See *PUSG*, 18, 301-2.

1868, July 4.   Joshua Morse, Ala. attorney gen., Montgomery, to USG. "A very respectful communication is this Day forwarded to you by prominent republicans of Ala, in reference to the removal of Gen Shepperd from the Command of of the District of Ala   I desire to add my own testimony to the truth of the statemnts set forth in the said protest,   In addition to that I am constrained to say that the proposed removal is designed for political effect alone and not because of any personal or official objections to Gen Shepperd by an Officer,   Besides that I take the liberty of saying that his *removal* was secretly agreed upon & determined by the late Democratic or Conservative Convention that assembled in this city, to appoint delegates to New York, and that they adopted a *secret resolution* in a *secret Caucus* to use all their influence and every means to secure his removal And the result proves that they have worked to some advantage   The whole republican party of this state feel outraged in this matter"—ALS, DNA, RG 108, Letters Received. The enclosure is *ibid*.

1868, July 11.   S. Y. McMasters, St. Paul, to USG. "I am an 'Officeseeker;' but not of a *President*. I have, for many years past, been projecting a large amount of literary labor, which I am not likely ever to accomplish while I remain in pastoral work. It has occurred to me, that, now I have finished my fine church, if I could get the chaplaincy of some military post, I might retire to it with a good conscience, and there find leisure to carry out my literary projects. I do not know wha[t] steps to take to effect such an arrangement; bu[t] if you know of any healthy post where a chaplain is wanted,—*not very far south*,—I shall be greatly obliged by your influence 'In this behalf.' I suppose I can do all the teaching that will be wanted, as I have been teaching, (mostly in college,) a great part of my life. I am sorry, My Dear General, that you have so strong an opponent; but I trust you are safe. I am not a politician; but I think the time has not yet come for the Democratic party to take control of matters. Begging your pardon for this intrusion . . ."—ALS, DNA, RG 94, ACP, M380 CB 1868.

1868, JULY 11.   James Reynolds, Lafayette, Ind., to USG. "I appeal to The in be halfe of John W Reynolds a private co F. 14 U. s. regiment now in confinement at fort point Sanfrancisco California   I as a father and a disabeld soldier appeal to the for pitty   my sone is insane at times having had fits at the age of one yeear old evry month until the year *1867* and never being used to hard labor not being capable of doing any thing as they hav confined him to hard labor & he will not stand hard work   he is not used to it   he was 18 years of age when he left home thare fore not being verry sensable the recruiting officer and some more drunken rufiens pursuaded him to go with out my leave   and know show pitty for hevens sake on me   can I live and know that my sone is Sentanced to too years hard labor with twenty four pounds ball to his leg   will one poor boy make any ~~profit~~ profit for the government or will he lessen the number   I hav given one sone of mine to mantain the the government   he lost his life in Tennisee and I was disabeled at Shiloh my self   Kow pitty me a hart broken father if you will releas my sone or if not write and let me know what you will do for me in this case   remember that I can not ever riccomepense you in this wourld for so great a deed of kind ness   you hav it in you power to release him so I am informed by our leading men in Lafayette   Know writte and let me Know what you y will do for me"—ALS, DNA, RG 108, Letters Received.

1868, JULY 11.   E. B. Williams, Columbia Cross Roads, Pa., to USG. "I interduce my Seff to you in Behalf of my Son Ashal F Williams   He is in Co. F 36 U S inft   He is A minar Enlisted with out my Consent or Knowledg was from A Child Subject to Convulsions   will you pleas giv him His discharg and Send Him Home . . ."—ALS, DNA, RG 108, Letters Received. Endorsements indicate that Ashal F. Williams deserted before this letter reached Fort Bridger, Wyoming Territory.

1868, JULY 14.   Judge Advocate Gen. Joseph Holt to USG. "The petition of Sarah Cowan for clemency in the case of her husband *Corporal John Cowan, Co. G. 7th. U. S. Infty.*, is herewith returned with the following observations—This man was convicted on a charge of desertion to which he plead guilty, and was sentenced 'To be reduced to the rank of a private soldier; to forfeit to the United States all pay and allowances now due or that may become due him, except the just dues of the laundress; to have one half his head shaved; to be indelibly marked with the letter D, one and a half inches long on the left hip; to be dishonorably discharged and drummed out of the service, and to be confined at hard labor at such place as may be designated by the Major General Commanding, for the period of two years.' He was absent from duty upwards of thirteen months. Neither by testimony or statement to the court, did he offer any excuse for or explanation of his crime. His pardon or some mitigation of his punishment is asked for by his wife, on the ground of the dependance of herself and two children upon him for support. The crime of the prisoner is wholly unredeemed by any extenuating circumstances, and the sentence therefore is not regarded as marked by too much severity. In accordance however with the recommendations heretofore made in reference to analogous sentences, it is believed that the shaving of the head and the marking with the letter D on the left hip, might well be remitted. He has but entered upon the two years imprisonment imposed by the sentence, and it would be premature to discuss at present the question whether this term of confinement may or may not hereafter be reduced."—Copy, DNA, RG 153, Letters Sent.

1868, JULY 15. Governor Harrison Reed of Fla. to USG. "I have the honor to transmit herewith copies of the record & papers in the case of Exparte W. J. Brennan [*Brannan*] a military convict from the State of Georgia, arrested in transit through Florida, and, in my judgment, improperly ordered released under Habeas Corpus, which order was disobeyed by the officer in charge."—ALS, DNA, RG 94, Letters Received, 353F 1868. On Aug. 13, D. P. Holland, attorney, Washington, D. C., wrote to USG concerning this case.—ALS, *ibid.*

1868, JULY 17. Bvt. Maj. Gen. George Stoneman, Richmond, to USG. "Enclosed please find a copy of a letter to me from Judge Alexander Rives, one of the ablest jurists and most consistent Union men in the State, upon a subject, the importance of which cannot be over estimated. I have to request that it may be laid before the Reconstruction Committee, for such attention as the Committee may think proper, with my endorsement of the statements and recommendations therein contained."—LS, DNA, RG 107, Letters Received from Bureaus. The enclosure is *ibid.* On Sept. 28, 1869, Stoneman, Wilmington, Calif., wrote to USG. "If I may be allowed I have the honor to call to your attention and favourable consideration the claims merits and distinguished abilities of my personal friend and your enthusiastic admirer Judge Alexr Rives—His well tested and long tried patriotism and devotion to the Govt of the Union is too well known to call for comment. A long and intimate intercourse with which he honored me while I was in Comd of Dist—No 1 enabled me to know him well, and appreciate him thoroughly as one of the most upright and capable of Judges; and whenever I had to refer to him for counsel or advice, which I often did, I felt that I could rely upon his counsel and follow his advice with the most implicit confidence. I know of no man in Va who possessed in a higher degree the confidence of the people of his State than Judge Rives; and I know that this confidence was based upon the strict integrity, distinguished ability, faithful services, long experience and unselfish patriotism he was known to possess—It would be well for the Govt. if the services of such men and such only could be secured, especially on the Bench"—ALS, *ibid.*, RG 60, Letters of Application and Recommendation.

1868, JULY 17. George W. Duncan & Co., Hiawatha, Kan., to USG and Schuyler Colfax, "Tanners." "Please ship us as soon as convenient two dozen of your celebrated old Democratic hides for immediate use . . ."—LS, USG 3.

1868, JULY 18. Lorenzo A. Phelps, Canyon City, Ore., to USG. "Allow me to state that at the first braking out of the rebelion in /61 I enlisted in the 5th Va. Vol. In a *private* afterward raising to the rank of *major.* Through the jealosy of officers in the same regiment a set of false and malicious charges were brought against me on which I was tried by a court which was strongly prejudiced against me and by sentence dismissed the service. Previous to the promulgation of the order of dismissal I was captured and taken to Richmond a prisoner being keept in different prisons in the south for 18 months. At Anapolis Md. in March /65, I first learned the decission of the court Brig Genl. R. B. Hays issued the orders under which I was acting at the time of my capture. I am refused pay for the time I was in prison. In fact there is nearly one years pay due me. Papers showing all the facts in the case are in the hands of Lawyer Enoch Totten Law Building Washington D. C, I come humbly and respectfully to request your aid in obtaining what is honestly and farely due me for services rendered in the army of the U. S. during the rebelion. This state went democratic at the state election. I am a republican and cannot be changed— Nothing gives greater pleasure than to learn of your nomination for the Presidency. I am determined to spend all my time and means to secure this state for you. I have not been here long but I have a pretty good tongue and mean to make good use of it. The money which is due me would be a great help just now General Schenk member of the House from eOhio knows me. I was Major under him in the Shenandoah vally. Genl, will you help me and in so doing heal a wounded feeling, and make glad a true soldier and a staunch Republican"—ALS, DNA, RG 108, Letters Received.

1868, JULY 20. Lucius S. Felt, Galena, to Elihu B. Washburne. "Genl Grant wrote me under date of 'Webster Grove July 13th' that he would be here about the 1st of Aug, his party consisting of himself wife 3 children 2 servants & old Mr & Genl Dent. 9 in all, & that they would remain here about 10 days. I had invited him with his family to stop with me which he said he would gladly do but for the number of his 'host' He says a part may stop at the Hotel or keep house but that this can be arranged after his arrival Altho I would like to have him & his family with me, giving me an opportunity of reciprocating his hospitality to me & mine, after consulting with Henry Corwith Col Stephenson & some others I wrote him we would have his own house in readiness for occupancy, he notifying us definitely as to the time of his arrival This we can do by a temporary loan of such articles of bedding linen &c as may be needed, renting some crockery & sending to the house the staple articles of provisions & engaging a cook with Mrs Richards. This will be as good as 'camping' & perhaps better than colonizing them in private or public houses. We will also have as on his former visit his first meal prepared if we know the train by which he will arrive   Having in mind what you told me of the extortion practiced on him in his other visit we have thought it best to engage a Carriage to be at his disposal while here at our expense. How does all this strike you & have you any improvements or change to suggest? It will perhaps look better for the 'insignificant' 'inland' town which has lost almost all its ~~other~~ claims to consideration except that it was the residence of the ~~future~~ General who put down the Rebellion (is such still when he is at home) & the future President. (I should not omit one other title to consideration intamately connected with this. namely that it is also the residence of the Hon E. B. W. My Wife regrets that Mrs W. is not here to assist or direct in putting the house in order. Will you be here with the Genl? Aint it about time for Congress to adjourn before appropriating all the Copperhead & Rebel 'Financial' thunder."—ALS, DLC-Elihu B. Washburne. On July [31], USG had written to Felt "that he and his family would be in Galena the following Thurs. or Frid., and all they would need to keep house would be a tea and dinner set as Mrs. Grant has her bed linens. Grant . . . adds that they will be in Galena no later than July 15."—*The Collector*, 842 (1975), p. 10. Whether this letter is dated July 13 or 31 (as listed in the catalogue) is unclear.

1868, July 31.   Charles H. Goodwin, New York City, to USG. "I don't know as you recollect my name, but I sent you a certificate of honarary membership, in behalf of our Sunday School, and would claim the liberty of writing to you. I would like very much to get my Brother in the Military Academy at West Point; and as I am not acquainted with either of the Senators from N. Y., I thought you would be kind enough to give me an appointment, if it is in your power, or if not, to use your influence with person who can. I wrote to Senator Doolittle, being a friend of my Fathers, but he being from another state, could not do it, I suppose. Sen. Ramsey is also a friend of ours. I know it is asking a great deal, at the time when you are so busy with other matters; but, as I said before, if you would be so kind as to trouble yourself with it, it shall never be forgotten; and I hope you may live to see the day, when you will know, you have not given that appointment in vain. His (my Brother) name is Francis Hatfield Goodwin, was (17) seventeen years of age on the 6th of July /68. With many thanks if you will be kind enough to answer this . . ."—ALS, DNA, RG 94, Unsuccessful Cadet Applications. On June 24, 1869, Mrs. E. H. Goodwin, New York City, mother of Francis H. Goodwin, wrote to USG on the same subject.—ALS, *ibid.*

1868, Aug. 1.   USG endorsement. "I think it would be well in the state of Miss. where the new Constitution has been rejected, to direct that all civil officers who cannot take the oath prescribed by Congress should be removed and men who could appointed to their places. For the high state offices I would adhere to the rule of appointing from the Army but for all county offices I would leave the appointments to the discretion of the district commander."—*The Collector*, 899 (1984), R-518. Written on a letter of July 24 from Peter P. Bailey, George C. McKee, and H. F. Fisher, Washington, D. C., citizens of Miss. ". . . fully conversant with the political condition of that State, having been actively engaged in aid of reconstruction, and knowing how little security there is there, for the persons and property of loyal men, under the present anomalous condition of affairs. . . . respectfully request and urgently press upon your attention the necessity of appointing officers for the civil government of that state . . ." The writers advocated replacing incumbents with Republicans and loyal men.

1868, AUG. 1. USG endorsement. "I am willing that you and the Sec. of War, or you without the advice of the Sec. of War, should give such instructions or suggestions as you think advisable."—AES, Richard Maass, White Plains, N. Y. Written on a sheet bearing an endorsement by Bvt. Maj. Gen. John A. Rawlins. "It might be well to suggest to Genl. Stoneman that where he can find an intelligent and capable colored men it would be well to appoint some of them to office. Such is That would answer the gist of this petition. They would make no objection to the payment of Taxes if their right to hold office is recognised even in these appointments be the most subordinate ones."—AES, *ibid*.

1868, AUG. 1. Vice Admiral W. Tegetthoff, Austrian Navy, Vienna, to USG. "I beg to introduce to you a brother-officer of mine, the Duke of Würtemberg, General, in the Austrian Army, who wishes most particularly to become personnally acquainted with the hero of the Great American War. My friend the bearer wants to see as much as possible of your army and his establishments and would like to visit the states, where your great battles were fought and won. I keep the kindness, which you have shown me during my stays at Washington to well in remembrance, not to feel fully confident, that you will kindly advise my friend how to undertake his tour, and adress him to some of your subordinate officers, who may be able to assist him in the different places he should visit."—ALS, USG 3.

1868, AUG. 5. USG endorsement. "Please ask the Sec. of War to make Kautz, leave 'awaiting orders,' and oblige . . ."—AES, DNA, RG 94, Letters Received, 158K 1868. Written on a letter of July 28 from Bvt. Maj. Gen. August V. Kautz, Omaha, probably to USG. "I see in the last Army & Navy Journal the order in my case. It gives me a leave of absence instead of authority to delay for six months. As this cuts down my pay one half, about which I spoke to you at the time, it will embarrass me a little in making arrangemts for my proposed trip to Mexico. As you assented to a delay I made my arrangements in anticipation of full pay. Of course I do not ask anything out of the usual way and if there is any objection to giving me a delay, I will try to get along on the Leave. A line or two addressed to me at the Fifth Avenue Hotel N y. as to whether the order as published in the Journal is final will be a kindness on your part for which I shall be greatly obliged"—ALS, *ibid.*

1868, AUG. 21. USG endorsement. "Respy. forwarded to the Sec of war— I respectfully recommend the full pardon and discharge of the within named deserters. They are the sons of respectable farmers, who sent—one 3, and the other 4 sons to the army, who all served during the rebellion, or until killed—these deserters were among the number who served during the rebellion."—DNA, RG 108, Register of Letters Received. Written on a letter of Aug. 13 from Uriel E. Harrison and Mrs. Mary Todd, Big Patch, Wis., requesting "pardon and discharge from confinement & service of sons, viz: *A. W. Harrison* and *William Todd*, privates in Co. "F" 22d Infantry convicted by G. C. M. of desertion and now incarcerated at Fort Randal, D. T."—*Ibid.*

1868, AUG. 22. Austin Barton, "colored Citizien of Charleston. S. C," Fort Macon, N. C., to USG. "I undersigned a Citizien take the liberty of addressing this few lines to you, and truly pray in them for your truly assistance. I wars tried by a Military Commission at Charleston S. C. on the Charge Larceny and sentenced to five years imprissment at this place. I anyt guilty of the crime I am charged with and also never wars punished before. I have a wife with six helpless children at home to support, them can not earn their daily bread and ~~are~~ verry near are starved to death. I allways conducted myself wrihgt from my childhood on and also I am able to show just as good a character in my native town as there can be showed to any man. Wars I guilty of the crime I am charged with I would not allow myself to ask you for assistance. Also wars I single I would be willen to serve my punishment. But now I humbly pray to you for pardon or remittance of my sentences and with that you will verry mutsh oblige my helpless wife and children . . ."—ALS, DNA, RG 94, Letters Received, 574B 1868.

1868, AUG. 22. Act. Asst. Surgeon Isaac G. Braman, post hospital, Watertown Arsenal, Mass., to USG. "2d Lt. Wm Magee of the 20th Infantry Stationed at Baton Rogue La. murdered my son Dr C. B. Braman Act. Asst. Surgeon at that Post on the 15th inst. As the particulars have been withheld from me, I have the honor to request, that you will take measures to procure them for me and forward them at your earliest convenience"— ALS, DNA, RG 94, Letters Received, 738S 1868. Additional correspondence is *ibid.*

1868, AUG. 24. To Bvt. Maj. Gen. John A. Rawlins. "Ask Sec of War to authorize Gen L C. Hunt to delay joining his regiment until December or if it can be done order him east to await orders until that"—Telegrams received (2—on Aug. 25, 9:00 A.M.), DNA, RG 107, Telegrams Collected (Bound); *ibid.*, RG 108, Telegrams Received; copy, DLC-USG, V, 55. On Aug. 13, Lt. Col. Lewis C. Hunt, Fort Sedgwick, Colorado Territory, wrote to Rawlins. "When General Grant was out here, he promised to get me ordered East, but yesterday my commission of Lieutenant Colonel, 20th U. S. Infantry, came along, with the usual order to join my regiment in Louisiana, without delay. I telegraphed General Grant at Galena, and he replies, 'I wrote from St Louis asking detail to retain you East. Ask them if orders are made.' Will you do me the favor to inform me on the subject. Any temporary duty will answer my purpose, preferably at New York, but would not object to a 'long job.' I hope you continue improving in health."—ALS, DNA, RG 94, Letters Received, 447H 1868. On Aug. 14, Col. Henry B. Carrington, Fort Sedgwick, telegraphed to Bvt. Brig. Gen. Adam Badeau. "What detail for Northern duty has been made for Gen. L. C. Hunt in accordance with Gen. Grants letter from St Louis? Answer by telegraph."—Telegram received (at 9:00 A.M.), *ibid.*, RG 107, Telegrams Collected (Bound).

1868, AUG. 24. S. C. Barker, Warrington, Fla., to USG. "Desirous of obtaining justice for myself and others who have served in the Fedal Army during the war, and knowing of no other way except through our old Commander I have the honor to address you on the subject It appeares that Bvt Col Prime Engineer in Charge of work on Fortifycations on the Gulf Coast is doing all in his power to crowd out Soldiers and espiecily Ex Officers of the Fedl Army. and putting men in responsible positions that bitterly opposed us during the Rebbelion. now I will ask you General is that doing justice to the Ex Fedl Soldiers Men, ex federal soldiers, more compitent to fill these places are put one side to make room for men who openly avow themselfs to be as good Rebbels to day as ever and who wer particularly noted during the Rebbellion for thier bitter secesh princapals. To draw a comparison General though a remote one, how humiliating would it be to yourself if Goverment. should suppercede you with Robbert. R. Lee To substantiate. this statement (although this is not the only case of this kind). Col Prime has sent a Mr Golay a well known rebbel to suppercede Mr Lorriagan an ex Officer who served in the U. S. service during the War, is a Civil. Engineer. has filled the place (that Golay now filles) for some time and is well known to be compitent for the position, made application for the position through Maj Sutter. (as well as myself,) was put in charge of the worke untill such times as Prime could hunt up a Reb to fill the place. now if that aint hell and repeat I am no soldier this appointment of Mr Golays places him over me, who am at presant Sub Overseer, (at Ft Pickens) this is humiliating to me. to put a man in charg of Goverment work over me. that is no more compitent than I am for the place, (and one at that, that don all he could to destroy. the same Fortifycations while I risked my life to save Goverment from being overthrown by just such men General as one of your old Officers, I ask you is this justice to the soldiers who stood by thier Country in the hour of need.

wee look to you the same now. as during the war. as our Leader. ~~and the~~ and the Soldiers friend. and are willing to abbide by your dicision. for myself and the veracity of these statements, I respectfuly refer to. Hon. Senitor Fessenden. and his son Brigr General James Fessenden. my former Captain in the 2d U. S. Sharpshooters. Hoping you will see justice don your old soldiers. . . . wee shall anxiously wait your dicision"—ALS, DNA, RG 108, Letters Received. On Aug. 25, Christopher J. Lorigan, Fort Pickens, Fla., formerly capt., 1st N. Y. Engineers, wrote to USG making a similar complaint about Prime.—ALS, *ibid.* On Sept. 19, Barker wrote a letter of apology to Maj. Frederick E. Prime.—ALS, *ibid.*

1868, AUG. 29. Edward M. McCook, U.S. legation, Honolulu, to USG. "Permit me to add my Congratulations to the many thousands you have no doubt already received from your old soldiers in all parts of the world, on being selected to lead them in another and I hope final campaign against the enemys of Union and peace. You have my most earnest wishes for your success, and though I may not be permitted to return to the United States in time to take part in the Presidential Canvas, yet I shall try to be of some service with my pen. Among other things, I send over by this steamer an article for the 'Overland Monthly' which I know will please you. Intelligence of the Democratic nominations have just reached here, and I was sorry to see that one of my name, (George W. McCook,) took part in that 'Convocation of Ex-Rebels, Copperheads, and Military failures, and gained an unenviable notoriety by presenting Seymours name to the Convention. *He is the only male member of our family who did not fight in the Union Army through the* war, and is the *only one* now, who *will* not *fight on your side* in the Presidential Contest. Comment is unnecessary; and so it will be through the whole Country; those who strove for the preservation of the nation during the war will support you now, while those who were hostile or indifferent then will be against you. The old soldiers will *vote* as they *shot*, against the Rebels! And I most fervently hope and believe that the American people will give future peace and prosperity to our country by placing you at the head of the Republic."—ALS, USG 3.

1868, SEPT. 5. George W. Brown, New York City, to USG. "I have this day made application to the Quartermaster General through Gen Ingalls Q M at this place, for the Command of the Steamer 'Newberne' soon to be taken from this port to San-Francisco. I commanded the Steamer (Gun-Boat) 'Forrest Rose' on the Mississippi and convoyd the Steamer 'Magnolia' at your request from Memphis to Vicksburgh when you went to Vicksburgh January 1863. Also commanded one of the Naval Batteries on shore at Vicksburgh. I also opend the Levee and with Lieut Col Wilson explored the Yazoo Pass. I mention these facts that you may remember me, or rather recognize me. I would be obliged to you if you could help me in procuring this situation. My references are Vice Admiral David D Porter, and some of the largest Shipping Merchants in this city. I have had about

15 years experiance as Master of Merchant & Government Ships. Hopeing you will excuse the liberty I have taken . . ."—ALS, DNA, RG 108, Letters Received. In Nov., New York City merchants and ship owners signed a petition to USG recommending Brown for consul at Havana.—Copy (press), DLC-Nathaniel P. Banks.

1868, SEPT. 10.   Mrs. Mary A. Deluc, New Orleans, to USG. "I embrace an opportunity to address you a few lines in regards to my position   I will inform you that I am in great distress   I have been sick for six-months and is not able to support myself therefore you will please render me a favor by having my husband discharged from the service   his name is Pierre A. Deluc and he is a sergeant in Company I 39th U. S. Infantry stationed at Fort Pike La   so please except to my request by letting him come to me for relief for the wages he is getting in the Army is not sufficient to give me any help. I have made application to that effect to the Secretary of war but of no avail so I take it on myself to address you   of the above request if excepted, you will please answer   address No 129 Thalia Street between Magazine and Constance Streets"—ALS, DNA, RG 108, Letters Received. On Oct. 13, Capt. James F. Randlett, Fort Pike, La., endorsed this letter. "Respectfully forwarded: with the remark, that it is believed that the facts set forth by Mrs Mary A Deluc, in the enclosed communication are true; and that she is the wife of Sergt Pierre A Deluc Co "I" 39th U. S. Inf   Sergeant Deluc is a reliable Soldier, and a very intelligent man. He knew at the time of enlistment, that he would be rejected, if he acknowledged himself a married man, to the Recruiting Officer. It is believed that he evaded giving such information to that Officer. He is now acting Com Sergt of his Company, and it will be difficult if he is discharged to fill his position well, from the material of which his Company is made up. I believe the interest of the Service require that this man serve the full period of his enlistment terms."—AES, *ibid.*

1868, SEPT. 13.   Bvt. Brig. Gen. Adam Badeau, Galena, to Cayetano Romero. "Knowing how great an interest both yourself and your brother take in American politics, and especially in whatever relates to my chief, I take the liberty of giving you some information in regard to Gen. Rosecranz, which I beg you will communicate as speedily as possible to Mr. Matias Romero. Gen. Rosecranz has been ever since 1862 the enemy of Gen Grant; especially since his great defeat at Chikamauga, and the success of Gen Grant immediately afterwards. His nomination to his present position was undoubtedly due to this fact; just as Gen. McClernand was certainly nominated for the same reason. Since his confirmation *I know* of his using language in regard to Gen Grant, which indicates the most decided personal hostility. His behavior in visiting the rebel generals lately in Virginia, with the avowed intention of thwarting the success of the republican party and of Gen Grant shows in what spirit he is ready to administer his functions at Mexico. Everything he does will be affected doubtless by his hostility to the general. It seems only proper that the peculiarity of his relations with Gen Grant should be known to your brother, under these circumstances . . . P. S. If you like to send this letter to your brother, I should not object; but I beg that you will consider it confidential, and that you will so request Mr. M. Romero to look upon it in the same light."— ADfS, USG 3.

1868, SEPT. 15.   Bvt. Maj. Gen. John A. Rawlins to John Russell Young, *New York Tribune.* "With this I send you an article which we have styled Reminiscences &c of Genl Grant, though if you publish it you can announce it by any heading you choose. I consider it a very well written paper & should be extensively circulated. It is from the pen of Brevet Maj Gen O. B. Wilcox Col of the 29th U. S. In'fy. He was one of the signers of the Cleveland Soldiers and Sailors Convention in 1866—Very much obliged to you for the telegram on the Maine election. It is great news. . . . P. S. I do not think it would be politic to give to the public the name of the author.—"— LS, DLC-John Russell Young. The article appeared with the title: "GEN. GRANT. REMINISCENCES AND OPINIONS OF THE GENERAL, BY A GRADUATE OF WEST POINT, LATE A MAJOR-GENERAL UNITED STATES VOLUNTEERS, AND NOW A COLONEL AND BREVET MAJOR-GENERAL IN THE REGULAR ARMY. I never shall forget one night that I spent with Grant. It was in the midst of the war, the battle of Chattanooga had been fought, the seige of Knoxville was raised, and Grant was passing on horseback through Tennessee, by way of Cumberland Gap, over steep and icy roads, in mid-Winter—the Winter of 1863–4—to look after affairs in the East. My quarters were scanty, and we occupied a room together. During the early part of the evening the General was engaged with his A. A. G. over some correspondence with his different field commanders. Grant wrote or dictated the more important letters, some of which were read in my hearing, and I was struck by the ease, conciseness, and clearness of his composition. Every sentence was simple and pithy, there was little repetition, no undecision, nothing to correct. Few men can equal him in putting orders or reports concerning complicated movements into intelligible English. Business over, the weary A. A. G. retired to bed, but Grant showed no signs of fatigue, and sat up with me long after the witching hour, smoking and talking over old times, and discussing the progress of the war, the characters of men, and, to a certain extent, the future movements of the several armies. I had known him casually for many years, but never till now had I enjoyed so good an opportunity to judge of his intellectual caliber. . . ."—*New York Tribune*, Sept. 28, 1868.

1868, SEPT. 17.   USG note. "It will be necessary to see Gn. Howard or the Sec. of War on the business named. The latter alone, if any one, can correct the mistake."—ANS, Gallery of History, Las Vegas, Nev.

1868, SEPT. 18. USG *et al.* to Bishop Matthew Simpson. "Having a great desire to hear your lecture on the 'Future of the Republic,' we most earnestly request that you will, should your health and time permit, favor the citizens of Galena with the delivery, on such evening as may suit your convenience, during your present visit to Galena."—*Galena Gazette*, Sept. 18, 1868. On the same day, Simpson wrote to USG *et al.* "Your note, requesting me to deliver my lecture on the 'Future of the Republic,' is just received. In accordance with your request, I will name to-morrow (Saturday) evening as the only time I shall be at liberty to do so, during my stay in Galena."—*Ibid.*

1868, SEPT. 19. William H. Reed, Boston, to USG. "I was Employed by Genrl O O Howard for the Government through the Impeachment Trial As Detective, was sent to Georgia by your order, as he Genrl O O Howard Said, and after Returning from Georgia I was detained In Washington by order of the War Department (Col Schofield) as Genrl Howard Said neglecting to Discharge Me. Genrl Mead Genrl Howard and Genrl Schofield Refuseing to pay Me Genrl Schofield Referring Me to you and Genrl Howard the Government owe Me Several hundred dollars which I am in want of will you, Genrl please tell Me who will Setle with Me"—ALS, DNA, RG 105, Letters Received. On Oct. 11, Bvt. Brig. Gen. Cyrus B. Comstock, Galena, endorsed this letter. "Respectfully referred to Gen. O. O. Howard, with the request from Gen Grant that if Mr Reed is the detective sent at his desire to Gen. Meade for the Ashburne case, the account may be settled."—AES, *ibid.* On Oct. 16, Maj. Gen. Oliver O. Howard wrote to Comstock. "What Reed says is part of the truth. He came back from Georgia and came to me for payment for services as detective. I sent him to Genl Meade at the request of General Grant. He received payment from Genl Meade's Disbursing Officer, but came on to Washington and claimed more. I asked him to make out his bill, which he did, and I transmitted it to Genl Meade with the request that he would settle it. Genl Meade reported against paying him the whole bill and gave his reasons which are endorsed on the account of Reed. I advanced him $70. because he was in want expecting a part of his account would be settled. I went to Genl Schofield, Secretary of War, and he replied to me that Genl Meade must settle the account. I never refused absolutely to pay Mr Reed what he demanded, although I was obliged to be governed by General Meades report. If he will send the same account back again I will pay every cent I have in my hands if you deem the account just and right. He owes me the seventy dollars I advanced him after his return."—LS, *ibid.*, RG 108, Letters Received. On Oct. 24, Comstock wrote to Howard. "Your letter of Oct 16 1868 is received. Gen. Grant in directing the endorsement which was put on Reed's letter & sent to you did not desire to express any opinion as to the amount to be paid to Reed, as he has no knowledge of the services rendered."—ALS, *ibid.*, RG 105, Letters Received.

1868, SEPT. 22.   John C. De Lany, Detroit, to USG. "When recently in Washington and other Cities of the East I have at diferent times and places heard parties offering to wager large sums of money 'that Genl, Grant *would not be* the next President of the United States',   In some instances these propositions being accepted under the supposition that the party making the proposition meant to bet that U. S. Grant would not be *elected*— when the conditions of the wager came to be put in writing the challenging party *declined* to bet that Genl, Grant *would not be elected*, but would stake a large amt, that 'Grant' would *not be the next President of the United States*'   I have also been informed that large sums have been offered in New York City on this same proposition,   There can be but two interpretations to this—Viz; It is simply bluster, or it means that the dying '*Slave Power*' dont intend that the general under whose loyal blows it was forced to yield—shall ever occupy the Executive Chair,   Is it probable that mere bluster should assume this new & tangible form at the same time in diferent localities—Whilst it is difficult from a stand point of reason and humanity to conceive that assassination would be again resorted to—it is well to remember, that the *murderous* spirit that opened Slavery's guns on Sumpter, has never been characterized by either *reason* or *humanity*,   Fort Pillow, Andersonville and the fearful tragedy at Ford's Theatre were only a few of its more prominent outcroppings—It is still rife & rampant, sullen & *revengeful.* The Loyal masses of the North feel assured of the safety of the life of their tried trusted & beloved General—in that they have the faithful, vigilant unswerving Colfax at his back,   But the spirit that would attempt assassination, cares but little whether it is two lives or one that is to be taken, This Slave-power does not stop to contemplate impossibilities—especially such as are only compassed by human life,   A Nations hope of liberty— order & 'Peace' with their consequent prosperity is to-day centered in you, For yourself you can afford to with our loved & lamented Lincoln to have your name go down to succeeding generations with a martyr's wreath upon your brow,   But to the cause of common humanity & liberty throughout the world—to this generation in our own land that asks that you shall preside over the government you have so nobly & ably defended—for the nex *eight* years—and to the future generations that shall fill its yet unpeopled realms *you owe it*—to guard with ceaseless and assiduous care all your surroundings and movements,   And only in the keeping of that God who holds the destinies of Nations in His hand is your life safe, as the successful leader of the battalions of liberty against the power that thwarted & crushed in its attempt to establish a goverment whose 'corner stone' was to be 'human slavery'—still seeks to *rule* or *ruin*,   Trusting that you will pardon this liberty taken by an humble citizen—. . ."—ALS, USG 3.

1868, SEPT. 23.   U.S. Senator Simon Cameron of Pa., Harrisburg, to USG. "While in Washington, Monday and Tuesday, so many inquiries were made of me regarding the vote of Pennsylvania that I fear you, like others, may doubt our ability and intention to carry ~~Pennsylvania~~ it. I write, therefore, to say to you, that it is just as certain for the republican ticket in October, as was Maine—and by about the same majority. In Oct. we will give from 15,000. to 20,000. and in November it will be doubled, when our people vote for you direct. The N. York & N. Jersey Senators assured me that a decisive majority here in Oct, will give both those states to you in Novr Morton says Indiana is entirely safe. So does Wade & Sherman of Ohio—So, I think you may as well begin to think over your 'Inaugural.' I start to day, with our Attorney Gnl. Brewster, on a trip of 10 or 12 days through the State, and when I return if I see anything worth telling will write again. It is agreed that Brewster, will make the speeches and I shake the hands of the men, talk to the Ladies and kiss the babies."—ALS, USG 3.

1868, SEPT. 24. U.S. Representative William A. Pile of Mo. and four St. Louis police commissioners to USG. "By reference to enclosed catalogue you will see that a large amount of small arms & ammunition is to be sold at the St Louis Arsenal October 5th There is much excitement & bad blood in the present political campaign. The old rebel element in this city are organizing & arming, threatening to over-ride the law, & carry the election by force. We deem it exceedingly imprudent to sell these small arms before the election, and have so telegraphed to Secretary Schofield, asking the postponement of the sale—We respectfully ask you to add the weight of your influence to our request, by telegraphing to Secretary Schofield immediately. We assure you there is great danger of a serious riot in this city, and much trouble in this state if these arms are sold, & pass into the hands of the desperate men of this city & state—"—LS, DNA, RG 108, Letters Received. On Oct. 1, USG telegraphed to Secretary of War John M. Schofield. "Would it not be well to stop all sales of arms and munitions of war by the Government for the present. I recommend such suspension"—Telegrams received (2—on Oct. 2, 9:00 A.M.), *ibid.*, RG 107, Telegrams Collected (Bound). On Oct. 2, Schofield telegraphed to USG. "I stopped the sale of small arms and amunition several days ago. Nothing is now being sold but canon powder and projectiles for the foreign market. Does your recommendation extend to these latter?"—ALS (telegram sent), *ibid.*; telegram sent, *ibid.*; telegram received (at 9:35 A.M.), *ibid.*, RG 108, Telegrams Received. On Oct. 6, USG wrote to Schofield. "Your telegram of Oct 2d is received and your action covers all that I thought necessary."—LS, *ibid.*, RG 107, Letters Received from Bureaus; copies, *ibid.*, RG 108, Letters Sent; *ibid.*, Telegrams Sent; DLC-USG, V, 47, 60.

[1868], SEPT. 26. "Boy in Blue" to USG. "Your old friend Hillyer is seeking a nomination for Congress in Fernando Wood's District and gives as a reason why Tammany should support him that you as President will *lean* on him as a Congressman and give him the control of the Government patronage in New York. If this is so, it will be a disappointment to all except those who say that you will be *run* by a few of your old associates for their own purposes. Hillyer is cheek by jowl with Rosecrans and unless you approve the riding of two horses at once in opposite directions, it is hard to see how you can promise the patronage to a zealous though new born democrat. If you have not given some assurances to Hillyer that he shall have the Ladle, would he promise soup to the hungry beggars of Tammany?"—AL, USG 3.

1868, SEPT. 29. USG endorsement. "Gen. Wessels should have some detail, either Supt. of Recruiting service or other, to bring him out of the field for two years. When it can be given without detriment to the service I would like him put on spl. service."—AES, DNA, RG 94, Letters Received, 797W 1868. Written on a letter of Sept. 11 from Bvt. Brig. Gen. Henry W. Wessells, Fort D. A. Russell, Wyoming Territory, addressed to "General." "General Grant in the multiplicity of business may forget the conversation with me whilst in my quarters a few weeks ago, and as you suggested, I now drop a line, to say that I am homesick, tired this kind of life, and wish for a change, that will give me better social advantages. I am too old for this kind of harrassing existence, and after thirty five years service, almost always on the fronteir, I think myself entitled to Consideration, Examine the Register & Records, and I am sure the General will feel no doubt, Let younger Officers have their turn, I have now been on this tour going on three years, changed six times from one post to another, both in heat of summer & dead of winter, wherever the authorities found that affairs had not been satisfactorily administered, My children are scattered about, and I have not seen them in the last three years—I have been over-slaughed, & compelled to serve under new Officers of recent date, & like a hermit am cut off from all my old associations—You can see how it is, and cannot fail to perceive that I have a just claim to consideration, as well from age as length of service—I do not know what to apply for, but there always seem to be openings in one way or another,—Boards of long standing, important Recruiting Depots, &c. &c., If the station at David's Island, is still in existence, it would suit me above all things, on account of my social relations in that vicinity It has been the station of a Field officer, and as Recruiting will probably be resumed, may be of importance—I do not care so much for a large command, but more to be where I can see my children and friends—The necessity of my always being here, dont seem to be very great, and if the General feels disposed to confer a favor, I am sure it will be fully appreciated—Were it not for reduced pay, I would ask for a leave of absence, but on half allowance, it is out of the question—This is all I can say, & hoping you had a pleasant trip with safe return . . ."—ALS, *ibid.*

1868, OCT. 2. Bvt. Maj. Gen. George Stoneman, Richmond, to USG. "Thinking that perhaps you may like to hear how we are getting along in Dist—No 1 I take the occasion to write you with the freedom which I could not well use in an official Communication As a general thing and as

far as I can learn all parties appear to be inclined to aid in every way
possible in carrying out my views & keeping things as quiet as possible—
An inclination was manifested by some persons soon after the adjournment
of Congress to raise questions for me to decide based upon the fourteenth
Art—and an effort has been made to open up the whole question by sueing
out a writ of Habeus Corpus—but I think or at least hope that the parties
pushing the thing may be induced to postpone the Case at least until after
the election—The questions that have been raised or attempted have been
started by republicans and an appeal to them as such has had the effect to
keep them quiet, and has prevented the manufacture of any democratic
material here in Va   There has been some talk about holding an election in
the state for Presdl Electors but the proposers having received no encouragement I do not think any effort will be mad to hold it—The principal
trouble I have to contend against is the want of competent and qualified
persons to fill offices as they become vacant—In some instances I have had
to *devolve the performance of the duties*, upon competent persons without
an actual *appointment*—with the understanding that the person so selected
is not disloyal or opposed to reconstruction though unable to take the Test
Oath. Unless this or some other expedient is adopted the taxes cannot be
collected and the wheels of the Govt must stop for want of fuel—The subject of the Rail Roads being the most important one in the state has had as
it deserves my most careful consideration—The question of Proxies & Directors on the part of the state is creating some nervousness on the part of
R R men and officials as the time has arrived for their appointment (Pro &
Drs) by the Board of Public Works—I hope I shall not be called upon to
interfere—I have as yet ordered no military commissions, thinking under
all the circumstances it would not be politic to do so—for the present at
least—If things remain in the future as quiet as they are at present more
trops can be spared from this Dept—should you have use for them elsewhere—The expenses of the Dept have been very much reduced, that in the
Q. M. Dept—being about $30,000 pr month, and we are carrying on re-
construction affairs now at an expense of less than sixteen hundred ($1600)
pr month, which will in all probability not be much increased until registration & elections are had—which cannot be for months to come—In my
administration of affairs I have endeavoured to do as little as I could consistent with the interests of those concerned and to keep within the limits
of the requirements of the laws and to not take the controle of affairs out of
the hands of the civil authorities but to hold them responsible for the due
execution of the laws and the enforcement of the same—with an assurance
of assistance from the mily—authorities when assistance is absolutely necessary—I have endeavoured also to keep out of politics feeling assured that
any thing like partizanship would do more harm than good, and not be in
accord with your views or wishes—& the result has been that Virginia
affairs have scarcely been noticed by the public journals—As there will in
all probability be no Legislature to meet and act this winter, some questions
of importance will arise which will require a solution and which will de-

mand serious consideration as they involve impotant interests affecting the
people in general—One of the most important if not the most important will
be the *Stay Law*—Upon these I may in all probability ask for your advice
or instructions *after election.* If there are other points upon which you
would like information I should be glad to give it . . . P. S. I expect the
information I have given you to be made use of officially if desireable—"—
ALS, DNA, RG 108, Letters Received. On Oct. 21, Stoneman wrote to
USG. "In my last letter I mentioned that the subject of R. Roads would in
all probability force itself upon me for consideration—I have written several
letters to Genl Schofield upon this question but he has as yet been unable
to give me any opinion or advice upon it or to indicate what course he would
have pursued had he remained   You perhaps are aware that in accordance
with the policy of consolidation inaugurated by this state by its last Legislature the three R. R. connecting Bristol and and Norfolk were consoli-
dated under the Presidantcy of Genl Mahone—This consolidation is thought
to act injureously to the interests of the Orange and Alexandria Road and
through it to the Baltimore or Garrett interest—An effort is now being
made to change the order of things by getting the controle of the road from
Lynchburg to Bristol ~~out of~~ away from Mahones ~~controle~~ and to put it under the controle of Garrett, and to deflect the trade from Norfolk to Balto
This can only be done through the Board of Public Works and with the
consent of the District Commander—Every effort is being made use of and
I am informed that money has been sent here to be used as an element
This is a question purely of local interests and not of a political character
further than that combinations are sought which it is thought may affect
the future interests of political aspirants—The question arises aught the
Dist. Comdr who is entrusted with the guardianship of the interests of the
state to remain inactive and assume the responsibility for the acts of the
military appointees whatever they may be in the matter—and whether he
approves of them or not—The last Legislative body that assembled in Va
recognised and inaugurated the general system of consolidation, and should
not that system be carried out until changed by the representatives of the
people in Legislature assembled?   in accordance with a principle I have thus
far observed and as I understand was observed by my predecessor to the
very general satisfaction of the people of Va I will remark that the private
stock holders are nearly unanimous in opposition to the Baltimore interference and appeal to me to protect them and their interests. I should be
glad to act in harmony with your views and to receive any instructions, or
if you do not choose to give them suggestions in this important matter—
The other question is the one connected with the Chesapeake and Ohio R. R.
This road is the result of a consolidation of the Covington and Ohio R. R.
now under construction, with the Va Central Road—This consolidation was
effected by the joint Commission from the two Virginias W—& E—last
Sept—The two Comns appointed by their Legislatures in accordance with
laws—met organized and arranged every thing to the satisfaction of every
one except a few disappointed aspirants for position, and placed the whole

road under the presidancy of Mr Fontaine the former Presdt of the Va
Central Road. An effort is now being made to have Fontaine removed an
Mr Wickham elected This is done purely upon political grounds—F—has
been Pt for fifteen or twenty years with the exception of one year when
W—was Pt W—was turned out & F—replaced it is said upon political
grounds—and an effort is now being made to replace Wickham ~~upon~~ upon
the same grounds—The Stock holders are nearly all in favour of retaining
F—The Commissioners on the part of West Va all republicans write urging
that he be retained—The N. Y. city moneyed men who are ready to advance
the money to complete the Road write asking what assurance can be given
that the funds they advance will be used in a proper manner and for legitimate purposes—The Board of Public Works are pressed to make ap-
points of State Proxies such as to ensure a change of Presdt & Directors
and I am pressed, ~~to prevent~~ by interferrence to prevent the change—This
road when completed will be one of the most important works in the whole
country—The interest of the republican party, (or the white portion of it)
demand that it should come under the controle of the party—the commissioners on the part of W—Va all say, though republicans, that the interests
of the Road demand that no change in the Presdt & Directors shall be made
for the present—The question is then simply which interest shall be made
subservient to the other. Whichever way I decide I shall be abused—Can
you give me any suggestions, or preferable instructions indicating the best
& most acceptable course to pursue? ~~or are you willing~~ I am willing to
decide the question and take the abuse—but would prefer waiting to learn
your views upon the subject in as much as in all probabilities you will be
appealed to whichever way I may decide—No other questions of any very
great importance than the above are pressing for immediate action—"—
ALS, *ibid.* On Oct. 25, Bvt. Brig. Gen. Cyrus B. Comstock, Galena, wrote
to Stoneman. "Your two letters in reference to Railroads in Virginia have
been received and the first sent to Washington. In reply Gen'l Grant desires me to say that as a general rule he would suggest keeping things of
this character as nearly in statu quo as possible, thus avoiding military
interference with local affairs, until reconstruction having been completed,
the state shall act on these matters as it shall deem best. He would also
suggest that the action of the board of Public works should not be interfered with unless that action was evidently injurious to the interest of the
State. As to the question what persons it would be for the interests of the
stockholders and the State, to have for the Presidents of the two roads he
has not sufficient knowledge to judge. All other things being equal his personal preferences would be for Mahone & Wickham, as he believes them
to be loyal to the United States."—Copies, DLC-USG, V, 47, 60; DNA,
RG 108, Letters Sent.

1868, OCT. 3. Bvt. Brig. Gen. Orville E. Babcock, San Francisco, to
Bvt. Brig. Gen. Adam Badeau. "Your long good letter from Galena reached
me yesterday, or we reached it yesterday on our return from Oregon. Many

thanks for the letter and all the news, and also for the kindness to Mrs B. I am sure she will feel well enough acquainted to call on you if you can be of service. We are quite well. as we can talk over minor things in W. in Nov. I will jot down a few items. This state is alive for Grant & Colfax, and will carry it by 10000. Nevada is also sure.—There are a lot of old 'sore head officers' here who 'bark' a little but do not 'bite'—They are '*so sorry* the *Genl accepted*' &c. Old Halleck heads the list, and a number of juniors follow. Ord is sound as a brick. All the 'Money' & 'patriotism,' out here are, for Grant. I was talking with a sound republican yesterday, representing nearly 2000000, gold, about the election, and he said 'I was disgusted yesterday. I met Geo W Dent, in the Club, and went up to him and said', 'We shall carry this state for Grant,' when Dent said 'I do not know, I am not so certain', &c, in a queer way, this gentleman then said 'yes we shall and shall elect him President.' Dent said 'I hope to God he will not be elected' bringing his hand down on the table with great force. He says such things hurt them very much for it seems to Confirm the thousand lies about drunkenness &c. Gov Haight, says he was told by men that cannot be doubted that Grant is so drunk in W. that he is not himself, except when in the hands of his friends &c. He says 'you know I Cannot hardly believe it but I am assured so by reliable people'—He did not tell me this but said so to a democrat who did tell me.—I sent you; or the Genl, some scraps from a paper on Old Nesmiths. He denounces the Genl as a 'drunken democrat,' and the people in Oregon—say, 'well Nesmith has been an intimate friend and in W. and knows'—He is a black hearted scoundrel—Oregon looks against us, but if Penn & Ohio, help us as Maine & Vt did, we may get Oregon yet. Oregon is a refuge for old 'Pap Prices Army,' and of course they vote as they fought. The *Jews* on this coast are doing no harm, they live upon the public patronage so much that they must be on the *winning* side. This coast can be fully redeemed in the next four years if a right policy is followed. I am glad the Genl remained so long in Galena, and has had such a nice time. Remember me to them all very kindly, and thank them for their kindness to Mrs B. We sail on the 6th and shall be due in N. Y. on the 28th—We have two splendid boats. We have some *thousands* or less invitations, that we have to decline, on accont of previous ones. We will have some long talks 'after the election' if not before. I must go and take a breakfast, if I can get Porter up. It is now 7 oclock."—ALS, USG 3.

1868, OCT. 3. President Andrew Johnson endorsement. "The endorsements upon the accompanying papers show that, in compliance with the request of John D. Freeman, Chairman of the Democratic Executive Committee of the State of Mississippi, they have been forwarded by Brevet Major General Gillem, commanding the Fourth Military District, to the General of the Army and the President of the United States; and that, in the absence of Genl Grant, they have been simply transmitted to the Secretary of War, who has submitted them to the President. Retaining in this office a copy of the correspondence between Genl Gillem and Mr Freeman, the original papers are herewith returned (through the Secretary of War) to the General of the Army, who, by the terms of the so-called reconstruction acts, is so intimately connected with their execution, and to whom Mr Freeman first directly appeals."—ES, DNA, RG 108, Letters Received. Related papers are *ibid.*, with copies in DLC-Andrew Johnson.

1868, OCT. 5. W. Marsh, consul, Altona, Germany, to USG. "As success attends all the acts of your life we may hope to see it realized at the Coming Presidential Election. In view of that event, and because I shall have no opportunity of being near you in Washington to address you personally, I beg you to allow me to do so now by letter, as it is upon a subject which mainly refers to myself. Six years ago the late lamented President (to whom I had lived neighbor several years at Springfield) appointed me Consul of the United States of America at Altona, to succeed a sympathizer with the rebellion who held the post of Consul at Altona previous to the Senate's confirmation of myself. I have employed the six years of my residence here in compiling and publishing an Emigrant's Guide, in the German and Scandinavian languages, which has passed through four editions of 20,000 copies. The publication of the book did not clear itself as a Commercial undertaking, but it did so much good in promoting an increased flow of respectable Emigration from Germany, Sweden & Denmark that, I continued it up to last year, and then suffered it to lapse into the hands of foreign publishers without realizing a profit from it. The ministers and Consuls in the beforenamed countries, appointees of the old Republican regime, who knew the value of the book, and the good resulting from it within their several districts, signed a Memorial to Congress asking an appropriation to cover the past and further distribution of it. This for want of friends to support it failed, and I then sought to be rewarded for my labor in promoting emigration, and with a view of continuing those efforts here, to be appointed Consul of the United States at Hamburg. That Consulate was vacant at the time I applied for it, but upon my application being presented to Mr Johnson he immediately nominated a brother of his private Secretary as Consul for Hamburg, of the name of Mr William's. This officer is a supporter of the politics of his patron, and looks foreward to the election of the Democratic candidate for President next month, and I have heard him denounce members of the Republican party in very harsh terms. Now, although I really merit a better office than Altona which is not worth $1000 a year, it being a fee'd office, I do not wish you to understand that I am an applicant for the Hamburg Consulate, but I do hope you will nominate a successor to Mr Williams, and I am certain the Senate (several members of which know something of his present politics) will confirm your nominee. I have sent you by Post copies of my 1866 and 1867 issues which will give you some idea of the usefulness of the book as a Guide to German Emigrants coming into the United States. I have sent copies of it to several members of Congress, and U. S. Senators, and I had

a letter from Mr Senator Sumner on the 21st of May in which he remarks—
'I am aware of your services in the cause of Emigration and am convinced
that it is from such men as yourself that our officers should be chosen.'
And Mr Sumner is also aware that, it would be absolute folly to attempt
to improve upon the appointees of Mr Johnson until we have a thoroughly
proved Republican President at Washington. This we shall have in the
person of yourself, and while I hope you will not forget the subject of these
remarks I trust you will pardon the freedom of my suggestions . . . P. S.
Please to observe on the yellow cover of 'Guide Book' the remarks of the
German Press. It is a very unusual thing for the German's to speak favorably of a foreigner writing in their tongue."—ALS, USG 3.

1868, OCT. 6. Mary Duncan, New York City, to USG. "I have recently
returned from Europe—after an absence of more than two years, & if you
have entirely forgotten me, these lines may perhaps serve as a reminder of
one to whom *your* kindness is still a very present & dearly-valued remembrance. I know, Dear General, that your time must be fully occupied at
this season,—& that you have so many friends to wish you success—that
my far-off whisper of good-will will be of no great interest or importance.
Nevertheless—as one who has no favour's to seek,—no office to crave—& no
other text for a letter than true friendship & grateful memories—my inky
souvenir will have at least the merit of sincerity   May you be as successful
in the coming campaign as you have been in other combats. & if kind
wishes can ensure good luck—you will be in the 'White House' on 4th of
March.—It is true that all *our* pecuniary interests are in the South,—& I
have many dear relatives there who are now suffering from the present
dreadful condition of things 'below the Line.' & I am not at all an advocate
for the Republican party or radical rule!—but, I know & have experienced
your justice & kindness in my own sorrowful history,—& have perfect &
absolute confidence in the noble nature which *proved* its integrity & sense
of right at the call of distress. So I feel convinced, Dear General, that you
will *never* 'to *party* give up—what was meant for *mankind*' but will rather
be a second Father of the country—to see that justice is done to every
state,—irrespective of political differences.—You are too good & too brave
to be tempted to yield to party spirit, & in the knowledge that you will be
to our distracted land what you have been to me,—viz—a friend & benefactor—. . . If Col' Badeau be with you—pray give him my warm regards."—ALS, USG 3. On Nov. 2, Duncan wrote to USG. "On my return
from Europe some few weeks ago—I sent you a letter which—in stupid
haste I carelessly addressed to 'Major Genl Grant,—Care of War Dep'mt.
Washington,' & I am quite persuaded that said missive can never have
reached its destination. Consequently—I now write again—(on this day
before the election) to offer my best hopes & wishes for your success.—It
may be that my truant epistle has finally found its wandering way to your
hands. in which case—*these* lines will seem quite unnecessary. but—as it
is more than probable that my mis-directed envelope has found a last home

in the dead letter office—I must be pardoned for giving a second edition of my desires in your behalf.—We have never belonged to the *radical* party, for with so many friends & interests at the South—it is impossible for us to pray for a continuance of the dreadful state of things in that region but we have always—(despite our interests & hopes) belonged to the *Union* side. & of *that* body, Dear Gen'l,—I regard *you* as the Head Centre. In my darkest hour of suffering & distress—I appealed—to *your* protection. & shall never forget with what justice & generosity our claims were answered. so I know that you will be equally just & true to the whole nation. & I have always hoped & wished for your command of the country's fate. *My* quiet aspirations for your success will hardly be remembered by you in the chorus of acclamation which will soon greet your ear. but I want you to know & believe that I have been *always* mindful of your great kindness,— that I have ever hoped for your victory in all things, & that I am & shall be—what I have ever been— . . . My kind regards to Col' Badeau."—ALS, *ibid.*

1868, OCT. 8.   To Secretary of War John M. Schofield. "The proprietors of the Stone Quarry known as 'Junction City Quarry,' Kansas, has put in a bid for furnishing 'Head Stones' for 'Soldiers graves' in accordance with Act. of Congress requiring Head boards of Stone or iIron. As the durability of the materal used is a matter of first importance I would suggest that Gen. L. Easton, Chief Qr. Mr. in the Dept. of the Mo. be required to examine the quality of the stone in the above named quarry, and report as to its fitness for the purposes required."—ALS, DNA, RG 108, Letters Received. Related papers are *ibid.*

1868, OCT. 9.   John W. Forney, Lancaster, Pa., to USG. "I am just completing my canvass of my native county of Lancaster and before starting out to address the people of the Southern end of the county I think it my duty to give you my impressions of the result of the October election. I have now been at work incessantly since your nomination having subordinated every other thing to the cause—not only in attending to my editorial duties on the Phila[d]elphia Press and Washington Chronicle but have addressed large masses of our people, and I feel therefore authorized to speak with some confidence of the coming election. There is some difficulty in Philadelphia owing to the immense number of naturalization papers issued by the Supreme Court—hundreds of which are known to be fraudulent. Hon. John M. Read, in a letter addressed to the two Democratic Judges who have permitted this great wrong, and who are the minority of the court, speaking for himself and his two col[le]a[g]ues Judges Agnew and Williams—gives the opinion that the election officers should disregard all naturalization certificates issued from that court, because the Clerk when called upon to testify a few days ago could not certify to his own signature, and one of the Democratic Judges admitted that the seal itself could be forged without difficulty. This opinion of Justice Read has created great excitement and will be obediently followed by the Republican election officers. It may lead to some trouble in the city but as our friends are firm and united, and will do everything to preserve the peace I do not apprehend any collision. My own beliefs is that we shall carry the city by a handsome majority. I have never known a campaign in which so many Democrats have signified their intention to vote with the Republicans—not even in 1864, when Mr. Lincoln was the popular candidate of our party. I think we shall reelect Myers, Taylor, Covode and Cake—representing doubtful districts. Now for the State itself, I have put three questions to every intelligent Republican I have met. 1. Will you do better in your district than you did in 1866, when we carried the state for Geary by 17,185? Do you know any Republican who voted for Geary that intends to vote for Seymour? Do you know any persons who voted for Clymer in 1866 who intends to vote for Grant? To the first question the reply is uniformly in the affirmative, to the second uniformly in the negative, and to the third uniformly in the affirmative. Indeed the number of accessions as I have said that we receive from the other side is without parallel. I think therefore I will telegraph you on Tuesday evening from Philadelphia that we have carried the State by from fifteen to twenty thousand, and if this is so you may look for a majority for yourself in November equal to that given to Andrew Johnson in 1832—fifty thousand. This county, the great empire Republican county of the state after Alleghany, will give over six thousand next Tuesday, and at least seven thousand for you on the third of November. . . . P. S. I will finish my canvass on Saturday night in the neighboring county of York, and will be in Philadelphia at my post, and prepared for the great struggle on Sunday morning the 11th inst."—ALS, USG 3.

1868, OCT. 11.   J. Russell Jones, Indianapolis, to [USG]. "Bass & myself left home Thursday P. M. spent a part of Friday here, went on to Vincennes stayed at V until yesterday noon, came up to Terre Haute & spent yesterday afternoon there & got back here last night—Think we shall stay here (in the State) until the fight is over, though I had hoped to spend next Tuesday eve'g with you, but I can do no good there & may perhaps do some here. My reccollection is that our Committee is to meet in, NYork on Thursday and if I am to be there I shall have to start Tuesday evening. About all that can be said about this State is that our frends seem full of confidence & pluck. I believe we shall carry the State on Tuesday and yet I can give no reason for thinking so except that on general principles I believe the Lord is on our side. I have seen quite a number of our prominent men, Morton, Conner, Shanks, Wallace & others—I have never seen so much excitement nor so much bad blood in any canvass. Not a day passes without somebody being killed—Every body goes armed, and there is reason to fear trouble on election day. In one Ward here where about 1000 is the highest vote ever polled, 1800 are now registered. Some fellow fired into the procession here last night from an Alley & killed one man. At

Lebanon about 20 miles from here there was quite a serious riot yesterday & the report is that some were killed, the authorities sent here for 100 armed men. I mention these things to show the feeling. In a conversation with Rose (late Marshal) this morning he said he would not bet one cent on Bakers Election, though he had a feeling of hope that he would get through—Morton says we ought to have 15000, Shanks thinks his election is pretty certain & that we shall carry the State—Conner is very sanguine— If I remain here, will telegraph you if not will have eConner do so. I was told at Terre Haute yesterday that Frank Blair was as drunk as a fool all during his speach. The crowd at the meeting there reminded me of the Steamboat loads of 'Refujesus' I saw at Cairo, sent up from below—Free- mont is here, with his wife. Wadsworth spoke here last evening—Freemont speaks here to-morrow eve'g—There is danger of Veach's defeat. though Conner thinks he will get through—One at your distance can form no sort of an idea of the appliances being employed in a fight like this, and you need not wish to know of them—"—ALS, USG 3.

1868, OCT. 12.   Thomas P. Ochiltree, Galveston, Tex., to USG. "I am arrested for vindicating your name and smiting the man that did it   Get me off"—Telegram received (on Oct. 13, 9:00 A.M.), DNA, RG 107, Telegrams Collected (Bound).

1868, OCT. 13.   Bvt. Brig. Gen. Frederick T. Dent to [USG]. "The en- closed order was given to the associated press Yesterday evening from the White House—leaving off the part marked in the copy sent you—on reading it in the Intelligencer this morning I saw the trick and gave a copy of the order in full—and Penn Ohio & Indiana by this time know the trick and can appreciate its littleness"—ALS, USG 3. Dent enclosed a printed copy of General Orders No. 82, AGO, Oct. 10. "The following order has been received from the President, and by his direction is published to the army:— 'The following provisions from the Constitution and Laws of the United States, in relation to the election of a President and Vice-President of the United States, together with an act of Congress prohibiting all persons engaged in the military and naval service from interfering in any general or special election in any State, are published for the information and gov- ernment of all concerned:—' . . ."—*Ibid.* Dent marked the first eighteen words.

1868, OCT. 15.   Bvt. Maj. Gen. William H. Emory, Washington, D. C., to USG. "Altho it was only a few days since, I had occasion to write you a note on my own business, I cannot at the risk of being considered officious, resist the temptation of congratulating you on the result of the late elec- tions, which I think makes your election sure, and saves the country from another revolution, or an attempt at one, which would have cost us more blood and treasure than the rebellion just ended"—ALS, USG 3. On the same day, Emory wrote to Maj. Gen. Philip H. Sheridan. ". . . We have just recvd the election returns and tho I have not drank a drop for many days on accont of the gravel and always expected that result I am absolutely drunk with joy. It saves the country from a counter revolution, which I think would have been more bloody and disastrous than any thing recorded in history. Hookers retiremnt makes a vacancy in the Brigadier Generals Stoneman, Buchanan & Granger are the three persons most pressed upon the President and it is thought the 1st or 2d will be nominated, but it is certain that a word from you or Genl Grant would stop any nomination not made by Genl Grant. In this connection, I will take it as a great favour if you would write to Gnl Grant my claims on the subject. I have been in more battles than any Colonel in the Army not promoted, and I have never had but one reverse and that was on the 19th of October 64 and was amply recovered before night and was in no way my fawlt, and would never have happened had you been present The flight of the 8th Corps and the failure of Gnl Wright to transfer the 6th Corps to my left, let the enemy Directly on my rear. Even then I was *the first* to reform and offer resistance. From motives of friendship & consideration for two brave & excellent officers, above me on that day, I have said but little or nothing on the subject. I hope Forsyth is doing well . . ."—ALS, DNA, RG 94, Generals' Papers and Books, Sheridan. On Oct. 21, Maj. Gen. Oliver O. Howard wrote to USG. "(Strictly confidential) . . . I have just had a long conversation with General Emory and I find he fears that his excellent record during the war may be over-looked and that others who are favorable to the present administration may, get the start of him in claims for the vacant brigadiership— Gen. J. J. Reynolds expressed similar fears with regard to himself when I was in Texas—I know your own good judgment will be the best to rely on in that selection & I know none will be confirmed whom you do not approve—I write this at my own option, because I find the modesty of Gen. Emory not adequate to the presentation of his own claims—We have been made happy & sanguine by the election just past & firmly believe the country will do *better* in *November.* I hope you are well & strong prepared for all the burdens an appreciative people may bestow leaning hard upon the arm of the Almighty for all additional strength you may need. With kind regards to Mrs Grant & the children . . ."—ALS (press), Howard Papers, MeB. On Jan. 20, 1869, President Andrew Johnson nominated Bvt. Maj. Gen. Robert C. Buchanan as brig. gen. to replace Brig. Gen. Joseph Hooker; the Senate tabled the nomination.

On Dec. 29, 1870, Orville E. Babcock wrote to Governor Oden Bowie of Md. "The President directs me to acknowledge the receipt of your letter of Dec. 27, 1870 and to say in reply that Gen. Buchanan has all the time had the option to retire or go out with one years pay. It is the opinion of the War Department, sustained by the President that it is not as hard for Gen. Buchanan to retire as the law provides he can, as to place some other worthy officer on the unassigned list who cannot be retired under the provisions of

the act of Congress reducing the army and thus force him out with one
years pay. The President requests me to communicate his kind regards."—
Copy, DLC-USG, II, 1. Buchanan retired on Dec. 31.

1868, OCT. 15.   William E. Chandler, Union Republican National Committee, New York City, to USG. "The smoke of Tuesday's battles has
lifted, and the result, although the contest has been closer than we wished,
has settled the Presidential election. After all, the result is as favorable as
we had any right to expect. The whole strain of the contest which was to
decide who should control the patronage and wield the power of the national administration for four years was on Tuesday in Philadelphia, in a
few counties in Pennsylvania and in the lower counties of Indiana. With
immense advantages to gain by success at those points, and with everything
to lose if they failed to carry them, it is no wonder the Democracy waged
a terrible contest. It is very fortunate that we have succeeded so decidedly,
although not overwhelmingly. The rest of the fight is easy. Heretofore there
has been some holding back; there has been too little money given us,
although our true friends have been very liberal, and the country has not
sufficiently aroused itself to the importance of the fight   Now, as I predicted, we shall get plenty of money—(sometimes in twenty-thousand-
dollar lumps!)   The timid and doubting will rally and fall into the line, and
we shall sweep the country like a whirlwind. In New York everything looks
promising; the party is thoroughly united. We have meetings of our Committee, ~~our~~ the New-York State Committee and at Gov Morgan's house
to-night to arrange for a vigorous prosecution of the war. I hope and believe
that New York will give her 33 votes for our ticket, but nothing can make
that result absolutely certain. If the Democratic leaders determine to cast
eighty thousand copperhead majority in this city, they will cast it. If they
only get forty-five thousand majority, it will be because they are discouraged and disheartened, and fail to perpetrate the frauds which they have it
in their power to commit. New Jersey looks well, and our friends from that
State are here to-day getting ready for the fight;—while we are assured that
we shall carry Connecticut. It really looks as if we should let poor Seymour
carry only Maryland, Delaware and Kentucky, with perhaps Georgia and
Alabama thrown in, but I have hopes even of these latter two. The article
in the *World* this morning is significant. It ascribes their prospective defeat
to your popularity and to Frank Blair's position in favor of breaking down
by force the reconstructed governments. It says *audacity* will save them,
and calls for a *bold stroke*, but leaves it indefinite whether it means that
the party leaders should declare that they do not mean to break down the
Southern Governments by force, or that Seymour & Blair or both should
withdraw in favor of other candidates. It evidently means one of these
propositions. Its admissions are significant and will be taken by the Democratic press throughout the country as an admission of defeat. I congratulate you, General, upon your certain election as President. I know you will
be true to the principles of the Republican party and to the best interests of

the country. I also hope and believe that you will appreciate, at their true value the men whom we have called to aid us and who have so nobly fought with us during the doubtful battles that have just been won; and will place the correct value ~~of~~ upon eleventh-hour adventurers and shysters who would have put the knife to our hearts at any time within the last six months, but who are now rushing to our side with loud-mouthed professions of friendship and devotion. We want their votes to help carry New York, New Jersey and Connecticut, and of course must not repel them; but—thank God!—we do not need them to elect Grant & Colfax. If we *did*, we should not get them."—ALS, USG 3.

1868, OCT. 15.   C. H. Hopkins, Savannah, to USG. "Permit me to Congratulate you, on your election. This County (Chatham) will give you a large majority. and we hope to carry Georgia, for you if our people. are allowed to vote."—ALS, USG 3.

1868, OCT. 17.   Maj. Gen. George G. Meade, Atlanta, to Bvt. Maj. Gen. John A. Rawlins. "I transmit herewith several communications from the Governor of South Carolina & one from the Governor of North Carolina in relation to the use of troops in sustaining the Civil Governments in these States. Similar communications both verbal & written, have been presented by the Governors of Georgia, Alabama & Florida. The sum & substance of all these communications are—that the present State Governments in these States, are powerless, & without the support of the military forces of the United States, are unable to exercise their functions or execute the laws. . . . Recently I visited Columbia, South Carolina & had a very full interview with Gov'r Scott from that State.—From the representations of Governor Scott I became satisfied, there is practically *no Government* in South Carolina, that what with those officers who from want of sympathy with the State Government & its origin, refuse to act,—& those who though in full sympathy with the party in power *are afraid* to act—there is really no Government at all. . . . Whilst in Columbia I had interviews with several prominent men of the Democratic party, who acknowledged the whites in the State were arming, but disavowed any intention of resisting either the State or General Government, but said the arms were to defend their homes & families in case of a negro insurrection which they deemed imminent from the incendiary appeals made to the negroes by political & partisan agents.— It was impossible to form any correct judgment from the very opposite statements made by each party—. . . I do not myself believe there will be any open resistance to the State Government & most certainly none to the General Government, but I have no doubt that any effort will be & is being made within what is considered the strict letter of the law, to paralyze & render impotent the several State Governments, & that in States like South Carolina, where the intelligent & active population, the whites, are almost unanimous against the Government it will be impracticable to maintain the same without military aid from the General Government.—Should the Gen-

eral-in-Chief not have returned to Washington on receipt of this letter, I
beg the same may be laid before the Honorable Secretary of War"—LS,
DNA, RG 94, Letters Received, A375 1868. Printed in full in *SED,* 41-
2-13, pp. 82–84. The enclosure is *ibid.,* pp. 84–85.

1868, OCT. 18.   Eugene Clover, unassigned recruit, Fort Harker, Kan.,
to USG. "I have the honor to make application for my discharge. You may
be aware of my motive name and connections from a former letter. *I was
formerly a resident of Springfield Illinois.* I entered the service from perhaps Quixotic motives; they are cured. I am also a married man with two
children and I apprehend that where the question is not asked of the recruit
in relation to his being married or single at the Recruiting Rendezvous the
enlistment is illegal. I was enlisted on the 22nd day of June 1868 and am
now attached to a Detachment of Unassigned Recruits 7th Cavalry U. S. A.
In any event as I sincerely intend and struggle to do my duty if it were
possible I would respectfully request to be transferred to some infantry or
other regiment, colored troops not excepted. I have assumed with the presumption that belongs only to a recruit to address you thus directly, my
ignorance must be my excuse for the informality. I am as I wrote before
the son of the Rv Dr Clover formerly of Springfield Ills and the husband
of a lady of that place. Miss Lizzy Edwards."—ALS, DNA, RG 108, Letters Received. On Dec. 6, Capt. Frederick W. Benteen, Camp Supply, Indian Territory, endorsed this letter. "Respectfully returned. This applicant
fell while gallantly charging with his company in the battle of the Washita,
Ind Ter. Nov. 27—1868, and thus, has gotten his discharge—"—AES,
ibid.

1868, OCT. 19.   Bvt. Maj. Gen. Edward O. C. Ord, San Francisco, to
USG. "I have the honor to enclose herewith a copy of the report of a scout
made by a party under the command of Second Lieutenant R. Somerby
8th US Cavalry, to which your attention is respectfully invited. Such success and zeal as is shown by Lieut. Somerby is so rare, and there are so
many inefficient officers in Arizona, that I should like to have the really
worthy, rewarded in some way—to show that they are appreciated and
distinguished. Major Clendenin exhibits skill and ability in the management of his Sub-District."—LS, DNA, RG 108, Letters Received. Ord
enclosed a letter of Sept. 14 from Bvt. Maj. John H. Mahnken, Fort Whipple, Arizona Territory, to Bvt. Col. John P. Sherburne. "During the absence of the Sub-District Commander (Major D. R Clendenin,) at Camp
McDowell, A. T. I have the honor to state that, Lieut Somerby, Comn'd'g
Troop "B" 8th US Cavalry, left this Post, August 30th, in obedience to
instructions from Bvt Brig: Genl. Devin. (then commanding the Sub-District,) to establish a camp on the Lower Agua Frio, and to scout from there
the country (surrounding the settlements.) North East through the Black
Mountains to Postals Ranch, and to the South West to the Hassyampa. On
the 5th of September, Lieut Somerby, with 17. men of his company and a

guide, left his camp on the Lower Agua Frio, to scout the Tonto Plateau—on the 9th of September, came upon a band of Indians near the Tanks, between Turret Mountain and Governore Gap, and succeeded in killing two warriors and capturing four women and children. On the morning of the 10th again surprised a band of ten Indians—killing four warriors and captured three women and children—two of the former prisoners escaped from the guard during a dense fog; Lieut Somerby, with his command also captured a number of bows and arrows, and destroyed a large amount of provisions and camp equipage—and returned to camp on the Lower Agua Frio on the evening of the 10th. September 12th in the evening, three Indians came in sight of the camp evidently for the purpose of stealing stock or watching the movements of the Cavalry.—Lieut Somerby with eleven of his men and five citizens, succeeded in surrounding them and killing all three of them. This make a total of nine warriors killed and five women and children captives now at this Post."—Copy, *ibid.*

1868, OCT. 20. Bvt. Maj. Gen. Lovell H. Rousseau, New Orleans, to USG. "Information has been received of the assassination of Judge Valentine Chase and sheriff Henry Pope at Franklin St Mary Parish Louisiana on the 17th of October 1868, an investigation of the attended circumstances is being made by a staff officer, Report will be sent as soon as received, Troops were sent to Brashear last night to prevent threatened disturbances a telegram from the Comdg officer of detachment since received says all is quiet at Brashear"—Telegrams received (2—on Oct. 21, 9:00 A.M.), DNA, RG 107, Telegrams Collected (Bound); *ibid.*, RG 108, Telegrams Received; copies, *ibid.*, RG 94, Letters Received, 353L 1868; *ibid.*, Annual Reports 1868; *ibid.*, RG 393, Dept. of La., Letters Sent; DLC-USG, V, 55.

On Oct. 24, Rousseau telegraphed to USG. "A fire occurred at Gretna, opposite New Orleans, on the night of the 22d. About thirteen houses were burnt. It was alleged by whites, and denied by negroes, to be the work of colored incendiaries. Two, or three negroes charged with plundering, were killed yesterday morning near the fire. I ordered General Buchanan to send a proper force to assist the Police to prevent disturbances and allay excitement, which was effected. The troops are still there. I had him take possession of the ferries, to prevent armed men from crossing from New Orleans to Gretna which [was being done,] which were released when the necessity ended. Quiet is not yet entirely restored. I do not think the matter serious. My action in the premises was in accordance with the wishes of the civil authorities."—LS (telegram sent—bracketed material omitted), DNA, RG 107, Telegrams Collected (Bound); telegram received (at 8:30 P.M.), *ibid.*; *ibid.*, RG 108, Telegrams Received.

On Oct. 26, Rousseau telegraphed to USG. "A riot occurred in parish St Bernard last night. A negroe was killed by a democratic procession in the afternoon and at night the negroes assembled killed a white man named Pablo Fellio, and his son and burned his house and the dead bodies. Other negroes have since been killed. Troops were sent to the parish to quell disturbance and are still there. Three 3 steamers filled with armed men destined for this same place of disturbance were stopped by me. Several hundred citizens were at city hall at seven 7 P. M. this evening to offer their services as police to the Mayor of the city who declined. At the same time about one hundred and fifty 150 roughs, armed with muskets entered the central police station, near the city hall, taking possession. General Steadman, Harry Hays and others addressed the crowd which dispersed. After this one 1 white man was killed While a democratic procession was marching through the street. All quiet now—eleven forty 11-40 P. M."—Telegram received (on Oct. 27, 11:30 A.M.), *ibid.*, RG 107, Telegrams Collected (Bound); *ibid.*, RG 108, Telegrams Received; copies, *ibid.*, RG 107, Telegrams Collected (Bound); *ibid.*, Letters Received from Bureaus; *ibid.*, RG 393, Dept. of La., Letters Sent; DLC-USG, V, 55.

On Nov. 30, Rousseau telegraphed to USG. "The publication of what purports to be my report in the New York Herald was surreptitiously made and without my knowledge or consent"—Telegram received (at 1:30 P.M.), DNA, RG 94, Letters Received, 416L 1868; (3) *ibid.*, RG 107, Telegrams Collected (Bound); copy, *ibid.*, RG 393, Dept. of La., Letters Sent. See *HED*, 40-3-1, part 1, pp. xxxiv–xxxix, 302–9.

In Dec., 1868, C. D. Ludeke, chief clerk, Board of Metropolitan Police, New Orleans, wrote to USG. "I am directed by the Board of Metropolitan Police Commissioners of New Orleans La, to lay before you the following statement, They learn from the public prints that Maj. General Rousseau in making to the War Department his annual report, made statements which if not contradicted, are calculated to reflect prejudicially on this Board; Among other things they learn from the public prints. that 'Keeler represents that up to the date of General Steedman assuming Command of the police, that body was entirely worthless, being composed of Two Hundred and Forty Three negroes, and One Hundred and Thirty Whites; that no riots have occurred since the change of police, and no City is more quiet and orderly than New Orleans since the change.' If the statement here quoted emenated from General Rousseau or Major Keeler his Chief of Staff, and if true, only one conclusion could be drawn from it viz: that the riots murders and assassinations which occurred in this City during the month of October was entirely brought about by the City of New Orleans employing colored men as police officers, The fact is General Rousseau never took any steps to inform himself anything about the matter beyond casually asking one of the members of the Board how many white and colored men were on the police. He answered from memory out of the office, without any official date, and events occurring since show conclusively that the gentlemen was misunderstood as he himself has since stated over his own signature. The public newspaper denied on behalf of this Board the truth of the statement of Genl Rousseau, and yet General Rousseau never made any application to this Board for a statement of the facts. The following table copied from the records kept in this office, will show the number of white and colored policemen on duty in the several precincts on Monday October 26th 1868 when the riot and tumult was at its height. . . . It will be seen that the statement of so large a number of colored men being on the police force is not true, but that there were more than two white men for each colored man on duty. Even had the statement been true, would that, with a peacably disposed community have been sufficient reason for shooting down policemen because they were colored, on the streets? Would that have constituted a good reason for breaking into peacable citizens houses, beating, and illusing them, and destroying their furniture? Does the alleged fact of a few more or less of colored men on duty justify bands of armed men parading the streets of the City, and shooting down white and colored who they knew differed from them politically? Did not General Rousseau lend himself to the turbulent element against the constituted authorities, and urge upon them compliance to the demands of the mob, instead of telling them plainly that the laws must be enforced by the proper authorities. Now why all this tumult about a few colored policemen? It was not a new thing. More than a year before Mayor Heath put colored men on the police force, but the same men who instigated and encouraged the riot in October 1868 never dreamed of getting up a riot on that account in 1867 when General Sheridan was here, After a number of colored policemen had been shot down on the public streets, by assassins who laid in wait of them, and with no probability of the discovery of their murderers, the Board of Police Commissioners came to the conclusion to withdraw from duty the colored men until quiet was restored. Major Keeler is reported to have said that the police were entirely worthless when Genl Steedman took charge, and since the change no city is more quiet and orderly, Why was this? not that the police were worthless, but because the mob had by means of the terror produced by killing and wounding policemen and private citizens compelled the Board so to speak, to temporarily relieve from duty the colored men: they had also with the help of General Rousseau forced upon the Board one of their political leaders as Superintendent. What did he do with this worthless force? With the exception of one officer he retained the whole of them, the Board appointing seventy eight more white men. General Rousseau is reported to have said that with the troops at his Command he could not preserve order. The troops at his Command were at least four times the number of police, They were all armed officered and disciplined, with the additional advantage of Cavalry and Artillery Now if General Rousseau could not preserve order with this force, are the Board of Police Commissioners to be blamed for not doing so, with not one fourth the force of unarmed and undrilled men. In conclusion General they are satisfied that a careful examination of all the facts will show that this Board is in no manner to blame for the scenes of riot and murder that disgraced this City."—LS (tabular material omitted), DNA, RG 108, Letters Received.

1868, OCT. 20.   Charles F. Peck, Georgetown Heights, D. C., to Bvt. Maj. Gen. John A. Rawlins. "PRIVATE . . . The late elections have left some of the most desperate men on the face of the earth nothing to hope for, as they think, unless it be the assassination of Gen. Grant—There are two intervals of time in which his death might greatly influence political results—First—if he were killed one or two days before the election, many voters who do not fully comprehend our system of electors would stay away from the polls, and many more would be unwilling to assist in the election of an unknown candidate—Secondly, if he were killed after the vote had been declared by the Chairman of the Senate and before his inauguration, there is no clearly defined constitutional mode of providing a successor to Mr Johnson. It may be that the Vice President elect should be inaugurated, but the constitution does not say so—. . . In consideration of all these circumstances and many more which have doubtless occurred to you, we have no right to take any chances which human foresight can avoid. The desperate fools and madmen are not all dead yet, and I sincerely hope you will not treat this matter too lightly."—ALS, USG 3. On Oct. 19, Ebenezer Peck, Washington, D. C., wrote to Governor Richard Oglesby of Ill. on the same subject.—ALS, Oglesby Papers, IHi. On Oct. 23, George H. Harlow, secretary to Oglesby, wrote to USG transmitting a copy of this letter.—ALS (press), *ibid.*

1868, OCT. 22.   A. Alderson, Natchez, to USG. ". . . To be qualified for the command of a position like this, demands a high sense of justice, great moral courage, and an indomitable will and energy to execute the law. These, with a quick perception and clear judgment to detect and unmask the hypocritical professions of loyalty, are essential qualifications for a commander at this time at the South. Such were the qualifications of the gallant *Sheridan*, and had he remained in command at New Orleans, the thousand murdered victims that have fallen by the hands of violence, would be alive today, and be so many living pillars in support of a loyal government. And these are the qualities that strongly mark the character of General *Dudley*, the present commander at this Post. He cannot be won by smiles nor deterred by frowns; and he is alike indifferent to praise or censure when right and justice points out the way he should go. They can neither buy nor sell him by fine dinners nor by flattering speech and therefore they curse him and seek his removal. But to remove him at this time would be a dire calamity to the Union element of this district. It virtually would be a condemnation of the General's course, that has given, to some extent, peace and security to the loyal men, and an invitation to the lawless disturbers of the peace, to new scenes of blood, where outrage, violence and murder would mark their course. Fully endorsing General *Dudley* as a gentleman, and as an officer, eminently qualified to command at this post, I earnestly hope he will be permitted to remain with us, to carry out the work he has so nobly begun, to restore peace and order to the community, and force the vicious to respect and obey the laws. . . . The foregoing letter having been submitted to the '*Grant Union Republican Club*,' of Adams county, held at Union Hall, 'Rose Hill,' Natchez, Miss, Oct. 22d 1868, for

their approval, on motion it was unanimously *Resolved,* That said club, consisting of over three thousand (3,000) members, do fully endorse said letter and request that it be immediately forwarded to *General Grant. . . .*"
—Copy, DLC-Nathaniel P. Banks.

1868, OCT. 23. A. Grant, Washington, D. C., to USG. "I have the honor to notify you, that the *'Boys in Blue of the District of Colombia'*—a loyal organization embracing an Engineer and Pioneer Battalion; a Battey of Artillery; one Cavalry, and eight Infantry Regiments,—propose to turn out, and appropriately celebrate your expected return, as *President-elect,* to the *National Capital*: . . ."—LS, USG 3.

1868, OCT. 26. Julia Bounetheau, Aiken, S. C., to USG. "Encouraged by your former courtesy and prompt attention in the application made for the discharge of private Comment and for whose valuable services I am truly indebted, I venture to lay before you my losses sustained owing to the inconsiderateness of one of the officers of the 5th. Cavalry quartered at my residence, Aiken, S. C. I refer to Lieut. Brady, who without my knowledge or or consent, instead of traveling by Rail Road took my carriage traveled in it to Greenville S. C. then to Flat Rock N. C. returned in it after an absence of a month the vehicle a perfect wreck—leaving it in the court yard besmeared with clay and mud, leather curtains cut out and thrown away, dash board destroyed, wheels broken so that the carriage is of no further use. . . ."—ALS, DNA, RG 94, Letters Received, 1066S 1868. Additional papers are *ibid.*

1868, OCT. 27. David Avery, Hampton, Conn., to USG. "I beg leave to introduce myself by pr[ese]nting you a copy of my 'poem' on the origin & 'suppression of the late [reb]ellion'; & also my parphrase of Gen. Blair's letter accepting his nomin[a]tion;—the latt[er] of which I ~~read~~ rehearsed at a late Republican Flagraisin[g] in this town. And I also send for your amusement a few lines in reference to your correspondence with Andrew Johnson con[cer]ning Mr Stanto[n's] restoration ~~to the war department~~ as Secretary of ~~war~~ the War department. Permit me to add that I am the father of Dr Geo. W. Avery, whom you so generously sustained in the office of Sheriff of the Parish of Orleans, New Orleans, La. last November. My son served as Surgeon in our army for nearly five years during the war & for some time after ~~the war~~ its closc. After he was honorably discharged said service, he settled in N. O. where he practiced his profession up to the day of his appointment as Sheriff. He attended over 80 of the victims of the great masacre of 1866, & treated between 3 & 4 hundred cases of yellow fever in the great epidemic of 1867. If what I have now done & am doing shall contribute as much as *the poor widow's two mites* towards your election as President of the United States; I shall feel that I have simply acknowledged the deep debt of gratitude I owe for what you have done for my *only* son & also for what you have achieved for our common country. I am older than our National Constitution by ten days; & I hope & pray that my dim eyes may be permitted to see you our Chief Magistrate safely guiding the goodly old Ship of State from confusion & trouble to the peaceful & happy seas of quiet & prosperity."—Copy, Princeton Theological Seminary, Princeton, N. J.

1868, OCT. 27. Bernard H. Nadal, professor, Drew Theological Seminary, Madison, N. J., to USG. "Enclosed you will find an attempt of mine to bring to light the mysteries of a very difficult theme Perhaps you may take time to read, & see how you look through my most thoughtful spectacles. I have been doing what I could, as the political Editor of the New York Methodist, to defeat the enemies of the country & of its peace. May heaven bring you into power, & guide & support you when in."—ALS, USG 3. Nadal enclosed a warning concerning USG's possible assassination.— *Ibid.*

1868, OCT. 28. Mary V. Duncan, Little Rock, to USG. "General Please Read this . . . my object in writing to you is to see if you could order the discharge of my husband Who is my Whole Suport my husband elisted in the 28th U S Regt and was Sworn in in last May I have been married nearly three years and have a child to carry in my arms and my husbands wages will not Suport me and I can not work to earn me an honest living my husband was formerly a Soldier in the 17th Army Corps Served in the 30th Ills Regt three years and was honorably discharged he is from Illinois and So ~~was~~ am I I lived in Coles Co and was well Respected by all my Husbands name is William Duncan and is a Private in Co C 28 USs Infantry I can Refer you to the Honorable H P H Bromwell who is Probaly aquainted with my folks an my husbands to my name before I was maried was Olmsted if you can do any thing for me while I am in distress please do so and my Prayers will allways be for the humane and just Please write to me and let me know what you can do for me"—ALS, DNA, RG 108, Letters Received. On Nov. 22, Capt. Albert H. Andrews, 28th Inf., wrote to 1st Lt. Samuel M. Mills. "I have the honor to respectfully return the within papers concerning the application of Mrs Mary V. Duncan for the discharge of her husband Private William Duncan of Company "C" 28th U. S. Infantry. With the statement that Private Duncan was assigned to my Company as an unmarried man, That he immediately consulted me about marrying, and asked me if he did so, whether I would appoint his wife a Laundress in my Company. I informed him that if he would get a good and respectable woman for a wife, I would do so with pleasure, but that if he got a bad woman she would not be permitted to stay with him at all. They were married and I appointed Mrs Duncan to be a Laundress, but she proved to be a very quarrelsome unchaste and disreputable woman and was in consequence turned out of the Company and Garrison. She may be a hard working woman for aught I know, but she certainly did not try to get an honest living, when she had a good opportunity of doing so as a Laundress. The statement made by Mrs Duncan that she had no Father is untrue, as she has one, who lives on a farm—which I am informed he owns,—and which is situated some eight or ten miles out from this city. Private William Duncan is a sober dutiful and good soldier,—although a very harmless and completely subdued man who is terribly in fear of and greatly abused by his wife. He does not want to be discharged the service, and so far as the support of his wife and the child is concerned, I would respectfully submit it, as my opinion, from what I know of the facts in the case, that all parties are better off as they are now situated—than they have ever been before, or are ever likely to be again during their lives should Private Duncan be discharged."—ALS, *ibid.*

1868, OCT. 28.   J. Russell Jones, Chicago, to [USG]. "I think Chandler is 'playing on his watch' I have written him to know by what authority he says the Natl Committee protests against Genl Kilpatricks speaking in Mass. I have no doubt about Chandlers being a tool of Butlers, and he is very improperly using his position to aid him. If it were not so late in the Canvass I would 'go for him.' . . . I have arranged for an operator at Mr Washburnes house on Tuesday night."—ALS, USG 3. On Oct. 26, William E. Chandler, New York City, telegraphed to Elihu B. Washburne. "I have informed Genl. Kilpatrick that if he goes to Mass to speak it will be against the advice & Protest of the National Committe that Gen. Butler is the regular Nominee of the Party and that his actions and statements are placing Genl. Grant in a false Position which I dont believe he is willing to assume—"—Telegram received (at 12:30 P.M.), *ibid.* On Oct. 29, Chandler wrote to Bvt. Brig. Gen. Adam Badeau. "I am off for NewHampshire to-night. Mr Claflin will remain here till Monday. Our Committee has finished its work. The New Yorkers are working with great energy, and with good prospects of carrying the State. I have written Mr. Washburne instead of to the General and yourself since he went to Galena; but I am reminded that he has been off speaking, and you may not have seen his letters. My worst annoyance during the campaign has been Kilpatrick; who has wanted to plunder everybody, and now must needs break his engagements in these States and go into Butler's District in order, if possible, to mix Gen Grant in the fight. I have written Mr. Washburne fully on this point. I trust I have not been mistaken in my judgment; at all events I have acted conscientiously and have tried to keep Gen. Grant from being embroiled in a District quarrel in such a way as to give Butler an excuse hereafter In return, Kilpatrick shows he is no gentleman and a low blackguard; he is notoriously an immoral man. All accounts agree that Butler will be elected A discriminating friend—who is no friend of Butler—writing from Massachusetts, well says that Hawley's & Kilpatrick's and much of the other opposition to Butler is flunkeyism towards Grant, hoping thereby to compel Gen. Grant to adopt and sustain them. That kind of business I will not engage in, and, if employed in serving a man, will do what I think is for his best interests, even if I run a risk that he will not exactly appreciate it

I have written Gen Grant a brief note to-day. I should really be gratified, considering my annoyances, to see a short note from him to lay away as a memento of the campaign. I shall be at Concord, N. H. till about a week after the campaign is closed, then shall go to Washington With high hopes of the election and much regard for you personally . . . P. S. Mrs Holmes has retracted her ridiculous charge against me, as per copy enclosed. I also send you copy of Kilpatrick's letter."—ALS, *ibid.* The enclosures are *ibid.*

1868, OCT. 28.   S. D. Kirk, Charleston, S. C., to USG. "I have read carefully your Speache, as sent me by Hon. Mr. Broomall, M. C. and as a citizen *born*, and *bred*, in *South-Carolina*, (and a lover of our union) I cannot for the life of me come to any other conclusion than to vote, and use my influence (what little I have) for *you* as *President* of the *United-States*. I shall hail with joy the 3d Nov. and feel gladdened the approach of the 4th march. Your noble sentiment, 'I shall have no policy to interpose against the will of the people,' is certainly strong evidence, of one of the golden rules of an upright and virtuous life, As one of the people, I shall feel bound by every insentive of a true republican, to give your ticke my undivided support. May I ask the liberty of a line from you, that I may hold it as a *keep sake*, and hand over to my children after me, as a treasured souvenir of the great past."—ALS, USG 3.

1868, OCT. 30.   William Frew, Pittsburgh, to USG. "As the Banner Republican County of the Nation, facetiously styled by Pres Lincoln the 'state' of Allegheny we expect you to do us the honor of a visit on your return to Washington—Permit me therefore to tender you the hospitalities of my residence 'Beechwood' in the 22d Ward. My claim is that I am the only man in this Congressional District who will vote for you, notwithstanding your great popularity! That this statement may not induce you to resign I will state that I represent my District in the Electoral College and my fellow citizens have delegated me to help cast the vote of Penna for yourself any my Friend Colfax. Further I claim a little relationship, very distant to be sure but yet worth speaking of. My Aunt Mrs Nancy Miller is I believe Cousin to Mrs Grant. However this may be, it will afford me much pleasure to entertain you and your Family during your stay in our loyal, Republican city. With much respect and congratulating you in advance over your next Great Victory on 3d prox . . ."—ALS, USG 3.

1868, OCT. 31.   Anonymous, Memphis, to USG. "Please pardon my presumption, but two ladies from New York, who board at the same house with me, say that you & I are very much alike, personally. The difference, however, between us is this—I was a poor, unfortunate rebel, who done his best for his cause, but finally had to knock under at Greensborough to Genl Sherman—while you in the matter of 'our little rebellion' came off with flying colors & have made yourself a second Napoleon. Under the circumstances, therefore, I don't know exactly whether the remark of the ladies is complimentary to you or me. But anyhow, Genl, you are a clever man or you would not have acted so nobly with Genl Lee & his boys. This alone stamps you a brave man for the brave are ever magnanimous to a fallen foe. Well, Genl, I am one of the disfranchised & can not vote for you or any body else or I would vote for Seymour—not on account of any dislike to you, but because you are the *Radical* candidate. But I believe you are going to be elected & I believe you will make us a very good President too & give every man his just rights, for you are not one to be turned & twisted about by any body. Genl, if this thing should happen couldn't you find it agreeable in the kindness of your heart to give a 'poor devil of a rebel' down here a bit of an office to keep body & soul together? True, I fought you my best while I was at it, but when 'old Joe' said lay down your arms at Greensborough I succumbed & ever since I have been as loyal as any body; but how I do hate these Tennessee Radicals. 'On consideration', Genl, I don't believe I want any office if it is all the same to you. I am poor its true, but I 'aint' proud much since you whipped us so & I lost every thing nearly I had. Please don't take offense at this . . ."—AL, USG 3.

1868, Nov. 3. Thomas P. Robb, Savannah, to USG. "At opening of the Polls this morning a collision occured between the Whites and Blacks— Police interfered *Killing* and *wounding* several *blacks*. Colored voters thereupon in a body left the polls, and refuse to attempt to vote. You will lose by this *over two thousand votes in Savannah*. I fear similar occurrences elsewhere, and thereby you will lose the State" "*Personal* . . . I prepared the dispatch hereto annexed, intending to telegraph it to you this morning, but since its preperation, I have learned that we Republicans in Savannah, sofar as this day is concerned, are in [the] *Enemys Country*, and that the dispatch if attempted to be sent, would probably never reach you, and for attempting to send it, *my life* would be endangered. This may seem almost incredible General, but it is true. I have the evidence of my senses. I will give you a very brief but correct history of the trouble. The Colored people, as is their custom, were first at the polls, and commenced voting. A body of men from the R. R. some two hundred—rebels to a man, marched up and instead of waiting their turn to vote, endavoured to push and drive the Colored men away. They endeavoured to retain their position. The police, another body of rebels, every one of them, commenced firing into the crowd of blacks. They were *unarmed* and believing, that it was part of a preconcerted plan to keep them from voting, retired from the polls in a body. Two colored men, and one white man were killed, and several dangerously wounded. They organized a meeting in an other part of the city, and after canvassing the matter, resolved to entirely absent themselves from the polls. At first I counselled them to act otherwise, but am now satisfied they acted properly, as I am further satisfied from what I have since seen and heard, that more blood would have been shed, if they had made further attempt to vote. The Rebels or Democrats, if you choose, had determined beforehand, to have the field to themselves. I advised the colored people to retire peaceably, and

quietly to their homes, which they did, adjourning their meeting after giving
three times three for Grant & Colfax. I fear that the scenes enacted in
Savannah today will be repeated in many portions of the South, and that no
fair expression of the peoples will, will be had here. We await with anxiety
news from the loyal North, to determine by *your election* that as American
Citizens we have rights in Georgia, or by by the election of Seymore & Blair,
that loyal men must leave their homes behind them and emigrate to a more
hospitable clime. May God defend the right: . . . P. S. While writing, word
is brought me that another man has been shot in coldblood, showing that the
colored men were right in absenting themselves from the polls. It is impossible to learn all the casualties at this time of writing—*4 o'clock P. M.*"—
Telegram received (at 8:00 A.M.), and ALS, USG 3. See *PUSG,* 5, 399.
On April 20, 1869, USG nominated Robb as collector of customs, Savannah.

On April 8, Cyrus Newlin, former maj., 7th Pa. Cav., Washington,
D. C., had written to USG. "In compliance with your request I have the
honor to submit the following statements of facts. Henry G. Cole now an
applicant for the Collectorship of the Port of Savannah. Geo. was in close
confinement as a civil prisoner at Atlanta, Macon and Charleston—for several months. He disbursed during that time at least twenty thousand dollars
($20000) among the Federal Officers confined there. He was a man of con-
siderable political influence and standing before the war, a wig elector in
the conventions which nominated Taylor and Scott, and I beleive his appointment to the post he seeks would be a merited recognition of valuable services
and rare charities in the cause of the Union—At least a hundred perhaps a
larger number of Federal officers owed to his generosity a material allevia-
tion of their sufferings—"—ALS, DNA, RG 56, Collector of Customs Applications. On April 14, Henry G. Cole, Marietta, Ga., had written to USG.
"I was in Washington last week, and would been glad to have paid my
respects to you, And asked of you in person, what I now will trouble you
with in writing I made application through the Treasury Department, for
the appointment of Collector of Customs at the Port of Savannah Ga, But
I wish to apply to you direct for this appointment, I have never befor asked
for an office, I was urged four years ago, by my friends to apply for this
position that I could get it, But I refused to take any appointment in the
gift of President Johnson And I felt too, that I had a higher and holyier
duty to perform And that was, To see to it, that all of the brave and good
men, who had sacrificed themselves on the alter of their country's good,
And whose bones were bleaching on the soil of Georgia, should have a decent burial, That duty has been preformed, And from the room which I
now write I look out upon the green Sod and delightful grove that spreads
itself over the remains of More than ten thousand Patriotic men that gave
their lives, that their Country might live—I do not wish to weary you, But
I feel that if I am qualified for the office which I ask, no one is more entitled
than myself, The present incumbent James Johnson Esqr, I have known
for thirty years our personal relations have alwase been good, He embraced
Secession, I did not—At the commencement of the war Johnson was poor—

held his own very well through the war, Since that time he has held office under the Government, and being a very good lawier he has advocated the claims of those who pretended to have been loosers some of whome have recieved large amounts, R L Mott of Columbus Ga has recived I understand $120,000, others a less amount, I understand Mr Johnson is now rich, At the begining of the war I was worth, exclusive of Negro property $120-000, Now I am not worth more than ¼ of that amount if that, My property has been destroyed mostly (not by the Union army) by the intolerant & visious rebels, My health has been greately impaire by long imprisonment, My Children are young yet to be educated, The office I ask would help me at this time My capasity to discharge the duties, My enemies who know me will not deny, I have left letter with Sect Boutwell that I think will satisfy you on this subject Hoping you will give my application due consideration . . ."—ALS, *ibid.*

On April 27, Governor Rufus B. Bullock of Ga., Albany, N. Y., telegraphed to Horace Porter. "I deem it of importance to the interest of the Administration and to the party that Colonel B. Robb should continue as Postmaster and Governor Johnson as Collector of the Port at Savannah No change should be made for the present at least and I therefore hope that Robbs commission as Collector will not be issued for a month or two 2 Please reply by telegraph"—Telegram received (at 7:00 P.M.), *ibid.*, RG 107, Telegrams Collected (Bound). On April 28, 1:45 P.M., Porter telegraphed to Bullock. "Robb's commission had been issued before your despatch arrived."—Copy, DLC-USG, II, 5.

1868, Nov. 6.   Lt. Gen. William T. Sherman, St. Louis, to USG. "Don Miguel Aldama of Havana, telegraphs me from NewYork, that he is going to Washington, and asks of me letters to my friends there. When we were on that Mexican Mission, you remember we spent a week in the Harbor of Havanna. All the Authorities and People were very kind to us, but none more so than Mr Aldama. He entertained us at his place in the City, and at his own expense took Alden, myself, and our officers, out to his Magnificent estate of Santa Rosa. Thence he carried us in carriages to several of the best sugar estates of the Island of Cuba. He manifested the most enthusiastic admiration of the actors in our Civil War, among them especially yourself, and I know that he will want to see you and talk with you. I beg you for my sake to see him and show him such marks of respect as are convenient, for I assure you he is every way worthy, and for anything you may do for him I will gladly reciprocate. Whatever is to be the destiny of Cuba, in the present Revolution that now prevails in Spain, or in whatever new relations may result to that Island in which we are so much interested, Mr Aldama must have great weight and influence, as he is a representative of the more wealthy class of native Creoles."—ALS, USG 3.

1868, Nov. 9.   To Secretary of War John M. Schofield. "I have the honor to inform you that the estimated sum required for expenses of the Commanding General's Office for the fiscal year ending June 30th 1870, is Five Thousand dollars ($5000.)"—Copies, DLC-USG, V, 47, 60; DNA, RG 108, Letters Sent.

1868, Nov. 9.   Secretary of War John M. Schofield endorsement. "Respectfully referred to the General of the Army."—AES, DNA, RG 108, Letters Received. Written on a copy of a telegram of Nov. 7 from Bvt. Maj. Gen. Joseph J. Reynolds, Austin, Tex., to Schofield. "Telegrams of yesterday announce my removal. The President has been imposed upon. Every act of mine has been demanded by the law and absolutely necessary to save life or property. I can prove this by the records and by men of all parties. General, I am no partisan and feel that I have a right to be heard in defence of my reputation and the supremacy of law."—Copy (marked as received on Nov. 8), *ibid.*

1868, Nov. 9.   "In the Ring" to USG. "My duty to my Country constrains me to inform you that there is a conspiracy against your life—A solemn covenent has been entered into by men accustomed to accomplish what they undertake—I would give their names, but from the nature of their position you cannot avoid meeting them or being thrown in their company and it is best for you not to manifest suspicion—I will however say—One of the men has a home in New York City and the other in California—Are well known, and would not be supposed capable of such intentions—They hope by secret means or the hands of others to accomplish the work, but by the terms of the oath will risk their own lives—This is positive.—I know whereof I affirm It is true, Alas too true—Reveal this, *not even to your wife,* Its publicity would be *fatal* to me and perhaps for you by the forming of a new combination DESTROY THIS PAPER IMMEDIATELY—I know not what more to say—"—AL, DLC-Horace Porter.

1868, Nov. 10.   USG endorsement. "Respectfully forwarded to Secretary of War, approved."—ES, DNA, RG 107, Letters Received from Bureaus. Written on a letter of Nov. 7 from Franklin J. Moses, Sumter, S. C., to Bvt. Maj. Gen. Edward R. S. Canby. "I had the honor of being elected by the Legislature, Chief Justice of the State. Before I can qualify, my disabilities must be removed by Congress. . . . It has been suggested to me, that a letter or certificate from you, in regard to my course, would be of service in my application, and I would be obliged to you for such a paper. . . ."—ALS, *ibid.* On Nov. 9, Canby endorsed this letter. "Respectfully submitted to the General of the Army. The writer was one of the Judges of the Court of Common Pleas and General Sessions of the State of South Carolina, and has lately been elected by the Legislature Chief Justice of the Supreme Court of that State under the new Constitution. Judge Moses was one of the first to accept the conditions of the Acts of Reconstruction and to act under them and soon after they went into operation he united with Judges Glover and Aldrich of the same court in making some practical suggestions in relation to the Jury system established by General Orders No. 32 of May 30th, 1867. The last named gentleman subsequently changed his course but the two former continued to act consistently. The election by the Legislature to the highest Judicial office of the State is regarded as a conclusive expression of the wishes of the people of South Carolina but it is proper that I should add that Judge Moses' course, official and personal, was of material aid to me as Commander of the District."—ES, *ibid.*

1868, Nov. 10.   USG note. "Upon a renewed verbal application to me on behalf of Horace L. Dunlap, late Captain 62d Regt. U. S. Colored Infantry, I respectfully recommend that the mitigated sentence of dismissal against him be revoked, and that he be honorably discharged of the date of his dismissal. This recommendation is based on the acknowledged gallantry of Capt—Dunlap, and that of other members of his family in the War, one of whom, his brother, lost an arm in service."—NS, DNA, RG 153, MM 1669. Upon charges including drunkenness on duty, Capt. Horace L. Dunlap, 62nd Colored, was cashiered as of Feb. 23, 1865, by General Orders No. 12, Dept. of the Gulf.

1868, Nov. 11.   Joseph J. Bartlett, U.S. minister, Stockholm, to USG. "Since the Election news has been received here by telegraph. I have been reminded of my interview in which I paid my parting respects to you before coming out on my mission. I then stated that the people would demand your Election, and that before the close of my diplomatic service I would be under your administration. I am very happy to be able to remind you of the fulfilment of my prediction, and of my earnest hopes for your success throughout the contest which has been so happily closed. The Government, diplomatic corps, and all the substantial people here, feel greater security in our affairs since your Election, and I am constantly congratulated upon the result. I add my own congratulations with the warmest assurances of friendship, and am happy to be once more under the command of my former chief. I have asked Mr Seward to send you a copy of my Despatch, No 24, of the 7th inst, relating to the Ancient Military System of Sweden, which is maintained to this date with but few modifications. If there should be anything more fully explanatory required I shall be happy to give it by return mail."— ALS, USG 3. On June 3, 1869, USG suspended Bartlett from his post.

On March 6, Alpheus B. Stickney had written to USG. "Genl. C. C. Andrews the late Republican candidate for Congress in the Second District of Minnesota who was defeated by a bolting faction headed by Ignatius Donnelly, is a gentlemen of integrity, ability and culture—a true Republican and a faithful soldier in the late war. Verry many Republicans of our District feel that his services entitle him to some recognition by your administration and that he is peculiarly adapted to do himself and the country credit in a respectable foreign appointment and should he be an applicant for such a position we take great pleasure in recommending him to your favorable consideration"—ALS, DNA, RG 59, Letters of Application and

Recommendation. Related papers are *ibid.* On April 6, Elihu B. Washburne, Galena, telegraphed to USG. "Hope you will send in General Andrews to Copenhagen whose nomination you directed me to make out"—Telegram received (at 6:30 P.M.), *ibid.*, RG 107, Telegrams Collected (Bound). On April 13, USG nominated Christopher C. Andrews as minister to Denmark; on Dec. 6, USG nominated Andrews as minister to Sweden. See letter to Mary Grant Cramer, March 31, 1869; Christopher C. Andrews, *Recollections: 1829–1922* (Cleveland, 1928), pp. 209–10.

On April 12, USG had nominated John S. Carlile as minister to Sweden; the Senate did not confirm this nomination. On March 10, Carlile, Clarksburg, West Va., had written to USG. "I respectfully ask the nomination and appointment of Minister to Brazil. My public record is part of the history of our country. I accompany this note with the letters of Senator Boreman and Representative McGrew of my state"—ALS, DNA, RG 59, Letters of Application and Recommendation. The enclosures and related papers, some protesting Carlile's nomination as minister to Sweden, are *ibid.* On April 26, Carlile telegraphed to USG. "I have mailed with a request to the Wheeling Intelligencer that it publish following correction but I have little hope of their doing it, The Intelligencer of this date in an article devoted to Governor Boreman and myself, is mistaken in its statements which refer to my past course, one or two of which I trust it will permit me to correct in its columns, In 1861 Mr Carlile het up to the work by his associates in this city who kept him supplied with both money and courage, and these assertions I deny and call for proof, also that I went over to Vallandigham, I also deny that I betrayed the people who elected me on the contrary I advocated our admission under the Constitution as we had adopted it I never met in conclave with Vallandigham, Equally false is the statement that I took the stump against the further prosecution of the war, The statement that I ever openly or secretly advised young men not to volunteer is also untrue directly the reverse was my whole action from the beginning to the end of rebellion: I never charged the state central Committee one cent for making speeches but obtained from the National Committee three thousand dollars, two of which was rec'd by the state Committee, one I disbursed, adding to it a portion of my own funds, The foregoing specimens show the animus of the Intelligencer as also its accuracy, It is the first and the last notice I shall take of it."—Telegram received (at 7:00 P.M.), *ibid.*, RG 107, Telegrams Collected (Bound).

On May 1, U.S. Representative James A. Garfield of Ohio, Hiram, wrote to USG. "I respectfully commend to your favorable consideration Hon A. W. Campbell of Wheeling WestVa, as every way worthy the appointment of Minister to Sweden. Mr. C. was a faithful and powerful defender of Republicanism and the union Cause before and during the dark days of the rebellion, in WestVa, and few men in that state have served the Country or the party so long and so well—The Wheeling Intelligencer of which he has long been the Editor, bears witness to his services I hope he may receive the appointment referred to—"—ALS, *ibid.*, RG 59, Letters of Application and Recommendation. Related papers are *ibid.* On May 14, Benjamin F. Wade, Jefferson, Ohio, telegraphed to USG supporting Archibald W. Campbell for minister to Sweden.—Telegram received (at 3:30 P.M.), *ibid.*, RG 107, Telegrams Collected (Bound).

1868, Nov. 17. Speech. "Gentlemen of the Bar of New-York: I thank you very kindly for the manner in which you have received this last toast which was intended to be complimentary to myself. I will say that there is no other community that I would receive such a demonstration of welcome from with any more gratitude than from the citizens I meet here this evening."—*New York Tribune,* Nov. 18, 1868; variant text in *New York Times,* Nov. 18, 1868. USG spoke at a New York Bar Association dinner for Attorney Gen. William M. Evarts. On Nov. 16, "General Badeau, of General Grant's staff, stated to-day, in answer to question as to whether General Grant intended to be present at Mr. Evarts,' that it would depend on whether Secretaries McCulloch and Wells or Postmaster General Randall would be among the guests; as the President elect did not desire to meet either of these gentlemen."—*Washington Star,* Nov. 16, 1868. See Howard K. Beale, ed., *Diary of Gideon Welles* (New York, 1960), III, 464–68, 512–13.

On Nov. 10 and 13, Henry E. Davies, New York City, had written to Bvt. Brig. Gen. Adam Badeau. "By this mail there goes an invitation to General Grant from the Bar of Newyork to attend the Dinner to Mr. Evarts the Attorney General on Tuesday Nov. 17. . . ." "Will you please say to the General that the Committee of Invitation of the Newyork Bar will Call upon him today at 2 oclock, if it will be agreeable to him. . . ."—ALS, USG 3. On Nov. 12, Thursday, Edwards Pierrepont, New York City, telegraphed to USG. "I hope that General Grant and staff will dine ~~with~~ at my house on Monday evening next at six oclock"—Telegram received (at 2:10 P.M.), DNA, RG 107, Telegrams Collected (Bound). On Nov. 16, Secretary of War John M. Schofield telegraphed to USG, Metropolitan Hotel, New York City. "I am going to New York tonight, and will call to see you in the morning. I am not quite sure as to the matter about which I wrote you"— ALS (telegram sent), *ibid.*, Telegrams Collected (Unbound); telegram sent, *ibid.*, Telegrams Collected (Bound). See Sherman Evarts, ed., *Arguments and Speeches of William Maxwell Evarts* (New York, 1919), III, 247–58; Chester Leonard Barrows, *William M. Evarts: Lawyer, Diplomat, Statesman* (Chapel Hill, 1941), pp. 165–66.

1868, Nov. 17. U.S. Senator Benjamin F. Wade of Ohio, Jefferson, to USG. "Permit me to ask a favor at your hands on behalf of my friend the Hon. B. Randall—He informs me that his son Brev. Major. G. M. Randall is now stationed at Fort Fetterman, Dacota Territory—He exhibits to me the statement of Doctor Treat, and he fully confirms that statement; and says that he confidently believes that the life of his daughter in law depends upon her husband remaining at home, during the present emergency. She goes into convulsions at the bare mention of his leaving The reason for asking so long an extension, is owing to the difficulty and danger of passing through the Indian Territory between Cheyenne and Fort Fetterman, during the winter season—The father has been many years a friend of mine and I confidently endorse any statement made by him, as entitled to full credit. And I ask as a personal favor that his Request may be granted, if not inconsistent with the Exigences of the service—"—ALS, DNA, RG 94, Letters Received, 495R 1868. Related papers are *ibid.*

1868, Nov. 20. Joshua Hill, Madison, Ga., to USG. "I have been informed that an effort is making to procure the presence of a company, or companies of colored troops, at the Municipal election in Augusta in this State—on the 2d proximo—I hope it will not succeed. Troops under a discreet and gentlemanly officer, may be of service, but they should be white— The election involves much personal feeling—as well as political—Firm, but prudent republicans prefer a company of white troops—as I am well informed. I think—they are right. That will insure a quiet election, if anything will."—ALS, DNA, RG 94, Letters Received, 1054S 1868.

1868, Nov. 21. To Bvt. Lt. Col. George K. Leet from Perryville, Md. "Please send my carriage to Depot at four fifty (4.50) today"—Telegram received (at 3:00 P.M.), DNA, RG 107, Telegrams Collected (Bound).

1868, Nov. 23. To Vice Admiral David D. Porter. "I will be at home tomorrow. Come directly to my house."—ALS (telegram sent), DNA, RG 107, Telegrams Collected (Bound). On the same day, Porter, Annapolis, had telegraphed to USG. "Will you be at your office tomorrow?"—Telegram received (at 1:00 P.M.), *ibid.* On Oct. 29, Porter had written to Bvt. Brig. Gen. Adam Badeau. "The note I wrote General Rawlins was in relation to General Grant. after that infamous attack on Negro passengers in Baltimore. I did not know what those scoundrels would not do, and I propose that General Grant and family should come from Havre de Grace by steamer to save annoyance—I see that the authorities in Baltimore promise to have a state police force kept on hand at all times, but I believe that the *father of lies* dwells in Baltimore, and the Plug uglys there know no law.—I am sorry to inform you that Ben Butler stands a good chance of election. the people in his district prefer to be represented by a *blackguard.*—I shall keep a steamer in readiness in case the General wishes to take advantage of her.— with kind wishes and regards to General and Mrs Grant . . ."—ALS, USG 3. On Nov. 11, Porter wrote to USG. "I suppose everybody is congratulating you on the result of the late election—now I will vary it and congratulate the *country* on the result of the vote, for I feel quite satisfied that it is going to bring us peace and prosperity. I cannot conscientiously, congratulate you, on having to give up so much, for I consider your position the best of any man's in the world. and you can scarcely be compensated for it by being made President. You will be subject to great annoyances but I know you are equal to the occasion and I don't believe your equanimity will be in the least disturbed. Mrs. Porter joins with me in kind wishes to Mrs. Grant and yourself . . ."—LS, *ibid*. On Nov. 12, Porter wrote to USG. "I would have been to see you when in Wn but I was not very well and after being with my Doctor two hours was not able to go up town again—. I have been quite under the weather for some time, tho no one gives me credit for being sick— I am quite amused at your want of influence with Uncle Gideon.   he has been trying to get on your side of the fence ever since the election, and has faint hopes that he may yet be retained—he has been so long in office that he thinks the Navy Dept belongs to him—they tell a story about him that when last sick, and expecting to die, he made a will and *left the Navy* to *Mrs Welles*, knowing that she could carry it on as well as he could. I think I can have the matter arranged without your appearing in it. I am glad you think of employing Ammen   he will make a good man in one of the Bureaus, particularly in the Bureau of equipment. I think there will be no trouble in getting Ammen ordered home tho Mr Welles is so vindictive that he would delight to disappoint you, especially if he thought Ammen would be called on to help clean up the Augean stable—. I will be up in a few days and will call and see you—you know where to find a a quiet retreat in case you are beset by office hunters, and that is here, where we are always glad to see you.   with kind regards to Mrs Grant . . ."—ALS, *ibid*.

1868, Nov. 24.   To Charles C. Fulton, publisher, *Baltimore American.* "I shall be unable to be in Baltimore tonight."—Telegram sent, DNA, RG 107, Telegrams Collected (Bound).

1868, Nov. 25.   To Bvt. Maj. Gen. George H. Stoneman asking him to appoint Samuel D. Williamson to some office in Lynchburg, such as Clerk of the Court.—Parke-Bernet Galleries, 1962. On Nov. 27, Williamson, Washington, D. C., wrote to USG. "By way of explanation I take leave to say, that a vacancy having occurred in the 15th Judicial district of Virginia —I became an applicant for the position and upon enquiry at Head Quarters, learned from General Stoneman himself that the Govenor's nomination was *necessary*, in order to procure an appointment from himself. He made the same statement to Majr Smith, who presented the name of a Mr Leftwich of Wytheville for the position. Majr Smith afterwards withdrew his friend's name in my favor, my nomination was made by the Governor, upon the Recommendations of Judge Underwood—Judge Rives, Judge Bond U. S. Attorney Chandler Dr Sharp & last by Chief Justice Chase who accompanied by Judge Bond went to him in person and said to him that 'had he the appointing power in this case he would appoint Mr Williamson'— General Stoneman after a delay of about a month, and in disregard of his declaration to Majr Smith & myself that the Govenors nomination was indispesable to secure an appointment, conferred without such *nomination* and upon *one*, not known as a union man, the office of Judge of the 15th Judical District of Virginia General, you will excuse me for adding, that since my nomination by the Govenor to a Judgeship, that,—which was *defamation* through the Press, from the date, of my election over a noted rebel officer to the constitutional convention,—has been converted into *persecution* by the courts, and during my absence, waiting for an interview with you here, by a recent decision of the Court I have been stript of every thing I possessed, and my wife and children turned out of her home by officers disqualified by the 14 Amendmt General, *proper investigation* before loyal men, will show, that this defamation of the Press, and this persecution of the courts,—both circuit, & Hustings of Lynchburg—is simply, and only, on the ground of my political sentiments, and my adherence to, and advocacy of the cause of the Union and I *invite* such investigation But my family, General are as lambs among these wolves, and I have not the means to extricate them, for they have stripped me during my absence of all—and my wife writes, come not back,—for many threats have gone out 'against your life'—"—ALS, DNA, RG 108, Letters Received. On Nov. 28, Bvt. Brig. Gen. Orville E. Babcock wrote to Stoneman. "General Grant directs me to inform you of a conversation I had today with the Secretary of War concerning the merits of Mr. Sam'l. D. Williamson. The Secretary thinks Mr. Williamson thoroughly loyal and a very worthy man, deserving the full protection of the military authority; that Mr. W. has been persecuted on account of his loyalty, and that had he, (the Secretary,) not afforded him protection through the military authority the rebels would have driven him from the State. He believes Mr. Williamson a fit person for an appointment as county clerk, and that he should be appointed county clerk in one of the richest counties in Virginia, and that he intended to give Mr. Williamson some such appointment. General Grant requests you to appoint Mr. Williamson to such a county clerkship in the place of one now occupied by a rebel."—LS, *ibid.*, RG 393, 1st Military District, Letters Received. On Nov. 30, Stoneman wrote to Babcock. "I have the honor to acknowledge the receipt of a letter from the General and also yours of the 28th instant, in reference to the appointment of Mr. Samuel D. Williamson, and to State that he has this day been appointed to the office of Clerk of the County Court of Campbell county, Virginia, vice William A. Clement, removed. In this connection I have the honor to enclose herewith a report from Brevet Major-General O. B. Willcox, to which I will thank you to call the attention of the General, as it may serve to explain why Mr. Williamson was not appointed to the responsible position of Circuit Judge. He has never been an applicant, nor are any recommendations on file in his favor for any other office or position. Please return the report of General Willcox for file in this office."—ADf, *ibid.*; LS, *ibid.*, RG 108, Letters Received.

1868, Nov. 28. Orvil L. Grant, Chicago, to USG. "Have you received my three letters particularly the first"—Telegram received (at 12:45 P.M.), DNA, RG 107, Telegrams Collected (Bound).

1868, Nov. 28.   Bvt. Brig. Gen. Cyrus B. Comstock to Bvt. Brig. Gen.
John C. Kelton. "I return herewith the list of names whose rejection for
brevets by the Senate, brings up the question of renomination. Opposite the
names you will find General Grant's recommendation, in each case, as to the
renomination written."—Copies, DLC-USG, V, 47, 60; DNA, RG 108,
Letters Sent. On Nov. 27, Kelton had written to Comstock. "This statement,
I think, explains itself. Shall the rejected be renominated? The Secy desires
the General will designate those he wishes renominated. Callaghan & Dudley, I suppose, there can be no doubt about as their rejection was evidently
under misapprehension."—ALS, *ibid.*, Letters Received. The enclosed list
indicated favorable recommendations for Capt. George W. Graham, 10th
Cav. (to maj.); Maj. Robert Macfeely, commissary (to brig. gen.); 1st Lt.
James B. Burbank, 3rd Art. (to capt.); Capt. Henry A. Du Pont, 5th Art.
(to col.); Surgeon Charles McCormick (to col.); Capt. William J. L. Nicodemus, 12th Inf. (to lt. col.); Capt. Leander S. Callaghan, 19th N. Y. Cav.
(to maj. and lt. col.); and Lt. Col. William W. Dudley, 19th Ind. (to brig.
gen.). The list included unfavorable recommendations for 1st Lt. Gustav
A. Hesselberger, 3rd Inf.; Capt. John C. Conner, 41st Inf.; 1st Lt. William
H. Clapp, 11th Inf.; Lt. Col. Charles F. Ruff; 1st Lt. Thomas Barker, 23rd
Inf.; Col. De Lancey Floyd-Jones, 6th Inf.; Capt. A. H. G. Richardson,
114th Pa.; and Maj. George F. Morgan, 155th Pa.—D, *ibid.*

1868, Nov. 30, 2:30 P.M.   Bvt. Brig. Gen. Adam Badeau to USG "Care
of Gen D. H. Rucker U S Quartermaster Philadelphia." "Mayor Bowen says
there will be no trouble"—Telegrams sent (2), DNA, RG 107, Telegrams
Collected (Bound).

1868, [Nov.].   To Eli A. Collins. "I have just been elected president of the
United States. There is but one office that I have thus far pledged myself to
bestow upon any man and that is the secretaryship of state to the Hon. E. B.
Washburne. You may name the man for the second office."—*Chicago Chronicle,* Dec. 8, 1902. This letter appeared in an interview with John H. Alden,
St. Paul, formerly of Galena, who explained that "Immediately after the
election of 1868 President Elect Grant wrote to Mr. Collins. I have handled
and read that letter, and as near as I recollect it was worded like this: . . ."—
Ibid. No additional evidence substantiates this letter or its implausible offer.

1868, DEC. 7.   USG, New York City, endorsement. "Respectfully forwarded to the Sec. of War with the recommendation that the two persons
named be allowed to purchase from commissaries at the proper price."—ES,
DNA, RG 192, Orders Received. Written on a letter of the same day from
Julia A. Graham, New York City, to USG. "The Ladies Missionary Association, organized to aid in sending the gospel to New-Mexico and Arizona
take the liberty of asking that you will kindly help them in their christian
efforts by obtaining from the proper Authority, permission, for two mis-
sionaries (who are to be sent to Arizona and to the Navajoe Indians—) to

purchase subsistence stores for their own use, from the military Posts near their stations on the same terms and conditions as Officers of the Army."— ALS, *ibid.*

1868, DEC. 7.   James H. Hardwick, Brooklyn, to USG. "Having seen a report from the Washington Express, (which I enclose,) relating to the Stay Law of Virginia I take the liberty to submit the following statement For many years previous to the late war I lived in Portsmouth Va where I was employed by the Government in the U S Navy Yard: and where I bought a small homestead borrowing a part of the necessary funds from a banking institution for which I gave mortgage on the property. I had just recieved the appointment of Master Caulker when the Rebellion commenced and on the evacuation of the Navy Yard I was constrained to leave my home with the Authorities (Naval) having been an opposer of secession I did not consider it safe to remain. I left everything (of property) behind and my family soon joined me here in a destitute condition. After ~~wel~~ I had left my house was despoiled of its furniture and rented, out on behalf of the Confederate Government: all the time they held possession of Portsmouth and in fact throughout the war my property was of no use to me, but at the conclusion of the war I paid all interest that had accrued on the note and have since curtailed the principal as fast as the support of a large family would admit. I have looked with satisfaction since I have left, ~~my~~ to the home which I mean to secure for my coming days, and if the Stay law is rescinded it will be sold at a sacrifice as I am unable to meet ~~meet~~ the demand which would be made, to me this would be peculiarly hard for I have tried to obtain redress for spoilation of my property through the courts of Virginia and though awarded a compensation by the jury the verdict was set aside by the Judge and reduced to a great extent and even then I have been unable to obtain the redress I have met other wrongs in Virginia in my affairs that could not have occured had I been a Rebel or sympathizer— I think General that rescinding the Stay law without proviso or exception would be a calamity to me and those like me that were Refugees from the South. I have been in the Employ of the Government since I have been here I have been considered worthy of confidence by my superiors they having appointed me Foreman in my department (Caulkers) and can bring evidence of the truth of the above"—ALS, DNA, RG 107, Letters Received from Bureaus. Related papers are *ibid.*

1868, DEC. 8.   John Bidwell, Chico, Calif., to USG. "For the position of U. S. Marshal, I recommend and endorse Maj. Wm G. Morris. He is eminently qualified and deserving—has ever been true to the country—true to the party—and true to you."—ALS, NNP. See *PUSG*, 16, 395–96.

1868, DEC. 8.   Mary Lincoln, Frankfurt-am-Main, to USG. "Permit me to present to your distinguished notice, Dr Bogen, formerly chaplain in our Army, and one of the most loyal Germans in America. He can explain the necessity, that attention should be paid to *the letter*, I troubld you with, a few days since. With my knowledge of your great nobleness of nature & your great affection for my deeply lamented husband, I feel, such a reminder, is not necessary. Under any circumstances, your ear would be ever ready to the cry of the widow, but to the loved wife, of the man, who regarded you, with such high favor, and with limited means & ill health upon her—It requires no assurance, but that you will use your powerful influence & succeed in having Congress, give me at least a pension of $3.000 a year— so that I may be enabled to obey the commands, of my physicians. Earnestly hoping, that in the midst of your duties, *this* petition, will be immediately remembered, as with my feeble health—time is precious, . . ."—ALS, USG 3. Frederick W. Bogen served as chaplain, 41st N. Y.

On March 16, 1869, USG signed a letter to Secretary of State Hamilton Fish. "The President directs ~~me to request~~ you to appoint J. & W. Seligman & Co. of New York the Disbursing Agents of the Government, as far as transmission of funds to Foreign Countries, is concerned in place of the First National Bank of New York."—LS, DLC-Hamilton Fish. On March 24, 1870, Joseph Seligman wrote to USG. "Enclosed letter of Mrs Lincoln was transmitted to me by my brother residing in Frankfurt, with the request to intercede with your Excellency in her behalf. My brother states that Mrs Lincolns means are apparently exhausted and that she lives quite secluded. If Your Excelency can consistently recommend to Congress to alleviate the pressing wants of the widow of the great and good Lincoln I have no doubt but what the bill now pending would pass to the satisfaction of the party and of all good citizens."—ALS, University of Oklahoma, Norman, Okla.

1868, DEC. 8.   Henry A. Smythe, New York City, to USG. "An old friend said the other day—*'before you were so great a man—you were very near to me*—& thus I say *to you*—my dear friend—(not that I was ever 'great'—but all things in this world go by comparison—) You were—and always will be *'near to me'*—for I have ever had a friendship for you—before I had the pleasure of your acquantn, or you were even *'a General'* My object in writing—is not to *bore* you—but to assure you I do not intend to do so at anytime—& while I have voted for you—& supported you—I neither *ask* or *expect* anything—should I hold any office when you assume the office to which you have been elected—my resignation will at once be placed before you—for in the first place, I have held office about as long as I wish to do so—& in the next—I never wish to run the risk of *being turned out*. My family being in Europe—& for other reasons—I would like an appointment abroad—from the present administration—& *especially* do I covet a confirmation from the Senate—Should I succeed in that—or still hold my present position—I shall expect to give either up—to those who are supposed to have 'stronger claims'—if I am abroad—of course I would like to retain the place for a short time under you—but never to the exclusion of anyone you wished to appoint—& rest assured my dear General—wherever I am—that either my 'portfolio' or my best services—shall be at your command. I would have been glad of a few words with you this evening—but being watched by jealous eyes—I have avoided intruding upon you at all times—& hope that noone—*yourself above all others*—will attribute to me, the least selfish motives—for they do not exist. With my kindest regards & best wishes for you & yours— . . ."—ALS, USG 3. See *PUSG*, 17, 386.

1868, DEC. 11.   USG endorsement. "Respectfully returned to the Secy of War with information that Gov. Bullock substantially submitted the same papers which were returned to him with the following endorsement 'Respectfully returned to Gov. Bullock as requested, attention being invited to Genl Meads endorsement thereon, and with the information that no additional or special instructions other than those referred to have been given to Genl Meade. The matter of the condition of Germany [*Georgia*] is now before Congress.' "—Copy, DLC-USG, V, 44. On Nov. 17, Governor Rufus Bullock of Ga. wrote a letter endorsed on Dec. 1 by Maj. Gen. George G. Meade. "There is nothing new in this com'n of His Ex. Governor Bullock, and that officer has been advised that if he is powerless to correct these evils—I am equally so under existing laws & orders of the War Dept. My letter of Oct 23 in relation to Warren Co. was sent for the purpose of obtaining explicit instructions. The fact is the civil authorities made no attempt to enforce criminal law, if they did and were met with resistance I would then intervene, but so long as no action is had on their part, and they permit themselves to be overawed, I do not see how I can intervene, unless instructed so to do. Besides to preserve order in this way the civil authorities seem to desire, and require me virtually to take charge of the five states under my command, and necessitate at much larger force than is now in the War Dept."—Copy, DNA, RG 108, Letters Received.

1868, DEC. 12.   To Secretary of War John M. Schofield. "About one year ago I recommended Capt. J. L. Graham, a wounded volunteer officer, for position in the Invalid Corps. If vacancy now exists I would respectfully renew my recommendation."—ALS, DNA, RG 94, ACP, 142 1872. On Dec. 2, 1867, Mayor Daniel Macauley of Indianapolis, former col., 11th Ind., wrote to USG. "If there are still vacancies of 2nd. Lieut. in the army for which it is desirable to obtain good and tried men I most respectfully call attention to the claims and qualifications of John L. Graham now I believe in service as Captain in 21st Regt. V. R. C. Having known him personally during the war I most warmly commend him as a gentleman, well qualified, honorable, and of such character and standing as will add to the efficiency and reputation of the Army if appointed. Being from another state than myself, a letter of recommendation may seem unusual but my knowledge of the man and interest in the welfare of the service prompt me to respectfully recommend the matter to your favorable consideration."— ALS, *ibid.* On Dec. 20, USG endorsed this letter. "~~File~~ f   Call special attention to this case for first vacancy occuring in Invalid Corps."—AES, *ibid.*

On Oct. 13, 1866, Jesse Root Grant, Covington, Ky., had written to USG. "Lieut John L. Graham V. R. C. at present Superintendent of Freedmen's Bureau at this place, desires to receive an appointment in one of the four new Regiments of Veteran Reserve Corps, authorized by a recent Act of Congress. On the 16th day of last August Lieut. Graham forwarded to the Secretary of War through the regular channels an application for such an appointment. It is believed that his application together with the accompanying papers have, through mistake, been mislaid, and it is a matter of interest and importance to him, as well as for the good of the service, that his application be taken up, examined and reported upon at the earliest practicable day. . . ."—LS, *ibid.* On Sept. 25, 1872, Jesse Grant wrote to USG. "Your attention is respectfully invited to the case of Second Lieut. John L Graham 13th U. S Inf'ty, who I have learned has been ordered before a General Court Martial convened in the city of Louisville by an Order of the War Dept. for trial—His trial has taken place and it is presumed that the records in the case including the findings of the Court have been forwarded to the Secretary of War for his action—It is confidently believed that the charges preferred against Lieut. Graham have not been sustained. It is most earnestly requested that you at the earliest practicable moment direct the Secretary to defer the issuing of any Order in his case, whether the finding of the Court be favorable or otherwise, till the record in the case of Major Ben. P. Runkle who is undergoing trial by the Same Court be also forwarded, as that record, it is believed, will contain important evidence very favorable to Graham, and which was not in the possession of and not known ~~to him~~ to him at the time of his trial— . . ."—LS, *ibid.*

1868, DEC. 13.   Bvt. Brig. Gen. Adam Badeau to Secretary of State William H. Seward. "In the absence of General Grant I have the honor to acknowledge the receipt of your communication of the 12th inst. addressed to him, with the cigar holders you have been so good as to transmit together with the copy of despatch No 234, dated Novr 27th, from the U. S. Consul at Dublin. I have the honor to present to you the thanks of General Grant for this act of courtesy."—ALS, Seward Papers, NRU.

1868, DEC. 15.   Jacob Ammen, Lockland Station, Ohio, to USG. "It gives me pleasure to recommend to your favorable consideration John P. Biehn Esq. of Georgetown, Brown County, Ohio, for the position of Consul to some German state—Mr. Biehn is a gentleman of intelligence and integrity, a Lawyer by profession a good German scholar, and would, in my opinion, discharge the duties with credit to himself, and advantage to the country—" —ALS, DNA, RG 59, Letters of Application and Recommendation. Carr B. White and five other citizens of Georgetown signed an undated petition for the appointment of John P. Biehn.—DS, *ibid.* On May 16, 1869, J. H. Marshall, Georgetown, wrote to USG. "Dear Cousin: Mr. Biehn has just called upon me and informs me that he will start to Washington to-morrow It gives me pleasure to say that I have been personally acquainted with Mr.

Biehn for Sixteen years and have universally found him to be a gentleman of strict integrity of good business habits a fair German and English Scholar and by profession a Lawyer. In short he is a plain unassuming practical common sense man. And speaking the English and German languages well and with the fair ability possessed by Mr. Biehn you could not make a much better selection of a gentleman for a german consulate—which he desires. Hoping that you may favorably consider Mr Biehn's application as well as Col. Loudons . . ."—ALS, *ibid.* Marshall was the son of Jesse Root Grant's sister Margaret. See *PUSG*, 15, 329; *USGA Newsletter*, VIII, 2 (Jan., 1971), 11.

1868, DEC. 21.   USG endorsement. "Respy. forwarded. to the Hon Geo. S. Boutwell, Chairman Committee on Reconstruction. It is recommended in view of this personal application that the disabilities be removed"—Copy, DNA, RG 108, Register of Letters Received. Written on a letter of Dec. 11 from Joseph Wheeler, New Orleans. "Application for pardon & removal of political disabilities—encloses letter of Genl McAlester recommendatory."—*Ibid.*

1868, DEC. 22.   USG endorsement. "If the object of this Association is to embrace now Soldiers of the Union Army, who fought in the late rebellion, I favor the recommendation of its President and other Officers."—Copies, DNA, RG 46, War Dept. Reports; *ibid.*, RG 107, Applications, Alex. M. Kenaday. Written on a letter concerning a soldiers' home on the Pacific Coast. See *ibid.*, RG 94, Letters Received, 72W 1869; *SED*, 41-2-34.

1868, DEC. 23.   To Secretary of War John M. Schofield. "I have the honor to recommend the transfer of 2d Lieut. Loyall Farragut, USA., from the 21st Infantry to the 3d Artillery."—LS, DNA, RG 94, Letters Received, 227M 1869.

    On March 21, 1869, 2nd Lt. Loyall Farragut applied to Secretary of War John A. Rawlins for transfer from the 21st Inf. to the 5th Art.—ALS, *ibid.*, ACP, 4027 1871. On April 12, Orville E. Babcock wrote to Rawlins. "Young Farraguts' case was not acted upon by the Senate. The President says he wants it sent in again. Will you do the *old Admiral* the kindness to speak to Senator Wilson, if you see him, and ask him to have it confirmed?"—ALS, *ibid.* On April 5 and 13, USG nominated Farragut for transfer.

1868, DEC. 23.   Robert T. Lincoln, Chicago, to USG. "I take pleasure in recommending to your favorable attention for Naval officer at Philadelphia, Dr Edward Wallace. Dr Wallace held the position under my father and was removed by the present Administration on account of his failure to fall in with its principles—His appointment would be very gratifying to a large number of sound Republicans in Pennsylvania and to myself both personally and politically"—ALS, DNA, RG 56, Naval Officer Appointments. Dr.

Edward Wallace of Reading, Pa., who was not reappointed, was the brother of Dr. William S. Wallace of Springfield, Ill., brother-in-law of Abraham Lincoln. Numerous other recommendations addressed to USG recommending Dr. Edward Wallace are *ibid.*

1868, DEC. 24.   To Henry C. Bispham. "During my absence, attending the Soldiers' Reunion in Chicago, the beautiful oil painting of the celebrated horse 'Dexter,' executed and presented by you, was received at my house. Please accept my thanks for a present which I prize very highly. I have seen the horse frequently, and think the likeness perfect."—*Washington Chronicle*, Dec. 31, 1868. Born in 1841, Bispham was best known for paintings of animals and landscapes.

1868, DEC. 26.   Anna Ella Carroll, Austin, Tex., to USG. "It is evidently the intention of some of the leading men in this Convention to prevent the formation of a Constitution of government so that the probabilities are that nothing will be done until after your inauguration. This intention of course is not avowed but there is no mistaking the fact that such is the wish of the Provisional government. . . . I believe it was unfortunate that Congress did not last session pass the bill authorizing the in laws the division of the State as it would have obviated all objection on the part of the as to the authority of the Convention, at the same time would have obviated the chief difficulty with the friends of the measure, which arises on the defining of boundaries on account of so many local competing interests. After diligent inquiry and a thorough investigation of this, whole subject, I am convinced that a division of Texas now would do more to to restore the people to their proper relations with the goverment of the U. S. than all other measures combined that Congress could possibly devise"—ADfS (17 pages), Carroll Papers, Maryland Historical Society, Baltimore, Md. On Dec. 28, Carroll wrote an eighteen page letter to USG.—Copy, *ibid.* The second letter may represent a revision of the first.

On April 19, 1869, Carroll wrote to USG. "*Personal* . . . Believing you place me in that class who have more earnestly and longest been devoted to your personal fortunes, I have refrained from being one to add to your annoyance at the present time—and I have naturally been more diffident on acct of the nature of the appeal, I feel you will pardon & appreciate. Will you my dear Mr President bestow on Hon Lemuel D Evans of Texas a first class position *abroad*—should you determine to change any one of the appointments you have made or any you propose to make. . . ."—ALS, DNA, RG 59, Letters of Application and Recommendation. Related letters from Carroll are *ibid.* On Dec. 14, 1874, USG nominated Lemuel D. Evans as marshal, Eastern District, Tex.

On May 15, 1869, Horace Porter wrote to Carroll. "I am directed by the President to acknowledge the receipt of the two volumes entitled 'Star of the West.', and 'Romanism.', and to convey to you his thanks for the same."—LS, Maryland Historical Society.

On June 26, Porter wrote to John L. Thomas, Jr., collector of customs, Baltimore. "I am directed by the President to say that Miss Carroll of Baltimore has been to see him a number of times to intercede for her father who was removed from the office of Pension Agent at Baltimore, but without effecting his restoration; she now says that her brother has been removed from his position in the Custom House. The President requests that you will examine into the case of the brother, and if it will not embarrass you in the organization of your office to endeavor to provide for him in some way."—Copy, DLC-USG, II, 1, 4. Carroll's father was Thomas King Carroll. See *PUSG*, 17, 391–94.

1868, DEC. 28. Bvt. Brig. Gen. Adam Badeau to Anson Burlingame, Chinese envoy. "Gen Grant directs me to write to you and say that Dr. Wm Martin Professor of International Law in the Imperial College of China has ~~applied to~~ enquired of him ~~to secure~~ whether Brvt Maj Gen Emory Upton an Officer of the American Army ~~who~~ would be a suitable person to instruct the Chinese Army in our tactics. Gen Grant has recommended ~~Brevet Major~~ General ~~Emory~~ Upton, very warmly and highly, and desires me to write to you on the matter. Gen Upton is the author of the System of tactics now in use in our army; he is a young man, not more than thirty years old, made a distinguished reputation for ability and energy during the late war; and Gen Grant though he would willingly recommend other young officers of equal merit and distinction would give higher recommendations to none than to him, and sees a peculiar fitness in him for this peculiar position. He also is favorably impressed with the plan in itself, and trusts that you may find equal advantages apparent to yourself with those which he perceives, both for China and America. I avail myself of this opportunity to say how closely your countrymen have watched your career in England, and how much admiration has been extorted by the sagacity and skill with which you have met and overcome peculiar obstacles."—ADfS, DLC-Adam Badeau.

1868, DEC. 28. Bvt. Maj. Gen. Montgomery C. Meigs to USG. "I have written to Mrs Montgomery notifying her of your wishes & saying that I presume she will under the circumstances decline the permanent position for which the appointment by the Secretary of War has lately been transmitted to her."—ALS, DNA, RG 92, Private Letters Sent (Press).

1868, DEC. 30. USG endorsement. "Respectfully returned to the Secretary of War. The resignation of Captain Mimmack having been accepted and his place filled by the promotion of the officer next in rank, it is my opinion that there is no place to which he can be reinstated. Before issuing the order here directed, I therefore respectly request the opinion of the Attorney General on this point."—ES, DNA, RG 94, ACP, M479 CB 1868. Written on a letter of Dec. 3 from Bernard P. Mimmack, Washington, D. C., to President Andrew Johnson requesting revocation of his acceptance of Mimmack's resignation as capt. and bvt. maj.—ALS, *ibid.* Johnson revoked the resignation, and the attorney gen. ruled on that action; on Feb. 15, 1869, USG again endorsed Mimmack's letter. "The order being, in my opinion, illegal, and being sustained in this view by the Atty. Gen. I decline to permit my name to be used in promulgating it. See Article of War No 9"—AES, *ibid.* On Feb. 11, 1869, and Feb. 18, 1873, Mimmack wrote to USG concerning this matter.—ALS, *ibid.*

1868, DEC. 30.   USG endorsement. "Respectfully returned to the Secretary of War, disapproved."—ES, DNA, RG 94, 681 ACP 1874. Written on documents recommending Lt. Col. Henry D. Wallen, 14th Inf., for promotion to bvt. maj. gen.—*Ibid.*

On Oct. 13, 1869, Secretary of War William T. Sherman wrote to Brig. Gen. Irvin McDowell. "The President wants General Wallen to be put on duty in NewYork so as to give him the allowance of fuel and quarters. You may assign him to duty for General Court Martial service, and this is your warrant. I prefer not to make this the subject of a General Order as others will apply for similar favors."—Copies, *ibid.*, RG 107, Letters Sent; *ibid.*, Letters Received.

On March 17, 1873, Wallen, New York City, wrote to USG. "I presented your letter to Mr Murphy, and he has promised to take favorable action upon it if the city charter passes. It is important that I remain here for a short time to await the current of events, and as I am not able to accept a leave of absence I have asked for *temporary* duty here, and trust that you will approve my application. If Mr Murphy can do nothing for me I must sell my property in the city and adjust my affairs to the best advantage—as I am pecuniarily embarrassed—this will take sixty or ninety days."—ALS, *ibid.*, RG 94, 681 ACP 1874.

1869, JAN. 5.   Speech. "I thank you for this manifestation of your sentiments. I do not know of anything more that I can say, than that I am glad to have had the support of all classes, and particularly of those who are finding employment under the Government. I hope there will be nothing in my course hereafter to make you regret the present you have seen fit to give."—*New York Times*, Jan. 6, 1869. USG received members of the Printers' Grant and Colfax Club who called at Hd. Qrs. to present him with a congratulatory letter. Charles E. Lathrop, foreman, Government Printing Office, also spoke.

1869, JAN. 7.   USG endorsement. "Respectfully forwarded to the Secretary of War."—ES, DNA, RG 107, Letters Received, B-1825 (131). Written on a letter of Dec. 13, 1868, from John Fisher, Vicksburg, to USG. "Here in I respectfully beg leave to report to you Some facts that I feel interested in   In applying to you as the last resort for justice if there be any due to me in your judgement of Said facts which I State   I live about

(20) miles from Vicksburg and was conscripted in to the Rebel army at
Port Hudson which Service I left in a few months and went in to Vicksburg
as soon as the surrender of that Place to the Fedral forces and there I renewed my allegiance to the Fedral Government by taking the recquisite
Oath of myown accord   While I was waiting in the Provo Martials office I
was aske whence I came my buisness &c and if I had any Cotton   I stated
that I had some cotton   After takeing the Oath of allegiance and my pass
obtained I went to labor in a quartermasters warehouse,   But I was so beset
about the cotton by the Provo Martial *Lieut Col* L. D. Waddell that by his
promises and with aid directed by him that I was influinced to go and get
(91) Bales of the Cotton and was assisted by a force of U. S. Cavalry troops
directed by the Said Provo Martial L. D. Waddell and I carried the cotton
in to Vicksburg with assurances that it was and should be my Property and
that I Shuld have the benefit of the Same and that by the assistance of Mr
W waddell could take it to New Orleans and there have the cotton sold and
get the money for the Same and hold it as of full wright for myself as my
Property   Mr Waddell loned me money to pay for labor in handling the
cotton which I paid back to him in his office Room   He allowed the Cavalry
force that he caused to assist and Protect me in mooving this cotton to keep
(28) Bales as Pay for their aid, the remaining (63) Bales I did go to New
Orleans with and by the advice of Provo Martial L. D. Waddell I went in
company with his chief of police a Mr T. B. Moorehous who was to be my
guard against the Military as to my right to the Said cotton,   Mr Waddell
sent Mr Moorehous with me on this Spcial buisness and also gave to me an
Official Sealed letter to Provo Martial General Bowen of NewOrleans which
letter was to Sustain me in my right to the cotton against Comodore Porter
if an interfearance was made by the Comodore   This letter was not to be
oped only by General Bowen   There being no trouble over the cotton this
Mr T. B. Moorehous takes charge of the Same and Sells it—the cotton in
the hous of Brott & Davis cotton brokers,   After this Mr Moorehous Col-
lects the money for my cotton he desires that we go to his room in the city
Hotell where he would let me have the money,   On arriving at his room
we enterd and he closed the door as for buisness   Mr Moorehous then gave
me all of the papers concerning the Sale of my cotton and demanded of me
all the papers and permits given to me at Vicksburg by Waddell *Provo
Martial*   After receiving those papers from me as he wished Mr Moorehous
then handed 2000.00/00 Two thousand dollars out of the Pile of money
and told me that if I contended for any more that he would have the whole
of it confiscated to the Government and that I would be put in Alton prison
Of cours I was much Suprised but seeing my cituation I said nothing to a
Rober   I returned to Vicksburg and complained to *Mr* Waddell Provo
Martial as my friend and he assured me that by his official authority that
he would force Mr Moorehous to give me the money that my cotton Sold
for amounting to the Sum of $18574-12/100 Eighteen thousand five hun-
dred and Seventy four dollars as my right and lawful property,   Mr Moore-

hous did not return with me to Vicksburg but did in 3 or 4 days come up from New Orleans,   After this time *Mr* Waddell would not give me any more attention the game being finished, . . ."—ALS, *ibid*. Related documents are *ibid*.

1869, JAN. 7.   To Vice Admiral David D. Porter. "Mrs. Grant and I will not be able to go to Annapolis to-morrow. We have company."—ALS (telegram sent), DNA, RG 107, Telegrams Collected (Bound). On the same day, Porter, Annapolis, had telegraphed to USG. "A special Car will be ready for you to leave washington at four 4 O'clock—"—Telegram received (at 3:00 P.M.), *ibid*.; *ibid*., RG 108, Telegrams Received; copy, DLC-USG, V, 55.

1869, JAN. 8.   To U.S. Senator Henry Wilson of Mass. "General Humphreys, Chief Eng'r US. Army, reports that the reservation line on the accompanying map is run on the south side of 'Bay Street' to prevent the citizens building into said street and then asking for the opening of a street in their front on the public lands, thereby reducing the reservation by the width of a street. There is at the same time no objection on the part of the military authorities to the use of Bay Street as a highway, but only to be used for that purpose."—LS, DNA, RG 46, 40A-E8. Related papers concerning Point San José, San Francisco, are *ibid*. See *PUSG*, 18, 433.

1869, JAN. 9.   Maj. Gen. Henry W. Halleck, San Francisco, to USG. "I have just been shown a letter from a prominent gentleman in Washington, in which it is stated that you will probably make one cabinet appointment from the Pacific Coast, and the name of F. Billings is given as one of the most prominent candidates. While I have no desire or intention to make any recommendations in regard to political appointments, I beg leave to say that I have known Mr. Billings very intimately for more than twenty years; he is a gentleman of great ability, high integrity, and the most scrupulous honesty."—LS, USG 3.

1869, [JAN. 9].   Calvin M. Brooks *et al*. to USG. "At a Caucus of the Republican members of the Legislative Assembly of Dakota Territory held at the Capitol in the City of Yankton on January 9th 1869 it was unanimously *Resolved*: That the members of this caucus do most cordially and earnestly recommend for the appointment of Governor of Dakota Territory Hon W W. Brookings of this Territory in place of Hon A J. Faulk. . . ."—DS (30 signatures), DNA, RG 60, Records Relating to Appointments. Related papers are *ibid*. On March 6, Nathaniel G. Taylor *et al*., Washington, D. C., wrote to USG. "We take pleasure in Stating that Hon. A. J. Faulk the present Governor of Dakota Territory is an honest competent and efficient public officer. . . ."—DS (3 signatures), *ibid*., RG 59, Letters of Application and Recommendation. Favorable endorsements attached to this item and related papers are *ibid.* On April 3, USG nominated John A. Burbank as governor, Dakota Territory.

On April 13, Wilmot W. Brookings, Washington, D. C., wrote to USG. "I have been acquainted with Hon John W. Boyle one of the associate Justices of the supreme court of Dakota for eight years, Mr Boyle was a supporter of Andrew Johnson's administration and policy having received his appointment from Mr Johnson, through Hon W. A. Burleigh, as a reward for Mr Burleigh's treason to the republican party, Mr. Boyle is not a republican nor has he in any way affiliated with that party since 1865. The republicans of Dakota do not desire his retention in office"—ALS, *ibid.*, RG 60, Records Relating to Appointments. On April 15, USG nominated Brookings as associate justice, Dakota Territory, in place of John W. Boyle. On Jan. 25, 1871, Arthur Linn *et al.* petitioned USG. "The undersigned citizens of Dakota territory ask the removal of W. W. Brookings from the office of associate justice of Dakota for the following reasons, . . . 6th He was one of the leading bolters from the Republican party at the last election and used all the power of his office to prevent the election of Hon W. A Burleigh as delegate to Congress who was the regular nominee of the Republican party, and is now doing all in his power to enable M. K. Armstrong the Democrat to obtain his Seat."—DS (5 signatures), *ibid.* Related papers are *ibid.* On June 22, Brookings, Yankton, wrote to USG. "Inclosed you will find certain papers which will conclusively show to you *who* caused the defeat of the republican party of Dakota last fall. . . ."—ALS, *ibid.*, Letters Received. Enclosures are *ibid.*

1869, JAN. 9. Ira Harris, Albany, N. Y., to USG. "An application will be made on behalf of General J. Merideth Read Jr of this city to appoint him to some second class European Mission—I desire to unite most earnestly with the friends of General Read in commending this application to your favorable consideration He is in all respects well fitted for such a position—a gentleman of fine talents—much culture and considerable literary distinction—In his social position he stands high and in the last presidential canvass he rendered valuable and efficient service—I sincerely hope he may meet with the success he so well deserves—"—ALS, DNA, RG 59, Letters of Application and Recommendation. Related papers are *ibid.* with copies in DLC-John M. Read. On April 13, USG nominated John Meredith Read, Jr., as consul, Paris.

1869, JAN. 11, 1:25 P.M. To Bvt. Brig. Gen. Joseph H. Potter, Fort Sanders, Wyoming Territory. "~~Your~~ It is optional with you whether to leave Fort Saunders or not."—ALS (telegram sent), DNA, RG 107, Telegrams Collected (Bound); telegram sent, *ibid.*; copy, DLC-USG, V, 56.

1869, JAN. 11. To Miss Mary Stillman, Richmond House, Chicago. "Come on with Miss Felt if you can, if not then come as early as convenient."—ALS (telegram sent—signed by USG as "Mrs. U. S. Grant"), DNA, RG 107, Telegrams Collected (Bound).

1869, JAN. 11.   Andrew D. White, Ithaca, N. Y., to USG. "Hearing that the Hon. Lewis H. Morgan of Rochester N. Y. is named in connection with the Legation of the U. S. in Sweden I take the liberty of saying that I know no one, and can imagine no one more admirably fitted for such a position. To a very extensive & honorable political & business experience Mr Morgan joins abilities & reputation as a scholar in various departments of Science— and as a writer, which would at once give him a position sure to redound to the credit of any administration which may appoint him to represent our country No appointment of the kind could meet with more general approval in this state"—ALS, DNA, RG 59, Letters of Application and Recommendation. On March 24, Joseph Henry, Washington, D. C., wrote to USG. "Hon: Lewis H. Morgan of the State of New York has devoted himself, for a number of years, to the study of Ethnology, and has acquired a wide reputation on account of his researches relative to the American Indians. He has, also, completed, after many years of labor, a work founded upon original investigations, relative to the different systems adopted by the various races of men for indicating blood-relationships. This work was presented to the Smithsonian Institution for publication, was referred to the American Oriental Society for critical examination, and, on their recommendation, was accepted and is now in the press. Mr. Morgan is a gentleman of great moral, as well as intellectual, worth, and, I am sure, would do honor to our country in any position which he might be called to occupy."— LS, *ibid.* On March 13, Isaac F. Quinby, Rochester, had written to USG. "I write this introductory letter for my old and tried friend Lewis H Morgan a member of the State Senate from this District. He is not a politician in the bad sense of the term. Still he takes an active interest in politics and his well deserved reputation for purity of character and for his scholarly attainments gives him a powerful and and wide spread influence in this section of the country—The position for which he asks is one that he will fill with credit to himself and to the country and I sincerely hope that you may be able to give it him."—ALS, *ibid.* On March 19, Lewis H. Morgan endorsed this letter to USG. "I intended to call upon you with this letter and pay my respects: but I find you have more than enough of this. and shall deny myself the pleasure."—AES, *ibid.* Related papers are *ibid.* No appointment followed.

1869, JAN. 12.   USG endorsement. "Respectfully forwarded to the Secretary of War."—ES, DNA, RG 107, Letters Received from Bureaus. Written on a letter of Jan. 9 from Bvt. Maj. Gen. George Stoneman, Richmond, to USG. "I have the honor to enclose herewith a copy of a telegram from Brevet Colonel Garrick Mallery, Captain 43rd U. S. Infantry, who was sent to Norfolk, Virginia, to take command there and investigate in regard to the disturbance in that vicinity."—LS, *ibid.* The enclosure is *ibid.*

1869, JAN. 12. William M. Byrd, Selma, Ala., to USG. "The state of our country—, your position and power, and the interest which every good citizen has in the early and permanent pacification and restoration of the late insurgent states, I hope will be a sufficient excuse for this intrusion upon your time and attention amidst the arduous and responsible duties upon and before you. Many persons in these states, like myself, have always been opposed to secession—denied the existence of any such *state right*—, were openly against its attempted exercise in 1861, *and* were uniform and consistent Union-men, *until* these states, in an evil hour, formed 'a government in fact', when they gave it a voluntary obedience and assistance under the belief that the law *excused* and *justified* a citizen *within its jurisdiction*, in doing so. I say '*voluntary*', because *in strict law* it was so. When the national authority was restored and was competent to protect us, we promptly resumed our allegiance. We had held office in the states prior to the rebellion and had taken an official oath to support the constitution of the state and national Governments. Hence, we are disqualified from holding office by the *14th Amendment*, thus putting us on the same footing with the disunionists who had held office; but not on the same, with those who had never held an office; for, *such men*, though they were members of the secession conventions and voted for disunion and freely participated in rebellion, *are not disqualified*. It seems to us hard, if not unjust, to proscribe the original Union-men who had held office, and to permit such disunionists to have precedence of them. In the case of *Mauran* vs *Insurance Company 6 Wal: Reps: 1*, the supreme court of the United States decided that the insurgent states did erect 'a government in fact'—Mr Justice Blackstone says, 'When therefore an usurper is in possession the subject is *excused* and *justified* in obeying and giving him assistance; otherwise, no man could be safe, if the lawful prince had a right to hang him for obedience to the powers in being, as the usurper would certainly do for disobedience.' *Com: Bk IV p. 78*. It is clear to me that a citizen who openly opposed secession and rebellion until 'a government in fact was erected,' and who then gave it obedience and assistance, cannot be *legally* held guilty of any offense therefor. The effect of the 14th Amendment has been to consolidate the white race of the south against it and the reconstruction measures; for it and they, put the leaders of all parties in the south under *the ban* of the national and state Governments. Besides, Congress in 1864 had passed a law authorizing the President to grant pardons; and under this act and the Constitution of the United States, he had as early as 1866 and before the adoption of the 14th Amendment, relieved *nearly* all persons in the south from the pains and disabilities incurred by participation in the rebellion. It, therefore, has the appearance of injustice to deprive them of the benefits of the Executive clemency, which in the language of ancient jurists makes 'a new man', and has the *legal* effect of blotting out the past. Not only so, but it imposes a disability on a class of persons who in *the eye of the law*, if not of the lawmaking power, are innocent of any transgression;—I mean—the original Union-men. I therefore respectfully ask you to favor and recommend *the removal of all disabilities imposed by the 14th Amendment,*—and if you think that Congress should not do so, then, that you would favor *the removal of such disabilities from all persons who openly opposed secession and rebellion until 'a government in fact was erected,' and who upon its overthrow promptly resumed their allegiance to the National Government.* We think that this should be done by a general act; and not by one which names us. We prefer not to be relieved at all, than to be by name, and thus hand us down to posterity on the records of our country as traitors and perjurers, *when we did all we could to prevent secession and rebellion, and were dragged into it against our earnest opposition, or carried away by its resistless current.* Hoping that you may give this communication a favorable consideration, . . ."—ALS, USG 3.

1869, JAN. 13. Bvt. Brig. Gen. Adam Badeau to U.S. Senator Edwin D. Morgan of N. Y. and George Bliss, Jr. "General Grant has authorized the press to deny ~~to~~ in toto the statement of the New York World. He has never made a remark derogatory to Senator Morgan in his life, nor expressed a preference for any one of the candidates now proposed for the United States Senate"—ALS (telegram sent), DNA, RG 107, Telegrams Collected (Bound); telegram sent, *ibid.*

1869, JAN. 14. USG endorsement. "Respectfully forwarded to the Secretary of War, with recommendation that Gen. Canby be authorized to employ two hundred Indian Scouts, provided the number allowed by law will not be exceeded thereby. The recommendation for authority to organize companies of volunteers is disapproved."—ES, DNA, RG 94, Letters Received, 1724M 1868. Written on a letter of Dec. 30, 1868, from Bvt. Maj. Gen. Edward R. S. Canby, Austin, Tex., to Bvt. Maj. Gen. John A. Rawlins. "I have the honor to report for the information of the General of the Army, that after a careful consideration of the situation, I have reached the conclusion that it will be necessary to employ the greater part of the Cavalry force and so considerable a portion of the Infantry force now in the District, in the interior of the State, that the frontier will be left inadequately protected, and it will be necessary to make other arrangements for the prevention and repression of Indian hostilities. To this end I recommend that Authority be given for the employment of two hundred Indian guides and Spies, under the Act of Congress, of July 28, 1866, Sec. 6, and for the organization of Four or Six Companies of mounted Volunteers, to be raised in the frontier Counties exposed to Indian depredations, and to serve only on the frontier, and in the Indian Country, and under the Command of U. S. Officers. I also recommend that the Cavalry companies serving in Texas, may be filled up by recruits as soon as the interests of the Service will permit."—LS, *ibid.*

1869, JAN. 16. USG endorsement. "I concur in the recommendation of Sgt. Moore to the Apt. of 2d Lt. and his retirement for long continued &

meritorious services."—AES, DNA, RG 94, ACP, R384 CB 1870. Written
on a letter of Jan. 15 from Sgt. Michael Moore, Fort Columbus, N. Y., to
Secretary of War John M. Schofield. "I have just re-enlisted in the service
of the United States after serving fifty six years and without reprimand
or reproach of any kind.   my son, Charles E. Moore of the 16th Infantry
is a graduate of the Military Acadaemy, and in good standing in the Army—
As a reward for my long continued and faithful services from and through
the Wars of 1812, Black Hawk & Florida, I respectfully ask that I may be
appointed a second Lieutenant, in the Army and immediately retired."—LS,
ibid. Moore received the appointment.

1869, JAN. 18.   U.S. Senator John Sherman of Ohio to USG. "Col. L.
Markbriet of Ohio will apply for the Columbia Mission. I most heartily
join with his friends in recommending him for that place: He is well qualified both from education, character & personal fitness for the place and he
has a peculiar claim to the kindly favor of your administration from his
service in the Army his long imprisonment in Libby Prison, the injury to
his health in consequence, and his influential political services and position
among our German Republicans in Ohio. I will be personally gratified with
his appointment"—ALS, DNA, RG 59, Letters of Application and Recommendation. Related papers are *ibid.* On April 12, USG nominated Leopold
Markbreit as minister to Bolivia.

1869, JAN. 19.   Hinton R. Helper, Asheville, N. C., to USG. "When I
was Consul at Buenos Ayres, under the administration of President Lincoln,
I had frequent occasions to meet the diplomatic and Consular representatives of all the great powers. It was then, and is now, a source of much
pride to me to find that the management of our State Department inspired
special and profound respect among the English, French, German and other
leading European diplomatists; and I have often heard some of the ablest of
them acknowledge that neither Palmerston, nor Russell, nor Thouvenel,
nor Drouyn-de-Lhuys, nor Von Buest, nor Bismarck, nor any other of their
astute statesmen, could more than cope,—and sometimes scarcely cope,—
with our own sagacious and versatile Seward. My object in mentioning
these facts is to to show in what estimation Mr. Seward is held abroad; and
an estimate of this sort is, it seems to me, eminently proper to be considered
in regard to a minister of government,—and more especially so in regard to
a minister for foreign affairs. I do not know whether Mr. Seward would, or
would not, be willing to remain at the head of the State Department, after
the 4th of next March; nor has he any knowledge of my having written this
note; but if he retires from office, I shall be heartily rejoiced if his place be
filled by a man who possesses equal fitness and ability for the position,—if,
indeed, it be possible to find such a man in the United States. With earnest
wishes that your own administration may contribute largely to the union,
peace, progress and prosperity of our common country, (but with a deep
and anxious distrust of a few of the more prominent pro-negro politicians,)

. . ."—Copy, Seward Papers, NRU. On April 6, Helper wrote to William
H. Seward enclosing this letter.—ALS, *ibid.*

1869, JAN. 20.   To Md. AG John S. Berry. "I am much obliged to the
Governor for his kind offer to order an Escort to conduct me from Depot
tomorrow But as I will be accompanied by several other of the 'Trustees of
the Peabody Fund' and as arrangements are probably already made to
conduct us to our respective stopping places, I think it best to decline.
Thank the Governor for me for his kindness"—Telegram received (at
10:00 P.M.), Hall of Records, Annapolis, Md. At 5:30 P.M., Berry had
telegraphed to USG. "I am directed by the Governor of Maryland to have
a Military Escort in readiness on your arrival at Camden St. Station to-
morrow, to attend you to your Quarters. Hoping it will be your pleasure to
accept the same, I respectfully await your answer."—Copy, *ibid.*

[1869], JAN. 22.   John C. Dent, St. Louis, to USG. "I learn from my
friend J G Gibbes of Columbia South Carolina that he is to be an applicant
for U S Marshall in his section,   during my stay at Columbia S C I found
Mr Gibbes a friend indeed, not only to myself but to all the Federal prisoners that called on him for assistance I learned during my stay as prisoner
at that place, that he was a high toned honorable gentleman, & I hope you
will favor his application & oblige one of many that would be pleased to
give Mr Gibbes this same endorsement"—ALS (dated 1868), DNA, RG
60, Records Relating to Appointments. On Feb. 25, 1869, James L. Orr,
Anderson, S. C., wrote to USG on the same subject.—ALS, *ibid.* On April
25, 1868, Dent had written to USG requesting the removal of the "political
disqualification" of James G. Gibbes; on April 28, USG endorsed this letter.
"Respy. forwarded to Chairman Committee on Reconstruction. [John] C
Dent was a number of months held a prisoner in [Colu]mbia S C. during
the rebellion. It was during that time, [when] he became acquainted with
the applicant—"—Copy, *ibid.*, RG 108, Register of Letters Received.

1869, JAN. 25.   Edward Salomon, Milwaukee, to USG. "I learn that Genl
F. J. Herron, at present of New Orleans, will be an applicant for the position of Collector of Customs at that place. While I was Governor of Wisconsin, in 1862 & 1863, Genl Herron was in command of troops in the
West & had several regiments from this State in his command. From the
acquaintance which I then formed with him & from what I then & since
heard & learned of him, I have no hesitation to endorse his application. He
would, in my opinion, be a compet[en]t & faithful officer."—ALS, NHi. On
April 12, James F. Casey, New Orleans, telegraphed to USG. "General
Herron is much concerned about another person being nominated for his
office, He leaves tomorrow to see you"—Telegram received (at 7:00 P.M.),
DNA, RG 107, Telegrams Collected (Bound). On the same day, Lt. Governor Oscar J. Dunn of La., Washington, D. C., wrote to USG. "Considering the interest of the colord race of whom I am one, in the state of

Louisiana and the necessity of having the chief Legal Executive office therein filled by one, in the execution of the laws of the united States, particularly those enacted in the interest of the newly enfranchised people, they can confide, I would most respectfully, in their behalf, solicit from you, the appointment of S B. Packard as unided states Marshal for the District of Louisiana, believing that no act on your part, would be more agreeable to them or give them greater reliance in your administration, He having the full confidence of the Republican party of that State."—ALS, Duke University, Durham, N. C. On April 13, Francis J. Herron, New Orleans, telegraphed to USG. "Please defer action on Louisiana Marshalship until I reach Washington"—Telegram received (at 11:20 A.M.), DNA, RG 107, Telegrams Collected (Bound). On the same day, USG nominated Stephen B. Packard as marshal, La., in place of Herron. For the April 2 visit by Dunn to USG, see *New York Herald*, April 3, 1869.

1869, JAN. 26. To Henry D. Cooke. "This will introduce to you Gn. J. Sullivan, now of Cumberland, Md. who desires an Agency, I believe, in the Insurance comp.y, of which you are president. Gen. Sullivan served through the rebellion as a Col. & Brig. Gen. a portion the time directly under me. His services then were satisfactory and I think he will prove to have all the qualifications requisite for the place he askes."—ALS, Albany Institute of History and Art, Albany, N. Y.

1869, JAN. 28, 10:00 A.M. To Governor-elect Joseph W. McClurg of Mo. "Gen. Johnson is not relieved from his present duties but is returned to his pay as a retired officer."—ALS (telegram sent), DNA, RG 107, Telegrams Collected (Bound); telegram sent, *ibid.*; copy, DLC-USG, V, 56. On Jan. 28, McClurg telegraphed to USG. "Let me beg the suspension until July first of the order relieving Maj Gen R. W Johnson from the duty to which he has been detailed as ~~professor~~ Professor in the University of the state, Will give reasons by mail."—Telegrams received (2—on Jan. 28, 9:00 A.M.), DNA, RG 107, Telegrams Collected (Bound); *ibid.*, RG 108, Telegrams Received; copy, DLC-USG, V, 55.

1869, JAN. 28. Edwin B. Babbitt, San Francisco, to USG. "Understanding that Mr. Wm Gouverneur Morris, late Captain & As'st. Qr. Mr. U. S. Volunteers, is or will be an applicant for the position of United States Marshall for California, allow me to say in his behalf that he served in the above capacity several years during the Rebellion, under my supervision in the Department of California, with credit to himself—zeal for the Gov'mt, and with firm, and loyal devotion to the Union cause. He is a son of the late Bvt. Brig. Gen'l. Morris, whose life was spent in the service of the country. Should Capt. Morris be a successful applicant, I believe the office will be worthily filled, and its duties faithfully administered."—LS, NjP. On April 8, U.S. Delegate Richard C. McCormick of Arizona Territory wrote to USG in support of William Gouverneur Morris.—ALS, DNA, RG 56,

Asst. Treasurers and Mint Officials, Letters Received. On Dec. 6, USG nominated Morris as marshal, Calif.

On Feb. 24, 1870, Horace Porter wrote to Morris, Washington, D. C. "The President directs me to acknowledge the receipt of the wine which was received yesterday, and to convey to you his thanks for sending it. They are his favorite wines and it was very thoughtful in you to present them."—Copy, DLC-USG, II, 1. On Feb. 25, 1873, Morris wrote to Orville E. Babcock. "I send to your address a couple of boxes of Manillas, commonly called 'Philopenas' which I imported myself from the Phillipine Islands, and beg to request, you will ask the President if he will honor me by accepting them."—ALS, Babcock Papers, ICN.

On Dec. 17, Morris, San Francisco, telegraphed to USG. "Before Issuing a commission to my successor I respectfully ask you will cause to be fully investigated the charges against me. Have been condemned without an opportunity to defend myself I can clearly show by undoubted testimony my innocence of any act warranting my removal. Have learned by telegraph recently for first time authentically of the cause of my removal"—Telegram received (at 11:20 A.M.), DNA, RG 60, Letters Received from the President. See *New York Times*, Feb. 19, 1884.

1869, JAN. 29. USG endorsement. "Respectfully forwarded to the Secretary of War."—ES, DNA, RG 107, Letters Received from Bureaus. Written on a letter of Feb. 7, 1867, from Capt. Charles H. Graves, Fort Snelling, Minn., to Bvt. Brig. Gen. Cyrus B. Comstock. "While stationed in Richmond Va, on the staff of Major General Terry, during the year 1865–6, I became somewhat acquainted with the affairs of a family there by the name of Van Lew, whom I believe to have rendered the most important and dangerous services to our cause, and to the Generals commanding in front of Richmond during the war, by furnishing information of events in that city, at a time when it was at the peril of their lifves to do so: I have seen some of the correspondence between them and our officials at that time, and have been told by other Union citizens of that city enough concerning the danger incurred by the family, and the amount of service rendered to our cause by them (, and particularly by Miss. E L. Van Lew) to be assured of their importance and of the duty of the government to handsomely reward such devotion and self sacrifice. Although I cannot give You particular statements in the matter, I know that they corresponded during 1864 and 1865 with General Butler and with some officer of General Grants at City Point; that their house was used as a concealing place for our spies when in Richmond, and was known as such by the Union people, though only suspected by the Rebels, For this service they have received but some little gratuity, while their business in that city has been ruined and the family reduced to poverty; partly, I believe, by the unusual expenses they went into on our account and the material aid furnished our prisoners of war, It seems to me that such noble service should not pass without ample reward from the government, sufficient to remove them from want, and put them in the easy financial position they knew before the war, I am not interested in any way in this matter, and write the above without solicitation from any person connected with that family,"—ALS, *ibid.* In Jan. 1867, George H. Sharpe wrote to Comstock. ". . . After the occupation of Richmond General Grant directed the Sum of Two Thousand Dollars to be paid to Miss Van Lew on a presentation of the case by Colonel Bowers and myself 'as a partial reimbursement to her or her brother from whose store the funds came.' This language I find in my letter to General Patrick of May 31, 1865 covering the order given me by Colonel Bowers, and which was made on Genl Patricks formal recommendation. . . ."—ALS, *ibid.* Related material *ibid.* includes a Feb. 22, 1869, USG endorsement. "Respectfully forwarded to the Secretary of War, inviting attention to papers in this case forwarded 31st July 1868."—ES, *ibid.* See Meriwether Stuart, "Colonel Ulric Dahlgren and Richmond's Union Underground April 1864," *Virginia Magazine of History and Biography*, 72, 2 (April, 1964), 180–81.

On March 17, USG nominated Elizabeth Van Lew as postmaster, Richmond. On May 27, Benjamin C. Cook, Grand Army of the Republic, Richmond, telegraphed to USG. "Miss Van Lew refuses to close the Post Office on memorial day It was closed last year If not closed many comrades will not be able to participate Will you order it closed Answer"—Telegram received (at 2:20 P.M.), *ibid.*, Telegrams Collected (Bound).

On March 24, 1881, Van Lew, Washington, D. C., wrote to USG. "The sending in the name of Dr. Gilmer—(he has never even lived in our city)—for Postmaster on yesterday—was a blow I had no strength to meet, for I have nothing earthly but sacrifice to fall back upon. The appointment of Judge Robertson for Col. in N. Y has made a great sensation here. I met at the Capitol to day a Readjuster—& I said it seemed your friends were not in favor—He laughed. at me—shook his head and said that *if you had cared* I would have had the place—that he was well informed & knew what he was speaking of—that he knew you spoke for me but that you did not want it much to be, or it would have been—that there were two ways of doing things & he knew—I was indignant & asked his authority—he said 'I cannot tell you' I told him 'I would write & tell you what he said—' he said well I could. I told him my faith in you was absolute—that you never went back upon a friend—& your word was truth—& if you had spoken for me it was in truth & sincerity—& that the Private Sec. of the P. M Genl. had told me you had spoken to Mr. James. To have such a story go out does distress me—The Private Secretary of the P. M. Genl—asked me to write to you—asking for a letter or line that he might put on file—I know you are good & will but I would have been glad if you had thought it best to do so. I cannot express the deep gratitude I feel for all your kindness to me—I have been here 3 weeks & always refused an interview by the President—& the Postmaster General has not permitted me to speak with him. If I ever live to see you I will tell you how *rudely* he treated me—& you know I would not tell a story—*I ask you as a favor specially not to mention this because it would only do harm—I have been careful to be any thing but pressing*—You did not see one third my papers and I am willing to stand or fall by this written record. A brave man is never rude to a woman. I saw Mr. Conkling only for a moment or two—gave him a written statement— He treated me like a gentleman—though he has his head & heart full of business & troubles   I saw Mr. Arthur—noble fine faced—& kind mannered Mr. Arthur.—on Tuesday P. M—he said 'I know you Miss Van Lew—& Mr. Conkling will do what is right'—I must believe that neither Mr. Arthur or Mr. Conkling knew Dr. Gilmer's name was to be sent in— May God bless you & your friends—if I were a man I would be able to stand by them publicly—I wish them success—If it seems right & proper to you to do so—I would be glad indeed—& more than glad—if before you leave ~~Amer~~ for Mexico—you would write one line to be filed among my papers—saying—I cordially recommend or recommended the appointment of Miss Van Lew as P. M. at Richmond—*I know you did*—I thank you for your thousand acts of goodness—This line need ~~never~~ not come to me only be sent to the office of the P. M. Genl—to be filed among my papers—as the Sec. said. I beg your kind excuse for writing so much—I put my hands upon my eyes, press back my tears, and know the time is coming when all human trials end.—"—ALS, USG 3.

1869, JAN.   Namik, minister of war, Constantinople, to USG acknowledging USG's letter of introduction, dated June 29, 1868, written for Gershom Mott, former maj. gen.—LS (in French), Munson-Williams-Proctor Institute, Utica, N. Y.

1869, FEB. 3.   Governor Rutherford B. Hayes of Ohio to USG. "Hon. John L. Thomas of Baltimore was a member of the 39th Congress and was throughout a firm and able supporter of the Republican measures of that Congress in opposition to the policy of Andrew Johnston. I am informed that his fidelity has cost him to a large extent his professional business and prospects in Baltimore. If in any proper way the patronage of the Government can supply to him what he has lost, it ought in my judgment to be done. I therefore respectfully urge his claims to the most favorable consideration."—Copies (2), DNA, RG 56, Collector of Customs Applications. Related papers are *ibid.* On April 8, USG nominated John L. Thomas, Jr., as collector of customs, Baltimore.

In [*April*], William J. Albert *et al.* petitioned USG. "The undersigned citizens of Maryland most respectfully and earnestly present to the President, the name of Judge H L Bond of Baltimore for the position of Collector of Customs at that port. Judge Bond is so well known that our certificate seems superfluous. From actual knowledge of his labors in the cause of the Union of the enfranchisement and Education of the colored people we know no one who has surpassed him in fearlessness and usefulness, while he has borne obloquy and persecution such as few have been called to endure. To a high order of ability—and personal integrity—he adds that power of will and practical executive force so conspicuously shown by his administration of the Criminal Court, which fitts him for the practical duties of the Collectorship We believe that the whole party would feel even if some of them preferred others, that in his appointment they had a faithful officer and that none would hesitate to say of him: 'There is a man.' "—DS (74 signatures), *ibid.* Related papers are *ibid.* On April 13, Hugh L. Bond, Baltimore, telegraphed to USG. "Can I see you tomorrow if I come to Washington? If yea at what hour?"—Telegram received (at 2:40 P.M.), *ibid.*, RG 107, Telegrams Collected (Bound). On the same day, Orville E. Babcock replied to Bond. "The President directs me to acknowledge the receipt of your telegram and to say that he is now very busily engaged all the time, and that he will be so busy until after the adjournment of the Senate that he cannot promise any special time for an interview"—Copies, DLC-USG, II, 1, 4.

1869, FEB. 5.   Bvt. Maj. Gen. Montgomery C. Meigs to USG. "A bed of coal or lignite suitable for fuel, is reported by General Holabird to exist about Two (2) miles North by East from Fort Stevenson, Dakota Territory. On the tenth of June 1868, an order, of which a copy is enclosed was issued by Bvt Maj Genl Terry, commanding the Department of Dakota, setting apart a large reservation. No action by the President approving this Reservation has yet been made known to this office. To prevent conflict of Jurisdiction and of titles it is very desirable that a sufficient reservation be set apart, and reserved from sale, by proclamation. Unless this reservation is thus made there is danger of the War Department finding the very site of this Fort, and the bed of coal which seems to be of great value to the Government as supplying fuel for the troops in this ~~waterless~~ timberless country, embraced in claims of settlers, who will probably soon enforce their rights and hold the War Department as trespassing. I have the honor to enclose the papers relative to the matter and request that you will bring the same to the attention of the Honorable Secretary of War at an early day—with a view ~~of~~ to establishing a reservation large enough to include the coal mine above referred to, should the large reservation proclaimed by General Terry not be ~~set apart~~ approved."—DfS, DNA, RG 92, Records Relating to Regular Supplies, Letters Received.

1869, FEB. 8.   USG endorsement. "Commanders of troops in the Department of the Missouri will please give Mr. Vincent Collyer facilities, when necessary, transportation and escort, to reach Fort Cobb and such other military posts as he may desire to visit in the Indian country."—*New York Herald*, Feb. 9, 1869. Written on the day USG met with Vincent Colyer, Peter Cooper, and LeGrand B. Cannon, members of the U.S. Indian Commission, at the Union League Club, New York City. On Feb. 6, Colyer, on Union League Club stationery, had written to USG. "As explained in the accompanying circular, I wish to start for Fort Cobb Ind. Territory next week—Will you not be pleased to give my Christian errand,—the sanction

& help of your great name—and on the plains, where I cannot get private conveyance, *Government Transportation.*"—ALS, Columbia University, New York, N. Y. On Dec. 8, Secretary of the Interior Jacob D. Cox wrote to USG. "I have the honor to submit, for your signature, the commission of Vincent Colyer, as a Member of the Indian Peace Commission. The Commission bears date, July 23. 1869,—the day upon which Mr Colyer was authorized to act as a member of said commission."—LS, OFH. A press copy of a letter of July 23 from Cox to Colyer is in the Jacob D. Cox Papers, Oberlin College, Oberlin, Ohio. On March 31, 1870, Colyer, secretary, Board of Indian Commissioners, wrote to USG. "I am directed by the Board of Indian Commissioners to call your attention to the recent bombardment of the Indian Village at Wrangel, Alaska, by the United States troops located at that Post. . . ."—ALS, DNA, RG 107, Letters Received from Bureaus. See *SED*, 41-2-67; *ibid.*, 41-2-68.

1869, FEB. 8.   John M. Harlan, Louisville, to USG. "I learn that the friends of Hon Bland Ballard of this city will present his name for the office of Judge of the Circuit Court of the United States for the Kentucky District under the law now pending before the Congress of the United States. It affords me pleasure to testify to the peculiar fitness of Judge Ballard for this position. In 1861 he was appointed by President Lincoln Judge of the District Court for Kentucky, which office he now fills. The duties of that position he has discharged with great fidelity and with marked ability. Such I believe to be the unanimous sentiment of the lawyers of this state who have had any opportunity to know the character of the labors which he has had to perform, and the manner in which he has discharge[d] his official duties. During that whole period he has discharged the duties belonging to the office of Judge of the Circuit Court of the United States for this District, except occasionally when a Justice of the Supreme Court was in attendance. As to Judge B's qualifications for the position in question my deliberate judgment is that he is the ablest lawyer in Kentucky and qualified for any judicial position within the gift of the President. The President elect would do a service to the country if he would nominate him for Associate Justice of the Supreme Court. The country believes that the President elect intends to purify the Revenue system, and put an end to the enormous frauds being perpetrated in that Department. The President may rest assured that the entire familiarity of Judge B, with the operation and administration of the Revenue laws and his incorruptible integrity will be of essential aid in effecting the contemplated reform."—ALS, DNA, RG 60, Applications and Recommendations. Related papers are *ibid.*

1869, FEB. 9.   Christopher C. Andrews, St. Cloud, Minn., to USG. "I take the liberty to represent that Maj. G. S. Alexander late of the 62d Ill. Vols. when a lieutenant in that regiment served for a considerable time as acting adjutant on my staff at the Hd. Qrs. Post of Little Rock, and at De

Vall's Bluff. He was a methodical quick and accurate business man; regular at his post of duty; courteous in address; perfectly trustworthy—an uncommonly fine gentleman and soldier. After the war he entered on the practice of law at Robinson Ill., and has acquitted himself with much credit. He is worthy of and would honor the office of Collector of Internal Revenue 11th Dist. of Ill."—ALS (press), Andrews Papers, Minnesota Historical Society, St. Paul, Minn. No appointment followed.

1869, FEB. 10.   James H. Godman, Ohio auditor, Columbus, to USG. "I understand Cooper K. Watson Esqr of Tiffin Ohio is a candidate for the appointment of District Atty of the U. S. for the Northern District of Ohio I have known Mr Watson for more than twenty years, practiced law at the same Courts with him, for ten or more years, and I know him to be an honest man, of superior talents; and an able lawyer. If appointed he will make an able successful and satisfactory District Atty."—ALS, OFH. On March 9, Ralph P. Buckland, Washington, D. C., wrote to USG. "Being about to leave for home, I desire to present the name of Hon Cooper K Watson for the appointment of District Attorney for the Northern District of Ohio. I practiced law at the same Bar with Mr Watson for more than twenty years and know him to be an honorable and incorruptible man. He is one of the best Lawyers in the State and will make an able honest and efficient District Attorney   I herewith present the recommendations of Several Members of Congress, Gov Hayes, Members of the Bar and other prominent gentlemen who have known Mr Watson many years."—ALS, *ibid.* On March 5, Governor Rutherford B. Hayes of Ohio wrote to USG recommending William C. Bentz as attorney, Northern District, Ohio.—Parke-Bernet Galleries, May 22, 1956, no. 83. No appointments followed.

1869, FEB. 10.   Sgt. Jack Magee *et al.*, 39th Inf., Ship Island, Miss., to USG. "I am Sir a Sargent of "A." Co 39th U. S. Infty.   the way that we have been treeted for the last yaear we cannot Stand it for the offersers treeteds us like dogs. knocks us down kick us and takes our money from us   I enlested to be treted lik a Soldier but they do not do as thy promes to. Sir I cannot Stand it. I will pubish it in All the papers in the United States and in the forn contres too.   you know that it is not wright to treet Men this way   Sir well you please do Some thing for us."—ALS, DNA, RG 94, Letters Received, 183M 1865. Related papers are *ibid.*

1869, FEB. 12.   To Secretary of State William H. Seward. "I have the honor to acknowledge the receipt of a copy of a letter from Mr Meylen, as well as of a copy of a volume of poems by the same person, which you have been good enough to transmit. I beg you to receive my thanks for this Courtesy."—LS, Seward Papers, NRU. On Feb. 9, Seward had written to USG. "In compliance with the request of the writer of the letter of which a copy is herewith enclosed, I transmit the enclosed volume to which he refers."—Copy, DNA, RG 59, Domestic Letters.

1869, FEB. 12. Governor Rutherford B. Hayes of Ohio *et al.* to USG. "Mr Luther A, Hall, of Tiffin, Ohio, desires appointment to the Governorship of Wyoming Territory. He was one of the Presidential Electors of Ohio, elected at the Presidential election in 1868, For over thirty years he has been a resident of Ohio, and now is a man of much vigor of intellect, a good lawyer, of high moral character, a most faithful and upright public officer, having been the first assessor of Internal Revenue in his District, and in every respect competant to fill the office desired."—DS (3 signatures), DLC-John Sherman. On March 9, Secretary of War John M. Schofield wrote to USG. "I have the honor to recommend Col. John A. Campbell, of Ohio, for Governor of the Territory of Wyoming or Montana."—ALS, DNA, RG 59, Letters of Application and Recommendation. On April 3, USG nominated John A. Campbell as governor, Wyoming Territory. On Jan. 5, 1871, Horace Porter wrote to Secretary of State Hamilton Fish. "Govr. Campbell of Wyoming Territory has been ordered here to settle his accounts as Indian Agent but feels a delicacy about coming without first obtaining permission of the State Department. The President desires me to say that, he will be pleased if you will telegraph Gov. Campbell, granting him the necessary leave of absence."—LS, *ibid.*, Wyoming Territorial Papers.

1869, FEB. 13. Kate Banks, Covington, Ky., to [USG]. "I write to you in behalf of my husband who has been a soldier in the army at the onset of the war and while there he contracted deseas which has disable'd him for over six years, he is now under treatment of one our best physicians and he thinks unless something can be done speedily he will lose both legs. . . ." —ALS, ICarbS. Jesse R. Grant endorsed this letter. "Gen Rawlings I know the facts herein stated—The case is one that really demands immediate & prompt attention—the within was written by the ~~affected~~ distressed wife of the afflicted soldier—It is a real case of distress"—AES, *ibid.*

1869, FEB. 13. Charles W. Ford, St. Louis, to USG. "This will be presented to you by my personal friend—Mr Jonathan Grimshaw of Jefferson City—He has been our agent at that place for about ten years past and my busines relations with him have been of the most intimate kind—He has been a firm friend of our Country & government throughout its recent Struggle for life—is intelligent—is honest and in all the relations of life— honorable, He tells me he desires to be Consul at Leeds, England, his native town—Should he receive such appointment, I have every confidence in his integrity and ability—that he will so discharge the duties pertaining to it—in a manner acceptable to both countries & crediable to himself—"— ALS, DNA, RG 59, Letters of Application and Recommendation. Related papers are *ibid.* On March 9, Chief Justice Salmon P. Chase wrote to USG. "Permit me to commend to you very earnestly my friend, Prof. Chas D. Cleveland, of Philadelphia, who would like to be appointed Consul at Manchester or Leeds, both places being now vacant. He has had experience in

Consular service and is admirably qualified by integrity, ability and patriotism. Very many good men would be gratified to see him in this Service."—ALS, *ibid.* Related papers are *ibid.* In March, U.S. Senator Alexander Ramsey of Minn. wrote to USG. "It gives me great pleasure to recommend Mr E. D. Neill for the vacant consulate at Leeds. He was my neighbor for many years, and was recognized as among the most energetic and public spirited of the citizens of Minnesota. He has culture integrity and experience in public affairs. The inclosed note from the Executive Mansion addressed to me a day or two before the burial of President Lincoln will shew that he faithfully discharged his duty as one of the Presidents secretaries As an opponent of Mr Johnsons measures I have been prevented from using my influence in his behalf until the preset time"—ALS, *ibid.* The enclosure, a letter of April 16, 1865, from John Hay, and related papers are *ibid.* On April 12, USG nominated Edward D. Neill as consul, Dublin.

On April 12, USG nominated Edward Stephens as consul, Leeds. On April 17, a columnist wrote from Washington, D. C. "The Senators are very busy to-day trying to figure out an adjournment by next Wednesday. . . . Some of the Consulates are exciting a great deal of feeling. At least, there is a tendency warmly to oppose not a few of the nominees. The principal ground of objection this morning is against the Consulship to Leeds, and the strife over it has become very animated. It is given on nomination to a young man named Edwin Stephens, a son of Mrs. Ann S. Stephens, the authoress, as our people call any woman hardy enough to write poor books of dwaddling fiction. Moreover, this same lady is not unconnected with the political scandals of Andrew Johnson's Administration, and her son, an inoffensive young man of no special ability, has been made to suffer on her account. It is not so unfair as it seems, as his mother, undoubtedly, procured him the nomination. The old lady has had her own demerits more canvassed than the son, and she has given the Committee of Commerce enough to do for a week to make plenty of local gossip for the Capital."—*Brooklyn Union,* April 19, 1869. On April 20, Ethan A. Allen, New York City, wrote to Secretary of State Hamilton Fish. "I had the pleasure of receiving your fav of 17th on 19th Inst. for which please accept my thanks. I perceive by *this* morning's N Y Herald that 'Edward Stephens' nominated for Consul at Leeds has been rejected. Should you still have this appointment open, I swould much like to have it. . . ."—ALS, DNA, RG 59, Letters of Application and Recommendation. On March 25, 1872, Stephens, Washington, D. C., wrote to Fish. "I have the honor to request that the letters recommending me for nomination to the U. S. Consulate at Manchester or Leeds England—be returned to me at your earliest convenience. The above were filed at your department March 1869—"—ALS, *ibid.*

On March 6, 1869, Governor DeWitt C. Senter of Tenn. wrote to USG. "Hon. F. S. Richards, Speaker of the House of Representatives of the General Assembly of the State of Tennessee, has been a leading Republican in that body since his accession to it in April 1865.—He took an active part from the beginning in securing the adoption of laws to establish the civil and political equality of all men. Although representing a constituency strongly hostile to liberal Republican measures, he firmly and fearlessly labored without ceasing, to open the Courts and the ballot-box to every citizen without respect to *race* or *complexion.* He was an out-spoken and uncompromising Republican, in the moust doubtful period in the history of the liberal party in Tennessee. He kept his seat in the Legislature for four years at a heavy pecuniary sacrifice, and greatly to the detriment of his private interest, giving his whole attention to the labor of establishing *good Government* in the State and restoring the supremacy of the law. While the Rebellion was in existence, he was a firm supporter of the *Federal Government,* and an advocate of whatever coercion was necessary to destroy the Confederacy, and on the cessation of hostilities he was among the first to advocate the establishment of a loyal *State Government,* and the restoration of civil law by the friends of the *National Government.* The enemies of the State Government have found him ever ready to oppose their schemes for its over-throw, while its friends have always been encouraged by his vigilance, industry and courage. At all times and amid all circumstances, he has been a consistent and efficient worker in the cause of Republicanism, and has earned the gratitude of all friends of the equality of human rights. As Speaker of Tennessee House of Representatives, he presided with signal success over its deliberations, and was universally popular, for his promptness, skill and uniform courtesy and knowledge of Parlimentary law. His fine business capacity and extensive knowledge of the world, and through acquaintance with men, could enable him to fill *any* position with credit to himself and profit to the *Government.*"—LS, *ibid.* Related papers are *ibid.* On April 20, USG nominated Richards as consul, Leeds. See *PUSG,* 5, 208.

1869, FEB. 14. Secretary of State William H. Seward to USG. "I have the great pleasure of informing you that Mr Cushing has safely arrived with a Treaty for the survey and construction of the Darien Ship Canal, which I hope will be found satisfactory, as it will assure the construction of the work and upon the best terms that could be secured"—Copy, Seward Papers, NRU.

1869, FEB. 14. Governor Joseph W. McClurg of Mo. to USG. "A white woman crazy and wandering on the plains, supposed to have escaped from the Indians has been sent here by Gen Sheridan from Fort Cobb for the Lunaetic Asylum. Her kindred are unknown. There is ~~no~~ in this state no law providing for such cases What shall be done with her?"—Telegram received (on Feb. 15, 9:00 A.M.), DNA, RG 107, Telegrams Collected (Bound); *ibid.,* RG 108, Telegrams Received; copy, DLC-USG, V, 55.

1869, FEB. 15. To Bvt. Maj. Gen. John A. Rawlins. "Mrs. Grant would like Mrs. Rawlins to stay with her for a few weeks."—ALS (telegram sent), DNA, RG 107, Telegrams Collected (Bound). On Feb. 16, Rawlins,

Danbury, Conn., telegraphed to USG. "Dispatch received, Mrs Rawlins will go with me to Washington Arrive there tomorrow evening train"— Telegram received (at 1:10 P.M.), *ibid.*

1869, FEB. 15. George P. A. Healy, Rome, to [USG]. "I beg to present to you my friend Dr Quackenbos who has not only laboured in the great work of your election, but is the gentleman I spoke to you of last June, who presented and read Badeau to me, this he did while I was designing my picture, no one encouraged me in this undertaking as did Dr Quackenbos. His knowledge of international law and the Italian language make him a highly proper person to be our consul in Rome. I pray you to look into his claims."—ALS, DNA, RG 59, Letters of Application and Recommendation. Related papers are *ibid.* No appointment followed.

1869, FEB. 16. To AG. "The Adj. Gn. will please order Lt. Ed. P. Daugherty, 5th U. S. Cav.y. to duty with that portion of his ʀRegt now serving on the plains."—ANS, DNA, RG 94, Letters Received, 47D 1869.

1869, FEB. 16. J. C. Aspinwall, Brodhead, Wis., to USG. "As my friends have the kindness to present my name as a candidate for visitor at West Point permit me to say that my only son expects to graduate there next commencement and I would like to be present I have often been employed as examining committee at our Colleges and Universities in Maine Vermont and Wisconsin Though we have had no personal acquaintance you may have heard of me for I resided in Platteville six years. Two on that station and four as Presiding Elder on that district. You may recollect meeting my daughter the wife of Samuel Rountree at his father's—Major Rountree's last fall—If you think the appointment would be useful and creditable to the Institution it would be a favor to me to have it made"—ALS, DNA, RG 94, USMA, Board of Visitors.

1869, FEB. 17. To Jane Tweed. "Mrs. Grant will be at home and glad to see you."—ALS (telegram sent), DNA, RG 107, Telegrams Collected (Bound).

1869, FEB. 18. Benjamin C. Foster, "Buenos Ayres," to USG. "As our advises:—of Jany 23 /69:—were principally based:—upon the Diplomatic Value:—of two thousand Pounds sterling:—Remitted, per order, of *President Lincoln*:—expressly:—to the End:—of defraying my '*Expenses*':—and '*to arrange, any small matter*':—that might be found pending:—'*Impending*':—with *the Government*':—to *which I am,* '*accredited*':—. . ."—ALS, DNA, RG 45, Subject File, Div. VI. On March 6, Foster wrote to USG congratulating him upon his election.—ALS, *ibid.*

1869, FEB. 18. Bishop Matthew Simpson, Philadelphia, to USG. "Having learned that Rev. J. B. Gould, of Bangor, Me., is an applicant for a foreign consul ship, and having been acquainted with him for several years, it gives me pleasure to say that I consider him well qualified for such a position, should there be a favorable opening."—ALS, DNA, RG 59, Letters of Application and Recommendation. On April 13, USG nominated John B. Gould as consul, Cork; on Dec. 6, as consul, Birmingham.

On May 6, U.S. Senator William A. Buckingham of Conn., Norwich, wrote to USG. "I am informed unofficially that Mr Stevens recently appointed U S Consul at Birmingham England has declined the appointment If so I beg leave to solicit the appointment of Elihu Burritt Esq of Conn to the position   Mr Burritt is known as the learned Blacksmith, is a gentleman of great modesty and purity of character, of undoubted patriotism, and in every respect would be an able & honorable representative of this administration—He has been acting for some time as Consular Agent, and was instrumental of sending more than one hundred thousand dollars in gold value to this country to aid in educating the freedmen   Has he not merited promotion—"—ALS, *ibid.* Related papers are *ibid.* No appointment followed. See Peter Tolis, *Elihu Burritt: Crusader for Brotherhood* (Hamden, Conn., 1968), pp. 273–78.

1869, FEB. 19.   John G. Mitchell, Columbus, Ohio, to USG. "Capt W. F. Wheeler, late of the 4th Minn Vols, I am informed, seeks a position under your administration   It affords me great pleasure to join his other friends in recommending to your special attentions the claims of Capt Wheeler. You could appoint no man to the position named, who would bring to the discharge of its duties more energy, character and integrity, and I trust that you may be enable to appoint him"—ALS, NNP. On Feb. 25, Bvt. Maj. Gen. Wager Swayne, Nashville, wrote in support of William F. Wheeler.—ALS, ICarbS. On March 6, George B. Wright, Columbus, Ohio, wrote to USG. "I know Wm F. Wheeler well. He is industrious, honest and capable, He served his country as a soldier faithfully and earnestly,   He has a family dependant upon him, and no means beyond his daily earnings for their support,   If any man living is worthy of a comfortable position under the Government I think Mr. Wheeler is, and I sincerely hope it may be given him"—ALS, William W. Layton, Millwood, Va. On Dec. 6, USG nominated Wheeler as marshal, Montana Territory.

1869, FEB. 20.   USG note. "The Adj. Gn. will please suspend S. O. No. 37 so far as it applies to Capt. E. R. Ames 7th U. S. Inf.y."—ANS, DNA, RG 94, Letters Received, 93A 1869. On April 20, 1868, Bvt. Brig. Gen. Orville E. Babcock had written to Maj. Gen. George G. Meade. "The General in Chief directs me to inquire whether an application of Captain Edwin R. Ames, 7th. U. S. Infantry, for six months leave of absence, has reached your Headquarters; and to say that if the application has not reached you, when it does Capt. Ames can be spared from his company—you are authorized to grant the leave without referring same to these Headquarters."—Copies, DLC-USG, V, 47, 60; DNA, RG 108, Letters Sent. In Nov. 1870,

Bishop Edward R. Ames wrote to USG. "I have the honor to ask that my Son, Capt E. R. Ames, now unattached, may be Assigned to a Regiment and placed upon Active duty—He first entered the Service as a ~~private~~ non-commissioned officer in the three months Volunteers from the State of Indiana and was engaged in the early Campaigns in West Virginia—In ~~July~~ March 1862 he was appointed a Second Lieutenant in the 7th Infantry, in which Regiment he Served until the Consolidation of the Infantry Regiments under the law of March 3d, 1869, attaining his present rank on the 7th October 1864—I may Safely Say that his Capacity and Attainments are greatly above the Average of Young Men of his age—that his habits are entirely Correct: that he is industrious and energetic and that he will always be Conscientious and faithful in the discharge of his duty—I am advised by those who have Served with him that his Service both in the Volunteer and Regular Army was highly Creditable and I can Refer for his character and Standing to General Canby, with whom he Served for Some time as an aid and to Col's Sprague and Flint, the former Colonel and Lieut Colonel of the 7th Infantry. I am the more Solicitous in this matter because my Son is strongly attached to the profession he has chosen and has labored diligently to make himself an useful member of it—"—ALS, *ibid.*, RG 94, ACP, A439 CB 1870. On Nov. 30, USG endorsed this letter. "Refered to the Sec. of War. I understand that Capt. Ames has proven himself one of the most efficient Indian Agts. If no special reason exists for keeping him on the 'unassigned' list I would like to see him placed on duty."—AES, *ibid.* On March 4, 1876, John P. Newman wrote to USG. "It is possible, in view of the *non-action* of the Secretary of War, that Captain Ames sent in his resignation. I do not know that this is so, but if he has, I hope you will not accept it, for the present, but grant him to 60 days leave as promised last evening."—ALS, *ibid.* On Jan. 10, 1877, former Capt. Edward R. Ames, Baltimore, wrote to USG. "I respectfully request that the order accepting my resignation as an officer of the army be revoked, and I be reinstated in that position. I enlisted April 16th 1861. in the 11th Indiana Volunteers, three months men, served my time. After discharge was engaged during part of the winter of 1861–2 in raising volunteers. Was commissioned a 2d Lieut 7th Infantry March 6th 1862. and served without loosing more than a day or two, except when on leave, until my health required me to resign. I was in the regular service fourteen years and nearly eight months. I consider my health restored and am therefore fit for duty. I was strongly recommended for the position of Asst Adjt Gen or Paymaster by very influencial parties   As the President did not see fit to make this promotion I hope will in lieu there of restore me to my position."—ALS, *ibid.* Related papers are *ibid.* and *ibid.*, RG 107, Applications for Positions. Reappointed, Ames soon resigned; after shooting a stranger in a boardinghouse, he died in an asylum in 1882.

1869, Feb. 20.   Maj. Gen. George G. Meade, Atlanta, to USG. "This mornings telegram states Battery E third (3d) Artillery is ordered to

Pensacola, In ignorance of the reasons causing this order, I feel I ought to inform you that this battery is now here, that this position is the best for a mounted battery, as in less than forty eight (48) hours it can be transported to any part of the Southern country, that it can be better and more economically supplied here than elsewhere—particularly Pensacola which is an out of the way place—without communications with any other, except a bi-monthly steamer from New Orleans to be discontinued after July first proximo, that this place is salubrious with grounds for practice, and that finally it has cost over five thousand dollars to locate the companies with stables &c—all of which will be lost, besides having to make a large expenditure at Pensacola, I beg leave to refer to Generals Porter and Babcock to confirm my opinion as to the eligibility of this point, for a mounted battery in the south and as to the quarters now occupied by battery "E." It may be that this company E is to be exchanged for another and the battery not moved, in which case the foregoing is unnecessary"—Telegram received (at 2:00 P.M.), DNA, RG 107, Telegrams Collected (Bound); (at 3:00 P.M.), *ibid.*, RG 108, Telegrams Received.

1869, FEB. 22. To Secretary of War John M. Schofield. "In consideration of the fact that Brevet Colonel J. B. Collins has already served out more than five months of his sentence, I would respectfully recommend that the remainder of his sentence be remitted and that he be restored to duty."— LS, DNA, RG 94, Letters Received, P90 1869. See *ibid.*, ACP, 2652 1871.

1869, FEB. 23. Michael J. Cramer, Leipzig, to USG. "Permit me to introduce to you my friend, *Hermann Frueauf*, Esq. the bearer of this note. Mr. Frueauf is a young gentleman of fine culture, and has spent several years in Germany to perfect himself in his studies. He is anxious to make your acquaintance, not for the sake of political affairs, but for the sake of knowing you whose career he has watched with great interest. Any attention you may show him, will be highly appreciated."—ALS, DNA, RG 59, Letters of Application and Recommendation. Related papers are *ibid.*

1869, FEB. 23. Francis J. Herron, New Orleans, to "The President," probably meaning USG. "Permit me to commend to you—Mr I. H. Douglass, of Erie, Penna, who is an applicant for the U. S. Disct Attorneyship of Western Pa: Mr Douglass is a gentleman of high legal and social standing, well known throughout the District, and would make a faithful and energetic officer. He will be strongly endorsed from this District, and I beleive that his appointment would be a good one for the Goverment interests."—ALS, NNP. On March 19, U.S. Representative Glenni W. Scofield of Pa. and nine others wrote to USG recommending John W. Douglass as U.S. attorney, Western District, Pa.—DS, DLC-Pennsylvania Miscellany. On April 5, USG nominated Douglass as deputy commissioner of Internal Revenue; on Dec. 7, 1871, as commissioner of Internal Revenue.

1869, FEB. 23. U.S. Representative James Mullins of Tenn. and eight others to USG. "the undersigned representatives in the congress of the United States from the state of Tennessee Take the liberty of introducing to you Mr H N Rankin a gentleman of Col' from Memphis Ten' It affords us pleasure to be able to say that Mr Rankin is recommended to us, by a large number of gentlemen of respectability as a man of integrity, polished scholar, and in every way an estimable gentleman, Mr Rankin will be an applicant for the appointment of minister to Liberia, and shudd you confer upon him the position; we have no doubt but he would acquit himself with credit to himself and race, and hope that you may be pleased to confer upon him the position"—DS, DNA, RG 59, Letters of Application and Recommendation. No appointment followed.

1869, FEB. 24. Maj. Gen. George G. Meade, Atlanta, to USG. "I take great pleasure in calling your attention to the services during the War of J. Warren Keiffer of Ohio—late Brevt—Maj—Genl. of Volunteers.—Genl. Keiffer commanded a brigade in the 3d Division 6th Army Corps on the campaign from the Rapidan to the James—and on this, as on previous campaigns—I had frequent opportunities from personal observation to note his efficient & meritorious services, and I am glad to be able to bear testimony to the same and to say they entitle him to the acknowledgement of the Government."—ALS, DNA, RG 60, Records Relating to Appointments. Related papers are *ibid.* No appointment followed.

1869, FEB. 25. To Bvt. Maj. Gen. William A. Nichols. "Order Gn. Forsythe to Washington."—ALS (telegram sent), DNA, RG 107, Telegrams Collected (Bound); telegram sent (at 3:00 P.M.), *ibid.*; copy, DLC-USG, V, 56. On the same day, Nichols, St. Louis, telegraphed to USG. "Genl J. W Forsyth Genl Sheridans inspector General has just come in from the Indian Country with important dispatches and to see Genl Sherman, The latter left yesterday for Washington, Forsyth desires to go to Washington to see Gen Sherman, Shall I order him there? The Cheyennes have broken faith and Genl Sheridan was to move a column against them the 12th inst; cause of breach of faith supposed to be outside influence the nature of which he gives in his letter, copy of which I sent to the Adjt General today—"—Telegram received (at 2:20 P.M.), DNA, RG 107, Telegrams Collected (Bound); (at 2:30 P.M.), *ibid.*, RG 108, Telegrams Received; copies, *ibid.*, RG 393, Military Div. of the Mo., Telegrams Sent; DLC-USG, V, 55.

1869, FEB. 25. Bvt. Maj. Gen. John Pope, Detroit, to USG. "I see that a bill for the reorganization the Supreme Court is before Congress and is likely to pass, and in this connection I beg to invite your consideration to the position & claims of the Hon John Erskine Judge of the U. S. District Court for the Two Districts of Georgia—If you know the Judge I can say little more to you than invite consideration to him; If not, I can only say that he is an accomplished Judge, a thorough gentleman & what is worth as much in that section of country, he is & has been always a staunch & uncompromising Union man—I know no man in that section of country in every way so worthy of the highest legal position & as the vacancy on the Supreme Bench has been occasioned by the death of Judge Wayne of Savannah Georgia & as Judge Erskine is also from Georgia & now holds the highest legal position as Federal Judge of that District, it seems eminently fit that he should be promoted to the Supreme Bench in place of Judge Wayne—I know of my own knowledge that his appointment would be most acceptable to every loyal man in Georgia Alabama & Florida"—ALS, DNA, RG 60, Records Relating to Appointments. Related papers are *ibid.* No appointment followed.

1869, Feb. 25.   Jacob D. Cox and Secretary of War John M. Schofield, Cincinnati, to USG. "Being informed that Col. W. E. Hobson of Kentucky will be an applicant for a consular appointment, I take satisfaction in saying in his behalf that both by meritorious services in the field during the war, and by a most unflinching support of true Unionism in Kentucky since the war, he deserves well of the Country & of your administration. He has been faithful in his patriotism when faithfulness required great courage & resolution, and is besides a gentleman of unexceptionable character & habits. He was the republican candidate for Congress in his District last year, & has never flinched from all the responsibilities attending a bold advocacy of Unionism in the most rebellious Communities of Kentucky. He served under my command in Gen. Schofield's army during the latter part of the war, & I do not in any way overstate his merits."—LS, DNA, RG 59, Applications and Recommendations. Related papers are *ibid.* USG appointed William E. Hobson as assessor of Internal Revenue, 3rd District, Ky. On Oct. 9, Jesse Root Grant, Covington, Ky., telegraphed to USG. "Telegrams announce W. E Hodsons Assessor 3rd Dist of Kentucky   Will you hold up commission until Col Campbell can be heard . . . answer"—Telegram received (at noon), *ibid.*, RG 107, Telegrams Collected (Bound).

1869, Feb. 26.   Henry R. de La Reintrie, Havana, to USG. "*Confidential* . . . When this reaches your hands, you will, probably, have been inducted into the office of President of our common country, in whose behalf you have amply done your full share of service as a soldier and a patriot. Your fellow citizens recognizing your services have placed you at the head of our government. I heartily wish you God Speed in your new career which I hope, with the aid of an All Powerful Providence, may be crowned with success.—You have heard, doubtless, of the revolution in Cuba and of its present status—It is the fight of Freedom against despotism. On the 16th instant, by telegram from Key West, I was *compelled* to resign my position as vice Consul general of the United States here, because I *could not* & *would not permit my countrymen to be shot down in cold blood by a lawless soldiery.*— . . . I trust you have not entirely lost sight of me, you will remember me as the firm friend of Mexico during her recent struggle. . . .*"*

—ALS, DNA, RG 59, Letters of Application and Recommendation. On March 13, de La Reintrie wrote to USG. "*Unofficial.* . . . I wrote you briefly a few days ago—The situation here is unchanged—General Dulce cannot control the volunteers, and should you adopt the course pointed out by Congress as to recognizing the Independence of Cuba, it would be well to have a strong force in this quarter to save the lives of our people. The feeling of the Spanish population is growing bitter against Citizens of the United States,—and so soon as they know the action of the Executive, there will be no safety for any of them. It was owing to my inability, (without the support of my Government) that I was compelled to resign: this measure has already had some good effect, which I trust my successor will avail of. I should like you to take a look at my correspondence with the State Department, and I am sure you will find that for at least four months I have been calling for aid, but in vain. The same call has also been made by all the United States Consuls in this Island."—ALS, *ibid.*, Miscellaneous Letters. On May 20, USG conferred with de La Reintrie.—*New York Herald*, May 21, 1869.

On Dec. 23, 1870, de La Reintrie, Baltimore, wrote to USG. "From the proceedings in the Senate, I learn that three Commissioners and a Secretary are to be appointed to proceed to St: Domingo and report on the condition, resources, &c, of that Island, with a view to its annexation to the United States. As, I believe myself to possess the required qualifications, both as a Spanish and French scholar, and of which you are doubtless aware, I respectfully request the appointment of Secretary to said Commission."—ALS, DNA, RG 59, Letters of Application and Recommendation. Related papers are *ibid.* See letter to Buenaventura Báez, Jan. 15, 1871.

1869, FEB. 26.   John H. Vincent, New York City, to USG. "I have not wearied you with communications, nor have I solicited any favors. Today, I have *one* request to make. This letter will be handed to you by Prof. Van Benschoten, a fine German scholar and familiar, from residence there, with the ins & outs of Germany. ~~life~~. He is Prof of Greek in our University in Middletown Conn. Having met with an accident on the railroad, the Prof. is compelled to spend a time in recruiting. He is no politician although an earnest republican. His friends believe that he would render most valuable service in some German consulate; and I write to ask that his request receive from you some attention; and if you can aid him you will have in your employ abroad, a worthy representative of our best American culture, and a true ~~loyal~~ American patriot. Hoping that you will pardon the freedom of my note, . . ."—ALS, DNA, RG 59, Letters of Application and Recommendation. Related papers are *ibid.* No appointment followed. See *PUSG*, 15, 302.

1869, FEB. 28.   Horace Rublee, Republican State Committee, Madison, Wis., to USG. "I am informed that Capt. W. S. Scribner, formerly of Wisconsin, & now a resident of Montana desires the appointment as Secretary of that territory. I have known ~~Mr~~Capt. Scribner intimately & can most cordially endorse him as a gentleman of integrity, with an excellent record as a soldier, & in all respects well qualified for the position in question."— ALS, DNA, RG 59, Letters of Application and Recommendation. Related papers are *ibid.* On March 30, Robert E. Fisk, editor, *Helena Herald, et al.,* Helena, Montana Territory, wrote to USG. "We the undersigned committee of Soldiers of the late volunteer union army, appointed at a convention of Soldiers & Sailors held at Helena in Montana Territory on the 9th day of Oct last, to represent the Soldiers & Sailors interest of that territory at Washington City at this time, beg leave to submit the following reasons why we ask the removal of James Tufts, the present Secretary of Montana Territory Mr Tufts was appointed Secretary by President Johnson, and is not in harmony with the Republican party, In the distribution of Government patronage he gives preference to democrats and disloyal men. He was not in the service at any time during the late war, but on the contrary went into the Territories to avoid its dangers,"—LS (3 signatures), *ibid.* Related papers are *ibid.* On April 3, USG nominated Wiley S. Scribner as secretary, Montana Territory. On April 15, 1870, U.S. Representative Amasa Cobb of Wis. wrote to USG. "I have the honor to enclose a telegram just recieved from Captain Scribner Secretary of Montana Territory. It is a reply to one from me notifying him that he was charged to you with having intermeddled in the matter of General Potts' confirmation and that he was likely to be removed therefor. I do not think that the Captain would tell a falsehood and unless the proof against him is clear I beg that his denial may be accepted"—ALS, *ibid.* The enclosure is *ibid.* On July 16, Governor Benjamin F. Potts of Montana Territory, Washington, D. C., wrote to USG. "I respectfully recommend Add. H Sanders of Iowa for Secretary of Montana Territory vice W. S. Scribne" —ALS, *ibid.* On July 19, USG designated Addison H. Sanders to replace Scribner. On Dec. 3, Potts, Virginia City, Montana Territory, wrote to USG. "Genl. A. H. Sanders Secretary of this territory goes to Washington on public business connected with his office, and I respectfully ask that leave be granted him for the period necessary for the transaction of his business"—ALS, *ibid.,* Montana Territorial Papers. On Dec. 14, USG nominated Sanders as register, land office, Helena.

[1869, FEB.].   John R. Cravens *et al.* to USG. "The undersigned members of the General Assembly and citizens of the State of Indiana, without any desire to interfere in so delicate a matter as the selection of your Constitutional advisers, would be gratified if, in making such selection, you could find it consistent with your duty to yourself and the country to appoint the Hon Samuel Galloway of Columbus, Ohio, one of them. You cannot be insensible to his high intellectual qualifications; which, added to his moral worth and undoubted integrity, fit him for any place of exalted trust under the government."—DS (74 signatures), DNA, RG 59, Letters of Application and Recommendation. On March 1, Samuel Galloway, Columbus, Ohio, wrote to Elihu B. Washburne. "This will be handed you by my friend

Genl B F Potts Member of the Senate of Ohio—Genl Potts is a noble man
and merits attention & kindness—The enclosed letter was sent to me & recd
this morning—It is rather a late movement—It is quite complementary &
therefore ought not be withheld—especially as from without any solicitation
or procurement—It will at least give Genl Grant an *inkling* of my position
outside of Ohio—I am intirely unconcerned as to his Cabinet appointments—
except to be saved from Dennison who was only plucked as a brand from
the Johnson flame by devoted friends. I admire Grant' reticence . . . *NB* It
is due to the Indiana Republicans of Senate & House that this paper should
be presented— . . . Will you be pleased to do so.—"—ALS, *ibid.* No appointment followed.

1869, [*Feb.*]. U.S. Senator John Sherman of Ohio to USG. "As this is
an application by a wounded ~~soldier~~ officer for service in your Presidential
office I enclose it to you now in the hope that you can comply with it"—
AES, NRU. Written on a letter of Feb. 20 from August Duddenhausen,
Washington, D. C., to Sherman. ". . . I would be most happy indeed to
have your endorsement on the enclosed application and would further consider myself very fortunate, if I perhaps could get through your aid the
assistance of your brother, Genl Sherman, in this matter. May I ask you,
whether you deem it necessary for me to get other recommandations to you
or Genl Sherman; the application to the President elect I would rather have
to go before him without any other endorsements. Permit me yet to give
you the following 'curriculum vitae' since I am out of the army. In May
1865 I was for a short time bookkeeper for a large german paper in St.
Louis (Senator Schurz is one of its proprietor's now). In June the same
year I removed to Evansville, Ind.a, accepting the invitation of the County-
Treasurer there, a friend of mine and fellow-soldier, to become his Deputy.
This position I held until April 1867 when I was elected a Justice of the
peace at the same place. Not finding this at all a remunerative occupation
however I accepted the assist.-editorship of the german republican paper
at Cleveland, Oh., at the same time teaching German and history at the
'Cleveland Institute'. Here (at Cleveland) I remained until April 1868
when through the kind assistance of the Honble Judge Spalding I received
the appointment as a Clerk in the 2d Auditor's Office, Dep. of the Treasury,
where I am still employed. For your kindness shown to me heretofore, Mr
Senator, please to accept my most heartfelt thanks; . . ."—ALS, *ibid.*

1869, FEB. Samuel Simpson, Bethel, Ohio, to USG. "Presuming upon
my relationship to you, I hereby respectfully recommend to your favorable
consideration, Mr. Wm. H. Fagley now of Manhattan Kansas who will be
an applicant for United States Marshal for the District in which he resides.
Mr Fagley was brought up in this community and is of good character, and
steady habits. He served as private and Captain in the late war until discharged on account of physical disability, afterward as assistant Provost
Marshal of this district until the close of the war, when, he removed to

Kansas. From personal knowledge of his character and ability I can cheerfully recommend him as a fit person for the position he seeks."—LS, NjP.
No appointment followed.

1869, MARCH 1.   U.S. Senator John Sherman of Ohio to USG. "As you
know I have carefully avoided giving you advice as to your Cabinet and
will not do so now—but upon one point the general sentiment of our Ohio
people is so strong that I feel it a duty to represent it to you—that is that
one member of the Cabinet should be from Ohio. You will feel this as
strongly as I do when you recall that we have about ½₂ of the population—⅛ of the Republican vote—and have furnished more than our proportion of the men—money—and intellect of the war. These considerations
together with a feeling of state pride in which you no doubt share—justify
an urgent desire that one member of your Cabinet should reside in Ohio. I
have personal reasons for sharing in this but will not trouble you with
them, nor with any expression of personal preferences"—Copy, DLC-John
Sherman.

1869, MARCH 2.   Governor Rutherford B. Hayes of Ohio to USG. "Gen
Theodore Jones of Ohio will apply for a place in the Civil Service of the
United States. I know him intimately as a soldier and a Citizen. He was a
most gallant and deserving soldier. He is an upright, reliable capable business man, and may be safely entrusted with any duty requiring honesty,
energy firmness and capacity. I recommend him strongly and confidently—"
—ALS, Jones Papers, OHi.

1869, MARCH 4.   Bvt. Maj. Gen. George Crook, Portland, Ore., to USG.
"May I solicit the appointment of Robert. G. Scott to the first vancancy in
the adjutant Generals Department,   He is very deserving—"—Telegram
received (on March 5, 9:25 A.M.), DNA, RG 107, Telegrams Collected
(Bound); copy, *ibid.*, RG 393, Dept. of the Columbia, Letters Sent.

1869, MARCH 4.   Bland Ballard, Louisville, to USG. "I understand, that
G. G Symes. of Paducah Ky is an applicant for the position of Associate
Justice of Montana Territory. Mr Symes is a lawyer of great industry. of
much professional pride and of excellent professional standing—He is too
and has been, at all times, a true lover of the Union. And I have no doubt
he would make an upright and an enlightened judge"—ALS, Slaughter
Papers, Western Kentucky University, Bowling Green, Ky. On March 26,
USG nominated George G. Symes as associate justice, Montana Territory.
    On March 26, U.S. Representative George W. McCrary of Iowa wrote
to USG. "Understanding that the delegation in Congress from Tennessee
will present to your Excellency the name of Maj John. L. Murphy of Knoxville for a territorial appointment, I beg leave to state what I know of him.
Driven from Tennessee by rebel persecution, he entered the Union service
as a private in an Illinois Regiment and served faithfully until his health

gave way, and he was sent to a Hospital in Keokuk. When partially restored he aided in raising a colored Regiment in Iowa, in which he was
appointed major, and served until the close of the war. I know Major Murphy to be a gentleman of good education, of fine mind of most excellent
moral character, and of earnest and devoted patriotism."—ALS, DNA, RG
60, Records Relating to Appointments. Related papers are *ibid.* On Nov.
25, 1870, Governor Benjamin F. Potts of Montana Territory, Virginia
City, wrote to USG. "The great dissatisfaction existing against. G. G.
Symes one of the Judges of the Supreme Court of this territory compels me
to ask his removal on the grounds of public interests. The Bar have asked
his removal because of incompetency of which charge they ought to the
best judges. I am confident that a change should be made and an able
Lawyer appointed in his stead. I recommend to Your Excellency the name
of Francis G. Servis of Ohio a lawyer of great experience and in every way
competent for the position. I refer you to Hon J. A. Ambler M. C. from 17.
Dist of Ohio and Hon John Sherman as to Mr Servis abilities   A. new
country requires a Judge of ability and nerve who will enforce the law and
punish offenders—We need a civilizer here and not a demoralizer as we
have now. An able Judge has more power for good here than all the Federal
Officers put together—and I earnestly hope you will send us. a civilizer—"—
ALS, *ibid.* On Jan. 9, 1871, USG nominated John L. Murphy to replace
Symes.

On March 23, 1872, U.S. Senator William G. Brownlow of Tenn.
wrote to USG. "I have learned with regret, that an effort has been made,
within the last few days for the removal of Hon. John L. Murphy Associate
Justice in Montana Territory. My long and favorable acquaintance with
him—the son of one of our best citizens; a Union officer during the war;
since, a lawyer, notary public, and U. S. Commissioner induces me to interpose. Dispatches from Montana inform me that there are on the way, by
due course of mail, memorials protesting against the change, from bench,
bar, citizens, including the great body of the community. My present request is that your Excellency will postpone action to give time for a hearing.
A few days delay can do no harm. A speedy decision on *ex parte* statements,
may work irremediable injury to an upright Judge and a worthy man."—
ALS, *ibid.* On Sept. 16, U.S. Representative Horace Maynard of Tenn.,
Knoxville, wrote to Attorney Gen. George H. Williams. "Your letter of the
12th gives me great pain. May I beg that nothing be done, until I can see
you in person, probably very soon; but at all events before Congress meets
in December, and not very long, No great harm can result, mean time
from non-action—When the attempt at removal failed last Spring, some of
the Judge's warm friends expressed apprehension of its ultimate success,
knowing, as they said, the character of the man who had undertaken it,
that if they could not accomplish it in way, they would find another. Shortly
before the session of Congress closed there came to Washington, on business, a gentleman from Montana, Mr. Black, spoken of on all sides as a
man of high character & standing in the Territory. He spoke to me so

warmly in behalf of Judge Murphy, that I felt constrained to invite him to see the President & to express his sentiments in person to him. We called & the President gave us to understand that nothing more would be done. Yet in view of what had been suggested touching the temper of the Judge's opponents, I requested Mr. Black to give me in writing, the substance of what he had said to the President at that interview. He complied & I enclose herewith his statement, addressed in letter form to me. Please examine it, & I think you will agree with me that there is great wrong somewhere. At any rate do not act until I can see you, I pray."—ALS, *ibid.*, Letters Received, Tenn. The enclosure, a letter of May 27 from L. M. Black, Washington, D. C., to Maynard, is *ibid.* On Sept. 21, USG designated Francis G. Servis to replace Murphy as associate justice, Montana Territory. See Clark C. Spence, *Territorial Politics and Government in Montana, 1864–89* (Urbana, 1975), pp. 83, 227.

1869, MARCH 4. John Evans *et al.*, Washington, D. C., to USG. "the undersigned most respectfully ask the retention of A. C. Hunt (present incumbent) ~~be returned~~ as Governor of Colorado Territory He is a long time resident and fully identified with the interests and acquainted with the needs and wants of the Territory Under the circumstances we depricate any change, and especially one that should fill the position with any one not a citizen of Colorado. We therefore most respectfully protest against any change in the office for the present"—DS (18 signatures), DNA, RG 59, Letters of Application and Recommendation. On April 15, USG nominated Edward M. McCook as governor, Colorado Territory, in place of Alexander C. Hunt. On April 16, Orville E. Babcock wrote to Secretary of the Interior Jacob D. Cox. "The President directs me to say that he wishes Gov. Hunt of Colorado nominated for Supt of Indian Affairs of New Mexico to fill the vacancy—"—Copies, DLC-USG, II, 1, 4. No appointment followed.

1869, [MARCH] 4. Governor John M. Palmer of Ill. to USG. "I take great pleasure in recommending to your favorable consideration Capt. Anton Neustadt as a man peculiarly qualified for the discharge of any important duties that might devolve upon him. He speaks several languages fluently, and possesses business capacities & habits of a high order. In point of patriotism, integrity, talents and general behaviour, he is well worthy of the consideration herein asked for."—LS (misdated Jan. 4), IHi. The letter is addressed to USG as "His Excellency," Palmer had not yet been inaugurated on Jan. 4 when the letter was sent from "Executive Office," and the letter is docketed "Mch. 1869"; all indicate misdating.

1869, MARCH 4. Petition. "We the undersigned Merchants and Ship Owners of the town of Deer Isle in the State of Maine would respectfully represent that we are included in the Castine Colective District and are largely interested in navagation which renews the appointment of Collector of the Customs at that Port a matter of great Interest to us and we therefore

humbly and respectfully reccommend Col Charles W Tilden of Castine as
a man eminently Possessing all the qualifications necessary for Collector
aforesaid and hope that when a new appointment is made your Excellency
will See fit to appoint Col Tilden to that Office"—Copy (unsigned), Revere
Memorial Library, Isle au Haut, Maine.

1869, MARCH 5.   Bvt. Maj. Gen. Oliver O. Howard, Washington, D. C.,
to USG. "My friend, Alexander P. Ketchum, who perhaps was known to
you while serving on my staff during some two years, as Assistant Adjutant
General, is a candidate for the appointment of Assessor of Internal Revenue,
for the 9th District of New York. Not being in sympathy with the Representative in Congress from that District (Hon. Fernando Wood) and knowing that I was more familiar with his excellent war record than any one
else, he has desired me at the proper time, to make known his wishes to
you, and that of his fitness, and his deserts, in such terms as I should see
fit. Among his qualifications for the position, many be mentioned his in-
variable courtesy of manner, his fine culture, (being educated for, and now
in the practice of law) a systematic ability and high toned moral character.
His personal habits are unexceptionable. In the recent political campaign,
he was active for the Republican party, devoting much of his time in public
speaking, and other services for the success of the cause. Confident that if
Colonel Ketchum shall recive the appointment, he will discharge his duties
to the satisfaction of the President, I shall be personally gratified if the
appointment can be made."—Copy, Howard Papers, MeB. On April 2, USG
nominated Alexander P. Ketchum as assessor of Internal Revenue, 9th
District, N. Y.

1869, MARCH 5.   Lt. Col. John C. McFerran, Washington, D. C., to
USG. "This will be handed to you by my friend Judge Turner of Arizona
Territory—whom I had the pleasure of introducing to you, at your Head
Quarters a few days ago. He was one of the first Federal Judges for that
Territory after its organization—and appointed by the late President Lincoln—has resided in the Country ever since and knows all of its wants &
interests. I take great pleasure in saying that I believe him to be thorougholy
identified with Arizona & its advancement, and as a most Excellent man for
the position of Governor of that Territory—"—ALS, DNA, RG 59, Letters
of Application and Recommendation. Related papers are *ibid.* On Dec. 10,
Henry A. Bigelow *et al.*, Prescott, Arizona Territory, wrote to USG. "Your
petitioners respectfully represent that William F. Turner, Chief Justice of
the Territory of Arizona, is most obnoxious to the people of the 1st Judicial
District, as a Judge, and pray that he may be removed. The said William
F. Turner was appointed first, by President Lincoln in 1863, and arrived
in Arizona in December of that year—In April 1864 he left his field of duty
and the Territory, and did not return hither until November 1865, having
been absent eighteen months, and having prolonged his stay for more than
a year after courts were established by law, greatly to the public detriment.

At the expiration of his first term of office, he was re-appointed by President Johnson. By the election to Congress of R. C. McCormick, Governor of Arizona, the office became vacant, and the said Wm F. Turner ambitious to obtain the appointment to the vacancy—again left his post in January 1869, and proceeded to Washington, D. C. to urge his claims, returning hither in August 1869, by reason of which action, no spring term of court was held in the 1st judicial district, much to the annoyance and loss of parties having cases then pending. With one member of the bar, the most successful of the attorneys practicing in his court, his intimacy is such, that it is commonly suspected and reported that the Judge assists said attorney in the getting up of cases, renders partial decisions and rulings in his favor, and shares in the fees received. The said William F. Turner has entered into business with different citizens, and by his operations has brought trouble upon his partners, and their business to unprofitable conclusions. He has contracted debts at gold prices, (as is the custom of the country,) and has settled them with greenbacks at twenty-five per cent. discount, and in consequence of such action, has been publicly posted in the streets of Prescott, as a swindler and a cheat. He has contracted other debts which he utterly refuses to pay, and as he holds all his property in the name of H. M. Turner, his wife, his creditors cannot enforce the collection of their claims by law. He has for two years carried on farming in partnership with a low mexican, who is married to a white woman the discarded mistress of a negro, and thereby scandalized himself before the whole people—He has had several lawsuits with citizens of this district, in all of which he has been plaintiff, one of which suits is of three years duration and is yet unsettled, and in these suits having testified as a witness in his own behalf, has been accused of perjury by the defendants and their witnesses. In consequence of the above recited facts, the said William F. Turner, Chief Justice of Arizona, has lost the confidence and respect of the community, to which his office should entitle him—and your petitioners pray for his immediate removal, and as in duty bound will ever pray—"—DS (8 signatures), *ibid.*, RG 60, Records Relating to Appointments. On March 30, 1870, William F. Turner, Prescott, answered these charges in a sixteen-page letter to USG.— LS, *ibid.* Related papers are *ibid.* On April 14, USG nominated John Titus as chief justice, Arizona Territory, in place of Turner.

On May 1, 1872, Milton B. Duffield, Tucson, wrote to USG. "Permit me the honor of addressing you this in behalf of the general Government, and the people of Arizona in particular—It is expected that good honest men are selected at Washington to fill the important offices of a Territory, but such is not the case in Arizona, I forwarded on the 20th day of March to the honorable Mr Williams, Attorney General U. S—charges, accompanied with numerous affidavits, against two Territorial officials of Arizona, viz— John Titus, Chief Justice, and James E—McCaffrey U. S. District Attorney for Said Territory, . . . My charges against them jointly, is a conspiracy to commit a premeditated, and cold blooded murder, by James E. McCaffrey slipping up behind me, and snapping a Derringer pistol close to my back,

so near that it touched my clothes as I was leaving the Court house on the
16th day of April 1870, the Court being in session at the time, and the act
perpetrated within ten feet and in plain view of Judge Titus's eyes, who
sanctioned, and justified the attempted assassination and prevented the
arrest of that said McCaffrey—there was no cause for the act, ~~as~~ as there
were no words passed between us, and had not been for perhaps two or three
months—Again—they made their Court a Court of Inquisition for the last
two years in persecuting, and trying to ruin and murder me through revenge I presume for compelling Judge Titus in the year 1863 to resign his
U. S. Attorneyship for Arizona (which appointment he had at that time)
after uttering in my presence that '*Valandingham of Ohio was as good and
honest man as Abraham Lincoln*'—I also charge John Titus Chief Justice
for Arizona with *Purjury* and *Forgery*, the *first*, in his Oath of Office to deal
justly, and *forgery*, by presenting to the Supreme Court held at Tucson in
January last a document in an appeal case purporting to be his charge to a
jury in the lower Court, but which has been proven by the Jurors who sat
on the Case below, to *not* be his charge— . . . I also charge John Titus with
being guilty of complicity in, or suppressing proceedings in a case of a U. S.
Mail robbery in Arizona of the U. S. Mail which was robbed in July 1869,
and proceedings instituted in February 1870 which was suppressed by said
Titus, and which has never yet been investigated— . . . There is no doubt
that some of their political friends who belong to the Same '*ring*' may
attempt through their position to screen those Officials above named and
charged as Arizona has its little political '*ring*' that can beat *Tammany* for
its size—they are all Republicans when in Washington, but Governors
staffs have *always* been filled with Democrats, and *all* the Offices in the
Southern part of the Territory is filled with the same material, with not one
at heart but dispises a Republican—And if there was a vote taken of the
Territory today, there would not be fifty votes cast in all Arizona for an
out, and out Republican, I mean a *true Republican* To be sure they have
their press and their Editor who is always ready to do their work—Mr
John Wasson the Editor at Tucson who is also Surveyor General of Arizona (yet I presume has never looked through a Surveyors Compass in the
Territory) is a very active man in sustaining the corruption of the '*ring*'—
I will ask Your Excellency to please excuse my plain manner of speaking,
as I have had experience long enough (over 61 years of age) to know that
truth and *facts* cannot be too plainly spoken, and I have been in Arizona
ever since its Organization, and know the people, and their political pro-
clivities—I had the honor of carrying with me a Commission from that
great and good man, President Lincoln, for the U. S. Marshalship of Arizona,—and I know that no man has ever been elected to any office under
the name of *Republican in Arizona*—We have just had a visit from that
noble gentlemanly Commissioner, General Howard who I presume left perfectly satisfied that our poor friendly Indians have been swindled out of all
the goods which the Government have sent them, with some small excep-
tions by dishonest and corrupt Agents, a subject with which I profess to

know something about, Arizona is a great way from home (Washington) and politicians play off on the Government—"—ALS, *ibid.* Related papers are *ibid.* On Nov. 30, 1875, Titus, Tucson, wrote to USG. "I hear that letters have been written from this place, to certain Members of the Federal Government at the Capital and probably to Youself, charging me with disloyalty to the Republican Party, disaffection to the National Administration and adducing as proof of this charge, my support of Mr. Hiram S. Stevens, last Year, as Delegate to Congress from the Territory of Arizona; and I beg leave to say that there is not a scintilla of truth in this charge of disaffection and disloyalty. I am, I have been, and I expect to remain in absolute sympathy and accord with the Republican Party of Pennsylvania and Philadelphia whence I hail, and to which I hope to return. I claim *no censorship* over Democracy or Democrats, but never though a voter forty odd Years have I voted for a Democrat per se, and I can conceive of no contingency that shall induce me to vote against the Republican Party. . . . You will probably not recognize the humble writer of this letter, nor do I know though I suspect my accusers, who as I am assured are doing their work of falsehood and calumny under convenient disguises. Permit me then to say, that I have twice held Your Commission as Chief Justice of Arizona, and as often that of the Lamented Lincoln for Utah, and I do not wish to stand as a silent Ingrate in the estimation of an Official Benefactor. . . ."— ALS, *ibid.*, Letters Received from the President.

1869, MARCH 6. Henry Dent, Louisville, to USG. "This will be presented to you by my friend the Hon. Boyd Winchester, I have never had the pleasure but *once* to meet you & then at Chicago yet I have known you for a long time, If consistent with the Public trust which is in your keeping, I shall be pleased to have the Appointment of U S. Marshall for the District of Ky I refer you to Genl W. T. Sherman, Genl H. Thomas, and Mr Winchester Please present my respects to old Mr Dent & say to him that I am the son of Major Alexander Dent of Charles County Maryland, my mother was also a Dent, and is Still living and in her 81st year & quite sprightly, and desires very much to see the old gentleman & speaks of visiting Washington for that purpose,"—ALS, DNA, RG 60, Records Relating to Appointments. On Feb. 2, 1870, Dent wrote to USG. "I have the honor herewith, respectfully to make application for a cadetship for my nephew Henry B Dent either in the Naval Academy at Annopolis, or in the Military Academy at West Point. . . ."—ALS, *ibid.*, RG 94, Correspondence, USMA. Related papers are *ibid.* No appointments followed.

1869, MARCH 6. George Gibbs, Washington, D. C., to USG. "I respectfully apply for the office of Governor of Washington Territory. As I am personally known to you, I do not enclose any references. I believe my appointment would be satisfactory to the people there, and that I could be of service to the Government. . . . Accompanying this is the application of my brother in law Professor d'Oremieulx, formerly of West Point, for a consulate."—ALS, DNA, RG 59, Letters of Application and Recommendation. On March 5, Theophilus d'Orémieulx, New York City, had written to USG. "I have the honour to submit to your kind consideration this my application for the office of United States Consul at Paris, France. Of my antecedents and Character I have nothing to say, having had the privilege to be known to your Excellency for the last 30 years. . . ."—ALS, *ibid.* D'Orémieulx was an instructor in French, USMA, 1839–56. Related papers are *ibid.* No appointments followed. For Gibbs, see *PUSG*, 1, 293–94.

1869, MARCH 6. Governor William W. Holden of N. C. to USG. "The Legislature of this state has ratified the fifteenth (15th) article by a large majority, official statement of ratification has been forwarded by Express—" "The reliable union element in this state would regret the assignment of Genl Sickles to this Department for reasons that will be given you in detail if the order be delayed a few days, I respectfully ask you to confer with our Senators on the subject and to suspend such order until I can communicate with you more fully"—Telegrams received (at 10:20 and 10:30 A.M.), DNA, RG 107, Telegrams Collected (Bound). On March 8, Holden wrote to USG. "Allow me to express my gratification at 'General Orders No. 10,' assigning Generals to the various departments. Our loyal people have special cause for gratification at that part of these Orders which assigns Maj. General Terry to this department. They respect him for his excellent personal character, and for his gallantry so conspicuously displayed on many fields in upholding the flag in the war to suppress the rebellion; and they have full confidence that he will acquit himself with satisfaction to the government and to all peaceable and well-disposed persons in his department."—LS, Duke University, Durham, N. C.

1869, MARCH 6. U.S. Senator Timothy O. Howe of Wis. *et al.* to USG. "The Representatives in Congress from the state of Wisconsin, respectfully ask that Horace Rublee of that state may be appointed Minister Resident to the Republic of Switzerland. Mr Rublee is a gentleman of high character, of fine culture, of great aptitude for affairs, and we believe would very much elevate the character of our representation there. Besides that, he has been for sixteen years the political editor of the Wisconsin State Journal, the leading Republican Newspaper of Wisconsin. During that time Wisconsin has been changed from a strong Democratic State, to a strong Republican State. For the last ten years he has been chai[r]man of the Republican State Committee. During that time, in spite of the defection of some individuals of influence in the party, the Republican majority has increased until last November the state polled a majority of about Twenty five Thousand for the Republican Ticket.—For what he has done for the Republican, not less than for what he can do for the National interests we earnestly ask for his appointment as above"—DS (6 signatures), DNA, RG 59, Letters of Application and Recommendation. On April 12, USG nominated Horace Rublee as minister to Switzerland.

1869, MARCH 6.   D. Wemyss Jobson, Philadelphia, to USG. "As a citizen of Texas since the year 1846, and of New York since the 5th of August 1854, I have to claim redress from you for the following outrages I have sustained from the British Government. The state of my health, and other private considerations, having compelled me to visit Australia in the year 1864, I was, in consequence of announcing my intention to deliver a Lecture in favor of the American Union, then endangered by civil war, marked for insult from the moment of my arrival, and that insult soon assumed the form of personal violence. . . ."—ALS, DNA, RG 59, Miscellaneous Letters. On April 10, 1871, Jobson wrote to USG. "General D Wemyss Jobson thinks it well to inform the President of the United States that his atttorney-general, Akerman, has yet taken no steps to investigate the brutal assault committed by the Marshal here, Sharpe, and two comrogues, his tipstaffs, and seemingly will taken none; the old rebel evidently acting in unison with that dastardly ruffian, and a U. S. Commissioner named Davenport, of this city, as well as Murphy of the Custom-house here, and the Democratic party, both Young and Old, to defeat General Grants' re-election"—Copy, *ibid.*, RG 60, Letters Received, N. Y., Southern District.

1869, MARCH 6.   U.S. Senator John Sherman of Ohio to USG. "Gen. Roeliffe Brinkerhoff is a fellow townsman at Mansfield Ohio and I have known him intimately for several years. At my suggestion he entered the military service at the beginning of the War & became Brig. Gen in his line of duty. He is a lawyer and a gentleman of character ability and integrity of good address & education. He is very competant to fill the position as a Minister of the second grade   I recommend his appointment to the Hague—a mission his studies taste & capacity fit him worthily to fill"—ALS, DNA, RG 59, Letters of Application and Recommendation. Related papers are *ibid.* See Roeliff Brinkerhoff, *Recollections of a Lifetime* (Cincinnati, 1900), pp. 188–90. On March 13, Governor John W. Geary of Pa. wrote to USG. "This letter will be presented to you by Hon: Benjamin Harris Brewster, Attorney General of Pa. and I beg the favor of its perusal by you in person, in consequence of the change in the Secretary of State. A few days ago, when I was in Washington City, I personally laid in the hands of Secretary Washborne, a letter in which I requested the appointment of Hon Lewis W. Hall of this city, to *Minister Resident at Brussels.* and stated that this appointment was the *only one I desired,* and that it was a *special and earnest request which I hoped would be granted. All of which I now reiterate. . . .*"—ALS, *ibid.* Related papers are *ibid.* On April 13, Geary telegraphed to USG. "I deeply regret that you have been unable to send my friend to Brussels,   Can not you give him either Copenhagen, Hague or Switzerland,   This will benefit me and the party in Pennsylvania."—Telegram received (at 11:20 A.M.), *ibid.* On the same day, Benjamin H. Brewster telegraphed to USG. "Can you not send Mr Hall to Copenhagen or the Hague"—Telegram received (at 12:30 P.M.), *ibid.*
   On March 17, Ellen E. Sherman, St. Louis, had telegraphed to USG.

"Please do not recall my brother Hugh Ewing now at the Hague   Three of my four brothers strongly favored your election. But one resided where he could vote and his vote and influence were for you   Three of the four 4 served throughout the war and were your sincere friends and admirers"—Telegram received (at noon), DNA, RG 107, Telegrams Collected (Bound). On Dec. 9, Governor James M. Harvey of Kan. *et al.* wrote to USG. "We the undersigned respectfully represent: that Kansas is Republican in fact and in deed— . . . In view of these facts, we respectfully call attention to the position occupied by *Genl. Hugh Ewing* now Minister to the Netherlands, and accredited to Kansas: when it is well known that he never was a citizen of Kansas, never was a voter in Kansas—has no interest with us—is politically opposed to us & is politically opposed to your administration of which we are warm, outspoken supporters—His whole political character and history are at open emnity with the State to which he is accredited—Of his moral character we know nothing, never having heard of him in Kansas but as a visitor—We respectfully, but earnestly pray for his removal—"—DS (5 signatures), *ibid.*, RG 59, Letters of Application and Recommendation.

On June 22, 1870, U.S. Senator Zachariah Chandler of Mich. wrote to Secretary of State Hamilton Fish. "Genl Charles. T. Gorham, Marshall Michigan, has elected the Mission to the Hague   The President gave him the choice. Please send in the name tomorrow . . ."—ALS, *ibid.* On June 24, USG nominated Charles T. Gorham as minister to the Netherlands.

1869, MARCH 6.   Lewis Wallace, "White House," to USG. "You have it in power to do me a favor. I have returned to the law, and by hard work and patience hope to win my way back to a good practice. The office of United States District Attorney for the District of Indiana has no political significance, and is at present filled by a gentleman notoriously incompetent; it would. nevertheless be a great help to me, by at once giving me the start in the profession which I so much covet. I make request for the appointment directly, as your knowledge of me makes recommendations and interference of others unnecessary. If you think me a proper person to discharge the duties of the position, and are free to give it to me, and are so disposed, I feel sure this direct asking will do me no harm. As to my qualifications I have no hesitation in referring you to Mr. Colfax. Having congratulated you before and after your inauguration, I leave you this note, and place the matter in your hands, and go home tonight."—ALS, DNA, RG 60, Records Relating to Appointments. No appointment followed.

1869, MARCH 7.   Mrs. William F. McLean, New Orleans, to Julia Dent Grant. ". . . I am one of those who espoused 'the lost cause'; who clung to it through its darkening days of adversity, until it culminated in total overthrow; and I must ever feel as I then felt, that their sufferings were my sufferings, their dead my dead, and their weeds of mourning are to me ever sacred—But, at the opening of that struggle, when we thought right and truth were on our side, I echoed from my heart the words of Jeff. Davis, and 'God for the Right!' The battle was decided against us, and without sitting down in useless repining, my heart instantly acknowledged the result as of God, and I set myself to work to harmonize with the result. The consequence has been that I am more than satisfied, I am glad that the Federal arms were triumphant, that the black was freed, and more than all, that the poor white has been liberated from a bondage which he hardly knew shackled him, and to-day knows not the value of his freedom— . . . When the tramp of twenty thousand men, most of them black, filed along our streets in their Republican procession previous to the election, I put on all the gas I could and made my little house blaze as cheery a welcome as possible, although knowing it would make me marked and hated of my neighbors, who with darkened houses, sullenly refused even to look at the passing jubilee of the long oppressed man—The next day was Sunday, and on Monday, my landlady ordered me out of my house, and issued a writ of ejectment to force me: at the shortest possible time. For this I knew no cause save my illumination. My husband was absent, I was very weak from a recent illness, and begged for respite in vain. My only answer was to leave— No one would rent to me, because I could not take a lease, and I was unable to communicate readily with parties on account of my health. However, by dint of legal strategy, I was enabled to remain where I was until my husband's arrival. Most of the leading Republicans, even, would not light their houses on the night of that procession for fear of persecution, and at my next house, I did not venture to put up my door plate, thinking it better to remain unknown. My husband, meantime was in the parish of Rapides attempting to establish a newspaper. Twice his press was thrown into the river, and his life threatened and his person assailed, so that he was forced to shelter himself as he could in New Orleans— . . ."—ALS, DNA, RG 107, Letters Received from Bureaus.

1869, MARCH 8.   John Carey, Wilmington, Ohio, to USG. "As I have felt deeply interested in the wellfare of the Aboriginese of Our Country and often remember the Covenant made by our worthy friend William Penn, with many of them, I have believed that if those in our day were approached in the same spirit he (Wm Penn) was led by ~~that~~ that a permanent treaty might have been obtained with less expense to our Government, than two months Cost of the war, if the faith of the Government & those sent to deal with them would adher[e] to strict justice   From statements I hear ~~of th~~ of thy feelings toward this class of people, I have rejoiced in the hope, and my prayers are that thou mayst be endued with a spirit of wisdom that may guide thee—in all things, that duty and justice demand   Please remember the destitution and sufering that is prevailing, from accounts now amongs many of the tribes. If thou shoulds see fit to make arrangement to alleviate their present need & encourage them in peaceable life I should be glad and heartily desire the success of each right effort. From one who desires that true wisdom may guide thee safely through the duties

& perils of life, and [p]eace and prosperity to Our Country, and the salvation of all mankind."—ALS, DNA, RG 75, Miscellaneous Letters Received,
1869, C144½.

1869, MARCH 8. David K. Cartter *et al.* to USG. "The undersigned
Judges of the Supreme Court of District of Columbia, understanding that
the Office of Marshal for this District is about to become vacant by the
resignation of the present incumbent; beg leave respectfully to recommend
for appointment to said Office Alexander Sharp of Richmond, Virginia."—
DS, DNA, RG 60, Records Relating to Appointments.

1869, MARCH 8. U.S. Senator Timothy O. Howe of Wis. *et al.* to USG.
"The undersigned respectfully recommend Hon Gerry W. Hazelton of
Wisconsin for the appointment of United States District atty for the District
of Wisconsin."—DS (3 signatures), DNA, RG 60, Records Relating to
Appointments. On April 5, USG nominated Gerry W. Hazelton as U.S.
attorney, District of Wis. On Dec. 1, 1870, Hazelton, recently elected U.S.
representative of Wis., wrote to USG resigning as U.S. attorney.—ALS,
ibid. On Dec. 12, U.S. Senator Matthew H. Carpenter, U.S. Representative Philetus Sawyer of Wis., and Howe wrote to USG. "We respectfully
recommend Hon Levi Hubbell, of Milwaukee to be appointed District Attorney of the United States for the Eastern District of Wisconsin, in place
of Hon G. W. Hazelton, whose resignation takes effect on the 1st January
next. Judge Hubbell is a good lawyer, fully competent to discharge the
duties of the office; and since the firing upon Fort Sumpter, has done as
much as any man in Wisconsin for the Union Cause and to promote the
interests of the Republican party"—DS, *ibid.* On Dec. 14, USG nominated
Levi Hubbell as U.S. attorney, Eastern District, Wis.

On May 28, 1875, U.S. Representative William P. Lynde of Wis.,
Milwaukee, wrote to USG. "It is reported here that Judge Hubbell is to be
removed or suspended from the office of U. S. District Attorney for this
District. I think this the general sentiment of the Bar and of the Public,
that his suspension at this time and under present circumstances would do
him great injustice. Judge Hubbell has held the office for more than four
years and has discharged its duties with more ability and fidelity than any
Attorney who has held the office prior to his appointmen[t] for many years.
If an opportunity was given to Judge Hubbell to meet any charges which
shall be made against him, there would be no cause of complaint, but his
suspension without an opportunity to be heard in self defence would cause
an imputation upon his character which would do him great wrong"—ALS,
ibid. On June 13, Charles S. Hamilton, Milwaukee, wrote to USG. "*Private* . . . I have just learned that an effort is being made to have G. W.
Hazelton, late M. C. made Dist Attorney for this District. Without consulting any one, other than Act'g Attorney McKinney, I regard such appointment as being so prejudicial to the Administration & to the successful
prosecution of the whiskey frauds, that I telegraph you in advance, & now

give my reasons. First. Hazelton is not a resident of this District. His home is Columbus in the Western District. His appointment would be regarded as a reward for political services, and would satisfy the public that the statements of Hubbell & Carpenter, to the effect that no respectable lawyer *in* the District will take it—are true. Second. We need all the sympathy we can get from the honest portion of this community. The population here is largely German—Nearly every distiller & rectifier are germans, and their bondsmen, are found among the best of our german business men. These business men to day are with us, if they can be made to believe that this prosecution of the ring, is for the sole purpose of breaking up the frauds, and is not a political move. They believe in making every man pay his just taxes. Their sympathy is with us now, but the appointment of Hazelton would change many in their sympathies, and we need all the sympathy we can get. . . . Mr Hazelton has always been friendly to me, and I would not willingly do him an injustice. He was appointed District Attorney in the Spring of 1869, & held the office until elected to Congress, taking his seat in March 1871. In all that time he paid scarcely any attention to the duties of the office. He lived about 80 miles from this City, rarely came here to attend Court, but hired an old broken down poverty stricken lawyer to do his work, and the consequence was, the interests of the government were either neglected or so poorly managed that they might as well have been neglected altogether. I write thus freely, because & only because of my desire to have this matter go right. Senators Howe & Cameron both live at extremes of the State, and in making up their opinions as to men here, are as apt to receive impressions from those who wish to ward off this prosecution, as from the honest republicans & Democrats who wish to see fraud punished. I do not believe they would for a moment think of Hazelton, did they know the facts, which I have written above."—ALS, *ibid.* On July 7, USG designated Hazelton to replace Hubbell. A lengthy unpublished oration by Hazelton on USG is in the Hazelton Papers, WHi.

1869, MARCH 8.   George B. McClellan, Hoboken, to USG. "Col R H Nodine, of the 25th Illinois, Army of the Cumberland, is anxious to procure an appointment for his son as a Cadet at West Point. I have known Col Nodine for more than 20 years: first, when he served under me in the Engineer Troops, & afterwards upon the Illinois Central R. R., and it affords me very great pleasure to bear testimony to his worth & merits. I trust that his character & his services with the western armies will prove sufficiently strong arguments to enable you to confer upon his son the appointment he desires. My strong interest in his welfare induces me to hope that our personal relations will induce you to pardon me for troubling you with a letter at a time when I know that you must be overwhelmed with business. With my earnest & sincere wishes for your welfare . . ."—ALS, DNA, RG 94, Correspondence, USMA. On March 15, Richard H. Nodine, Washington, D. C., wrote to USG requesting his son's appointment to USMA.—ALS, *ibid.* On March 16, Maj. Gen. George H. Thomas endorsed this letter. "I remember Col Nodine as Col of the 25th Ill which served in the Army of the Cumberland from 61. till it was mustered out of service. He had an excellent Regiment & he was universally esteemed by his brother Officers as a gallant and efficient Officer."—AES, *ibid.* Charles H. Nodine did not attend USMA.

1869, March 8. U.S. Senators Oliver P. Morton and Daniel D. Pratt of Ind. to USG. "We recommend that Col. John W. Foster be appointed Deputy Post Master at Evansville Indiana"—DS, ICHi. On March 31, USG nominated John W. Foster as postmaster, Evansville.

1869, March 8. U.S. Senator John Sherman of Ohio to USG. "I add to the very strong recommendations made by others my earnest hope that Gen. Benj F. Potts of Ohio be appointed Governor of Montana. His services in the Army from Colonel to the command of a Division—must be known to you—He possesses rare Executive abilities is now prominent as a Member of the Ohio Senate—and is a Republican leader—No one of my acquaintance is better fitted to be Governor of that ~~turbulent~~ important Territory & I trust he will be appointed"—ALS, DNA, RG 59, Letters of Application and Recommendation. On the same day, General William T. Sherman endorsed this letter. "I cheerfully concur in the within. Genl Potts was one of my very best young Division Commanders in the closing campaigns of the War. He possesses high merit, & character, and would do justice to any official Station."—AES, *ibid.* Numerous letters of recommendation are *ibid.* On March 19, U.S. Senator Oliver P. Morton of Ind. wrote to USG recommending Nathaniel P. Langford for governor, Montana Territory.—ALS, *ibid.* Related papers are *ibid.* On March 23, Lester S. Willson, National Republican Committee for Montana, *et al.*, Washington, D. C., wrote to USG. "In submitting finally, what we have to say of the Governorship of Montana in behalf of the honorably discharged Soldiers and Sailors of the United States there, we do not care to say more of the political deservings of Mr N. P. Langford, than that while our Collector of Internal Revenue, more than half his patronage went to Democrats, in sympathy with the Rebellion, that he was used by them and condescended to trade with Democrats and corrupt Republicans, whereby he procured in January last, the nomination to this office from the late President, Johnson. In his official career, he paid at least two Men, $2400 each, who were ornamental attaches of the Revenue Service of the United States and offices were rented by him, for twice as much as the whole buildings were worth and the amount thus paid out by the Government, without receiving an equivalent, was from Five to Seven thousand Dollars per annum. Mr George M. Pinney inspires and marshals all the opposition to Col Sanders. He is a mercenary candidate for Office, corrupt to a lamentable extent and ready to support any one, who will promise to bolster up his failing fortunes and continue him in his mercenary career; and with two or three exceptions, the opposition to Col Sanders from our Territory, is from men who believe the Government is to used, not served; plundered, not protected by its guardians. Having endorsed Col Sanders for this position, we abide by our recommendation and by it, stand or fall— . . ."—DS (4 signatures), *ibid.* Related papers are *ibid.*

On April 5, USG nominated James M. Ashley as governor, Montana Territory. On June 25, Harry Chase, Toledo, wrote to USG. "It is believed, that you are not aware that Hon. J. M. Ashley, appointed Governor of Montana, has not gone to the said Territory at all; but that he is and has been spending his time since his appointment, in this District holding and attending public & private meetings, ostensibly for the purpose of inducing citizens from here to Emigrate with him to Montana, but really for Electioneering purposes, tending to perpetuate strife and division in. the Republican parrty of this District.—"—ALS, *ibid.*, Montana Territorial Papers. On Dec. 16, USG nominated Benjamin F. Potts to replace Ashley.

On Dec. 17, Robert E. Fisk, editor, *Helena Herald, et al.*, Helena, telegraphed to USG. "We most respectfully request of you a hearing from Hon James M Ashley in the matter of his removal from the Governorship of Montana"—Telegram received (at 3:50 P.M.), *ibid.*; (press) *ibid.*, RG 107, Telegrams Collected (Bound). On the same day, Andrew J. Smith *et al.*, Virginia City, Montana Territory, telegraphed to USG. "The republican party of Montana protest against the removal of Gov Ashley desire his retention in office and ask time to be heard 'Let us have peace' "— Telegram received (on Dec. 18, 9:20 A.M.), *ibid.*, RG 59, Montana Territorial Papers; (press) *ibid.*, RG 107, Telegrams Collected (Bound). On Dec. 21, Francis M. Case, Denver, wrote to USG. "You have done a wise thing in removing *J M Ashley* Gov of Montana The letters, which the telegrams, of this morning, say you have read, do not show the *whole arrangement.* nor will I take your time to detail it—for I seek no redress for my own wrongs in the matter—He is unfit for any official trust and I am most heartily glad you have sent him to private life, where his Constituents in Ohio sent him the last time he was before them for their suffrages"—ALS, *ibid.*, RG 59, Montana Territorial Papers.

On Dec. 20, Ashley, Virginia City, wrote to USG. "The telegraphic report of my removal was the most unexpected, and the hardest blow I ever received. Conscious that no *private* or official act of mine since I entered public life in 1858 would, unless misinterpreted, receive the condemnation of a republican administration, I am unable to devine the cause of my removal. Anticipating that a few men, who for years have made a bitter personal war upon me, might enter into a secret combination to do, by unscrupulous means, what they could not do by fair, I asked and obtained before leaving Washington a promise, from the Honorable Secretary of State Mr Fish, that if an effort were made to remove me after my arrival in the Territory, I should have timely notice and a fair hearing. With this assurance, I felt confident in my new position, and at an expense greater than I could afford I removed my family to this distant country and had but just unpacked my furniture when without previous warning, the telegraph announces my removal. You have been so unscrupulously & scandalously maligned, that I felt safe in your hands as against all maligners. Relying

with confidence upon my official record to successfully vindicate me, I have
seldom noticed those who for years have pursued and maligned me with a
vindictiveness which even time and distance seems unable to soften. As
against secret political combinations no man is safe, unless an oppurtunity
be given him to meet and reply to the charges made against him. Believing
that your sense of justice will accord me a fair hearing, before final action
is taken. I telegraphed such a request this morning. From the year 1852, to
this writing, the best years of my life have been devoted to securing the
triumph of the republican party. If in all that time I have ever given a vote
or done an official act which your administration, disapproves, I do not
know it. On my arrival here, my first official act was to appoint well known
repulicans to the Territorial offices, which were held by democrats and as
I believed illegally. The case went before the Court—Chief Justice H. L.
Warren [who is a democrat] presiding, and the right of the Governor, to
make the appointments was affirmed. In my message which I sent you some
days ago, you will find a reference to the case. For fear the copy of the
message sent may have been mislaid I enclose herewith another copy. In
whatever I have done since I came to the Territory I have had the hearty
cooperation and approval of the great body of leading republicans, and so
far as can be learned no one has asked for my removal. In coming to Montana I staked whatever of political hope or ambition I had for the future,
on making it a republican state. I had faith that I could do it, and for that
reason preferred the office you gave me to any other in your gift. It seemed
to me a laudable ambition. Observation since I came to the Territory confirms me in the belief that I could succeed if sustained at Washington. But
I would rather fail in this, and in all the prospective hopes of political success which I may have had, than dim in the least ~~the~~ a record which I regard
as the brightest I shall ever make; I mean my ten years record in Congress
in favor of the Negro and the freedom of all men. If however my views on
'immigration' as set forth in my message are disapproved by the administration, and I am to be removed for their utterance, I can only say that
they are views which I honestly entertain, and that while I shall regret my
removal as the greatest misfortune which could befal me politically, I could
not change them to retain any office however honorable or desirable or however necessary its emoluments might be for the maintance of my family. As
I have not the most distant idea why I have been removed, I have referred
to the only matters on which I supposed it possible I might differ with you
or any considerable number of republicans. I do not know but what you
and a majority of the party hold substantially the same views which I have
expressed in my message on 'immigration'. I know by some comments which
I have seen, that a few of our journals do not. As soon as I can hear from
you or the State Department, I shall be ready to respond to any questions
asked or charges made or to obey any order you may on a consideration of
the case, be pleased to make. With this statement, I submit the whole
matter to you, confident that you will do me the justice, to award me a full
and fair hearing."—ALS (brackets in original), *ibid.*

On Jan. 5, 1870, Israel Gibbs *et al.*, Virginia City, wrote to USG. "The Legislative Assembly of Montana is now about to adjourn *sine die*. As the only Republican members of that body, we desire to state to you, and to the cabinet, that, during the session, we have severally been in daily consultation with Governor Ashley, and our experience with him and his administration, satisfies us that he is the man we want for our Governor.— . . . Strictly temperate in his habits, he is never seen in Saloons, gambling houses, or other improper places, something which could not be truthfully said of his predecessors. Under the lead of Governor Ashley, with the programme which he has marked out, we believe that we can reclaim this Territory from the control of the 'left wing of Pap Price's Army' . . ."—DS (8 signatures), *ibid.*, Letters of Application and Recommendation. On March 29, Fisk, Washington, D. C., wrote to USG. "Your attention is respectfully called to the newspaper extract herewith appended, clipped from a late number of the Helena (Montana) Daily Herald, bearing upon the case of Governor Ashley. The assurance is given your Excellency that Governor Ashley wholly disclaims having ever unfavorably or unkindly criticised your appointments. . . ."—ALS, *ibid.* The enclosure and related papers are *ibid.* See Robert F. Horowitz, *The Great Impeacher: A Political Biography of James M. Ashley* (New York, 1979), pp. 162–63; Clark C. Spence, *Territorial Politics and Government in Montana, 1864–89* (Urbana, 1975), pp. 58–71.

1869, MARCH 9.   To Senate. "I transmit to the Senate, in compliance with its resolution of the 5th instant, a report from the Secretary of State, communicating a list of the public and private acts and resolutions passed at the third Session of the Fortieth Congress, which have become laws either by approval or otherwise."—DS, DNA, RG 46, Presidential Messages. See *SED*, 41-1-2.

1869, MARCH 9.   Robert W. Flournoy, Pontotoc, Miss., to USG. "When this communication reaches you it may find you too much engaged to give it any consideration: if so I pray you to lay it aside, and take it up when you have time. I need offer no excuse for addressing you; it is the privilege of one American citizen to politely address another. I might however place it upon another ground, which consist in the fact, that it was upon my motion you received the nomination by the Republican Convention of Mississippi, for president, And although we were not permitted to proceed farther in aiding you, to the extent of our power we did go. Another reason is, that I claim to be a disinterested friend of yours, ⱥNever since I first heard of you having my confidence in your destiny or integrity shaken. I will mention an incident, understand me, I am a southern man by birth. Soon after the battle of Pittsburg landing, better known as Shiloh—From some cause you seemed to be under a cloud, during that period, a friend and myself's waṣre speculating upon the war, and as to who would prove the master spirit in that contest. We mentioned over the names of all the

Fedral and Confederate generals, many of them filling a larger space in the public mind than was occupied by yourself. I then decided, that in my opinon you were destined to rise above all and finally terminate the war gloriously for the Union. I now believe your civil adminstration will be as beneficial as your military record is brilliant. And if there be any who doubt it, I am not to be counted among them. It is possible that in fixing the status of this state; it may become your duty to appoint a civil governor. I think it due to the loyal people here who amid so many trying circumstances have never faltered in their devotion to the Union; to have themselves the appointment of that officer, ʰBut Congress may determin otherwise. Should that duty devolv upon you, may I be permitted to slocit your favourable consideration of the claims of Gen Eggleston for that appointment,   He was run by the loyal people and we believe fairly elected,   His firmness and patriotism is a guarantee for the faithful performance of the trust if confided to him. There are also other reliable and distinguished men, who ~~were~~ if either of them should be appointed, would be acceptable to the loyal people, among them are Col Perse, Gen Tarbell, Gen McKee, and Gen Alderson, Mr Mygatt, Maj Castello; and Judge Brown. They are true men. But I respectfully protest against Gen Alcorn's being appointed. I do not look upon him as sound in the present condition of affairs here. And I also respectfully protest against, the appointment of any demacrat, or bolter like Wofford, Tindall, Field, and others from the Republican Party. I have been solicited to permit my name used in connexion with the office; but have declined. But I will now say, that if you think it better, for the interest of the state and the cause of loyalty, and the establishment of peace and order; that, I should accept the position although I have no aspirations in that direction I would not under a sense of duty feel authorized to decline. I possess beyond dispute a larger share of the confidence of the loyal people than any man in the state, though I say this myself, yet upon investigation out side of a few restless politicians, you will find it confirmed. I would too, be acceptable, to many dema[c]rats, who from my known liberal views in reference to amnesty, would prefer me; still I am considered as an extreme Radical, upon the rights of every citizen black, or white, to the full enjoyment of their privileges, equal and unrestricted. Above all I beg for the removal of Gen Gillem"—ALS, DNA, RG 107, Appointment Papers.

1869, MARCH 9.   William C. Graham, Cairo, Ill., to USG. "I shall be an applicant for the position of Collector of this Port—Many of my old army friends have promised me their support but we are so widely separated that I am delayed in procuring such credentials as I desire to accompany my application.   this fact, together with your uniform kindness to me in former days. prompts me to ask that the nomination for the place be witheld for a few days, when I hope to be able to satisfy you that my claims are worthy of your favorable consideration."—ALS, DNA, RG 56, Collector of Customs Applications.

1869, MARCH 9.   U.S. Senator Richard Yates of Ill. *et al.* to USG. "We respectfully and earnestly recommend the appointment of Governor William Jayne of Springfield Illinois as Pension Agent at that place."—Copy, DLC-Lyman Trumbull.

1869, MARCH 10.   To Attorney Gen. Ebenezer R. Hoar. "Please inform me whether the President of the U. States, is authorized by law to advance an officer in the Navy, in the grade to which he belongs, for distinguished conduct in battle?"—LS, DNA, RG 60, Letters Received from the President. On March 11, Hoar wrote to USG. ". . . Upon examination, I find that by the 6th section of the act of April 21, 1864, (13 Stat., p. 54,) 'any officer in the naval service, by and with the advice and consent of the Senate, may be advanced, not exceeding thirty numbers, in his own grade, for distinguished conduct in battle, or extraordinary heroism.' . . ."—Copy, *ibid.*, Opinions.

1869, MARCH 10.   U.S. Senator Richard Yates of Ill. *et al.* to USG. "The undersigned respectfully request that Hon. E. P. Ferry of Illinois be appointed Governor of the Territory of Washington. Mr. Ferry is an accomplished lawyer, a thorough Republican of long standing, a fine scholar, and a thoroughly honest and reliable gentleman."—Copy, DLC-Lyman Trumbull. On April 5, USG nominated Elisha P. Ferry as surveyor, Washington Territory. See *Calendar,* Jan. 9, 1872.

1869, MARCH 11.   Speech. "BARON GEROLT AND GENTLEMEN OF THE DIPLOMATIC CORPS: I heartily thank you for the kind expression of your good wishes for my welfare and the nation which has chosen me as its Chief Magistrate. You may be assured that it shall be my constant endeavor to maintain those relations of peace and friendship which now exist between the United States and the countries which you respectively represent, a purpose which I am happy to learn from you will be fully reciprocated."— *Washington Chronicle,* March 12, 1869. The address of Baron Gerolt is *ibid.*

1869, MARCH 11.   To Robert W. Tayler, 1st Comptroller. "Under authority of the Act of January 31. 1823 'concerning the disbursement of public money' permission is hereby given, that needful advances of money be made to disbursing Officers in the Civil Service of the Government, who may have given bonds as required by law, to such military and naval officers as may by law be authorized to disburse the same; and to the Bankers of the United States in London; as requested in your letter of the blank instant."— LS, DLC-Finance Miscellany. On March 10, Tayler had written to USG requesting this authority.—LS (press), DNA, RG 217, 1st Comptroller, Miscellaneous Letters Sent.

1869, MARCH 11.   Columbus Delano and Edward A. Rollins to USG. "The legal services of Benjamin F. Tracy have been of great value to this Department. His knowledge and familiarity with the revenue laws acquired by a large practice render it very important that he be continued in the employment of the government where such services are most frequently required. In view of these facts we respectfully suggest for your consideration the propriety of giving him the District Attorneyship for the Southern district of NewYork, provided the person intended for this place if there be any such person, shall be willing to accept the Northern District. This is respectfully submitted merely as a suggestion for your consideration."—LS (press), Delano Letterbooks, Illinois Historical Survey, University of Illinois, Urbana, Ill. On Jan. 9, 1871, Orville E. Babcock wrote to Attorney Gen. Amos T. Akerman. "*Personal* . . . The President directs me to inform you that the time of service of the U. S. District Attorney for the Eastern District of New York, Mr. Tracy will expire during the present month, and that he thinks an early nomination will prevent any pressure for a change." —Copy, DLC-USG, II, 1. In Dec., 1866, President Andrew Johnson had nominated Benjamin F. Tracy as attorney, Eastern District, N. Y., a position for which he was renominated on Jan. 9, 1871.

1869, MARCH 11.   Charles C. Fulton, publisher, *Baltimore American*, to USG. "I respectfully endorse the application of Brig. General Felix Agnus for a French Consulate. Gen. Agnus is a native of Paris, and a gentleman of education, good character, courteous and pleasant manners, and excellent business qualifications. He entered the service as a private in 1861, rose through all the grades on merit alone, and left the service at the close of the war as Lieut. Colonel. He was wounded at Harrison's Landing, his right shoulder shattered and maimed for life; Whilst recovering raised another regiment and participated in the siege of Port Hudson on the Mississippi, where he was again wounded. He has the strongest letters from Generals Emery, Dix, Kilpatrick, Warren, Sherman, Logan and Denison, as to his military services and capacity. He is but thirty years of age, and as a Frenchman would take pride in returning to his native country in the service of his adopted country   It is proper for me to add that when wounded at Harrison's Landing I found him in a dying condition, brought him to my house. My daughter nursed him, and the result was marriage."—ALS, DNA, RG 59, Letters of Application and Recommendation. No appointment followed.

1869, MARCH 11.   Marshall O. Roberts, New York City, to USG. "Hon Freeman J Fithian of this City, will as I understand, be named to your Excellency as a suitable person to fill the office of District Attorney of the United States for the Southern District of NewYork. I desire to bear cordial testimony to the eminent fitness of Judge F. for the place both by legal ability and personal character; and to express the opinion, that, if the appointment be conferred upon him, it will be most satisfactorily received."— LS, RPB. No appointment followed. See *New York Times*, Aug. 5, 1884.

1869, MARCH 11.   U.S. Senator Carl Schurz of Mo. to USG. "If you desire to recognize, and to do honor to, the patriotic Germans of this country,
you can, in my opinion, do so in no better way, than by appointing to a high
official position Ex-Governor Salomon. who is a candidate for a foreign
mission. The eminent services rendered by Gov. Salomon during the most
trying period of our history, are highly appreciated by all and remembered
with particular pride by his German fellow-citizens, while his patriotism,
great ability and high character excellently fit him for such a position as he
desires. There is no German-born citizen in this country whose elevation
would give satisfaction so general. He has hosts of friends every where, and,
as far as I know, no enemies. I would, therefore, most cordially and earnestly recommend him for a European mission and at the same time suggest, that an appointment like this might be charged to the account of the
German-born element in this country instead of that of a particular State."—
LS, DNA, RG 59, Letters of Application and Recommendation. Related
papers are *ibid.* No appointment followed.

1869, MARCH 12.   To William P. Brayton, sheriff, Fulton County, N. Y.
"Whereas, it appears, by information in due form by me received, that Benjamin Miller and Clay Mathews charged with the crime of robbery, are
fugitives from the justice of the United States in Canada, . . . Now, therefore, you are hereby authorized and empowered . . . to take and hold them
in your custody . . ."—Copy, DNA, RG 59, General Records. On March 10,
Brayton, Johnstown, N. Y., had written to USG. "on the 23 of Febuary
1869 I sent the enclosed papers to the Attorney General to get a Requisition
on the Canadian Athority for two desperate high wayman who are now near
the Falls on the Canada side   the papers was returned to me saying the
Attorney General has no Athority in the matter,—but dont say who is the
proper person to attend to it   I am informed that a Requisition can be obtained under the ashburton Treaty"—ALS, *ibid.*, Miscellaneous Letters.
On March 27, Brayton wrote to USG. "On the 13 March I received the
requsition for Clay Mathews & Benjamin Miller in Canada   since then I
have caused them to be arrested and examined at St Catharine in Canada
the papers have been sent to the Govonor General   the name of Wm P.
Brayton was mentioned to receive them from the British authorityies,   would
it be wise to name one other person with me in case of Sickness or death
My Attorney advised me to write to you and has sent on the name of S. V. R.
Brayton to the Govonor General   he would only act in case I was unable to
do so,   the authoritys in Canada have shown a very friendly feeling in the
matter and rendered me all the assistance I needed . . . P S. Pleas name
S V R. Brayton"—ALS, *ibid.*, RG 60, Letters From the President.

1869, MARCH 12.   Bvt. Maj. Gen. Montgomery C. Meigs, Washington,
D. C., to USG. "Some unknown person has sent me these specimens of the
manufactured products of the no longer ever faithful Isle of Cuba. I do not
smoke myself but I understand that they are worthy to solace the hours of

the greatest General of the age & the elected President of forty millions of freemen. Please accept them . . ."—ALS, OFH.

1869, MARCH 12.   Jesse Bishop to USG. "I am informed that Col. Robt. G. Ingersoll is an applicant for the position of District Attorney for the Northern Dist. Illinois and I take great pleasure in testifying to his eminent ability and fitness for said position. Col. Ingersoll has been very active during the severe trials through which our Country has lately been passing and in all of them has been true and faithfull. His ability and energetic activity in behalf of our country certainly entitles him to high favor in the distribution of the offices."—Van Nosdall, List 1,240 (Jan., 1954), no. 367, copied in OFH. No appointment followed.

1869, MARCH 12.   U.S. Senator Matthew H. Carpenter of Wis. to USG. "I respectfully recommend Col Charles Dillingham for appointment as Naval officer of the Port of New Orleans   I have known Col Dillingham from childhood, he is a son of Gov. Dillingham of Vermont, was in the war as Lt Col of 8. Vt. Regt. and has resided in New Orleans since the close of the war, . . ."—ALS, DNA, RG 56, Naval Officer Applications. Related papers are *ibid.* On March 22, U.S. Senator William P. Kellogg of La. and three others wrote to USG. "We respectfully and earnestly recommend the appointment of Major Wm G. McConnell to the Naval Office of New Orleans. The present incumbent is a democrat and is not an active & efficient officer—Major McConnell was a good soldier throughout the entire war on the Union side—He has resided in New Orleans since the close of the war and is a *bona fide* and deserving citizen of the state of Louisiana. As a republican he is active, self-sacrificing and influential, and as a man possesses the confidence of the people—"—DS, *ibid.* On April 3, USG nominated Charles Dillingham as naval officer, New Orleans. On April 7, Horace Porter wrote to Secretary of the Treasury George S. Boutwell. "The President requests that you will examine the case of Dillinghams nomination for Naval Officer at New Orleans La with reference to the propriety of withdrawing his name from the Senate. He is objected to by the Senators and others from his State."—LS, *ibid.* On April 9, Dillingham was confirmed.

1869, MARCH 12.   James Speed, Louisville, to USG. "Judge. B. Lr. Du Guffy of Butler County is applying for a judgeship in one of the Territories—Judge Guffy is well qualified to fill such a place—He is honest & capable & a true man in all the relations of life—His appointment would gratify all republicans who know, & be especially grateful to those who know him intimately as I—"—ALS, MH. On March 8, Bayless L. D. Guffy, Washington, D. C., had written to USG. "I herewith present this my application for the position of Associate Justice of Wyoming Territory— . . ."—ALS, DNA, RG 60, Records Relating to Appointments. Related papers are *ibid.* No appointment followed.

1869, MARCH 12.   Peter J. Sullivan, U.S. minister, Bogotá, to USG. "The Honorable Antonio Ferro, late Secretary of the National Treasury of the United States of Colombia, admiring your exalted patriotism, and unselfish love of country, has requested me for this letter of introduction to you, for the sole purpose of making your acquaintance. Mr Ferro is a gentleman of refinement; a Statesman of much culture; and an eminent lawyer. He is an avowed friend of our country; and hence I beg leave to commend him to your favorable notice."—Copy, DNA, RG 59, Diplomatic Despatches, Colombia.

1869, MARCH 12.   Timothy Winn, New York City, to USG. "I have the honor to recommend to you through our Representative the Hon. N. P. Banks, Mr G. W. M. Hall of Woburn. Mr Hall has been personally known to me for a number of years. and I can testify to his ability, integrity and morality,   If he should be appointed by you Consul at Toronto, I feel confident the selection would be a good one, and prove acceptable to the large body of Republicans in our District"—LS, DNA, RG 59, Letters of Application and Recommendation. Related papers are *ibid.*; DLC-Nathaniel P. Banks. No appointment followed.

1869, MARCH 13.   Governor William H. Smith of Ala., Washington, D. C., to USG. "After full consultation with a number of gentelemen from Ala, prominent in the Republican Party, I have come to the conclusion that it is a duty I owe to myself, as well as to the people of Ala, to address you upon a subject of great interest to them, & one upon which to a great extent, the Success of your administration must depend in that State,   I men a just distribution of the Federal Patronage,   I would not be understood as desireing to dictate to you or even injudiciously to press my views upon you in the premises,   But I trust that the interest I feel in the earnest you are making to give peace to the whole Country; particularly to the South, will be accepted as a sufficient apology for my present action. The condition of Alabama is *Anomalous.* The two Senators & six Representatives, whose terms of office have ~~expired~~ just expired, with one exception, are residents of the State only since the War & consequently cannot be presumed to have a sufficient knowledge of the long resident population of the state to make that just distribution of the offices, which the public interest demands, without consultation with those who know. I have been informed that these Senators & Representatives hold meetings & determin by ballot whom they shall recommend for, the various ~~offices~~ positions without conference or consultation with any one, save perhaps, a few of the office seekers. Prominent gentlemen whose counsels are certainly of the greatest moment to the permement success of the Republican Party in the State, have been excluded from their ~~debate~~ deliberations, and when enquiry has been made of these senators & Representatives, they have treated with indifference by some and by others told 'you will be informed in due time'   This injudicious course upon the part of Senators & Representatives, in this to us now critically important matter will promote discord in the Republican Party, that will seriously threaten its overthrow in the state,   Already it has caused many to believe that these men regard these offices as so much Stock in trade to be used for ~~suess~~ selfish purposes, either in returning themselves to Congress or some other such end. I trust that this may not be so—but candor compelse me to say that I fear their apprehensions are not entirely without foundation   I have been for more than thirty years a resident of the State— opposed the rebellion for which during the war, I was driven from ~~my~~ the State,   Since the war opposed the reconstruction policy of President Johnson, and Continuously advocated the reconstruction measures of Congress, & in carrying them out the people elected me Governor,   Since my election every official & private act of mine have have been intended to promote the successful reconstruction of the State,   I have spent much of my time during the Winter at Washington, yet not one of these Senators & Representatives has consulted with me in relation to Ala affairs: But on the Contrary when I have spoken to them of matters I deemed of importance I was manifestly treated with indifference—I respectfully submit Mr President, as an ardent friend of your administration that this condition is calculated to excite just apprehension as to the wisdom of the policy which dictates it. If you think that these suggestions are worthy of your consideration & would like to be more fully informed I would be pleased to have you indicate a time when I may see you and converse with you on this subject"—ADfS, Smith Papers, Alabama Dept. of Archives and History, Montgomery, Ala.

1869, MARCH 13.   U.S. Senators William M. Stewart and James W. Nye and U.S. Representative Thomas Fitch of Nev. to USG. "We most earnestly request from you the appointment of Hon Charles E De Long of Nevada to be Minister to Japan   Mr De Long has been for a long time a most effective and earnest worker for the Union cause   He was for years a member of the California Senate from Yuba County. He removed to Nevada in 1863, was elected a member of the State Constitutional Convention in 1864, and was invaluable in aiding to procure the ratification of that instrument by the people. He was elected a delegate to the Chicago Convention, was one of the Committee on Resolutions, and is one of the National Executive Committee   He was one of the Presidential Electors of Nevada last fall and was chosen Electoral Messenger. He has been on two occasions a candidate for United States Senator from Nevada supported by a numerous party of earnest friends, and recieved a large vote for that office. He is a lawyer of ability and industry and a man of general learning and information. He would be a jealous capable and effective guardian of the interests of this nation at the Japanese court, and we know of no man who would be more earnest or effective in forwarding and fostering the vast commercial interests, which, on the completion of the Pacific Rail Road, are expected to grow up between our country and the Japanese islands   The appointment of Mr De Long to this position would be entirely acceptable to the people of the Pacific coast, and would be peculiarly gratifying to the Union men of Nevada, as some recognition by you of their devoted and effective labors for the Republican cause   We again urge upon you Mr President to make this appointment"—DS, DNA, RG 59, Letters of Application and Recommendation. Related papers are *ibid.* On April 15, USG nominated Charles E. De Long as minister to Japan.

1869, MARCH 15.   To Senate. "I invite the attention of Congress to the accompanying communication of this date which I have received from the Secretary of the Interior."—DS, DNA, RG 46, Presidential Messages. On March 11, James Brooks, Jesse L. Williams, Daniel L. Harris, Joseph D. Webster, and Hiram Price, "Government Directors of the Union Pacific Railroad," had written to Secretary of the Interior Jacob D. Cox reporting legal actions taken to obstruct the election of company officers and requesting legislation "to protect the interests of the United States, and to keep on uninterrupted this great national work."—Copy, *ibid.* See *SED,* 41-1-4.

1869, MARCH 15.   Vice President Schuyler Colfax to USG. "I take pleasure in introducing to you Hon Thos H. Nelson of Indiana, who has been recommended to you for an European Mission by the Republican Senators & Representatives from Indiana, the Republican Electors, State Officers, & members of the Senate & House of Representatives, of that State; & I cordially join with them in this earnest endorsement. Col Nelson, as I have heretofore stated to you, served the country faithfully as Minister to Chili for nearly five years, canvassed our entire State as the head of our Republican Electoral ticket, and is a gentleman of culture and ability who would honorably and successfully represent the United States at any Court to which he might be accredited."—ALS, DNA, RG 59, Letters of Application and Recommendation. Other letters to USG on this subject are *ibid.* On April 12, USG nominated Thomas H. Nelson as minister to Mexico.

1869, MARCH 15.   Capt. John De Camp, Philadelphia, to USG. "Not having received my promotion agreeable to a law passed during the session of Congress of 1866 which provides for the promotion of officers according to their war record of the late war, and believing my record during the war to be equal to either of the eight Captains, who were junior to me, but promoted over me in 1866, and having complied with the requisitions of the law, which provides for an examination by a board of examiners, a copy of a certificate of qualification and recommendation for promotion from whom is, herewith, enclosed I most respectfully request you to consider my case and see that justice is done in securing me my legitimate rank."—LS, DNA, RG 45, Subject File, Div. NI. The enclosure is *ibid.* On the same day, Vice Admiral David D. Porter, act. secretary of the navy, wrote to USG. "This officer was recommended by a Board of Admirals to be promoted ten (10) numbers for gallant conduct at the capture of Forts Jackson and St. Philip. That would have made him a Commodore on the Active List of the navy.

The recommendations of the Board in his case and in that of many others, were set aside by the Secretary of the navy for reasons that do not appear to be satisfactory. This officer was finally sent before an Examining Board and placed on the retired list for disability and lost his promotion. I respectfully request that this act of justice may be done him at this late day."— Copy, *ibid.*, Letters Sent to the President. A nomination for De Camp as commodore on the retired list, prepared for USG's signature and dated March 15, is *ibid.* On April 5, Porter wrote to USG. "The enclosed letter refers to the case of Captain John de Camp, of the Navy, who was nominated recently as Commodore on the retired list. He was placed on the retired list for disability, and has given no evidence to the Department since, that he is fit for active duty."—Copy, *ibid.*

1869, MARCH 15. Alton R. Easton, St. Louis, to USG. "Thos E. Tutt Esq of this City, wishes to be a Director of the Union P. R Road—I have known him for twenty years, he is a gentleman of high standing, of unblemished character, and worthy in every way, and would make a good and faithful officer—He is in no way pecuniarily interested in said Road— but would Desire to have a Rail Road connection between S Louis and the gold mines of Montana. Mr T. is on the *list* of your old friends, which has been revived and published for the edification of the public. Please give his claims a fafvorable consideration"—ALS, DNA, RG 48, Appointment Div., Letters Received. Charles W. Ford favorably endorsed this letter.—AES, *ibid.* See *PUSG*, 1, 349.

On March 5, Chauncey H. Snow had written to USG concerning the progress and condition of the Union Pacific Railroad.—*National Intelligencer*, April 30, 1869. On the same day, Horace Porter wrote to William T. Otto, act. secretary of the interior. "The President directs me to request that you send him Commissions for the following named persons, to be Government Directors of the Union Pacific Rail Road Company for the unexpired term. Hiram Price of Davenport Iowa vice S. McKee of Pa   J. D. Webster, of Chicago, vice Chauncy Snow of Washington   D. L Harris of Springfield. Mass—vice S. Temple of Tenn. Jesse L Williams of Fort Wayne Indiana reappointed."—Copies, DLC-USG, II, 1, 4. On April 5, Elihu B. Washburne, Galena, telegraphed to USG. "Friends want Nathan Corwith director Pacific Road Vice Webster resigned"—Telegram received (at 3:20 P.M.), DNA, RG 107, Telegrams Collected (Bound). On the same day, William F. Coolbaugh, Chicago, had telegraphed to Washburne. "Telegraph president Immediately appoint Corwith Vice General Webster or it may be late. This appointment will give great assurance to Bond Holders & is important"—Telegram received, DLC-Elihu B. Washburne. On April 6, Secretary of the Treasury George S. Boutwell wrote to USG. "In accordance with your directions I transmit herewith the nomination of J. D. Webster as Assessor of Internal Revenue 1st District of Illinois vice M R M Wallace to be removed"—Copy, DNA, RG 56, Letters Sent. On May 31, 1867, USG had endorsed a letter of May 22 from Joseph D. Webster, Chicago. "Respy. referred to the Q. M. G. there is no more honest man living than General Webster—has had experience during the war in managing R. Roads—and was as efficient in that as he is honest."—Copy, *ibid.*, RG 108, Register of Letters Received.

1869, MARCH 15. Mrs. C. A. Jameson, Lewisville, Tex., to USG asking for help in reclaiming property in Ark. and concluding: "Mrs General Thomas Dockery is a friend of mine, you made her acquaintance near Vicksburg, she can vouch for my veracity,"—ALS, DNA, RG 60, Letters from the President. See *PUSG*, 8, 482–83.

1869, MARCH 15. James Sinclair, Raleigh, N. C., to USG. "I take the liberty of enclosing to your Excellency a certified copy of certain Preamble and Resolution introduced by myself and adopted by large majorities in both branches of the Legislature of North Carolina. When in 1868 the County Convention of Wake in this state nominated Judge Chase for the Presidency of the United States, I had the honor to preside over the Republican Convention of Robeson County, called by myself, and nominated you to the exalted position which you now occupy. This was on the first day of February 1868, ten days after the nomination of Judge Chase by the Republicans of Wake Co. I simply refer to these facts as a key to the enclosed Resolutions. Having the honor to be the first man in my state to nominate you for the Presidency of the United States I deemed it proper to be the first to move to untrammel the President of my choice & allow him under the constitution of our fathers an opportunity, to render his administration in history, as illustrious as his achievements in the field already are. In preparing the Preamble and Resolution I am indebted for valuable assistance to Ex Senator Clingman who though he disagrees with me in politics, has been a warm personal friend ever since we served as Colonels of our respective Regiments in the rebel service. I am happy to state here that Senator Clingman will warmly support your Excellencys administration"—ALS, USG 3. The enclosed resolution, dated March 13, commended USG for "extraordinary ability and varied talent, as well as exalted patriotism" and called for the N. C. congressional delegation to vote for repeal of the Tenure of Office Act.—Copy, *ibid.* On April 16, USG nominated Sinclair as assessor of Internal Revenue, 3rd District, N. C.

1869, MARCH 15. Stephen Walker, New Berne, N. C., to USG. "Mr. Stephen Walker hav taken it a pound him self to rite you aBout the laber I Don at little Washington N. C. . . . & We beleav here in this destresed place it the lord hav place you in a place for as a father for We poor colred people . . ."—ALS, DNA, RG 107, Letters Received from Bureaus.

1869, MARCH 16. To Secretary of State Hamilton Fish. "I desire that H. Kriesmann, consul at Berlin, should be retained."—ANS, DNA, RG 59, Letters of Application and Recommendation.

On May 19, William E. Dodge and three others, New York City, wrote to USG. "John Austin Stevens, Esq. of this City, at present sojourning in Europe with his family, desires the position of United States Consul at Berlin. . . ."—DS, *ibid.* Related papers are *ibid.*

1869, MARCH 16.   To Secretary of State Hamilton Fish. "You will please take no steps towards the removal of Ja's Monroe Consul at Rio Janeiro without bringing it to my attention & the attention of the Secretary of the Interior"—L (initialed), DNA, RG 59, Letters of Application and Recommendation.

On April 13, U.S. Representative James A. Garfield of Ohio wrote to USG. "I desire to recommend to your favorable consideration—Col Ralph Plumb of Streator Ill for appointment as Consul at Rio Janerio, which position I understand is shortly to be resigned by Mr Munroe. Col Plumb has been well known to me for many years. He served with marked faithfulness and ability as a Quartermaster in the Army for nearly five years—is an accomplished Lawyer and a business man of much experience and rare ability. He has been a Member of the Ohio Legislature and a prominent and influential Member of the Republican Party from its organization. I cannot too strongly express my confidence in the eminent fitness of Col Plumb for this appointment and my hope that it may be given him."—LS, *ibid.*

On June 24, 1870, U.S. Representatives Alfred E. Buck, Charles W. Buckley, Charles Hays, and U.S. Senators George E. Spencer and Willard Warner of Ala. wrote to USG. "We beg leave to respectfully and earnestly recommend to your consideration the appointment of C. T. Thweatt, publisher of the Alabama State Journal, as Consul to Rio de Janeiro, Brazil. Mr Thweatt is a gentleman of ability and experience in public affairs. He is respected by all who know him for his private worth and high standing. He was an earnest working Republican in Alabama when it required independence of character and courage of heart to be a member of that party. In obloquy and proscription he has adhered to his principles and asserted his opinions. His appointment will be regarded by the entire Republican party of the State, as a fitting reward and recognition, by the Administration, of the valuable services of a worthy and capable citizen."—DS, *ibid.* On July 1, USG nominated Charles T. Thweatt as consul, Rio de Janeiro.

1869, MARCH 16.   USG endorsement. "Approved."—AES, DNA, RG 60, Records Relating to Appointments. Written on a letter of March 12 from James Lawrenson, Washington, D. C., to USG. "I respectfully ask the favor of a renewal of my Commission as a 'Justice of the Peace for the County of Washington, DC.' *to take effect on the 22nd instant.* Twenty six years ago, Sir, I accepted this little office at the request of, and for the special accomodation of our Postal Department, of which I am the oldest Clerk under the Government. The services of a Magistrate, *on the spot*, in the settlement of accounts, have long been found quite important in the prompt despatch of business.—"—ALS, *ibid.* Postmaster Gen. John A. J. Creswell and four others favorably endorsed this application.

1869, MARCH [16]. USG endorsement. "Suspend present Commissioners."—Copy, DNA, RG 107, Orders and Endorsements. Written following the March 13 request of the "Indiana Delegation in Congress" for "the removal of the present Commissioners, appointed by the late President, to settle the Indiana War Claims, and, until the same can be done, a suspension of their operations as such."—*Ibid.* See *PUSG,* 17, 558.

1869, MARCH 16. To Senate. "In compliance with the Resolution of the Senate of the 11th instant, asking if the first instalment due from the government of Venezuela pursuant to the Convention of April 25, 1866, has been paid, I transmit a Report from the Secretary of State to whom the Resolution was referred."—DS, DNA, RG 46, Presidential Messages. On March 15, Secretary of State Elihu B. Washburne had written to USG. "The Secretary of State, to whom was referred the Resolution of the Senate, of the 12th instant, requesting The President to inform the Senate, if compatible with the public interest, whether the government of Venezuela has paid the first instalment due to American citizens under the award recently made by the Mixed Commission of the two governments, has the honor to report that no intelligence of any such payment has been received at this Department. A correspondence has taken place with the representative of Venezuela accredited to this government in regard to the proceedings of that commission, a copy of which is hereunto annexed."—LS, *ibid.* The enclosure is *ibid.* See *SED,* 41-1-5; *Calendar,* March 1, 1870.

1869, MARCH 16. Taylor Blow, St. Louis, to USG. "I leave this afternoon for Washington"—Telegram received (at 3:35 P.M.), DNA, RG 107, Telegrams Collected (Bound). Blow, brother of former congressman Henry T. Blow, had supported USG's bid to become county engineer of St. Louis County in 1859. See *PUSG,* 1, 349. Taylor Blow's obituary noted: "In former years he won the friendship of Capt. U. S. Grant, once an humble farmer on the Gravois, and now President of the United States. The kindness received from Mr. Blow in those days has never been forgotten by the President, and we have seen letters from the latter, in which he spoke of the years of his adversity and the friendship of Mr. Blow in a manner that showed the goodness of his own heart and the noble qualities of his friend." —*Missouri Democrat,* Aug. 21, 1869.

On April 12, Logan U. Reavis, St. Louis, wrote to USG. "Allow me though unknown to you, in the interest of StLouis and the Commerce of the Great Mississippi River to make th Hon. Henry T. Blow Minister to Brazil. He capable politically and Commercially. Nothing ~~is~~ can be more valuable to our future Commerce than the [exc]hange of the trade of the Amazon and the Mississippi and it will be one of the best works of your administration to develope that trade. Hoping that you will consider this matter in the true light of the notional interest, . . ."—ALS, DNA, RG 59, Letters of Application and Recommendation. On April 27, U.S. Senator Charles D. Drake of Mo., Philadelphia, wrote to USG. "I should be unmindful of your consideration in purposing to give the Brazilian Mission to a citizen of Missouri, did I not endeavor to aid you in selecting the best person for that post. In my interview with you before I left Washington I mentioned to you the name of Major Henry Hitchcock, of St Louis, as a suitable person, and I desire thus to reiterate my views on that point. . . . He was a member of Gen. Sherman's Staff during the war, and my impression is that Gen. S. would corroborate all I have said. Though I would acquiesce in the appointment of Mr Blow, I should rejoice in that of Major Hitchcock; believing him very much the superior."—ALS, *ibid.* On May 1, S. N. Reavis (probably a telegrapher's error for Logan U. Reavis) telegraphed to USG. "You are the child of the Great West Give to St Louis the Brazillian mission Give it to Hon Henry T Blow"—Telegram received (at 6:30 P.M.), *ibid.*, RG 107, Telegrams Collected (Bound). On the same day, USG designated Henry T. Blow as minister to Brazil. On July 6, James B. Eads, St. Louis, telegraphed to USG. "Minister Blow's friends tender him a complimentary banquet on Tuesday next at 8 o'clock and they direct me to say that they will feel highly honored by your presence. Will mail formal invitation tomorrow. Can we hope for a favorable reply?"—Telegram received (at 2:20 P.M.), *ibid.* USG did not attend the banquet of July 13. See *Missouri Democrat*, July 14, 1869.

1869, MARCH 16. Henry L. Burnett, Cincinnati, to USG. "I am an applicant for District Attorney here. Please delay any appointment until my late partner Governor Cox can present my papers to you and to the Attorney General"—Telegram received (at 3:25 P.M.), DNA, RG 107, Telegrams Collected (Bound). No appointment followed.

1869, MARCH 16. Benjamin Eggleston, Cincinnati, to USG. "Our people are clamerous for the retention of Thomas for Postmaster. cannot some other good place be assigned for Foulds"—Telegram received (at 2:00 P.M.), DNA, RG 107, Telegrams Collected (Bound). On March 29, Thomas H. Yeatman, Cincinnati, telegraphed to USG. "Public sentiment of our city is in favor of C W Thomas for Postmaster"—Telegram received (at 7:00 P.M.), *ibid.* On March 24, USG nominated Thomas H. Foulds as postmaster, Cincinnati, in place of Calvin W. Thomas. On March 31, Jesse Root Grant, Covington, Ky., wrote to Foulds. "Allow me to introduce Mr John Elstner—The son of and old acquaintance of mine Also his friend Charles Reader These young men would like to get a situation in your Post Office If you need any aditional Clerks, Please give them a favorable consideration"—ALS, NjP.

1869, MARCH 16. E. Macé, Nantes, to USG recommending a metric system for navigational purposes.—ALS (in French), DNA, RG 77, Explorations and Surveys, Letters Received.

1869, MARCH 16. Alexander T. Stewart, New York City, to USG. "I take pleasure in calling your attention to the accompanying letter referring to the application of Mr *John N. Brown* of Baltimore. He is a Nephew of my friend Mr *James Brown* of the firm of *Brown Brothers* & Co of this City. I would consider the appointment to office of such gentlemen as the beginning of a new era in our Government;—the Selection of men for capacity and integrity; rather than for their political influence, or position in the party. I trust the application will meet with your favor."—LS, DNA, RG 56, Appraiser of Customs Applications. On April 12, John N. Brown, Baltimore, wrote to USG. "About the 23d of last Month I informed you by letter that I was an applicant for the position of appraiser in the Custom House of this City Mr A. T. Stewart of New York sent me word that he had written you in my behalf & requested me to call upon you at Washington. I spent two days in the attempt but the press upon you was too great to obtain the interview My object *now* is merely to remind you of my application . . ."—ALS, *ibid.*

On April 10, George W. F. Vernon, Frederick, Md., had written to USG. "I would beg leave to respectfully State to your Excelency that I have been maimed for life in my country's service, during the late Rebellion, (haveing had my left eye shot out in Battle) That I have ever been a consistent Republican and have represented my County (the only 'Grant' County in Rebel Maryland) in every County, State or National Convention of the Republican Party for the past four years; That I have been endorsed by 'Judge Weisel' late Rep Cand for Cong in my Dist, The 'Hon F. Thomas' late Rep Cong from same, the Rep County Committee, and the Hon Wm J. Albert of Balto Md, which reccommendations according to a long established custom, relevant to the dispensation of Federal patronage, has almost the same effect as common Law, and deemed sufficient to make an appointment, and surely should occasion a retention nevertheless I have been turned out of the Post Office at Frederick Maryland, (although two years of my time remain unexpired) at the instance of Mr J. A. J. Creswell Post Mast. Gen in consequence of my not haveing endorsed him, in one of our State Conventions; for the 'Vice Presidency,' with the ultimate object in view, of secureing a place in your Cabinet. I would therefore respectfully pray that the persecution of 'Mr Creswell' may be staid, and that I may be either reappointed to the position from which I was ejected, *or appointed to one of the Appraisorships in the Baltimore Custom House, in the place of a Civilian named 'Hicks'* I think (with all due deference) that rather than ostracism and degradation, that I am entitled to some consideration at the hands of the present Administration."—ALS, *ibid.*, Naval Officer Applications. On April 15, Orville E. Babcock wrote to Secretary of the Treasury George S. Boutwell. "The President directs me to inform you that he had inadvertently removed Geo. W. F. Vernon from the Post Office at Frederick, Md. Col. Vernon served faithfully during the War, losing one eye,—Col. Vernon now wishes the position of Appraiser of Customs at Baltimore, Md. The President requests this be given him if compatible with the good of the service. In case this appointment cannot be given him, the President wishes some equally good one be given him."— LS, *ibid.* On April 20, USG nominated Adam E. King as appraiser, Baltimore, in place of Hooper C. Hicks.

On May 19, Arthur Rich, Baltimore, wrote to USG. "I present myself to you as an Applicant for one of the *Appraisers* for the Port of Balto—Mr Meredith has had the place for 8 years rendered no party service, and has not made any sacrifice   Col. Anderson has had His place 4 years—I was one of your original friends in Maryld as a copy of note enclosed will show when I solicited your autograph—at the same time, those now filing the Federal offices here were in correspondence with Colfax—and some others assisting Chase to stain His Judicial ermine   I regret that the able and venerable Frank Thomas was not more consulted in relation to Mayld Appointments as he knows all the true men—As you so well, and ably, flanked Johnson and His whole Cabinet so do I hope that you will flank others, should it appear that for their own personal ambition, they are making Grant and the Republican party a secondary consideration—I hope Mr Presidt by the close of the fiscal year Sect.y Boutwell will see the propriety of making one or two new *Appraisers* with my freind Genl King   In the event Mr Presdt of Dr Nicolls vacating the charge of the Hospital for the Insane—I could present testimonials for your consideration"—ALS, *ibid.*, Appraiser of Customs Applications. Related papers are *ibid.*; *ibid.*, RG 48, Appointment Div., Letters Received. See *PUSG*, 17, 532–33.

1869, MARCH 18.   USG endorsement. "Respectfully refered to Sec. of State for such action as may be deemed proper."—AES, DNA, RG 59, Miscellaneous Letters. Written on a letter of March 13 from Thomas T. Crittenden, Warrensburg, Mo., to USG. "On the 16th of August 1851— William L Crittenden—(my brother) in company with others was shot in Cuba—by the authority of the Spanish Government,   My mother (an aged and venerable lady—residing in Kentucky) desire—if possible—to recover his remains—and remove them to our quiet family Grave Yard—where repose those, of my Father—Brothers and Sisters   Our affection cover his errors—with the charity natural to our positions—and we fondly cherish the hope of sooner or later—removin[g] the remains—from a common and dishonored grave, to the kindred circle of our dead—: To accomplish our desire—w[e] solicit the influence of your name—and position; I have already addressed a letter to the Captain Genl of Cuba—thro the Spanish Minister at Washington   My Bro'—was a graduate of West Poin[t.] He entered Mexico with Gen Taylor—served his Government with commendable gallantry throughout that whole Wa[r.] I think Gen J J Reynolds now Com-

manding the State of Texas was a classma[te] and a warm associate: The
long years that have elapsed since his murde[r] have borne heavily upon my
mothe[r] & the prostrating grief will soon convey her to the grave—I fear—
and nothing would have the same refreshing effect upon her—as the possession of his remains: I hope my dear Sir—that you will give us the poten-
tial assistance of your name and position—if compatible with your views
of propriety:"—ALS, *ibid.*

1869, MARCH 19.   Horace Porter to Secretary of War John A. Rawlins.
"The President directs me to request that the guard now on duty at the
Executive Mansion be relieved, and in its place to have detailed daily, one
~~corporal and three men~~ extra man with gun at War Dept for duty at the
Pres[i]dents."—LS, DNA, RG 94, Letters Received, 183P 1869. On March
20, Porter wrote to Rawlins. "The President directs me to countermand
the instruction communicated to you on the 19th inst in regard to retaining
a Corporal and three privates on duty at the Executive Mansion. Hereafter
no guard whatever will be required."—LS, *ibid.* On June 3, 1872, U.S.
Senator Matthew H. Carpenter of Wis. stated that when "General Grant
took possession of the White House it was patrolled by sentinels day and
night; . . . The first night General Grant slept at the President's House,
after retiring, he heard the tramp of soldiers in the hall below, and pres-
ently the command, 'Halt; order arms,' and the crash of muskets on the
floor. The General, not knowing what it meant, ran down stairs to ascertain. There he found an officer in command of a squad of soldiers; and on
asking an explanation, the General was informed that it was the night
guard of the Executive Mansion, which for a long time had been stationed
there every night. But General Grant informed the officer that he could
take care of himself, and ordered him to take his soldiers to their quarters.
He waited till his armed friends had left, then locked the door and went to
bed. The next day the whole business of sentinel service was discontinued,
and not a soldier has been on duty at the White House since."—*CG*, 42–2
(Appendix), p. 557.

1869, MARCH 19.   U.S. Representative Nathaniel P. Banks of Mass. and
fifteen others to USG. "We cheerfully recommend to you, for appointment
to the Mission of Resident Minister to Equador, South America exCon-
gressman *James Thorington* of Iowa as being competent and worthy."—
Copy, DLC-Nathaniel P. Banks. On April 15, James Grant Wilson, New
York City, wrote to USG. "More than a year since I was recommended by
the Senators from NewYork, and by many prominent gentlemen, for the
mission to Ecuador, made vacant by the death of Mr Coggeshall. My claims
and fitness for the position were recognized, but your predecessor declined
appointing me, on the ground that I was a pronounced Republican, a warm
adherent of yours for the Presidency, and the author of a campaign *bro-
chure* intended to aid your Election. During the past month I was again
strongly recommended for the position of Resident Minister to the Republic

of Ecuador by the NewYork Senators, by Admiral Farragut, by James. W. Beekmen, and many other well known gentlemen, who believe my appointment would be satisfactory to the Party and to the Country. I very respectfully and most Earnestly solicit this favor at your hands, and ask it among other reasons, because my health requires a change of climate which my limited means will not admit of my otherwise obtaining."—ALS, DNA, RG 59, Letters of Application and Recommendation. Related papers are *ibid.* William Cullen Bryant wrote to USG in support of Wilson.—Copy (undated), *ibid.*, RG 56, Appraiser of Customs Applications. Neither applicant was appointed. See letter to Hamilton Fish, Nov. 6, 1869.

1869, MARCH 19.   Peter Cooper, New York City, to USG. "Having heard that Mr E W Wynkoop is a candidate for the position of Superintendant of Indian Affairs and from the strong and earnest manner in which he is recommended by men to whom the welfare of our country is a consideration paramount to every other and from what I have known of himself personally and of his services among the Indians I consider him eminently fitted for the post of Superintendant of Indian Affairs and have no hesitation in commending him to your favorable notice"—ALS, Museum of New Mexico, Santa Fe, N. M. No appointment followed. See *PUSG*, 17, 164.

1869, MARCH 19.   Governor Robert K. Scott of S. C. to USG. "It gives me pleasure to introduce to your acquaintance Maj. Martin R. De Laney, an officer in the 104th Regiment U. S. colored troops, during the war, and subsequently Sub Assistant Commissioner under me in the Freedmens Bureau for three years, during which he served with intelligence, efficiency, and fidelity. A physician by education and profession, and of highly respectable acquirements, he has improved the advantages derived by a large intercourse with society, and still further by extensive travel in foreign countries, among them the continent of Africa in the service of a British Benevolent Society. He possesses a power of influencing his own race which is rarely equalled, and admirably qualifies him for filling any position, at home or abroad, in which such influence may be exercised with honor to himself and advantage to his country."—LS, PHi. On Oct. 18, Martin R. Delany, Washington, D. C., wrote to USG. "The undersigned, late Major of the 104th U. S. C. Troops, resident of Wilberforce, near Xenia, Green County, State of Ohio, most respectfully makes Application for the Mission of Minister Resident and Consul General, to the Republic of Liberia. He has explored extensively on the Coast and in the Interior of Africa, reporting on its commercial importance before the Royal Geographical Society, London, and other Institutions in both England and Scotland, as well as before distinguished members of the British Government. For his knowledge and experience in commercial developments, he would most respectfully refer to Major Gen'l Rufus Saxton, under whom he served ten months in South Carolina; also Major General Robert K. Scott, now Governor of South Carolina, under whom he served three years, assisting in the restoration of the Industrial and Agricultural productions of the State; also to Major General Daniel E. Sickles, now Minister to Spain, under whom he received the appointment by Special order (No 148, series of 1865,) of Inspector, with direct reference to the Commercial and Domestic relations of the Sea Islands in the southern part of the State, and around about Charleston."—LS, DNA, RG 59, Letters of Application and Recommendation. Related papers are *ibid.* No appointment followed.

1869, MARCH 20. Alexander T. Augusta, James Wormley *et al.*, Washington, D. C., to USG. "We the undersigned believing that the interest of the colored people of the District of Columbia demands that they should be represented upon the magisterial bench; and having full confidence in the education, integrity, and judgement of the Rev. D. W. Anderson a citizen and property holder of Washington City, respectfully request that your Excellency will appoint him a Justice of the Peace for the District of Columbia. He was educated by the lamented President William Henry Harrison, because of the brilliant conduct of his father at the battle of Tippacanoe Nov. 7th 1811, and we pray that this consideration, aswell as the great benefit such an appointment would bestow upon the colored people, will have its due influence in guiding your Excellency in this particular."—DS (7 signatures), DNA, RG 60, Records Relating to Appointments. U.S. Senators Charles Sumner of Mass. and Samuel C. Pomeroy of Kan. favorably endorsed this petition. On April 1, USG made this nomination.

On April 5, Augusta *et al.* petitioned USG. "We the undersigned having the greatest confidence in the education, judgement and integrity of Mr John F Cook a Citizen an property holder in this city, most respectfully request that your Excellency will appoint him a Justice of the Peace for the Dist. of Columbia His standing among the colored people with whom he is identified, will make such an appointment both popular and beneficial."— DS (4 signatures), *ibid.* On July 9, James A. Magruder *et al.*, Georgetown, D. C., petitioned USG. "The undersigned members of the Executive Committee of the Republican party of Georgetown D. C. respectfully recommend, (and ask for) the appointment of John Cornell as a Magistrate—A large proportion of our population are Coloured people, they desire one of their own race to try their cases—and we are Satisfied from our own knowledge of Cornell that he is an intelligent, upright man, and a good Citizen, we feel sure his appointment will give great Satisfaction to the Republicans of this town."—DS (10 signatures), *ibid.* On Dec. 6, USG nominated John F. Cook and John Cornell as justices of the peace.

1869, MARCH [22]. USG endorsement. "I have no doubt but Gn. Biggs would make a most efficient Auditor"—AES, Herman Biggs Papers, University of North Carolina, Chapel Hill, N. C. Written on a letter of March 19 from Herman Biggs, Washington, D. C., to USG requesting appointment as auditor, Treasury Dept.—ALS, DNA, RG 56, Records Relating to Appointments. No appointment followed. See *PUSG*, 11, 38.

1869, MARCH 22.   To Senate. "I, herewith, lay before the Senate, for the constitutional action of that body, a treaty, concluded in this city, on the 9th instant, between Thomas Murphy and Hampton B. Denman, on part of the United States, and the Miami tribe of Indians, of Kansas, by their duly authorized delegates. A letter of the Secretary of the Interior of the 20th instant, together with the papers therein referred to are also herewith transmitted."—LS, DNA, RG 46, Presidential Messages, Indian Relations. Related papers are *ibid.* A copy of the letter from Secretary of the Interior Jacob D. Cox is *ibid.*, RG 48, Indian Div., Letters Sent.

1869, MARCH 22.   Judge Mark W. Delahay, U.S. District Court, Kan., Washington, D. C., to USG. "In January last I was induced to write out my resignation as United States District Judge for the District of Kansas, and placed the same in the hands of Hon John P Usher, to be delivered to your Excellency on the first of next June—Having reconsidered my purpose I do now hereby revoke and recall said letter of resignation.—I have by letter notified Mr Usher of this act, of revocation—"—ALS, DNA, RG 60, Records Relating to Appointments. On May 29, John P. Usher, Leavenworth, wrote to USG. "*Private* . . . On yesterday I mailed to you certain papers affecting Judge Delahay. I could not with those papers express to you the great regret I felt that the promise I had made compelled me to perform the duty of sending them—That regret grows out of the great distress that will be inflicted on the Judge and his most estimable family— Mr Lincoln had but a very limited number of relatives upon whom he could bestow any favor,   The office to Delahay was one of those—I dont want to be an instrument in breaking down or injuring in any way an object of his affections—& hope you will not accept the resignation but have it recalled and revoked as I really suppose it to be, thus giving Judge Delahay a further opportunity to ~~have~~ make amends for the past and have the office which the best man on Earth bestowed upon him"—ALS, CSmH. On June 2, Attorney Gen. Ebenezer R. Hoar wrote to USG. ". . . I am of opinion that the contemplated resignation of Judge Delahay has not taken effect, and that no vacancy exists in his office. Mr. Usher was not deputed by you to receive the paper containing the resignation, and was only the agent of Judge Delahay for that purpose. Until the paper was delivered to you, it had no operation and the power to deliver it to you has been revoked. I think it has no more effect as a resignation than if it had been written and remained on the desk of Judge Delahay, and transmitted to you without his consent. . . ."—Copy, DNA, RG 60, Opinions. With impeachment impending, on Dec. 4, 1873, Delahay, Topeka, wrote to USG resigning his judgeship.—LS, *ibid.*, Records Relating to Appointments. See *HRC*, 42-3-92; *CG*, 42–2, 3926; *New York Times*, March 4, 1873.

1869, MARCH 22.   Lewis Dent, Washington, D. C., to USG. "I would most earnestly recommend Mr F. C Clarke of Pennsylvania for the U. S. Consulship at Callao Peru S. A. I have long known him as a gentleman, accomplished and respected and think him peculiarly well fitted for the position believing that should he be appointed, he will discharge the duties of the office in a manner that will prove honourable to himself and creditable to the Government. My knowledge of the character of Mr Clarke extending as it does through a series of years especially through the dark hours of the late Rebellion was such as to commend itself to the esteem of all for the zeal manifested in the support of loyalty, and the soldiers in the field: his means which then were large being lavished to that end in the various channels that an unostentatious and unassuming gentleman would select. Now that his circumstances are less prosperous, his health failing, I trust that his application, influenced as it is for a change of climate, will meet with favor, and that you will give to my endorsement of Mr Clark the same consideration you would grant to any other person,"—LS (signed as Louis Dent), DNA, RG 59, Letters of Application and Recommendation. Related papers are *ibid.* No appointment followed.

1869, MARCH 22. U.S. Senator Lyman Trumbull of Ill. to USG. "I have been too busy to call on you for some days, but before you finally decide upon the persons to be appointed to Territorial and foreign positions from Ill. I should be glad of an opportunity to present the names of a number of worthy & deserving Gentlemen, whose applications have been filed in the proper departments. Quite a number of Illinoisans are in the city importuning personally and through friends for outside appointments, & I think it but just to equally deserving Gentlemen who have been less pressing, that their names should not be overlooked when you come to make your selections—I annex a list of several applications for territorial appointments, which I hope may be favorably considered . . . Gen. J. H. Howe for Judge in Wyoming James Strain for Judge in Montana C. M. Hawley for Judge in Utah Dr. Geo. T. Allen for Gov. Wyoming E. Washburne for Sur. Gen. New Mexico Dr. F. R. Payne—Land office Washington—Besides these there are applicants for positions abroad whose names I desire an opportunity to present before final action is had—"—ALS (tabular material expanded), DNA, RG 59, Letters of Application and Recommendation.

On March 6, U.S. Representative John A. Logan of Ill. wrote to USG. "Allow me to present the name of Judge J H Howe of Kewanee Ills. who is an applicant for the position of Judge in the Territory of Wyoming You may remember him as Col of the 124th Ills. Vols. He was in my command & I take pleasure in endorsing him as an honest, faithful brave and judicious man, and eminently fitted for the position having been upon the Bench for many years. I will be glad if consistent if you will appoint him"—ALS, *ibid.*, RG 60, Records Relating to Appointments. Related papers are *ibid.* On April 3, USG nominated John H. Howe as chief justice, Wyoming Territory.

On Nov. 2, 1868, John M. Palmer, Springfield, Ill., wrote to USG. "I request the appointment of Hon James Strain of Monmouth Ills to the position of Judge of the United States Court in the Territory of Montana I ask the appointment of Mr Strain to this postion upon the ground that he is Capable and honest and that he has always true to the Country   I am satisfied that the interests of the people of the Territory and of the United States may be promoted by his appointmt"—ALS, *ibid.* Related papers are *ibid.* On Jan. 1, 1869, Governor Richard J. Oglesby of Ill. wrote to USG. "Allow me to call your attention to the Subject of appointment of Judge for the United States for the Territory of Montana. Such an appointment will I suppose be made during the Spring months. I hope you will consider the qualifications for that responsible position of Hon James Strain of this State, an excellent lawyer a good citizen and a gentleman possessing every qualification for the Office   Mr Strain has been a State Senator for four years, has been a strong Union man and will be devoted to the Union. He desires to move to the Territory will take his family and become a citizen there   I earnestly recommend his appointment as one in every respect suitable to be made"—LS, *ibid.*; (press), Oglesby Papers, IHi. No appointment followed.

On April 15, USG nominated Cyrus M. Hawley as associate justice, Utah Territory. See letter to John M. Thayer, Dec. 22, 1870.

On Feb. 26, 1869, George T. Allen, Springfield, Ill., wrote to USG. "I have the honor to request from you the appointment of Governor of Wyoming Territory, and would respectfully refer you to the accompanying recommendations and to your knowledge of me as Medical Inspector, U. S. A., during the late war."—ALS, DNA, RG 59, Letters of Application and Recommendation. Trumbull endorsed this letter. "I have known Col. Geo. T. Allen for many years, & can bear testimony to his high character, integrity & ability—He is a physician of eminence, & possesses all the qualifications requisite for an able & efficient Governor of Wyoming for which I cheerfully, & earnestly recommend him—"—AES, *ibid.* Related papers are *ibid.* On April 12, USG nominated Allen as consul, Moscow.

On March 26, U.S. Senator Oliver P. Morton of Ind. wrote to USG. "I personally desire the success of Elmer Washburne, of Alton, Illinois, in his application for Surveyor General of New Mexico. Allow me to call attention to his application,"—ALS, *ibid.*, RG 48, Appointment Div., Letters Received. No appointment followed.

1869, MARCH 23.   Archibald Buchanan, Camden, Maine, to USG seeking payment from the Spanish government for confiscation of the "Bark Georgiana" in 1850.—ALS, DNA, RG 59, Miscellaneous Letters. See *HED*, 32-1-83.

1869, MARCH 23.   Mrs. George T. Hardcastle, "formerly Miss A. Case," Boonville, Mo., to USG. "I addressed a letter to you on the 15th inst, enclosing it in a letter to Mrs Nellie Sharp. at Richmond, Va. and requested her to forward it to you. A few days afterwards, I noticed that Dr. Sharp had been appointed Marshal at Washington, and I am fearful, from this fact. my letter may be detained at Richmond, and consequently, take the liberty of writing you again—My object in addressing you as stated in my previous letter is to ask for the Office of 'U S. Marshal' of this district or 'Receiver' or 'Register' of the Land Office here. for my husband or in case these should be already filled, An Office in St Louis or Chicago or Washington that you might think more desirable and *more profitable*, would be greatly preferred by me, Your assistance in this last request, my dear friend! I assure you would be greatly appreciated by me. As regards my husbands integrity and capacity for filling an Office he would refer you to the following Gentleman. William H. Trigg Boonville Mo Capt Joseph L. Stephens Boonville Mo Hon Erastus Wells Representative St Louis Chs. W. Ford. St Louis and also your brother in law Dr. Alexander Sharp—who is an old acquaintance of ours. I cannot forget the very pleasant call we had from you while we were liveing on Olive Street next door to your friend Judge Moody—I fear you have forgotten it, as I have never received your Photograph you then promised to send me—but it is not yet too late, and I must again beg for one of yourself and wife. Will you not send them to me? I trust my friend! you will pardon the liberty I have taken of addressing you now while your time is so much employed: but if you will spare me a *few moments* of your time and thought on this subject you will fill my heart with the deepest gratitude, and I can never forget your kindness—Please present the kindest regards from my husband and my self to your wife . . ." —ALS (tabular material expanded), DNA, RG 60, Records Relating to Appointments. No appointment followed.

1869, MARCH 24. To Senate. "I transmit to the Senate, in answer to their Resolution of the 1st. instant, a report from the Secretary of State, together with accompanying papers."—LS, DNA, RG 46, Presidential Messages, Foreign Relations, Spain. On the same day, Secretary of State Hamilton Fish had written to USG. "The Secretary of State to whom was referred the Resolution of the Senate, of the 1st instant, requesting the President, 'if in his opinion compatible with the public interest, to transmit to the Senate copies of all correspondence on file in the State Department between the Minister of the United States at Madrid, and the Secretary of Legation at the same place within the last two years,' has the honor to lay before the President all the correspondence on file in this Department upon the subject of the Senates call as specified in the accompanying list. I deem it proper in submitting these papers, to invite especial attention to the concluding paragraph of Mr. Perry's communication, dated March 2nd. 1869, in relation to the impropriety of giving publicity to the accompaniments of his despatch."—LS, *ibid.* Related papers are *ibid.* Horatio J. Perry's letter accused John P. Hale, minister to Spain, of improper duty free importation of textiles. Printed in *New York Times,* April 10, 1869. See Howard K. Beale, ed., *Diary of Gideon Welles* (New York, 1960), III, 518–19, 553, 578; Richard H. Sewell, *John P. Hale and the Politics of Abolition* (Cambridge, Mass., 1965), pp. 227–30.

On April 7, Perry, Madrid, wrote to Fish. "Yesterday morning at about

9 o'clock I received from you a telegram in cipher which I read as follows. 'Your resignation will be accepted. Please inform me by telegraph if you do resign.' To which I immediately replied as follows. 'Under calumnious accusation and having fulfilled my whole duty, I do not resign, and hope from your justice not to be dismissed.' The motives for such an answer will not be hidden to your penetration. I trust to have proved by my long record at the Department now in your worthy charge that whenever the service of the country has needed any sacrifice at my hands it has received it. The election of General Grant to the Presidency was a cause of sincere satisfaction to me, and the new administration could have asked of me every sacrifice except one. I cannot by any voluntary act of mine leave the least shadow of a doubt upon the mind of any body as to the falsity of the charges brought against me by my superior officer and his abettors. . . . What I would willingly have done at your request in ordinary circumstances I am not free to do now; nor ought the President to ask it. I ask from him & from you *justice*, and due consideration for what affects my honor & good name. The President may claim from me any sacrifice except that. I cannot yield him that. And when you call his attention to this aspect of the matter I am certain that General Grant will have no wish to dishonour me."—ALS (press), DNA, RG 46, Papers Pertaining to Executive Nominations.

On April 17, Charles W. Stewart, Covington, Ky., wrote to USG. "At the urgent request of many friends it is thought expedient to direct your attention to the papers of Maj. James L. Foley of this City, which were filed for a 'Consulship.' Being assured that his claims have been overlooked and forgotten through the pressure of business and other duties of office, . . ."—ALS, *ibid.*, RG 59, Letters of Application and Recommendation. Jesse Root Grant endorsed this letter. "In a conversation this morning with Maj Foley I told him that you had probably forgotten his case, & suggested the expediency of writing & calling your attention to the subject—I know you intended when I left to to give the Maj an appointment—Mr Stwart is his half brother—"—AES, *ibid.* Related papers are *ibid.* On April 19, 1:00 P.M., Horace Porter telegraphed to Jesse Grant. "Does Foley speak the spanish language? Would secretary of Legation to Spain be agreeable to him."—Copy, DLC-USG, II, 5. On the same day, Jesse Grant telegraphed to Porter. "Foley does not speak Spanish, Could easily acquire the language, The position would be very acceptable"—Telegram received (at 7:00 P.M.), DNA, RG 107, Telegrams Collected (Bound). On April 20, USG nominated James L. Foley as secretary of legation, Madrid, in place of Perry; the Foreign Relations Committee made no recommendation and the Senate took no action. On June 28, USG suspended Perry. On Nov. 20, Perry wrote to the Senate seeking reinstatement.—ALS, *ibid.*, RG 46, Papers Pertaining to Executive Nominations. On Dec. 6, USG nominated John Hay for the position.

On Aug. 30, 1870, Hay, Washington, D. C., who had resigned as secretary, wrote to USG. "I take the liberty to add a word to the recommendation which Gen. Sickles has made in favor of Mr Alvey A. Adee to be Secretary of Legation at Madrid. He is thoroughly qualified for the post, possessing a good knowledge of the French and Spanish languages, and is a gentleman of the highest character for integrity and industry. Gen. Sickles is very anxious for his appointment and I venture to say that in doing this favor for one of your strongest friends and supporters you will obtain a valuable officer for the diplomatic service."—ALS, *ibid.*, RG 59, Letters of Application and Recommendation. Related papers are *ibid.* On Dec. 6, USG nominated Alvey A. Adee as secretary of legation, Madrid.

1869, MARCH 24. Christopher C. Andrews, St. Cloud, Minn., to USG. "I beg leave cordially to recommend the appointment of Hon. Charles T. Brown of St. Peter, Minn as Surveyor General for the District of Minnesota. The ability and integrity of Mr. Brown in my opinion specially fit him for that office. He is one of our prominent and highly respected citizens; has served with distinction in the legislature, and was chosen Presidential elector last fall by some 16.000 majority. I think the appointment would be quite popular, as well as beneficial to the public."—ALS (press), Andrews Papers, Minnesota Historical Society, St. Paul, Minn. On April 6, USG nominated Charles T. Brown as agent, Chippewas and other tribes; on Dec. 14, 1870, as surveyor gen., Minn.

1869, MARCH 24. William H. Reed, Richmond, to USG. "Much dissatisfaction prevails here—wheels of State Government stopped Stoneman refuses to appoint State officers until Canby arrives. Further delay injurious We hope you will order immediately appointments No disbursements can be made Sheriffs, are delayed"—Telegram received (at 10:55 A.M.), DNA, RG 107, Telegrams Collected (Bound). Bvt. Maj. Gen. George Stoneman endorsed Reed's telegram. ". . . The writer of this telegram is a drunken, debased worthless fellow, whose statements under any circumstances are unworthy of credence."—ES, OFH. On April 3, Secretary of War John A. Rawlins endorsed the telegram. "Respectfully returned to the President"—ES, *ibid.*

1869, MARCH 24. William W. Webb, Lunenburg, Va., to USG. "The war has been at an end for nearly four years, we have had all sorts of governments in this our beloved old Commonwealth, we have born up under them in every shape & form, but at last the machine has run off of the track, and we are left without any government of any shape or form.—If a man is shot down in our Streets, there is no one to arrest the murderer. we don't know what to do with criminals now in Jail, having no Jailer. Our young men are applying to me, as late clerk, for marriage license. I can do nothing for them. we are certainly in an awful, fix.—Mr President.—we hope, and are anxiously waiting to hear one word from you in our behalf. is there nothing that you can do for us? what would you have is do? we have prayed congress to remove our political disabilities, but they have as yet

turned a deaf year to our entreaties. all that we ask for is *Peace*. we are
placed in that anomalous position, that we are required to ask the removal
of Political disabilities where none exist, that we may get rid of the *Iron-clad*
oath.—I know there is not a man in my County, that can take it, that has sense
enough to issue a marriage license, and no respectable man will come down
here, and hold office, when he knows the people don't want him, most especially the small offices, in the Country, that pay but little.—Mr President.
we anxiously wait, and look, to you, for deliverance.—"—ALS, DNA, RG
107, Letters Received from Bureaus. Variant text in *New York Herald*,
April 1, 1869.

1869, MARCH 24. William M. Wood, Owings Mills, Md., to USG. "I
respectfully apply for a nomination to the Military Academy at West Point,
for my son C. Erskine Scott Wood, aged 17 the 20th of last February, and
a native of Erie, Pennsylvania The Navy Register shews that I have been
in the naval service forty years within two months; In that time it has been
my duty to render service in every naval war in which we have been engaged—Seminole—Mexican Chinese and Civil; having been in the last, Fleet
Surgeon of the North Atlantic Squadron. My naval service, almost, necessarily debars me from the claim of a Congressional nomination, but I would
not compete with any other applicant for an appointment at large, but that
I have a family either from age or sex dependent upon my life, and I believe
the boy to be morally & physically fit for the demands of the service"—ALS,
DNA, RG 94, Correspondence, USMA. Related papers are *ibid.* Charles
E. S. Wood graduated USMA in 1874. See *DAB* (Supplement 3).

1869, MARCH 25. Commander John H. Upshur, "Off New London,"
Conn., to USG. "I have the honor to ask that, in the event of any one of the
late appointees to the Naval Academy failing to pass the requisite examination, my son, Custis P. Upshur, may be appointed in his stead. I would
submit to your Excellency, if it may have any weight, that the grandfather
of my son lost his life in the regular army of the United States while storm-
ing Monterey; that his father has fought through one foreign and one domestic war for the government; that he is a grandson of Mrs. General
Washington, and that he has been for three years praying through me for
an appointment as midshipman."—HED, 41-2-308, p. 25. A similar letter
of March 9 is *ibid.* Custis P. Upshur was appointed midshipman as of
Sept. 24.

1869, MARCH 25. William L. Burt, postmaster, Boston, to USG. "I have
taken the liberty to recommedn to your most favorable notice Major Thomas
L. White formerly of this City now residing in the State of Mississippi—
Major White was in my office & a practicing attorney when the war broke
out and he enlisted as a private soldier was promoted and finally after being
severly wounded was transferred to the South and became an officer in one
of the Colored Regiments—He was energetic brave and reliable securing

the confidence & esteem of his superiors and the greatest devotion on the part of those under him—After the war closed he continued in the South with a view to a permanet home and has labored amid the greatest difficulties & sacrifices to assist in saving his adopted State and restoring her to the Union—His labors have been in every political field there for the past three years—and now he finds himself with impaired health and exhausted means—the only rewards for his labors and sacrifices—He has been an extreme and active supporter of reconstruction—one of the earliest organizers of the Republican party there and were his health equal to the task proposed to labor on in the same field till full success was reached—Knowing him as I do & his labors and merits no one better than he can have favorable recognition by the Governmt in that State—for the good of the cause—I trust it may be consistent with the public interest to grant him the position he now seeks—a consulate on the South American Pacific Coast. He will be a faithful & excellent officer who can be trusted to any extent and will win friends constantly in any position he may be placed for the Governmt and for himself—"—ALS, DNA, RG 59, Letters of Application and Recommendation. On March 22, Lewis Dent, Washington, D. C., had written an endorsement. "I have known Major Thomas L White for some time, (over a year,) and cheerfully bear testimony to his eminent fitness for any position to which h[e] can aspire, being a gentleman of character and ability. He has done good service in the Republican party and canvassed the State of Mississippi during the last election, with great ability." —AES (signed as Louis Dent), *ibid.* Related papers are *ibid.* No appointment followed. See *PUSG,* 18, 571–72; letter to Lewis Dent, Aug. 1, 1869.

1869, MARCH 25.   Juan N. Navarro, Mexican consul gen., Washington, D. C., to USG. "I have received by the last steamer from VeraCruz a letter of President Juarez, charging me with the agreeable commission of congratulating you on behalf of the Government of Mexico, for your well merited appointment by the popular voice, as first Magistrate of this great Republic. I request from your courtesy the honor of an interview for the aforesaid purpose, . . ."—LS, ICHi.

1869, MARCH 26.   Secretary of the Interior Jacob D. Cox to USG. "I have the honor, to submit, herewith, for your signature, a commission for the appointment, by and with the advice and consent of the Senate, of Dudley. W Haynes of New York to be Pension Agent at Brooklyn New York."— LS, OFH.

1869, MARCH 26.   Governor Rufus B. Bullock of Ga., Washington, D. C., to USG. "I respectfully invite favorable consideration to the application of Dr Felix Petard, Dr Petard is an American citizen by adoption & one who actively aided & thoroughly sympathized with the Union cause during the Rebellion, His Republicanism has prevented him from profitable practice of his profession in Georgia."—ALS, DNA, RG 59, Letters of Application

and Recommendation. Related papers are *ibid.* On Dec. 6, USG nominated
Felix C. M. Petard as consul, Strasbourg.

1869, MARCH 26.   Jonathan E. Cowen, Galveston, to USG. "I have the
honor to request of you the appointment to the Office of United States
Marshall, for the Eastern District of Texas. I most respectfully refer you
to the annexed statements and recommendations."—ALS, DLC-Nathaniel
P. Banks. The enclosures are *ibid.* On April 8, USG nominated William
E. Parker as marshal, Eastern District, Tex.

1869, MARCH 26.   John Pendleton Kennedy, Baltimore, to USG. "My
friend Mr Wm Thomson, I understand desires to return to the Consulate at
Southhampton in England, which post he filled for several years with great
credit to himself and with the universal esteem of his countrymen. . . ."—
ALS, DNA, RG 59, Letters of Application and Recommendation. Related
papers are *ibid.* On April 12, USG nominated William Thomson as consul,
Southampton, in place of John Britton.

On May 4, W. L. Palmer, Stonington, Conn., wrote to USG. "Yesterdays N. York 'Tribune' contains an account from its London correspondent
under date 17th Apl. of the removal from the office of 'Consul of Southampton' of Capt John Britton and appointing in his place William Thomson, and who was appointed to the same office by James Buchanan, which
of itself is sufficient reason, why he should not be put on guard for the
reason I have not known the first Buchanan Democrat who *was* true & stood
by his country in the hour of danger—I am satisfied you were wrongly informed as to this appointment and that you will (As stated in your inaugural) put none but 'true and good men on guard,' and that Capt John Britton
a good and true man to his country, and known to every merchant in the
city of New York, will be reinstated to the office Mr Lincoln appointed
him"—ALS, *ibid.* On May 5, Horace Porter wrote to Secretary of State
Hamilton Fish. "The President directs me to send you herewith a slip cut
from the New York Tribune of the 3rd instant, and to request that you
have the case investigated."—LS, *ibid.* Related papers are *ibid.* Thomson
retained his position.

1869, MARCH 27.   Bvt. Maj. Gen. Joseph A. Mower and Maj. Amos
Beckwith, New Orleans, to USG. "The appointment of Doctor Peterson as
postmaster will be satisfactory to the business community here and we
recommend it"—Telegram received (at 3:00 P.M.), DNA, RG 107, Telegrams Collected (Bound). No appointment followed.

1869, MARCH 27.   David Davis, U.S. Supreme Court, to USG. "I take
pleasure in introducing to you the Hon Charles A Ray of Indianapolis—
who desires to see you on business, the nature of which I am not apprised
of—Being unable to go personally and present Judge Ray, I have taken the
liberty of giving you him this note of introduction. Judge Ray is a gentle-

man of character, and high standing in Indiana ~~as is evidenced by the fact,~~
~~that he is~~ and is Chief Justice of the Supreme Court of the State   Regretting
my inability to present him in person ~~to you~~ . . ."—ADfS, David Davis
Papers, IHi.

1869, MARCH 27.   George P. Fisher, D. C. Supreme Court, to USG.
"Joseph M. Carey, Esquire a native of Delaware but for five years a resident
of Philadelphia and a member of the bar there desires to be appointed District Attorney for Wyoming Territory. . . ."—ALS, DNA, RG 60, Records
Relating to Appointments. Related papers are *ibid.* On April 3, USG nominated Joseph M. Carey as U.S. attorney, Wyoming Territory. On Dec. 3,
1870, E. Schwiger *et al.*, Evanston, Wyoming Territory, wrote to USG.
"We the undersigned citizens of Uinta Co. Wyoming Territory do hereby
petition your Excellency to appoint Hon M. C. Brown Now residint of
Laramie eCity Wyoming as associate Justice of the supreme court for
Wyoming Territory to fill the vacancy caused by the election of Hon W. T.
Jones as delegate to Congress from Wyoming"—DS (107 signatures),
ibid. Related papers are *ibid.*

On Jan. 16, 1871, William T. Jones, associate justice, Wyoming Territory, resigned.—ALS, *ibid.*, Letters Received, Wyoming. On Feb. 3, USG
nominated Joseph W. Fisher as associate justice, Wyoming Territory. On
Sept. 23, Governor John A. Campbell and Jones, U.S. delegate, Wyoming
Territory, twice wrote to USG. "Having been informed that Hon J. H.
Howe has tendered his resignation as Chief Justice of Wyoming, to take
effect on the 31st of October, we have the honor to recommend as his successor Hon J W. Fisher, Associate Justice of the Territory—Judge Fisher
has fulfilled his duties on the Bench since his appointment ably and acceptably—he has had a long experience at the Bar—is well versed in the law,
and is in every respect a man of ability and undoubted integrity—His
appointment as Chief Justice would be heartily endorsed by the people, the
Bar and the Republican party of the Territory, and would be a just recognition of his merits—"   "We have the honor to respectfully recommend
that Hon Joseph M Carey, United States Attorney for the District of Wyoming may be appointed Associate Justice of this Territory vice Hon J. W.
Fisher, in case the latter is promoted to the Chief Justiceship vacated by
the resignation of Hon J H Howe— . . ."—LS, *ibid.*, Records Relating to
Appointments. Related papers are *ibid.* On Dec. 6, USG nominated Fisher
as chief justice, Wyoming Territory, and, on Dec. 13, nominated Carey as
associate justice.

On Dec. 21, 1875, Fisher, Cheyenne, wrote to Attorney Gen. Edwards
Pierrepont. "I have the honor to call your attention to the subject of my reappointment to the position which I have filled for the last four years. When
I was in Washington during the latter part of October last I was favored
with interviews both with the President and yourself, and in those interviews I was led to beliveve that my reappointment was an assured fact. I
came home to attend a term of court with the fullest confidence, that I had

given almost entire satisfaction, so much so, that I was told by the President
and yourself that there never had been a complaint against me. Recently
however I have learned that efforts have been made to have some one else
take my place, and that some efforts have been made by persons from this
territory to have me replaced by some friend of Gov Thayer. Why this is
done I cannot conceive, since my appointment first in 1871 I have endeavored by every act and thought to discharge the responsible duties of
my office with the strictest fidelity, that I may have made mistakes I have
not vanity enough to attempt to deny, but that I have done an intentional
wrong I do not believe that my worst enemy will dare to say. There may be
men who will be more subservient to other parties than I have been or ever
will be but I challenge any man to show wherein in any single instance I
have done an intentional wrong. I know very well that there have been
efforts made with the President by unscrupulous men to affect in his mind
something predjudicial to me, knowing that I cannot very well be on hand to
meet any direct charges or even mean inuendoes, but I have this to say that
there can be no charge made that I cannot in the most triumphant manner
meet, and I think overthrow by the testimony of the person making it. I
would not degrade myself by begging for any office, but to have the President refuse to confer upon me a reappointment, through the slanderous
statements of men who have failed in their efforts to use me for the accomplishment of their dishonest purposes, without giving me a chance to be
heard would be an unkindness that I cannot believe possible, When I
speak of a friend of Governor Thayer, I would not for a moment have it
inferred that I am his enemy, far from it, I entertain the kindest feelings
for him, but I mean his friend in a peculiar or political sense. I am now no
politician, previous to my coming here I was very active in support of republican measures and republican men but in Coming on to the bench I left
politics for others. I should be glad if you would show this letter to the President"—ALS, *ibid.,* Letters Received, Wyoming. See Lewis L. Gould,
Wyoming: A Political History, 1868–1896 (New Haven, 1968), pp. 24,
32–33, 46–47, 75–78.

1869, MARCH 27. Lamprecht, Halle, Prussia, to USG. "Strange as this
petition may seem to you, stranger circumstances have prompted it. Out of
ten sons, brought up in tender care, nine have found homes in the United
States. Three of them fought in the war against the South, and are now
buried in American soil; the others are trying to earn an honorable living
at their various callings. Otto served in the 7th U. S. Inf. and was killed in
1867, in a fight with the Indians. Carl died of cholera, at Freeport, in the
year 1850. Rudolph was wounded in battle near Richmond, and died of his
wounds at Raleigh, N. C., in 1868. Of the remaining six *August,* with 7
children, is now a minister of the gospel at Washitaw, in Minnesota. *Robert*
is sergeant in the 12th US. Infantry Band. *Max,* from whom I have not
heard for many years, is living in Illinois, as I am told. *Frederick* left the
Navy last year and bought a parcel of land near San Francisco, in Cali-

fornia, but has no means to cultivate it. *Herrmann* is in the 7th US. Infantry band, at San Augustine, in Florida. *Richard* is in the 2d US. Cavalry band, at fort McPherson, in Nebraska. All my wealth is in these six sons and I can do nothing for them. Therefore I approach Your Excellency, in manly candor, with this petition: 'I beg you will be a father to my six living sons, especially to the preacher, and the one with 7 children; assist them in their temporal affairs, as they now have no body to depend upon but you and their adopted country. I hope you will give me a favorable answer, that will serve to sweeten the last days of my declining years, And now Mr President, I beg you to accept the exprssion of my highest esteem."—ALS (in German), DNA, RG 107, Letters Received from Bureaus; translation, *ibid.*

1869, MARCH 27. Thomas J. Mason, Loudon, Tenn., to USG. "you may think it impertinent for me to write you this note but from reports I feel in duty bound to do—so—and I will refer you to the Hons Horace Maynard R. R. Butler and others for my veracity   I see from report that Andy Knott has been appointed United States Marshal for East Tennessee —which I am surprised and ~~and~~ pained to learn—Capt Evans of Roane County—also other good mem were applicants   Capt Evans's application was in the hands of Mr Maynard and I suppose were presented. Capt Evans is a meritorous deserving Honorable man he served over three years in the late war and lost one of his legs below the knee while on shermans raid through Georgia at the Battle of Resaca and to think that a meritorious soldier should be ignored for such a man as Mr Knott   Andy Knott is nothing more than a drunken blackguard and a by word . . ."—ALS, DNA, RG 60, Records Relating to Appointments. On April 12, USG nominated Samuel P. Evans as marshal, Eastern District, Tenn. A letter recommending Evans is *ibid.*

1869, MARCH 27. F. Marion Shields, Macon, Miss., to USG. "I would most respectfully ask for the removal of my *disabilities*—I always opposed the war—but was forced in the Army of the C. S. A—served a short time and was legally discharged by Jeff. Davis & Secty of War—at the *surrender* I applied for *parole* but was refused upon the *fact* that none but soldiers *defacto* was *paroled*—I am now appointed Surveyor of this Co—by Maj Genl Ames & have my Commission—but am sorry to say I can not take the Oath of office prescribed by act Congress July 2nd /62   please remove my disabilities and accept with assurance my highest Esteem"—ALS, USG 3. On March 17, Bvt. Maj. Gen. Adelbert Ames, provisional governor, Vicksburg, had telegraphed to Horace Porter. "Many offices become vacant tomorrow by operation of joint resolution of Congress which has not been received here   Time is needed to make proper appointments"—Telegram received (at 6:00 P.M.), DNA, RG 107, Telegrams Collected (Bound). On March 20, 12:30 P.M., Orville E. Babcock telegraphed to Ames. "Have you issued your order for removal of all officers who cannot take the test oath, in accordance with the Act of Congress."—Copy, DLC-USG, II, 5. On March 22, Ames telegraphed to Babcock. "No official notification of act of Congress mentioned has been received, I had so informed Porter, Please instruct me"—Telegram received (at 2:00 P.M.), DNA, RG 107, Telegrams Collected (Bound).

1869, MARCH 29.   To Senate. "In compliance with the request contained in the Resolution of the Senate of the 17th instant, in regard to certain correspondence between James Buchanan, then President of the United States, and Lewis Cass, Secretary of State, I transmit a Report from the Department of State which is accompanied by a copy of the correspondence referred to."—DS, DNA, RG 46, Presidential Messages. The enclosures are *ibid.* U.S. Senator Zachariah Chandler of Mich. had introduced the resolution, presumably to vindicate Lewis Cass, also from Mich. See *New York Times*, March 18, 31, 1869; *CG*, 41–1, 102–3; *SED*, 41-1-7.

1869, MARCH 29.   Secretary of the Treasury George S. Boutwell to USG. "Pursuant to your request I have examined, with reference to the application for pardon, the papers in the case of Arthur Ballou, against whom certain indictments are pending for an offence against the Internal Revenue laws for which his property has already been forfeited. I am of opinion that it is not a case requiring the present interposition of executive clemency."— Copy, DNA, RG 56, Letters Sent to the President. On March 16, Boutwell had written to USG about the same case.—Copy, *ibid.*

1869, MARCH 29.   Vice Admiral David D. Porter, Washington, D. C., to USG. "When I made an application for Mr H S Wetmore as Consul to Queenstown or manchester I omitted to state his qualifications. those how-ever are all set forth in his recommendations now in the hands of the Sec-retary of State.—in the first place he Served with me three years of the Rebellion, was promoted three times for good conduct.—since the war he has been attached to the custom house in several capacities—he has been in the merchant service as supercargo. he is a good penman and a good accountant. having been clerk in a large mercantile house—he is an *honest man* and a gentleman, perfectly qualified to perform all the duties of Con-sul—his object in going to England, is because his wife's family reside at manchester—I hope I shall not regret having asked of you this favor. which I would not do did I not know that the gentleman will give you great satis-faction"—ALS, DNA, RG 59, Letters of Application and Recommendation. Related papers are *ibid.* On April 13, USG nominated Henry S. Wetmore as consul, Manchester. On April 20, Porter wrote to USG. "An opposition having sprung up against my esteemed, loyal and gallant friend H. S. Wet-more whom you were so kind as to appoint to the Consulate at Manchester, England, I this morning requested Secretary Fish to do me the favor to withdraw his nomination for the present. The epithet of 'Copperhead' has been libellously applied to Mr Wetmore by people who have no *real* charge to prefer against him, but *who want his place*. Senator Cameron has sworn that he will have it and Senator Scott intimates 'that there is no use in fighting Cameron'! Responsible for Mr. Wetmore's good war record and steady loyalty, I regard these attacks—although made from interested motives—as levelled at myself, and I do not like to be beaten in any kind of fight. If therefore the Secretary of state shall prevail on you to withdraw Mr Wetmore's nomination, I shall consider it a high personal favor if you will see that the place is not filled. This will give the Department ample time to see how unjust are the aspersions against your nominee and give him a chance to defend himself. Hoping that you will keep this thing open, . . ."—LS, *ibid.* On April 20, USG withdrew Wetmore's nomination and nominated Charles H. Branscomb as consul.

1869, MARCH 29.   Coles Bashford to USG. "I respectfully make application for the appointment of Secretary of Arizona Territory in the place of James P. T Carter. Mr Carter was appointed a few years ago by President Johnson *as his personal frind, and partizan.* He is violently opposed to the Republican party, and abusive of General Grant personally. I have been a resident of Arizona since 1863. And have held the offices of Attorney General, and President of the Legislative Council. In the year 1866 was Elected Delegate in the 40th Congress. I am Endorsed by the Delegate in the Present Congress, by Jno N Goodwin late Delegate in the 39th Congress, And by the whole Delegation in Congress from the State of Wisconsin my former home. I expect to make Arizona my permanent home."—ALS, DNA, RG 59, Letters of Application and Recommendation. Related papers are *ibid.* On April 3, USG nominated Bashford, former governor of Wis., as secretary, Arizona Territory.

1869, MARCH 29.   Lewis C. Rochester, New York City, to USG charging that U.S. diplomatic officials failed to respond properly after the captain and mate of a merchant ship harassed Rochester's pregnant wife.—ALS, DNA, RG 59, Miscellaneous Letters.

1869, MARCH 29.   David Wagner, Mo. Supreme Court, *et al.*, St. Louis, to USG. "The undersigned have great pleasure in recommending Hon. George P. Strong of this city, to your consideration as a suitable person to be appointed United States circuit judge for the judicial district embracing the State of Missouri. Mr Strong has had a high standing at the bar for many years, taking rank among the leading minds of the profession in this state. His professional attainments are unquestionable, and his patriotism without reproach—His services in the interests of the country during the war, in public and private stations, were such as become the character of a loyal and devoted citizen—"—DS (3 signatures), MoSHi. No appointment followed.

1869, MARCH 30.   Secretary of War John A. Rawlins to USG. "In transmitting the accompanying nomination list for promotions in the Cavalry, Artillery, and Infantry for your signature and reference to the Senate, I have the honor to state that the greater part of these officers were originally nominated during the third session of the 40th Congress, but failed to receive the action of that body. Other nominations, however, of officers junior to some of these, for promotion to vacancies of later dates were confirmed by the Senate at their last session, and unless these nominations likewise receive the favorable action of the Senate, great disadvantage will result to the officers, whose promotion is again respectfully submitted for your approbation. As one instance of this, Captains La Motte and Hambright entitled to promotion, December 3, 1868 and January 27, 1869, respectively, are still Captains, while their juniors, Captains Dallas, Mizner and Rathbone whose nominations were submitted subsequently have been confirmed as Majors. The names of 1st Lieut. Andrew S. Bennett 15th Infy 2d Lieut. Thomas Dunn, 15th Infy. & 2d Lieut. Fred'k M. Lynde, 22d Infy. were not before submitted to the Senate, but as the vacancies to which these officers are nominated, occurred *before* March 3. 1869, the date of the act stopping promotions in the Infantry, it has been thought proper that the list should also embrace their names."—Copies, DNA, RG 94, ACP, W101 CB 1869; *ibid.*, Letters Sent, Nominations; *ibid.*, RG 107, Letters Sent to the President.

1869, MARCH 30.   Bvt. Maj. Gen. Oliver O. Howard to USG. "I desire to commend to your kind attention Col. T. S. West formerly Comdg. 24th Wisconsin Infantry in the 1st Brigade, 2nd Divn 4th Army Corps, and for some time commanding the Brigade, whilst I was in command of the Corps— Col. West has a good record as a gallant soldier and a fine officer. I recollect particularly his regiment as being one of the finest in the service—He was taken prisoner at Chicamauga and was one of the few who escaped from Libbey Prison by the tunnel in February 1864. He was afterwards wounded at Resacca when he was obliged to leave and I lost sight of him from that time. He is I understand an applicant for the position of Consul at Manchester England, and I trust his recommendations may be favorably considered."—Df, Howard Papers, MeB. No appointment followed. On June 26, 1868, USG had disapproved a request to promote Theodore S. West as bvt. col. and brig. gen.—ES, DNA, RG 94, ACP, W124 CB 1868.

1869, MARCH 31.   To House of Representatives. "In compliance with a resolution of the House of Representatives, of the 30th of January last, calling for the papers relative to the claim of Owen Thorn and others against the British Government, I transmit a report of the Secretary of State, together with copies of the papers referred to in that Resolution."— Copies, DNA, RG 59, General Records; *ibid.*, RG 130, Messages to Congress. See *HED*, 41-1-3.

1869, MARCH 31. Governor William Claflin of Mass. *et al.* to USG. "The undersigned having learned with regret of the resignation of General O. O. Howard as Commissioner of the Bureau of Refugees, Freedmen and Abandoned Lands beg leave to request that, if not inconsistent with the public service, he may be retained in that office; and to present the following considerations. 1st, The existence of the Bureau is to terminate in so short a time that it will be very difficult for any successor to become sufficiently acquainted with Bureau affairs to carry to a successful termination the work already begun. 2nd, The benevolent Associations that have so heartily coöperated with him, employing a large corps of laborers, and expending a great amount of funds, in the work of educating the Freedmen, can not expect to become acquainted with a new Commissioner in the few months that remain, so as to mak[e] their coöperation as effectual as under General Howard. 3d, We believe that General Howard has wisely and efficiently carried on this great work under adverse circumstances and we respectfully request that now under a favorable administration he may be permitted to carry it through to the end. In view of these considerations and the great interests involved may we not hope for a favorable consideration of this petition and the retention of General Howard in the position of Commissioner of the Bureau of Refugees, Freedmen and Abandoned Lands."—DS (8 signatures), DNA, RG 107, Letters Received from Bureaus. See John A. Carpenter, *Sword and Olive Branch: Oliver Otis Howard* (Pittsburgh, 1964), pp. 178–80.

1869, MARCH 31. Thomas Clow, Lockport, N. Y., to USG promoting "Egyptian spirit cement" for naval construction.—ALS, DNA, RG 45, Letters Received from the President.

1869, MARCH 31. James Longstreet, Washington, D. C., to USG. "The continuous delay of my case by the Senate leads me to apprehend that action may not be taken before adjournment. In view of this contingency I am induced to speak for the appointment of Commissioner for the settlement of claims between citizens of the U. S. and Mexico. I understand that most of the Senators who cause delay, in my case, desire that I should be assigned a national position, so as to avoid the great influence that I might have in a particular locality."—ALS, DNA, RG 59, Letters of Application and Recommendation. On March 11, USG had nominated Longstreet as surveyor of customs, New Orleans. See *PUSG*, 17, 115–17.

[*1869, March*]. USG note. "Please call attention to application of Francis Frapps, Springfield Mass. for Consulship when distribution of these offices takes place."—AN (initialed), DNA, RG 59, Letters of Application and Recommendation. Written on papers requesting an appointment for Francis Fraps.—*Ibid.* No appointment followed.

1869, MARCH. USG endorsement. "Refer to Atty. Gn."—AE (initialed), DNA, RG 60, Records Relating to Appointments. Written on a letter of March 11 from James H. Orne, Philadelphia, to Secretary of the Navy Adolph E. Borie. "I take some little interest ain the appointment of some of our Soldiers. Major Genl Horatio G. Sickel of the Penna Reserves was also Col of the 198th which I sent out for the League, I believe no man has a better record and I desire to have him appointed Marshall for the Eastern District of Penna. Will you please inform me when this class of appointments will be made, as I desire to present his name to Genl Grant—We must pay the debt we owe these men and when I enlisted our Ten Regiments I pledged myself to do all I Could to look after their future, Will you try and help me to redeem that pledge."—ALS, *ibid.* Borie endorsed this letter. "Jas H. Orne Gen H. E. Sickles for marshal E. Dt Penna would be a good appt"—AES, *ibid.* Related papers are *ibid.*; *ibid.*, RG 107, Telegrams Collected (Bound). On Dec. 6, USG nominated Horatio G. Sickel as collector of Internal Revenue, 4th District, Pa., and, on Dec. 5, 1871, as pension agent, Philadelphia.

On March 8, 1869, John A. Hiestand, *Lancaster Examiner & Herald*, wrote to USG. "I am an applicant for *United States Marshall* of the Eastern District of Penna. Am *forty-four* years of age, have had considerable experience in public positions of trust and responsibility, and consider myself fully competent to discharge any duty connected with the office, and if appointed will attend to the duties in person. At the proper time the Hon. O. J. Dickey, and others, pwill present you with such recommendations as to my claims and fitness, as I hope will be satisfactory to you."—ALS, *ibid.*, RG 60, Records Relating to Appointments. On March 15, James L. Selfridge, chief clerk, Pa. House of Representatives, wrote to USG. "I desire to recommend Col J G Frick of Schuylki[ll] County for Marshall of the Eastern Distric[t] of Pennsylvania—Col Frick served wit[h] credit in the late war and is in every respect qualified to discharge the duti[es] of said office—His appointment would be most satisfactory to the solders of our state to whome he is most favorabl[y] known—"—ALS, NNP. On March 16, Samuel P. Bates, Pa. state historian, Harrisburg, wrote to USG. "The appointment of Colonel Jacob G. Frick, who served faithfully and with marked ability in the 96th and 129th Regiments, Pennsylvania Volunteers, to the position of Marshal of the Eastern District of this State, would be received with great favor by his constituents, and be highly conducive to the best interests of the public."—ALS, *ibid.* On the same day, John W. Forney, Washington, D. C., wrote to USG recommending George M. Lauman for that position.—LS, DNA, RG 60, Records Relating to Appointments. Related papers are *ibid.* Also on March 15, John Ely, Attleboro, Pa., wrote to USG. "I have the honor to apply for the Office of US Marshal for the Eastern Dist of Penna and beg leave to refer you to my military rRecord; reports letters & Endorsement of Major Genl John Sedgwick of the operations of the 6th Corps A of the Potomac in the Chancellorville campaign, captureing Mayries Heights &ct and also from Maj Genls D B Birney, Hooker & Meade as to the value of my services in the Field; and from Bvt Maj Genls C B Fisk Jeff C Davis, O. O. Howard & Maj Genl G H Thomas in regard to my services in the Freedmens Bureau in Kentucky *all* on file in the War Dept together with the accompanying papers in favour of my claims & fitness for the post I seek   I am also permitted to refer you to my friend the Hon A E Borie Secy of the Navy to whom I gave a short synopsis of my military history in a letter bearing Even date herewith"—ALS, *ibid.* Additional letters of support are *ibid.* See *PUSG*, 18, 347.

On March 25, Mary E. Calhoun, Reading, Pa., wrote to USG. "Seeing in public print the name of John A Hiestand strongly Represented for United States marshall for the Eastern district of Penna I feel it my duty as a mother to let you know about his Character   he is a politition of the blackest die   he is a man of no Principle   he will spend any amount of money to Seduce a poor young Girl from fifteen to twenty five years of age and will treat all the young men that visit the haunts of Ill faim   he has plenty of money at his Command   he is wealthy from home and is an Editor of the Lancaster Examiner and Herald. I know him personally   a worse man is not living   yet with all that he is popular with polititions   for God Sake dont appoint Such men to Office   keep Such men out of power and you will have the Prayers of all good Order loving Christian Church Peoples.   he will go any distance and spend any amount of money   I have known him to bring poor young Girls to Lancaster and keep them in houses of ill fame till he was tired of them and send them home to afflicted Pearents do I Pray put good Christian men in Office and God will bless you and your Administration   you have my Prayers and will Continue to Pray for you and the Over through of Vice and Immorality."—ALS, DNA, RG 60, Records Relating to Appointments. Other denunciatory letters are *ibid.* On April 3, USG nominated Ely as U.S. marshal, Eastern District, Pa.

On May 5, Hiestand telegraphed to USG. "General Jno Ely Marshall for this District I learn died last night   I am again an applicant for the position"—Telegram received (at 11:30 A.M.), *ibid.*, RG 107, Telegrams Collected (Bound). On the same day, Wade Hampton Morris, Philadelphia, wrote to USG. "The death of my Brother in law, John Ely (creating a vacancy in the marshallship of this district, I write you at this time for the purpose of assertaining whither in the event of my producing such credentials as may prove to your satisfaction my fitness in every respect for the position, It would be worth my while to do so,   Trusting you may give a favorable responce . . ."—ALS, *ibid.*, RG 60, Records Relating to Appointments. Letters to USG recommending Frederick S. Stumbaugh are *ibid.* Correspondence in favor of John M. Moriarty is *ibid.*; *ibid.*, RG 107, Telegrams Collected (Bound). On May 6, George H. Stuart, Philadelphia, wrote to USG. "The sudden death of Genl Ely causes a vacancy in the office of the Marshall of the Eastern Dist of Penna and among the names I

hear mentioned for the place I consider that of Genl Gregory to be preeminent,   I have no knowledge of his military ability, but a *personal* knowledge of his high character and Executive ability leads me to believe he is
the very man for the place,   His appointment would give great satisfaction
to all Except the '*Whiskey Ring*' who would have justly cause to fear,   I
shall take the liberty of introducing to you this week or next ROBERT
MACKENZIE Esqr of Scotland a merchant who wrote '*America & Her Army*'
and thereby did more for the UNION than almost any other man in Britan,
He has a great admiration for you, & I hope he may be so fortunate as to
have a few minutes quiet talk with you,   His Brother in-law holds a high
position in the British Govt   Mr. Mackenzie will likely be accompanied by
Mr Fox the European partner of A. T Stewart Esqr."—ALS, *ibid.*, RG 60,
Records Relating to Appointments. Related papers are *ibid.*; DLC-Pa. Miscellany.

On Dec. 6, USG nominated Edgar M. Gregory to replace Ely. See
PUSG, 18, 384, 481. On April 18, 1871, USG nominated Hiestand as
naval officer, Philadelphia. On Nov. 10, Joseph A. Nunes, Louisville, wrote
to USG. "You may perhaps recollect that about the time Gen'l Gregory was
appointed Marshal of the Eastern Dist of Penn, you were kind enough—
after an examination of my papers—to give me a note to Judge Hoar, favoring my application for the same position. Judge Hoar also examined my
papers, spoke most encouragingly to me on the subject, and intimated that,
if the administration was not committed by previous action to Gen'l Gregory, I would be appointed. He afterwards, as I understood him, mentioned
to me that there had been such a committal, (when Genl Ely was first
appointed,) and offered me any other position in his department, stating
however that the best he then had was the Marshalship of Montana, which
he did not think worthy of my acceptance. I have just read, with regret, the
announcement of Gen'l Gregory's death, and suppose that circumstance
leaves the administration untrammelled in regard to the position he held,
and I therefore again take the liberty of presenting myself to your consideration in that connection, and to ask for the appointment,—referring to
papers on file in the State Department, and the Attorney Gen'ls Office,
attesting services somewhat influential in the states of Pennsylvania, California and Kentucky, and also in Pay Department of the Army. . . . P. S.
The financial reverses which induced my original application have constrained me to take up a tempory residence in this City."—ALS, DNA, RG
60, Records Relating to Appointments. Related papers are *ibid.* On Dec. 6,
USG nominated James N. Kerns as U.S. marshal, Eastern District, Pa.

1869, MARCH.   [Andrew J. Faulk], Yankton, Dakota Territory, to USG.
"I have the honor to recommend for appointment *George W. Bible. Esq:*,
believing him fully capable of filling, with credit and ability, any position
you may be pleased to confer upon him.—I knew Mr. Bible in Pennsylvania,
as a gentleman of Education, unspotted character, and commercial expe-

rience,—and believe that he merits your most favorable consideration."—
AL (incomplete), Coe Collection, CtY. No appointment followed.

[*1869, March*]. U.S. Senator Samuel C. Pomeroy, U.S. Representative
Sidney Clarke, and Governor James M. Harvey of Kan. to USG. "We respectfully state that Thomas Murphy of Atchison, Kansas, has served as
Superintendent of Indian Affairs, for the Central Superintendency, for the
last three years: that he has proven himself to be a faithful and efficient
officer: and believing that a change in his office, at this time, would be
injurious to the public service, we respectfully ask that he be continued in
office until the expiration of his commission in March A. D. 1870."—DS,
DNA, RG 48, Appointment Div., Letters Received. On April 21, USG
nominated Enoch Hoag as superintendent, Indian Affairs, Central Superintendency, in place of Thomas Murphy.

[*1869, March*]. U.S. Senators Samuel C. Pomeroy of Kan., James W.
Nye and William M. Stewart of Nev., Orris S. Ferry of Conn., Frederick
A. Sawyer of S. C., Waitman T. Willey of West Va., Henry W. Corbett of
Ore., Oliver P. Morton of Ind., John Sherman of Ohio, and Cornelius Cole
of Calif. to [USG]. "The undersigned Senators respectfully recommend
the appointment of Hon: Lot M. Morrill, of Maine, as circuit judge for the
circuit of which he is a resident."—DS, DLC-James G. Blaine. A similar
petition from thirteen U.S. representatives is *ibid*. No appointment followed.

1869, [MARCH]. Benjamin M. Prentiss to USG. "Gen. Logan will present for consideration my Endorsement for an Appointment from which
you will perceive I desire position as Minister to one of the South American
States my preference is Brazil In addition to the papers forwarded I have
assurance from most of the Illinois Delegation in Congress of their influence
in my behalf also the same from Iowa. I have not sought to obtain their
signatures but have numerous letters from them assuring me of their cordial
support and if further Endorsements are required will obtain them. I confess my Anxiety concerning success is great made particularly so by my
Condition having a large family and but small means and if successfull shall
feel greatly relieved I should have called again to have seen you previous
to Inauguration but considered that you were engaged in business more
important, therefore have refrained until now in presenting my Application"—ALS, DNA, RG 59, Letters of Application and Recommendation.
Related papers are *ibid*. On April 6, USG nominated Prentiss as pension
agent, Quincy, Ill., in place of James M. Rice.
    On April 9, John Wood, Quincy, telegraphed to USG. "Removal of
Major Rice Pension Agent here would outrage the general republican loyal
sentiment He is a true republican badly crippled for life in the Wilderness
and most efficient officer. Please investigate before confirmation of change"

—Telegram received (at 12:30 P.M.), *ibid.*, RG 107, Telegrams Collected (Bound).

1869, [MARCH].   John B. Young *et al.* to USG. "The undersigned members of the bar and officers of the courts of Beaver County Pennsylvania and within the western District thereof. Do respectfully reccommend that Genl William Blakely of the city of Pittsburgh be appointed District Attorney for the said Western District. Gen. Blakely has rendered his country efficient service in the late war for the suppression of the rebellion and is a gentleman of fine legal attainments,"—DS (15 signatures), NNP. One concurring endorsement was dated March 10.

1869, APRIL 1.   James M. Scovel, New York City, to USG. "The position I would be glad to have if General Grant thinks me entitled to either is consul to Liverpool or Marshall of New Jersey"—Telegram received (at 9:00 P.M.), DNA, RG 107, Telegrams Collected (Bound). No appointment followed. On Oct. [9], Samuel Archer, president, Republican Invincibles, Philadelphia, telegraphed to USG. "T[h]e fight going on in Camden County N J for the senate on the part of Hon James M Scovel is for your administration not against it. The ring of office holders ought to be made to say 'Hands off' and the secy of the Navy ought to keep out of it—"—Telegram received (at 12:45 P.M.), *ibid.* On Oct. 12, Scovel, Philadelphia, telegraphed to USG. "You won your spurs from the people. We are fighting the peoples battle against the ring in Camden County and are for you heart and soul. Call off Wm P Tatem Collector, who is interfering in every way with a fair election"—Telegram received (at 12:30 P.M.), *ibid.* On Nov. 16, Scovel, Camden, N. J., telegraphed to USG. "Private, I was snowed under at the recent election by your handsome & ingenious Secretary of the Navy and by A G. Cattell but I was true, Through much tribulation to you & your administration"—Telegram received (at 2:30 P.M.), *ibid.*

1869, APRIL 2.   Secretary of the Interior Jacob D. Cox to USG. "I have the honor to submit, herewith, for your signature, a commission for the appointment, by and with the advice and consent of the Senate, of Charles Lafollet of Oregon, to be Agent for the Indians of the Grande Ronde Agency in Oregon."—LS, OFH.

1869, [APRIL 2].   A. Alpeora Bradley *et al.* to USG. "Your humble petitioner comes and prays your Excellency to *remove* from Office *Edward* C. *Anderson* the Alderman and *Chief* of Police Levie S Hert, & Phillip M Russell Jr of Savannah as they now hold Offices in violation of the Constitution of the United States Article 14 Sec 3 Amend and also the Omnibus *bill* Section 3 in these words 'no person prohibited from holding OFFICE under the United States or under any State by Section 3 of the amendment to the Constitution known as article 14th, Shall be deemed ELIGIBLE, to any office in either of said States': And Section 6 of the act supplementary to ant act passed 2 day of March 1867 and also an act of the 23 said month, where 'Executive or judicial officers in any State shall be construed to include all civil officers created by law for the administration of justice':— Therefore your humble petitioners pray that these laws be *Executed*; and that the Honorable E. C Anderson, Levie S Heart, and other *ineligible* persons in the city of Savannah Ga be Removed and that Thomas P Robb be appointed Mayor of Savannah Ga with instructions to have one half colored Officers with him, that we may have peace."—ADS, DNA, RG 107, Letters Received from Bureaus. On April 5, Gen. William T. Sherman endorsed this letter. "Respectfully returned to the Secretary of War. This case does not fall under the Generals supervision as Georgia has a Civil Govt & is no longer a Military District under the 'Reconstruction act' "— AES, *ibid.* On [Sept. 29], Bradley addressed a similar petition to USG requesting the removal of Mayor Edward C. Anderson of Savannah to "save the loyal White and Colored people from *outrages* and *Murders.* The colored people have all been disarmed and the disloyal have all been armed and ordered to be Patroles over us."—ADS, *ibid.*, RG 60, Letters from the President.

1869, APRIL 2.   U.S. Senator Samuel C. Pomeroy of Kan. *et al.* to USG. "We have the honor to present for appointment to a Consulate in Italy, Mr. Robt. L. Ream, of Washington City, & to ask for him your favorable consideration. We ask for him a salaried Consulate, either at Rome or Florence, or as near to one of those Cities as possible. Mr Ream is a gentleman of education, & of good business capacity & habits. He speaks German & French, is a man of excellent moral character, & we believe is well qualified to discharge the duties of any of these positions ~~with~~ to the entire satisfaction of the Government"—DS (25 signatures), DNA, RG 59, Letters of Application and Recommendation. On March 22, James S. Rollins, Columbia, Mo., had written to Secretary of State Hamilton Fish. "I take the liberty of commending to you, Messr Robt. L. Ream as an applicant for a consulate in Europe. . . , His main inducement to ask this appointment, is, that he may accompany his daughter, a young lady of fine accomplishments, and wonderful genius in the Art of Sculpture, and who proposes to complete her marble statue of President Lincoln, for which work, she has been commissioned by Congress, in one of the best schools of Art in Europe. This young lady struggling with many disadvantages, was educated in this place, and is a person of great moral worth, and extraordinary promise. It would be a source of great satisfaction, to the numerous friends of Messr Ream and his gifted daughter, in Missouri to know, that the place which he asks, has been awarded to him by the State Department; . . ."—ALS, *ibid.* Related papers are *ibid.* See *PUSG*, 16, 583.

On May 20, William Cullen Bryant, New York City, wrote to USG. "James Lorimer Graham Junr Esq. now residing at Florence has been recommended to you for the appointment of Consul General at Florence in Italy. I beg leave to add my testimony in his favor to that of his other friends. He is every way worthy of the appointment and I hope will recieve it."—ALS, DNA, RG 59, Letters of Application and Recommendation. Related papers are *ibid.* On Dec. 6, USG nominated James L. Graham, Jr., as consul, Florence.

1869, April 2. U.S. Senator Thomas W. Tipton of Neb. *et al.* to USG. "I hereby recommend for the position of a messenger in the Departments W. H. Bowman of Omaha He is has been in the Navy during the war, and we believe him worthy of confidence."—DS (3 signatures), DNA, RG 107, Appointment Papers. On April 5, Grenville M. Dodge, Washington, D. C., wrote to Secretary of War John A. Rawlins. "William Bowman (colored) was one of our servants while on the trip on the Plains During the war he served in the navy & he is desirous to obtain a situation in one of the Departments I recmmd him for such position as his ability and fitness makes it proper for him to fill"—ALS, *ibid.*

1869, April 3. To Secretary of the Treasury George S. Boutwell. "It will best suit my convenience to have the Presidents salary deposited monthly with the First National Bank of Washington D. C.—"—Copies, DLC-USG, II, 1, 4. On Jan. 23, 1870, Horace Porter wrote to Henry D. Cooke, president, First National Bank. "Will you please place the amount of the enclosed draft to the President's Credit, and Send him a new bank book. He has lost his again"—ALS, CSmH.

1869, April 3. To House of Representatives. "In answer to a Resolution of the House of Representatives of 28th January last requesting information concerning the destruction during the late War by rebel vessels of certain merchant vessels of the United States, and concerning the damages and claims resulting therefrom, I transmit a report from the Secretary of State, and the tabular statement which accompanied it."—Copy, DNA, RG 130, Messages to Congress. See *HED*, 41-1-4.

1869, April 3. To Joseph S. C. Taber. "Under Section 4, of 'an act making appropriations for the Legislative, Executive, and Judicial Expenses of the Government for the year ending the thirtieth of June 1867 and for other purposes', you are hereby appointed Steward of the Presidents household—"—Copies, DLC-USG, II, 1, 4. On April 13, Orville E. Babcock wrote to Secretary of the Treasury George S. Boutwell. "The bearer James L Thomas has been relieved from duty as Steward at the Executive Mansion by the appointment of Mr Taber. Mr Thomas when appointed Steward held a place as Messenger in the Treasury Dept.—his conduct having been uniformly good, it is the wish of the President that he be appointed a Messenger again—"—Copies, *ibid.*

On March 5, James M. Ashley, Washington, D. C., had written to USG. "I learn that Mr Geo. H. Platt of my State is an applicant for the position of Stewart at the White House under your administration. I take pleasure in saying that I have known Mr Platt for a number of years, and believe him to be competent and worthy to fill the place. He ha~~ds~~ had some experience as a *Caterer* and dealer in groceries and produce and also as a butcher and green grocer Mr Pratt served in the army during the war and was honorably discharged after *two* enlistments. He has been employed, since the close of the war, at the White House by the Commissioner of Public Buildings."—ALS, OFH. Benjamin F. Wade and U.S. Senator John Sherman of Ohio favorably endorsed this letter.—AES, *ibid.* On the same day, John Holzt, "Consul Genl. of Switzerland and late President of the German Relief Association," Washington, D. C., wrote to USG and Julia Dent Grant. "The undersigned having been informed that Mr Wm Rullman of this City has applied for the appointment of Steward at the Executive Mansion, he takes great pleasure in stating that apart of Mr Rullmans un-questionable fitness for the position, his application would seem furthermore entitled to favorable consideration from the fact of having been during the late war a most active member of the German Relief Association and particularly indefatigable in his personal attention to the wounded on the field after the memorable battles of the Wilderness, Spotsylvania C. H. and Whites House—"—ALS, NN. On Dec. 11, Secretary of the Interior Jacob D. Cox wrote to USG. "I have the honor to inform you that Mr. Valentine Melah, appointed Steward of the President's Household, has filed his oath of office and an official bond in the sum of Twenty thousand dollars, which I have this day approved."—LS, NNP.

1869, APRIL 3. Secretary of the Treasury George S. Boutwell to USG. "Senator Harris of Louisiana recommends Mr. Napoleon Underwood in the strongest terms, and says that if there is any person in Louisiana, native born, who is thoroughly republican and loyal Mr. Underwood is that. I therefore transmit herewith his nomination which I took yesterday upon the suggestion of Gen. Porter that there was some question about Mr. Un-derwood's position."—Copy, DNA, RG 56, Letters Sent to the President. On March 31, USG had nominated Napoleon Underwood as assessor of Internal Revenue, 2nd District, La., then withdrew his name on April 5. On April 12, USG renewed the nomination.

1869, APRIL 3. Secretary of the Interior Jacob D. Cox to USG. "I have the honor to submit, herewith, a nomination for the appointment of Jared. W. Daniels of Minnesota as Agent for the Sisseton and Warpeton bands of Santee Sioux Indians in Dakota Territory, vice Benjamin Thompson, removed. The nomination of Dr Daniels is submitted at the earnest request of the Right Revd H. B. Whipple, Bishop of Minnesota, who is designated by law to expend the sum of $60,000, appropriated by Congress for the support of these Indians, and who is responsible for its expenditure—for which he has filed the requisite bond."—LS, OFH. On April 5, USG nomi-nated Jared W. Daniels as agent, Sisseton and Wahpeton Sioux, Dakota Territory. See *HED*, 41-2-1, part 3, pp. 768–71.

1869, APRIL 3. Governor Ambrose E. Burnside of R. I. to USG. "The bearer of this letter Mr Amos Perry was consul and minister at Tunis under President Lincoln's administration—He was a most excellent representative of the government, and would probably have held the position until now, but was, like Mr Motley, a victim to the McCracken correspondence—As a gentleman, and good loyal citizen, he felt ~~him~~ himself called upon to tender his resignation—He now seeks a position as minister resident to some one of the foreign courts, and I am free to say that I regard him as every way qualified for such a position—He has ~~been~~ always been on the advance line in his loyalty to the government—"—ALS, DNA, RG 59, Letters of Application and Recommendation. Numerous related papers are *ibid*. No appointment followed.

1869, APRIL 3. Ceburn L. Harris, deputy U.S. marshal, Raleigh, N. C., to USG. "The nomination in the U S Senate C J. Rogers for P m at this place creates considerable excitement, Mr Rogers is a defaulter at the N C Depot as Agent for some two thousand nine hundred (2900) dollars and said to be incompetent for the place. for proof of both of the charges I refer you to the President of the N C R R, W A Smith Company Shops N C"—Telegram received (at 11:20 A.M.), DNA, RG 107, Telegrams Collected (Bound). On April 2, USG had nominated Calvin J. Rodgers as postmaster, Raleigh.

1869, APRIL 3. Henry Pilkington, St. Louis, to USG. "*Private* . . . May your old friend ask appointment as gauger for Saint Louis"—Telegram received (at 11:45 A.M.), DNA, RG 107, Telegrams Collected (Bound). No appointment followed.

1869, APRIL 3. John A. Sutter, Jr., Washington, D. C., to USG. "I take the liberty to remind you of a promise you gave to my grandfather some time before your election, to give me an appointment to West Point. I think I will be able to pass the examination required. I would be very much pleased to receive it."—ALS, DNA, RG 94, Correspondence, USMA. Docket entry states: "Appointed, July 16, 1870 for Sept, 1870, vice Spiegel under age."—AE, *ibid*. Sutter did not attend USMA. Despite his signature, the writer was the son of John A. Sutter, Jr., commercial agent, Acapulco, and the grandson of John A. Sutter of Gold Rush fame.

On Feb. 8, 1870, USG nominated Sutter, Jr., as consul. On May 5, George E. Mills, San Francisco, wrote to USG. "last December I left this city for Port Angels Via Acapulco Mexico on my arrival at Acapulco I stopped with Judge Filipe Salas of Acapulco I inquired of our so called American Consul John A Sutter for the most direct passage to Port Angels he told me he had a small whale boat and he would send me to the above Port in from 3 to 6 days that he would put 3 Mexicans in he boat to row when no wind and would charge me $75 and have the boat ready in 6 hours when I went to his swindling grocery or dry good and variety store where he does all kinds trading he told me to pay him his bill $97,68 cts I had Judge Salas with me to go my security for my passage to put me in Port Angels so all the papers was properly sined I went to sea and remained on the Pacific Ocean 14 days and the men could not find Port Angels the provisions was full of worms the men had never been to Port Angels we got out of water and provisions and returned to Acapulco I had the fever very bad by eating his provisions that was not fit for a dog on my arrival at Acapulco I engaged the Government Pilot who put me in Port Angels in 2 days before I left Acapulco Sutter could only get one Judge out of 6 to sue me for the passage money and done all he could to stop me from going on my Journey to see Luis Rivas Gongora of Mexico on my return to Acapulco this Sutter done all he could to prevent me from and to stop me at Acapulco from getting aboard the steamer for this city on inquiring at Acapulco I soon found out who this Sutter is he was run out of San Francisco for going to blow out his fathers brains he has a respectable Mexican lady for his wife but soon as she heard of Sutter and his doings she left him Sutter gave her such a awfull beating that she was at the point of death this so called American consul now lives with as low a Mexican Prostitute as ever lived in Acapulco he is engaged in all kinds of business and speculations and expects the brave old Flag to protect him in all he does he has been wiped in the streets of Acapulco and is hated by all Americans & Mexicans his office or ranch is graced by a Prostitute where Americans that visit Acapulco from the steamers take their wives send some Gentleman whom you know to fill that situation and let him investigate who this Sutter is he will soon find that John A Sutter is not a proper person for that position and please send one soon to inquire and investigate his career . . ."—ALS, *ibid.*, RG 59, Letters of Application and Recommendation. Related papers are *ibid.* On June 29, 1872, P. O. Wells, San Francisco, wrote to USG. "Having just arrived from Panama and on the way up having business at Acapulco Mexico I was much surprised when at that place to hear that the American Consul. J A Sutter was canvassing among the Steamer passengers for. Horace Greeley. . . ."—ALS, *ibid.*

1869, APRIL 4. Bvt. Maj. Gen. Oliver O. Howard to USG. "I wish to recommend to your special consideration a worthy citizen of Hartford Connecticut for the Post Office there—He has done much for the soldiers & much for the freedmen—He solicits no office—but his friends write urging to take this one for the public good—He recently gave me $5.000 dollars for the education of the poorer students—"—ALS (press), Howard Papers, MeB. On April 2, Edward W. Whitaker, Hartford, had telegraphed to Horace Porter. "Please say to the President that I solicit delay in nomination to Hartford Post Office until Wednesday. Genl's Rawlins and Wilson will vouch"—Telegram received (at 7:10 P.M.), DNA, RG 107, Telegrams Collected (Bound). On April 8, Judson Kilpatrick, Newton, N. J., telegraphed to Secretary of War John A. Rawlins. "I beg of you to stand by Gen Whitaker in his fight for Post Office at Hartford. He has done more for General Grant than all the politicians in Connecticut"—Telegram received (at 7:00 P.M.), *ibid.* On April 13, Marshall Jewell, Hartford, telegraphed to Porter. "Will you please see that the following dispatch sent to President Grant last evening reaches him at once. . . . I strongly urge the appointment of Henry T. Sperry as postmaster at Hartford believing it will give greater satisfaction to the public than any other"—Telegram received (at 2:15 P.M.), *ibid.* On the same day, USG nominated Whitaker as postmaster, Hartford.

1869, APRIL 5. USG endorsement. "Respectfully refered to Com. on reconstruction with recommendation that the disabilities of Mr. Duncan be removed."—AES, DNA, RG 233, 40A-H21.2. Written on a letter of March 27 from Bvt. Maj. Gen. Adelbert Ames, provisional governor, Vicksburg, to USG. "The bearer, Mr. John Duncan, a resident of this state, desires to have his political disabilities removed. I wish to make him State Treasurer. The bonds for the office are heavy and few who are qualified can give them. Aside from these considerations Mr Duncan is a thoroughly upright and honest man and in full sympathy with the present administration. He will be of assistance to me in reconstructing the state. He is a southern man already endorsed by you. The material I have is quite limited in quantity. It is to be hoped that Congress will act in the cases of applicants for removal of political disabilities. Though men's disabilities be removed I shall not use them unless they possess the requisite qualifications."—ALS, *ibid.* On Dec. 12, 1865, USG had written a note. "I believe from the evidenses in Mr. John Duncan's behalf that he has been a Union man so far as such a position could be maintained in the State of Mississippi throughout all the rebellion. He is therefore entitled to all the consideration due to loyal citizens residing within the rebel lines during the existense of war"—Copy, *ibid.* Related papers are *ibid.*

1869, APRIL 5. Orville E. Babcock to Secretary of War John A. Rawlins. "The President requests that the Surgeon General be directed to contract for medical services at fifty dollars per month with Dr Jno. G. F. Holston of Zanesville Ohio, who has been assigned to duty as Physician to the Executive Household. Dr. Holston will report to Genl. Horace Porter, Secretary." —LS, DNA, RG 94, Personal Papers, Medical Officers and Physicians, Holston. Related papers are *ibid.* See *PUSG*, 6, 178; *ibid.*, 7, 248–49.

1869, APRIL 5. Secretary of the Navy Adolph E. Borie to USG. "I have the honor to return herewith the letter referred by you to the Department from E. McD. Reynolds, late a Captain in the Marine Corps, and submit for your information the papers recently presented in his behalf, together with a copy of a general order of the Department dated December 7, 1864, stating the grounds of the dismissal of Capt. Reynolds from the service. The Department communicated to Mrs. Reynolds a copy of the opinion of the present Attorney General in the case of her husband, and informed her that in view of that opinion, it had no power to afford relief in the case. It is respectfully requested that the papers now submitted may be returned by your order to the files of the Department."—Copy, DNA, RG 45, Letters Sent to the President. On Dec. 16, 1873, Secretary of the Navy George M. Robeson wrote to USG restating this position.—Copy, *ibid.* See *HMD*, 48-2-15, p. 262.

1869, APRIL 5. Admiral David G. Farragut, New York City, to USG. "I take great pleasure in uniting with Captain Rodgers and others in recommending for an appointment to the U. S. Military Academy, William H. Coffin, the son of an old shipmate and friend, Professor J. H. C. Coffin, of the Navy. Professor Coffin has trained so many officers for the naval service and having a son possessing a natural turn for the army, it seems but natural that he should desire to have a representative in that branch   I should be happy to hear of his son's success—"—LS, DNA, RG 94, Correspondence, USMA. Enclosed with a letter of May 13 from John H. C. Coffin, Washington, D. C., to USG.—ALS, *ibid.* William H. Coffin graduated from USMA in 1873.

1869, APRIL 5. Commodore James F. Schenck, Dayton, to USG. "Presuming upon our former acquaintance I take the liberty of asking that my Grand-son James F S. Crane be appointed a Cadet, his application, with accompanying recommendations, is on file at the war Department, I know but little of the form of applications of this kind, but if you can comply with my request, I will consider myself under great personal obligations to you," —ALS, DNA, RG 94, Correspondence, USMA. James F. S. Crane, who entered USMA in 1870, did not graduate.

1869, APRIL 5. Henry W. Andrews, Philadelphia, to USG. "I respectfully solicit the position of U S Consul at Bordeaux or should that be already disposed of, then any other in France; My qualifications as to fitness from mercantile experience, character, & Knowledge of the French language are vouched for by many influential fellow citizens. warm supporters of the Administration, The warm friendship Henry Clay ever evinced for my father in law Henry White of Phila, based on his long & faithful services in his cause, (Mr White never would accept any office from the party), would make my appointment particularly acceptable to the old Line Whigs of the Republicans.—During the war my brother Col J W Andrews of Delaware raised the first Regt in his state & his only two sons were officers in the Army of the 'Union', my remaining brother fell a victim to exposure while serving in the 23 Penna Vols. My time was devoted to the providing for the wants of the sick & wounded at 'Mower Hospital' not in an *official* capacity but as a volunteer at the solicitation of Dr Hopkinson Surgeon in Charge. & it is my pride that the Dollars expended by me bought only of *the best* & went further than any other Hospital in the state, Should I receive the appointment sought I shall fulfill its duties faithfully

& to the best of my ability,"—ALS, DNA, RG 59, Letters of Application and Recommendation. On March 20, Lt. Col. James H. Wilson, Keokuk, had written to Horace Porter. "My wife's uncle, *Henry W. Andrews Esqr* born at Bordeaux, for many years a successful commercial broker in Philadelphia, well known by Mr Borie, and highly recommended by *all* of the leading Merchants *of our side*—An educated, upright Christian Gentleman is an applicant for the consulship at Bordeaux. You met him at my wedding as did the General (Genl is more sweeter to my ears than President), and may therefore remember him. I should say that no man could fill a consulate more creditably than Mr A. & that if there is to be any change, I hope you may be able to do something in his favor—not as a favor to me— but to a most worthy man."—ALS, *ibid*. On April 9, Andrews wrote to USG. "When I made my application for the Consulship of Bordeaux, I was not then aware that the appointment of Mr C J Church [*Clinch*] was particularly requested by A T Stewart Esq of New York, As neither my friends nor myself desire for a moment seemingly to conflict with such deserving claims as Mr Stewarts, I beg leave to withdraw my application for that post, & respectfully submit that of either Nantes, Lyons, Boulogne, La Rochelle or Nice to your favorable consideration in my behalf"—ALS, *ibid*.

On April 15, Alexander T. Stewart, New York City, wrote to USG. "Allow me to remind you, that Mrs. Stewart through me and our mutual friend Judge Hilton, requested you to nominate for the Consulship at *Havre*, her Nephew Chas I. Clinch, a gentleman who has resided three years in Paris, and two in Havre, speaking the french language as fluently as english, surely this request you will not refuse or neglect,"—ALS, Kevin J. Weddle, Eagan, Minn. Related papers are in DNA, RG 59, Letters of Application and Recommendation. On April 12, USG had nominated Charles J. Clinch as consul, Bordeaux. On April 17, Stewart wrote to USG. "Mr. Chas. I. Clinch respectfully declines the appointment of Consul to Bordeaux, whose nomination your private Secretary informs me by note dated the 16th inst. was made on the 13th, as it was for HAVRE, not for Bordeaux that application was made, and Judge Hilton desires me to add that you promised him to nominate Mr. Clinch for the Consulship at Havre"—ALS, *ibid*., Letters of Resignation and Declination. Clinch served as consul, Bordeaux.

1869, APRIL 5. William E. Chandler, Washington, D. C., to USG. "I have the honor to request that Dr M. T. Willard Post Master at Concord New Hampshire be not removed. He was appointed only two years ago upon the recommendation of the entire Congressional Delegation from New Hampshire, has always been an earnest Republican and is entitled by every rule to remain in office two years longer, until the expiration of his commission. He is the personal friend of Senator Cragin, is my intimate personal friend and his retention is earnestly desired by Hon Onslow Stearns our Governor elect and several hundreds of leading citizens who have remonstrated against his removal—In case a change should be made public sentiment is divided upon the question of his successor. A large majority—probably four fifths of the active Republicans and business men of the city would desire the appointment of *Col. P. P. Bixby,* an old resident of Concord and a gallant officer wounded during the war—Col. James E. Larkin is recommended by a few leading Republicans but is not the choice of the working Republicans of the city. The removal of Dr Willard, the ignoring of Col Bixby and the appointment of Col. Larkin would be exceedingly detrimental to the interests of the Republican party, would gratify few and would displease the great body of active Republicans of the city of Concord Under these circumstances it is unquestionably correct policy to allow Dr Willard to remain. His removal would be unprecedented Such action should be reserved for copperheads unless the Republican has been long in office and refuses to resign in order to give place in rotation to some more deserving Republican That Dr Willard ought to remain is the judgment of the Senators from New Hampshire Messrs Cragin and Patterson. Genl Stevens the member from the district feels committed to Col. Larkin and desires to serve his friend which is creditable to him. But I conceive it would be a mistake for the Republican party and for General Stevens himself, for him to give Col. Larkin a place by removing Dr Willard and passing over Col Bixby who would be the overwhelming choice of the people if a change should be made. For these reasons as well as for my personal interest in a warm personal friend in my own native town I respectfully and urgently urge that Dr Willard may be returned as Postmaster"—LS, New Hampshire Historical Society, Concord, N. H. On April 13, USG nominated James E. Larkin as postmaster, Concord. On April 18, Moses T. Willard, Concord, wrote to Chandler. "The deed is done; Stevens, Fogg & Co. have triumphed. I presume my friends have done all they could, but if Gen. Grant was thoroughly posted, relative to the case, he has acted very different, from what has always been said of him. It is a new thing in the history of Political parties, to remove one of their own men, because another one wanted the place,—especially, unless the change should he deemed a public improvement. Rumor has it, that Larkin frequently said while getting up his petition that if they didn't give him the P. O. he would never vote with the Republican Party again. At any rate, he has no established political character as a citizen, and while in the army, he always acted on the principal, that he had rather be a *live coward,* than a *dead hero* It does seem to me, that if Mr Cragin had shown Grant the remonstrance, and explained to him its character, as representing the leading and business men here, adding that he and Senator Patterson were opposed to a change, that the Pres. would have said to Stevens, the Public good requires no change . . ."—ALS, *ibid.* On March 15, 1873, USG nominated Willard as postmaster, Concord, to supersede Larkin, and on April 4, 1876, USG nominated Larkin in place of Willard.

1869, APRIL 5. U.S. Senator William M. Stewart of Nev. *et al.* to USG. "I have received a large number of letters of leading republicans in the

Territory of Idaho urging m[e] to do all in my power to secure the appointment of the Hon E J Curtis of that territory for the position of secretary, . . ."—DS (3 signatures), DNA, RG 59, Letters of Application and Recommendation. On July 6, Bvt. Maj. Gen. George Crook, Portland, Ore., wrote to USG. "I have been advised that Territorial Secretary S. R. Howlett, of Idaho has been suspended from his office through misrepresentation on the part of his Enemies. . . ."—LS, *ibid.* Related papers are *ibid.*; *ibid.*, Idaho Territorial Papers; *ibid.*, RG 46, Executive Nominations, Miscellaneous Papers. On Dec. 6, USG nominated Edward J. Curtis as secretary, Idaho Territory.

1869, APRIL 5. Governor Henry C. Warmoth of La. to USG. "Considering the probable action of Congress, increasing the number of Judges of the Circuit Court of the United States, I beg leave to recommend to you, the name of the Hon R. K. Howell Associate Justice of the Supreme Court of this State, as a man peculiarly fitted to fill a position of that character. The system of the civil law, peculiar to this State, suggests the importance of having on this Circuit, a Judge, conversant with its principles, and familiar with its practice. Judge Howell is well qualified as a lawyer and his integrity is unimpeachible, I found him on the Supreme Bench when I came into power and have retained him in that position I think his appointment would be commended by the entire Bar of this State."—LS, Warmoth Papers, Louisiana State University, Baton Rouge, La. On March 30, John Ray, Monroe, La., had written to USG recommending Judge Rufus K. Howell, La. Supreme Court.—ALS, DLC-USG, 1B. No appointment followed.

1869, APRIL 5. James R. Wheeler, Boston Highlands, to USG. "The undersigned respectfully requests that he may be appointed Consul for the Port of Queenstown Ireland. And he begs leave to represent that he entered the Naval Service of the United States in the Year 1861; that he was attached to the United States Steamer Kearsarge, and was Acting Master on board the same at the time of the destruction of the Rebel Steamer Alabama; that on the return of the Kearsarge in December 1864 he was promoted to Acting Lieutenant and ordered to the Command of the Gunboat Preston on the West Gulf Squadron and assisted at the taking of Mobile and also at the taking of Galveston—He farther represents that at the time he entered the Service he was and had been for some Years in lucrative employment as Master of ships sailing from Boston and New York; and that he was honorably discharged in February 1867 in consequence of being disabled by injuries received while in the line of duty on board the Kearsarge . . ."—ALS, DLC-Nathaniel P. Banks. A copy of this letter and related papers are in DNA, RG 59, Letters of Application and Recommendation. On Nov. 12, USG suspended Aaron Gregg as consul, Kingston, Jamaica, and on Dec. 6, USG nominated Wheeler in his place.

1869, APRIL 6.   Orville E. Babcock to Secretary of State Hamilton Fish. "I forward today the papers in the case of Dr Julius Skilton who is an applicant for the position of Consul in the City of Mexico, which I believe is now vacant, there being only a vice-consul.—I passed two months in the City of Mexico during the winter of 1867 & 8 and had an opportunity to judge of the character of the man and his associates there. I found him always the perfect gentleman, and with the very best people in that city. His true Union principles are so well known there that he is much opposed by the great number of rebels from the Southern States, who fled to Mexico after the surrender of the rebel army.—I know that for his outspoken republican principles he has at times endangered his own personal safety,—During the last Campaign the rebels there swore that if Seymour was elected the rebellion would be renewed, and they would commence shooting Union men there, when he told them they would find the Union men would shoot as soon as the rebels. I feel certain that the appointment of Dr S. will please all the good Americans in the City of Mexico, and at the same time be a just recognition of the services of a gallant soldier. This letter is written Mr Secty. by permission of the President."—LS, DNA, RG 59, Letters of Application and Recommendation. Related papers are *ibid.* On April 13, USG nominated Julius A. Skilton as consul, Mexico City.

1869, APRIL 6.   Secretary of the Treasury George S. Boutwell to USG. "An error was committed in this Department in the nomination of J. B. Couillard for Collector of Customs at Pembina, Dakota Territory. I therefore respectfully request that the nomination made to the Senate of Mr Couillard may be with drawn."—Copy, DNA, RG 56, Letters Sent. On April 7, USG withdrew his nomination of J. B. Couillard as collector of customs, Minn.

On Nov. 27, 1867, J. B. Couillard, Saint Joseph, Dakota Territory, had written to USG. "I beg leave to entertain you succinctly upon a subject of a mere importance for the progress of the settlement of tho United States Territory. Your humble servant has the honor of having been introduced to you just after the end of the war, at the time of your visit to Montreal (Canada). Being then one of the officers of the Montreal institute, an institution well known by its liberal principles, I was happy of being honored by the reception of the saviour of his country. . . . A few months after your visit to Montreal, I left my native country to join the children of liberty. I started a french journal last summer (1866) at Chicago, always in the republican sense, & having been unsuccessful in the undertaking, I have directed my steps in a place where I can yet be useful to the party that I have always served. Therefore confident that you will condescend to my vows, I shall ask you to take notice of the petition of the inhabitants of Pembina relative to a demand of a military protection, in the hands of the Hon. Alexander Ramsay, U. S. Senator, for the State of Minnesota & to pay a favorable attention to it. . . ."—ALS, *ibid.*, RG 94, Letters Received, 606R 1867. Related papers are *ibid.*

1869, APRIL 6.   Cyrus K. Osgood *et al.*, Washington, D. C., to USG. "The undersigned Citizens of Georgia and members of the Republican Party respectfully solicit the appointment of Thomas P Saffold Esq. of Morgan Co Georgia to the office of United States marshall, for the state of Georgia. Mr S. has resided in the same Community all his life—and no Citizen is more generally respected or universally known by the intellegent people of the state—He was one of the most active and Efficient friends of reconstruction and one of the most prominent members of the late Constitutional Convention. In that body he was the most intimate and valued ally of the Hon A. T. Akerman the most useful of its members. For personal character pecuniary responsibility and Every necesary qualification for the office of Marshall—it would be difficult to find a superior any where"—DS (8 signatures), DNA, RG 60, Records Relating to Appointments. On April 9, James Atkins, Washington, D. C., wrote to U.S. Representative William H. Upson of Ohio. "This will be handed you by my friend P. M. Sheibly of Rome Ga. who is an applicant for the position of U. S. Marshall for our state. . . . While Mr. Sheibly drinks some times and occasionally has been 'tight,' he will not disgrace himself nor dishonor his office. I will bind myself to be an informant against him and to bring charges in case he obtains the appointment and afterwards gets drunk. I make it a special request that you lend him your influence."—ALS, *ibid.* Upson endorsed this letter. "I am well acquainted with Col Atkins the writer of the within. He is a man of undoubted integrity & a true Union man."—AES, *ibid.* On April 10, Horace Porter telegraphed to Bvt. Maj. William H. Smyth. "Will you resign and accept the U. S. Marshalship of Georgia if appointed? This is confidential."—Copy, DLC-USG, II, 5. On April 16, USG nominated Smyth as marshal and, on Dec. 17, P. M. Sheibley as postmaster, Rome, Ga.

1869, APRIL 7.   To Senate. "In answer to the resolution of the Senate of the 27th of May last, in relation to the subject of claims against Great Britain, I transmit a report from the Secretary of State and the papers which accompanied it."—Copy, DNA, RG 130, Messages to Congress. See *SED*, 41-1-11.

1869, APRIL 7.   Horace Porter to Attorney Gen. Ebenezer R. Hoar. "Commissions for the following named persons were received at this office and signed by the President this morning. Saml C Mills. Justice of the Peace. Wash. DC. Converse W. C. Rowell Atty US. Arizona   As these names do not appear on the records of this office, it is presumed they were appointments under the last administration,   under the circumstances the Prest directs me to inquire if the Atty Genl desires that the Commissions issue."—Copies, DLC-USG, II, 1, 4. On the same day, Hoar wrote to USG. "The commissions of Mills and Rowell were in pursuance of appointments by the last administration, but examined since in this department and found to be suitable, and recommended by me—"—ALS, OFH.

1869, [APRIL 7].   J. C. Baker, Philadelphia, to USG. "I hope you will remember Your *true friends* in Your distribution, here is Mr J. L. Southwick one of *Your best friends* and a Neighbour who greatly Contributed to Your home Comforts in fixing Your house. he and his lady are and ever will be to You friends why not to a man so capable as Mr Southwick give him Directorship of Mint or Some other good position within Your gift I hope You will remember *Your friends* at 2025 Chestnut St Southwick is a Gentleman, and a scholar, remember him, . . ."—ALS, DNA, RG 56, Asst. Treasurers and Mint Officials, Letters Received. On April 16, USG nominated James Pollock as director, U.S. mint, Philadelphia.

1869, APRIL 7.   Reverdy Johnson, London, to USG. "The medal of the late Richard Cobden, which you will receive with this, was placed in my hands by the Cobden Club with a request to forward it to you. Mr Cobden's high character, his great ability, and his long devotion to the interest of his own country; and his inculcation of doctrines calculated to advance the prosperity of all nations, and to maintain them in peace, the Club naturally suppose will cause you to accept with pleasure a medal of him. I am gratified to be the medium to place it in your possession, . . ."—LS, OFH.

1869, APRIL 7.   U.S. Senator Alexander McDonald of Ark. to USG. "In behalf of the Arkansas delegation feeling a deep regret in being Compelled to do so—We submit to you the following facts About 3 weeks since our delegation filed in the office of the Atty Genl an application for Marshall of a Territory We waited untill it was understood that all appointments of this class had been made and then called upon you in person when you told us that our man for Marshall had not been presented to you, but that you would give us a judgeship—and asking us to file our papers that day for the Same which we did—Supposing all would be right We then called upon the Atty Genl and told him what we had done he then Said he would submit our Case and that we should be represented with the balance We Called on yesterday morning Calling his attention to the Same When he answered in a way as we thought was not becoming a Cabinett officer that Arks was not Entitled to any such appointment I told him we would not have persue this except on a promise we had from *you*—his reply was you generally did what you said—but that he said we should not have *Either* and said it in such a way as to attract the attention of all parties present to our extreme mortification—Nothing but our great Anxiety for the Complete success of your administration and personal feeling for yourself would lead us at this time to mak this Complaint—in conclusion we think no citizen or constituent however humble could have been more rudely treated than was we by ~~his~~ the attey Genl"—ALS, USG 3.

1869, APRIL 8.   USG endorsement. "Approved"—AES, DNA, RG 45, Letters Received from the President. Written on a letter of the same day from Secretary of the Navy Adolph E. Borie to USG. "Authority is requested to further regulate the pay of Petty officers, Seamen, Ordinary Seamen and Landsmen in the Navy. By law the pay of seamen is fixed by the President (act of april 18. 1814.) It is proposed to issue 'Continuous Service Discharges' to seamen, to induce American Seamen to enlist and continue in our Navy   It is recommended that one dollar per month additional be allowed enlisted who after being shipped for three years reenlist continuously. This with the bounty allowed by Congress and the Honorable Discharge it is thought will enable us to secure the best class of men for the Navy. I strongly recommend this and request your approval."—LS, *ibid.* See *HED*, 41-2-1, part 1, pp. 21–23.

1869, APRIL 8.   John W. Andrews, Wilmington, Del., to Horace Porter. "Is it necessary for me to come down. I can tell the President something that ought to be known"—Telegram received (at 10:00 A.M.), DNA, RG 107, Telegrams Collected (Bound). On the same day, Porter wrote to Andrews. "Could you not write the President. He has refused nearly all interviews for several days."—Copy, DLC-USG, II, 5.

1869, APRIL 8.   Frederick T. Frelinghuysen, Newark, to USG. "I feel an interest that Thos. H. Dudley should be continued as Consul at Liverpool—Liverpool as a commercial centre was a most important point during the war, and the earnest loyalty of Dudley subjected him then to insult and social ostracism—In giving information, in seizing rebel property, and in his returns to the Government he has been very faithful—On Mr Dudley making a visit to New Jersey last fall, his political friends manifested their appreciation of his service to the country by giving him a dinner, at which such enthusiastic approbation of his course was manifested, that I think considerable disappointment would be created by his removal. My views are thus plainly expressed with all deference to those of the President—"—ALS, DNA, RG 59, Letters of Application and Recommendation. Numerous related papers are *ibid.* On the same day, Frelinghuysen wrote to Thomas H. Dudley. "The President casts the toil of hearing representations as to appointments on his Secretaries, & to *talk* to him as to claims of any one for a consulate wd go in one ear & out of the other—*The better* to get your case before the President I have written him that it is a matter in wh I am interested— . . ."—ALS, CSmH. On April 24 and June 10, David A. Wells, special commissioner of the revenue, wrote to Dudley. "I have written you already about the efforts ~~being~~ which were made to secure you in your present position. I had a talk with Cattell this morning on the subject. He detailed to me the result of a conversation he had with Grant last night in which your matter was introduced by his thanking Grant for having not interfered with you. Grant's reply was in accordance with the common run of affairs now. He did not seem in the least degree to recognize or know of your services during the rebellion, although the thing has been very carefully explained to him, and the credit given to you of preventing the sailing of the ironclads, and other rebel cruisers. He simply remarked that you have had the place eight years, and he thought that an officer who had held a good fat place for that length of time ought to be ready to give way. At the same time I think that your matter is, for the present, settled, and that he will not venture to disturb you; and you must not consider this as any thing personal to yourself, for the disposition is to ~~strike~~ thrust every body out of office and commence anew; Republicans and Democrats, Radicals, and conservatives. I want to tell you in this connexion that the Adams family have omitted no opportunity to do you good service, and Henry Adams I know has been your earnest champion, and has exerted a good deal of influence with Hoar the Atty Genl   I heard him tell Hoar the other night at a dinner table that your services and qualifications entitled you to be appointed Minister, rather than to have been obliged to struggle to keep the place you are in. . . ." ". . . In regard to your retention in office I have ploughed considerably & with the following results. Fish and the Ast. Secretary are warm friends of yours & appreciate your services. They will not allow you to be removed if they can help it: & I think they can. Grant has no feeling of dislike to you, but has the idea of rotation on the brain: and it may break out at any time, as respects you, or others. In this status, I think unadvisable for you or your friends to agitate the matter, as you dont want Grant to have the subject brought before him. I think my relations with Fish are such, that I shall have warning of any danger—and then it will be time to influence Grant. For the present I belive, whatever you may hear to the contrary, that you are entirely safe . . ."—LS and ALS, *ibid.* On Sept. 16, Secretary of the Navy George M. Robeson wrote to Dudley. ". . . The fact is I was reminded of my duty to reply to your letters ~~but~~ by seeing, the other day, on the Presidents table, a paper, purporting to be signed by about 20 masters of American Ships trading at Liverpool asking for your removal on various general grounds (nothing in particular in the way of charge)—As the President is constantly pressed with applications for your place and as he has a strong idea 'that a person who has been abroad 8 years ought to come home' &c &c, it would not be amiss for you to get up some counter statements & evidence &c &c & send them to me to be used, if the subject ever comes up—I think it had better not be stirred as long as it is quiet (which as Fish is your friend I think, it will ~~not~~ be, unless some ~~busy~~ body stirs it from abroad) but to be prepared in case of an emergency—This is of course, *confidential*—& in any counter papers no allusion should be made to the source of your information— . . ."—ALS, *ibid.* In Sept., 1872, F. W. Brown *et al.*, Liverpool, petitioned USG. "We the Owners & Masters of American Ships now in the Port of Liverpool sincerely congratulate ourselves, and all interested in American Commerce on the departure of T. H. Dudley, Consul of this Port, and would hope in the selection of his Successor, that some person of a more suitable Character, may be sought for. . . ."—DS (31 signatures), DNA, RG 59, Letters of Application and Recommendation.

On May 9, 1869, U.S. Senator Timothy O. Howe of Wis., Green Bay, had written to USG. "I beg to obtrude upon your time for a single moment with a suggestion on behalf of Gov. Fairchild—I believe you know him—you have no truer friend—He was one of the very first Co. mustered into the service from this State in 1861, & he was a democrat of the straightest sect. He left his politics at home & soon left one arm in the field—Since the war ended he dont seem to care to resume his politics & he cant *regain* his arm. For four years he has been Governor of this State, & is very popular. But it is a usage here not to re-elect but once—It never has been disregarded & I fear will be enforced in the case of Gov. F. If so he will be left with out fortune, with out a profession—& with but one arm—Now if there is in your gift a Mission or Consulate which you can afford to him—or if you have any place at your bestowal for which you want fearless integrity & first class Executive ability all your friends in this State would be very glad to have you provide for Gov. Fairchild. And of your friends I beg you will count me one"—ALS, *ibid.* Related papers are *ibid.* On Dec. 3, 1872, USG nominated Lucius Fairchild as consul, Liverpool.

1869, APRIL 8. Andrew J. Hamilton *et al.*, Washington, D. C., to USG. "The undersigned, citizens of Texas, respectfully petition you to request a delay in the confirmation of J H Lippard as Marshal of the Western Dist. of Texas until you telegraph to Bvt Majr Genl Reynolds, Comdg 5th Mil. Dist., as to the propriety of the nomination. Some fifteen months since a serious riot occurred in Hill and Navarro counties between the whites and blacks, caused by the murder of Capt Culver of the Freedmens Bereau, in which Mr L. was actively engaged as a leader of the blacks. Genl. Reynolds sent Capt Hills to investigate the affair and this officer freely charged Mr Lippard with great blame for the riot. Such was the opinion of Genl Reynolds, who refused to countenanse Mr Lippard in his turbulent course, and regarded him as a breeder of discord and trouble. Mr L. has ever since been bitter in his denunciations of Genl Reynolds, and we are satisfied that his nomination will give much pain to an excellent officer. We respectfully request that he be consulted before it is too late. Genl. Reynolds desired and recommended that the present incumbent, Mr A P. Blocker, should be retained, as the papers on file in the Attorney General's office will show."—DS (9 signatures), DNA, RG 60, Records Relating to Appointments. A related petition is *ibid.* On April 9, Governor Elisha M. Pease of Tex. telegraphed to USG. "Lippart is not qualified by education or character for the office of Marshall"—Telegram received (at 11:50 A.M.), *ibid.*; *ibid.*, RG 107, Telegrams Collected (Bound). On April 8, USG had nominated John H. Lippard as marshal, Western District, Tex.; on April 20, the Senate tabled his nomination. On Sept. 25, USG suspended incumbent marshal Abner P. Blocker and, on Dec. 6, nominated Thomas F. Purnell. Bishop Edward R. Ames had written to USG in support of Purnell.—ALS, *ibid.*, RG 60, Records Relating to Appointments.

1869, APRIL 9. Horace Porter to Gen. William T. Sherman. "I have just read your letter from Reverdy Johnson, and will show it to the President, as I know he would like to read it. I can say, however, to you that a cipher dispatch was received from Mr. Johnson, more than a week ago, asking this question; and he was answered, by cable, that a change would be made, ~~and~~ but that action would be delayed till his resignation reached this office."—ALS, DLC-Reverdy Johnson. On March 25, Reverdy Johnson, U.S. minister, Great Britain, had written to Sherman asking him to ascertain whether USG would name a new minister to Great Britain.—LS, DLC-William T. Sherman.

1869, APRIL 9. Bvt. Maj. Gen. Oliver O. Howard to Frederick T. Dent. "I wish you would introduce to the President Gen. J. Harlan—who commanded a Cavalry force during our war—called the 'Harlan brigade' or regiment afterwards embraced in Penn. troops as 11th Penn. He has lived some twenty years in Asia—had a national reputation as a Comdr. of Division in [—]. Gen. Grant may remember his visit to West Point when he Gen. Grant was a cadet."—ALS (press), Howard Papers, MeB. For Josiah Harlan's unsuccessful efforts to secure diplomatic appointment, see DNA, RG 59, Letters of Application and Recommendation.

1869, APRIL 9. Louisa Lynch Burke and Maria Anna Lynch, Chicago, to USG. "May it please your Excellency your memorialists beg leave to represent to your Excellency that our beloved brother Robert B. Lynch, late of Louisville, Kentucky, who was seized by the Canadian Authorities while acting as reporter for the Louisville Currier, during the Fenian raid of June 1866, and not thinking that he was committing any acts of hostility against the Canadian Government or people, he was nevertheless condemned to an imprisonment of twenty years, in the provincial Penitentiary, Kingston, Canada. We now hope that the Government of his adopted country will interceed in his behalf. . . ."—Copy, DNA, RG 84, Instructions, Great Britain. See *HED*, 41-2-170; *New York Times*, Jan. 15, 1884.

On April 28, 1870, Robert B. Lynch, Kingston, wrote to USG. "The undersigned approaches your Excellency with feelings of Much respect for your exalted Station as chief Magistrate of his adopted Country, and respectfully represents. That he is incacerated in the Penitentiary at this place for the last *four years*, for an alledged participation in the Fenian Raid into this Province in the Summer of 1866. That he was Correspondent of a public Journal, and had no *Military Connection whatever with* that *expedition*, and that he never belonged to the Fenian organization, That he was faced to trial at a time of Much excitement and tried by a Jury Composed *exclusively* of *British* Subjects, That he was denied a Safe Conduct for his Witnesses, Neither was he permitted to have their testimony taken in the U S. before a Commissioner, and as a Matter of Course was Convicted, Sentenced to Death which was Subsequently Commuted to an imprisonment for 20 years in this Institution Subject to all the degrading humiliations of a Common Felon,   That he is an adopted Citizen of the U S. 28 years—and Served during the War in the *Army* of the *Union* and under the Flag he had Sworn to Support,   That if an Irish naturalized Citizen have any rights in the U. S. I respectfully appeal to you that I may have the Benefit of those. I am Suffering a Cruel Penal Servitude. My Health is failing very Much   My offence is purely Political and I ask your Kind intercession in my behalf,   I am held as a Hostage for the acts and Conduct of a few Political adventurers in the City New York who are Misguiding My Honest but too Confiding Countrymen threatning to disturb the Peace of this *Country* and interrupt the friendly & Commercial relations with the U S. and endangering the Peace of their adopted Country by a violation of the Neutrality Laws. That I have every Confidence in the desire of the Canadian Govt to extend the Executive clemency to the Political Prisoners, Could they do So with Consistency & honor. But this Continued excitement, and the avowed determination of those reckless Men to again invade this Province alone prevents this clemency being extended least it should be Considered to proceed from Fear, I am fully Satisfied that if your Excellency would make a Special application in My behalf to the Canadian Govt with an assurance that the Neutrality Laws would be Strictly enforced that My release would be obtained . . . Please refer to Hon Matt. H. Carpenter Senator—Hon Genl Halbet Paine M. C. Hon Charles Eldredge *M.* C. Hon W. H. Seward"—ALS, DNA, RG 59, Miscellaneous Letters.

1869, APRIL 9.   U.S. Senator Charles D. Drake of Mo. to USG. "The nomination of George Smith for ~~the~~ Marshal of the Western District of Missouri takes me so much by surprise, that I am constrained to suppose that it was made without a full knowledge on your part of all the facts. . . . Last year Mr Smith was the Democrat's candidate for the Republican nomination for Governor of Missouri, but he was unsuccessful in getting it. That paper is still his champion. Of course, he is hostile to me; & I am satisfied that, for that reason, he was put forward for this office. I deem it my duty to state these facts to you, in the hope that they may lead you to reconsider this nomination. I ask as a personal favor that it be withdrawn."—ALS, DNA, RG 60, Records Relating to Appointments. Related papers are *ibid*. On April 8, USG had nominated George Smith as marshal, Western District, Mo.

1869, APRIL 9.   John B. Richardson, Auburn, N. Y., to USG. "Rumor says another is nominated for Auburn Post Office   Am I forgotten. . . . Answer"—Telegram received (at 2:15 P.M.), DNA, RG 107, Telegrams Collected (Bound). On April 12, USG nominated Clinton D. MacDougall as postmaster, Auburn, and on Feb. 26, 1873, nominated Richardson for this post after MacDougall's resignation.

1869, APRIL 9. Harry Runge, Chicago, to USG. "You may remember an effort made by my friend the Hon. Mr. Morris of Quincy to procure for me the Consulate to Glasgow, Scotland. Depending entirely upon his representations of your assurance that I should have the position, I failed to call to my aid other influential friends in the Illinois Indiana and Ohio delegations who proffered their assistance. Feeling secure in what Mr Morris said I hesitated to annoy you with a multitude of references. I am now in [r]eceipt of a telegram from Mr Morris to Orville, stating that I have no prospects for the place. I have depended upon this so confidently that my mortification and dissappointment is extreme. If your decision in regard to my application to the Glasgow Consulate is final—may I hope that there is yet a place in any of the German or French ports which I may be tendered"—ALS, DNA, RG 107, Letters Received. James E. McLean, business partner of Orvil L. Grant, endorsed this letter. "It gives me pleasure to state that Mr Runge is by education capacitated to fill a position in a German or French port, being conversant with both languages,—as well as having had a polished collegiate education. I can vouch for his intelligence, ability, sobriety & gentlemanly bearing. He has served his country in the War as a private—and since been Editor of a Republican Newspaper. His Wifes maiden name was Kate Thornton—who is cousin to Orvilles wife, and she being an invalid—a change of climate would doubtless be to her of great benefit."—AES, *ibid.* On Nov. 9, 1868, Orvil L. Grant, Chicago, had written to Isaac N. Morris. "I hope you will pardon me for intrudeing on your time with a business letter. Mr Harry. Runge of Clayton Ills commenced business as a news boy, and by his own efforts has acquired a good education and has done some good work in the Union ranks. I would like for Runge to have some position, a consulship in Europe would be one for which he is well qualified; if you will recommend him to my brother I would consider it as a personal favor and would be happy to reciprocate if in my power. I write to you instead of my brother knowing the position you occupy and the influence you have, that a recommendation from you will be all that is necessary. I write this voluntarily and not at the suggestion of any one knowing Runge to be worthy of the position. When you come to our city I would be pleased to have you make our house your home Hoping that you will comply with my request" —ALS, Morris Family Papers, IHi. No appointment followed.

1869, APRIL 9. S. S. Turner, Washington, D. C., to USG. "The Independent Order of Odd Fellows will celebrate the Fiftieth Anniversary of their organization in the United States at Philadelphia on the 26th instant, and the Fraternity in this jurisdiction propose to take part in the ceremonies. Therefore, as Chairman of the Committee of Arrangements on the part of the Grand Encampment of this District, I have the honor respectfully to request your Excellency to direct the Heads of the different Executive Departments to grant leave of absence to members of the Order serving under them, who may desire to participate in said celebration, where it can be done consistently with the interests of the public service. This is desired in order to procure uniformity of action in the Departments in regard to such leave and is the course generally pursued by your predecessors, in behalf of organization in this District where so many are in the government service."— Copies, DNA, RG 45, Subject File, VA; *ibid.*, RG 56, Letters Received from Executive Officers; *ibid.*, RG 77, Gen. Administration, Letters Received; *ibid.*, RG 92, Letters Received from Depts. and Bureaus; *ibid.*, RG 94, Letters Received, 279R 1869; *ibid.*, RG 107, Letters Received from Bureaus; *ibid.*, RG 153, Letters Received.

1869, APRIL 10. Horace Porter to Secretary of State Hamilton Fish. "The President directs me to request you to nominate Mr Jay for the Austrian Mission in place of Geo Wm Curtis—"—Copies, DLC-USG, II, 1, 4. On March 22, Charles Butler, New York City, had written to USG. "Presuming that Mr Motley would be restored to the Austrian Mission which he filled with such distinguished honor the expression which I now take the liberty of making in behalf of Mr John Jay has been withheld—In case that Mission is to be filled by another than Mr Motley, as intimated in public quarters, I do not know of any gentleman who would represent his country more usefully and acceptably than Mr Jay: indeed his pursuits & studies have qualified him eminently for such a position—The history of our country—its constitution & the principles which underlie it—politics in their higher relations, to government & the development & progress of the country have been the subjects of special interest & study with him—His appointment to the Austrian Mission I am sure would be regarded with satisfaction by all citizens who feel a pride in having our country represented at foreign courts by gentlemen distinguished for their intelligence, virtue, culture & patriotism—To this class Mr Jay belongs—I sincerly hope that you may deem it in the interest of the Government & country to appoint him to the mission named . . . P. S. It is proper that I should add that this note is written without the knowledge of Mr. Jay & without ever having conversed with him on the subject matter"—ALS, DNA, RG 59, Letters of Application and Recommendation. Related papers are *ibid.* On March 26, Charles C. Terry, Hudson, N. Y., had written to USG. "In the appointments made to represent the United States in foreign coutries, I would respectfully ask if the name of George William Curtis of New York has been mentioned in regard to such position Need I say such an appointment would be honorable to the country"—ALS, *ibid.* Related papers are *ibid.* On April 12, USG nominated John Jay as minister to Austria.

1869, APRIL 10. Horace Porter to Attorney Gen. Ebenezer R. Hoar. "The President directs me to call your attention to the marked portion of the enclosed letter from Gen Ames, Commanding the Dep't of Mississippi and to say that in consequence of representations made to him of the necessity of a District Attorney in Mississippi, he requests that a nomination be made with out delay."—Copies, DLC-USG, II, 1, 4. On April 12, USG nominated G. Gordon Adam as U.S. attorney, Southern District, Miss.

On July 7, Alston Mygatt, Vicksburg, wrote to USG. "In December last I was appointed a Delegate to visit Washington for the purpose of Representing the Interests of the Republican Party of the State of Mississippi. At that Time there Existed against me a Revenue Bill for Special Tax upon my Business as Commission Merchant, for a Fractional part of the Year amounting To $29,17—I called on Major Carey the Collector and arranged with him to allow my acct to remain unpaid until my return from Washington He very cordially consented and made an entry to that effect upon his Books— Immediately upon my return from Washington I made the payment according to Agreement—During my absence I was Indicted by the Grand Jury at the instance of G Gordon Adam now U. S. Dist Atty for this District, upon the charge of 'Defrauding the Revenue'—I was Indicted for $10 00 while the True Bill was $29,17 showing conclusively that the action was not taken at the Instance of the Collector, but on the contrary that it was done by parties who had no access to his Books The Bill was not handed in by the Collector, I was not notified, nor was my agent whom I left in Vicksburg. The whole affair seems To have been gotten with a direct intention To be used against me in Washington in order to impair my Influence as a Republican Delegate and through me other Republicans who had gone there to represent our Interests G Gordon Adam is not in Sympathy with the Great Republican Party, Neither Does he enjoy the confidence of the Party nor of the people of this community—He is now a '*Bolter*' deep in the Interst of the Wofford & Jeffords Faction, In Virginia he would Support Walker, In Tennessee Senter, In Georgia He would have Turned the Negroes from Office and in Mississippi he is lending his Influence to lead Disguised Rebels on to Victory, And using his *official* power to break down more than one leading Republican. Had the present Administration known the Political Character of the man I feel Confident that he would not have been made *Dist Atty* His removal would be very acceptable to the Republican Party I recommend that he be relieved by the Appointment of Edwin Hall"—LS, DNA, RG 60, Records Relating to Appointments. On July 15, Judge Robert A. Hill, U.S. District Court, Jackson, Miss., wrote to USG in support of Adam.—ALS, *ibid.*

On Aug. 10, Adam, Washington, D. C., wrote to USG. "I respectfully tender my resignation of the Office of attorney of the United States for the Southern district of Mississippi. Though the Office is not one of much importance, I cannot retain it without being identified to some extent with an administration, whose acts, so far as they relate to my own state, I do not approve. Major Wofford, an Officer in the late rebel Army, who in defiance of the contumely and reproach heaped upon him by the Southern People, supported bravely, and almost alone in this district, the reconstruction policy of Congress, has been removed from Office. From the late approved published statement of your views, I am justified in the belief that this is done in accordance with the established policy of your administration. From the same source I learn your confidence in and support of Genl: Ames, an Officer who has degraded his position as Military Commander of the 4th military district by exercising its functions solely in furtherance of his own personal and partizan ends, unhesitatingly avowing that he desires to use the high Office of Senator from my State as a stepping stone to the appointment of Brig: Genl: in the regular army, and whose whole course in that state has been marked by a tyrannical exercise of power, utterly antagonistic to the spirit of the reconstruction laws. As a resident of Mississippi, and one of the founders of the republican party in that state, though never a political aspirant, I would be false to my state and to the republican princibles, which I always have maintained, if I longer retained the Office to which your kind preference has assigned me."—ALS, *ibid.*, Letters from the President.

On Aug. 11, USG suspended Adam's appointment and named Armistead Burwell to replace him. On March 7, 1870, Burwell, Jackson, resigned this position and, on May 2, wrote to USG. "Some weeks since I tendered my resignation of the Office of District Atto: of So: Dist of Miss: I have no reply. The Judge is sick and Court will not be held until next monday. I ask to be relieved from this Office, which pays no salary, & involves an immense amount of labour. Some young man ought to fill it. I am too old. . . . N. B. As Miss: has no good men, and Officers must be imported I suggest the name of my son Charles Blair B, as my successor; He is with Chapman Scott & Crowell No 33. Wall Street. Alas for our State! Alas!! Alas! Miss: is not fit to be in the union. A Negro and Soldier are her Senators & she has not furnished a single representative in Congress. God may have mercy on her, but no man will."—ALS, *ibid.*, Records Relating to Appointments.

1869, APRIL 10. Grenville M. Dodge, Washington, D. C., to USG. "Gen S. L. Glasgow Elector at Large from the State of Iowa, is an applicant for a consulate at any point you see fit to give him. It is the only appointment for a foreign position asked from the 5th Dist of Iowa the other Elector from that District withdrawing in favor of Gen Glasgow: My successor Mr Palmer has made this appointment a speciality on account of the labors of Gen Glasgow for the party and for the Country. He entered the Service in 1861 as a Lieut of my Regimt, 4 Iowa Inf was Promoted to Maj. 23d: Inft then Col. and commanded that Regiment [in] the fight at Milikens bend which you have personal knowledge of his regiment also led the charge at Black River Bridge and was mustered out with his regiment He is a *Gentleman* a *scholar*, able, and will do credit to himself and his government in this position"—ALS, DNA, RG 59, Letters of Application and Recommendation. Related papers are *ibid.* On April 13, USG nominated Samuel L. Glasgow as consul, Havre.

On Aug. 25, 1873, Elihu B. Washburne, Paris, wrote to USG. "There is nothing I dislike more than to feel constrained to write you in regard to *offices*, but you must bear testimony that I do not often trouble you. I might, however, be justified in saying a word in regard to the official position of our countryman in the country to which I am accredited. General Glasgow, our Consul at Havre, was a brave and excellent soldier who served under your general command in the West and under the immediate command of my brother on the Gulf. In his service he contracted a camp diarrhoea, which used him up for years, and his friends in Iowa got you to make him Consul to Havre in 1869. He is a very honest, capable man and has made a most excellent Consul. Having suffered so much from disease contracted in the service (from which he has now happily partially recovered,) having made so creditable a consul and having been so very kind to my family, when in Havre in consequence of the Commune, I feel anxious that he might be retained, particularly as I believed that the public service could not be benefitted by any change. When in Washington last fall, I explained to you the case of the General and you was pleased to say to me that he would not be disturbed unless for *cause* and that I might say so to him. He now writes me that he has just received a letter from the Secretary requesting on your behalf his resignation, and it adds that the request is 'not caused by any dissatisfaction with his official conduct.' In view of what I wrote him and told him, it rather takes him 'between wind and water.' I have written him to forward his resignation, without delay, as a matter of course, and that it was possible that you and the Governor, might on a reconsideration of the matter, conclude not to accept it and let him hold on, at least for a time. I shall enclose this letter to the Governor that he may read it and enclose to you.—"—ALS, *ibid.* On Dec. 2, USG nominated Glasgow as consul, Glasgow.

1869, APRIL 10.   P. J. Kaufmann, Huntsville, Ala., to USG. "permit me to call your attention in regard to Office. Inasmuch as our State is intitled for representation abroad I had the honor to aspire for such an Office acording to this fackt. I left an application highly recomanded in care of our present hon: Senators of the State applying for a Consulship to Bremen, Antwerpe, Basle or Rotterdam. Well Knowing that your Exilence is willing to do Justice to every friend of You, I beg you kindly for this appointment.   you wouldt oblige me very much and when appointed I will endeaver to fill the Office to the honor of my adopted Country and to the my fellow citizens. Dont force me to believe that there is no Justice in our Partie but Ungreatfulness   In the last Elecktiones I did all in my power to see your Ticket sucessful and I thank God for the results. I am proud to say I supported your Ticket with my heardt blood, and I saw the muzle of a Pistol aimed at me for Elecktionering   Hoping your Exilence will appoint me to one of this hon: Possitiones and not dissappoint my expecktations."—ALS, DNA, RG 59, Letters of Application and Recommendation. On March 10, 1872, Kaufmann wrote to USG. "May it please your Honor to listen to a voice in the ranks. For the last ten years I have been afilliated with the Republican Party. I have dispursed over $1000 cash in Your Electorial Campaign and my public spirit dind't prove andvantagious to my Confectionary. During your three years Administration my Hon: Friend G. E Spencer was't able? to obtain a Consulate for me for wich I have been an Applicant. Our State has a verry poor Representation abroad. . . ."—ALS, *ibid.* Related papers are *ibid.*

1869, APRIL 10. Stephen P. Purdy, Detroit, to USG. "The pensioners and soldiers of Michigan will send you protest against removal of Colonel H. Barnes Pension Agent here and appointment of A. Kaichen a jew recommended by the Michigan Delegation from personal and official intercourse with them. Shall be able to satisfy you that such an appointment would be obnoxious. Please defer any appointment until you hear from them."—Telegram received (at 8:00 P.M.), DNA, RG 107, Telegrams Collected (Bound). Similar telegrams from Detroit to USG concerning this matter are *ibid.* On April 12, USG nominated Arnold Kaichen as pension agent, Detroit.

1869, APRIL 12. Secretary of the Navy Adolph E. Borie to USG. "As the time approaches for the examination of Midshipmen at the Naval Academy for graduation (June next) the Department desires that you will inform it of the names of such persons as you may select to constitute a Board of Visitors to be present at the examinations."—Copy, DNA, RG 45, Letters Sent to the President. On April 14, Horace Porter wrote to Borie. "The President directs me to request you ask Admiral Porter to call with you at the Executive Mansion to consult with him in regard to the appointments of the Board of Visitors to attend the examinations at the Naval Academy"—Copies, DLC-USG, II, 1, 4.
On April 21, Vice Admiral David D. Porter wrote to USG. "I have the honor to inform you that Judge D. C. Humphreys of Huntsville, Ala. notifies the Department of his acceptance of the appointment as Member of the Board of Visitors to the Naval Academy. Cornelius Vanderbilt, Esq. informs the Department that he regrets to find that his engagements are such that he cannot accept the appointment."—Copy, DNA, RG 45, Letters Sent to the President. Notice of Simeon B. Chittenden's acceptance of his appointment is *ibid.* See *HED,* 41-2-1, part 1, pp. 136–41.

1869, APRIL 12. Bvt. Maj. Gen. Joseph A. Mower, Lt. Col. Romeyn B. Ayres, and Maj. Amos Beckwith, New Orleans, to USG. "In view of the recent Law creating an additional Judgeship of the Supreme Court of the United States, our interest in the able and fair administration of the Law, leads us to urge upon your attention the Name of the Honorable Edward H. Durell for that place. In the opinion of those friendly to the Government here, Judge Durell is eminently qualified for the place—In this opinion we heartily concur— . . ."—DS, DNA, RG 60, Records Relating to Appointments. Related papers are *ibid.* On April 20, Mark Hoyt, New York City, telegraphed to USG. "I am informed that Judge E H Darrell of New Orleans is a candidate for the new circuit Judgeship. He is unfit for the place for the reason that he is corrupt, A citizen having the interest of the public service in view I ask that Gen Sheridan may be asked to state his opinion of the man, I will state my objections in writing and furnish abundant reasons why he should not be promoted, Senator Sumner knows me well"—Telegram received (at 4:30 P.M.), *ibid.*, RG 107, Telegrams Collected (Bound). No appointment followed.

1869, APRIL 12. Rowland Cromelien, Washington, D. C., to USG. "Referring to the proceedings of the Honorable Senate on the Pacific Railroad matters of national interest, 'that five eminent persons qualified,' should be by you appointed to investigate and report of the general compliance of their charterd priveleges and perfection for their travelling use, that I take the privelege and timely opportunity to offer my self as one for such task, I am no way owner of Railroad securities or connected with the present companies in the U. S. My fidelity to my country, and government, are of trust you cannot be mistaken in. I beg leave to refer, as I am well known to the Honorable members generally of both branches of our Representatives, and as being disengaged, and delayed again untill next session, in my own Petition for a railway charter to Annapolis M., *on my Centre Patented track method* for general improvement and much greater security in travelling, that I shall consider myself, highly honoured if you will confer on me my request."—LS, DLC-Nathaniel P. Banks. Related papers are in DNA, RG 107, Letters Received, C220 1869.

1869, APRIL 12. Jesse Root Grant and Mortimer M. Benton, Covington, Ky., to USG. "We earnestly recommend Hon John A. Prall of Lexington for U. S. Assessor for Seventh 7 District of Kentucky as a staunch union man every way qualified for the office by intelligence integrity and business habits"—Telegram received (at 2:00 P.M.), DNA, RG 107, Telegrams Collected (Bound). On April 16, USG nominated John A. Prall as assessor of Internal Revenue, 7th District, Ky., after withdrawing P. Burgess Hunt.

On May 5, John T. Croxton, Paris, Ky., telegraphed to USG. "A telegram from Washington advises me that the Assessor for this the Seventh District has not been appointed, I trust you will not consider me importunate if I again urge the appointment of Col Hunt, The contest has engendered much feeling and the office has been lost sight of in the struggle between the professional fireside politicians on the one hand and the soldiers who followed your flag on the other"—Telegram received (at 9:00 P.M.), *ibid.*

1869, APRIL 12. William B. Matchett, Washington, D. C., to USG. "The undersigned respectfully asks an appointment as Consul to Jerusalem and refers to accompanying commendations. In April, 1861 I applied to Mr Lincoln for a Consulate, but the Rebellion breaking out, I entered the service of the Union. I now repeat a request then made, confident of some little consideration for services I have tried to render my country; as also to carry out an old desire to visit the sacred Places, and lay in store for future use knowlege of the Ancient Lands of the Bible."—ALS, DNA, RG 59, Letters of Application and Recommendation. On May 3, Matchett wrote to Secretary of State Hamilton Fish. "Some four or five weeks since, I filed an Application with you for the Consulate at Jerusalem, and soon after, in an interview with President Grant, was informed by him that 'if any causes of removal were found against the present incumbent, I should be favored.' —I find, as I stated to him, not only that the party rec'd. his appointment at the hands of Mr. Johnson; but, that he is a Frenchman, & can in no way sympathize with our country and its institutions; neither is he prepared to carry out its spirit abroad, & has consequently laid himself open to censure, & the country to reproach by some injudicious acts. . . ."—ALS, *ibid.* Related papers are *ibid.*

On Jan. 21, Victor Beauboucher, consul, Jerusalem, had written to USG. "Amputated of the left leg in consequence of wounds received at Coal-harbor the 4th June 1864, afterwards employed at the War department (Subsistence dept) I am Consul at Jerusalem since the 30th August 1865: The copies here annexed testify how I discharged this last function. I rise from a serious and long sickness caused by great fatigue resulting from my forced journies to Jaffa, by almost impossible roads, in the interest of our poor families there; and my physician strongly recommends a change of climat for the complete recovery of my health. I am not rich, what I advanced to our poor families at Jaffa to prevent them from starvation in 1866 and 1867 has not been repaid me (it cannot be done but by Congress to whom this exceptional case has been submitted by the State-dept. All my ambition is to obtain in case of a vacancy a post in Italy, Spain or Germany if your Excellency and our honorable Secretary of State will judge me worthy."— ALS, *ibid.* On July 9, Benjamin A. Finkelstein, Jerusalem, wrote to USG. "I have the honour most respectfully to solicit your protection. It is about three years since I am in the U. S. Consular Career as Deputy Consul at Jerusalem, under Consul V. Beauboucher Esqr. During this period he has not paid me as he had agreed and promised, has broken his promises, has tyranised over me, declares everywhere that I have been dishonorably discharged from the U. S. service, and is trying all in his power to ruin my reputation, do me materiel injury and blast my future. . . ."—LS, *ibid.* Related papers are *ibid.*

On Feb. 15, Ind. Senator Anson Wolcott *et al.* petitioned USG. "The undersigned members of the General Assembly of the State of Indiana respectfully recommend Richard Beardsley, late a Purser of the U. S. Navy, as a suitable and worthy person to be appointed a Consul of the United States to some port on the Mediterranean."—DS (76 signatures), *ibid.* Related papers are *ibid.* On Dec. 15, USG nominated Richard Beardsley as consul, Jerusalem.

1869, APRIL 13.   Orville E. Babcock to A. C. Richards, police superintendent, Washington, D. C. "The President directs me to request that you detail for duty at the Executive Mansion, one policeman to assist at Every

Tuesday Afternoon reception, between the hours of 1½ & 5 P. M."—Copies, DLC-USG, II, 1, 4. On April 3, newspapers reported "that Mrs. GRANT will hold public receptions at the Executive Mansion on every Tuesday afternoon from 2 to 4 o'clock."—*New York Times*, April 4, 1869. See John Y. Simon, ed., *The Personal Memoirs of Julia Dent Grant* (New York, 1975), pp. 174–76.

1869, APRIL 13.   William Cullen Bryant, New York City, to USG. "As many of the prominent merchants of New York who are engaged in the trade between this country and Germany have recommended Otto Wilhelm Pollitz Esq. for the post of American Consul at the port of Hamburg in Germany I take pleasure in seconding the application. I know Mr. Pollitz well and know that every thing said in his favor in the paper signed by the Merchants is strictly true and cannot but hope that the appointment will be made, confident as I am that no man fitter for the place in every respect cannot be found."—ALS, DNA, RG 59, Letters of Application and Recommendation. Related papers are *ibid*. On April 15, USG nominated Edward Robinson as consul, Hamburg.

1869, APRIL 13.   A. P. Curry, sheriff, Memphis, to USG. "Appointment of Salter Collector is an outrage to community and your friends   He is not known here at all"—Telegram received (on April 14, 9:10 A.M.), DNA, RG 107, Telegrams Collected (Bound). On April 12, USG had nominated Francis Salter as collector of Internal Revenue, 8th District, Tenn.; on April 19, he withdrew this nomination in favor of Robert F. Patterson.

1869, APRIL 13.   Morton McMichael *et al.*, Philadelphia, to USG. "At the recent interview, which we had the honor of holding with you at the Presidential Mansion, you were good enough to say that at a proper time you would appoint our fellow citizen George H. Boker to a foreign mission. In order that Mr Boker's name may be placed on the files of the State Department in this connection, we respectfully present him to you as a candidate for Minister to Spain, Italy or any similar position, with the expression of an earnest hope that it will not be long before you will be able to realize your good intentions towards him."—DS (7 signatures), DNA, RG 59, Letters of Application and Recommendation. Related papers are *ibid*. On Dec. 6, 1871, USG nominated George H. Boker as minister to Constantinople.

1869, APRIL 13.   U.S. Senator Oliver P. Morton of Ind. to USG. "The name of my son John. M. Morton has been sent to you by the Sec of the Interior for the Register of a Land Office in Dacotah. This was done by my friends without my intervention. I cannot afford to have him appointed even if it suits your convenience and pleasure. I will not ask the appointment of another relative by blood or marriage, and for what you have done I am grateful. If you can give an appointment to Gen Terrell who has rendered great service to me in the government of Indiana & who has qualifications of the highest order I shall esteem it a great favor. He was the first person for whom I made an application and in whose success I feel the deepest interest. I would not again mention the matter but for the intimate relations existing between us, and what he has a right to expect ~~of~~ from me."—ALS, OFH. On Jan. 10, 1870, USG nominated William H. H. Terrell as 3rd asst. postmaster gen. See *PUSG*, 16, 559; William Dudley Foulke, *Life of Oliver P. Morton* (1899; reprinted, New York, 1974), II, 523, 531.

1869, APRIL 13.   Bishop Matthew Simpson, Philadelphia, to USG. "I beg leave to recommend to you, in reply to your note through yr Secretary, the Rev. Albert S. Hunt, of Brooklyn NewYork. Mr Hunt is a gentleman of good address scholarly habits and is a faithful and devoted Christian minister. I can freely and fully commend him as being in my judgment every way suitable for Chaplain. I think he will be respected and beloved by young men. I thank you for your courtesy, and I pray that in all your acts you may be so guided and directed that the best interests of the country may be advanced. I hope to be in Washington in a few weeks, when my pressing duties are over, and will hope to see you when your hurry of appts is through."—ALS, DNA, RG 94, ACP, H90 CB 1869. On April 5, Simpson had telegraphed to Horace Porter. "Yours is received   Please say to President I will answer as soon as possible"—Telegram received (at 2:30 P.M.), *ibid.*, RG 107, Telegrams Collected (Bound). On April 15, USG nominated Albert S. Hunt as post chaplain, USMA.

1869, APRIL 14.   Secretary of the Navy Adolph E. Borie to USG. "I have the honor to submit, herewith, for your information, copy of a despatch, with enclosures, received from Commander Thos. Scott Fillebrown, commanding the U. S. Steamer Narragansett, dated Havana, April 8th relative to the boarding of the American schooner 'Lizzie Major,' by the Spanish Frigate 'Fernando Catalico,' and the removal therefrom of two persons said to be passengers."—Copy, DNA, RG 45, Letters Sent to the President. On April 15, 19, and 22, Secretary of State Hamilton Fish wrote in his diary concerning the passengers.—DLC-Hamilton Fish. See *New York Times*, April 11, 1869; Message, Dec. 6, 1869; *SED*, 41-2-108, p. 156.

1869, APRIL 14.   U.S. Senators Arthur I. Boreman and Waitman T. Willey of West Va. to USG. "On yesterday you sent to the Senate a nomination for the Mission to Costa Rica—This, if confirmed, removes the present Minister, Hon. Jacob B. Blair, of West Va,—Mr Blair is one of the best men in our state—is a true and very active Republican—and we trust that you can allow him to remain where he is, as we feel sure that the country will be as ably & faithfully represented by him as by any one who may be appointed his successor—He is the fellow townsman, of one of us (Senator Boreman) and the personal friend of both. of us & we shall feel the blow seriously if he is removed from his present position—which he has only held for a very few months—In all that we have done to secure positions for others we did not design to interfere with the interests of Mr Blair."—LS, DNA, RG 59, Letters of Application and Recommendation. Related papers are *ibid.* On April 12, USG had nominated Charles N. Riotte of Tex. as minister to Costa Rica. Letters recommending Riotte are *ibid.* On April 17, Horace Porter wrote to U.S. Representative Horace Maynard of Tenn. "The President directs me to request you to recommend some one from Tennessee for the office of Minister at Nicaragua"—Copies, DLC-USG, II, 1, 4. On April 20, USG withdrew Riotte's nomination and named him as minister to Nicaragua.

1869, APRIL 14.   Jesse Root Grant and John S. Nixon, Covington, Ky., to USG. "Please suspend appointment of Dobyns Assessor Eighth 8 District until advised by mail"—Telegram received (at 12:40 P.M.), DNA, RG 107, Telegrams Collected (Bound). On April 9, Horace Porter had written to U.S. Senator John Sherman of Ohio. "The President directs me to request that action be suspended for the present in the case of George H. Dobyns nominated to the Senate 8th instant for the office of Assessor of Internal Revenue for the 8th Dist Ky"—LS, *ibid.*, RG 46, Papers Pertaining to Executive Nominations. On April 8, USG had nominated George H. Dobyns as assessor of Internal Revenue, 8th District, Ky.; on April 9, the Senate Finance Committee reported Dobyns's nomination without recommendation.

On Feb. 12, 1873, Dobyns, Washington, D. C., wrote to USG. "I have the honor to apply for the appointment of *Inspector* of Indian Agents . . ."—ALS, *ibid.*, RG 48, Appointments Div., Letters Received. No appointment followed.

1869, APRIL 14.   U.S. Representative James S. Negley of Pa. to USG. "I simply yield to the repeated solicitations of my constituents including many of the most prominent Republicans of Western Pennsylvania in stating to you that the greatest dissatisfaction prevails in consequence of the omission of a single Foreign or Territorial appointment being credited to Allegheny County. This County as you are aware gave over 10.000. majority, saving the State, and thus securing your election. I have recommended the Hon. P. C. Shannon for the Ministry to Portugal—Jay. T. Howard Consul to a French Port—and John H. Stewart Consul to Leeds England. The Secretary of State informs me that there are no vacancies and no possibility of making either of these appointments, or providing for them otherwise. I know of no answer to make to our people that will explain this seeming oversight to their political claims. I am therefore induced to state this fact and make one more appeal in behalf of the desires of my constituents."—LS, DNA, RG 59, Letters of Application and Recommendation. On April 20, USG nominated Jay T. Howard as consul, Leghorn; on Dec. 6, John H. Stewart as consul, Turks Island; on March 15, 1873, Peter C. Shannon as chief justice, Dakota Territory.

1869, April 14.   U.S. Senator Thomas W. Osborn of Fla. to Julia Dent Grant. "I take the liberty of saying that the bearer, Mrs. Hutchens, has my sympathy in ~~any~~ the matter she may lay before you, & I think I may say also, the sympathy of the entire Congressional Delegation from Florida. I beleive her to be a most worthy & estimable lady. She lost a fine property at the hands of the rebels, during the war, & has since been compelled, though formerly in affluence, to earn bread for herself and little daughter in the Treasury Department. Her fidelity to the country & the administration has never been questioned."—ALS, OFH.

1869, April 15.   USG order. "All persons holding 'continuous service' certificates, will be entitled to receive for each continuous re-enlistment for three years within three months from the date of their discharge one dollar per month in addition to the pay prescribed for their several ratings."—Copy, DNA, RG 130, Executive Orders and Proclamations. See *HRC*, 51-1-2836.

1869, April 15.   William S. Harney, Washington, D. C., to USG. "I have never asked a favor of a President of the United States, but I am going to ask one of you.—My son John M Harney wishes to go as Consul to Nice, France, Geneva, Switzerland or to Geno Italy—He speaks & writes the French & Italian languages as well as the best educated natives. His character is unexceptionable and is one of the most popular young men in Saint Louis.—If General, my long & hard services entitle me to any consideration, I will consider myself fully repaid by granting this request & it will place me under a great obligation to yourself—I received my sons letter on this subject this morning—. . . P. S. I assure you that John will be a credit to your Administration—I wish to spend a year too in Europe when I get through with the Indians. I have not seen my two Daughters for nearly five years.—"—ALS, DNA, RG 59, Letters of Application and Recommendation. On Feb. 8, 1873, Harney wrote to USG on the same subject.—ALS, *ibid.* Related papers are *ibid.* No appointment followed.

1869, April 15.   Elvira G. Baxter, Jonesville, Mich., to USG. "A gross injustice has been done my husband If you had ever seen the papers which ought to hve been sent to you with the names of all our prominent Michigan men in behalf of my husband we are just confident that Mr J. E. Bennet would neve[r] have received the appointment of Marshall for the Eastern district of this state Mr Beaman promised my husband he should surely have the position and it was by surporting Mr Beaman in our last election when there were other candidates that he lost his place as register of deeds in Hillsdale County My husband was the Col that command the seventh Michigan or the little band of forlorn hope in the crossing to Fredricksburg and was wounded in crossing . . ."—ALS, DNA, RG 60, Records Relating to Appointments. Related papers are *ibid.*, RG 59, Letters of Application and Recommendation; *ibid.*, Reports to the President and Congress. On

April 15, USG nominated Henry Baxter as minister to Honduras. See USG Documents, Brigham Young University, Provo, Utah.

1869, APRIL 15. John H. Foy, Atlanta, to USG. "Allow me on behalf of 80.000 colored people of this State to lay before you for favorable consideration, the name of Henry M. Turner of Macon. I know him to be a man of rare intelligence vigorous and unceasing in educating his people in political science, morals and industry, he championed the cause of Freedom and Liberty throughout this State, was the ablest advocate in our Legislature, and did more to give tone and stability to Republican principles in this State than any three men in it. We feel that he should have recognition at the hands of your Excellency by the appointment of Minister to Hayti. Turner is keen, far seeing, judicious and educated The appointment of such a man would be an act of simple justice to a large class of worthy citizens and do much to strengthen their confidence in your administration."—ALS, DNA, RG 59, Letters of Application and Recommendation. On May 18, USG nominated Henry M. Turner as postmaster, Macon, Ga. On June 9, J. Clarke Swayze, editor, *American Union*, Macon, *et al.*, telegraphed to USG. "Telegram published this morning says you have [yie]lded to Republican pressure in case of Turner, Please keep the matter open un[til] Republicans can be heard from by mail"—Telegram received (at 10:30 A.M.), *ibid.*, RG 107, Telegrams Collected (Bound). On Aug. 10, USG suspended the appointment, possibly because Turner had been accused of misconduct.—*Ibid.*, RG 59, Letters of Application and Recommendation. See *PUSG*, 12, 461–65; E. Merton Coulter, "Henry M. Turner: Georgia Negro Preacher-Politician During the Reconstruction Era," *Georgia Historical Quarterly*, XLVIII, 4 (Dec., 1964), 386–96; Edmund L. Drago, *Black Politicians and Reconstruction in Georgia* (Baton Rouge, 1982), pp. 66–67. On Dec. 6, USG nominated James H. Washington to replace Turner.

1869, APRIL 15. Samuel F. Miller, U.S. Supreme Court, to USG. "I do not know if it is in contemplation to remove the Hon Hiram Knowles appointed Associate Justice of Montana last fa Summer. At all events I wish to say that Judge Knowles was born and raised in my town and studied law in my office and I know him well He is now and always has been a thorough anti Johnson republican. He was appointed with any knowledge that he was thought of for the place and was surprized when he saw it in the newspapers. He was confirmed on my dispatch to Senator Harlan and left a growing practice to accept the place. Under these circumstances and as he unobjectionable as a judge I hope he will be permitted to serve out his term"—ALS, DNA, RG 60, Records Relating to Appointments. On April 17, Henry R. Horr *et al.*, Washington, D. C., wrote to USG. "The Undersigned Members of the Republican Party, residents of Montana, now in Washington City, Earnestly petition for the removal of the following Federal Officers of our Territory—viz: Chief Justice Warren and associate Justice Knowles of the

Supreme Court—Both of these officers are appointees of Mr Johnson—Justice Warren is an avowed Democrat; while Justice Knowles has used the patronage of his Office in the appointment of a Clerk for his court who was a rebel soldier, when an equally competent person and a Union Soldier, applying for the place was disregarded—The United States District Attorney, Mr Mahew, is a known Democrat, and was last year Speaker of the Democratic House of Representatives of the Territory—United States Marshall Howie, has repeatedly employed rebels and Democrats as his Deputies, and is neither qualified for or deserving of the office he fills—"—DS (8 signatures), *ibid.* On April 22, S. T. R. Edwards and 12 others, Virginia City, Montana Territory, telegraphed to USG. "*Private.* Chief Justice Warren just arrived with family learns by telegraph that S. M Burson' name sent to Senate yesterday for his office, all parties wish Warren retained and dont want Burson,"—Telegram received (on April 23, 9:00 A.M.), *ibid.*, RG 107, Telegrams Collected (Bound). USG retained Henry L. Warren as chief justice and Hiram Knowles as associate justice and removed Alexander E. Mayhew as U.S. attorney and Neil Howie as marshal, Montana Territory.

1869, APRIL 15. Alfred T. A. Torbert, Milford, Del., to USG. "I trust that you can give me the appointment as Minister to Portugal; such a position has been my aim and ambition for some time and it would be my endeavor to represent the Government with that honor & dignity which would be pleasing to your Administration. As you expressed to me your intention, to distribute these appointments as near equal as possible to the different States I would call attention to the fact that *now* Delaware has not a *single foreign appointment.* You know my position here and I have not asked my friends from other States to support me because I thought they were bored enough at home. My case rests entirely on its own merits, with which I hope you are sufficiently acquainted to grant my request."—ALS, DNA, RG 59, Letters of Application and Recommendation. On April 17, USG nominated Torbert as minister to Salvador.

1869, APRIL 15. Jerome W. Turner, Baltimore, to USG. "(Confidential) . . . On this day of the month, and in this year *Anno Domini* I have been in the City of Washington for the first time in my life. I came over a thousand miles to see the town, and staid just three hours by the clock! It was long enough, however. If any freindly Rail Road train could have taken me sooner, I should have gone. The only thing I regret is, that I could not have seen you—about the only specimen of nobleness I think, that there is in your delectable City. I came to Washington to ask an appointment as a great many are doing at present, but in a *very different manner.* I did not suppose it was necessary to stand around the door of the Senate while in Executive Session. As no Seats were provided, I got tired in about an hour, and left. I was not taken with the *manner* adopted by ~~applications~~ applicants, and in short, came off disgusted. I never could stand it, to *stand long* on my feet. When I had reached this place on my return it struck me that it would do no harm to write a letter to *yourself*, and let *Heads* of *Departments* go to the dogs! I rather prefer (as I know you do) a *Head* with *Departments in it*! I might tell you a good many things I have done & what I am but that is the ordinary way & I despise it—I send you inclosed a letter from the Chairman of the Michigan, Republican, State Central Committee. It was designed for Senator Chandler, but I did not have time to give it to him. I have not spoken either to him or Howard about the matter, but refer you to them should you take any interest in this letter—If you accede to the request I shall be pleased—if not I shall have to be satisfied."—ALS, DNA, RG 59, Letters of Application and Recommendation. The enclosure is *ibid*. No appointment followed.

1869, APRIL 16. To Senate. "I transmit to the Senate for consideration with a view to ratification, a Convention between the United States and the Emperor of the French, signed this day by the Plenipotentiaries of the Parties, for the mutual protection of trade marks of their respective citizens and subjects."—DS, DNA, RG 46, Presidential Messages, Foreign Relations, France.

1869, APRIL 16. Orville E. Babcock to Columbus Delano, commissioner of Internal Revenue. "The President directs me to say that on the representation of the Senators from Arkansas—he thinks Mr Oliver should be removed"—Copies, DLC-USG, II, 1, 4. On the same day, USG nominated Joseph Brooks as assessor of Internal Revenue, 2nd District, Ark., in place of John M. Oliver; on April 17, USG withdrew the nomination to allow Oliver's resignation and, on April 20, renominated Brooks.

1869, APRIL 16. Horace Porter to Isaac N. Morris. "The President directs me to inform you that after an examination of the terms of the treaty in regard to the Cherokee ~~Indian~~ lands, he has decided that it involves questions which the Senate should properly decide upon and therefore prefers not to give an opinion upon the subject—"—Copies, DLC-USG, II, 1, 4.

1869, APRIL 16. Attorney Gen. Ebenezer R. Hoar to USG. "I have considered the questions proposed by E. H. Smith, Esq., whose communication of the 13th inst. with the accompanying papers, you were pleased to refer to me, relative to certain rules and directions promulgated by the Commissioner of Patents concerning proceedings in his bureau for the extension of patents. . . ."—Copy, DNA, RG 60, Opinions.

1869, APRIL 16. John Binny, New York City, to USG. "In regard to the Alabama difficulty, the wisest course to be adopted appears to be this.—Since the treaty negotiated between our Minister Reverdy Johnson and Lord Clarendon has been rejected by the Senate, it is the duty of the American government to take the initiative and open up new negociations for the settlement of those disputed claims.—Two Commissioners should be appointed by

the American Government to meet with two Commissioners from England to adjust a new mode of settlement. It would be advisable to select Washington as the seat of the new negociations. The Commissioners to be selected for this purpose by the American Government ought to be preeminent lawyers, of sterling integrity & undoubted patriotism—Mr Bingham the Chairman of the Judiciary Committee in the House of Representatives and Mr Evarts the late attorney General ~~would~~ are admirably qualified for this important work.—The chief points to which their attention should be directed are these:—1. To shew precisely the ~~injuries~~ criminality of England—in granting belligerent rights to the rebels of the south at the time she did—in allowing the Alabama & other piratical vessels to leave her ports—and in not taking active measures to prevent their depredations on the Commerce of the United States.—2. To shew whether this is, or is not, in violation of the present established usages of civilized nations or in violation of international law.—3. If the code of international law is defect[iv]e as to the rules of neutrality, to point out how it should be amended.—4. To indicate *the extent of damages* done to America by these piratical vessels—by the connivance of the English Government,—or through their criminal neglect.—Although I have often to condemn the political editorials in the 'World', there is a sensible & judicious article in yesterdays paper which I send you a Copy of,—treating on this subject. If you think proper, you may submit this note, with the newspaper, to Mr. Fish the Secretary of State . . . P. S. The difference between this Country & England concerning the North Eastern boundary was satisfactorily adjusted in a similar manner to the one above proposed.—"
—ALS, DNA, RG 59, Miscellaneous Letters.

1869, APRIL 16.   James F. Casey, collector of customs, New Orleans, to USG. "Some days ago I recommended Nevill's appointment as Appraiser in place of Stanford who should be removed. In any event I desire to retain James Jackson the other Appraiser whose services at this time are indispensable and I hope the appointment of West does not remove him"—Telegram received (at 7:30 P.M.), DNA, RG 107, Telegrams Collected (Bound). On April 14, USG had nominated Julian Neville as pension agent, New Orleans. On April 15, USG nominated Joseph R. West as appraiser, New Orleans, in place of William L. Stanford; on April 19, he withdrew West and, on April 20, nominated Thomas Ong.

1869, APRIL 16.   Andrew J. Smith, Washington, D. C., to USG. "I have the honor to apply for the appointment of Post Master of Syracuse N. Y. I base my application upon the accompanying letters and military endorsement of Gen. officers with whom I have served and petitions &c of citizens of my native city— . . . And beg leave to call your attention to the interview had this morning—and to the fact that the appointments of assessor and collector of Internal Revenue have already been made in our district and the soldiers claims have not been recognized—"—ALS, DNA, RG 46, Papers Pertaining to Executive Nominations. Related papers are *ibid.* On April 19, USG nominated Smith as postmaster, Syracuse. On April 20, U.S. Representative Dennis McCarthy, Syracuse, telegraphed to USG. "It is going against the wishes of a great majority of Republicans and a great injury to myself & unjust to the Post Master who has served the country well, His term not having expired to send in Col A J Smith for Post Master here, Hold it until I reach Washington"—Telegram received (at 10:00 A.M.), DNA, RG 107, Telegrams Collected (Bound). On April 21, McCarthy, Jersey City, telegraphed to USG. "Hope nomination for Syracuse Post office is held over Shall be in Washington this evening"—Telegram received (at 9:35 A.M.), *ibid.* On April 22, USG withdrew Smith's nomination; on Dec. 10, 1873, he nominated Smith as surveyor gen., Montana Territory.

1869, APRIL 16. Dick Watts, Louisville, to USG. "My excessive modesty has prevented me from asking for an office up to this time, but I find that every body else has presented claims, and therefore I now come forward Have you a consuship at your disposal that has not been applied for? If you have please remember your humble servant I have the city directories of Chicago, St. Louis, Cincinnati, and Louisville before me, and could, if so disposed, present as grand an array of names as any applicant now in Washington. I 'have done the Country some service' whether she knows it or not, having been a member of the Tenth Ky. Regiment, which fought for the Government Mr. President I am in earnest about this little matter. It requires about $5000 to keep me going each year, for I dabble considerably in elections. But should the Government need my services abroad I could get along on Considerable more or less I can confidently refer to General Geo. H. Thomas as to my social status. And as to my honesty I will only say that I was a Quartermaster during the war, and came home in debt. Small favors thankfully received . . . P. S. Senator Ross is not a friend of mine"—ALS, DNA, RG 59, Letters of Application and Recommendation. No appointment followed.

1869, APRIL 17. Secretary of the Interior Jacob D. Cox to USG. "The Senators from Nebraska, agree that the nomination of C. H. Gere, for Register of the Land Office be withdrawn, and I therefore recommend your action in the premises—Mr Gere's name was sent in for the Land Office at 'Lincoln,' Nebraska."—ALS, OFH. On April 19, USG withdrew this nomination.

1869, APRIL 17. James H. Boucher, Iowa City, to USG. "*Personal* . . . Y'r letter recommendatory was duly received, for whch please accept my most profound thanks It was properly presented to the Board with others and thro' its influence I will secure the position The Trustees, however, at their last meeting decided not to fill the Medical Chairs during the next two years inasmuch as the Iowa Legislature at its last Session failed to make the necessary appropriation for this Department and the Trustees did not deem it prudent to withhold any funds from the other Departments for this purpose . . ."—ALS, DNA, RG 59, Letters of Application and Recommendation.

1869, APRIL 17. William S. Wilcox, Toledo, to USG. ". . . I will now send you My Name as an Applicant for Collector of Customs at The Port of Toledo. I used to know you when you was at Sackets Harbor. I was at that time Master of a Vessel for S. T. Hooker . . ."—ALS, DNA, RG 56, Collector of Customs Applications. No appointment followed.

1869, APRIL 19. USG order. "The reservation of Fort Arbuckle, Indian Territory, and Fort Bayard, New Mexico, as described in the accompanying plats and notes of survey, approved by the Secretary of War, are made for military purposes; and the Secretary of the Interior will cause the same to be noted in the General Land Office, to be reserved as Military Posts."—Copy, DNA, RG 107, Orders and Endorsements. Similar orders relating to military reservations, *ibid.*, will not be printed. On April 27, USG endorsed a letter from Bvt. Maj. Gen. Edward O. C. Ord, San Francisco, to the AG. "A reservation at Camp Wright, Round Valley, California, of one mile square, with the flag-staff for a centre, as recommended in the accompanying letter of the Commanding General Department of California; approved by the Secretary of War, is made for military purposes; and the Secretary of the Interior will cause the same to be noted in the General Land Office, to be reserved as a military post."—Copy, *ibid.*, RG 153, Military Reservation Files, Calif. Ord's letter of Jan. 16, with enclosures, is *ibid.*

1869, APRIL 19. U.S. Representative Sidney Clarke of Kan. to USG. "I have the honor to call your attention to the fact that it was in evidence before the Committee on Public Lands of the House of Representatives, that Mr. Robinson, Southern Supt. of Indian Affairs, held a Power of Atty from the Absendte Shawnee Indians for the transaction of business for said Indians. This was regarded as very improper conduct on the part of a Public Officer. I have heard the same facts from parties in which I have confidence, and I deem it my duty to make known the same to you. I veiw of the well known combinations for corruption purposes existing in the limits of the Southern Superintendncy I earnestly urge that a new Superintendent be appointed at an early day."—ALS, DNA, RG 48, Appointments Div., Letters Received. Congress closed the Southern Superintendency as of July 1, displacing L. Newton Robinson as superintendent.

1869, APRIL 19. Anonymous, Bangor, Maine, to USG. "I cordially recommend and endorse the recommendations already given for the appointment of Capt. Alpheus T. Palmer to the position of Special detective under the Secretary of Treasury; to be assigned to any locality in New England, . . ."—AL, Chamberlain Papers, MeB.

1869, APRIL 20. Secretary of the Interior Jacob D. Cox to USG. "I have the honor to invite your attention to the accompanying copy of a letter from the Commissioner of Indian Affairs, dated the 19th instant, in relation to the indebtedness of nearly $100,000, incurred by General Harney prior to Octr 1st 1868, on account of certain Sioux Indians with whom treaties were made by the Indian Peace Commission, and for debts incurred subsequently to said date, which is in excess of the amount appropriated to satisfy said liabilities. . . ."—Copy, DNA, RG 48, Indian Div., Letters Sent.

1869, APRIL 20. S. B. Avery, D. F. Underhill, and Charles Wickes, Rochester, N. Y., to USG or U.S. Senator Reuben E. Fenton of N. Y. "At large meeting held this evening by citizens Brockhart following resolutions were unanimously passed: That no person should be appointed to the charge of a post office who is not acceptable to those who resort to the office for its accomodation and benefit. Resolved, that this community received with much joy and satisfaction the news of the nomination by the President of Mrs. Mary E. Baker to the charge of the Post office in this village—she being the decided choice of a very large majority of persons having intercourse with the office. Resolved, that we have since learned with deep regret that the President has been induced to withdraw Mrs Bakers name and substituted the name of Horatio N. Beach whos confirmation and appointment will be most unacceptable to this community and is desired by a very few if any. . . ."—Telegram received (on April 21, 9:45 A.M.), DNA, RG 107, Telegrams Collected (Bound). On April 16, USG had nominated Mary E. Baker as postmaster, Brockport, N. Y.; on April 19, he withdrew her nomination in favor of Horatio N. Beach; on April 21, he withdrew Beach's nomination and renominated Baker.

1869, APRIL 20. Louis C. d'Homergue, Washington, D. C., to USG. "Recommended by Gov E. D. Morgan of N. Y, and Senator Howard of Michigan, and politically, as well as personally endorsed by Lieut-Gov Oscar J Dunn of Louisiana, as well as by Messers B. F. Joubert, F. E. Dumas, J Clay, C. S Souvinet and T. C. Thomas prominent Republicans of N. O. I have respectfully solicited a European consular position, having a large family acquaintance and connection, both in France and in Greece. During the war I served part of the time with the old 69th of N. Y. and when family duties required my presence, I placed a substitute who served until its termination. At New Orleans, I have always been known for my Republican sentiments, and open hospitality extended to Union people and to the Army and Navy. My late father was from 1830 to 1842 French attaché and consul at Philadelphia, through him I owe my knowledge of consular duties. I speak French fluently, and in my immediate family (wife, son and mother) we speak English, French, Spanish, Italian and Greek. . . ."—ALS, DNA, RG 59, Letters of Application and Recommendation. Related papers are *ibid.* No appointment followed.

1869, April 20. N. M. Sneed, Griffin, Ga., to USG. "In the distribution of favors to the original Union Men of the Southern States I beg leave to submit my case. I am the Son of an old U. S. officer in the war of 1812 a native of Granville Co. North Carolina, Paymaster of the army of South Carolina & stationed at Fourt Moultrie with the rank of Major. After the death of my father in 1830. I returned to N. C. as a repersentative of what a Georgia boy was, with my uncle. When the late war began I was a resident of Memphis Tenn, and did all in my humble way to stop the tide of Secession there, as will more fully appear when reference is made to Hons Jno. W Leftwick, Horace Maynard, Hon. W. G. Brownlow, Hon Garnett Andrews Washington Ga and many others in the States aforesaid. Were I not in feeble health with a family I would not wish an appointment; as it is I do, as consul to South America, or Cuba, or Scotland or Ireland, or where a southern man can take his family & recuperate his health and at the same time serve his country. I first met you at Memphis in July (I think) 1862, at the gate of the Residence of Wm R Hunt your then head quarters, making application to go with my family to my place in the country which was granted me. There are many other citizens of Tenn & Ga to whom I could refer Hon A. H. Stephens an old & valued friend, but I have said enough: if you can send my name to the Senate for any position as aforesaid it will be confering me a favor, and doing justice to one who has been a consistant union man from first to last."—ALS, DNA, RG 59, Letters of Application and Recommendation. No appointment followed.

1869, April 21. To Senate. "I transmit to the Senate, in answer to their resolution adopted in Executive Session on the 16th of February last, requesting copy of the official correspondence of Mr Buchanan, during his residence at St. Petersburg as Minister of the United States, a report from the Secretary of State, with the accompanying papers."—DS, DNA, RG 46, Presidential Messages, Foreign Relations, Russia. The enclosures are *ibid.*

1869, April 21. Severin A. Barthoulot, Philadelphia, to USG. "I have the honor to ask you the position of *Attaché* in the Ambassade of the U. S. to the Court of St Petersburg. I am a frenchman, got a diploma as french Teacher, was 1st Lnt of Genl N. P. Banks Body-Guard, Senior Capt of Collis's Zouaves, 1st Lnt in the Vet. Res. Corps and now Capt Comdg Co B. Zouaves d'afrique, Penna militia and in the Court of Russia French language is adopted. . . . P. S. One of my Uncle *Evard* was Governor of Tombour Russia"—ALS, DNA, RG 59, Letters of Application and Recommendation. No appointment followed.

1869, APRIL 21. Robert L. May, Washington, D. C., to USG. "I would be pleased to act as one of your Assistant Private Secretaries, if they are not all yet permanently appointed. Should there be no vacancy, I would respectfully solicit a Consulship at some European port. I do not know as it would be in good taste to mention our personal resemblance as a recommendation for some foreign appointment, but that circumstance can certainly be no objection."—ALS, DNA, RG 59, Letters of Application and Recommendation. The file contains a photograph. No appointment followed.

1869, APRIL 22. To Senate. "I transmit to the Senate letters from the Commissioner of Indian affairs, and Graham Rogers and others, Delegates of the Shawnee Indians, and in accordance with their request, do hereby withdraw the Shawnee treaty concluded on the 4th of March 1867."—DS, DNA, RG 46, Presidential Messages, Indian Relations. On April 19, Graham Rogers, Charles Tucker, and Henry F. A. Rogers, Washington, D. C., had written to USG. "We the undersigned Delegates, duly elected by the Shawnee tribe of Indians of the State of Kansas, have the honor to request on behalf of our people, the withdrawal from the United States Senate, the Shawnee treaty concluded on the 4th day of March 1867. for the following reasons, towit. . . ."—DS, *ibid.*

1869, APRIL 22. R. D. Badger, "Colored and others," Atlanta, to USG. "We pray you to nominate Captain Daniel S. Snyder Assessor Fourth 4 District Georgia vice L. D. Brady rejected by the Senate this day. He is worthy and competent. His letters and recommendations are on file with the Commissioner"—Telegram received (at 6:30 P.M.), DNA, RG 107, Telegrams Collected (Bound). On April 21, USG nominated Luther B. Brady as assessor of Internal Revenue, 4th District, Ga.; on April 22, the Senate rejected this nomination. On Dec. 6, USG nominated Daniel D. Snyder for this post; on Dec. 8, he withdrew Snyder's nomination; on Dec. 16, he nominated William Jennings. On May 4, John W. Forney, Knoxville, telegraphed to USG. "I beg most respectfully to suggest that the protest of our Republican friends at Atlanta against the appointment of J. H. Caldwell as assessor of fourth District of Georgia be favorably considered and that action be withheld until they can be heard."—Telegram received (at 3:30 P.M.), *ibid.*

1869, APRIL 22. William R. Crane, New Orleans, to USG requesting appointment as judge, Eastern District, La., and relating his political services amid local factional strife and corruption.—ALS, DNA, RG 60, Records Relating to Appointments. Related papers are *ibid.* On March 8, U.S. Representative Benjamin F. Butler of Mass. forwarded a petition to USG of Charles Depasseau and two others, "Delegates and members of the late Constitutional Convention of Louisiana of 1867–68"—AES, *ibid.*, RG 56, Collector of Customs Applications. "The petition of the undersigned Radical Republican citizens in the City of New Orleans, State of Louisiana; Represent that they opposed the nomination of H. C. Warmoth for Governor and State Ticket headed by him; made by a corrupt rotten Republican (so called) State Nominating Convention as well as the election thereof on the 17th and 18th of April 1868 and still oppose his venal and profligate administration and corrupt 'Ring' of pretended Republicans, enemies to equal rights, justice, reform, economy, retrenchment, and official integrity, of which said 'Ring,' said H. C. Warmoth is the chief tactician and official head, successor of official predecessors in said office since 1863, less conspicous in degree, but similar in action each and all professing more and better official conduct and Republicanism, but practically friends of the Union per se and a free white man's goverment with extravagance and waste less conspicuous, yet all have have proved little Andrew Johnson apostate's to true Republicanism, justice and honest men. . . . Now declaring and testifying our firm belief that W. R. Crane justly and truly enjoys and possesses the unbounded respect regard and confidence next to T. J. Durant of the entire colord population above and greater than any white Republican citizen as well official as ex-official in Louisiana representing or claiming to represent her in the councils of the nation or elsewhere and of all honest men of all parties, citizens and inhabitants thereof. And desiring to add from our personal knowledge our unbounded confidence that he possesses the requisite capacity, integrity, incorruptibility, intelligence and qualifications in addition to his sacrifices and services in the cause of justice, equal rights and his sincere and arduous labors therein and therefor and under a profound sense of our obligations our gratitude and our bounden duty to him for ourselves as well as the race we represent, as well as the cause of justice and philanthropy; We a few and as types of thousands of others whom we represent do sincerely beseach your Excellancy not to visit and inflict as has heretofore been done for the and in regard to civil-official positions and places neither a Copperhead, nor by his antecidents a comparative stranger to our population, but to appoint the said W. R. Crane Esq. to the office of Collector of Custums for the Port of New Orleans."—DS, *ibid.* No appointment followed.

1869, APRIL 22. U.S. Senator Lyman Trumbull of Ill. to USG. "John W. Smith Esq. of Springfield Ill, is a gentleman of high character & one of the most active & efficient Republicans of Sangamon Co. He was formerly Collector of Int. Rev. from which office he was removed by the late administration. He is not an applicant for any office that we are aware of but there are many places in which his energy, activity, & integrity might be of service to the government & we especially recommend him as fitted for some position of confidence & trust."—Copy, DLC-Lyman Trumbull.

1869, APRIL 23. USG note. "In the absence of the Sec. of the Navy, if absent, please call special attention of Adm.l Porter to the inclosed papers."—ANS, Kohns Collection, NN.

1869, APRIL 23. Secretary of War John A. Rawlins endorsement. "Respectfully forwarded to the President of the US."—ES, USG 3. Written on a letter of April 19 from Edward Hulbert, Atlanta, to Lt. Col. William M. Dunn. "PRIVATE. . . . Inclosed please find telegraphic notice of the death, *by assassination*, of Dr. Benjamin Ayer, Republican Representative in the Legislature from Jefferson County, Georgia. Dr Ayer was about 70 Years of age—an Unobtrusive, highly-intelligent Christian gentleman;—*a good man.* A few days before the adjournment of the Legislature, he remarked to me that he should return home, although he felt fully convinced that his life would be in danger; and that he would, in all probability, be *murdered;* 'Yet,' said he, 'I will do my duty, and leave the result with GOD!' This old, and really estimable gentleman, was one of the Republicans in Washington City when the following appeared in an Editorial in the New Era of this City: 'As a GRANT Republican we loathe these monsters in human shape, *and hope they may perish by the Wayside,* and that the State may never again be cursed by their presence.' *The italics are mine.* Thus has another good Union man fallen, ('PERISHED BY THE WAYSIDE',) a victim to the terrorism which is hunting Republicans to the death. Several members of the Legislature from the negro belt are here, not daring to return to their homes. How long, O LORD, *how long*, are the true Union men of Georgia to be thus hunted down, and mercilessly shot?"—LS, *ibid.* Dunn endorsed this letter. "Col. Hulbert (writer of the within) was Genl. Pope's Supt. of registration. He was the President of the first 'Grant Club,' organized in Georgia, and is now Supt. of the Western & Atlantic Rail Road."—AES, *ibid.* In 1869, Foster Blodgett wrote, probably to USG, regarding Ayer's murder and other outrages in Ga. and recommending that USG call a special session of Congress to protect loyal citizens.—William Evarts Benjamin Catalogue No. 42 (March, 1892), p. 4. See *Atlanta Constitution,* April 21, 22, 1869.

1869, APRIL 23. James Otis and Caspar T. Hopkins, San Francisco, to USG. "At a special meeting of the Chamber of Commerce of San Francisco this day holden the following memorial was unanimously adopted and ordered to be telegraphed to the President of the United States, . . . The chamber respectfully but urgently prays that Your Excellency will take such actions in the premises as will protect this coast and the country at large against the calamity of stopping at this juncture, the stoppage of the mint upon which the country depends for three fourths of its coin supply and upon which the coast is wholly dependent"—Telegram received (on April 26, 9:00 A.M.), DNA, RG 56, Letters Received from Congress; (press) *ibid.*, RG 107, Telegrams Collected (Bound). William A. Richardson, act. secretary of the treasury, endorsed this telegram. "Answer by Telegram as follows April 27th 1869 . . . The Commissions of the new Officers have not been issued & the mint will not be stopped at present."—AES, *ibid.*, RG 56, Letters Received from Congress.

1869, APRIL 23.   Isaac F. Quinby, Buffalo, to USG. "Please authorize
Judge Hall to correct clerical error in my commission by telegraph"—Tele-
gram received (at 1:20 P.M.), DNA, RG 107, Telegrams Collected
(Bound). On April 2, USG had nominated Quinby as marshal, Northern
District, N. Y.

1869, APRIL 24.   Secretary of the Navy Adolph E. Borie to USG. "I beg
leave to acknowledge the receipt of the papers in relation to Paymaster
Eldredge, signed by Rev'd H. Ward Beecher and others. I have to state for
your information the following facts: Paymaster Eldredge has been in
charge of the office of Purchasing Paymaster at New York for four years—
which is one year longer than the regulations of the Navy allow. He has
not been to sea since 1864. Paymaster Bradford, whose term of sea service
has expired, was detailed to relieve him. When Paymaster Eldredge received orders to turn over his duties to another officer he importuned the
Department with numerous letters from influential persons, which action,
he was told, was offensive to the Department. A General Order was issued to
prevent the bringing of such influence to bear on the Department, to which
Paymaster Eldredge has paid no attention. He has no claims whatever
upon the indulgence of the Department and it would be doing manifest
injustice to others and to the Government to retain him in his present position. The interests of the service require that he should vacate his present
office at as early a day as possible."—Copy, DNA, RG 45, Letters Sent to
the President. On July 24, Henry Ward Beecher, Brooklyn, wrote to USG.
"At West Point I spoke with you briefly respecting Paymaster Eldredge, &
you said that on returning to Washington, I might recall your attention to
the matter, by letter. On the 10th April, I addressed a request to you that
Paymaster Eldredge be allowed to retain his present position in New York,
. . . When he was appointed to New York, the place ~~was~~ was laboring under
a bad reputation   Upright & honorable business men refused to bid upon
government ~~contracts~~ proposals, and those who had sold goods made bitter
complaint of delays, and vexatious impositions, until it was a widespread
impression that no man could do business with government through this
department, without becoming partners in swindling the government. Under Mr Eldredge the service has regained its good name. Every suspicion
of connivance with fraud has passed away; . . . I had but two motives a
desire for the public good, and my personal pride that a personal friend,
and a member of my church, had set so laudable an example, in a responsible position which had been formerly used for selfish ends, & through
which the governmt had largely suffered.—In my conversation with you at
West Point, you gave me to understand what Admiral Porter meant by
saying that '*justice to the Government*' required Mr Eldredges removal—I
understood from you that Admiral Porter stated to you that Mr Eldredge
had been in the habit of holding back large sums of money, & tho' not dishonest, yet, using them to his advantage. Now, it is to this point that I beg

leave to put in an emphatic & indignant denial. . . ."—ALS, OFH. On July 30, Horace Porter wrote to Beecher. "I am directed by the President to acknowledge the receipt of your letter of the 24th inst, and to say that he has directed the Secretary of the Navy, to retain Paymaster Eldredge at his present station, if by so doing no injustice be done to other officers."— Copy, DLC-David D. Porter. On Aug. 3, Vice Admiral David D. Porter wrote to USG. "In the absence of the Secretary of the Navy, the papers of Paymaster Eldredge came to me. He claims to remain a longer time in the office of Paymaster at New York after receiving official notice of his detachment from the Secretary of the Navy. His successor has been ordered home from the Mediterranean to relieve him and may be expected at any moment. I have read Mr Beecher's letter in which he rather calls in question my statement in regard to Paymaster Eldredge, . . . Mr Eldredge came on to see the Secretary of the Navy, Mr Borie, and as the latter was absent he stated his case to me shewing me many letters of recommendation from persons outside the Navy, urging his retention in office. This was in violation of a positive order of the Department forbidding officers from using outside influence in matters relating to duty. When told by me that he had a large amount of money on hand and that it must be deposited to the credit of Contingent Navy, Mr Eldredge asked for a month's time in which to deposit the funds, saying that he did not know to what appropriations the money belonged in. This statement did not agree with his summary statement of receipts and expenditures, which gave the items of appropriations and it was from this that the Department discovered that monies to a large amount had remained in Mr Eldredge's hands for so long a time as four years. His asking for an extension of time was a very unusual course for an officer to pursue as all Paymasters should be ready to pay over government funds at a moment's notice when called upon to do so. The communication of the Department directed Mr Eldredge to pay the money into the treasury, and from the fact that he asked an extension of time to get the fund out of his hands, he could not have complied with the law which requires that all Paymasters shall keep the government funds in the nearest sub treasury. . . . I trust Sir, for the sake of the service that you will not accede to Mr Eldredge's exhorbitant claims. It would be establishing a precedent that would result in injury to the Navy. In my opinion the public interests and the discipline of the service require that Paymaster Eldredge be detached from his present duty."—Copy, DNA, RG 45, Confidential Letters Sent. On Aug. 27, Beecher, Peekskill, N. Y., wrote to USG. "In reply to your order dated, July 30th I have received from the Navy Department, a copy of a reply from Admiral Porter, in which reply he makes a charge against Mr Eldredge which if true, should ~~cha~~ cashier him, & which if not true, should make a gentleman's cheek tingle, for having ignorantly brought it against an honest man. I enclose the statement of Paymaster Eldredge, in which, it will be perceived, he shews by documents, that Admiral Porter's statement, that he asked for a month's time to make a transfer of money in his hand, was simply absurd—as the money was not, nor had ever been, in his hands, but was all the time, & always in the sub treasury—Is it against me, or against Mr Eldredge that admiral Porter has a grudge? . . ."—ALS, DLC-David D. Porter. The enclosure is *ibid.*

1869, APRIL 24. William Finkler, Augsburg, to USG. "Permit me to adress you still as General and not as President, because I know that General Grant never will forget his old comrades, who were with him during the darkest, but also the glorioust time of the war. You will recollect that during the siege of Vicksburg, I was Assistant to Colonel Bingham and afterwards Depot Qr Mstr there. I remained in the service until may 1865 when I was compelled to resign on account of ill health. To restore my health and to have my four motherless children educated, (my wife died in Vicksburg) I went to my relations in Germany.—Since that time I am residing in the city of Augsburg: my health has been restored and I could return to my home, Milwaukie Wisc. if I would interrupt the education of my sons. . . . My respectfull solicitation therefore on General Grant is, to implore the President to have the undersigned appointed as consul for the city of Augsburg.—"—ALS, DNA, RG 59, Letters of Application and Recommendation. Related papers are *ibid.* On Dec. 8, 1874, USG nominated Finkler as consul, Ghent; on Feb. 25, 1875, he withdrew this nomination.

1869, APRIL 24. U.S. Senator George H. Williams of Ore. to USG. "Allow me to ask of you the personal favor of giving Mr. Mercer of Oregon an inteview at your earliest convenience, as to the question of emigration to the Pacific Coast. He is thoroughly posted in all that relates to this subject, and his statements are entirely reliable. At the present time he has a proposition before the Secretary of War asking the transfer of two or three Government transports to the Pacific with the privilege to him of filling them with emigrants for Oregon. The expense to the Government will be trifling, and in my opinion the movement will be a wise one in a military point of view, there being no Quarter Master's Steamers on that side. With the hope that you may find time to see Mr. Mercer, and give him the necessary order, . . ."—ALS, DNA, RG 107, Letters Received, M183 1869. See *PUSG*, 15, 595–96.

1869, APRIL 25. Emanuel Smith, Apalachicola, Fla., to USG. "Excuse the liberty I take in addressing you on business matter. I desire the appointment of *Weigher & Gayager* of this port—Appalachicola Fla. I am a *Coulord man*, age forty two, with a fair English Education—During my days of Servatude I was employed in Marking & Branding cotton which gave me considerable experience in business matters. Our Representative Hon. Mr. Hamilton I presume has left Washington—is why I make direct application to you—Hoping to receive a favorable reply. . . ."—ALS, DNA, RG 56, Collector of Customs Applications. No appointment followed.

1869, APRIL 27.   Secretary of the Navy Adolph E. Borie to USG. "I respectfully request that the Executive files and records may be examined for
the purpose of ascertaining whether in March 1868, or the following April,
O. K. Bernbaum, late Acting Master in the Navy, made any, and if any,
what, application to the President under the Act of March 3, 1865, sec. 12,
relating to summary dismissals."—Copy, DNA, RG 45, Letters Sent to the
President. On July 15, Secretary of the Navy George M. Robeson wrote to
USG. "I have the honor to return the application of O. K. Bernbaum, late an
Acting Master in the Navy of the U. S., for a Court Martial, which has been
referred by you to this Department. After a careful examination of the case,
I beg leave to state that in my opinion, the request of Mr. Bernbaum should
not be granted"—Copy, *ibid.*

1869, APRIL 27.   Isadore Blumenthal, Washington, D. C., to USG. "I
have come from the State of Florida to see you on a matter concerning a
brother of mine. He has his hearth sett upon going to West Point to receive
from his adopted country a military education and he prays you that you
may appoint him from at large as a Cadet. He without flattery is a fine youth
19 years of Age, received his preliminary education at High School in
Segnitz Bavaria and if appointed by you I am certain will do credit to his
country. I failed to get an audience with you this morning and I am compelled to leave for New-York this evening on Business. It is seldom that a
youth of the jewish faith has any inclination for a millitary education but he
seems to be all military. He is now in this country about 3 years. His name
is Max Blumenthal and resides with me in Fernandina Fla   Please to consider this request of mine and that of my brother and afford him this opportunity. This matter alone has brought me to the Capitol and I am confident
if I could have seen you would have made a favorable impression on you. I
my self served during the war in the 24th Regt Ills Vols and have been engaged in the Lumber Business since the War in Fla.—Mr President. I would
feel greatly obliged to you if you would inform me by letter to New-York
care Heckess—Forchheimer 472 Broadway your pleasure in the matter so
I may know what steps to take to secure for him a military schooling.—"—
ALS, DNA, RG 94, Unsuccessful Cadet Applications.

1869, APRIL 27.   B. A. M. Froiseth, Washington, D. C., to USG. "I have
the honor to enclose herewith a copy of the Daily Skandinavisk Post' of
New York City, together with a translation of two Editorial articles which
appeared in the same on the 22nd inst which will speak for itself   I wish to
call your attention to the fact that this is the only Daily paper printed in the
Scandinavian language that is published in this Country and representing
a population of over one million souls; it is therefore not deemed inappropriate to call the attention of the Executive to the fact in order that such
public Advertisments as can be given with propriety may be extended to
it, especially the publication of the Laws of this Country, of interest equally
to the Scandinavian population as that of any other people. Trusting that

you will see the propriety of extending to the *Post* a fair share of the public Advertisements and gave direction for the same . . ."—ALS, DNA, RG 59, Miscellaneous Letters. Enclosures are *ibid.* See Secretary of State Hamilton Fish to Froiseth, May 5, and Froiseth to Edward McPherson, May 8, in DLC-Edward McPherson.

1869, APRIL 27. John T. Jenkins, New Brunswick, N. J., to USG. "*Strictly Confidential.* . . . I have seen that the appointment of J Holmes Grover of South Carolina has been ~~appointed and~~ Confirmed by the Senate as U S Consul. This J Holmes Grover is a native of this place and has resided here or in Philadelphia, where he was in the state business for a time, since which time and up to within a year he has been exhibiting himself as an Irish Comedian. The love and respect I have my Country and the regard I have for You, and the desire for your success in the high place Your people has placed You, induces me to beg you to have an interview with the Consul, that you may test his qualities before he sails."—ALS, DNA, RG 59, Letters of Application and Recommendation. Related papers are *ibid.* On April 15, USG had nominated J. Holmes Grover as consul, Ancona. See *New York Times,* Jan. 19, 1879.

1869, APRIL 28. Horace Porter to J. C. Bancroft Davis, asst. secretary of state. "I am directed by the President to request a copy of the Spanish proclamation of neutrality between the Federal and Confederate States of America, of June 1861; also, of Carl Schurz' dispatch to Secretary Seward on the subject and Secretary Seward's reply."—LS, DNA, RG 59, Miscellaneous Letters.

1869, APRIL 29. William Cullen Bryant, New York City, to USG. "Allow me to give my testimony in favor of the merits and qualifications of Alfred B. Street Esq. whose friends have applied for his appointment as Surveyor of the port of Albany in this state. Mr. Street is a man of excellent personal character, of no little distinction as a man of letters, educated to the bar, and for twenty years Librarian of the State Library at Albany. He is in all respects competent to the duties of the office, and it could not be given to a worthier or more upright man. I learn that his appointment is supported by such men as Senator Sumner, Lyman Tremain; Thomas W. Olcott, George William Curtis, H. Greeley and Mr. Harris of the U. S. Senate. Mr. Street was a warm friend of the Union during the war and his martial songs were read all over the country. I sincerely hope, that he will recieve the appointment."—ALS, ViU.

1869, APRIL 29. Edwin D. Morgan, New York City, to USG. "If in looking for a suitable man for any place abroad, of responsibility and importance, your mind should be directed to John Bigelow our late Minister in France, You will I am sure find an excellent Diplomatist, and a careful and prudent man. I have no authority for saying that such an appointment, would gratify some other men, that you would be glad to please, yet in a conversation a day or two since, with the Senior Editor of the Evening Post, Mr Bryant, I found that he entertained the same opinion, as myself concerning Mr Bigelow's eminent fitness for a Foreign Mission—"—ALS, DNA, RG 59, Letters of Application and Recommendation. No appointment followed.

1869, APRIL 30. Horace Porter to Moses H. Grinnell, collector of customs, New York City. "The President directs me to state that the bearer Edward Fitzgerald, served faithfully through the war as a soldier in the General's bodyguard & during a portion of the time as his personal orderly— He can commend him to you as a very deserving person—"—Copies, DLC-USG, II, 1, 4.

1869, APRIL 30. Henry Boehm, Jersey City, to USG. "It will be a gratification, & personal favor to me, if you will appoint Cadet to West Point, Charles H. Cragin son of Dr Cragin of Georgetown D. C. I met the great Grandfather of the young man, some time in 1790, his name was Henry Foxall, he had a Foundery in Philadelphia, for the purpose of making Cannon for the government, Robert Morriss was connected with him I think In the early part of 1800 he (Mr Foxall) went to washington for the same purpose, was the friend of Jeffersons &c &c. In 1813 the writer was present at the marriage of Mr Foxalls only Daughter, the Grandmother of the young man, the ceremony performed by Bishop Asbury who was a dear friend in the family—Mr Foxall built & gave to the M. E. Church, the Foundery M. E. Church in washington, & was in all respects a great friend to his adopted country. Mr Foxall & Mr Renshaw (Wrenshall) (the latter Grandfather of Mrs Grant I believe) came over together from England, & were warm personal friends to each other & to myself—May God guide you, & bless you in your trying position is the prayer of your friend"—ALS, DNA, RG 94, Correspondence, USMA. USG endorsed the envelope. "Call spl. attentn to this when apts. come to be made"—AE (initialed), *ibid.* Charles H. Cragin did not attend USMA.

1869, APRIL 30. Chaw-kan-dais, Centralia, Wis., to USG. "Be it known, That I, Chaw-kan-dais, the oldest son of the late chief Way-me-gis-e-co, deceased, of the chippewa tribe of Indians, (from which his Portrait or likeness, is to be seen in one of the rooms in the House of assembly, at Madison, It having been presented to the State of Wisconsin, by the late Solomon Juneau.) I Chaw-kan-dais, do represents (in the name of said chippewa tribe of Indians) that a certain person by the name of Johnston surnamed by the Indians Wosh-ka-bo, residing at Lake Shawayno. Said Johnston, being Interpreter to the Menominee tribe, of Indians, with an associate of the same tribe named Weikaye, they both intend to proceed to Washinton D. C. with a petition, to be presented to our Great Father the President, so that he may stop our annual payment from our land sold to the Government of the United States of America, some years ago. My father Way-me-gis-e-co, was at the time, Head chief of the chippewa, Menominee, and Potowahtomie tribes of Indians, when the treaty was made, concluded and signed by both parties. The oldest men of our tribe cannot exactly name the year, the treaty was made—but recollects that the annual payments were to be paid and agreed to for Three generations to come. The last annual payment made to the chippewas, was in 1836, at Chicago Ills. As near as they can remember, was the 20th annual payment, which would bring the treaty made with the Government, at or about the year 1816— . . . In this last war, many of us, were in your Army and helped you all we could fighting for the Union, and we shall be ready at any time you want us. Therefore we hope you will take our interest, so that we may hereafter receive our annual payments if proved fairly due to us. In being informed by our Great Father the President the result in this case, I shall (in behalf of my brothers chippewa) ever pray &: . . . P. S, Please address me care of Eugene A. Juneau Centralia Wood Co. Wisconsin"—L (signed by mark), DNA, RG 75, Letters Received, Chippewa Agency. See *HED*, 41-2-1, part 3, pp. 874–75.

1869, APRIL 30.   James L. Crane, Springfield, Ill., to U.S. Senator Richard Yates of Ill. "More than a week ago I wrote a letter to Genl. Grant through you asking for an appointment to a foreign mission, & mentioned either Switzerland or Belgium. I thought as Grant had indicated ~~the~~ in the Postoffice matter that he was willing to confer upon me something of the kind I felt that I might, without impropriety, ask for *something*. . . . I had a talk with Cullom yesterday in regard to the Postoffice here. He tried to fix the affair up smooth on his side. He made his boast that he had made Grant break all the promises he had made, where said promises conflicted with his (Cullom's) arranged plans. Let me hear from you at your Earliest Convenience If you have a favorable opportunity, ask Grant if there is any chance, or probability of ~~Changing~~ moving Keyes from the P. O. From what I can see here Keyes is quite unpopular Three fourths of the Republicans in this city would have prefered me to Keyes. Numbers called upon me & so expressed ~~himself~~ themselves to me."—ALS, DNA, RG 59, Letters of Application and Recommendation. On March 31, USG had nominated Isaac Keys as postmaster, Springfield; on Dec. 6, USG nominated Crane for this position to replace Keys.

1869, APRIL 30.   B. F. Sanford, Covington, Ky., to USG. "(private) . . . Having understood that it was your intention to make a change in the Collector of Customs Savannah, Ga. I have herewith made formal application for the office named. Appended to my application is the recommend of your father whom I have known intimately for many years as well as the other members of your father's family. Although I have never had the pleasure of a personal acquaintance with yourself. . . ."—ALS, DNA, RG 56, Collector of Customs Applications. Jesse Root Grant endorsed a letter of April

29 from Sanford to USG. "I have been intimatly acquainted with Mr Sandford for 14 years, and know him to be a man of good business qualifycations of unexceptionable habits, and every way strictly reliable"—AES, *ibid.* No appointment followed.

1869, APRIL 30. Thomas Webster and five others, Union League House, Philadelphia, to USG. "The Committee which organized the grand demonstration of this community in favor of suffering Cuba instruct us to inform you that the meeting has been marked by unbounded enthusiasm. There is much congratulation among all shades of both parties. Universal faith is centered in you Please see papers"—Telegram received (on May 1, 9:15 A.M.), DNA, RG 107, Telegrams Collected (Bound).

1869, [APRIL]. USG endorsement. "Now applies for the place of appraiser of Merchandise in New York City. Refer to Sec of the Treas."—AE (docketed as received on April 28), DNA, RG 56, Appraiser of Customs Applications. Written on a letter of March 27 from T. Dean, New York City, to USG. "I am informed that the friends of Col. J. A. Bridgland are intending to ask of you his appointment to the office of Collector of Internal Revenue in the 32d District—New York. I am in no sense a politician and know but little of the machinery and appliances used in this matter of obtaining office, As a business man and large tax payer, I am deeply interested in having good, honest and competent men placed in office, Without such men, all your good intentions and admirable purposes, to faithfully collect the revenues, and put an end to the wholesale plundering of the Treasury, which has characterized the past three or four years, must fail, So cunning & powerful have the plundering rings become, it is absolutely necessary to place in the prominent offices, such as that of the 32nd District of N. Y., men who are not only *honest*, but those who possess a *thorough knowledge of men*, with energy and executive ability, in addition to honesty— . . ."— LS, *ibid.* On April 20, Henry J. Raymond, *New York Times*, telegraphed to USG. "Confidence in the integrity and merit of Mr McElrath is universal. Nobody here doubts it, politically and personally no objections can be urged against him, His retention as Appraiser would please all our friends and the public at large"—Telegram received (at 4:30 P.M.), *ibid.*, RG 107, Telegrams Collected (Bound). On the same day, USG nominated Thomas McElrath as appraiser, New York City, in place of Charles A. Dana, who had refused the office.

1869, APRIL. USG endorsement. "I have no objection to Pile going to Brazil."—AE (initialed), DNA, RG 59, Letters of Application and Recommendation. Written on a telegram of April 9 from E. W. Fox *et al.*, St. Louis, to USG. "The undersigned having entire confidence in the ability uprightness and fidelity to public interest, of Gen W. A. Pile most respectfully yet earnestly request his appointment as minister to Brazil. We believe his appointment would greatly facilitate in development the Commercial intercourse and trade of Brazil with the Mississippi valley which was destroyed by the war"—Telegram received (on April 10, 9:00 A.M.), *ibid.*; *ibid.*, RG 107, Telegrams Collected (Bound). On April 12, USG nominated William A. Pile as minister to Venezuela, then withdrew the request and nominated him as minister to Brazil, but the U.S. Senate tabled the nomination. On April 22, Pile, Washington, D. C., telegraphed to USG. "Senators Schurz Harlan Pomeroy and others are confident of my confirmation by decided majority if no change is made in nomination"—Telegram received (at 11:50 A.M.), *ibid.* On Dec. 6, USG nominated Pile as governor, New Mexico Territory. On April 30, 1870, Pile, Santa Fé, wrote to USG. "I am informed that urgent representations are being made to you intended effect my removal. I do not know how much truth there is in these Statements nor the grounds of objection but they come to me from So many Sources I cannot longer disregard them I desire respectfully to State That removal now with expenses incurred in comeing here and losses involved in again moving my family, would *ruin* me financially and leave me in debt. If any representations are made affecting my party fealty I can; and desire an opportunity to refute them *fully* and *completely.* If such accusations are based on movement in this Territory to form a State goverment I can establish beyond question that Such movement only contemplated uniting all the friends of the movement in its favor; *and no* sacrifice of *principle* or *division* of Offices. I distinctly announced to the 'State Central Committee' and all with whom I conversed that the moment either of these things were attempted I should withdraw and oppose the whole thing I refer to this for the reason that I can think of nothing else upon which accusations against me can be founded I *earnestly request* that *no* adverse conclusions be reached nor action taken until I can be heard Thanking you for uniform Kindness . . ."—ALS, *ibid.*, RG 59, New Mexico Territorial Papers. On Sept. 25, Pile wrote to USG explaining that opposition from Alexander P. Sullivan, editor, *Santa Fe Post,* "commenced when I declined to interfere in the matter of his removal for opposition to the Indian policy of your administration and the incendiary character of his editorials: and has continued with great bitterness to the present time. He is an adventurer seeking to establish a '*paper*' but does not represent the Republican party in the Territory. All the party conventions since its establishment have ignored his paper. No Republican of character in the Territory so far as I know joins him in this opposition. In reference to the allegations said to be urged upon your consideration as grounds for my removal, I only desire to say 1st The Attorney Genl of this Territory although a rebel officer, has acted with the Republican party since its close—supports earnestly your administration and moreover is the only Republican lawyer in the Territory (not a whiskey) bloat) who understands the Spanish language and will take the office. He is a good *efficient* officer. 2nd While it is true that Mr Bond made a mistake in selling some old Papers without properly assorting them it is also true that he has put the Library in better condition and keeps it better than ever before in the history of the Territory 3d. The accusation of unfaithfulness to the party I pronounce a base falsehood. I always announced in committee and out of it that if the Democrats would not unite with us for a Slate on a clean republican ticket that we must run two tickets and if a joint ticket was attempted I should withdraw and oppose the whole thing. If this is doubted abundant proof will be furnished. 4th I have had nothing to do with Missouri Politics since I left the State. I have believed for years that sound *party policy* and the interest of the whole Country alike demand the renfranchisement of *all* disfranchised Classes of our Citizens. Whether the so called '*Missouri bolters*' had justifiable cause for their action is quite another Question. With reference to that point I have expressed no opinion further than to express surprise at and disapprobation of their failure to endorse your administraiton. I may have erred in allowing my name to be used in reference to the Peña Blanca convention, and I certainly committed a personal indiscretion in the Heath affair, and for all seeming want of deference to you (I assure you none was intended) I beg your pardon. I have remained constantly in the Territory attending to my official duties. and Respectfully claim that my administation has made a marked improvement in the affairs of the Territory. I am just commencing to save something from my Salary with which I am paying off previous obligations. I desire to come to Washington for the purpose of confering with you about public matters, and if after such conference my continuance in office is not entirely satisfactory to you I shall at once resign. I have telegraphed the Secretary of State asking a leave of absence."—Typescript, USGA. On May 18, 1871, USG nominated Pile as minister to Venezuela.

1869, [APRIL].   USG endorsement. "Refered to the Sec. of State. McC. was a Col. of Cav. during the rebellion, and a very good man."—AE (initialed), DNA, RG 59, Letters of Application and Recommendation. Written on a letter of March 26 from La Fayette McCrillis, Grafton, Ill., to Charles E. Hovey. "If you can not secure to me the appointment of the Counsulership to Rio Janeiro, Strike for that of New Zealand—If you can see President Grant yourself he will do something for me,—he knows he has never had a better or truer friend, than I have been to him during the whole war and since. 'Dont give up the ship' you will win in the end"— ALS, *ibid.* Related papers are *ibid.* No appointment followed.

1869, [APRIL].   USG note. "Refer to State Dept."—AN (initialed), DNA, RG 59, Letters of Application and Recommendation. Written to accompany a petition of Michael Hahn *et al.* "We, the undersigned citizens of Louisiana, at present sojourning in Washington, having learned that the Hon. Michel Vidal, recently a member of Congress from our State, is an applicant for the mission to Constantinople, or an appointment as Consul, do most respectfully and urgently request that his application will receive the most favorable consideration. Mr. Vidal is a gentleman of education and refinement, speaks and writes several languages fluently and correctly. His appointment will reflect credit on the government, and meet with the hearty approval of every republican in Louisiana."—DS (15 signatures), *ibid.* Related papers are *ibid.* On March 25, 1870, USG nominated Michel Vidal as consul, Tripoli.

[1869, APRIL]. John Boyle *et al.* to USG. "We whose names appear below would most respectfully request your Excellency to appoint Col. Jackson M. Sheets of Paris Illinois, Consul Resident at either Melbourne, Australia, Bueonas Ayres, or Valparaiso Chilli South America—"—DS (13 signatures), DNA, RG 59, Letters of Application and Recommendation. On April 7, U.S. Senator Richard Yates of Ill. wrote to Secretary of State Hamilton Fish. ". . . Genl Sheets was a member of the President's regiment of Ills troops, and no man in the service, did more faithful service. He is brave, intelligent and earnest, and was wounded almost unto death for our salvation—The President made request that the Genls papers should come before him through your office, and I beg of you this favor in his behalf"— ALS, *ibid.* On Dec. 7, 1870, USG nominated Jackson M. Sheets as postmaster, Paris, Ill.

[1869, APRIL]. Mrs. C. B. Lasell, Orange, N. J., to USG. "I would like very much to have my husband appointed—minister to Greece. My father is the Revd Jonas King. I have not the means of visiting my home unless you can do this favor for me—We are no politicians, & never intend to be, but have always been Republicans Senator Hamlin can tell you who, The Lasells are as his daughters were at one time under Mr. Josiah Lasells charge. One favor please grant me. If you decide negatively let me know it soon so that I may not be hoping."—ALS, DNA, RG 59, Letters of Application and Recommendation. A related letter is *ibid.* No appointment followed.

1869, MAY 1. Horace Porter to Secretary of War John A. Rawlins. "The President requests that Bvt Major General S S. Carroll—Lt Col. 21st U S Infantry be appointed Governor of the Soldiers Home"—Copies, DLC-USG, II, 1, 4.

1869, MAY 1. Horace Porter to Joseph D. Webster, assessor of Internal Revenue, Chicago. "I am directed by the President to acknowledge the receipt of your letter of the 28th ult—, and to say that there is no particular individual he desires to have appointed in your office but hopes that in your selections you will give the preference to disabled soldiers where they are found competent."—Copies, DLC-USG, II, 1, 4.

1869, MAY 1. Jerôme Fischer, Aarau, Switzerland, to USG seeking financial assistance to patent and manufacture an ironclad artillery wagon.— ALS (in German), DNA, RG 156, Correspondence Concerning Inventions.

1869, MAY 1.   Justus McKinstry, St. Louis, to USG. "The proceedings
of the Court Martial before which I was tried in the autumn of 1862 upon
a charge of 'Neglect and violation of duty to the prejudice of good order
and military discipline' is a part of the history of the late war. The operations of the army of the United States—especially its organization and
movements in the Department of the West in the early stage of the rebellion,
came in review during the progress of that protracted trial.—You have personal knowledge of the disturbed and peculiar condition of affairs in this
Department at the inception of the rebellion—therefore I need not stop to
narrate in detail the peculiar embarrassing difficulties which then surrounded me and which I encountered at every step in the discharge of my
duties as Chief Quarter Master in this Department—Discord and Excitement ruled the hour.—The exigency of the public service devolved upon
me not only incessant labor, but also duties of the gravest character. The
testimony adduced in the course of my trial showed with what zeal and
ability I discharged the duties of my office. It would tax your time and patience too much were I to attempt any thing like a review of that evidence—
I content myself with a reference to the Record of it. Although several
months intervened from the time I was placed in arrest and the Convening
of the Court Martial, the discord, strife and contention, so wide spread at
the inception of the war, had not passed away, when I was placed at the bar
of the Court and then for the first time I was informed of the charge against
me. This was the condition of things and such were the surroundings of
the Court during the time of the trial. Time and cool reflection have demon-
strated, that I became the victim of prejudice as well as of influences, which
were exerted against me—partly of a personal, partly of a political character to accomplish ulterior purposes. In support of this statement, I refer
you to the record of the evidence and to the finding of the Court Martial. I
challenge the most critical examination of that evidence to find one jot of
proof, which reflects upon my honor or integrity. I may have erred in
judgment, but you will search in vain through that voluminous record for
proof which reproaches me with dishonor or dishonesty. I have the satisfaction to refer you also to the opinion of the Court of Claims in the case of
Child, Pratt & Fox vs the United States, lately decided by that Court. In
the trial of that case the whole ground was reviewed and the most important
portions of the same evidence was heard, that occupied the attention of the
Court Martial during the time I was on trial. The opinion of the Court of
Claims in the case referred to, is a full and complete vindication of my
official conduct. I take the liberty of placing before you a copy of the Record
in the case of Childs, Pratt & Fox and a copy of the opinion of the Court,
which reviews the testimony in connection with the manner I discharged
my duties as Quarter Master. The record of the War Department will show
you, how many years I was in the public service and the reminiscences of
the Army will disclose the manner I performed my duties—both in time of
peace and in war. Conscious of my own innocence and my conduct having

been vindicated in the manner before mentioned, I appeal to you and to your sense of justice and ask to be re-instated in the Army of the United States."—ALS, DNA, RG 94, Letters Received, G508 1861. Numerous letters to USG requesting McKinstry's reinstatement are *ibid.*; *ibid.*, ACP, 1959 1872. No action followed.

1869, MAY 3.   George W. Howland, Fort McPherson, Neb., to USG. "Having been retired by a Board of Officers as announced in Special Orders No 82. Dated April 8th 1869. HdQrs Army; I would respectfully solicit your patient perusal of my statement and position, And hope that it may result in your favorable reconsideration of my case, with the view of having me reinstated in the Army at an early day. I was arraigned for habitual intoxication, and though I do not deny having induldged, but not to excess, still I did not do so to a greater extent, than by the Officers who appeared against me. . . ."—ALS, DNA, RG 94, Letters Received, 320H 1869. On Dec. 6, USG nominated Howland as postmaster, Santa Fé.

1869, MAY 4.   James H. Markell, York, Pa., to USG. "Excuse my liberty in thus addressing you but I am in great need of aid for myself and family and can not help it. When the Rebbelion broke out I was a citizen of Winchester Virginia and belonging to a Volunteer Company was ordered to Harpers Ferry much against my will, but Seeing I could do no better I determined to go and make the best of a bad bargain, and so I went and after being in the rebel service a short time I deserted at the first opportunity and came to Baltimore where I stayed without even being enrolled for the draft but on coming to Gettesburg I was enolled for the draft of 18 and drafted and not being disposed to risk my chances in the Union Army after deserting the rebels I had to pay the three hundred dollars even in the face of ample proof which I had to show that I was a deserter from the rebel Army besides ample proof of my loyalty which it will give me great pleasure to show any time. as well as important information which I gave President Lincoln in regard to affairs at Harpers Ferry a short time before I went there with the rebel Army. Being in great need of aid for myself and family I hereby most respectfully petition His Excellency for the return of the three hundred dollars which I paid for said draft beleiving that when His Excellency takes a fair and impartial view, will order its return immediately. . . ."—ALS, DNA, RG 110, Enrollment Div., Letters Received.

1869, MAY 4.   Thomas P. Robb, collector of customs, and John Milledge, U.S. attorney, Savannah, to USG. "I am receiving numerous communications by telegraph from candidates for the position of Postmaster at Savannah requesting my influence in their behalf, therefore please pardon this liberty. If the Postmaster General finds it difficult to decide between the different candidates pressed upon him, allow me to recommend Judge George D. Dees now assistant Postmaster here. I have known him for many years intimately   He is capable and trustworthy and honest to a fault. His appointment would be joyfully hailed by the whole community here both colored and white of all parties, and would add great strength and popularity to your Administration in South western Georgia and Florida."— Telegram received (at 12:30 P.M.), DNA, RG 107, Telegrams Collected (Bound). On May 17, Cyrus K. Osgood, Savannah, telegraphed to USG. "A petition of citizens will be forwarded tomorrow urging my appointment as Postmaster"—Telegram received (at 2:15 P.M.), *ibid.* On Dec. 6, USG nominated Walter L. Clift to replace Robb as postmaster, Savannah; on Feb. 15, 1871, USG nominated Osgood as postmaster in place of Clift.

1869, MAY 5.   Caleb H. Blood, Brownsville, Tex., to USG. "Permit me to tender to you, my only son, Daniel R. Blood, now at New London Institute N. H. fitted for college, eighteen yrs old last Oct a stedy, well grown Boy, a member of the church, stands at the head of his class, He has made his selectiontion to be a soldier, for years, has asked my consent to go to *West Point.* I yield to his wishes, feeling he will be an honor to the service, Shall he be appointed (this Spring) I was a persecuted Refugee from Fla 1861, U. S. Consul to Monterey Mexico 1862—contributed about $4000.— in raising 1. & 2d Texas Regt's U. S. Vols 1863 & 4 Am robbed, and left poor by the late Wicked Rebellion— . . ."—ALS, DNA, RG 94, Unsuccessful Cadet Applications.

1869, MAY 5.   George Francis Train, New York City, to USG. "The Government stopped the Fenians on the Canadian Frontier I demand in the name of one million 100,0000 Irish voters that you send a fast war steamer to seize the Cuban Fillibuster which sailed yesterday. The Expedition is an English intrigue to checkmate Irelands freedom The Cuban Mass meeting was a Tammany officer in English interest."—Telegram received (at 3:20 P.M.), DNA, RG 107, Telegrams Collected (Bound). See Willis Thornton, *The Nine Lives of Citizen Train* (New York, 1948), pp. 194–95.

1869, MAY [6].   USG endorsement. "Reappoint Alex. H. Adams Pension Agt. and apt Goodloe Mail Agt. for Ky."—AE, IHi. Written on a telegram of May 6 from William O. Goodloe, Lexington, Ky., to Alexander H. Adams, Washington, D. C. "I agree to your proposition Make it sure Answer"—Telegram received, *ibid.* On Aug. 1, Goodloe was listed as special agent, Post Office Dept., Lexington.

1869, MAY 6.   Walbridge A. Field, act. attorney gen., to USG. "I have examined the petition of Sophia E., Alexander. and Amelia C. Robinson, of Cook Co., Ill., which you were pleased to refer to this office on the 4th inst. The petitioners represent that they are the heirs of Alexander Robinson, deceased, an Indian reservee, under the Treaty of July 29, 1829, (.7 Stat. 321,) according to the provisions whereof the lands to which they have succeeded cannot be alienated without the permission of the President; and the object of their application is to obtain such permission to make a conveyance of part of the property in trust to secure a loan to them of $1000, which they desire to employ in building. I perceive no objection to the scheme proposed, and recommend that permission be granted in accordance with the request—which may be done by merely signing your name under the endorsement written on the back of the petition."—ALS, DNA, RG 60, Letters Sent.

1869, MAY 7. Frederick Eaton, Toledo, to USG. "I notice by the papers that Nunn of Tennessee declines mission to Ecuador My brother, General Eaton is risking everything for that State, Has incurred debts, injured his health Friends in Ohio New England and Tennessee have written and seen him for permission to present his name for some appointment but he is so absorbed in saving affairs there that he does not consent. I take the liberty to suggest you could give the appointment to no more devoted friend there and after the crisis in Tennessee is passed we may induce him to accept particularly should a useful place like that at Constantinople be offered him"—Telegram received (on May 8, 9:20 A.M.), DNA, RG 59, Letters of Application and Recommendation. On Jan. 27, 1870, USG nominated John Eaton, Jr., as commissioner of education. See *PUSG*, 15, 463–64; John Eaton, *Grant, Lincoln and the Freedmen* (1907; reprinted, New York, 1969), pp. 248–50, 258–59.

1869, MAY 8. James W. Taylor, St. Paul, to USG. "Although slavery, the great cause of sectional strife, is abolished, still you will find it expedient to guard against future dissensions of a sectional character. Something like an equilibrium of sections will be the best assurance of national harmony. The North and West cannot be indifferent to the indications of territorial expansion beyond the Southern frontier. If these lead to results, the Republican party will expect the most vigilant and determined measures for the acquisition of territory on the North—especially the interval between Minnesota and Alaska. The newspapers propose the annexation of Canada. Although in 1866 Gen Banks presented a bill, drawn by me, for the voluntary admission of the English Provinces as States and Territories; still I am not sanguine that the Confederation has run its course. The annexation of the Eastern Provinces can hardly usher your administration, although it may be consummated before your retirement from the Presidency. Not so, I submit, with the British Territory west of the Great Lakes. As to Selkirk, Saskatchewan and Columbia—the great grain and mineral districts northwest of Minnesota—these few months of 1869 present the golden opportunity for its peaceful acquisition. I entreat your attention to a few reasons for this opinion. . . ."—ALS, DNA, RG 59, Miscellaneous Letters.

1869, MAY 10. To Ellsworth Zouaves, Co. A. "I have to acknowledge the receipt of the card of honorary membership of the Ellsworth Zouaves, and accept the same, with thanks."—*Chicago Times*, May 18, 1869.

1869, MAY 10.   Secretary of the Interior Jacob D. Cox to USG. "I have the honor to transmit, herewith, five copies of the Pamphlet laws of the 3d session of the 40th Congress—a small supply of those statutes having just been received at this Department."—LS, OFH.

1869, MAY 10.   Joseph E. Brown, Atlanta, to USG. "I do not know what representations interested parties may have made to you in reference to my position, with a view to prejudice your mind and secure to one extreme faction here the control of the appointmts for Georgia. I am as decided and determind a supporter as you have in Georgia, and my wish and aim is to build up a strong party in the state to sustain your adminstration. If those in authority with patronage in the state, would act with moderation and wisdom nothing is easier than to split the democratic party, made up of very antagonistic elements, and banded together on the single issue of opposition to reconstruction, and carry one wing of it to your support. As matters now stand with 45,000 majority of democrats the republican party can have no power or control, till the democrats are divided. Any person at all acquainted with political affairs must see this on a moments reflection. But unfortunately there is a faction of extreme ultra men in the republican party in this state, determind to rule or ruin, with no experience in the managemt of political affairs, and I fear but little love for any party longer than the spoils last; who seem bent on driving from the party now greatly in the minority, all the most conservative and best material of which it is composed; and who denounce evry one who wishs to split off a wing of the democracy, as in favor of a new party and an enemy to the present republican party. Thus far by misrepresentation detraction, and abuse of better men and truer republicans than themselves, they have secured for their extreme wing nearly all the appointmts for this state, and I will say that ~~three fourths~~ a majority of these appointees add not the influence of a dozen votes other than their own, to your support: and ~~none~~ never can if they remain years in office. I make these remarks in no spirit of fault finding, but as a friend who has had large experience in matters of this nature and who is well acquainted with the people of this state. I am no disappointed office seeker. I am no applicant for any place within your gift. My only ardent wish is to see your adminstration a triumphant success. I have no specal friend for whom I ask an office. But I want you to know the truth about matters here, and I write you plainly and without reserve, believg you prefer such a statement, to one of false flattery. One after another the heads of Conservative republicans fall in Georgia, and their places are filled by extreme men, who have neither influence nor experience to add any thing to the party. I have just heard today that efforts are being made to secure the removal of Col A N Wilson of Savannah and Col James Atkins of this City, both Collectors of internal Revenue. They are both men of moderate views but they are two of the most intelligent and influential republicans in Georgia. They are worth ~~the~~ to the party in future ~~in the state~~ more than the whole faction who now seek to destroy reconstruction in the State, and to resume military Governmt angry strife, and anarchy. I trust there is no foundation for this rumor, but their friends are alarmed judging from the faete of others of our truest and best men. Let me beg you to stop this movemt if it be on foot, and to give the moderate true and influential portion of the republcans at least some little share in the offices. I do not believe their removal will cause one of them to abandon the party, but you destroy their influence, and prejudice the popular mind against your admstration, by proscribing them. It is through the moderate wing alone that strength can be brought to the party from the democracy. Please pardon the plainess and frankness with which I have written, and accept assurances of my friendship and support . . ."—ALS, University of Georgia, Athens, Ga.

1869, MAY 10.   Samuel G. French, Greenville, Miss., to USG protesting Bvt. Maj. Gen. Adelbert Ames's suspension of the Miss. Board of Levee Commissioners.—ALS, DNA, RG 94, Letters Received, 142F 1869. On May 17, Horace Porter telegraphed to Ames. "Would it not be well to suspend order vacating the offices of Levee Commissioners 'till present high water recedes or successors to old Board are appointed."—Copy, DLC-USG, II, 5. On the same day, Ames telegraphed to Porter. "Successors to old board of Levee Commissioners have been appointed and qualified, river has fallen, no danger whatever.   fear misrepresentations have been made to you"—Telegram received (at 7:25 P.M.), DNA, RG 107, Telegrams Collected (Bound).

1869, MAY 10, NOON.   Leland Stanford, Thomas C. Durant, John Duff, and Sidney Dillon, Promontory Point, Utah Territory, to USG. "We have the honor to report that the last rail is laid. The last spike driven. The Pacific Railroad finished"—Telegram received (at 4:00 P.M.), DNA, RG 107, Telegrams Collected (Bound). On the same day, Grenville M. Dodge, Promontory Point, telegraphed to USG. "The time to which you have looked interested has today arrived,   It is now all rail across the Continent, It gives me great satisfaction that the work was completed during your administration"—Telegram received (at 8:30 P.M.), *ibid.* See Grenville M. Dodge, *How We Built The Union Pacific Railway and Other Railway Papers and Addresses* (n. d.; reprinted Denver, 1965), pp. 29–31.

1869, MAY 10.   B. F. Williams, El Paso, to USG. "In the dispair of the moment, I have resolved to address you personally upon a subject of the most vital interest to the oppressed people of this Country—The ends I have in view are those of justice and this is my apology for thus addressing you—There is a man holding the office of Collector of Customs at El Paso del Norte by the name of W. W. Mills—He has been charged with corruptions of the basest character, but still he holds his position—The frauds he may have committed do not effect the happiness of our people, but the terrible tyranny under which he rules this Country, as brought wretchedness, to hundreds of poor and defenseless people—He holds all civil and judicial officers of this Country in his hand—He controls even the decisions of Judges—All the property of this Country was illegally Confiscated during the war, and the Supreme Court of the United States have so decided—Yet Mills, who made our Judge controls him, and prevents poor and homeless people from getting the possession of property to which they are legally entitled. He has openly boasted that, he would continue to do this for years to come—We implore you to remove him from power, and to save us from this terrible future. We do not ask that any particular person be appointed in his stead—All we desire is to *be rid of him*, Certainly no change could be for the worse—I have known Genl. Longstreet well, and was his first and warmest supporter, when he in New Orleans, ~~when~~ announced himself your political friend and adherent—"—ALS, DNA, RG 56, Collector of Customs Applications. On April 15, USG had nominated Dwight C. Marsh as collector of customs, El Paso, to replace William W. Mills; on April 19, he withdrew this nomination; on Dec. 7, he renominated Marsh for this post.

1869, MAY 11. USG proclamation announcing the ratification of "an additional article to the convention for the surrender of criminals, between the United States and his Majesty the King of Italy."—(Printed), DNA, RG 84, Spain, Commercial Treaties, Conferences, and Conventions.

1869, MAY 11. Lt. Governor Oscar J. Dunn of La., New Orleans, to USG. "If the position of Minister to Liberia is not filled, the appointment of Capt James H Ingraham of this city would give satisfaction"—Telegram received (at 3:45 P.M.), DNA, RG 59, Letters of Application and Recommendation; (press) *ibid.*, RG 107, Telegrams Collected (Bound). On April 9, 1872, USG nominated James H. Ingraham as surveyor of customs, New Orleans.

1869, MAY 11. Montague S. Hasie, Vicksburg, to USG. "I would respectfully call your attention to the manner in which discharged Colored Soldier[s] entitled to bounty are imposed on in this city, it is a subject of common remark here—And the fact has become notorious, that a Soldier seldom leaves the Store where the bounties are paid with more than one third of his money. The manner in which it is done is known to but few outside of the ring which has been formed—for the purpose. but everyone knows it is done from the frequnt complants which are constantly made. The bounties are paid by B. A. Lee, Cashier of the Freedmens Bank which is situat[ed] in the back, part of the Store of G. M. Barber & [Co] after the Soldiers have signed their vouchers, and their money is here Mr. Lee refuses to pay the[m] putting them off, from time to time, but Mess G. M. Barber & Co. offer to relieve their necessities—by advancing them on their bounties, at 50. per cent most persons having $300—bounty due them seldom receive more than $200 in that way—And if a soldier refuses to accept of this he is

kept out of his money sometimes longer than Six months,   this poor soldier
is made drunk and evry other means employed, to cheat him out of his
bounty—Mr. Lee affords Mess Barber & Co the necessary facilities for collecting whatever they claim sometimes paying it over at once of B & Co.
These facts have been reported to the Bureau at Washington, but to my
knowledge no notice was taken of it—An investigation will fully substantiate this statement,   The appointment of an officer of the army, to the duty
of paying these bounties—would I think, be entirely satisfactory to all the
parties most interested, and remove the present evil. Hoping this will meet
with the prompt attention it merits . . ."—ALS, DNA, RG 105, Letters
Received. See *PUSG*, 2, 91, 126.

1869, MAY 11.   Lewis McKenzie, Alexandria, Va., to USG. "I hope you
will come down on the nine oclock boat in the morning to go up on a special
train on the Alexandria and Loud[o]n road to the Blue Ridge Mountains,
This train will leave as soon as you arrive,   Bring any Gentlemen or Ladies
along you desire,   Perhaps Mrs Grant would like the trip to the Catoctin
valley where you will see a splendid country,   Will have you back by five
or six oclock,   Reply yes or no."—Telegram received (at noon), DNA,
RG 107, Telegrams Collected (Bound). On the same day, 12:35 P.M.,
Horace Porter telegraphed to McKenzie. "The President will not be able to
accept your polite invitation."—Copy, DLC-USG, II, 5.

1869, MAY 11.   Hugh White, Cohoes, N. Y., to USG. "The Freed men of
the city of Palatka having solicited me to request the interposition of your
executive mercy in behalf of the man whome they elected Mayor of their
city during last month, but who is unable to qualify in casequence of disabilities incured during the Rellion, I do now cheerfully comply, and earnestly request the exercise of that clemency, which will enable Mr Henry
R Teasdale to qualify as Mayor of the city of Palatka Florida acording to
Law & usage as he is a good citizen, just & honorable, capable, & willing
to perform the duties of the Office of Mayor without prejudice or partiality
& is the best and most suitable individual in that city as well as the most
acceptable to the Loyal people in all the region around & about Palatka
The Offence for which He is disqualified was serving as an Officer in the
confederate army, which position he was compelled, against his better
judgement & wishes to adopt, in order to save his life & property but now
he desires to be honest & true, to the Loyal people of his city & State   I pray
your Excelency to grant this favour to the Freedmen & right Loyal people
of Palatka, and assure your Excelency that it will be an act of great utility,
& Service & well worth performing on account of the good & useful results
to flow therefrom."—ALS, DNA, RG 59, Miscellaneous Letters.

1869, MAY 12.   USG note. "Will the Sec. of the Treas. please see Col.
Ayers? I think he will make a good Supervisor for the dist. embracing Va

if none has yet been selected."—ANS, Doris Harris Autographs, Los Angeles, Calif. Ira Ayer served as special agent, U.S. Treasury. See *New York Times,* Feb. 4, 1903.

1869, MAY 12.   U.S. Delegate José Francisco Cháves of New Mexico Territory to USG. "I had the honor to recommend to you Judge Perry E. Brocchus for the position of Chief Justice of the Territory of New Mexico. I did so because, during a service of some years on the Bench of our Territory, he had commended himself to the confidence, respect, and affection of the public, as the ablest, most diligent and impartial Judge ever sent to preside over the Courts of New Mexico. Contrary to my earnest hope and confident expectation, he was not only not appointed Chief Justice, but was superseded as Associate Justice, a position which he had dignified and honored. This course was taken, as stated to me by Mr. Attorney General Hoar, solely on the ground of his absence from the Territory without leave. That absence was occasioned by the serious illness of one of his daughters, who had been in a critical condition of health for some months, as shown by certificate of her physician, which was on file in the office of the Attorney General at the time at which the name of his successor went to the Senate. —I regard it as my duty to trouble you with this statement, in justice to Judge Brocchus, whose official fidelity and exemplary private life have endeared him to the people of New Mexico. He has uniformly & cordially sympathized with the Republican party of our Territory and I desire that he may be properly known to you, as a gentleman in every way worthy of your confidence and esteem.—"—ALS, DNA, RG 60, Records Relating to Appointments. Related papers are *ibid.* No appointment followed.

1869, MAY 12.   James M. Smith, Charlottesville, Va., to USG seeking to regain property in Alexandria, Va., vacated during the Civil War and sold at an allegedly unconstitutional tax sale.—ALS, DNA, RG 107, Letters Received from Bureaus. Related papers are *ibid.*

1869, MAY 13.   USG note. "Please call special attention to this case when apts come to be made."—Copy, DNA, RG 94, Correspondence, USMA. Filed with a letter of April 17 from Charles E. Joyce, Washington, D. C., to USG. "I have the honor to apply for an appointment as a cadet 'at Large', to the Military Academy.—I would state that I entered the military service on the 21st of Sept 1861, as a drummer in the 88th N. Y. Vols, and served throughout the entire war; having been mustered out of service July 15th 1865. I am at present 22 years and 9 months of age, and am now employed as a detailed clerk in the Adjt Genls Office War Department. Of my immediate family, my Father and two brothers served in the army during the war,—the former dying of disease contracted in the service, and one of the latter (Capt Joyce 88 NY) was killed at the battle of Antietam. The attention of Your Excellency is invited to the enclosed recommendations"—

Copy, *ibid.* Related papers are *ibid.* Joyce did not attend USMA. On Feb. 27, 1874, Col. Nelson A. Miles, Fort Leavenworth, wrote to USG requesting Joyce's appointment as military storekeeper.—LS, *ibid.*, Applications for Positions in War Dept.

1869, MAY 13.   William G. Collier, Lincoln County, Ky., to USG protesting the seizure of his whiskey distillery for alleged internal revenue violations.—LS, DNA, RG 56, Letters Received.

1869, MAY 13.   William F. Harvey, Plainfield, Ind., to USG. "I take the liberty of saying to thee through this medium, that I am afraid that thou hast been wretchedly imposed upon by designing Quaker polititians, in a large number of the persons who have been recommended to thee for appointment as Indian agents; Now I want simply to say, give them a fair trial and if they fail to bring peace among the Indians, turn them out, and look to the west for persons to fill the places, but take none from any place, who do not belong to the regular *line* of Orthodox Friends, who are in regular correspondence with London Yearly Meeting, as the Mother Yearly Meeting. . . ."—ALS, DNA, RG 75, Letters Received, Miscellaneous.

1869, MAY 14.   U.S. Representative Jesse H. Moore of Ill., Decatur, to USG. "Allow me to ask you to appoint one of Rev. J. L. Crane's sons to West Point the ensuing Summer. You stated to me, I remember, when I was in Washington, the rule you expected to adopt in making your selections But I hope, *under the circumstances* You can conclude to accommodate Your Old Friend in this thing. Crane has five sons, promising boys they are, if they can be educated, But so large is his family and so limited his means that he is going to find it difficult to do all for them that he could desire in this direction. His oldest son Will, is now a little over sixteen, and a smart lad. Can you appoint him? May I hope to hear from you in reference to this application."—ALS, DNA, RG 94, Correspondence, USMA. William Crane did not attend USMA.

1869, MAY 14.   Alonzo V. Richards, Galena, to USG. "Herewith I have the honor to hand you a petition, in favor of my Brother. Perhaps you will remember his calling on you here just before you left. He is a good student, and I think would improve all the opportunities offered by a cadetship should you see fit to honor him with an appointment. I would most respectfully add my voice to the prayer of accompanying petition"—ALS, DNA, RG 94, Correspondence, USMA. On May 10, S. K. Miner and four others, Galena, petitioned USG to appoint William A. Richards to USMA.—DS, *ibid.* Richards did not attend USMA.

1869, MAY 15.   E. S. Barnes, Nebraska City, to USG announcing his patented ship propulsion mechanism.—ALS, DNA, RG 45, Letters Received from the President.

1869, MAY 17. USG endorsement. "Accepted,"—AES, DNA, RG 60, Applications and Recommendations. Written on a letter of May 12 from T. Lyle Dickey, Washington, D. C., to USG. "To carry out your suggestions to me on the subject—I ask leave to withdraw my immediate resignation heretofore tendered & now I tender to you—to take effect on the 1st day of December next—my resignation of the office of Assistant Attorney General—which I now hold—& ask that you accept the same. . . ."—ALS, *ibid.*

1869, MAY 17. Samuel A. Duncan, Grand Army of the Republic, Washington, D. C., to USG. "Saturday, the 29th inst., having been selected by the Grand Army of the Republic for the annual ceremony of decorating the graves of the Union soldiers and sailors who lie buried in the environs of the National Capital, I have the honor to ask that, if it be not inconsistent with the public interests, the day be made a public holiday for the officers and employés of the executive departments in Washington. It is believed that all whose hearts beat in sympathy with the Union cause during the late terrible war, and who now hold dear the memory of our patriot dead, will desire to participate in the beautiful and solemn ceremonies of this national anniversary. The course proposed will aid in this, will add new dignity to the occasion, and would seem a fitting recognition by the Head of the Nation of the illustrious virtues of those by whose dread sacrifice the Republic lives."—ALS, DNA, RG 59, Miscellaneous Letters. On May 18, Secretary of State Hamilton Fish endorsed this letter. "The President directs that the request of the within application be granted, & that each Department give the necessary order so far as relates thereto—An order will accordingly be made as to the Department of State"—AE (initialed), *ibid.* Copies were sent to other departments.

1869, MAY 17. John A. Parker, New York City, to USG. "In the hope that you may now be relieved in a measure from the pressure of that private and partisan interest, which has burdened the commencement of your administration, I desire to ask your attention to some particular views on another matter, in which if private interest should seem to be the motive for this application, it is nevertheless of such public moment, as will undoubtedly, in some form or other receive your early and very special consideration. I allude to the individual claims for loss by the Alabama captures. I represent for the Great Western Insurance Company of this city, claims to the amount of near Three hundred thousand Dollars, the property of upwards of Two hundred Stockholders of the Corporation; and the enquiry which suggests itself is, by what means, can a present remedy be affo[rd]ed the sufferers. . . . Although more than seven years have elapsed since the depredations of the Alabama began and two or three years have elapsed since filing of proofs of such depredations with the Department of State, there has yet no movement been made towards determining the amount of such claims, or which, or how many of them are well founded; in the mean time the government is holding our claims against the counter claims of England to our great injury and loss."—LS, DNA, RG 59, Miscellaneous Letters. See Adrian Cook, *The Alabama Claims: American Politics and Anglo-American Relations, 1865–1872* (Ithaca, 1975), pp. 145–47.

1869, MAY 18.   Orville E. Babcock to U.S. Senator Henry Wilson of Mass. "The President directs me to acknowledge the receipt of your letter of the 14th upon the outrages in Georgia, and to say that he has already directed the Sec. of War to have the matter investigated. as action could not well be based upon newspaper reports"—Copies, DLC-USG, II, 1, 4.

1869, MAY 19.   USG endorsement. "Mr. Jewell is a loyal Mississippian and unless there is reason for retaining the present incumbent at Amoy I would like his appointment to that place"—AES, DNA, RG 59, Letters of Application and Recommendation. Written on a letter of May 18 from James G. Jewell, Washington, D. C., to USG. "In accordance with your Suggestion to me, to day, I have the honor to make direct application, for the position of Consul of the United States of America, at the Port of Amoy, in China."—ALS, *ibid.* On May 16, Jewell had written to USG. "I have the honor to solicit an appointment under your administration, and to say, that being from the State of Mississippi, which State is, unfortunately, without representation in Congress, I am compelled to place my case before you in person. My residence in Mississippi, is of more than twenty years duration; I left there because of persecution for my principles, in 1861; I came to Washington, and recruited the first troops to defend the Government, and commanded a Battalion at the outbreak of the rebellion. I have been fortunate in being among the first to suggest your present position, which I did in 1864, immediately after the fall of Vicksburg, in a letter to the N. Y. Ev'g Express. More recently, before and after your nomination, I have taken an active part in that direction, as some copies of my correspondence (herewith enclosed,) with *four* leading Journals of the country will show,—and that without pay. I shall not presume to bore you with a long story, but this, I may say, the property of myself and family was destroyed by Gen. Grierson on his raid thro' Mississippi; and within the last ninety days the Rebel Ku-Klux Klan destroyed the Store and Warehouse of my brother and self, by fire. Our home is thus left unto us desolate, because of adherence to principle. With these few remarks I leave it to your own estimate, as to whether I am deserving of your patronage. I feel that I need it."—ALS, *ibid.* On May 22, Jewell wrote to USG. "During an interview with the Honorable Secretary of State, this day in regard to the position of United States Consul, at Amoy, China, for which you were kind enough to recommend me, the following facts transpired: *First*: The Secretary desires to see the President before he makes the change. *Second*: The present incumbent is a Frenchman. *Third*: He exposed himself when the Chinese pirates attacked Formosa, and protected the property of American citizens, as was his duty. *Fourth*: He is a good officer. To these objections to making a change, I beg leave to make the following reply. *First*: I am a Native American. *Second*: I exposed myself, when the rebels attacked my government, in the late war, and raised eleven companies of troops, for that purpose, and defended and protected the millions of government property in this city, when others refused to do so, *as was my duty*. *Third*: I propose, if appointed, to make as energetic, competent and faithful a public officer, as the present incumbent, as I presume any American, of ordinary intelligence would do. *Lastly*: I advocated U. S. Grant for the position he now fills. I respectfully beg leave to refer yourself and the Honorable Secretary of State, for further information to my papers on file."—ALS, *ibid.* Enclosures and related papers are *ibid.* On May 27, USG designated Jewell as consul, Singapore.

1869, MAY 20. Sallie Adkins, Warren County, Ga., to USG. "Pardon a heart broken outraged woman, who feels that in all this broad Land she can appeal to no one save you, who are the head of this mighty nation with any good hope of redress, I am the widow of the late Joseph Adkins, who was Senator in the Georgia legislature for the counties of Warren Green & toleferro & who in broad day light was on 10th of this Instant fouly and brutaly murdered, for no other reason than, that, since 1861 he has constantly been the friend of the United States & since 1865 a friend & supporter of Reconstruction under the Laws of Congress. My late Husband was over fifty five years of age,—During the late *Rebelion* he was one of the very few who dared to let his devotion to the Union be known & for that devotion, he was seized & imprisoned at Augusta,—He was a minister of the Gospel, a good kind generous, brave out-spoken man,—firm & decided in his own views upon all subjects, but tolerant & charitable to-wards others, He was a member of the Convention of this State in 1867 & 1868 & did not hesitate to avow his approval of the Emancipation & admission to citizenship of the *blacks* . . . We have long known that his life was in danger—time & time again have we been warned of it—nay notified of it by those whose skirts are now spotted with his blood,—Since January of this year he has been afraid to stay about Home, He remained at his duties at Atlanta untill March, He then visited Washington called upon you & then returned to Georgia, But did not dare come Home—We are farmers & needed greatly his presence but we did not fell it safe & he remained a refugee. I joined him at Augusta & by the aid of friends we have there—we exiles, out-cast, refugees waited events,—At length through our inability thus to live on our own means and an unwillingness to bear down on our friends in an evil hour, we determined to go home hoping that time & reflection, had per haps made it safe,—We ordered our Buggy to meet us at Deering Station on the Georgia Rail Road—We got the carrs at that place on the 10th Instant The coming of the Buggy seemed to have given notice of our return & our Enimies were on the spot—Hardly had we arrived when we were assailed—Sour looks—snears—insulting side talk & at length open abuse & threats of my Husband were commenced,—We thought of giving up the attempt to go Home and taking the next train back to Augusta, but was denied any place to stay at untill its arrival & ordered out *doors*—We then determined to start for Home at all events and were denied permission of our own Buggy and we started on foot leaving the Buggy & got away from our persecutors, when we had thus gone about a mile, two of the crowd from Deering overtook us, & told me if I would return I could get my buggy so I returned leaving my Husband & the driver to go on foot, till I could overtake them,—I got the Buggy the crowd having dispersed & started for Home, By some mistake either of theirs or mine I took a different road home from the one they took.—When I arrived there the driver who accompanied my Husband had reached Home telling that my Husband had been Killed shot in the *Public Road* by an *assasins.* We hasten to the spot some 8 miles from Deering and 3 miles from Home & found him lying in the Road mortaly wounded, weltering in his blood, though not dead,—He died before we reached home with him, though he lived long enough and was conscence to tell us how & by whom he was murdered—We poor women a few relatives & some negroes burried him— The (*so much prated*) good people of county still shunning & scorning us nay even in our agony they passed & laughfed at us in this our saddened event,—No inquest was held *though* (*coroner was sent for*) no steps taken by the civil authorities to arrest the foul crew—who murdered him—His murderarrs are now at large openly, no body moves, no body cares—The officers the magistrates the bailiffs, the men of influence are either over-awed or are in sympathy with the assinsins,—This Sir is in Georgia Nor is it a solitary case my Husband is the 2nd member of the convention & the 8th member of the Georgia Legislature who has been murdered in 20 miles of my *Home* by a *mob* for opinions sake and the number of negroes thus dispatched is legion—what say you are the people of Georgia all murderars —God forbid,—But when the very first men in the country stalk over the Land crying out against Radicals every vile epithet Eloquence and passion can invent, when every Newspaper in the State fills its colums with every epithet of vituperation that four years of constant practice has accumu-lated—When it is well know that at the death of a Radical the Land is glad & there is no danger of punishment—what hinders any ruffian from his vengeance—I am no Statesman—no Lawyer,—I am only a poor woman whose Husband has been murdered for his divotion to his country—I may have very foolish ideas of Governments, States & Constitutions But I feel that I have claims upon my country,—The *Rebels* imprisoned my Hus-band,—*Pardoned Rebels* murdered him There is no law for the punish-ment of them who do deeds of this sort the men who set the law in motion the magistrates the Juries the baliffs dont care, tho most of them are *Glad*— no body moves,—tho murderers go unpunished,—I do not know that you can help this—It may be that Republics have no remdy for such a state of things,—If so Republics are bad *things* and there may arrise a doubt if Republics had not better be done away with,—General Grant your pledge is unredeemed there is a spot in America,—yes in Georgia where men can not be Republicans with safety—I believe from the statements of my Husband who meet with many other refugees when we were in hiding & while he was at Atlanta that this is a common thing I believe—I say this is common in Georgia.—Can it be helped—Will forms & shams & newspaper—honey-hush-up even this outrage God Knowns I am done my Husbands blood calls upon his country for vengeance upon his murderers—I have no hope of redress from the effete, helpless over powered thing called the Goverment of Georgia—It is a sham, a mockery, a mere modification of the Confedercy—The law making power having been taken, and placed in the hands of disloyal *Rebels*—The Ku Klux control it, they having been allowed to take possession of it and they are but what the people are—Why nine in ten of them *Glory* in my Husband murder & I have no hope in them—I appeal to the United States—I demand that you *President Grant* Keep the pledge you made the *nation*—make it safe for any man to utter boldly & openly his devotion to the United States & his confidence in you."—ALS, DNA, RG 60, Letters Received from the President. See *HED*, 41-2-288, pp. 2–39; *SRC*, 42-2-41, part 7, pp. 1023–26.

1869, MAY 21. Governor Rutherford B. Hayes of Ohio to USG. "Enclosed please find the Prison Record of Smith Still—who has just been discharged from the Ohio Penitentiary to which he was sentenced by the Circuit Court of the U. S. for the Southern District of Ohio, for the crime of Counterfeiting. By the laws of Ohio, restoration to Citizenship is given discharged prisoners, sentenced by our State Courts, who have committed no infraction of the rules of the Prison. I have to request your Excellency to grant to this young man a Pardon or other paper that will restore him to his Civil rights, his prison conduct being unexceptionable."—LS (press), Hayes Letterbooks, OFH.

1869, MAY 24. A. Bridgewater, Stanford, Ky., to USG. "Please excuse my boldness in writing to you upon a subject which may be of little interest to you but when you hear my object you shurly will think that I have grounds for appealing to you I am living in a den of those midnight murders that has caused so much distress in Kentucky and unless we get Protiction there will not be a union man in this Part of the Country in one year from this date we have been told all along to try and hold out that when you took your seat as President you would give us Protection we have been waiting and have heard nothing therefore we have concluded to write Personly to you and I hope that you will not turn a deaf ear to us if you cannot help us any other way Please give us you advice while I write you this I am in the woods with some others for no other cause only our adhearance to the government last week they made a charge on our neighborhood and shot a man 40 times for saying that he had stood gard before your tent at Vicksburg no general that is so beyand a doubt and the sheriff of our county upholds them for yesterdy he came to my house with others and told my family that if those fellows was ever fired on they would burn houses old men & women   he was a colonel in the Rebel army   the mob here has already been killing weomen & children shooting down union men in there yards with out any cause whatever   thearefore we have caled upon you for advice or help   if you will condesend to answer my letter and require it, I can send you proof that there has been three hundred men kiled and made to leave in the last two years   I think that it is time that we had some thing done for us   there is not an office in our county that is not a Rebel nor will they allow a man to hold office without he is one and it is so in all the ajoining counties   will you Please let us hear from you   we have some claim I think for we have fought all through the war and done evry thing that we could for the government we could"—ALS, DNA, RG 107, Letters Received from Bureaus.

1869, MAY 24.   Charles H. Rogers, New York City, to USG. "Permit me to call your attention to the application of Captain Wickam S. Havens for a reappointment to the office of collector of customs in the port of Sag Harbor. Long Island which office he now fills with credit to himself and advantage to the goverment—Capt. Havens is a retired Ship Master, a man of ability and integrity, fitted to fill a much more important office—He has from boy hood been my intimate friend, or rather *we* have been firm and intimate friends and comrads—and therfore ventur to ask for him ~~myon~~ *my account* ~~to~~ your favourable consideration."—ALS, DNA, RG 56, Collector of Customs Applications. On Feb. 15, 1870, USG nominated Wickham S. Havens for reappointment.

1869, MAY 24.   U.S. Representative Robert C. Schenck of Ohio to USG. "I ask the President most respectfully to take up this question & revise it, & if he deems it proper refer it for opinion to his Cabinet. I beg to refer him for full explanation to Vice Admiral Porter, as well as to the Secy of the Navy. It is of the utmost importance to my brother Commodore Schenck that the question should be settled definitely *before the 11th of June.* I hardly think that Mr Johnson's cabinet could *change the law* of the land."—ANS, OFH. On May 27, Commodore James F. Schenck, Dayton, wrote to USG. "I have the honor respectfully to appeal from a decision made by the Hono Attorney General through which decision Rear Admiral Goldsborough, in my opinion contrary to law, is retained upon the active list, thereby depriving me the Senior Commodore on the active list, of the promo[ti]on to which I am legally entitled, and I ask that a fuller investigation may be made of the case, either by submitting the question to your Cabinet, or in such other way as you may deem proper,"—ALS, DNA, RG 45, Subject File, Div. NI.

1869, MAY 24.   Joseph Ward, Washington, D. C., to USG. "I enlisted as a Volunteer in 1st District of Columbia Colored Troops in 1863 at the City of Washington, And was sent to Masons Island, to do duty.   was there taken Sick and was sent to Washington until I emproved and was again sent to Masons Island to Join my Regiment. When I got there the Regiment had moved and I was sent to Alexandria, And from there to City point, there I was again taken Sick and lost my eye sight, being unable to do duty I was sent again to Alexandria from there to freedmans Villiage then to Armory square hospital under the Charge of Dr Bliss from there to Campbell hospital wher I staid until last fall when I went home to my family. I have never received a discharged from the Army And I humble aske that the President will order the Same to be made out"—L (signed by mark), DNA, RG 94, Colored Troops Div., Letters Received, M29 vol. 9 CT1869.

1869, MAY 25. Secretary of the Interior Jacob D. Cox to USG. "I have the honor to Enclose for your Consideration, the invitation of Mr Gallaudet, to attend the Commencemt Exercises of the National Deaf-Mute College, on the 23d of June next."—LS (press), Cox Papers, Oberlin College, Oberlin, Ohio. USG did not attend.

1869, MAY 25. Charles Dillingham, naval officer, New Orleans, to USG. "I take great pleasure in stating that the recent appointment of Charles Clinton Esq. to the position of Treasurer of the Branch Mint and assistant Treasurer of the United States at New Orleans, is a selection which can but strengthen the confidence of honest and loyal men in the wisdom of your administration. The character and ability of Mr Clinton are such as to emintly fit him for a representative of the Governmt in the faithful discharge of the trust you have confided to him"—ALS, DNA, RG 56, Asst. Treasurers and Mint Officials, Letters Received. Related papers are *ibid.* On June 3, U.S. Senator William P. Kellogg of La., New Orleans, telegraphed to USG. "Mr Charles Clinton is a good business man of excellent standing here, Under the circumstances I hope he may be allowed to file his bond,"—Telegram received (at 3:00 P.M.), *ibid.*, RG 107, Telegrams Collected (Bound). On the same day, Orville E. Babcock wrote to Secretary of the Treasury George S. Boutwell. "The President directs me to say that as Mr. Chas. Clinton's appointment has been made and sent to him, and his bonds executed, that he will be pleased to have him placed in possession of the office."—LS, *ibid.*, RG 56, Asst. Treasurers and Mint Officials, Letters Received.

1869, MAY 26. George W. Balloch, Bureau of Refugees, Freedmen, and Abandoned Lands, to USG. "I have the honor to request that the usual Executive order may be issued giving a leave of abscence on June 5th 1869, to such clerks and Employees in the various departments as are connected with Sabbath Schools and wish to participate in the celebration of the Washington City Sunday School Union, which is to be held on that day—" —ALS, DNA, RG 59, Miscellaneous Letters. Copies were sent to other depts.

1869, MAY 26.   George H. Butler, Port Chester, N. Y., to USG. "Pardon
the liberty I take in addressing these few lines to you in reference to the
Missippie ~~claims~~ Prizes money   I noticed some time ago in the papers that
they were to be paid. I am a Colord man. I served three years in the U S.
Navy. in admiral Farrigut fleet   I Joined U S Sloop of war. Pencola at
Washington 1861 and served one her untill volenteers were wonted up the
river to take Port. Hudson   I then volenteered and Joined the Mortar vessel
Sarah Bruren, and served my term of three yeargs and I received injuries
while while on her from the heavy firing of the mortars—for I spitting
blood more or less Every since my discharge and for the past year back it
has intirely disabled me from doing any kind of work   I have a family and
they are suffering for the wont of means, and I knew that you could tell me
in what way to Obtain my prize, if it was ready for Payment   I have my
honorable discharge which can be presented at any sesson   any information
which you will please to send me will be most thankfully received"—ALS,
DNA, RG 45, Letters Received from the President.

1869, MAY 26.   U.S. Senator Cornelius Cole of Calif. to USG. "Learning
that the U. S. Land Office at Los Angeles, Cala is about to be reorganized
I recommend Matthew Keller as a most suitable person for the office of
Receiver. Mr Keller is an old Resident of Los Angeles & a man of the highest respectability, & cultivation."—ALS, OFH. On the same day, Cole wrote
to USG recommending Henry C. Austin as register, land office, Los Angeles.—ALS, *ibid.*

1869, MAY 26.   John Speer, editor, *Kansas Tribune*, Lawrence, to USG.
"I am personally acquainted with Charles H. Langston, of Kansas, and
take pleasure in recomending him as a most suitable man for the appointment of Minister Resident in Liberia. Mr. Langston is a colored man of
finished education and great ability, a popular orator of power, a man of
the strictest integrity and the truest patriotism, and a most worthy and
acceptable representative of his race. He has been a most useful man during
the recent Rebellion, in defence of the Union."—ALS, DNA, RG 59, Letters
of Application and Recommendation. Related papers are *ibid.* No appointment followed.

1869, MAY 26.   Joseph B. Will and J. Daniels, Washington, D. C., to
USG. "The undersigned respectfully request that an order be issued to the
Executive Departments of the Government, granting the Knights Templar
therein, who desire to attend the semi-centennial anniversary of the Knights
Templar at Philadelphia, a leave of absence for four days, commencing on
the 14th proximo."—LS, DNA, RG 107, Letters Received from Bureaus.
Copies were sent to other depts.

1869, MAY 27.   William E. Dodge, New York City, to USG. "The public
parade on the next Sabbath is very distasteful to many of our citizens, but

their protest and that of our General Assembly's now in session has failed
to prevent it. The papers now state that General McDowell has ordered
the guns in our forts to be fired every minute for hours on the Sabbath. I
am urged by many of our best citizens to ask you to see that this is stopped
We are all axious to do honor to the dead but can̶n̶o̶t̶ see no propriety in
such a desecration of the Sabbath Let it be done on Monday as they do in
Brooklyn and elsewhere"—Telegram received (at 11:20 P.M.), DNA, RG
107, Telegrams Collected (Bound). On the same day, Frederick S. Winston
had telegraphed a similar protest to USG.—Telegram received (at 2:45
P.M.), *ibid.*

1869, MAY 27.   Isaac Seeley, Savannah, to USG. "In the absence of General Terry permit me to send to you direct the following information
During the year past there has been within the police barracks of this city
a daily, secret drill of men armed with rifles and cartrige box. Said drill
has been conducted in military style, according to the '*Manuel of Arms*'
And on one occasion this militia has had a public parade, and is composed
of the police of this city,   I cannot say whether or not the fire companies
constitute a portion of the force to be arrayed against the government,   Nor
is it for me to decide whether this organization comes within the meaning
of term militia as used in the following law, Act of March 2nd 1867 2nd
Sess of 39 Cong Statutes at Large page 487 . . . Affidavits can be readily
procured sustaining the above facts, which I communicate to you in the
hope that you will make such an investigation as will enable you to decide
whether the organization comes within the prohibition of the '⍺*Act*' above
cited,   I am actuated by a desire to be of service to my country and to the
present administration, and would like to be advised if any further statement of facts, (as to Georgia matters) from me, would be agreeable or
useful, to your Excellency,   '*I am a plain man that loves my friends*' and
trust you will overlook any violations of official etiquette, . . ."—ALS, DNA,
RG 107, Letters Received from Bureaus. A subsequent investigation identified the men drilling as members of the Savannah police.—*Ibid.*

On April 14, Seeley, Washington, D. C., had written to USG. "I am
informed since making my written statement that a record appears in the
Treasury Department connecting a person bearing my name, with a cotton
claim. *Knowing* that I have never been connected with *any* claim, I feel
certain that the record refers to some one else, as I *know* it cannot refer to
me,   And as I do not like to be crushed out for the acts of other people, I ask
as an act of simple justice access to the record, and time to explain the mys-
tery, or coincidence,"—ALS, *ibid.*, RG 60, Letters from the President.

1869, MAY 30.   Governor James M. Harvey of Kan. to USG. "The indians have again commenced hostilities on our western frontier murdering
citizens at various points. More troops are urgently needed"—Telegram
received (at 11:00 A.M.), DNA, RG 94, Letters Received, 744M 1869;
ibid., RG 107, Telegrams Collected (Bound). On June 5, Harvey tele-

graphed to USG. "The plains swarm with hostile Indians   Shall we raise
volunteers for the united states service. Prompt action is necessary"—Telegram received (at 1:50 P.M.), *ibid.*, RG 94, Letters Received, 744M
1869; *ibid.*, RG 107, Telegrams Collected (Bound). On June [9], Harvey
wrote to USG. "On Sunday, the 30th ult. I addressed a telegram to you
announcing that the Indians had again commenced hostilities against
our western frontier. They had then already attacked the settlements
at various points, killing men women and children, torn up the railroad track, murdered and mutilated an employee of the road and, in
utter defiance and contempt of the Government of the United States, on
that Sunday afternoon they attacked the settlements on the Saline River,
killing some thirteen men, women and children, within a mile of the camp
of the troop of U. S. cavalry sent there for the protection of the people. As
your [Ex]cellency must be aware, this is but a continuation of a long series
of the most dastardly and horrible outrages which year after year have been
perpetrated upon our people, until those beautiful valleys are dotted with
their graves, and the plains made ghostly with their unburied bones. And
yet these people are citizens of the United States—the most powerful nation
in the world and as fully [en]titled to its protection as though they were
denizens of the Atlantic sea-board or any other favored portion of our common country. A solitary instance of the perpetration of even a single one of
such outrages upon a community in any of the older states, would [l]ead to
a war of sufficient magnitude and duration to secure 'indemnity for the past
and security for [the] future' no matter w[ho] or what the aggressor might
[be.] England sent a large army into the center of Abysinia, killed the Emperor, destroyed his army and devasted his country, because a few British
subjects were held under [—]. The United States permits a barbarous foe
to roam at will in the center of its territory, murdering, mutilating and
outraging, in every conceivable manner, its best and most loyal citizens, at
their own homes, in their own fields. I am told that this is because the
number of troops at the disposal of the Government is inadequate to afford
the protection to which our citizens are entitled. This I believe to be true;
and, therefore, in the name of outraged humanity and humiliated loyalty,
I ask that you call for a sufficient number of volunteers to protect our frontier and to pursue and punish the murderers of our people. I make this
appeal with the knowledge that you have the power, and in the full faith
that you have the will, to put a stop, at once and forever, to scenes which,
from their continued repetition, are [bring]ing reproach upon the Government we fought to save[. H]oping that at least it would in return protect us
from murder and mutilation in our own homes."—LS, *ibid.*, RG 94, Letters
Received, 744M 1869. On June 14, Harvey telegraphed to USG. "Hostile
Indians still continue their work of murder and devastations on our western
frontier, I wish to know whether the United states will provide for the
protection of our people and the punishment of their murderers"—Telegram
received (at 10:45 A.M.), *ibid.*; *ibid.*, RG 107, Telegrams Collected
(Bound); copy, *ibid.*, RG 94, Letters Received, 744M 1869. On the same

day, Horace Porter wrote to Harvey. "In the absence of the President your despatch has been referred to the War Dept."—Copy, DLC-USG, II, 5.

On June 20, Carmi W. Babcock, Lawrence, Kan., wrote to USG. "Gov Harvey was in Town yesterday for the purpose of consulting with *Supdt Hoag* upon Indian matters—The Supdt was absent so he did not see him though they have had one or two interviews, before—The Gov has spent the most of his Time during the last 3 weeks on the Frontier, and has visited in person all the settlements where the Indians have been and has collected all the information he could—*He says* he *thinks* there *has been fully 30 persons killed* in *all*—To day I have had an interview with *Supdt Hoag* and his information is about the same as the Govs though he thinks not more than 20 persons have been killed in all—At the time of the outbreak there was 4 surveying parties in the field—They have all come in—Two of the parties Report *that they saw no Indians*—One party Reports that they saw several small Bands but were not disturbed—The 4th party Reports that they were attacked by a small Band but they soon left after 4 or 5 shots had been fired at them—The surveying parties are all frightened and do not like to go back into the field at present—From talking with these men I get the impression that there are *several* small Bands of Indians scouting over that country for *mischief* and intend to kill and plunder all they can without taking too many chances—I get the impression that the Indians are not combined to any great extent and do not mean to bring on a Regular War—Though I think the chances are that many of the Tribes know that their young men are out on a '*Bushwhacking*' expedition—My judgement is that the settlers and Trains are in great danger from these parties for the reason that they are out for the purpose of doing mischief and not mearly hunting or passing through the country—Gov Harvey told me he was going to write you again for more Troops or allow him to raise a Regt and asked me to join him in the request—While I am in hopes the Indians do not mean real and combined War I do believe that they have several Bands out who mean to do all the mischief they can—I am also of the impression that Genl Schofield has but few Troops for the scope of country he has to look after and hope you will allow the Gov to raise a Regt if you have no troops which you can send here—*You* can *place* the *utmost confidence* in *Gov Harvey*—Of course he may be mistaken in his judgement but he will not *knowingly deceive you*—I can also testify that Supdt Hoag is working hard and doing every thing he can but the trouble he has is *he cannot reach these stragling Bands*—He also tells me that he wishes the Gov had more Troops to protect the settlements until he can make an effort to get these Bands back &c."—ALS, DNA, RG 75, Letters Received, Miscellaneous.

On June 21, Harvey wrote to USG. "Having returned from the scenes of the recent Indian outrages on the western frontier, I feel impelled to write to you again, to correct any false impression which may have been made by the representations of parties who are prone to 'cry peace when there is no peace.' Some two weeks since I met Friend Hoag and several of the Indian Agents of his Superintendency, the Agent for the Cheyennes being one of the party. They all admitted the evident fact that the Cheyennes, Sioux and Arapahoes were at war with the whites, and said it was folly to expect them to accomplish anything until the Indians were constrained to go upon their Reservations, and were kept there 'as within the walls of a penitentiary'—to quote the simile of the Agent for the Cheyennes. They further said that they could not and dare not approach the Indians under the present state of affairs. Of course, I was surprised to hear that, at a subsequent date, Friend Hoag telegraphed from Atchison on the Missouri River, a very safe distance from the scene of hostilities, that the reports of Indian depredations were exaggerated and conflicting—that some eight or ten 'remote settlers' had been killed, &c &c. Now I wish to say that *I know* that thirty or more men, women and children have been killed, wounded and captured, these outrages being accompanied by acts of the most revolting atrocity. And I will state further, and be responsible for the statement, that the plains on our western frontier are infested with numerous bands of these hostile savages from north of the Platte and south of the Arkansas, and that I believe nothing will end this disgraceful state of things but the sending of a large military force against them, with orders to chastise them thoroughly, and force their survivors upon their reservations, retaining them there by military power. I have written earnestly concerning this matter, and feel justified in having done so from the fact that, to a considerable extent, I am responsible for the protection of the citizens on the frontier of this State, while it is the manifest and imperative duty of the Government of the United States to keep these Indians in subjection."—LS, *ibid.*, RG 94, Letters Received, 744M 1869. Related papers are *ibid.*

1869, MAY 30.   Thomas Wentworth Higginson, "Lately Col. 1st S. C. Vols. (33d U. S. C. T.)," Newport, R. I., to USG. "I take the liberty to introduce to you my friend Mrs. Chamberlin of Boston the excellent wife of the Quartermaster of my late regiment. She wishes to obtain for her husband, (Lt. G. B. Chamberlin) a continued appointment in Georgia, where he has been on duty in the Freedmen's Bureau. Though a Quartermaster, Lt. Chamberlin is an honest man, & thoroughly trained in business affairs. He deserves well of his country, & so does she, for she taught my black soldiers & was a blessing to my whole camp when she lived in it."— ALS, DNA, RG 105, Hd. Qrs., Letters Received.

1869, May 31.   U.S. Representative John Cessna of Pa., Bedford, to USG. "I learn that young Mr Washington of Franklin County Pa (in my District) desires a Commission in the regular Army—He is a son of the late Capt Crawford Washington who fell at Vicksburg—It will afford me great personal gratification if you can comply with his request—"—ALS, DLC-Charles Ewing. On May 19, Alexander King had written to USG on the same subject.—ALS, *ibid.* See *PUSG*, 17, 408.

[*1869, May*].   USG note. "William Griffith.—If possible, I wish the Secretary of the Treasury would give the bearer a watchman's place. He met with the misfortune from which he suffers under my eyes, and I feel a sympathy for him."—*New York Herald*, May 25, 1869. William Griffith, appointed watchman, had lost both arms while firing a salute in honor of USG.

1869, [MAY].   USG note. "The Sec. of State may substitute S. H. M. Byers, of Iowa, as Consul to *Zurich* Switzerlan[d] in place of C. A. Page, same state, unless reasons exist for"—AN (incomplete), DNA, RG 59, Letters of Application and Recommendation. On April 13, U.S. Representative William Loughridge of Iowa had written to USG. "I respectfully reccommend and earnestly request the appointment of S. H. M. Byers, as Consul to one of the following places, Zurich, Naples, St Petersburg, Funchal, or Geneva, or Some other Similar grade of Consulship, in case a change cannot be made in either of those. Mr Byers is a Lawyer, of talent, he lost his health by suffering during Sixteen months in Rebel prisons during the war, and his Surgeon advises travel and change of climate as necessary to his restoration to health—He is well qualified to discharge properly the duties at any of those places, . . ."—ALS, *ibid.* On April 14, Gen. William T. Sherman endorsed Loughridge's letter: "I found adjutant Byers a prisoner of war, at Columbia, S. C. in February 1864, and took him on my staff by reason of his Zeal and inteligence as far as Fayetteville NC whence I sent him with despatches to Washington. I have not seen him since, but I feel great interest in his behalf, and would be glad if he receive such an appointmt as would tend to restore his health, shaken I am told by his long imprisonmt in the ill fed 'Camp Sorghum' "—AES, *ibid.* Related papers are *ibid.* On Dec. 6, USG nominated Byers as consul, Zurich.

    On Sept. 29, Elihu B. Washburne, Paris, wrote to USG. "This will be handed to you by our young friend Chas. A. Page, of Dixon in our Congressional district and recently our Consul to Zurich. Mr. P. desires to talk with you about his recent 'suspension' and to see if you cannot do something for him. I believe the record of the departments will show that he was a most excellent Consul Mr. P. is a young man in whom I have ever felt a great interest, and I would be most glad to see him gratified. All his relative and friends live in the old Third District and they are strong friends of us both."—ALS, *ibid.* On Dec. 17, suspended consul Charles A. Page, Washington, D. C., wrote to USG. "I desire to be reinstated as Consul at Zürich, and I think that on a full presentation of the facts in the case you will be disposed to annul the letter suspending me. 1/ Passing through Paris I was handed by Mr. Washburne a letter to you, on showing which to you I was told to hand it to the Secretary of State. This I did, when the Secretary said that he could not open the case of any suspended officer. . . ."—ALS, *ibid.* Related papers are *ibid.* No reinstatement or appointment followed.

[*1869, May*].   Thomas A. Mitchell to USG petitioning for U.S. protection of his Caribbean guano islands.—ALS, DNA, RG 59, Letters Received Relating to Guano Islands.

1869, JUNE 1.   Admiral David G. Farragut, New York City, to [USG]. "Having a full knowledge of the facts herein set forth by Com. McKinstry U. S. N. who was one of my most distinguished officers on the Mississippi I take pleasure in recommending the within applicant to your consideration for an appointment as a cadet at the Military Academy"—AES, DNA, RG 94, Correspondence, USMA. Written on a letter of May 25 from Commodore James P. McKinstry to USG. "Towson Caldwell is desirous of an appointment as a Cadet at the Military Academy. He is the grandson of the late distinguished Paymaster General Towson U. S. Army. His Father and paternal Grandfather were highly meritorious officers in the U. S. Navy   From my personal knowledge of the qualifications and character of the applicant I take great pleasure in recommending him to your favorable consideration."—ALS, *ibid.* Towson Caldwell did not attend USMA.

1869, JUNE 1.   William T. Clark, Norwalk, Conn., to USG. "Mr Henry Betts of Norwalk Conn claims to be the original projector of the Pacific Rail Road, and has filed evidence of that fact with the Sec'y of Interior—It is his desire that you should become acquainted with his project and plans, inasmuch as he claims in the construction of these Roads, superiority of material, removing of time, and safety of travel—I have only to say that the perusal of his document would reward the effort in your moments of leisure —"—ALS, DNA, RG 59, Miscellaneous Letters.

1869, JUNE 2.   USG endorsement. "Special attention of the Sec. of State invited."—AES, DNA, RG 59, Letters of Application and Recommendation. Written on a letter of May 24 from S. Newton Pettis to USG. "By the answer I received to my card last Friday morning, by the politeness of Genl. Dent, I infered that you misapprehended the nature of my business. Two weeks previously you had not only honored me with a protracted interview, but listened to a detailed history of the condition, past & present of the organization, and its future wants and securities, with great patience. The only recollection connected with that interview unpleasant to me, is found in the mortification I felt in dwelling upon a state of affairs in which I had for years been so conspicuous, but in the necessity of telling you *all*, if I said any thing, I found an apology for the discharge of what I deemed a very unpleasant duty,   My object then in visiting Washington last Thursday and Friday was simply in the interests of Mr Henderson, which I considered the interests of the party,   Remembering the remark that fell from your lips when I told you the truth, that although he was in Washington with friends to press his appointment immediately after the inauguration, so thoroughly disgusted was he at the rush, importunity and clamor for office at your hands, that he left the city for home, sending word to our

M. C. Mr Gilfillan not to file his papers but to return them to him here, as well as the willingness expressed by you to appoint him to Antwerp, I urged Mr Henderson to visit Washington with me, that you might see and know that he was both a *man* and a gentleman, He was there, and had your time admitted, you would have been glad I have no doubt, to have seen for a moment one who labored with others so arduously for the country, in placing you in the Presidential Chair. After my interview with you and my return home, I told the workers of the organization the result of our interview *touching Mr Henderson & Antwerp only.* One and all felt more than gratified—Our District (the 20th) is the great oil District and Antwerp of all other Ports I am informed Mr Gilfillan, our M, C, ascertained our oil producers were interested in, and filed Mr H's papers in, after Mr Henderson directed their return. . . ."—ALS, *ibid.* No appointment followed.

1869, JUNE 2. Secretary of the Navy Adolph E. Borie to USG. "I have the honor to submit to you my opinion regarding the further continuance of Surgeon P. J. Horwitz as Chief of the Bureau of Medicine and Surgery. At the death of Surgeon Whelan, during the administration of Mr Welles, Dr Horwitz was placed at the head of the Bureau he being at the time a young Surgeon although a gentleman of ability and good administrative qualities. His appointment at the time of the Rebellion might have been very proper under the circumstances, as it was necessary for the Secretary of the Navy at that time to retain about him persons in whose business capacity he had confidence. The appointment of Surgeon Horwitz was not acquiesced in by the senior medical officers of the Navy, many of whom were his equals in every respect, and it was due to them that they should have been tendered the appointment. Surgeon Horwitz has for four years past enjoyed advantages not belonging to his rank, although he has performed his duties in a faithful and satisfactory manner. The senior medical officers hopefully expect a change in the Bureau of Medicine and Surgery, on the expiration of Surgeon Horwitz's term of four years and it is really due to the Corps that this change should take place. While so young a Surgeon remains in the Bureau it is looked upon as a reflection upon the older Surgeons, who as a body, are a very intelligent set of men. It is the opinion of officers of the Navy, well qualified to judge, that no officer should remain in a Bureau longer than four years, and it would relieve the Department of much importunity if the President would decide this matter by an order. I will here observe that the practice of officers obtaining outside influence in relation to securing positions afloat and ashore, is highly injurious to the discipline of the Navy and is very embarrassing to the Secretary. The Department is anxious to do all in its power to oblige the officers of the Navy, but so numerous have the applications from influential persons become, that I have been obliged to issue a general order forbidding it. Surgeon Horwitz has tendered strong recommendations ect, but I beg leave to suggest that these should in no way influence his case which stands on its own merits."—Copy, DNA, RG 45, Confidential Letters Sent. On April 15, U.S. Representatives Thomas W. Ferry of Mich., Aaron F. Stevens of N. H., Glenni W. Scofield of Pa., Eugene Hale of Maine, and Henry H. Starkweather of Conn. had written to USG recommending Phineas J. Horwitz's reappointment as chief, Bureau of Medicine and Surgery, U.S. Navy.—DS, OFH. On April 17, U.S. Senators Aaron H. Cragin of N. H., Henry B. Anthony of R. I., Charles D. Drake of Mo., James W. Nye of Nev., and John R. Stockton of N. J. wrote to USG on the same subject.— DS, DNA, RG 45, Subject File, Div. VA. On May 14, U.S. Representatives Charles O'Neill and Leonard Myers of Pa., Philadelphia, wrote to USG in support of Horwitz.—LS, *ibid.* On May 24, William E. Chandler, Washington, D. C., wrote to USG urging Horwitz's retention.—ALS, OFH. On Dec. 6, USG nominated William M. Wood as chief, Bureau of Medicine and Surgery, U.S. Navy.

1869, JUNE 2. James May, Washington, D. C., to USG. "The enclosed letters will show that I have been an humble instrument, in an endeavour, to have my friend Genl. R. E. Lee favoured with a *quiet* social interview with you. I presented the kind regards of Genl Lee, his excellent wife, two sons, & two of his Daughters to you some weeks *before* Genl Lee called on you. I informed you, that Genl Lee desired me to say to you that he would be much pleased to entertain you at his Home, or shew his kindness to you, in any way that might be presented to him. But that he did not deem it proper for him, *under existing circumstances*, to either write to you or call on you. There was *no response from you to that message.* Having more than forty years acquaintance with my old friend Frederick Dent Esq. & a slight acquaintance with Genl Dent, I presumed to persist in my endeavour to procure an interview. Hoping it might eventually be a *national benefit* to have *you two representative* Gentlemen on social, friendly terms. There- fore, I had a conversation with F Dent Esq. & one with Genl Dent. They both encouraged me to hope that you was kindly disposed towards Genl Lee, *notwithstanding you had given no response to the kind message sent to you through me by Genl. Lee, his good wife, his two daughters, his son Robert, and a special kind & greatful message from his son young* Genl *Lee,* to *you for a favour* he recd at *your hand when he was at your mercy,* for which *he said* 'as long as I live I will feel greatful to Genl Grant' (Genl Lee instructed me to be *cautious not to have any notice* of his arrival &c) Being well convinced of the *kind* feelings of the *whole Lee family* towards *you,* & hoping my old friend F. Dent Esq. & his son (the Genl) was *not* mistaken, I with some assurance, *persevered* in my humble exertions to have my valued friend Genl Lee, favoured (as I sanguinely hoped he would be) with a social, friendly, *private* half hour, with you in the White House and hoped, that, that meeting, would be the means, of making you perma- nent reliable confidencial friends whilst you both lived. I have been more than thirty years acquainted with Genl Lee & his Family, and *know* his character from his acquaintances who have known him from *boyhood.* I feel safe in the assercion that not withstanding his Age, experience, education, & the exalted positions he has held continuously nearly all his life, He is a difident cautious, unpretending Gentleman. The situation he has been in the past few years, must necessarily render him *sensitive. That* circumstance, (in my humble opinion), gives him *a just claim* on any *friend* he may have, who is *now* in an *elevated* position for a *little more courtesy* than he might look for *under ordinary circumstances.* Genl Lee *did not say one complaining word to me in reference to his few* minutes with you, in the *presence* of *several* Gentlemen, but I believe he was deeply mortified that the interview was *so short & formal.* He *told me* he very much regretted that he had *not* the pleasure of paying his respects to Mrs. Grant & the Family. I make this intrusion on you without authority from Genl Lee. I hope when you give the matter a few moments consideration, you will see that I am only performing my duty. . . . I desire that there may be *no publisity given to any thing pertaining to Genl. Lees friendship with you* if *real friendship does exist as I hope it does.*"—Copy, USG 3. On April 28 and 30, Robert E. Lee, Baltimore, wrote to May. "I have recd your letters of the 24th & 26th & shall certainly respond on my route through Washington to the kind sentiments of Pres: Grant as expressed through Genl. Dent to you—There is some important business detaining me here which prevents my stating the day that I will be in Washington, but I will try & inform you the evg previous to my departure. It is possible that I may have to go to N. Y. which I wish to avoid, but if I am obliged to go I cannot be in Washington before next week. I wish no notification of my arrival in Washington to be given & desire to be as quiet as possible, I hope therefore you will not mention it. I will drive from the R. R. to the Pres:'t mansion & send my card to Genl Dent, who can, inform me whether it will be convenient for the Pres: to see me. I shall be very glad to accept Mrs Kennons invitation to her house if it will not inconvenience her—The arrangements mentioned above will I think divest my visit of all unnecessary publicity, which will I think be the more agreeable to Pres: Grant as well as myself—I rely upon your discretion. . . . P. S. Letters directed to Mr S H Tagart 84 Madison St. Baltimore will reach me—I will be in the Country for the next two days" "I have just returned from the country & found your letter of the 27th I regret that I shall be unable to accept Mr Montgomery Blair's kind invitation to his house, but I have promised to stay with my relative Mrs Kennon who expects me. Please express to him my regrets—I hope to visit Pres: Grant tomorrow as I stated in my former letter. You must come to Mrs Kennons to see me if I should miss you in Washington—"—Copies, *ibid.* See Douglas Southall Freeman, *R. E. Lee: A Biography* (New York and London, 1934–35), IV, 382–85, 401–2, 520–21.

1869, JUNE 4. Henry D. Cooke, Washington, D. C., to USG. "I beg to commend to your favorable attention, Col. W. Yates Selleck of this City. Col. Selleck is well known to the citizens of Washington, as the Agent for the State of Wisconsin during the War, in which capacity he rendered invaluable services to our soldiers in Camp and Hospital. I believe he is known to you personally as a Trustee of the Gettysburg and Antietam National Cemeteries, in connection with Hons. John Jay, James T. Blaine, Senator Ramesyay & others. Much of the executive part of the work of constructing those Cemeteries has fallen upon Col. Selleck, and the Cemeteries themselves attest his Efficient services. In business, I know him to be Energetic, capable, and thoroughly trustworthy. His appointment to the position which he seeks, would gratify a large circle of friends, and would secure for the Government, services of Exceptional worth."—ALS, DNA, RG 59, Letters of Application and Recommendation. On June 8, W. Yates Selleck wrote to USG. "I most respectfully request of you the appointment of Consul or Commercial Agent of the United States at Bradford, England, in place of Mr. George M. Towle the present incumbent—Mr. Towle supported General McClellan for the Presidency in 1864 in opposition to Mr. Lincolns reelection and was appointed to the position that he now holds during the year 1868 by President Johnson—In regard to my merits and claims for the position that I ask and of my ability to fill it in a mnner creditable to the Government, I most respectfully refer you to the enclosed letters of commendation from General Hawley, Senators Carpenter, Howe, Fenton, Ramsey and others personally acquainted with me recommending my appointment. Trusting that the application may receive your early and favorable consideration . . ."—ALS, *ibid.* Related papers are *ibid.* On Oct. 12, USG appointed Selleck as commercial agent, Bradford, England. On May 29, 1873, Selleck, Bradford, wrote to Dr. Alexander Sharp. "A week ago last Tuesday I received a notice from the Hon. J. C. B. Davis, Acting Secretary of State, that William W. Douglass of Virginia had been appointed United States Commercial Agent at Bradford, and directing me to turn over the Archives of the Office to him on his arrival, &c—I was taken by surprise; having been an earnest supporter of the Administration from first to last, and having contributed last summer $50—(in Gold) to aid in the reelection of General Grant, having full faith to in his fitness for the high position of President; deemed that I would not be removed without good cause—As far as I can learn there is no cause, unless it be that my place is wanted, and the pressure for places has made a sacrifice of me— The enclosed copy of a letter from General Badeau will show with what amount of fidelity I have performed the duties of the office—On the 6th inst when the appointment was made, General Grant was away from Washington; and it may be that he is not aware that I have been removed—I have such faith in his desire to do justice to all, men, that I believe that if he knew the facts connected with my case—that he would do me justice in the matter— . . ."—ALS, *ibid.* The enclosure is *ibid.* On April 12, USG had appointed William W. Douglass as commercial agent.

1869, JUNE 5.   George Wilson, New York City, to USG. "By direction of the Chamber of Commerce I have the honor to transmit for your consideration, the enclosed resolution on the subject of commercial relations with Canada, which was unanimously adopted by the Chamber at a meeting held on Thursday last."—LS, DNA, RG 59, Miscellaneous Letters. An enclosure requesting "reciprocal trade" with Canada is *ibid.* On July 5, H. B. Willson, New York City, wrote to USG. "I have the honor to enclose you a correspondence between the Right Honorable W. E. Gladstone and myself, on the subject of Canadian Independence, which appeared in the Herald of the 21st Ultimo. The subject of my letter will not be less interesting to American than to English Statesmen. The correspondence has been copied and commented upon by the leading journals of Canada—praised by some and denounced by others. Independence is the stepping stone to annexation, and a wise policy on the part of your administration may lead to important results. I am acting in concert with many prominent Canadians, whose opinions I fully represent, and would be glad of an opportunity of making suggestions bearing on the case. It is easy to perceive that the labor expended in [e]fforts to influence the policy and ripen the public [o]pinion of England, in reference to Colonial Independence will be thrown away, if the Government of Washington, as it did on a former occasion, when it entered into an unwise Reciprocity Treaty, plays into the hands of the pro-British party in Canada. I wish to apprize you of facts, of which you are possibly, not cognizant, respecting the efforts now making to secure another similar treaty. The Canadian Government has had for more than a year, and still has, a secret agent in Washington, whose business it is to watch and report on events bearing on this much coveted object. Some fifteen or eighteen months ago, he managed to secure the good offices of Secretary McCulloch, through the influence of the Hon. John W. Forney, who was paid by the Canadian Government a large sum of money for his services—a fact made public in the NewYork Herald and the Canadian papers. A bill drafted by the Secret agent was introduced into the House of Representatives in May, [or] June 1868, and referred to the committee of Ways and Means. The Chronicle, worked it up in several elaborate articles, during that and the following Session, and the committee at length made a report, suggesting that the President open negotiations with the Dominion through the British Minister for a new treaty of commerce. The same committee, composed mainly of the same men, and having the same chairman, reported a similar resolution during the first Session of the present Congress, and I notice by the papers that the Secretary of State has commenced acting on the recommendation of the committee, and has given notice to the British Minister that he is prepared to enter upon negotiations for a new Treaty. I also notice by the Canadian papers that the Honorable John Rose, the Finance Minister of Canada has been designated on the part of the Dominion Government to conduct these negotiations on behalf of Canada, and is shortly expected to visit Washington for that purpose. Mr Rose was once an annexationist, but the allurements of office and emolument have converted him to high British principles, and he now persecutes all his old associates who have resisted the temptations, to which he has fallen an easy prey. I

do not propose, at present, to tender advice, or make suggestions, feeling assured that you are too able a general to do, or sanction, what your antagonist most desires you to do. Mr Seward 'diplomatized' the French out of Mexico, and no doubt would do the same with regard to the British in Canada, if he could hold the Seals of the State Department another four years. If Mr Fish is a sincere advocate of the Monroe Doctrine, I presume he will lose no favorable opportunity to promote it, and one is about to offer itself, and I presume he will endeavor to master the whole question. I prepared a Bill, and an argument on subject of ‡Trade, ‖Navigation and the Fisheries, between and common to the two countries, and handed them to Governor (now Senator) Fenton, las[t] Winter and asked him to give the matter his attention. As I have heard nothing from him, except a verbal acknowledgment, I presume his time has been too much engrossed in the everlasting question of patronage, to examine these papers. That bill forms the only true American base for a treaty, or for legislation. It is not what the pro-British party in Canada want, or will accep[t] but it is just what the great mass of intelligent people in both countries desire and *would* accep[t.] I would send Mr Fish a copy, but it requires explanation from some one, well versed in the international relations of this Country and Canad[a] and perhaps it will be time enough after Mr Rose has 'filed his appearance,' in response to Mr Fish's declaration that he is ready to 'treat.' "
—ALS, *ibid.* On July 25, "W. Ulhf," St. Louis, wrote to USG. "The annexation of the Canadas seems not to be advisable because neither the English language can be spread by it and made more generally honored nor will the greatness of the Anglosaxon races be extended by it as the United States are Anglosaxon themselves. It would rather cause the Anglosaxons to appear jealous, quarrelsome and unsociable. The liberties in both countries are equal enough to make both to live happy—The assistance of the Canadians is not needed by the Americans as they are strong enough against all enemies they may have to fear. But the possession of Canada adds greatly to the splendor of the British throne and nation as to remain one of the great powers of Europe. Natural friendship must be upheld anyhow by the always weaker Canadians in their cold climate. But it seems to be wise to initiate th[e] annexation of as much of the West Indi[es] as possible: first because the Americans need thu[s] not learn the Spanish language so much, the knowledge of which language is a[ll] wise altogether unnecessary as the roo[ts] of it are contained in the Latin; second if South America will speak English too the English language wi[ll] be the most important in the world, taught then on the European Universi[ties] and spoken readily by the courts; third, after a country is thickly settled, a new language can hardly [be] introduced any more and the new ra[ce] is hated for the new language; fourth, if a people is to deem itsel[f] the same with another, it must seem to have commenced from and throug[h] it, partaken of its first glories, fin[d] its first forefathers mixed up, attach[ed] to the same cause and unrecogniza[ble] or wars of races will follow; fifth, nothing

would add more to [the] glory of the Anglosaxon races. Inde[ed] this would commence a new era in the world and would make the President who accomplished this Union; illustrious and immorta[l.] The Alabama affair may be better forgotten. The English had reasons to fear the Americans and to hope a division in order to have place for politics. The best revenge is to make the United States still stronger yet. The Southern generals may be used equally with the Northern generals for the accomplishment of the purpose if the objections are not made too strong Both are of the same blood. To hatred will cease. The nigger is better moved as much southward as possible in order to avoid future wars of races or Mexican affairs. His blood and color is too different and the difference all the time recognizable. We can foresee, he will deal unfair therefore we deal unfair and prevent it.—The possession of the South American States may beforehand be held nominally rather and treated like Indian territories in order to press the old population more back and avoid future wars of races. For the effectual ᵽPacification of the South Pacific coast it will become necessary to complete the canal of Daria as quick as possible. . . ."—AL, *ibid.*

1869, JUNE 7.   G. W. Barber, Jacksonville, Fla., to USG. ". . . I will here insert acopy of an order to a poor harmless old Gentleman to leave the country which he will be compelled to Do or he will be in all probability murdered soon and to go it is next thing to murder he being a poor farmer to give up his comfortable home and what little property he has at such a hard time of the year will Bring him and his hole house to starvation for it must Be remembered that a man has to have a capital to support on if he gives up all he has and gets nothing for it But a Bad name where is a subsistance to come from.   and I will insure you that he gets nothing for his substance for that is the whole object in making him go is to obtain what he has without paying for it . . . But is it not escential that such conduct should be put Down and that at once and upon my honor I Dont see any other way to stop it But to send a lot of troops here immediately and Breakup thes clans of miserable robers and Law Breakers   their are crowds that hold secrete meatings I find out through others   what the intention is I can not guess   I Don't mean Masonic or odfellows   But from what I can gather it is something like these clans of murders and robers I have Just Been speaking of   I have been told By sevral that these fellows are a sworn Band to protect each other even to spilling of Blood and swearing of lies in the Defence of each other, from any other partys Bringing them to Justice   I pray your honor Just thhink how miserable a man can Be made by these villains   Just think how hard it is for an honest man to be Drove with a family of helpless children on the world without purse or protection or even a hut to stay in from a comfortable home and a plentiful subsistance if you could only see the sufferance that is caused By it you would say hang the last one of them without Judge or jury   a short time since I am told a party went at a late hour at night took the man out beat him to such a shamefull rate that he expected Death and as soon as he got so he could be left to save his life   some Days since his wife was met toating a small Bag of moss to sell to try to obtain something to eat and said that her little children had not one mouthful of vituals of any kind all caused By her husband Being Beat and Drove from home and numbers of other cases to tedious to worry you with   I can not answer for the honour of all these familyes that have Been Brought to Distress for I am not personaly acquainted with them all But some of them I can vouchsafe are good honest citasens and realy Deserve protection . . ."—ALS, DNA, RG 94, Letters Received, 457B 1869. Related papers are *ibid.*

1869, JUNE 7.   John Sheahan, County Cork, Ireland, to USG. "I most respectfully and humbly beg to address your dignified personage, in the name of, and for the numerous Irish Friends in this District of those Countrymen, who served under your Banners and displayed under your Command that Chivalry, for which they have become proverbial, and which aided your Excellency in obtaining those Signal Victories which have gained World-wide Fame, and an additional wreath for your untainted Crown. Sanctioning their intreaties therefore, and confidentially trusting on your Exalted generosity, I request for their & the public pleasure, a Subscription for the Freemount-Races, which is to come off, in September next, and *which* is the most favored public Amusement not only in this district but through all Ireland. And permit me to state that if agreeable to your Will, that the *Wager* shall be nominated from your Excellency. Hoping that I may be favored, with a Kind and Speedy response to this transatlantic appeal, . . ."—ALS, DNA, RG 59, Miscellaneous Letters.

1869, JUNE 9.   Horace Porter to Secretary of State Hamilton Fish. "I am directed by the President to request you to furnish him with Five hundred dollars ($500) from the Secret Service Fund"—LS, DLC-Hamilton Fish. Fish endorsed this letter. "Received the above for the President from Geo. E. Baker Agent June 9 1869"—ES, *ibid.*

1869, JUNE 9.   Secretary of the Interior Jacob D. Cox to USG. "I have the honor to submit, herewith, a commission designating Howard White of New Jersey, a member of the Society of Friends, to perform the duties of Agent for the Winnebago Indians on the Missouri River, vice George. W. Wilkinson, who has been suspended."—LS, OFH. On April 21, USG had nominated Howard White as agent, Omaha Agency, but the Senate rejected the nomination. On Dec. 21, White was confirmed as agent, Winnebago Agency.

1869, JUNE 11.   Elihu B. Washburne to USG. "At the request of Genl. Cluseret I have the honor to transmit you herewith the enclosed communication on the subject of his recent arrest in this city."—ALS (press), DLC-Elihu B. Washburne.

1869, JUNE 12.   Secretary of State Hamilton Fish to USG. "The ratification of Consular Convention, negotiated last winter with Belgium, was to have been exchanged in Brussels on or before the 5th instant. Owing to the Senate of Belgium not being in session they could not be exchanged within the time limited by the Treaty. Consequently it becomes necessary to negotiate an additional article to continue the time within which the ratifications may be exchanged. As the Belgian Legislature is understood to be now in session, I have instructed Mr Sanford to negotiate such additional article. He will require for this purpose a new power from you which I send by the bearer for your signature if it meet your approval. If you approve, the instruction and power will go out by the steamer of Wednesday and may reach Brussels before their Senate adjourns."—Copy, DNA, RG 59, General Records. Instructions to Henry S. Sanford, U.S. minister, Brussels, are *ibid.*, RG 46, Presidential Messages, Foreign Relations, Belgium.

1869, JUNE 13.   Norman McLeod, Chicago, to USG. "Please find enclosed few Slips of the many that I could Send, but a few is better than none (as an honest man and no politician I Send you the Slips to let you See them and if these contents are true as I have no reason to doubt it is horrible & disgracefull that poor men and women Should be killed by an Indian or any other man, I tell you with me there is no excuse allowed for Such out rage why Sir dont you See that life is protected in every Sphere of life in all new Settled Sections of our country, . . ."—ALS, DNA, RG 75, Letters Received, Miscellaneous.

1869, JUNE 14.   James F. Casey, collector of customs, New Orleans, to USG. "Permit me to introduce to your favorable consideration Mr. Arthur McArthur, a gentleman of most excellent merits, whose acquaintance I made during his visit to this city last Spring. Mr McArthur is proposing to locate here and identify himself with the interests of this State, and understanding that he is an applicant for the position of District Attorney for this District, I take pleasure in expressing the hope that he may receive the appointment, feeling assured that he would do credit to your administration, and from his known energy of character, be of great service to me."—LS, DNA, RG 60, Records Relating to Appointments. On July 15, 1870, USG nominated Arthur MacArthur as justice, Supreme Court of D. C.

1869, JUNE 14.   Elihu B. Washburne to USG. "The bearer, Mrs. Linton, of Louisiana, but who has lately resided in this city, is about returning to the United States. She is the daughter of the late Doctor Perkins, of Louisiana, who was one of our firm friends during the rebellion. Mrs. Linton was equally loyal and devoted to our cause. She proposes to visit Washington and desires an introduction to you, which it affords me much pleasure to give and to commend her to your kind consideration as a most estimable lady."—*HRC*, 43-2-142, part 2, p. 93.

1869, JUNE 15.   Gilbert P. Bennett, collector of Internal Revenue, Grant, Dakota Territory, to USG. "With pain I learn of the suspension of Hon, *Geo*, H, Hand, from office of U, S, Dist, Atty, Dist, of Dakota, I am aware that one Walter. A. Burleigh late Delegate ofrom Dakota, an *unscrupulous* and *untruthful* polititier of the *opposition stripe*, has prefered serious charges against Mr Hand, which have no foundation in fact, and could have been prompted only by desire to weaken and injure the *Republican cause* in *this Territory*, in the removal of one of the most sound and consistant men of our party, Mr Hand, and Mr Spink (present Delegate) were the only federal officials in the Territory who supported the Republican ticket last fall, I am well acquainted with Mr Hand, and know his private as well as official character to be above reproach in the estimation of *fair minded men* of all parties, and it would be a source of deep regret to them that the *machinations* of a *bad man* should succeed in robbing him of a position that he *merits* and *honors*,"—ALS, DNA, RG 60, Records Relating to Appointments. Additional letters to USG opposing the removal of George H. Hand are *ibid.* On Feb. 17, 1870, U.S. Delegate Solomon L. Spink of Dakota Territory, Washington, D. C., wrote to Secretary of State Hamilton Fish recommending Hand as territorial secretary.—ALS, *ibid.*, RG 59, Letters of Application and Recommendation. Related papers are *ibid.* On Feb. 19, Horace Porter wrote to Fish. "I am directed by the President to say that, if you have not already requested the Arkansas delegation to name a Secretary for Dakotah, he requests that you will not do so, but nominate the person recommended by the delegate from that territory."—ALS, DLC-Hamilton Fish. On Feb. 21, USG nominated Hand as secretary, Dakota Territory, but withdrew the nomination on March 21. On May 22, 1872, USG nominated Hand as register, U.S. land office, Yankton, Dakota Territory, and, on Dec. 9, 1874, again nominated Hand as secretary.

1869, JUNE 15.   Charles Little and James B. Chase, Jr., Congregational Association of Neb., Fremont, to USG. "Believing that you are heartily interested in the temporal and spiritual welfare of the Indians; as a religious body in the immediate presence of these Indians, we venture unasked to make to you a few suggestions as to what to our religious body seems a practicable, just and Christian method of dealing with them. You are doubtless aware that a strong political pressure is now being exerted to remove the Indians from our State and to plant them on lands further removed from the white settlements;—and to this end strong arguments are found in the following facts—I. The Indian reserves in Nebraska are now nearly surrounded by white settlers. II. These Reserves embrace some of the best lands in the state and their opening for settlement by whites would add somewhat to the Wealth, population & prosperity of the state III. The Indians are unpleasant neighbors even when at peace—IV. Their national feuds are continually provoking bloody conflicts among themselves, even in the case of these Indians who are located on reserves, and in these quarrels

the rights of the adjacent white settlers are often too little respected—V
The proximity of the Reserve Indians to the white settlements gives a
plausible excuse to the wild Indians of the plains to come within striking
distance of the white settlers—thus producing continually a feeling of distrust and danger in the border settlements, which is very prejudicial to the
rapid increase of these settlements through immigration. While these facts
above stated are indisputable, we would respectfully request your careful
consideration of the following facts, which we believe to be equally true
and indisputable I. The foregoing facts are all the natural results of the
heathen character and customs of these uncivilized peoples, aggravated
largely by the vices contracted and exaspirations received at the hands of
unprincipled White men II. These vices contracted and exaspirations received have been so productive of fatal results, because thus far the motives
which have prompted intercourse on the part of the whites with the Indians
have been so largely of a mercenary and vile character—and because the
extreme border settlements are often not a fair representation of the morals
or manners of our Christian nation—III. If the Indians are now removed
for reasons given above it will be but a short time befo[re] advancing immigration will again bring about the same state of affairs—and with equal
force call for a continued series of removals. IV. It is manifest that might
does not make right in our dealing with the Indians any more than with any
other people—and as a powerful Christian people we should while giving
them every just due, manifest such a spirit of true benevolence as to lift
them up to a Christian civilization—V. It is a fact that the present condition
of these Indians is becoming every day more favorable for their evangelization and civilization—and that this work is already being prosecuted with
prospects of success among the Omahas, the Pawnees and some tribes of
the Sioux. VI. It seems possible to obviate almost entirely the difficulties—
certainly all the dangers—already spoken of, which come from a near residence of these Indians, by stringent laws laws keeping them on their Reserves—forbidding all warlike and theiving demonstrations by one tribe on
another—and the occupation of the country by such posts of cavalry as shall
form an efficient protection from all evil disposed persons. In consideration
of these things, we ask your Excellency to pass by all arguments for the
removal of these unfortunate peoples based on selfish territorial financial or
political reasons—We believe that the new system which your Excellency
has recently adopted will succeed if it be supported by a military arm sufficient to awe down the dissatisfied and lawless—and if the policy be held
without wavering for a time sufficient to shew its reasonable results. And
we pledge ourselves as a Religious Body to cooperate so far as we can
consistently in every effort for the evangelization and civilization of these
Indians. Praying that the Lord would guide your Excellency to adopt and
execute the best plans for the welfare of all races found within the borders
of our nation, be they white or black or red—And that He will keep you and
strengthen you to accomplish all His Holy Will—with great joy to yourself

and a full assurance of everlasting life—We have the honor to remain your true friends and Staunch Supporters."—DS, DNA, RG 75, Letters Received, Northern Superintendency.

1869, JUNE 16. USG speech. "*Mr. Governor:* It affords me great pleasure to visit the Capital of the State which has done so much for my support and for the support of the Union in the time of the great rebellion—a State whose principles did so much to give me whatever political position I have attained, and a State where I have received such a hearty welcome in other days."—*Boston Evening Transcript*, June 16, 1869. USG spoke in response to a welcoming speech by Governor William Claflin of Mass. On June 1, Claflin had written to USG. "I have the honor to introduce to you Brvt Major Genl Underwood and Brvt Brig. Genl Bates, members of my personal staff, who visit West Point, for the purpose of tendering to you the courtesies and hospitalities of the State during your expected visit to Boston the coming week, and if agreeable to accompany you to this city. They will lay before you the suggestions that have been made as to a review which it is my desire and the desire of all the authorities should be conducted in the manner most in accordance with your feelings. I trust that you will honor the State and city by your presence, on the occasion and that you will see no objection to this public reception, for I assure you that nothing would be so gratifying to the people of the State as the opportunity of greeting the President, to whose election, they have given the largest majority of any State in the Union, and whose course since meets so fully their cordial approbation. I beg to commend Genl Underwood and Bates to your kind regard."—Copy, Massachusetts State Library, Boston, Mass. On June 14, USG, West Point, N. Y., telegraphed to Governor Onslow Stearns of N. H. "Will not be able to visit Concord at this time. Can only spend one day in Boston."—Sotheby Sale, May 23, 1984, no. 136. USG arrived in Boston on June 16 and, the next day, traveled to Worcester, Mass., and New York City.—*Boston Evening Transcript*, June 17, 1869. On Friday, June 18, USG, New York City, telegraphed to Horace Porter. "Please see Superintendent of RailRoad and get special car for me on train from here Monday morning next"—Telegram received (at 12:15 P.M.), DNA, RG 107, Telegrams Collected (Bound).

1869, JUNE 16. To Secretary of the Navy Adolph E. Borie. "You are authorized to direct that the pay of Machinists in the Steam Department of the Navy, on board Sea going vessels, be fixed at fifty-five dollars ($55.) per month."—Copy, DNA, RG 130, Executive Orders and Proclamations. On June 24, USG wrote to Borie. "You are authorized to establish the following rates in the Navy. Seaman Gunner at $32. per month Boiler Maker at 40. per month Coppersmith at 40. per month"—Copy, *ibid.*

1869, JUNE 16. Loudin Mullin, Denver, to USG. "Knowing no better way of having wrongs made right where there has been and is now a great abuse of power and position than to apply to you the highest power known for the remedy I have the honor respectfully to represent the following facts In the fall of 1865 A B Smith and G. W. McClure both brought suit in the District Court by Attachment against John Henry. The property was sold under the attachment and the money placed in the hands of Judge Eyster then and now Judge of the District Court for this District and he deposited it with the said G. W. McClure an officer in the U. S. Mint to whom the said John Henry afterwards confessed a judgement fraudulently as it has since fully appeared, leaving Mr Smith and Mr McClure to decide the matter in law. Mr Smith has all the time been ready to try his rights, but Mr McClure has continually asking for time which Judge Eyster has granted upon any frivolus pretexts for a motion from 1865 to the October term of 1868. At that term Mr McClure by his Attornies made a motion to dismiss on the ground that the said John Henry had been discharged from all liabilities, by the Bankrupt Act which benefit the said John Henry did apply for and obtain long after Mr Smith had attached his property, hence Mr Smith by his Attorney demurred. It was argued and the demurrer sustained and so *entered of record.* After the time and unknown to Mr Smith's Attorney, he Judge Eyster by some influence ordered the clerk to change the record to read *took under advisement* and since that time and through two terms of Court held by Judge Eyster in Denver he has been called on by the Attornies divers and sundry times and up to this date he has refused and failed to make any decision. The favoritism to the said G. W. McClure is a financial one, the Judge having his suit of rooms for Offices in McClure's building free of rent, and other like favors as I am credibly informed and verily beleive and for the correctness of this writing I refer to the records of the Court and the papers in the case and for my truthfulness &c I refer to my record as Capt & A. Q. M through the late war. Hence as a friend to Justice and right I must sincerely ask you to apply the proper remedy, by giveing this people a Judge that will act promptly and not be easily corrupted and a Mint Officer that will not seek to corrupt Judges"—ALS, DNA, RG 60, Records Relating to Appointments. On July 13, 1870, Horace Porter wrote to Attorney Gen. Amos T. Akerman. "The President directs me to ask you to inform him when the term of C. S. Eyster, Asso. Justice Sup. Court of Colorado Ter. expires."—Copy, DLC-USG, II, 1. The next day, Akerman wrote to USG. "In reply to your inquiry of yesterday I have the honor to state that the term of C. S. Eyster, Associate Justice of the Supreme Court of Colorado Territory will expire March 2d 1871."—LS, Free Library of Philadelphia, Philadelphia, Pa. On May 4, U.S. Representative Hamilton Ward of N. Y. had written to Frederick T. Dent. "I saw the Attorney General after my interview with the President with regard to the Appointment of the Hon Horace Bemis as Associate Justice of Colorado Territory Please advise me by letter what is the probability of Mr Bemis receiving an Appointment this summer or fall or earlier Please direct your Communication to me at Belmont Allegany Co NY as soon as practicable I think there will be no difficulty in giving him the Colorado appointment as the President says he is not Committed to any one for that position"—ALS, ICarbS. On Dec. 15, 1869, Ward had written to USG recommending the appointment of Horace Bemis as associate justice, Montana Territory.—ALS, DNA, RG 60, Records Relating to Appointments. On Jan. 25, 1871, U.S. Delegate Allen A. Bradford of Colorado Territory and Jerome B. Chaffee, delegate-elect, wrote to USG. "We very respectfully aske the appointment of Col E T Wells of Central City Colorado, Associate Justice of the Supreme Court of Colorado in the place of Hon C. S. Eyster whose term expires on the 2nd March next. Col Wells is a graduate of Knox College Ill was admitted to the Bar in 1856 and practiced law at Rock Island until 1862 when he entered the Army as 1st Lieutenat in a company raised in his own County, served on the Staff of General Johnson until the close of the War rising to the rank of Colonel was seriously wounded in battle, and served with great credit being constantly in the field. He has now been a resident of the Territory over five years and is well acquainted with the law & practice of the Territory and is in every way qualified for the position. His appointment will be quite satisfactory to the Bar & people and we believe will also be very creditable to the Administration."—LS, NNP. On Dec. 19, 1869, Thomas J. Wood, Dayton, had written to USG. "Captain E. T. Wells, late of the 89th Illinois Volunteers, served during the war for the suppression of the rebellion in the Army of the Cumberland—a part of the time on my staff—Therefore in speaking of him I speak from conscious knowledge—Captain Wells was a gallant, faithful, and intelligent officer, and deserves well of his country for his good services. I need not enumerate them all in detail. I understand he is an applicant for the office of Post-master in Central City, Colorado Territory. I feel that I may safely say he fully comes up to the standard fixed in the earlier days of the Republic—he is 'honest and capable'—"— ALS, *ibid.* On Feb. 3, 1871, USG nominated Ebenezer T. Wells to replace Christian S. Eyster as associate justice, Colorado Territory.

1869, JUNE 17. Governor Henry G. Blasdel of Nev., San Francisco, to USG. "There is much ill feeling existing on the Pacific coast against our Chinese population, which in several instances has resulted in violence; they are peaceable, industrious and very usefull in the developement of our resources; they have in the County of Humboldt in this State been driven from their homes, and now there is a large number employed in building a Rail Road from this place to Virginia City, the largest town in this State. It has come to my knowledge that organised bodies of men are threatening to drive them from the State; I will do all in my power to prevent such an outrage upon a peaceful and inoffensive people, but it is difficult to command sufficient force, in case the movement should be made. Many of our young men, belonging to the Military Companies, also belong to the organizators of the movement against the Chinese. There will be less danger of an outbreak if it is known that there is sufficient force to suppress it. I have deemed it necessary to inform your Excellency of these facts; for the necessity may arrise in a few days when I may be compelled to call on the United States forces to aid the civil authorities of the State to preserve the peace. In order that assistance may be within reach in case of an emergency I have to request that the Military authorities on this Coast be instructed to render the necessary assistance on my requisition. It would be well to instruct by telegraph as it may be too late to wait for instruction by Mail. The outbreak is expected early in July; but I hope to prevent even the attempt of violence by making it known that the laws will be enforced."—LS, DNA, RG 94, Letters Received, 499P 1869.

1869, JUNE 20. Eldridge McArthur, Shieldsboro, Miss., to USG. "as there now exists and has Existed for more than amonth a vacancy in the Custom Collection and Light House Pay Master and Superintendent Depterment at this Port of Entry, by the death of the late incumbent, Dr Robt Eager which you are likely ~~you~~ aware of ere this time, and it being generally entertained by some of the citizens, from, what I learn that there is some doubt whether but very few if any can Establish Sufficient Proof of Loyalty or not, and not being contaminated, or restrained by any of those unnatural fears, as I can show up a record entirely advarse to Some of my neighbours therefore no, other arrangements having been contemplated or adopted by yourself, Gen'l, I respectfully Solicit the appointment Provided there is any to be made—at present the office is temporari[ly] occupied by the family representatives of the Late Dr Eager (Females) to the best of my knowledge there being no male survivors, but I wish not the appointment to the Exclusion or injury of any person what ever Especially the weaker Sex. Gen'l an Early answer will Elicit many heart felt thanks etc"—ALS, DNA, RG 56, Collector of Customs Applications. M. B. Avery, "late Pastor of. M. E. Church Shieldsboro," Goodman, Miss., endorsed this letter. "The applicant is Well Known to me & is connected With the M. E. Ch—at Shieldsboro, is a *Native Mississippian*. He is the only Colored Man fully competent in every respect, to fill the office With credit to himself & honor to our Party—Consistant, energetic & honest and free from those intrigues so common among men—"—AES (undated), *ibid.* No appointment followed.

1869, JUNE 21. Mary E. McKay, Covington, Ky., to Julia Dent Grant. "I have been induced to send you this few lines by A publication. I saw in the newspapers, You stated if you had any influence you would use it in favor of the soldiers that defended the goverment, My husband was one among the first to take up arms, he joined the ram fleet under the Command of Col. Ellet he was in every battle from the mouth of the Ohio to New Orleans, he was at the siege of Vicksburgh. when it surrendered to Gen Grant, he was acting as Pilot, he ran the Queen of the West, past the batterys several times, he has prize money due him from the gunboats Gen Price Queen of the West and Switzerland, he has proved up his claims in regular form and forwarded them to the secatary of the Navy

many months ago   we have heard nothing from them   would you please
be so kind as to use your influence to induce him to send part of it immediately if not all,   My husband on account of disease contracted in the war
has not been able to do any thing sinse, bsede he recieved A severe gunshot
through one of his limbs   he is now fifty six y six years of age   we live in
one of the meanest rebel states in the union and they would be glad to take
our little home from us for taxes.   we ask for nothing onely what is justly
due us   what would congressmen think of the goverment if they had to
wait four or five years after rendering services. I here enclose you A line
from J R. Grant. your fatherinlaw.   for any kindness I will render up my
prayers to Almighty God for your hapiness and wellfare.   please excuse
any error I may have commited in writing these few lines."—ALS, DNA,
RG 45, Letters from the President. The enclosure is *ibid.* On Feb. 12, 1874,
the Senate reported adversely on the petition of Rowley S. McKay.—*SRC,*
43-1-87; *SJ,* 43-1, pp. 241–42.

1869, JUNE 21.   Yardley Warner, Germantown, Pa., to USG. "The enclosed with many other similar goads to duty, brings my mind to a point
of decision; viz to offer my services in the gap between the Indian and the
Govt. I presume it is too late to go through the forms of application specified by our 'Friend's Andian Aid Assn of Philada' of whose representative
Comtee I am one. Besides I frankly confess that I would prefer working in
a direct channel of *authority from the President & the Indian Dept* (looking to Philada Friends only for *supplies*) to any other complicity whatever;
making my *reports and pledges just as any other Agent,* but responsible
for my policy and management only to the Govt through its lawful representatives. . . . Genl Howard (O O) & E. Whittlesey know me by my work
in the South; where, immediately upon the retreat of Johnson out of North
Carolina, I organized the circuit of schools in that state, known as the
Friend's Circuit; and was its first Supt. . . ."—ALS, DNA, RG 48, Appointments Div., Letters Received.

1869, JUNE 22.   USG order. "The Secretary of the Interior is hereby instructed to cause to be laid before me, in accordance with the provisions of
the Indian Appropriation Act of Congress, approved April 20th 1869, such
evidence as shall be satisfactory, that certain Indians, heads of families,
and single women of adult age, belonging to the Pottawatamie tribe, have
conformed to the requirements of the treaties of November 15th 1861, and
March 29. 1866. thereby becoming citizens of the United States, to the end
that I may be enabled to direct that such monies as may be due said Indians
shall be paid to them and patents to issue for lands as required by the aforesaid treaties and Act of Congress."—Copy, DNA, RG 130, Executive
Orders and Proclamations.

1869, JUNE 22.   Secretary of the Navy Adolph E. Borie to USG. "The
enclosed papers, sent to this Department by the Commissioner of Internal

Revenue, are respectfully submitted to the President. The Department has no authority to comply with the request of the Commissioner to use the Marines for civil purposes, without orders from the President of the United States."—Copy, DNA, RG 45, Letters Sent to the President.

1869, JUNE 22. William A. Richardson, act. secretary of the treasury, to USG informing him of gifts held at the customhouse, Georgetown, D. C., from " 'a poor and very humble Mexican in his transports of satisfaction at the abolition of slavery . . .' "—Copy, DNA, RG 56, Letters Sent to the President. USG received a twenty-eight piece silver coffee set.

1869, JUNE 22. Cyrus A. Eastman, San Francisco, to USG. "I take the liberty of writing to thank you for the appointment of Asst. Treasurer—I am the more grateful as I believe I owe it entirely to your kind remembrance and belief in my integrity & capacity, and not to any outside influence It took me by surprise, & found me on a sick bed—from which I have now recovered, but shall not be fit for active business for two or three weeks—I also hear a rumour that charges have been made against me—but I cannot ascertain what they are, nor can I find any one to father them—I am perfectly willing that anything I may have done should be laid before the Department—~~but~~ but I object to garbled statements lies and slander—and if there are any charges against me I would like copies of them—if they are such as you deem worthy of notice—Under these circumstances I have asked the Hon. Secy. of the Treasy. for time to decide on the acceptance for the office will require my whole undivided time to the exclusion of private business & I will not accept unless I can do full justice to the Government and to you, who have so kindly honored me with the appointment—"—Copy, DNA, RG 56, Collector of Customs Applications. On May 12, USG had designated Eastman as treasurer, branch mint, and asst. treasurer, San Francisco. On May 19 and 25, Col. Rufus Ingalls, New York City, telegraphed to Orville E. Babcock. "Do not understand me as endorsing what Ben Holladay says of C. A Eastman. I believe the latter to be an honorable man" "C A. Eastman of San Francisco telegraphs me as follows: Who was appointed Assistant Treasurer here. I should like it Please inform me if any appointment is made and if so who is the man. I supposed Eastman was appointed"—Telegrams received (at 1:15 P.M. and 11:50 A.M.), *ibid.*, RG 107, Telegrams Collected (Bound). On June 24, Eastman wrote to USG. "Since mine of the 22d Inst. a copy of which I enclose—I have understood that Genl. Miller. Collector of Customs here, has or will soon resign. Now if you have no one on whom you wish to bestow it—it is a position that I would much like to have—I must say however that I have no shadow of a claim on you—for in advocating your election with spech, purse & vote I only carried out my own party views—acted for the good of my country—and followd the dictates of esteem & friendship—Neither will it advantage, much in future—for in any event the administration will have my cordial though humble support—I can only promise—I think a competent, I am sure an honest & faithful administration of Custom House affairs—I know it looks like presumption after having been honored with an office of trust and responsibility to ask for a change—but I must confess that I dislike—what is a great charm in the eyes of most—the charge & disbursement of such large sums of money—Now about $9.000.000 & increasing—while as Collector I can deposite daily—And I am not so poor as to have nothing to loose nor so rich as to be able to stand great losses—"—ALS, *ibid.*, RG 56, Collector of Customs Applications. See *PUSG*, 16, 146.

1869, June 23.   To Vice Admiral David D. Porter, superintendent, U.S. Naval Academy, and act. secretary of the navy. "This will be handed to you by T. B. Howard, a Galena boy who I have appointed to the Naval Academy, and in whom I take great interest. The boy has never been much from home and may be a little home sick at first, but I have faith in his proving well at the end. I hope you will find it convenient to give him a word of encouragement. . . ."—Christie's, June 9, 1993, no. 174. On March 15, Orville E. Babcock had written to Lucius S. Felt, Galena. "The President directs that you send the full name of young Howard, applying for appointment as Cadet at the Naval-Academy"—Copies, DLC-USG, II, 1, 4. On March 22, Horace Porter wrote to Secretary of the Navy Adolph E. Borie. "The President directs me to request that the following named persons be appointed Cadets at large in the Naval Academy John M Robinson Jones M Jackson NewYork Edmund B. Underwood NewYork Frederick Van Vliiet Thomas B Howard Illinois James Duane and requests that the Secretary of the Navy name four additional cadets from the sons of Naval officers—"—Copies, *ibid.* On March 23, Horace Porter wrote to Borie. "The President directs me to inquire whether there is not an additional Naval Cadet appointed from the District of Columbia, making the whole number appointed by him eleven?"—LS, DNA, RG 45, Letters Received from the President. On March 24, Horace Porter wrote to Borie. "The President directs me to say that he promised an appointment of Naval Cadet to Chas. F. Holder, and had endorsed an order for his appointment on his application, but overlooked it in making up the list of names. He therefore requests that the name of Mr Holder be substituted for that of James Duane, and that conditional appointments be sent to James Duane and Jones M. Jackson entitling them to admission to the Naval Academy in case vacancies should be created by any of the ten appointments at large being found deficient."—Copies, DLC-USG, II, 1, 4. On June 26, Admiral Porter wrote to USG. "I notice by the papers, that a son of General Robinson is mentioned as having been appointed at West Point. This young man was also appointed in the Navy and has passed a creditable examination at Annapolis. So there is one more vacancy at West Point. I also beg leave to inform you that Charles F. Holden, whom you appointed to Annapolis in your letter of March 24. has been rejected. You also directed that conditional appointments be sent to James Duane and Jones M. Jackson in case of rejection. Will you please inform me to which of these young men the appointment should be sent. I would state that James Duane originally received the appointment which was revoked by your order and sent to Holden."—LS, OFH.

1869, JUNE 24. Chief Justice Salmon P. Chase, Richmond, to USG. "An old friend of mine, an earnest & faithful Republican, & a zealous supporter of yours is anxious to have a letter in his behalf & one written by himself meet your eyes; and has asked me to aid him in the accomplishment of this wish. I therefore enclose these & shall be gratified by any good that may befall the writer. With best wishes for the success of your administration & for your personal happiness, . . ."—ALS, DNA, RG 59, Letters of Aplication and Recommendation. The enclosures are *ibid.* On June 9, Chambers Baird, Ripley, Ohio, had written to USG. ". . . I can refer you to Chief Justice Chase, Ex. Gov. Dennison of Ohio, & most of our Ohio, Representatives & Senators Sherman & Wade: to your frinds Messrs S. Hemphill, W. B. Campbell, O. F. Shaw, of our Town: to Col. White & others of Georgetown, & to your father, who has known me for many years. If you think I would be faithful & competent, & you have any use for me in any capacity for which I am competent, I shall be pleased to receive your appointment, & will *try* to do my duty. Accept my kindest regards & best wishes."—ALS, *ibid.* No appointment followed.

1869, JUNE 24. "Solders of 25 Inft," New Orleans, to USG. "We the Solders of the 25th U S. Inft. stationed at Jackson Barracks make the following statement to you knowing you are our Friend. our time is out in about three weeks and we should like to enlist again—when it is out. but the bad treatment we receive from our officers will not allow us to do so. we know you do not know about it. weare tied up by the thumbs and are not allowed to take any exercise outside the barracks. for the reason that we must spend all our money with the Sutler who charges double the price for his thrash he has got to sell us to what the stores out side charges for better goods. and when we are paid off we cannot get any passes out side untill all our money is spent with the Sutler and the offices gag and court martial us if wedo not pay him. he claims more money than we owe him. they wont even let the women that comes in to sell us Milk & Eggs. sell us cakes and bread. we must trade with the Sutler and no other person. We hope you will do something for us and then we will enlist if we get better treatment from our officers—"—AD, DNA, RG 94, Letters Received, 295L 1869. Lt. Col. Romeyn B. Ayres, 19th Inf., investigated the complaint.— ES, *ibid.*

1869, JUNE 26. William E. Dodge, New York City, to USG. "The 'Suez Canal' One of the great Works of the Age is approaching completion and in the month of October next the Event is to be celebrated by very Extensive cerimonies which will occupy several days, and all the Nations of the World will be represented—When the Work was fairly commenced in

April 1865 there were appropriate ceremonies and 'the chamber of the State of [N]ew York sent Cyrus W Field Esq one of its members to represent the Commerce of New York who made a very interesting report which was published—In conversing with several of our Members it has occured to us that the Completion of this great work demanded that our Nation should be represented and as I am informed Mr Field will be in Europe at the time it Would be very gratifying to the Merchants of New York if he should be appointed by the Government . . ."—ALS, DNA, RG 59, Letters of Application and Recommendation. Related papers are *ibid.* See Samuel Carter III, *Cyrus Field: Man of Two Worlds* (New York, 1968), p. 280.

1869, June 28.   Governor John W. Geary of Pa. to USG. "No act of yours could have afforded me more personal gratification than the appointment of my son a *Cadet to West Point.*—I tender you my most ardent thanks as an instalment of my gratitude."—ALS, PHi. William L. Geary graduated from USMA in 1874.

1869, June 29.   John W. Garrett, president, Baltimore and Ohio Railroad, Baltimore, to USG. "I have completed the arrangements for the visits tomorrow,   a special train will await yourself, the members of the cabinet & friends at the Washington station to start at 9 A. m. The train will be run directly to mount Claire and after the inspection of the works there proceed to Locust Point   The steamship Baltimore will sail at two PM,   I have so arranged that the party will return by the chesapeake to reach Balto about seven P. m. I have also arranged in accordance with your desire that the special train shall return to Washington immediately after your arrival in Baltimore"—Telegram received (at 12:10 P.M.), DNA, RG 107, Telegrams Collected (Bound). See *Washington Chronicle*, July 1, 1869.

1869, June 29.   W. McLan and two others, Manassas, Va., to USG. "Will members elect to the Legislature be required to take iron clad oath before taking their seats"—Telegram received (at 9:30 A.M.), DNA, RG 107, Telegrams Collected (Bound). On July 31, U.S. Representative John F. Farnsworth of Ill., St. Charles, wrote to USG. "I see that the question is agitated, 'what oath shall be administered to the members of the Virginia Legislature. I gave that subject considerable thought in connection with the reconstruction of some of the other states—It is not now presented for the first time—The members of the legislature were elected in peursuance of the provisions of the constitution of Virginia—They can only legislate in accordance with its provisions—that constitution prescribes the qualifications of the members and the oath to be taken by them—Shall they take that oath, or should they take the '*Test oath*' which is prescribed by congress for 'officers of the United States'?—Every one I believe, admits that after the state is fully 'restored' to the Union the 'Test oath' cannot be administered to the legislature; but only the oath required by their constitution—Can different qualifications be required of members of the same legislature, at different periods, under the same constitution, and without *any change of laws*?! . . . "—ALS, *ibid.*, RG 60, Letters from the President. On Oct. 4, Attorney Gen. Ebenezer R. Hoar endorsed this letter. "Came rather too late to be of service—but seems to agree very well with our views—"—AES, *ibid.*

1869, JUNE 29. Governor Robert K. Scott of S. C. to USG. "My attention has been called to an associated press telegram of the 27th inst. from Washington, announcing that Dr A. G. Mackey, Collector of the Port of Charleston had been removed, and G. W. Clark Esqr of that City appointed in his stead. While I would not presume to interfere in the Federal appointments in this State; I beg leave to express my views in regard to this change, whether it has been already made or is only contemplated. . . ."—LS, DNA, RG 56, Collector of Customs Applications. On July 7, Henry Beecher, Charleston, wrote to USG. "The change you have made in our Custom House meets the approval of all respectable people whether Southern or Northern. Mackay who you has displaced from office of Collector of Port has the Custom House filled with soldiers of the Confederate Army. . . ."—ALS, *ibid.* Related papers are *ibid.*

1869, JUNE 29. J. W. Thomas, alderman, Wetumpka, Ala., to USG. "Parkinson has come, is not a Republican a right to live in South"—Telegram received (at 12:13 P.M.), DNA, RG 107, Telegrams Collected (Bound). Democratic candidate for Congress J. C. Parkinson canvassed Wetumpka on June 29. See *Montgomery Daily Advertiser*, June 24, 30, 1869.

1869, [JUNE]. "Widow Klein," Villefranche, to USG. "I take the liberty of having the honor of addressing the present to you. I have recourse to you Mr President because there now are many letters which I have addressed to my Son Louis Marick, at Mr Dressers, Druggist, at Killsboro (Ohio) and always I have not be been able to get any answers and this is what ails his poor mother; very old and without property; by keeping her in the sorrow of not knowing what has become of him. (whether dead or alive). at any rate I do not forget him, and commend him to Divine Providence, and to you Mr President, in case he he is in existence, praying you with all my heart to be pleased to allow me to recommend him to you if you please; He is a good son to his Mother, if you can Mr President find out where he is, if living, in the United States. . . ."—ALS and copy (docketed as received on June 17—in French with translation), DNA, RG 59, Miscellaneous Letters.

1869, JUNE. E. B. Payne, Waukegan, Ill., to USG requesting an appointment as special treasury agent in a western territory. ". . . I . . . was the first man in my county to advocate the nomination & election of Gen. Grant

for President which I did in a Public Speech during the fall of 1867."—
Harold R. Nestler, 1984, no. 124. No appointment followed.

1869, JUNE. T. F. Tukesbury, Brentwood, N. H., to USG. "Having
obtained more favorable impressions of your views in relation to Peace than
of any former president, by such expressions as, '*Let us have Peace*' and
the like, and by appointing Friends to settle Indian difficulties without
bloodshed, I take liberty to present you a copy of my little work 'Book of
Essays,' and forward in company with this line for your examination, and
hope it may meet your approval. We feel truly glad to know that you
render your influence and executive power to favor Peace. Such a course
will not only secure the approval of the most virtuous in community; but
what is far more Peace is in accordance with the eternal truth and commands of God our Creator.—I wish to do good and benefit my fellowmen.
Is there not some one or more whom you know would be good canvassing
agents to make sale of my little books?—If this shall not too much intrude
upon your already multiplied duties, will you please to favor me with a
reply at your earliest convenience?—May the blessing of God attend you."
—ALS, Ford Collection, NN.

1869, JULY 2. Horace Porter to Walter Harriman, naval officer, Boston.
"The President has been informed by Gen'l John A. Dix that his brother
has been removed from the position of Deputy Naval Officer at Boston. I
am directed by the President to request that if you can find it consistent
with your sense of duty you will restore Mr Dix to the office formerly held
by him. This request is made at the earnest solicitation of Genl. Dix who
feels a deep interest in his brothers restoration."—Copy, DLC-USG, II, 1,
4. Replaced by Hiram Smart as deputy naval officer, T. Brown Dix served
as storekeeper in the Boston customhouse.

1869, JULY 2. Frederick Dent Grant, New York City, to USG. "I leave
here tomorrow night. Send the carriage to the Depot for me"—Telegram
received (at 11:45 A.M.), DNA, RG 107, Telegrams Collected (Bound).

1869, JULY [3]. USG endorsement. "Gen. Quinby, the writer, is U. S.
Marshal for the Northern dist. of N. Y. He would not be likely to make a
recommendation which he did not think well merited."—AES, DNA, RG
56, Collector of Customs Applications. Written on a letter of July 1 from
Isaac F. Quinby, U.S. marshal, Rochester, N. Y., to USG. "Permit me again
to invite your attention to the matter of the appointment of Colonel William
Emerson as Collector of Customs for the Port of Genessee. As I told you
last saturday the present incumbent belongs to the class of low politicians
and his social and political Standing is such that his continuance in office
will certainly reflect no credit upon your administration and in my opinion
and that of many other earnest members of the republican party will seriously injure the future of the party in this Congressional District For

these reasons and because Colonel Emerson is a deserving soldier whose
claims are urged with great unanimity by his fellow soldiers as well as by
a large number of prominent citizens (republicans) of this district Judge
Davis, our representative gave him a strong but well merited recommendation the disregard of which in this case I am sure he would deeply feel.
Judge Davis is one of the most able men in the State of New York upon
whom the nomination for Congress for this District (28th) was almost
forced and whic[h] he finally consented to accept only in the hope of recon-
ciling the party feuds which threatened to result in the election of a democrat   He is a man who will make his strength felt in whatever position he
may be placed and in him you will find a firm and valuable friend at all
times   I hope for the good of your administration and for the good of the
party in this District that you will not disappoint his expectations in respect
to Colonel Emerson."—ALS, *ibid.* Additional recommendations are *ibid.*

1869, JULY 5.   To Secretary of the Navy George M. Robeson. "Will the
Secty of the Navy please see the bearer, J D Baltimore. I think it would be
well to appoint him at once as apprentice in one of the govt machine shops
where he can be employed on machinery. Please see statement of what he
has done without instruction."—Copy, USG 3.

1869, JULY 5.   Lewis V. Hollyfield, Dadeville, Mo., to USG. "I Enclose
to you a Letter from the Commissioner of Pensions to myself Suspending
the Pension Claim of Matilda James Simply because her husband belonged
to the Enrolled Missouri Militia   General John. B. Sanborn of your City
will Testify that—the Enroll Missouri Militia was in Joint Service with the
U. S. forces By order of the General Commanding this District and under
the Ninth Section of the act of July 4. 1864 She is Entitled to a pension if
Justice is done her and I want you to Se that this Claim is Caled up and
proper attention is paid to See that this widow gets her pension alloud   I
have got Severl Pensions alloud for widowes that their husbands Served in
this Same Service   I believe this Class of Claimes was Suspended by president Johnson and his Set of Clerks   I have Severl Claimes rejected in this
way of this Class   please attend to this and oblige your friend . . ."—ALS,
DNA, RG 48, Miscellaneous Div., Letters Received. The enclosure is *ibid.*
On the same day, Hollyfield wrote to USG concerning other pension claims.
—ALS, *ibid.*

1869, JULY 5.   Maurice Langhorne, Washington, D. C., to USG. "The
reason I wrote to you on the 26th ultimo was that I had seen no reference
made to any of the matters (herewith enclosed) in either our press or the
correspondence with England in relation to the differences arising out of
the war—and from my knowledge of the facts—I judged that the regular
channels upon which this government had to rely for information in regard
to this matter were not sufficiently uninterested to report fairly upon the
subject, and taking an article that appeared in the Atlantic Monthly of July

1865 purporting to be from the records, as a fair sample of such reports, I know if any similar are to be found on file in any of the Depts, that the channels aforesaid were corrupted to an extent that the best interests of the government were set aside—Now I can convince you or any fair minded man that that article is untrue and that if it had been taken as true, one of the consequences would have been that it would have resulted in the arraignment of both Genls Sweet & Hill by the Gov't.—I have always thought General, if there was anything that appeared irregular in my conduct at the time the government as the recipient of my services should have notified me and requested an explanation, particularly as I had been a rebel, and had gone off quietly about my business without seeking any office or reward until I was so poor and satisfied beyond a doubt that my prospects of engaging successfully in any business were materially impaired by the use my personal enemies made of these very services, then I accepted a clerkship in the Treasury, supposing the government had given it to me on this account, and you can judge my humiliation when I discovered a few months later (and your conversation with my attorney confirms my impression) that it had been gotten for me under a total misapprehension of the facts—Now General as I was the only person in the country who could have furnished the government with a statement covering the scope of these expeditions, you will perceive, that not only sound policy; but the positive interests of the country required that my testimony should be kept unimpaired for the purpose of fully protecting the interests of the nation as against Canada & England—Now however the government can only use my knowledge of these affairs, and I offer that, because it is my duty, and again if I did not and these matters should be brought to light some day my personal enemies would claim that I remained here in Washington, without making an effort to have the record straitened when I knew the public interests demanded it—I beg leave to refer you to the accompanying synopsis of these several expeditions fitted out in Canada against the U. States during the war, and ask leave to file in the War ~~Dept~~ and State Departments my version or history of them—and most respectfully represent that I have never connived at concealing any of the facts from the government, and do not hesitate to say that I believe if the government had been kept correctly informed in relation to the aid and comfort extended the confederates by Canadians its armies would have been turned northward at the close of the war   I beg leave to call your attention to the fact that my testimony before the Cincinnati Military Commission was never corrected because it was impossible for me to do so without interlining it to such an extent that it would have rendered it unintelligible—2nd That the statement I furnished the State Department in October 1864—was made, at the request of Mr. Seward to be informed as to the status of certain parties then living in Canada, and when I was under the impression that the details of these matters which had occurred previous to that time, had been laid before him—"—ALS, DNA, RG 59, Miscellaneous Letters. The enclosure is *ibid.* In 1864, Langhorne accompanied C.S.A. agent George St.

Leger Grenfell from Canada to Chicago, informed U.S. authorities about Grenfell's plans to release prisoners there, and eventually testified against him.—*HED*, 39-2-50, pp. 77–101.

1869, July 6. Secretary of the Navy George M. Robeson to USG. "I have the honor to enclose herewith the resignation of Paymaster H. Bridge as Chief of the Bureau of Provisions and Clothing; and to request the appointment of Paymaster Edward T. Dunn to fill the vacancy. Paymaster Dunn is the senior officer of his grade on the active list, and combines all the qualifications requisite for the fulfilment of the duties of the office."—Copy, DNA, RG 45, Letters Sent to the President. On July 14, Robeson wrote to USG. "I have the honor to submit, herewith, for your signature, a commission for Paymaster E. T. Dunn, as Chief of the Bureau of Provisions and Clothing, vice H. Bridge, resigned."—Copy, *ibid.*

1869, July 8. Charles B. Norton, Paris, to USG. "I have the honour to ask your kind attention to enclosed Circular. Since leaving the army I have served as United States Commissioner to the Great Exposition and at that time commenced the publication of the Journal referred to. It is my object to make a national Paper for Europe and I have the support of Mess Washburne, Burlingame Curtin and others—I shall value your aid in this plan most highly."—ALS, Ford Collection, NN. Norton, formerly a noted publisher and book dealer in New York City, published the *Continental Gazette.*

1869, July 9. James T. Fulton, International Hotel, Niagara Falls, N. Y., to USG. "Will you stop here on your way west, Answer"—Telegram received (at noon), DNA, RG 107, Telegrams Collected (Bound).

1869, July 9. Cornelia T. Russell, Mare Island, Calif., to USG. "I wrote you a few weeks since in regard to the promotion (by a few numbers) of my husband Comndr Russell I presume your absence from home has deterred you from writing. I yesterday received a paper recently published containing a short account of an expedition Commanded by Capt Russell and will forward it for your perusal You will I trust be kind enough to let me know what you will do towards the advancement of Capt R to his proper position on the *List* explained in my previous letter—I would not trouble you thus, did I not know I was writing to my friend. I cannot tell you how very much you will oblige me by attending to this matter & informing me of the result—"—ALS, DNA, RG 45, Subject File, Div. HA. The enclosed clipping is *ibid.* Vice Admiral David D. Porter endorsed this letter. "This case has been considered by the Department and for the present it is not advisable to reopen it."—AES (undated), *ibid.*

1869, July 10. Secretary of the Interior Jacob D. Cox to USG. "I have the honor to submit, herewith, a letter, dated the 8th inst., from the Commissioner of Indian Affairs, and accompanying papers including a petition asking Executive clemency in behalf of one David Ross, a native Cherokee, recently convicted of murder, in the U. S. District Court for the Western District of Arkansas, and respectfully invite your attention to the suggestion of the Commissioner."—Copy, DNA, RG 48, Indian Div., Letters Sent. On Aug. 7, John H. B. Latrobe, Newport, R. I., wrote to Secretary of State Hamilton Fish. "Availing myself of a personal acquaintance, which has always been most agreable to me, I am going to ask a favour which your presence near the President, just now, may enable you to grant. Sometime since, I was applied to by the friends of an unfortunate Indian under sentence of death as accessory to a murder committed in his presence. The trial took place in Western Arkansas, and application was immediately made to the President for a pardon, or, at least, commutation of the sentence, signed by the bar, members of the Court and jury and a large number of most respectable persons, as I was assured, both white and Indian—I addressed a letter to the President which reached Washington, I am told, the day he left for Long Branch, and which he has probably not seen. The letter was but the addition of my voice to those that had been already raised in the Indian's favour. The case went, of course, to the attorney Genl—and I am, to day, in receipt of information, that the papers which seem to have been sent to the District Atty for Westn Arkansas, have been returned, with the opinion, previously expressed by him, that Dave Ross, the Indian in question should not be hung, but that his sentence should be commuted. . . . Under these circumstances, I have thought you would not take it amiss, if I asked you to call General Grant's attention to this matter. I know the President personally but, notwithstanding, I dislike excessively to intrude with business upon a leisure that he has well earned. If a life were not, possibly, at stake I would not do so—But the worst of hanging is, that the party cannot be *unhung*. I have addressed, enclosed, a few lines to the President, his endorsement on which, if he should see fit to reprieve the party till this matter can be looked into, will make it certain, when forwarded to the proper department in Washington, that a reprieve will be had, by the postponement of the execution, at all events. . . ."—ALS, DLC-Hamilton Fish. On Aug. 11, USG commuted the sentence.

1869, JULY 10. Charles W. Dabney, consul, Fayal, Azores, to USG. "I have the honor, Sir, to acknowledge the receipt of your despatch announcing my suspension from the Office of Consul of the U. S. for the Azores. Being proud of my record, I can only ascribe my removal to the same cause, that occasioned it in 1846, when Mr Haight appeared here as Consul of the U. S. appointed by President Polk, but was so disappointed that he returned by the first opportunity and resigned his commission. Representations were made in my favor by some of the principal commercial cities and the Honble Caleb Cushing (who had been here on his way as Ambassador to China, and was then Attorney Genl of the U. S.) giving his testimony, there was no difficulty in convincing President Polk of the advantages to be derived from my reappointment. Since then I have twice been the recipient of the thanks of the King of Portugal for relief afforded by me and through my exertions and co-operation in crises of famine, and from the local authorities and inhabitants I have received the strongest expressions of gratitude. My long residence here as U. S. Consul, while rendering my services more valuable, also renders the stigma of removal more trying, for this is now my home and I cannot break up my business here which has required so many years to establish. Were your time not so valuable, I should beg an investigation into my action throughout the late war, by which I cheerfully lost much money from patriotic motives. Permit me to lay before you copies of four dispatches from the Department of State, together with copies of Mr Cushing's letter to me on his departure from Fayal and of the copy of his letter addressed to the President, enclosed in mine, written 20th August *1843*."—LS, DNA, RG 59, Letters of Application and Recommendation. Enclosures and related papers are *ibid.* On June 1, USG had designated John C. Cover to replace Dabney. On Sept. 11, U.S. Senators Matthew H. Carpenter and Timothy O. Howe of Wis., Milwaukee, wrote to Secretary of State Hamilton Fish. "Our friend J. C. Cover Esq of Wis. who was appointed by you Consul at Fayal Azores, has been sorely persecuted and beset by the friends of his predecessor to resign in his favor; and having been offered, as we are informed $12.000 gold if he would do so, which he declined to consider, Mr Cover was then threatened with removal by you before he could reach his post; that is he was threatened that they would procure you to revoke his appointment. We understand that the predecessor of Mr Cover and his father have held that position, together, for over 60 yrs. and the willingness to pay $12.000 gold to prevent removal from an office with $1800 salary, would seem to suggest that it was high time for a change. Mr Cover is every way a fit appointee, and we trust he will not be disturbed"—LS, *ibid.* On Sept. 19, Manning F. Force, Paris, wrote to USG. "At the risk of being forward, I beg leave to say a word about Mr. Dabney, U. S. consul at Fayal. I have known of him as consul since I was a student at college, and have some personal acquaintance with him. He is a man of extraordinary purity of character, an accurate man of business, a gentleman of more than ordinary accomplishment, and a true American. In the war, he and his family were all ardent in the national cause. The son living in Boston served as an officer in a Massachusetts regiment.— Mr. Dabney has lived so long in Fayal and has such commanding influence there, that I do not see how any other person could fill the office with equal credit and service to the government. While writing, I cannot refrain from saying that Gen. Rawlins looked so well when I saw him in Washington only last July, that it was a shock to hear from Mr. Bancroft in Berlin of his death. His large head, his great warm heart, his burning patriotism, were felt and known by every man in the Army of the Tennessee. We all knew how close and dear he was to you—and the telegram that conveyed the news of this bereavement set every one, at least of that old army, living over again ~~the~~ from the time when Captain Rawlins was your adjutant till he became, under you, the war minister of the nation."—ALS, *ibid.* On

Feb. 9, 1870, Sarah M. Hills, North Easton, Mass., wrote to USG. "I take the liberty to address you at this time in order to express my gratification at the removal of Mr Dabney from the Office of American Consul at Fayall, and I hope it will be consistent with your views not to reinstate him, for the reason, *that* when he chartered the Portuguese Brig Everista, which sailed from that Port 13th Nov. /67 for the purpose of bringing those 87 unfortunate Seamen to Boston, *he knew she was not Sea Worthy.* I have reliable information from his Brother in Law who resides in this vicinity, that the Brig was built and owned by Dabney and Co. was called at that time the News Boy, She was a very fast Sailer, but on account of her sharp build they did not consider her safe for Sea; and they subsequently sold her to a company in Fayall. He mentioned it in a casual manner, without any appearance of unpleasant feelings towards the Consul, I do not know why Mr Dabney was removed, but in my opinion he not only deserved removal, but public censure, for permitting ~~those~~ those poor Sailors to *attempt* to cross that boisterous and trackless waste, in the winter season, in a vessel that he *knew* could not live in a storm, I hope an efficient Officer is appointed who will fill that high Office of trust with honor to himself, and his country, and will feel sympathy for those who are left in his Charge, in a Foreign land, . . ."—ALS, *ibid.* On Dec. 3, 1872, following the death of Cover, USG nominated Samuel W. Dabney as consul.

1869, JULY 11. U.S. Senator Carl Schurz of Mo., St. Louis, to USG. "Last week I received a telegram from Mr. George Earle, first Assistant Postmaster General, stating that 'the President would appoint Mr. James Hunter postmaster at St. Joseph unless I could make good my objection to him on the ground of personal hostility.' I replied by telegraph, that I would personally meet the parties concerned and then write to you. I telegraphed to several prominent Republicans of St. Joseph to meet me at Kansas City on the 3d inst., but they failed to do so, and not having time to go to St. Joseph, I returned to this city without having received any further light on the subject. I should have written to you at once, had I not fallen sick and been unable for several days to attend to my correspondence. As I stated in my last letter, I should not have raised any objection to Mr. Hunters appointment on *puerely personal* grounds, had I not been convinced that a majority of the Republicans of St. Joseph wanted somebody else. When Mr. Asper submitted to me affidavits intended to show that my impressions of Mr. Hunters personal hostility to me were unfounded, I wrote to some of the leading men at St. Joseph and received replies of which the enclosed letters ~~is~~are a specimens. I had several from Col. Strong and other prominent Republicans of the same tenor. I send these merely to show you, that I acted in good faith when I objected to Mr. Hunter on personal grounds. I send these letters confidentially and shall be obliged if you will cause them to be returned to me. If my impressions of Mr. Hunters conduct were wrong, they at any rate proceeded from the representations of gentlemen on whose statements I had good reasons to rely. As to the Republicans of

St. Joseph strongly desiring the appointment of somebody else, I refer to a petition in favor of Major Drumhiller recently sent out from St. Joseph and signed by a majority of the Republican voters of that place. That petition must be on file in the Post office Department. I write this letter merely for the purpose of justifying my own position in this controversy. I may add that I had nothing in view but the desires of a majority of the Republican voters of St. Joseph. I have no personal interest, no axe to grind in this matter. Although I naturally prefer my friends to my enemies, it is after all of little consequence to me whether the postmaster at St. Joseph loves or hates me. Had I not had reason to believe that I was doing a service to the Republicans of St. Joseph, I should never have raised any objection to Mr. Hunter on my own account. If Mr. Hunter has it in his power to satisfy the Republicans of St. Joseph, no personal objection on my part shall stand in his way. It is more their affair, than mine."—ALS, MoSHi. On May 11, Schurz had telegraphed to USG. "I with hundreds of St Joseph republicans earnestly object to Hunter's appointment, papers will be forwarded"—Telegram received (at 11:30 A.M.), DNA, RG 107, Telegrams Collected (Bound). On April 17, USG had nominated James Hunter as postmaster, St. Joseph, Mo., withdrew the nomination on April 20, then renominated him on Dec. 6.

1869, JULY 12.   Jesse Applegate, Yoncalla, Ore., to USG. "As the politicians are making great exertions to cause you to change your policy in respect to placing the Indians under the care of army officers, and as one of our Senators has gone to Washington specially to inform you that your change will be injurious and detrimental to the Indians and the States and Territories in which they reside, I have ventured to address you on that subject. I believe a large majority of the people of the United States approve of placing the Indians entirely under the care of the military and the change will be followed by the best results and none of the evils predicted by those having an interest in maintaining the old system. I have spent a long life on the frontiers, the last twenty six years in Oregon. My experience has taught me to prefer military to civil officers in all positions consistent with their profession, the management of the Indians is in strict accordance with it, and they would have been placed under their care years ago, had it not been for the opposition of those interested in maintaining the old order of things. . . ."—ALS, DNA, RG 48, Appointment Div., Letters Received.

1869, JULY 12.   Virginia Grant Corbin, New York City, to USG. "Many thanks. Father will return therefore I cannot leave home"—Telegram received (at 1:20 P.M.), DNA, RG 107, Telegrams Collected (Bound).

1869, JULY 13.   USG endorsement. "I hereby rescind the executive order of March 20, 1867, referred to, and direct the restoration of the lands withheld, to market."—*HED*, 45-3-1, part 5, p. 743. Written on a letter of July 6, from Ely S. Parker, commissioner of Indian affairs, to Secretary of the Interior Jacob D. Cox. "I have the honor to transmit herewith a letter from the Commissioner of the General Land Office, dated the 2d ultimo, asking information relative to the Santee Sioux Indian Reservation, situated between the Big Sioux and James Rivers, and between the forty-fourth and forty-fifth parallels of north latitude, in Dakota Territory, and suggesting that if those lands are no longer occupied by Indians, necessary steps should be taken to restore them to the public domain. This office has informally obtained from the General Land Office the inclosed copy of a letter and indorsements, by which it appears that Louis V. Bogy, as a special commissioner, selected the above-described reservation, and that upon the recommendation of Hon. O. H Browning, then Secretary of the Interior, the said lands were withdrawn from market by order of the President, dated March 20, 1867. The Santee Sioux Indians have never occupied this reservation. They have a reservation on the Niobrara River in Nebraska, where I deem it proper they should remain. It is not practicable for them to be located upon the reserve above described. I therefore respectfully recommend that the order of the President withdrawing the above described lands from market may be rescinded. Please return the accompanying papers."— *Ibid.* On Aug. 31, Cox wrote to USG. "I have the honor to transmit, herewith, a report of the Commissioner of Indian Affairs, of the 28th instant, and accompanying papers, in relation to proposed changes in the Santee Sioux Indian Reservation as therein suggested, and respectfully recommend that the President order the restoration to market of certain lands designated in the Commissioner's report, and the withdrawal from sale of the lands therein described."—Copy, DNA, RG 48, Indian Div., Letters Sent. On the same day, USG endorsed this letter. "The within recommendation of the Secretary of the Interior, is hereby approved, and the necessary action will be taken to carry it into effect."—Copy, *ibid.* On Dec. 31, 1873, USG amended this order "to exempt from its operation lots . . . previously patented to Thomas J. Quinn, on Sioux half-breed script No. 349 D."— *SED*, 48-2-95, p. 477; *HED*, 49-2-1, VIII, part 5, p. 560.

1869, JULY 13. T. G. Messervy, Roubaix, France, to USG. "Being one of the Protestant Ministers of the Roubaix's parish, I have from time to time to visit and evangelize the protestant prisonners, of the general prison of Loos, near Lille, in the north of this country. There is in it an American of the United States, (who has been an officer,) of the name of W. H. Lewis. He has been sentenced to five years imprisonment. As he regrets having behav'd improperly in the past and conducts himself very well in the said prison; and besides as he is confin'd, through a serious sickness, to the prison's hospital, where he may die before three months are elapsed, I have the honor to beg of you[r] Excellency to be so kind as to interced[e] by a letter, either to His Majesty, [the] Emperor, or to the Minister of the Int[e]rior in Paris, in behalf of Mr Lewis in order to obtain on the 15th of Augus[t] next, (which is the Emperor's *fête* day, either ~~the~~ his grace of̶r a diminnution of his imprisonment. Be pleased to allow me Sir and honor'd Presiden[t] to think and hope you will have the goodness to comply to my request; a[nd] to assure you that your before mentioned countryman, as well as mysel[f] would feel thankful towards your Excellency for granting such a favor"—ALS, DNA, RG 59, Miscellaneous Letters.

1869, JULY 13.   James J. Miller, *Farmers' Home Journal*, Lexington, Ky., to USG. "To your Father I refer you. for. my position in Ky as well as my devotion to the party of which you are the head. as well as the active part I have taken in late Presidential canvass and my early advocacy of your claims to the Presidency   I was Special agt P. O. Dept apponted by Mr Lincoln. which office I held for more than sevn years. was removed by Johnson because of my advocacy of your Election last Sept   I ask. nothing now. but I have a brother. who has been a clerk in Quarter Master Genl Office &. with the reduction of the force. hee with a large number of others. were. dispensed with. I understand. some are to be reappointed. and I ask it as Special favor. that my brother E. P. Miller may be restored to his Office   he has a large family *dependent* is a faithfull clerk. has the approval of Genl Meigs & all ovr him. This favor. will be considered. a personal favor to me. & I believe to your father for my sake. and will secure for you the Everlasting gratitude of my brother & his family."—ALS, DNA, RG 107, Appointment Papers. Related papers are *ibid.* E. P. Miller received an appointment as clerk, q. m. dept.

1869, JULY 13.   Nathaniel G. Whitmore, Mansfield, Mass., to USG. "I have the honor and the pleasure, herewith, to submit to your Excellency, a letter from Senator Sprague of R. I. endorsed by Representative Ames of Mass, recommending me for appointment as Master Armorer in some U S. Arsenal, and I respectfully make application for such position. I should prefer a situation at Springfield Mass. but willingly leave the designation to your Excellency. I have confidence that my skill; in any department pertaining to arms, would be of service to the Government, having had much experience in their manufacture. The reference made by Senator Sprague is a fair specimen of my work. During the late war, Gen. R A. Peirce, Chief of Ordnance, of Mass, several times employed me to inspect and test the fire arms in his Department. Recommendations from Gen. Peirce. Gov. Andrew and other competent authority, are on file in the War Department."—Copy, DNA, RG 156, Letters Received. The enclosure is *ibid.* No appointment followed. See *PUSG*, 17, 416.

1869, JULY 14.   Gustave Reiche, Warrenton, Mo., to USG. "I beg leave to forward the enclosed recommendation of Mr. J. Fogg to your Excellency's kind consideration. . . . I rank among the 'Hungry Office seekers,' so troublesome to your Excellency. I make the most solemn promise, that, if I should be favored with an appointment, I will exercise my utmost diligence, to become an addition to the public proof by facts, that your Excellency is successful in His noble zeal, to give to the country able and honest officers."—ALS, DNA, RG 59, Letters of Application and Recommendation. Related papers are *ibid.* No appointment followed.

1869, July 15.   USG endorsement. "The within recommendations of the Secretary of the Interior are approved, and the Secretary of the Treasury and himself are hereby directed to carry the same into effect."—Copy, DLC-Charles Ewing. Written on a letter of the same day from Secretary of the Interior Jacob D. Cox to USG. "I have the honor to transmit herewith, for your action, five reports dated the 9th ultimo, of the Commissioners, Messrs. Gouverneur K. Warren and James F. Wilson; also the report of Isaac N. Morris, the other Commissioner, dated May 28th 1869, appointed by you to examine and report upon a section of 85 $\frac{88}{100}$ miles of the road and telegraph line constructed by the Union Pacific Railroad Company, . . . I therefore respectfully recommend the acceptance of the same and the issue of bonds and of patents for lands due on account of said section, . . ."—Copy, *ibid.* Printed in *HED*, 46-2-1, X, part 5, p. 161.

On May 13, Isaac N. Morris, Omaha, had telegraphed to USG. "Expected to meet Mr Watson here but disappointed Mrs Morris and Mrs Broadwell are with me. Can I go on now or must I wait. Would like to go [n]ow. Answer"—Telegram received (at 6:30 P.M.), DNA, RG 107, Telegrams Collected (Bound). On May 28, Morris wrote to USG. "On the 13th day of March last your Excellency tendered me an appointment as one of the commissioners 'to examine and report to the President of the United States upon the road and telegraph line of the Union Pacific Railroad Company as contemplated and specified by an act to aid in the construction of a railroad and telegraph line from the Missouri River to the Pacific Ocean, and to secure the Government the use of the same for postal, military, and other purposes.' . . . I will add, in conclusion, that on my return to Omaha, I was shown a prepared report, gotten up by an officer of the company, on the first section of twenty miles of the road west of the last accepted section, setting forth it was constructed in strict compliance with law, and was told that other similar reports for the remaining sections were in progress of preparation; that such was the accustomed way for reports to be prepared for the commissioners, and then they signed them. Not being satisfied that I could, without violation of duty, adopt the usual form and sign such a paper, I have prepared this report for myself, as expressive of my own views. PERSONAL. I regret being compelled to go over the road without my associates, in consequence of a misunderstanding of the time the commission was to meet at Omaha, growing out of an unexpected delay in instructions. I should have been highly gratified to have accompanied General Warren and Hon. James F. Wilson. As that pleasure was denied me, I was obliged to perform my duty by making the necessary examination alone. Not even the privilege of consulting either of these gentlemen before

this report was prepared was afforded me. I therefore submit it for myself."
—*HED*, 44-1-180.

1869, JULY 15. "de Mativier de Valz," Paris, to USG. "Convinced that
the powerful american nation over whose destiny you have been called to preside, is ever desirous to civilize the various small states of central America by
inducing them by friendly measures to connect themselves with your institutions, by a broad spread confederation, and having no doubt of the
success of such noble views by the employment of a system of penetrative
expansion, through the acquisition of the centre of those republics, I venture
on the freedom of offering to your government, the purchase of two millions
of acres of land of the greatest fertility, which, reduced to french measure,
represents an expanse of six thousand square kilometers. It seems very probable, General, that a strong Colony of your countrymen, established on this
vast property would soon induce, by insensibly percolating, the neighboring
populations, so that they altho for the moment recalcitrant, would soon
hasten to solicit the honor of taking part in your immense power through
the world. The vast property in question, is admirably located as the seat
of one or more ~~several~~ colonies, it belongs by title of inheritance to Madame
the widow Willock, native of France, and dwelling in the bosom of her
family in one of the departments of France—she was the wife of the deceased Sir Matthew Henry Willock, an English captain of a merchant
vessel, who in association with another captain of the same nation obtained
from the King of the Mosquitos, upon the payment of a certain sum of
money to his government, ~~and~~ authentic act of conveyance in perfect order,
of certain lands mentioned above, carrying with it besides many privileges
which constitute this domain to be an independent country. . . . I think I
should add that the English Government has formally abandoned its pre-
rogatives on that portion of the Mosquito Kingdom, given to the Republic
of Honduras by the treaty of 28 November 1859. the Willock property is
locked in by the portion ceded, which includes all the district from Cape
Gracias a Dios."—ALS and copy (in French with translation), DNA, RG
59, Miscellaneous Letters. Related papers are *ibid.*

1869, JULY 16. Cummings Hale, Heston, Vt., to USG. "I want ~~to tel~~ to
lay my case befour you, but as I have never seen you I hope you will forgive
me for troubling you at this time. now dont think it is office that I want
for it is not. but I am going to state a few fax in my case I will begin
with the war when that begun my son Almon. H. Hale tho young only 16
years old thought it his duty to go to his cuntryes cause he went on board
the Portsmouth at first afterwards he enlisted in the 10 vermont Co H and
he was transfurd from that to Co I 10 vt in which on the 1 day of June in
the Battle at Coal Harber he was wounded and carred to Richmond a
Prisnor where he died the 24 of march now since that time theire has
bin an act for the benifit of dependent Fathers and I thought that I was as

dependent on that Son as any Father could bee   I made application for a
Pencion and they rejected my claim on the ground that the mother was Still
living   now I want to know if a man aint as dependant when he has wife
that is out of helth to support as one that hath not any   now Friend Grant
I will tell you the truth about my afaires   in the first Plaice. I am a criple
for life and are unable to support my Family which consists of my wife
which has been troubled with a cansar for more than 7 years two little
girls one 12 and the other 3 years old and my mother She is 84 years old
and Sick   it costs me from 4 to 5 dollars a week to take care of her.   now
unless I am entitled or my wife is entitled to a Pencion I Shall have to ask
help from the Town to help me take care of that mother who had 2 Sons
killed in the war Daniel Hale in the 1 Mass and James Hale in the 10 vt
and Sewall Heald which was out through all the war and wounded has
since died leaving me along to strugle through this wourld   it seems rather
Hard to have to ask help of the Town when I think that we ought to have a
Pencion from the Govement that my son and Brothers died to support.
tho if I was well and smart I would not ask even the Govement to help
me   I hope you will read this and if you think I ought to have any thing,
let me know how to Proseed   I think I can Prove all I have riten . . . P S I
know you was a good general and I hope by the Blessing of God you will
Prove a good President   my hope and trust is alone in God   may his Blessing attend you in all your labours for the the People"—ALS, DNA, RG 48,
Miscellaneous Div., Letters Received.

1869, JULY 16.   Jean-Antoine Lascaris, Florence, to USG. "The Prince,
Jean Antoine ange Flave, Comnene, Paleologue, Lascaris, whose ancestors,
after having been compelled to abandon their Imperial Thrones at Constantinople have always been, through centuries which have passed away,
received with great honor near all the Princes of Christendom, and notably
by the German Emperors, whose letters confided to the archives of the
Senate of Ratisbon affirm it, as well as those of the twelve Pontiffs, kept in
the archives of the Senate, and Roman People in the Capitol. In his quality
as decendant of Flavius Augustus, the Undersigned, in following the usage
of his ancestors, who have always demanded their inscription as Roman
Senators, and although that ~~Inscription~~ usage has suffered an interruption,
the Undersigned has believed it to be his duty to cause the revival of this
right of his Family. The Undersigned has therefore the honor of communicating to your Excellency that having presented in due form to the Roman
Senate the authentic documents which constitute in sequence the genealogy
of his family; and which after having been recognized in good and due
form, the Senate at its session of the 18th February of this current year
1869 by unanimous vote in his favor, and in favor of all his descendants,
redintegrated, in all its rights titles and honor formerly decreed to the
Paleologues, and particularly named by the said Senate on the 16th may
1817   This last event the undersigned deems it a duty to make known to
your Excellency, as well in his own name, as in that of his Spouse, and

Daughter the Princess Maria and to present to Your Excellency the marks of their high consideration"—ALS and copy (in French with translation), DNA, RG 59, Miscellaneous Letters.

1869, JULY 17.   Maria L. Abington, Wentzville, Mo., to USG. ". . . The year before the war broke out, my husband died. leaving me with two children. both very young, and I had to stru[ggle] very hard to support them but with the [serv]ice of my only two negro boys I did make out to live, and if I could have kept them three years longer, I could have had a good start: but [i]n :62. they were enlisted in the army, I was then left to my own feeble efforts: (I still [own] a small house and lot in Wentzville,) I resort [to] keeping boarders and so by hard labor manage to make a support.   in the mean time, the [soldiers] that stoped at different called on me for their meals, which I gave not grudgingly but each meal reduced my little store, moreover, when the train was shot into by the detestible bushwhackers: the soldiers came to my house and took my best bed for the wounded to lay on, they however promised to pay for it. . . . I scarcely expect now the p[ay] for my negros, although [several promises to persons] less loyal than myself got pay for theirs   Mr Orie of St Charles [s]aid that he [would] attend to getting mine but ha[s] failed to do so, from what cause I have not assertained. My deeds were sent on to Washington city and that is the last   but expecting at this late day to recover the pay for my boys. I appeal to *your individual benevolence* as the Supreme ruler of States in this part of the terrestrial globe   If you doubt the verity of my condition or statement. I will tak the liberty of, refering you to Senator John B. Henderson, who is well acquainted with our family, and former circumstances. My father was his guardian. . . ."—ALS, DNA, RG 107, Letters Received, 479A 1869.

1869, JULY 20.   Ellen Brown, Thomasville, Ga., to USG. "Having been torned from my home in West Virginia while the war was going on, and brought to this country and sold, and since freedom I have not been able scarcely to support my self & children that I have with me, and when I was taken from Virginia I there left some of my children who were not older than five & 7. years of age and I have been laboring hard to make money enough to take my self and two children back to my native State Virginia where I was raised and where all my relations are, but my age and infirmities has caused me to fail   Therefore Honored President: I beg of you to be so generous as to give myself and two children, free transportation back to our home, for which kind sir you will ever have the humble gratitude of a poore feeble colored Woman.   if you will be pleased to grant her request will you be so kind as to let her know, and at what time it will please your Honor, to favor her request"—ALS, DNA, RG 107, Letters Received from Bureaus. On July 31, Bvt. Maj. Gen. Oliver O. Howard endorsed this letter. "Respectfully returned to Hon Secretary of War   Transportation for Refugees and Freedmen is no longer issued by this Bureau, the appropriation for that purpose having been exhausted. & now the Educational branch only remains"—ES, *ibid.*

1869, July 20. Thompson McKinley, Irish Union Republican Association, Nashville, to USG. "By direction of the above Committee I have the honor to enclose herewith copy of Preamble and Resolutions, attested by the Secretary and adopted on the 19th instant, relating to recognizing as belligerents the people of Cuba by Your Excellency on the part of the Government of the United States."—ALS, DNA, RG 59, Miscellaneous Letters. The enclosure is *ibid.*

1869, July 21. Secretary of the Navy George M. Robeson to USG. "I have the honor to submit for your decision the report of a Naval Retiring Board in the case of 1st Assistant Engineer A. Dunbar of the Navy, who is found by the Board to be 'incapacitated for performing the duties of his office because of disease contracted in the line of his duty.' I respectfully recommend that the judgment of the Board be approved."—Copy, DNA, RG 45, Letters Sent to the President.

1869, July 21. Secretary of the Navy George M. Robeson to USG. "I have the honor to submit for your decision the record of proceedings of a Naval General Court Martial recently convened at the Navy Yard, Mare Island, Cal., in the case of Third Assistant Engineer John K. Stevenson, of the Navy. This officer is found guilty of the charges of 'absence without leave,' and 'scandalous conduct tending to the destruction of good morals;' and is sentenced 'to be dismissed from the service of the United States and to forfeit all pay and emoluments which are now or may hereafter become due him, the said money to go to the payment of Edward Harrington and George Hubbard as far as may be.' I respectfully recommend that the sentence be approved."—Copy, DNA, RG 45, Letters Sent to the President.

1869, July 23. Louis Moreau and Co., Houston, to USG promoting "Condensed juice of beef for soup."—Copy (in French), DNA, RG 107, Letters Received, M443 (1869). Related papers are *ibid.*

1869, July 28. To Napoleon III. "I cordially reciprocate your good wishes, and trust that the liberal policy of the United States, pursuant to which this cable has been landed, may result in many such means of communication—especially between this country and its earliest ally and friend."— *New York Times,* July 29, 1869. On the same day, Napoleon III, Paris, had telegraphed to USG. "I am highly gratified to inaugurate the new line of telegraph which unites France with the United States by sending to you the expression of my good wishes for you and for the prosperity of the United States."—*Ibid.*

1869, JULY [28]. Anson Burlingame to USG. "See that Howard has declined am sorry. important to have a man who understands our policy How would George Wilkes do?"—Telegram received (on July 28, 9:20 A.M.), DNA, RG 107, Telegrams Collected (Bound). On April 13, USG had nominated William A. Howard to replace J. Ross Browne as minister to China. Papers recommending Howard are *ibid.*, RG 59, Letters of Application and Recommendation. On Aug. 10, George F. Seward, consul, Shanghai, cabled to USG. "If mr. Browne resigns I request promotion"— Telegram received (on Aug. 28, 9:00 A.M.), *ibid.*, RG 107, Telegrams Collected (Bound). USG appointed Frederick F. Low to replace Howard. On Sept. 29, Vice President Schuyler Colfax *et al.*, San Francisco, telegraphed to USG. "Ex Governor Lowe's appointment to the Chinese Mission is a high compliment to the Coast, eminently satisfactory to our people And gives the nation a representation at that Ancient Empire whose ability and acquaintance with their customs commerce and industries will vindicate the fitness of his selection. We join in congratulations to the President on this excellent choice."—Telegram received (on Sept. 30, 9:00 A.M.), *ibid.*

On Oct. 28, 1871, Horace Porter wrote to Low. "Gen Upton in regard to whom we had some correspondence a year ago has been talking to Gov. Seward and others who have visited China and they tell him that there now seems a better prospect of his meeting with success in an attempt to secure an appointment as Instructor of the Art of War in that Empire. The President feels a deep interest in Gen. Uptons success and it is by his direction that I ~~renew~~ make the request ~~formerly made~~ that you will write me upon the subject and advise me whether your views upon the subject have changed since your last letter ~~in regard to the matter~~. Gen. Emory Upton as you remember ~~at~~ is a lieut. Col of infantry, and Bvt Maj. Gen. and is at present Commandant at West Point, ~~and~~ Having commanded artillery, cavalry and infantry at different times during the war, ~~and~~ having ~~see~~nrved for four years in the field ~~he has~~ and being the author of the tactics now ~~used~~ adopted in our service he enjoys a higher military reputation than any one of his age in ~~the Army~~ our country. In case you see ~~a possibility of a desire~~ any desire on the part of the Chinese authorities to introduce the American Art of war into their armies will you please ascertain if you conveniently can what salary they would give and what the prospects will be generally. By writing me your views at present on this subject ~~at present~~ you will greatly oblige a number of your friends here. Should there be a prospect of an opening for Gen Upton he will be furnished with an official recommendation from our Government in regard to his qualifications"— ADf (initialed), USG 3.

On Feb. 5, 1873, Governor Newton Booth of Calif. wrote to USG. "I understand that in the event of the resignation of Hon F. F. Low, U. S. Minister to China, Mr G. F. Seward, will be an applicant for the position— Mr Seward is tolerably well known to the leading business men of this State, and his fitness for the position he aspires to is so generally recognized, that I believe his appointment would be approved by the most intelligent public sentiment here."—ALS, DNA, RG 59, Letters of Application and Recommendation. Related papers are *ibid.* On Jan. 7, 1876, USG appointed Seward as minister to China. On March 22, USG wrote to the House of Representatives. "In answer to a resolution of the House of Representatives of the 23d of February ultimo, I transmit herewith a Report of the Secretary of State and the papers which accompanied it. . . . Subject.— Charges against Geo. F. Seward lately Consul General at Shanghai and now U. S. Minister to China."—Copy, *ibid.,* RG 130, Messages to Congress. See *CG,* 44–1, 1236, 1997; *HMD,* 45-2-31, part 2.

1869, JULY 28.   Horace Binney Sargent, Boston, to USG. "Will my sincere friendship for Fitz John Porter, and the profound respect, with which I should bow to your opinion, save me from a charge of officiousness, if, as a Republican in politics, I add my entreaty to many, in furtherance of his 'Appeal' for a full revision of his case? Dear, *radical* Governor Andrew, my most honored and beloved Friend, was well disposed to believe, that, under the fierce excitements of the hour, grave injustice to a soldier of gallant elder record, and one who had suffered enough to make a bad man a traitor, had been done, and ought to be undone; though there might be doubt as to the method. The army of the Potomac was undoubtedly affected by General Porter's disgrace; as the British Navy was affected by the trial of Byng, who, as Voltaire wittily said, was shot 'to encourage the others—' *pour encourager les autres*'—But now that this terrible encouragement is not required any longer, I think that the just common sense of *Massachusetts desires* a full reconsideration of the proceedings which exclude, forever, *one* man from all possible share in the great National rejoicing. No heart— not vindictive—could fail to welcome a sober second judgement, which should make the agonized life of General Porters wife and family less miserable—The public mind is not satisfied with the *present* position of the question; and anxiously awaits the judgment of such soldiers as now do enjoy the unbounded love and confidence of the nation, whatever that judgement may be—"—ALS, ICHi.

On Nov. 3, Gen. William T. Sherman wrote to Secretary of War William W. Belknap. "I now have the honor to submit to you a printed Pamphlet entitled an Appeal to the President of the United States for a Re-examination of the Proceedings of the General Court Martial in the case of Major General Fitz John Porter, and I send with it a letter dated October 27th from Governor Randolph of New Jersey to the Hon. Mr. Robeson, Secretary of the Navy, and referred to me by him, with one from General Thomas of October 18th to General Porter, and another from General Porter to me, of October 27th last. I beg you will lay these papers before the President of the United States, for his action and decision. The matters herein referred to have long been agitated, and have been mixed up with other considerations that I need not now refer to, and I will confine my attention to the two distinct propositions contained in General Porter's letter to me of June 10th 1869, as modified by that of October 26th,—both herewith. These are—1st To remit the sentence or so much of it as disqualifies him 'forever to hold any office of trust or profit under the Government of the United States' 2nd. To be nominated to the Senate for restoration to his rank in the Army, 'under the late Act of Congress allowing that mode of redress of wrong by a Court Martial.' Influenced by the high reputation of General Porter anterior to this dreadful sentence, and the respect and affection of his old associates of the Army as illustrated by General Thomas' letter of the 18th of October, I venture to recommend to the President that he remit so much of the sentence as disqualifies him from holding civil office. With regard to the second proposition, I know of no 'late Act of Congress' that allows the restoration of an officer for trial anew, or the review of an old case. The Act approved July 20, 1868, is construed by me to mean that no officer dismissed by a Court Martial can be restored to the Army, except by a new nomination and a new confirmation. That a new nomination be possible there must be a vacancy. There are no vacancies in the Army, of Colonel,—or of any grade save that of 2d Lieutenant; but, on the contrary, there are twenty Colonels of Infantry without regiments, and therefore a compliance with the 2d proposition seems to me, impossible."—LS, DNA, RG 94, Letters Received, R574 1867. The enclosures and related papers are *ibid.*

On Dec. 3, Bvt. Maj. Gen. John Pope, Detroit, wrote to USG. "I learn from sufficient authority that certain influential persons are again pressing on you the case of Fitz John Porter; this time only asking that the disabilities imposed on him by the sentence of the Court Martial in his case be remitted. This, of course, is only the first step toward his restoration to the service. I beseech you General for your own sake, for the honor of the Army and in justice to honorable officers who performed their duty with zeal and fidelity, to do nothing in Porters case without long consideration and careful examination of all the facts. Porter committed the most enormous & disgraceful crime known to the military Profession viz desertion from the field of battle with the strongest & best corps of the Army, without firing a gun & in positive disobedience of orders to attack the enemy, abandoning his comrades to defeat & disaster which he says himself he believes they were sustaining & which, wonderful, indeed astounding to say, he gives as one of his reasons for deserting the field. It would not be surprising if your constant occupations have prevented you from examining this case fully. Indeed it is a difficult matter to eliminate the exact facts from the clouds of witnesses & words in which such cases are always enveloped but I submit to you herewith a brief printed statement of the case, stripped of all reference to the mass of testimony which was introduced & recorded. I beg you in justice to yourself & to all concerned that you read it carefully before you do any thing in relation to Porter. In this statement the only testimony referred to to prove Porters guilt is his own written testimony. The only testimony as to its consequences to the Army & the country, is the testimony [written] of stonewall Jackson, Longstreet & J. E. B. Stuart who commanded in front of us on the day of that battle. If Porter's guilt is not made clear on this testimony alone I am willing that he shall have all the benefit of any doubts on the subject. But if he shall appear guilty, his crime cannot be pardoned, nor any portion of his sentence remitted without wrong of the deepest kind to the Army & the country. His sin was the unpardonable sin in war & his sentence, as I think you will yourself admit, the very mildest that could have been pronounced. I beg you General to read this printed statement carefully. The documents quoted can be verified in the War Dept. where the originals are kept. I can say no more & I will not ask nor suggest more. What I do ask is reasonable enough and I feel sure will be complied with."—LS (bracketed material in original), *ibid.* See *PUSG*, 16, 550–51; *ibid.*, 17, 327–40; *SED*, 46-1-37.

1869, JULY 30.   USG endorsement. "The within recommendation of the Secretary of the Interior is hereby approved, and, within the limits of the tract reserved by Executive Order of June 14, 1867, for the Indians of Southern Idaho, will be designated a reservation provided for the Bannocks, by the 2d Article of the treaty with said tribe of 3d July 1868."—Copy, DNA, RG 48, Indian Div., Letters Sent. Written on a letter of July 29 from Secretary of the Interior Jacob D. Cox to USG. "I have the honor to submit, herewith, a communication from the Commissioner of Indian Affairs, dated the 23d inst., and accompanying papers, relative to the designation of a Reservation in Idaho, for the 'Bannock' Indians as provided by the 2nd Article of the treaty of July 3d 1868, with that tribe, and, for the reasons stated by the Commissioner, respectfully recommend that you direct that the lands reserved by an Executive Order dated June 14th 1867, for the Indians of Southern Idaho, including the 'Bannocks,' be designated as the reservation provided for said tribe by the 2nd Article of the treaty referred to, dated July 3d 1868."—Copy, *ibid.* See *HED*, 45-3-1, IX, part 5, pp. 746–47.

On Jan. 31 and March 30, 1870, USG favorably endorsed similar reports designating land in Calif. for Indian reservations.—Copies, DNA, RG 48, Indian Div., Letters Sent. *HED*, 41-2-296, p. 12; *ibid.*, 42-2-224, p. 14. On Feb. 17, 1871, USG approved a recommendation of Ely S. Parker, commissioner of Indian affairs, to revoke the order of Jan. 31, 1870.— *SED*, 48-2-95, pp. 226–27. On Dec. 27, 1875, and May 15, 1876, USG also set aside land in Calif. for reservations.—*Ibid.*, pp. 227–28.

On April 12, 1870, USG approved a report designating reservation lands for the Arickaree, Gros Ventre, and Mandan.—Copies, DNA, RG 48, Indian Div., Letters Sent; *ibid.*, RG 94, Letters Received, 4461 1871. Related papers are *ibid.*; *ibid.*, RG 48, Indian Div., Letters Sent. See *HED*, 45-3-1, IX, part 5, pp. 740–42.

1869, JULY 30.   Samuel Ligon, Little Rock, to USG. "Your Petitioner Samuel Ligon—Colored—would humbly represent that he was formerly a

Slave, owned by Doct—Wm Ligon of Aberdeen, Miss—and highly esteemed for his good conduct—that he was there living quietly with his
family until the 7th of July 1867 when he, togather with one Jefferson
Wood (Cold) was seized by two citizens named Hatch and hurried off 400
miles to Vicksburg, when civil courts were open, and tried by a Military
Commission on a charge for stealing a Mule, and on a finding of guilty was
sentanced see copy of proceedings of Court Martial, with said Wood to
three years each, at hard labor in the Penetentiary at Little Rock Ark—
which sentance he is now, and has been for nearly two years serving out—
the other, Jeff—Wood having died on his way to prison.—That he was hur-
riedly tried, being entirely ignorent of the law, and had no Attorney or
friend there to advise—That he was entirely inocent of the crime charged,
the evidence made against him, as will appear from the record now in the
Attorney Generals Office at Washington D C—was all secondary and not
competent or safe to convict—neither was it true in fact, except that Wood
stayed at his house one night with the mule said to be stolen . . ."—D (signed
by mark), DNA, RG 153, OO248, Samuel Ligon. On Aug. 21, Maj. William Winthrop, act. judge advocate gen., endorsed this letter. ". . . The
conviction in this case is regarded as fully justified by the testimony. . . . It
is believed that, as a general rule, the sentences of these courts should be
accepted by the Executive as just and final; and no reason is perceived for
departing from such rule in this instance. A pardon is not, therefore recommended."—AES, *ibid.* Related papers are *ibid.*

1869, JULY 30.   Augustus I. Newsome, Clarksville, Tenn., to USG. "I
hope you will excuse ~~these~~ these lines, but we colored People, of this county,
at least, Some of us, are very anctious about those lands in Kansas. those
home Stead lands, that the government has Set apart, for the purpose, of
inducing us to go to, and Settle, where we will have, what we cannot get
Here and that is homes.   we want to raise as large a company, to go there
as we possibly can.   we are very anctious, to know, all, of the particulars,
about it, if you please, and, as Soon as possible; for as Soon as our Guber-
natorial Election is over, we want to go to work, to form A company, of
Emegrant, to go out, and lead the road for others, to follow in our tracks.
No more at presant, . . ."—ALS, DNA, RG 48, Lands and Railroads Div.,
Miscellaneous, Letters Received.

1869, [JULY].   A. H. Broome, Baltimore, to USG. "In the year ending
the war my husband was imprisoned six weeks. from which imprisonment
he died in Dec—of the same year. The imprisonment so involved him in
debt that since his death myself & children have been obliged to give up
our home & are now struggling for a livelihood which it seems hardly possible for us to obtain   My object in addressing you is to ask if it may not
be possible, (as there never was any charge made against my husband.
but simply imprisoned & released on his parole of honor to appear when

called for by the government—& that imprisonment causing his death & pecuniary loss) the government may ~~not~~ be willing & able to bestow a compensation (as far as such can compensate) on me, to secure my declining years from want—I ask you, because you are the head of the government & because I believe you will befriend the widow & fatherless—"— ALS (docketed as received on July 30), DNA, RG 60, Letters from the President.

1869, AUG. 1.   Mary Witham, LaGrange, Ga., to USG. "I trust you will pardon my claiming the attention of one of your superior intellect To matters of minor importance While I am satisfied It requires your whole time to look to the interest of the government,   However I shall not expect sencure from you. When I say I am at a loss where to look for redress unless you will sympathise with us,   My husband and myself are northen persons by birth   we adopted this State as our home years prior to the war,   When the troubles of /61 commenced, we went North. But our interest being left in the South. When the war closed, we in common with all others whose interest was here found ourselves reduced to poverty in old age. My husband physically unable to labor was forced to do something to support himself and family,   It being a very difficult matter to get teachers for the colored people that my husband in sympathy to them in their destitution and ignorance took a school for their benefit with the promise of the government agent that he would see that he was compensated.   he can prove by the citizens that he made an efficient teacher, taught day and night And has never received one cent for his servises,   he furnished house fuel and lights. And what we would ask of you Is to know if you will not see that he is paid for his labor to subsist from while too feeble to work.   he is in the last stage of Consumption.   very thankfull for all former kindnesses to the destitute I will close"—ALS, DNA, RG 105, Letters Received.

1869, [AUG. 4].   USG endorsement. "Refer to Gn Terry."—AE, DNA, RG 94, Letters Received, 583W 1869. Written on a letter of July 20 from D. Woodruff, Tuscaloosa, to USG. "I hate to encroach upon your time; but in the absence of our Senators, I feel it is the duty of Some one to advise the Govt occasionally of the progress of this war, now of eight years continuance, and is more unsafe for Union Men in this county to day, than it was at any time during the war.—Kansas people are protected against Indian massacres— Why cannot we be protected against these enemies of the U. States ('Ku-Klux Out Laws')—Is not war against loyal U. States citizens war, against the U. States? Our puny State Govt it seems to me, Should not be allowed any longer, to Stand betwen us & Federal protection. The 16th inst. I wrote to Governor Smith in Substance as follows, which Mr. President, covers pretty much what I wish to Say to you—'The marked lines in the enclosed Slips, are Suggestive, & Significant—The question arises, *Why there is not Safety*—Answer; because the teachings of this Editor, as he very well knows, has Stimulated the lawless & blood thirsty to acts of violence, blood-shed, & murder, until his "Schooled Klans" have become inured, & hard-ened in crime to that degree, that he knows there is no Safety for the life of any *decided* Union Man. It is time this war had ceased—Union Men have been thus threatened, & exposed for eight years, & in this Co. there is more danger *now—to day*; than there was any time during the war—I hope to be understood; my own personal Safety is a matter of moonshine, life is too far Spent—but as a citizen, I am anxious for the welfare, honor, & peace of our State—Its reputation is being called in question—Some 26, murders in this County already within a few months, besides other outrages, and as yet, *not a Single arrest.* Your Excellencys' letter to our Shff. Apl. 24th Says, "This State of things is *intolerable* These lawless bands, must be put down at all hazards . . . It is my Sincere wish that this be done by the local authorities of the County; but, if they are unable to accomplish the desired end, it *must*, & *Shall* be *done by Some other means.*" I must be permitted to Say to your Excellency, that I believe that nothing Short of "those other means" will restore peace & Safety in this County—' If Tuscaloosa County, which is the head center of Ku-Klux outrages, was put under Martial law, it would arrest outrages all over the State, & command Some respect for our State Govt—as it now is, the civil State authority is openly defied—If Genl Terry would call upon the Commander of this Post for a Report, Capt. Mills would no doubt furnish one that could be relied upon, and I doubt not Genl Terry would do so, at the Suggestion of Govr Smith, or perhaps more cer-tainly, if made by the Sec. of War. May the God of Heaven, Give to the President of our choice wisdom, prudence, & firmness, & bless him for time, & for Eternity."—ALS (ellipses in original), *ibid.*

1869, AUG. 6. Dotson Seybold, Quitman, Mo., to USG. "I have forbore writeing you knowing that your mental faculties must be severely taxed, but vast public intrust will excuse, sir I have lately traveled through a portion of the west and find eighty per cent of the lands unocupied and in the hands of Speculators who are asking from five to fifty dollars per acre Justice requires that Legeslation and law Shall be for the intrust of the many, insted of Speculators, Public lands being braught in market are son monopolised by capitalists thus depriveing the poor of homes the masses love and protect their Government! the speculator dollars and cents, being your zealous Supporter I feel excused for requesting you to advise the proper official department to order that no more public land be entered until Congress have time to act on the Subject and I hope you will advise and even urge Congress to pass a law that all public lands may be entere[d] by homesteds only, Justice and Government policy demands it and if you be the instrument by which this great object is accomplished it will increase your popularity more than the greatest victory you ever gained this law would do away with the present expensive land office cystem and I suppose that homesteds might be registered even in Post offices. the isolation and barroness of the public lands will not more than Justify the Seller though they be given them,"—ALS, DNA, RG 48, Lands and Railroads Div., Letters Received.

1869, Aug. 10. Judge Advocate Gen. Joseph Holt to USG. "Edward M Yerger, citizen, was arraigned before a Military commission convened at the Post of Jackson, Miss. on the 10th of June last, under the charge of Murder To this charge were four specifications, setting forth in legal phraseology, that the accused, with malice aforethought did in the City of Jackson, on the eighth day of June, 1869, inflict certain wounds upon the body of Captain Joseph G. Crane, commissary of subsistence and Brevet Major U. S. Army, with a large knife, which said wounds caused the immediate death of Major Crane. After a trial continuing up to and including July 22d the accused was found guilty and sentenced 'to be hanged by the neck until he be dead at such time and place as the President of the United States of America may direct; two thirds of the commission concurring therein' The proceedings, findings and sentence have been approved by Bt. Major Gen. Adelbert Ames, commanding the Fourth Military District; who forwards the record for the action of the President. After a careful study and review of the testimony adduced in this case for the prosecution and in defence, this Bureau is firmly of opinion that the verdict of the Commission was warranted and demanded, and that the sentence should be enforced. . . . The testimony of leading citizens Shows that while accused has been an overbearing person quick to take offence and assume intended insult, prone to get into quarrels and think himself of great importance; yet his sanity has never been questioned that he has transacted his business as other men; that he was possessed of more than average ability; and that for some years he has been drinking freely In a legal view, had the commission accepted the evidence submitted to them of the singular conduct of the accused, as proof of his insanity on those occasions, they would not have been justified in acquiting him of legal responsibility. His acquittal could only have been warranted by clear and sufficient proof that he was insane at the time he committed the homicide. Upon this point the Judge advocate of the commission submitted an exhaustive presentation of the law, and the leading cases decided in this country and in England. That the accused was in the full possession of his reasoning powers on the day of the homicide is conclusively proved; that his course in demanding satisfaction from Major Crane for a conceived indignity was a usual one in the locality, is argued by his counsel; that he was thoroughly aware of the nature of the act is shown by his remark at the instant of its consummation, calling attention to the fact that he had been struck by deceased as justification of his crime. There are no palliating circumstances in the case calling for any mitigation of the sentence. On the contrary, it is marked by features of peculiar atrocity and cowardice. The accused, knowing Major Crane to be unarmed, sought by every taunt and insult, while he himself stood clutching his weapon prepared for its instant use, to force him into a fight. As he saw his intended victim taking his departure, he seized upon him and said, 'go you damned dog.' For this he received a blow from a cane that, used as it was, could not inflict serious injury, and then gave full vent to his malignant, murderous passion. It was known by members of his family and by many people on the street that the 'difficulty' was threatened, yet no measures were taken to prevent it; and a faithful officer, who had been honestly striving to dis-charge his duties, was sacrificed without any arm being raised in his defence The protection owed by the Government to its officers engaged in duty amid their enemies, and the requirements of justice, demand that a sentence so clearly warrented and deserved should be rigidly enforced"—Copies, DNA, RG 60, Letters Received from the President; *ibid.*, RG 153, Letters Sent. On Feb. 5, 1870, Secretary of War William W. Belknap endorsed this report. "Respectfully returned to the President with a copy of the report of the Judge Advocate General upon the trial of E. M. Yerger; the proceedings of the court by which he was tried having been laid before the President and not returned to this Department. It is believed that the Honorable Attorney-General can supply the information desired by the House of Representatives."—ES, *ibid.*, RG 60, Letters Received from the President. On Jan. 31, the House of Representatives had requested that USG furnish information concerning the Edward M. Yerger case and "state what has taken place in regard to said case since the finding of the military commission, and what has been the occasion of the delay in the promulgation and execution of any sentence rendered against the accused, and what agreement; if any, in regard to the same has been made with any person by the Attorney General of the United States to suspend action in the case, and by what authority or with what object."—DS, *ibid.* On Feb. 1, Attorney Gen. Ebenezer R. Hoar endorsed this resolution. "It does not seem to me consistent with the public interest to communicate the information asked—"—AES, *ibid.* On Feb. 7, Orville E. Babcock wrote to Hoar. "By direction of the President, I transmit the report of the Secretary of War in answer to a resolution of the House of Representatives requesting information in regard to trial by Mil. Com. of E. M. Yerger of Miss. for murder of Maj. Crane U. S. A. for reference, should you desire it, in making up your report in answer to the same resolution. You will please return it to the President when you transmit your report."—Copy, DLC-USG, II, 1. See Charles Fairman, *Reconstruction and Reunion, 1864–88* (New York and London, 1971), I, 564–91.

1869, AUG. 14. R. S. Denny, Fredericksburg, Va., to USG. "In reply to yours of the 21st ult addressed to me, by the Adjutant General I have to say that at the time I received it I thought the refference of the subject of mine to you of the 10th ult, was just what I did not want—Since that time I have had the pleasure of meeting Genl Canby & am disposed to beleive him a verry fair man & not likely to be biased by any political views he might have as against any *official* act. He would be much more likely to be governed by the *law* & *your* orders than by what he might conceive to be

political policy & therefore I am satisfied with the refference I hope there
will be nothing inconsistant in replacing Mr Mallam in the Mayors chair—
which act I am sure would be much more likely to be satisfactory to the
inhabitants of this place than as it now is—I am also quite sure that if the
people should ever, have an opportunity to vote upon this question Mr
Mallam will be replaced by an overwhelming vote—The prevailing sentiment of the land is conservatism or conservative & quite as much so at the
north as at the south—For instance the state of Mass. which gave you a
majority of from 80.000 to 90.000 votes will this fall come verry near
making choice of John Quincy Adams as a democratic Governor—It is true
there are some local causes tending to produce this result but the main
feature is opposition to radicalism If by any mistake the other election
should be ordered in this state (& of course if the test oath is applied there
would be) the same result would be obtained only much more strongly—I
beg of you to avoid radicalism as you value the peace & comfort of the
people of the United States & do not be deceived by the voice of obstinate
politicians—I do not ask any thing for myself but am desirous that we
should 'have peace' & a united people & free & then we shall be prosperous—
So fix matters that the business community can be successful & all is done
& that can't be done without a Union of all the states with equal rights to
all in their government"—ALS, DNA, RG 107, Letters Received from
Bureaus. On July 21, Bvt. Maj. Gen. Edward D. Townsend had written
to Denny. "Referring to your communication of the 10th instant addressed
to the President of the U. S. urging the retention of Colonel Mallan as
Mayor of Fredericksburg Virginia, you are respectfully informed that the
same has been referred to the Commanding General 1st Military District,
for proper action."—Copy, *ibid.*, RG 94, Letters Sent. On April 11, 1870,
Charles E. Mallam, Fredericksburg, wrote to USG. "I have the honor most
respectfully to ask to be appointed to one of the Consulates named in the
list attached.—my claims to this favor are that I rendered some service to
the Country during the late war, my record is attached, and since the close
of the war I have spared no labor or expense to aid in the 'reconstruction' of
this state."—ALS, *ibid.*, RG 59, Letters of Application and Recommendation. The enclosures are *ibid.* No appointment followed.

1869, AUG. 17. W. G. Kephart, Kossuth, Iowa, to USG. "As you will of
course have no personal knowledge of the one who addresses you, I will say
that I am a Presbyterian minister, having charge of a congregation in this
place; Served as Chaplain to the 10th I. V. R. Inf., through the Vicksburg
campaign, at Chattanooga, and through Sherman's campaign in Georgia,
and the Carolinas, till the close of the war. I suppose this will be sufficient
for an introduction . . . I resided in Santa Fé, N. M. for near three years;
in the three-fold capacity of Misssionary, Agent for the American A. Slavery
Soc., and Editor of the *Santa Fé Gazette*, . . . I have watched with some
interest your Quaker policy. I confess to some skepticism in regard to its
success, simply because we do not live in the days of Wm Penn, when the

Indian had not wholly lost all confidence in the *white race*, and in the *government*. While acting, as editor of the *Santa Fé Gazette*, in 1852, I wrote an editorial article upon the subject of our Indian policy, which Gov. Lane was pleased to indorse by incorporating it in his annual Message. I have never seen reason to change the views there expressed, which I will give you in epitome, and if it suggest a thought worthy of further consideration, I shall be *fully* repaid. 1st The great impediment to the Indian's civilization and christianization being undoubtedly his nomadic habits, I propose that the government take an exact census of every tribe, and from the public lands or those still held by the Indians, apportion to every man, woman and child a sufficient amount of land to constitute an ample farm. I would then say to the Indians: now here is your land, you must cease your roving, hunting, predatory habits, *go to work*, and earn your living honestly, as all honest men do. 2nd Create officers of justice among them; (of their own number when practicable,) and extend over them salutary laws, and *require obedience to them*. An Indian has no more right to be a vagabond, thief and murderer, than a white man. 3rd Pay them an honest equivalent for all lands in their possession not thus appropriated, and let them become the property of govt This will give them enough to go on until they can get a start in the world, if traders are kept from plundering them. 4th Let the work of literature and evangelization be turned over to the churches and missionary Societies. They will do it much better than govt agents, if they are protected in the work. 5th Let a sufficient number of trading posts be established among them under the supervision of Govt 6th Furnish them, for a time, with agricultural instruments; and competent instructors in the business of agriculture or the mechanic trades. There are but two feasible objections, so far as I can see, to this policy, viz: 1st The Indians would not *consent* to it. My only reply to this is, *they must be made to* ACQUIESCE in it. It will be in the end a far more *humane* policy than our present slow but sure *extinction*. 2nd It would be expensive to the government. Admitting (what is very doubtful) that it would be more expensive *in its inception* than our present policy, it will become less so every year, and at least gives us some other hope of a future solution of our Indian troubles than their *entire annihilation*. . . . P. S.—The Spanish government adopted a policy somewhat like that above indicated toward what are now known as the 'Puebla Indians' of N. Mexico. The result was, that while all the roving bands remain wild and Savage, the 'Pueblas' have at least as high a state of civilization, and *better morals* than their Mexican neighbors."—ALS, DNA, RG 75, Letters Received, Miscellaneous.

1869, AUG. 18. U.S. Senator Lyman Trumbull of Ill., Helena, Montana Territory, to USG. "Being here on a visit to my son I have learned some facts in regard to Indian matters, which I think ought to be brought to your notice. Three or four weeks ago two Indians, an old man and a boy were killed by white men in the streets of Fort Benton without cause or provocation as I am told. There are no troops at Fort Benton, and the civil authorities from inability or some other cause have failed to arrest or take any steps to bring to justice the guilty parties. Since then the Stage company between here and Benton have lost several horses, and the stock of some of the settlers has been run off as is supposed by Indians. Last night a party of Indians killed a man by the name of Clark residing some twenty miles from here on the Benton road and wounded his son. These outrages are creating excitement and unless a larger military force can be stationed in the Territory to hold in check hostile Indians, & to restrain & bring to justice bad white men who are committing outrages upon friendly Indians, there is great danger of an Indian war; the consequences in loss of life and expense in this far off country would be fearful   Some of the friendly Indians are said to be very destitute and greatly disappointed at the non-ratification of treaties—Cannot more troops be sent to Montana and a part of the two million appropriation to be set apart for the relief of the suffering & disappointed tribes? Something should be done speedily—"—ALS, DNA, RG 75, Letters Received, Montana Superintendency.

1869, AUG. 24.   John W. Caldwell, Tarata, Bolivia, to USG. "Personal, private, confidential. . . . I write the more freely and frankly, to you, because I know, that, the proper public servant, can never attain such elevation, as to be inaccessible, by one of the Sovereigns of our beloved country. And, also, because I know, that, you, having the power, will, in a proper case, exercise it, when it will conduce to the best interest of our country, to do so. I wrote to you, by the last mail, the 17th inst. frankly suggesting, and respectfully requesting a diplomatic appointment, and I now write, renewing my request. My mission here, has been to me, no sinecure. First, the journey is some 7000 miles of sea and land, not the smoothest, very tedious, laborious, trying and expensive, and not to be undertaken, lightly, or frivolously. Second, I have written, an average, of more than two official letters, per day, counting copies, besides translating the Spanish letters I received from the Government of Bolivia; have held extensive correspondence in the necessary work of recovering the Archives and property of the U. S. Legation to Bolivia, scattered to the four winds, ever since Col. McClung, a quarter of a century or more ago, as U. S. Minister to Bolivia, left at Cobija, what he had; have held, also, extensive correspondence, for the recovery of the estate, of the late. Hon. Allen A. Hall, my predecessor as U. S. Minister, who died at Cochabamba, on the 17 May 1867, and from whose infant orphan daughters in Boston, Mass. U. S. A. I have today received a letter acknowledging the receipt of my first remittance of funds, a second being on the way, and others yet to be made; have held, also, extensive correspondence, in efforts to collect from Bolivia, the claim of Mr Colton of N. Y. of near $50.000 00, not yet collected. Third, I have made, more intimate, the relations of amity subsisting between the U. S. and Bolivia, by securing personal respect, by introducing our National music, some of which, the Prest, in whose company I am, day and night, orders, daily, to be played in the hearing of himself and myself, by his military bands; and by accepting, for myself and daughter, the cordial invitation of the Prest and his family, to accompany him, as his guests, on this extensive excursion to the Departments of the South of Bolivia. Fourth, I have magnified my office, in that I have been thought, by the Government of England, worthy of receiving their thanks, tendered through the Govt of the United States, for my official and personal care of the person and estates of the late Doctor Cook, a British subject, who died in La Paz Bolivia, in February last, in the absence of any Representative of Great Britain, (I have nothing from my Govt on this subject, but information from England, through letters of a friend). Fifth, in the [w]ar, I was the bold defender, and ardent supporter, of the despised and slandered West Pointers in the front, one of whom was my brother Lieut Col. Jas N. Caldwell 18th Regular Infantry (a cotemporary with yourself in the U. S. M. Academy), during the Rebellion; and sacrificed, business, property, every thing but honor, in support of the great party of the Union and yourself, devoting myself, exclusively, without fee or reward, to the work of raising, instructing and equipping recruits for the front. I was slandered, and you was imposed upon, when your nomination of my successor was procured, and I, consequently, recalled, before I was fairly warm in my seat of office. In my last, I named some of my classmates; I can name others, among them, Gens Cullum and Barnard, at New York, who, not polititians, will tell you the truth, of me. I am not a politician. The Prest. of Bolivia, and family, and Cabinet, and Officers, are as kind as possible; and, daily, we converse freely, about the U. S.; our Govt; National progress; &c. &c. The U. S., yourself, and myself, are, daily, the toast of the Prest, at table; and, all present, never less than twenty five to thirty persons, enjoy the palpable manifestations, of respect and confidence, in expression of which, the Prest himself, always, is first; and, in which, they, all participate, with whole-souled frankness, and national spirit. The Prest requests me to present to you, his personal regards, in most sincere expressions of respect. Please address me at Cochabamba, Bolivia. . . . Ex-Minister resident U. S. to Bolivia"—ALS, DLC-Hamilton Fish.

1869, AUG. 25.   Elihu B. Washburne, Paris, to USG. *"Personal.* . . . Mr. de Catacazy, the new Russian Minister, has done me the honor to call and see me, and we have had a talk in regard to what is known as the 'Perkins Claim' against Russia. Mr. de C. desires to have an unofficial talk with you on the subject, as it has assumed a matter of some international importance, and I have assured him that you will be glad to have a frank conversation with him on the subject. While in Congress I had some knowledge of that claim, which was very vigorously pushed by the Lobby, and they managed to get a Resolution through the House giving some direction to the Secretary of State. I am not certain but it is now being urged without regard to its real merits, and as a mere matter of speculation, and even to the extent of creating differences between two most friendly nations.—Such being the case I have no doubt you and Gov. Fish will desire to have the views of Mr.

de C. in relation to this claim. to the end that you may have an insight into its character as regarded by Russia. As you know I have seen so much of 'claims' against our own Government that I have not much faith in them. I cannot say that I have more faith in claims of this character against Foreign Governments than I have of them against my own Government."—ALS, DLC-Hamilton Fish. On Sept. 24, Constantin de Catacazy, Russian minister, presented his credentials to USG.—*New York Herald*, Sept. 25, 1869. The claim of Benjamin W. Perkins is discussed in Allan Nevins, *Hamilton Fish: The Inner History of the Grant Administration* (New York, 1936), 503–9.

1869, SEPT. 1.   Mary C. Saunders, Whittle's Mill, Va., to USG. "I am constrained to appeal to you for some compensation for what I have done for sick People of Color.   the year after the surrender I took care of a sick woman with three small children.   for ten months, I fed them, furnished her with medicine and clothed her children. Another I took care of, for twelve months, another was very sick here for eight months   She died here I nursed her as if she had been my own family. Several men have been sick here for months at a time.   in every case I have furnished Food and medicine such as there case demanded and have never recieved one cent for what I have done for them.   a man came here last March sick.   he had been driven from sever other people house's, because they said they were not able to take care of him. I could not drive a sick man from my door so I took care of him as long as he lived   he died during the summer   I now ask of you, The *Head* of our great *Nation*, some recompence, for what I have done. I would not ask any thing if I was not reduced to it   I have not a barrel of corn or a single piece of meat and am pressed for debt I was oblige to incur I have no money at all.   if you will only give me a few hundred-dollars it will place my busyness in such a situation that I hope I can get on comfortably I hope. *Please* do not refuse me only think of the milians at your disposal, and *you* the *Greatest man* in the *whole known World*—let *not* a *woman* PLEAD to *you in vane*   I am very needy at preasent and my health is very bad   I have two small children to educate. I have ever been true to the Union   my sympathy was with the Union during all of the war   if it is necessary I can prove every word I have written   please aid me I must and will hope, for it is our great Ruler Genrral *Grant* that I entreat.   the address of your suplient is . . . P S you know the termination of the War freed my Slaves and left me with very little money   I think with the experiene I now have if I can get a start I can make out very well"—ALS, DNA, RG 105, Hd. Qrs., Letters Received. On Sept. 30, Bvt. Maj. Gen. Edmund Schriver, inspector gen., wrote to Saunders. "The President has referred to this Dept your letter of Sept 1st, requesting to be recompensed for aid rendered by you to needy colored people, and I am directed to inform you that there are no funds at the disposal of the Government out of which payment for such services could be made—"—Copy, *ibid.*

1869, SEPT. 6. Maj. Gen. John M. Schofield, St. Louis, to USG. "I am informed by the officers of the Kansas Pacific Railroad that it will be necessary to change the location of a portion of their line betwen Sheridan and Denver so far as to render valueless, to the road, the withdrawal of public lands heretofore made. It is therefore very important to this road that no sale of public lands should take place in that part of Colorado until the permanent location of the road can be made and the maps filed at Washington. The lien which the Government holds upon the property of this road seems to me to make its interest in this matter identical with that of the railroad company, while the great public importance, especially in a military point of view, of the proposed extension of the Kansas Pacific road into Colorado and New Mexico should I believe induce all practicable aid and encouragement on the part of the Government. For these reasons I respectfully recommend that any public sales of land in Colorado be suspended until the permanent location of the railroad to Denver."—ALS, DNA, RG 48, Lands and Railroads Div., Letters Received.

1869, SEPT. 6. Columbus Delano, commissioner of Internal Revenue, to USG. "I have just rece[ive]d from Supervisor Tutten the following Telegram 'Detective J. J. Brooks was shot through the lung at Keenans liquor store at one O'Clock P. M. Assassin, escaped, unknown A. P. TULLEN Supervisor . . .'"—LS (press), Delano Letterbrooks, Illinois Historical Survey, University of Illinois, Urbana, Ill.

1869, SEPT. 21. Mrs. Timothy Smith, Olive Branch, Ohio, to USG. "I take the libetery of wrighting a few lines with the intention of laying before you a statement of the tretment and outrages that has bin comitted on the person and property of Timothy Smith formely of Hawesville Hancock Co Ky I believe you promised the pople that they should be proteted boath in person and property of naturlized sitizens as well as native born and that the laws should be inforsed and exicuted but it has not bin dun as far as this case is conserned the sitezens of Hancock Co Ky has robed him and comitted outrage upon outrage and drove him from his home and he dare not go back for feer of his life he was taken out of his bed at midnight to be hung a way in the woods miels from home and threttend if he reported on one of them they would kill him and wife and burn his house and destroy every thing he had and they comitted severel other outrages to teages to mention he appled to the Judg of the Co and the athoritys for protection and they told him to go over in to the state of Ind a mong his friends they refused to protect him and his property but dun every thing to in courage and protect the thieves and that robed him every office in the Co was filed with rebels and gerelers and what could a union man do he has appled to the covener and every place in the state for redress wher he thought he could get something dun in his case he has bin told time a gane that he can make them pay all dameges but he cannot get a lawyer ore an officer in the state to take hold of the case   can not this case come befor the united States court   he can produse plenty of evidence and the names of them that robed and outraged him   I his wife who wright this can ~~as~~ testify to all and every thing   do in the name of just God and the name of humanity do something in this case ore is their no law to remedy such a case as this   must a naturlized sitizen now and old gray headed man be outraged robed and driven from his home to end his days in poverty is this a reward for a loyal man that stud up for the country in a time of need while thoes that robed him dun every thing in their power to distroy this goverment and now are enjoying what they have robed him of   he has tryed untill he has got discouraged and is going back to Old Englan their to lay his case and make his troubls known and detur others from coming to a countery wher their is no protection   this I think would be a great disgrase to eny country   this is the third letter that has bin sent to your exlencey and no return but hope this will meet with better sucksess   he asks a dameg of fifteen thousan dolors in the Co of Hancock Ky for non protection   pleas to ansur this"—ALS, DNA, RG 107, Letters Received from Bureaus.

1869, SEPT. 25. Speech. "Mr. Bille, you are peculiarly welcome as the Minister Resident here of your Sovereign, from our knowledge of your character and of your goodwill towards the United States hitherto during your sojourn in this country. It seems to me that you cannot be charged with partiality or exaggeration in your description of Denmark. The high qualities which you attribute to the subjects of that kingdom are generally acknowledged, and are confirmed by the not inconsiderable experience of such of us as have had the advantage of seeing them on their native soil. The kind wishes which you express on behalf of his Majesty are cordially reciprocated by me, especially as I consider that he has afforded a delicate proof of his sincerity, and of a regard for the continuance of the friendly relations between the two countries by selecting you as his representative." —*New York Herald*, Sept. 27, 1869. On the same day, Frantz E. Bille, Danish minister, had presented his credentials to USG.—*Ibid.*

1869, SEPT. 25. Appleton Oaksmith, Brussels, to USG. "After eight years of exile, at the solicitation of some who are near and dear to me, I venture to appeal to your Excellency for that justice which I have well nigh given up all hope of ever obtaining. As this is the only appeal *I* have ever made, or ever shall make in the premises, I hope it will meet with that grave consideration which so serious a thing demands. In the year 1860 I was engaged in business as a ship broker at No 29 Cedar st in the City of New York. In the course of my operations in that and the following year I negotiated the charter and purchase of many vessels for other people, but *not one* for my own account. One of these vessels called the 'Wells' was chartered by a merchant in Cuba, who was properly introduced to me, but whose name even I cannot now remember, to convey a legitimate cargo to

Africa. I had not one farthings interest in her, I only negotiated the charter, and as she was owned chiefly by a very respectable gentleman, whose son commanded her, I had every reason to believe she sailed only on a legitimate voyage. Unfortunately her commander *died* on the coast of Africa, and I have been informed that, *after his death*, the charterer took advantage of that calamity to turn her into a Slaver. I negotiated the purchase of another vessel called the 'Augusta' for a party now residing on Long Island, to be fitted out as a Whaler, in which Trade she had been previously employed. This vessel in 1861 was seized and condemned by the United States Courts in New York, on the allegation that she *was going* into the Slaving business. The representations made to me by the party interested were entirely at variance with the judgement of the Court, and my knowledge and beleif of the facts. I am writing only from memory, and I trust your Excellency will pardon me for not being more exact as to details. In the same year, I introduced a man by the name of Samuel P. Skinner a ship master residing in New Bedford, whom I had known for a long time, to the firm of J. P. Piedra-hita & Co, a Spanish house who occupied an office in the same building as my own. He was engaged by them to purchase and fit out a vessel for the whaling business to be employed on the Coast of Brazil, for some of their correspondents. This was her ostensible business, but from some conversation which I afterwards heard, I have always beleived that she was intended as a coal vessel for some of the Confederate Cruizers, or as a Blockade runner. I acted only as an interpreter and negotiator between Piedra-hita and Skinner. Subsequently a vessel called the 'Margaret Scott' was purchased by Skinner in his own name, Piedra-hita & Co supplying the money. A man named Landre was appointed to command this vessel, and he and Skinner proceeded to fit her out. I don't think I ever saw her, and it is needless therefore for me to say that I had nothing to do with 'fitting her out.' When the ship was about ready for sea she was seized by the U. S. authorities on the charge of being intended for the Slave Trade, and, I beleive, condemned. Skinner and Landre were also arrested and I beleive tried and convicted in Boston of having fitted her out for that purpose. Pending the case of the 'Augusta', the owner decided to '*Bond*' the vessel, and to prove that she was going on a legitimate voyage, by performing one. And now commenced a series of illegal acts on the part of certain persons in authority, that would not be tolerated in any civilized country that I was ever in. While endeavouring to get the Augusta off, on what I beleived was a legitimate voyage, I was arrested by an armed force in Suffolk county, New York, near my residence, under what purported to be an order by Telegraph from William H. Seward, Secretary of State, and dragged to Fort Lafayette, where I was kept in close confinement. My arrest and incarceration were without warrant or just cause and in direct violation of the Constitution of the United States and the highest law of the land. . . . Resistance being in vain, I was carried by force without warrant, or any legal authority whatever, from the jurisdiction of my own state of New York to Massachusetts, and there thrown into Fort Warren.

After having been kept a long time in this prison I was taken out and carried on board a steamer, which conveyed me to Boston, where upon landing
on the wharf the *legal form* was gone through, of arresting me on a charge
of fitting out the Barque Margaret Scott as a slaver. On this charge I was
carried to Boston jail where I remained till September 1862 when I succeeded in making my escape; and, feeling that under the then existing state
of things there was no use for me to seek to obtain justice, I fled the country. . . . I am told that the only means of removing my disabilities are, that
the President should cause the proper Law Officers of the Government to
enter a 'Nolle Prosequi' in the case of 'The Margaraet Scott' at Boston, and
make some *final* disposition of any other indictments that might have been
procured against me in the matters before referred to, either in Boston or
New York. This would settle the Slave Trade charges. If no general law,
or 'decree of Amnesty' exists, which would releive me from liability on
account of my Confederate experiences, I beg respectfully to ask your
Excellency's clemency in that respect. I have nothing to advance in ex-
tenuation except the circumstances herein related. I was driven from the
Government which should have protected me—most unjustly accused, and
most cruelly imprisoned. For the one matter I ask at the hands of your
Excellency for justice; for the other I humbly ask your clemency."—ALS,
NHi. On Nov. 9, 1872, USG pardoned Oaksmith. See *SED*, 37-2-40; John
J. TePaske, "Appleton Oaksmith, Filibuster Agent," *North Carolina His-
torical Review*, XXXV, 4 (Oct., 1958), 427–47.

1869, SEPT. 27.   USG endorsement. "Respectfully refered to the Sec. of
War to take such action upon as the case seems to demand."—AES, DNA,
RG 94, Letters Received, 270D 1868. Written on a letter of Sept. 22 from
Conrad C. Dumreicher, Washington, D. C., to USG. "In accordance with
the sentence of a General Court Martial, convened at San Antonio, Texas
on the 13th of April 1868. I have been dismissed the service as Assistant
Surgeon in the U. S. Army, which office I held for seven years. Honestly
and deeply convinced, that the sentence of that Court inflicted upon me a
heavy and a cruel wrong, I have, from the time it was made known to me,
been vainly endeavoring to obtain a re-hearing of my case. After flattering
promises from your predecessor, Ex-President Johnson, I failed to obtain
before him, or through his order, any opportunity to have my reasons for
such an application considered. All that was done for me was to refer my
papers to the Judge Advocate General's office, where unfortunately and
for what reasons I am utterly ignorant, I have been so misunderstood and
misrepresented, as to fail entirely in my object. I assure your Excellency,
that I am an innocent and injured man, and I appeal to you as an honored
and brave soldier, and as the distinguished head of a great nation, to allow
me to encroach so far upon your valuable time and your wonted generosity,
as to lay before you the facts and circumstances, which substantiate my
allegation. I promise to be concise and brief, and earnestly request, that
you will appoint some hour of some day, when you will kindly hear my

statement."—ALS, *ibid.* On Oct. 5, Secretary of War William T. Sherman endorsed this letter. "Case of AssSurgeon Dumreicher—called for by the Presdt Oct 5, 1869—In Cabinet meeting the Presdt examined this case, and was satisfied ~~the ease~~ it was one that had no just claim on his clemency —or further notice"—AES, *ibid.* Related papers are *ibid.*

1869, SEPT. 27.   Bvt. Maj. Gen. Adelbert Ames, provisional governor of Miss., to USG. "I have not yet received reply to my telegram making inquiries about the applicant for Collectorship of third District, on the 29th the republican Convention will meet   I can the[n] be able to give you the name of a fit person"—Telegram received (at 1:45 P.M.), DNA, RG 107, Telegrams Collected (Bound). On Sept. 28, Ames telegraphed to USG. "I recommend Wm W. Bell of Pontotoc, Pontotoc County for Collector of Third Dist   he is highly recommended and I believe Will prove a valuable officer"—Telegram received (at 2:40 P.M.), *ibid.* On Oct. 7, Horace Porter wrote to Ames. "A Collector for third District has been appointed."—Copy, DLC-USG, II, 5. USG appointed Benjamin B. Emory as collector of Internal Revenue, 3rd District, Miss., to replace William C. Vernon Hicks. On June 14, Orville E. Babcock had written to Ames. "Your letter is at hand. I told the Prest. what you said about Mr Hicks, and also told him what you said about a removal. He said nothing that would lead me to any such conclusion. I have never heard him say one word against you or your administration. Some man may have been to him with some story, and he said if such should be true, he would relieve the commander, We are all pleased at the promp manner in which you have brought Mr Yerger up to trial. Nothing but a mil commission would cover such a case. I am delighted that you put the wretch in irons—It is a good lesson for the 'Chiv,' . . ."— ALS, CSmH. On June 23, 1870, USG nominated William W. Bell to replace Emory, then withdrew the nomination on June 28. See *Calendar,* Aug. 10, 1869.

1869, SEPT. 28.   USG endorsement. "Please call special attention to this application when appointments come to be made."—AES (photocopy), USGA. Written on a letter of Sept. 28 from Mrs. J. R. McGunnegle, Annapolis, to USG. "I most respectfully renew my application for one of the Naval Academy Appointments 'at large' for 1870, for my Son G. Kennedy McGunnegle. My Claims are the services of my husband the late Lt W. McGunnegle U. S. N. who lost his life from exposure during the late war."—ALS (photocopy), *ibid.*

1869, SEPT. 28.   USG endorsement. "Direct special attention to this case when appointments come to be made."—AES, DNA, RG 94, Correspondence, USMA. Written on a letter of July 21 from Capt. William Thompson, 7th Cav., Fort Harker, Kan., to Lt. Gen. Philip H. Sheridan. "This will be handed you by my wife, who joins me in anxiety to obtain your influence in getting our son Charles an appointment to West Point. You must remember the boy very well as having been with me down in Texas and during our campaign last Fall & Winter. Should he receive the appointment we are vain enough to believe he would make a good officer. Any aid you may feel able to give us in this desirable end will be remembered with great gratitude."—ALS, *ibid.* Related papers are *ibid.* Charles W. Thompson, who entered USMA in 1871, did not graduate.

1869, SEPT. 29.   Jesse Root Grant, Covington, Ky., to USG. "The accompanying papers were forwarded to me by Dr Ames, with the request that I would add a note & forward them to you—I have but a slight acquaintance with Dr Ames, enough to know that he is a man of education and abilaty. And that he & his wife (then but two years married) served 4 or 5 years in the Army—that she has been for several hours at a time under fire, & often sighted the guns & ordered the firing—I told the Dr I did not think there was any vacancy, or chance for the appointment, but if there is I think he would be a suitable man to appoint"—ALS, DNA, RG 59, Letters of Application and Recommendation. The enclosures recommending Dr. Fisher W. Ames for a consulship are *ibid.* No appointment followed.

1869, SEPT. 29.   Henry Johnson, Louisville, to USG. "I must address you with a few Lines the Following   Spectments Is the Entergasion of these Entovews Wich I Hope you Will Be Very Willing to Grant Is this We Collord People of Louisville air Trying to Get Up a Company for Pretectsion and We Write to you for Permisson to get a Company up   it Is for the Benfict of the Collord Man of Louisville Ky Wich it Will be very Usefull here   thay Can Not Walk the Streets anless thay being Shot Down thay has been Serval Casses of that kind here & We Want to Get Our Company Complected Just Soon as can   We Will Dress the Men In Blue Very Man will funish thir ~~Col~~ Clothing themSelves and Bye thir gunes and Every thing We Need   All We Want Is to Get Permission to Get a Company Up and the Company Will be Called the Young Gentlemens Militray assocation of Louisville Ky"—ALS, DNA, RG 107, Letters Received from Bureaus. On Oct. 6, Maj. Oscar A. Mack wrote to Johnson. "The President has referred to this Dept your letter dated Sept 29th, requesting permission to raise a military company for the protection of the colored residents of Louisville, and to inform you that your application ~~shall~~ should have been addressed to the Adjutant General of Kentucky, at Frankfort, for the consideration of the Governor of the State, who, alone, has the authority to grant your request"—ADfS, *ibid.*

1869, SEPT. 30.   USG endorsement. "Refered to the Qr. Mr. Gn."—AES, NHi. Written on a letter of Sept. 28 from Eliza C. Swan, Washington, D. C., to USG. "I would respectfully state to your Excellency that I have been very unjustly dismissed from the Qr. Mr. Generals Office upon charges made by the Acting Lady Supt. of insubordination and having other means of support, which charges can be proven to be utterly false. she does not like me—she has always been a rebel sympathiser and I am an outspoken radical and will not tamely or silently hear her in my presence call the one who has saved our country a 'horse Jockey, a drunkard and no gentleman' My brother Major Swann 16th Pa. Cavy. went into the fight at the firing of Fort Sumter & remained until the fall of Richmond. he was rendered a cripple for life at Cold Harbor. another brother languished in Southern prisons until he lost his health forever—My young brother Eugene fought gallantly in the 6th. Corps as a private—My cousin Wm B— Cushing of Albemarl notoriety also fought well—I was appointed by Secy' Stanton per recommendation of Gov. Andy Curtin, I am from Erie Pa. Gen. Thomas, Dana &c, know of my ability as a clerk. Therefore I humbly ask your all powerful aid in restoring me to my place—which was so unjustly taken from me. Hoping you will favorably consider my case."—ALS, *ibid.* On Oct. 1, Bvt. Maj. Gen. Montgomery C. Meigs endorsed this letter. "Respectfully returned to the President of the United States. Miss Swan was discharged upon report of insubordination, such that her remaining here, was inconsistent with the proper discipline of the Office. The lady against whom she makes such accusation, is a near relative of the late Gen'l Sedgwick well known to the President—of a family of undoubted loyalty and whose own loyalty, conduct and conversation, are above reproach. She utterly denies the gross accusation made against her. Miss Swan was not discharged because she had other means of support or because she had relatives in Office, but simply because she did not behave with necessary respect and obedience to those in charge of the branch of the Office in which she was employed. No injustice was done her."—ES, *ibid.* On Oct. 4, Ellen E. Janney, Washington, D. C., wrote to USG. "I wish to call your attention to the fact that within a few days past the only two *outspoken* loyal women in the Quarter Master Generals' Office were dismissed without a moments notice. Of those who remain secure in their positions there, nearly all were friends and supporters of Andrew Johnson and his policy and as a matter of course are opposed to Congress and the present administration. They are also unfaithful and inefficient to the last degree. Of all the Departments of the Government, I presume there is not one in which merit is so little regarded, loyalty of so little consideration. I received my appointment from Secretary Stanton in 1863, since which time I have remained in the Office up to the date of my dismissal on the 24th of last month. Not the shadow of a charge was brought against me. I am alone in the world and am entirely dependent upon my own exertions for support. My Father and brothers died before the war. My nephew Jos. Janney was in the Army of the Potomac while you were in command, and was wounded. My Cousin Wallace Hughes was Surgeon in the Army. I also had two other Cousins who enlisted. These are my nearest male relatives. Believing my discharge to have been brought about through the influence of a woman, who is to say the very least, a southern sympathiser, I earnestly request an investigation of the case. I am a relative of Saml M. Janney who is at present engaged as Superintendent of the Indian agency."—ALS, IHi. USG endorsed this letter. "Refer to Qr. Mr. Gn."—AE (initialed), *ibid.*

1869, Oct. 1.   USG endorsement. "Refered to the Sec. of War. If there is a vacancy now I would like to have the writer of this letter fill it. If not then I will name him for the first vacancy occuring."—AES, DNA, RG 94, ACP, S253 CB 1869. Written on a letter of Aug. 21 from Samuel D. Smith, Fort Walla Walla, Washington Territory, to USG. "I have been urged by many of my Army friends to apply for the appointment of Military Storekeeper, Qr Mas. Dept, in order to have my application on file in the war dept. when a vacancy occurs, I am assured by my old Army friends (and they are numerous) of your kindness and desire to do something for me, as expressed by yourself to them, . . . you Sir, well know my capability and fidelity, in times past to the Officers, under whom it was my honor to serve, I have had an experience of almost thirty years in the Qr. Mas Dept, . . . Should the President in his kindness consider my application favorably and reccomend or name me, for the first vacancy that may occur in the position asked for, it will be conferring a last benefit on one who is proud of having served under you in the position of Qr Mas Sergt. . . ."—ALS, *ibid.* On Oct. 4, Secretary of War William T. Sherman wrote to Smith. "The President referred to this office your letter of Aug 21st with his most flattering endorsement. I regret to inform you that Congress on 3d March last just before adjournment passed a law providing that until otherwise directed no new appt should be made in the Q. M. Dept. Until this law is repealed no appt can be made of a Storekeeper at Vancouver's or indeed any where in the Army. I will cause your letter to be filed so that if Congress repeals this law, meant of course, to be temporary if a vacancy occurs in the number of Storekeepers now full, your case will be favorably considered—"—Copies, *ibid.*; *ibid.*, RG 107, Letters Sent.

1869, Oct. 2.   To Secretary of War William T. Sherman. "Please have the case of Dr. Dunbar examined and a just & legal settlement made."—Copy, DNA, RG 107, Orders and Endorsements. On the same day, Sherman authorized the q. m. gen. to pay $25,000 to veterinarian Alexander Dunbar. ". . . If he makes claim for more let him petition Congress."—Copy, *ibid.* See *PUSG*, 16, 54–58; *ibid.*, 17, 11–13.

1869, Oct. 4.   USG endorsement. "Respectfully refered to the Com. of Int. Rev. I think on the whole the change in Assessor had better be made. Dr. Smith is a native of the South and the facts he states I have been cognizant of myself having seen a good the Dr. frequently since /65 both in Richmond & Washington."—AES, DNA, RG 56, Appointments Div., Heads of Treasury Offices, Letter Received. Written on a letter of Oct. 3 from Dr. Edwin H. Smith, Willard's Hotel, Washington, D. C., to USG. "The circumstances attending my application for the office of Assessor of

Int. Rev. for the 3rd Dist. of Va are sucinctly these—Viz: Mr Hudson the
present incumbent was appointed by Mr Johnson, and certainly not in the
interest of the Government as we understand its interests—He is a stranger
in our community and has enjoyed the emoluments of this office for more
than four years—Having ample means, he has never made any investments
in our midst, nor given any other evidence of his desire to become one of us.
He is reputed to own a large estate in New York, has only three in family,
and can receive, if desired by the Government, an official position in his
own section of country.—On the OTHER hand I have been a victim of
oppression for opinions sake at my own home, by my old friends and neighbors & my own kindred. I and my family have been snubbed, humiliated
and ostracised by equals and inferiors—and have been deprived of earning
the means of a livelihood from my profession in which by a laborious devotion of my time & energies for a quarter of a century I have acquired a
reputation. The property of myself & family was either lost or rendered
profitless by the late war & its results. Thus bereft, isolated, persecuted &
maligned what earthly recourse is left to me & mine but to lay the whole
matter before you marked out and appointed by Providence as I firmly
believe to heal the wounds & to right the wrongs of our late horrid war—
and not less to succor the otherwise friendless victims of loyalty at the
South, who for conscience sake have remained steadfast & unswerving in
their love to the union. The condition of my affairs, (for which no relief
can be had under our present state government,) has deeply impressed
that able, noble & good man Genl Canby and induced him to interpose in
my behalf, and commending itself to other noble-natures, it presents itself
as the very element in which General Grant lives & moves. It would be a
crowning joy & pride of my line to occupy a position by which I could add
my mite to what will be the world wide renown of your administration. God
knows for myself *alone* I would not venture a word on this subject; but
when I reflect that a large family—put in being by me, and dependent upon
me, is writhing under unmerited contumely and suffering caused by my
persistent & immoveable pursuance of principle and a sense of duty I would
be more or less than mortal were I to remain silent. May an unerring Providence counsel and direct you in this matter, and I will be content. Please
excuse fervor of feeling on my part and allow me to subscribe myself your
earnest, sincere & grateful friend under all circumstances . . ."—ALS, *ibid*.
Smith received the appointment.

1869, OCT. 4.   John F. Hartley, act. secretary of the treasury, to USG.
"I have the honor to transmit herewith for your information copies of letters
addressed to the Secretaries of State and of War, concerning Steamer
'Lady Sterling' alias 'Hornet' reported by Collector Rumley at Wilmington
N. C. as being at Smithville taking in coal and provisions. A copy of Col-
lector Rumley's telegram conveying this information to the Department is
transmitted with the above."—Copy, DNA, RG 59, Miscellaneous Letters.
The enclosures are *ibid*. On Oct. 3, Denard Rumley, collector of customs,

Wilmington, N. C., had telegraphed to Secretary of the Treasury George S. Boutwell. "The Steamer Lady Sterling, alias 'Hornet' with one hundred and Sixty (160) men and officers, and Eight (8) guns, is at Smithville, mouth of the Cape Fear River, touching there for coal, and provisions. Officer of Customs Boarded for papers and they produced only commission of Cuban Government. She is lying under Fort Caswell, and with the aid of the garrison at Fort Johnson, she can be stopped—I await your instructions—"—Copy, *ibid.* On Oct. 5, Boutwell wrote to Rumley. "I telegraphed you to day that your conduct in the case of the 'Lady Sterling' alias 'Hornet' was approved by the Department, I also directed you to hold the steamer under the 11th section of the Act of 1818 until you are directed by the President to release her. This you will do without reference to the action of the Commissioner in the case now pending. The Attorney General will communicate with the District Attorney, and also with the special counsel, who has been employed by you, as I understand from your despatch of the 4th inst received to day. The legal proceedings for the purpose of ascertaining the character of the vessel will be probably conducted by the Attorney General through the District Attorney, and Counsel associated with him. I desire you, however, to keep me advised either by letter or telegraph of the progress of proceedings, and of any facts which you may deem important to a proper understanding of the case by the President."—Copy, *ibid.* Boutwell's telegram of the same day to Rumley and related papers are *ibid.* On Oct. 7, George Francis Train, Indianapolis, telegraphed to USG. "I protest against release of Hornet She is another alabama"—Telegram received (at 2:00 P.M.), *ibid.*, RG 107, Telegrams Collected (Bound). On the same day, Secretary of State Hamilton Fish wrote in his diary. "Called upon the President on the subject of the Hornet—mentioned the receipt of a telegram from Marshal Barlow expressing apprehension that it was intended to run her out—President sd order had been given to Commanding officer in Ft Casswell, (under whose guns she lies) to watch her, & not allow her to sail—I suggested the embarassment that wd result from her escape—however vigilant we may be, we should be suspected of negligence, or collusion—He replied, if she escaped he would order the Navy to pursue & capture or sink her—but that if any additional precautions could be taken they should be—I suggested that a vessel of war be ordered there to watch & prevent her sailing—He immediately sent for Admiral Porter, who said the Frolic was in N. Y. ready to sail at an hour's notice President directed that she be ordered to sail immediately for Smithville, & lay along side the Hornet, & prevent her sailing at any hazard"—DLC-Hamilton Fish. On Oct. 7, Vice Admiral David D. Porter wrote to USG. "The enclosed telegrams have been sent in different directions."—LS, DNA, RG 59, Miscellaneous Letters. Copies of three telegrams from Porter ordering naval officers to intercept *Hornet* (renamed *Cuba*) along the N. C. coast are *ibid.* On Oct. 8, Porter wrote to USG. "I have the honor to send herewith a copy of a telegram received this A. M, from Rear Admiral Godon, Commandant of Navy Yard New York, dated 7th Inst, and copies of two telegrams from Commander Queen, Senior officer at Key West."—LS, *ibid.* The enclosures are *ibid.* See *New York Times,* Sept. 29, Oct. 1–23, 1869.

On June 1, 1870, William E. Chandler, New York City, wrote on behalf of his client to USG. "The undersigned, Mr Fernando Macias, Merchant, resident in NewYork and a naturalized citizen of the United States, respectfully calls your attention to the case of the steamship 'Cuba' commonly known as the 'Hornet' now pending in the United States District Court for the District of North Carolina, and requests the discontinuance of proceedings against the vessel and her cargo, tackle and apparel, and her delivery to the undersigned   The Hornet was purchased by the Undersigned in July 1869 of the United States Navy Department for the sum of about thirty three thousand dollars; and is now under seizure together with her cargo, apparel and tackle, at Wilmington and libelled for forfeiture for alleged violation of the neutrality laws of the United States, by leaving the United States for the purpose of committing hostilities against Spain. . . ."—LS, DNA, RG 59, Miscellaneous Letters. Related papers are *ibid.*

1869, OCT. 8.   Proclamation. "The painful duty devolves upon the President of announcing to the people of the United States the death of one of his honored predecessors, Franklin Pierce, which occurred at Concord, early this morning. Eminent in the public councils and universally beloved in private life, his death will be mourned with a sorrow befitting the loss which his country sustains in his decease. As a mark of respect to his memory it is ordered that the Executive Mansion and the several Departments at Washington be draped in mourning, and all business suspended on the day of the funeral. It is further ordered that the War and Navy Departments cause suitable military and naval honors to be paid on this occasion to the memory of the illustrious citizen who has passed from among us."—DS, DNA, RG 59, Miscellaneous Letters.

1869, OCT. 11.   USG endorsement. "Let special attention be called to this recommendation when appointments come to be made."—AES, DNA, RG 94, Correspondence, USMA. Written on a letter of Oct. 8 from Otis Bisbee, principal, Riverview Military Academy, Riverview, N. Y., to USG. "Your very kind, and very full letter in reference to Gen. Rawlins' son I received. I am glad, and proud of my country, when I see her generous sons, who have risked all for her, borne up in the hour of their need, by an appreciative people. Now, My dear sir, may I crave your indulgence for a moment. I have, in my employ a young man by the name of *James Conlisk,* who acts here as drill master and instructor of Tactics. His common sense is large; his aptitude for study, good, his habits, regular. He has a strong desire to get an appointment to *West Point* for next year, or, in case that cannot be, for the year after—as his age will then be suitable. Allow me to bespeak for him your kind attention. If it is in your power consistently to give him a place, I am confidant, you will, by so doing, not only benefit him, but put into the military service, an efficient member. Begging your pardon for this intrusion, . . ."—ALS, *ibid.* No appointment followed.

1869, OCT. 12.   USG endorsement. "Let special attention be called to this application when appointments come to be made."—AES, DNA, RG 94, Correspondence, USMA. Written on a letter of the same day from Col. Samuel D. Sturgis, Washington, D. C., to Secretary of War William T. Sherman. "I have the honor to apply for the appointment of Cadet to the Mil. Academy—West-Point, for my son Jas. G. Sturgis—to enter in June 1871—at which time he will be seventeen and a half years of age—"—ALS, *ibid.* James G. Sturgis graduated from USMA in 1875.

1869, OCT. 13.   USG endorsement. "Respectfully returned to the Hon: the Secretary of the Interior, whose recommendation is approved"—ES, DNA, RG 59, Miscellaneous Letters. Written on a letter of Oct. 12 from Secretary of the Interior Jacob D. Cox to USG. "On the 1st October 1863, a treaty was concluded with the Western Bands of Shoshone Indians, at Ruby Valley, Nevada. The treaty was laid before the Senate, and that body advised and consented to its ratification, with amendment; which amendment has been presented to the Indians and received their assent. The treaty and the Senate Resolution, together with the paper signed by the Chiefs and principal men of the Western Bands of Shoshones, in which they agree and assent to the amendment of the Senate, are herewith submitted, with the recommendation that the treaty be ratified and proclaimed."—LS, *ibid.* On Feb. 3, 1870, Cox wrote to USG concerning a treaty with the Seneca and, on Feb. 14, concerning a treaty with the "Klamath and Moadoc tribes and the Ya-hoos-Kin band of snake Indians . . ."—Copies, *ibid.,* RG 48, Indian Div., Letters Sent.

1869, OCT. 14.   Speech. "I have great pleasure in visiting for the first time the City of Frederick, of which I have heard so much during the period of the late rebellion, and which, too, stood up manfully for the maintenance of a whole Union. I expected to visit this city some years ago, but found myself unable to do so; but now that I have found so many friends, and have been so gratified with what I have seen of your fair and enjoyed of your hospitality, I hope at some future time to visit you again."—*New York Times,* Oct. 15, 1869. USG attended the Frederick County (Md.) Agricultural Fair.

1869, OCT. 14.   R. D. Harrison, chairman, Republican Committee, Columbus, Ohio, to USG. "Hayes and state ticket elected by ten thousand (10.000) majority Legislature House three (3) Senate one (1) Republican"—Telegram received (at 11:00 A.M.), DNA, RG 107, Telegrams Collected (Bound).

1869, OCT. 19.   William D. W. Barnard, St. Louis, to USG. "Charles B. Smith is applicant for Supervisorship this District,   papers leave tomorrow, appointment would be good one and give satisfaction"—Telegram received (on Oct. 20, 9:10 A.M.), DNA, RG 107, Telegrams Collected (Bound). No appointment followed.

1869, OCT. 19.   James M. Deems, Baltimore, to USG. "Permit me to call your attention to the application of my son Clarence Deems, handed to you last spring by P. M. Genl Cresswell—it is recommended by all the Electors of Maryland, also by the most prominent men, military & civil of our own party. I would simply state that in August 15 /61 I, with others commenced raising the 1st Md Cavalry, and received my commission as 1st Major from Mr Lincoln the President, and served until discharged at from the Hospital at Annapolis.—commanded the Regt as Lt Col. under Generals Stoneman & Pleasanton in all those heavy cavalry fights previous to and including Sharpsburg which occurred soon after Gettysburg. when I was sent to Hospital with Rheumatism. My Grand Father served in the Revolutionary war and my Father in the war of 1812. No Union will ever be appointed from this state unless by the President as our party is in an almost hopeless minority from the number of rebels coming here from the southern states. Many who now hold lucrative offices here did not know upon what side they stood in 1861, and had Johnson or Seymour been elected instead of yourself would have been among the best rebel sympathizers. As I have lost much and gained nothing but the approval of my own conscience by going into the army I hope you will favorably consider my sons application."—ALS, DNA, RG 94, Correspondence, USMA. Related papers are *ibid.* Clarence Deems graduated from USMA in 1874.

1869, OCT. 19.   "Committee of arrangements," Virginia City, Nev., to USG. "The first pick in Sutro Tunnel was struck to day,   may this great and noble work be completed during your administration."—Telegram received (on Oct. 21, 9:00 A.M.), DNA, RG 107, Telegrams Collected (Bound). On March 30, Horace Porter had written to Adolph H. J. Sutro. "The President directs me to express to you his thanks for a copy of your work entitled 'The Sutro Tunnel'."—Doris Harris, Catalog 36 [June, 1987], no. 75. See Robert E. Stewart, Jr., and Mary Frances Stewart, *Adolph Sutro: A Biography* (Berkeley, 1962), pp. 68–69, 81–85.

1869, OCT. 20.   To Dorothea L. Dix, Washington, D. C. "Please accept my thanks for the photograph of the Monument in memory of the Union soldiers who perished during the rebellion, which in such great measure by your energy has been erected in the National Cemetery near Fort Monroe." —LS, MH. On Oct. 12, Dix had written to USG concerning a soldiers' monument.—William Evarts Benjamin, Catalogue No. 42, March, 1892, p. 8; Stan. V. Henkels, Catalogue No. 1194, June 8, 1917, p. 91. See

Francis Tiffany, *Life of Dorothea Lynde Dix* (Boston and New York, 1890), pp. 344–48.

1869, OCT. 25. Secretary of the Interior Jacob D. Cox to USG. "I have the honor to transmit, herewith, a deed executed to Nicodemus Chilcote by the children of Maria Christiana DeRome, conveying a portion of the land reserved to them by the provisions of the Miami Indian Treaty of Octo 23. 1826, forwarded to this Department by the Commissioner of Indian Affairs, with letter dated the 20th instant, and respectfully recommend the approval of the same by the President."—Copy, DNA, RG 48, Indian Div., Letters Sent.

1869, OCT. 28. To Secretary of the Treasury George S. Boutwell from Philadelphia. "Your letter rec'd. Your pleasure will be mine. I do not advise delay."—ALS, IHi.

1869, OCT. 28. U.S. Delegate James M. Cavanaugh of Montana Territory, Washington, D. C., to USG. "I desire most respectfully to call your attention to the enclosed proceedings of a meeting held by the Citizens of Bitter Root Valley, in the Territory of Montana, at Stevensville, September 4th 1869, and to ask your careful consideration of the same. I further beg leave to call your Excellency's attention to article XI, Stevens Treaty Statutes at Large, Page 978, Vol 12, and ask that you may be pleased to order a survey of the lands in this Valley, with a view to a final adjustment of the difficulties."—ALS, DNA, RG 75, Letters Received, Montana Superintendency. The enclosure is *ibid.*

1869, OCT. 30. Governor John W. Geary of Pa. to USG. "I take pleasure in bearing testimony to the high personal character for integrity and business capacity of George W. Andrews, Esq., of Brookville, Pa. Mr. Andrews is now, and has been for a number of years, a member of the bar at Brookville, and stands among the most respectable and competent in his locality. He has always had an extensive practice, and possesses, in an eminent degree, the confidence of the citizens of his region of the State. Mr. Andrews is an applicant for the appointment of a Judgeship in one of the Western Territories, and I feel assured that this appointment would not only be peculiarly suitable, but that it would meet with great satisfaction, especially among his professional brethren of Pennsylvania."—LS, NNP. No appointment followed.

Index

All letters written by USG of which the text was available for use in this volume are indexed under the names of the recipients. The dates of these letters are included in the index as an indication of the existence of text. Abbreviations used in the index are explained on pp. xv–xix. Individual regts. are indexed under the names of the states in which they originated.